RESEARCH METHODS IN PSYCHOLOGY:

Evaluating a World of Information

RESEARCH METHODS IN PSYCHOLOGY:

Evaluating a World of Information

BETH MORLING

University of Delaware

W. W. Norton & Company, Inc.

New York • London

Copyright © 2012 by W. W. Norton & Company, Inc.

First Edition

Editor: Sheri L. Snavely

Developmental Editor: Beth Ammerman

Ancillaries Editors: Matthew Freeman, Callinda Taylor

Editorial Assistant: Mary Dudley

Project Editor: Christine D'Antonio

Copy Editor: Jackie Estrada

Design Direction: Hope Miller Goodell

Book Design: Lisa Buckley

Marketing Manager: Andrea Matter

Composition and Layout: Prepare

Manufacturing: R. R. Donnelley, Crawfordsville

Production Manager: Eric Pier-Hocking

Library of Congress Cataloging-in-Publication Data

Morling, Beth.
    Research methods in psychology : evaluating a world of
    information / by Beth Morling. — 1st ed.
        p. cm.
    Includes bibliographical references and index.
    ISBN 978-0-393-93546-2 (pbk.)
   1. Psychology—Research—Methodology—Textbooks. 2. Psychology,
Experimental—Textbooks. I. Title.
    BF76.5.M667 2012
    150.72'1—dc23

                       2011036533

W. W. Norton & Company, Inc., 500 Fifth Avenue, New York, N.Y. 10110
www.wwnorton.com

W. W. Norton & Company Ltd., Castle House, 75/76 Wells Street, London W1T 3QT
5 6 7 8 9 0

For my boys

About the Author

Beth Morling is Associate Professor of Psychology at the University of Delaware. She attended Carleton College in Northfield, MN, and received her Ph.D. from the University of Massachusetts at Amherst. Before teaching at Delaware, she held positions at Union College (NY) and Muhlenberg College (PA). She has taught research methods at Delaware almost every semester for 8 years. In addition to research methods, she also teaches undergraduate cultural psychology and a seminar on the self-concept, as well as a graduate course in the teaching of psychology. Her research in the area of cultural psychology explores how cultural practices shape people's motivations. Dr. Morling recently returned from a year as a Fulbright scholar, teaching and conducting research in Kyoto, Japan.

Brief Contents

Contents

Seeing Red Affects Achievement

(Intelligence, 2010)

More Than 2 Million U.S. Youths Depressed

(Reuters, 2008)

"Should I buy these boots? They got four out of five stars on Zappos."

*Happy people
cut the
chit-chat*

(*Washington Post*, 2010)

**Feeling Cold?
Maybe You're
Lonely**

(CBS News, 2008)

Should Cell Phone Use by Drivers Be Illegal?

(*New York Times*, 2009)

People who
are extroverted
like upbeat,
conventional
music

(Rentfrow & Gosling, 2003)

Preface

The psychology major prepares students for a tremendous variety of careers—not only for advanced study in psychology. Indeed, very few psychology majors go on to be active researchers. At my institution, fewer than 5% of our graduating psychology majors pursue Ph.D. work; even fewer eventually have careers as scientific psychologists. Perhaps that is why many students consider the research methods course "dry" and "boring" compared with courses in cognition, abnormal psychology, or social psychology. Often students tell me they find the content irrelevant to their future goals: Why do they need to learn how to do research when they want to be therapists, social workers, teachers, lawyers, or physicians?

I once told such students that by learning to plan and conduct research, they would be able to read and apply research later, in their chosen careers. But then I reviewed what we know about the difficulty of transferring learning across contexts. I realized that at the undergraduate level, it is unlikely that the skills involved in designing one's own studies can be transferred to understanding and critically assessing others' studies. If we want students to explain whether a study supports its claims, we have to teach them how to do so. That is the approach I started using in my own classroom, and that is the approach this book attempts to teach.

The book was written with an audience of liberal arts psychology majors in mind—students who are taking their first course in research methods (usually sophomores or juniors). These students may never become researchers, but they need to navigate the world of information they live in. They deserve a book that can hone their skills as *consumers* of research. Of course, this book can also be used to teach the flip side of the question: How can *producers* of research design better studies? The producer angle is presented so that students will be prepared to design studies and collect data in courses that prioritize these skills. However, unlike most other research methods books, which emphasize the research producer over the research consumer, this book emphasizes the consumer over the producer.

To be effective consumers of research, students need to be systematic, quantitative reasoners who can find, read, and critically analyze the relevant research (Lutsky, 2008). This book is therefore designed with quantitative reasoning skills at its core. It teaches students how to interrogate the quantitative information that they will encounter—not only in the empirical journal articles they will read in their psychology courses, but also in online magazines, print magazines, newspapers, blogs, and wikis. They will learn when, why, and how to ask questions such as "Compared to what?" "Could there be a confound?" "Is a causal claim justified here?" "Is that difference significant?" "What do other studies say?" or "Do these data support the theory?" Students learn to ask for empirical evidence behind a writer's claims ("What is the evidence?") and learn how to evaluate that evidence when it is provided.

Critical thinking is also integral to this book, but of course thinking "critically" does not mean simply adopting a skeptical mindset. Thinking critically means knowing what to prioritize when assessing a study. Sometimes large or random samples matter, and sometimes they do not. Sometimes we ask about random assignment, and sometimes we do not. Students benefit from having a set of systematic steps to help them prioritize their questioning when they interrogate quantitative information. To that end, this book presents a framework of "three claims and four validities," introduced in Chapter 3. There are three kinds of claims that researchers (as well as journalists, bloggers, or commentators) might make: frequency claims (some percentage of people do X), association claims (X is associated with Y), and causal claims (X affects Y). The four validities are generally agreed upon by methodologists: internal, external, construct, and statistical.

To consider the evidence for one of the three claims, good quantitative reasoners prioritize different validity questions depending on the claim. For example, for a frequency claim, we should ask about measurement (construct validity) and sampling techniques (external validity), but not about random assignment or confounds, because the claim is not a causal one. For a causal claim, we prioritize internal validity and construct validity, and external validity is generally less important. The idea is for students to hone skills as *systematic interrogators*. They need to know what validities to prioritize, how to ask the questions in a meaningful way, and how to assess the answers. The "three claims, four validities" scaffold provides a simple structure that is reinforced throughout the book. These features should help students remember the steps of information interrogation even years after they take the research methods course.

The 13 chapters in this book are arranged in six parts. The first two parts contain introductory chapters on the scientific method, the "three claims, four validities" scaffold, measurement, and ethics. Next come parts that correspond to each of the three claims (frequency, association, and cause), followed by a final section about balancing research priorities. Most of the chapters will be familiar to veteran instructors, including chapters on external validity, experimentation, and factorial designs. However, unlike some methods books, this one devotes two full chapters to correlational research (one on bivariate and one on multivariate studies). These two chapters help students learn how to interpret, apply, and interrogate different types of association claims, one of the common types of claims they will encounter.

The book's pedagogical features emphasize active learning and repetition of the most important points. Each chapter begins with high-level learning objectives—major skills students should expect to remember even "a year from now." Important terms in a chapter are introduced in boldface. The Check Your Understanding at the end of each major section provides basic review questions that allow students to revisit key concepts as they read. Each chapter ends with a set of Learning Actively questions that encourage students to apply what they learned (answers are provided at the end of the book). I wrote the Learning Actively questions to enable students to test themselves on the material in new examples.

The questions also help students recognize how they can apply what they have learned in the chapter to real-world, high-fidelity headlines and examples. A master table of the three claims and four validities appears on the book's inside cover to remind students of the scaffold for the course.

I believe the book works pedagogically because it continually reinforces the three claims, four validities framework, building in repetition and depth. Although each book chapter addresses the usual core content of research methods, students are always reminded of how a particular topic helps them interrogate the key validities. The ever more detailed iterations of a simple message will help students remember and apply this questioning strategy in the future. My hope is that by using this book in a course, students will sharpen the way they read and think about psychological information in their daily lives.

In addition to the book itself, Norton offers a carefully designed support package for instructors and students. The combined Instructor's Manual/Test Bank contains detailed teaching notes based on my own experience with the course, extra student activities, and a full test bank. Students and instructors can find additional examples and critical thinking questions on the book's blog, Everyday Research Methods (www.everydayresearchmethods.com; no passwords or registration required). The blog, curated by me and, occasionally, other contributors, offers an often-updated bank of teachable moments from the web: blogs, newspapers, research studies, online video, speeches, and so forth. The book comes with a number of other ancillaries to assist both new and experienced research methods instructors; a full list is available on page xxiii.

Acknowledgments

The past years of working on this textbook have been more fun and less painful than I expected, thanks to the many people who have helped. To start, in my first foray into textbook writing, I feel fortunate to have worked with an author-focused company and an all-around great editor, Sheri Snavely. She was optimistic, realistic, savvy, and smart—and good at reminding me when to smile. She also made sure I got the most rigorous reviews possible and that I was supported with great Norton staff: Christine D'Antonio, Mary Dudley, Callinda Taylor, Matthew Freeman, Eric Pier-Hocking, and Hope Miller Goodell. I have felt very lucky to be working with the Norton team, but by far my closest partner has been Beth Ammerman, who spent months revising the book with me. She recrafted the casual sentences, organized the messy parts, and kept track of every detail. Each day that we worked together I felt grateful for her talent, tact, and energy.

I am also thankful for the early support and enthusiasm I have received from the Norton sales management team; Michael Wright, Annie Stewart, Dennis Fernandes, Lib Triplett, Allen Clawson, Katie Incorvia, Kym Silvasy Neale, Jim Gibson, and Jordan Mendez. I especially thank my marketing manager, Andrea Matter, for her creativity and enthusiasm. Her efforts made sure a wide range of research methods instructors learned about our approach to the course, generating early interest in the book that motivated us in the final stages.

The present book owes some core examples and explanations to Doug Mook's 2001 research methods textbook, and Doug's counsel shaped early drafts of the chapters, especially those on scientific reasoning, null effects, and external validity. Educator and author Dana Dunn provided encouragement and support right from the beginning. I am fortunate and thankful that Mark Sciutto, my former colleague at Muhlenberg College, agreed to comment on *every* chapter. He gave his own experienced perspective about where students struggle and advised me on how to help readers through those difficult topics. (The sample paper in Appendix C was written by Mark's student Kristina Ciarlo.) My friend Carrie Smith shared my vision for assessment and helped make this book's test bank an authentic measure of quantitative reasoning. Many thanks, also, to Christine Lofgren at the University of California, Irvine, for taking great care in writing the exercises for StudySpace. The book was reviewed, re-reviewed, and fact-checked by a cadre of talented research method professors, and I am grateful to each of them. Their students are lucky to have them in the classroom, and my readers will benefit from the time they spent in improving this book:

Kristen Weede Alexander, *California State University, Sacramento*
Gordon Bear, *Ramapo College*
Brett Beston, *McMaster University*
Kenneth DeMarree, *Texas Tech University*
Jessica Dennis, *California State University, Los Angeles*
Rachel Dinero, *Cazenovia College*
Dana S. Dunn, *Moravian College*
C. Emily Durbin, *Michigan State University*
Christina Frederick, *Sierra Nevada College*
Timothy E. Goldsmith, *University of New Mexico*
AnaMarie Guichard, *California State University, Stanislaus*
Andreana Haley, *University of Texas, Austin*
Deborah L. Hume, *University of Missouri*
Kurt R. Illig, *University of Virginia*
W. Jake Jacobs, *University of Arizona*
Christian Jordan, *Wilfrid Laurier University*
Victoria A. Kazmerski, *Penn State Erie, The Behrend College*
Heejung Kim, *University of California, Santa Barbara*
Greg M. Kim-Ju, *California State University, Sacramento*
Carl Lejeuz, *University of Maryland*
Christopher Mazurek, *Columbia College*
Daniel C. Molden, *Northwestern University*
J. Toby Mordkoff, *University of Iowa*
Elizabeth D. Peloso, *University of Delaware*
M. Christine Porter, *College of William and Mary*
Joshua Rabinowitz, *University of Michigan*
James R. Roney, *University of California, Santa Barbara*
Silvia J. Santos, *California State University, Dominguez Hills*
Mark J. Sciutto, *Muhlenberg College*
Elizabeth A. Sheehan, *Georgia State University*

Mark A. Stellmack, *University of Minnesota, Twin Cities*
Eva Szeli, *Arizona State University*
Lauren A. Taglialatela, *Kennesaw State University*
Alison Thomas-Cottingham, *Rider University*
Christopher Warren, *California State University, Long Beach*
Charles E. (Ted) Wright, *University of California, Irvine*
Nancy Yanchus, *Georgia Southern University*
David Zehr, *Plymouth State University*

Gifted statistics teacher Gordon Bear's line-by-line comments and helpful correspondence are responsible for making the statistical appendices much better. I have tried to make the best possible improvements from all of these able reviewers.

My life as a teaching professor has been enriched during the last few years because of the friendship and support of many colleagues, including, but not limited to, Brian Ackerman, Ryan Beveridge, Larry Cohen, Mike Kuhlman, Susan Fiske, and Steve Heine. In addition, some chapters of this book were revised during a sabbatical year that I spent as a Fulbright Lecturer/Researcher in Kyoto Japan. I am grateful to the Fulbright organization for its support of international exchange, and I am also thankful to my colleagues at the Kokoro Research Center at Kyoto University for hosting me: Yukiko Uchida, Kai Hiraishi, and Kosuke Takemura, and also Vinai Norassakkunkit. I received much practical help during my sabbatical year from Mizhuo Iwata, Miki Nakaji, and Yuri Yano.

My boys Max, Alek, and Hugo ensured that I never had to work on the book for too long at a stretch (thanks, guys . . . I think). I owe special thanks to my mother-in-law, Janet Pochan, for graciously helping with so many tasks on the home front. Finally, I want to thank my husband Darrin for reminding me that it's worth the effort.

Media and Print Resources for Instructors and Students

Instructor's Manual

Beth Morling, *University of Delaware*

The text's Instructor's Manual contains teaching guides to the textbook's key pedagogical features, a discussion of how to design a course that utilizes the textbook, sample syllabus and assignments, and chapter-by-chapter teaching notes and suggested activities.

Test Bank

C. Veronica Smith, *University of Mississippi*

The Test Bank provides over 450 questions using an evidence-centered approach designed in collaboration with Valerie Shute of Florida State University and Diego Zapata-Rivera of the Educational Testing Service. The Test Bank contains multiple-choice and short-answer questions that are classified by section and difficulty, making it easy for instructors to construct tests and quizzes that are meaningful and diagnostic. The Test Bank is available in print, Word RTF, PDF, and *ExamView®* Assessment Suite format.

Instructor's Resource Disc with PowerPoints

The *Research Methods in Psychology* Instructor's Resource Disc contains the Instructor's Manual as a PDF and all of the art and tables from the textbook in JPG and PPT formats.

The *Research Methods in Psychology* Blog:
Everyday Research Methods, Interrogating the Popular Press

www.everydayresearchmethods.com

The *Research Methods in Psychology* blog offers an often-updated bank of teachable moments from the web—blogs, newspapers, research studies, online video, speeches, and more—curated by Beth Morling and occasional guest contributors. Each blog post connects with material students encounter in the textbook and includes critical thinking/discussion questions that an instructor may discuss in lecture or assign as homework. The blog is easily searchable, and each entry is tagged with a learning objective from the textbook and appropriate keywords.

StudySpace

wwnorton.com/studyspace

Christine Lofgren, *University of California, Irvine*

The Norton StudySpace is a free and open resource designed using the analytical framework of the text for students who want extra practice. StudySpace includes quizzes, chapter outlines created by the textbook author, and review flashcards. The APA style guidelines appendix from the textbook will also be available on StudySpace, reformatted for ease of use on desktop and mobile browsers.

To access the APA style guidelines through StudySpace or on your mobile device, use the code APAS-TYLE.

PART 1

Introduction to Scientific Reasoning

NEW RELEASES

Mozart Effect— Shmozart Effect

(Intelligence, 2010)

Seeing Red Affects Achieve- ment

(World Science, 2007)

1

Psychology Is a Way of Thinking

Learning Objectives

A year from now, you should still be able to:

1. See psychology as a way of thinking and understand what it means to reason empirically.
2. Appreciate how an understanding of psychological research methods is crucial not only for producers of information but also for consumers of information.
3. Describe four cycles in psychological science.

Thinking back to your introductory psychology course, what do you remember learning? You probably remember studies about dogs salivating at the sound of a bell or about people failing to call for help when the room they were in filled up with smoke. Or perhaps you remember the studies in which people administered stronger and stronger electrical shocks to an innocent man although he seemed to be in distress. Or you remember studies about how we learn best, why we sleep, and how well we can trust our memories. As you continue your study of psychology, you can anticipate learning about other landmark studies—research about the brain, cognition, social behavior, child development, and clinical disorders.

Psychological science is based on studies—on research—by psychologists. Like other scientists, psychologists are empiricists. To be an empiricist means to base one's conclusions on systematic observations. Psychologists do not simply think intuitively about behavior, cognition, and emotion; instead, psychologists know what they know because they have conducted studies on people and animals acting in their natural environments or in specially designed situations. If you are to think like a psychologist, then you must think like a researcher, and taking a course in research methods is crucial to your understanding of psychology. This book explains the types of studies psychologists conduct and some of the potential strengths and limitations of each type of study. As you read, you will learn not only how to plan your own studies but also how to find research, read about it, and ask questions of it. You will gain a greater appreciation for the rigorous standards psychologists maintain in their research, and you will learn how to be a systematic and critical consumer of psychological science.

Research Producers, Research Consumers

Some psychology majors are fascinated by the research process and intend to become *producers* of research information. Perhaps they hope to get a job studying brain anatomy, observing the behavior of pigeons or monkeys, administering personality questionnaires, observing children in a school setting, or analyzing data. They may want to write up their results and present them at research meetings. These students may dream about working as research scientists or professors.

Other psychology students may not want to work in a lab, but they do enjoy reading about the structure of the brain, the behavior of pigeons or monkeys, the personalities of their fellow students, or the behavior of children in a school setting. They are interested in being *consumers* of research information—in reading about research so that they can later apply it to their work, hobbies, relationships, or personal growth. These students might pursue careers as family therapists, teachers, sales representatives, guidance counselors, or police officers, and they expect a psychology education to help them in these roles.

In practice, many psychologists engage in both roles. When they are planning their research and creating new knowledge, they study the work of others who have gone before them. Furthermore, psychologists in both roles require a curiosity about behavior, emotion, and cognition. Research producers and consumers share a desire to ask, answer, and communicate interesting questions. And they share a commitment to the practice of empiricism—to answer psychological questions with direct, formal observations and to communicate with others about what they have learned.

Why the Producer Role Is Important

For your future coursework in psychology, it is important to know how to be a producer of research. Of course, students who decide to go to graduate school for psychology will need to know all about research methods. But even if you do not plan to do graduate work in psychology, you will probably have to write a paper in APA style before you graduate, and you may be required to do research as part of a course lab section. To succeed, you will need to know how to randomly assign people to groups, how to measure attitudes accurately, and how to interpret results from a graph. Perhaps more important, the skills you acquire by conducting research can teach you how psychological scientists ask questions and how they think about their discipline.

As part of your psychology studies, you might even work in a research lab as an undergraduate (see **Figure 1.1**). Many psychology professors are active researchers, and you might have the opportunity to get involved in their laboratories. Your faculty supervisor may ask you to code behaviors, assign participants to different groups, graph an outcome, or write a report. If such an opportunity arises, take it! Doing so will give you your first taste of being a research producer. Although you will be supervised closely, you will be expected to know the basics of conducting research. This book will introduce you to what you need to know. In turn, by participating as a research producer, you can expect to deepen your understanding of psychological inquiry.

FIGURE 1.1
Producers of research.
As undergraduates, some psychology majors work alongside faculty as producers of information.

Why the Consumer Role Is Important

Although it is important to understand the psychologist's role as a producer of research, most psychology majors do not eventually become researchers. But regardless of the career you choose, you will need to become a savvy consumer of information. In your psychology courses, you will read studies published by psychologists in scientific journals. You will need to learn how to read about research with curiosity—to understand it, learn from it, and ask appropriate questions about it.

Even in everyday life, we are constantly bombarded by information on the Internet, on TV, in magazines, and in newspapers, and much of this information is based on research. For example, during an election year, Americans may come across polling information in the media almost every day. In addition, many newspapers have special science sections that present stories on the latest research, and lifestyle magazines such as *Self*, *Men's Health*, and *Parents* summarize research for their readers. Entire websites are dedicated to psychology-related topics, such as treatments for autism, subliminal learning tapes, or advice for married couples. However, only some of this information is accurate and useful; some of it is dubious, and some is just plain wrong. How can you tell the good research information from the bad? Knowledge of research methods enables you to ask the appropriate questions so that you can assess information. So research methods skills apply not only to research studies but also to much of the other information you encounter in your daily life.

Finally, being a smart consumer of research could be crucial to your future career. Even if you do not plan to be a researcher—if your goal is to be a social worker, a teacher, a sales representative, a family therapist, a human resources representative, or an entrepreneur—you will need to know how to read research with a critical eye. Clinical social workers and family therapists read research to know which therapies are the most effective. Teachers use research to find out which teaching methods work best. And the business world runs on quantitative information: Research is used to predict what sales will be like in the future, what consumers will buy, and whether investors will take risks or lie low. Once you learn how to be a consumer of information—psychological or otherwise—you will use these skills constantly, no matter what job you are in.

In this book, you will often see the phrase *interrogating information*, because a consumer of research needs to know how to ask the right questions, determine the answers, and evaluate a study on the basis of those answers. This book will teach you systematic rules for interrogating research information that will make you a better consumer of information.

The Benefits of Being a Good Consumer: An Example

What do you gain by being a critical consumer of information? Psychology is full of well-run studies that you can apply to your workplace and life. Imagine, for example, that you are an occupational therapist (a person who helps people with physical and mental disabilities find solutions to daily living challenges), and you work in private practice. You are considering taking an expensive training course in a treatment called facilitated communication (FC), in which therapists help clients communicate by guiding their hands as they type sentences on a computer. This treatment is billed as a breakthrough for people who have autism, a disorder that appears early in childhood and is characterized, in many cases, by reduced language abilities and impoverished social interactions. The technique is also used for patients with cerebral palsy and other developmental disorders that limit the ability to speak. Before you invest your money in a weekend-long course, you decide that it is your professional responsibility to look into the effectiveness of this technique.

The organizers of the training course claim that people with disabilities—even if they cannot or will not speak—are able to type coherent messages on a keyboard if their hands and arms are supported by a sympathetic adult "facilitator" as they use the keyboard. Proponents of FC believe that the facilitator develops a relationship of trust and helpfulness with the client. The intent is for the clients to independently create written messages in which they express thoughts that they ordinarily cannot, because of the disability.

When you do further research, however, you learn that some psychologists suspect that the alleged successes of FC could be cases of "unconscious cuing": While supporting the client's hands, the facilitator has many opportunities to influence what the client types (Twachtman-Cullen, 1997). Psychologists have used controlled research to test the claims about the technique. In one study, a patient and a facilitator were each presented with a drawing of a common object, and the client was asked to type its name with the help of the facilitator (Klewe, 1993). Neither the client nor the facilitator could see the other's drawing, so neither person knew that they had been shown two different objects. (For example, in one trial the client was shown a picture of a key, while the facilitator saw a picture of a sandwich.) Sure enough, the client typed out a name that fit one of the drawings—but always the drawing that the *facilitator* saw (that is, the sandwich). Obviously, the typed responses had been determined by the facilitators, who must have been cuing the clients in some way, even if they were not aware they were doing so—and even if they were trying *not* to do so. (For a summary of this research and an explanation of why FC may still be practiced today, read Twachtman-Cullen, 1997; Jacobson, Mulick, and Schwartz, 1995; see also **Figure 1.2**.) Indeed, the American Psychological Association (APA) resolved that FC has "no scientifically demonstrated support for its efficacy" (American Psychological Association, 1994). But the controversy continues, and current proponents of FC maintain that at least some clients can communicate independently by typing (e.g., Janzen-Wilde, Duchan, & Higginbotham, 1995).

FIGURE 1.2 Facilitated communication. One behavior that led some researchers to doubt FC was that clients were observed to type with one finger while looking away from the keyboard. (If you try it yourself, you'll notice that it is virtually impossible to type coherently with one finger without looking.) Such observations meant that the facilitators, not the clients, were probably creating the typed words. Current users of FC say they ensure that clients always see the keys.

To return to our scenario, because you are a careful consumer of information, you would probably decide to save your time and money for training in therapies and techniques that are backed up by empirical evidence. But without some ability to find, read, and understand the research on this topic, you might not have learned that FC is an unsupported technique. Training in research methods should motivate you to ask questions about this and other therapeutic techniques that you encounter.

Even if you choose a career that is not part of the field of psychology, you can benefit from reading psychological research. Consider a study on the impact of the color red, conducted by Andrew Elliot and his colleagues (2007). These researchers observed that the color red could become associated, over time, with messages of danger, caution, and avoidance. Red is the color of stop signs, stoplights, and warning signs, and teachers often use red ink or pencil to correct homework and tests. Do these associations matter for student achievement? When Elliot and his colleagues gave college students a cognitive skills test, students scored lower if their test booklets had a red paper cover rather than a green or white one. In a second study, the students solved fewer anagrams when their participant ID number was written on each page in red ink rather than green or black ink. Elliot and his co-authors thus demonstrated that using red ink or a red cover as part of a cognitive test can inhibit people's performance. In a third study, students with a red-covered test (compared with students given a green or gray one) decided to solve more of the easy problems instead of the more challenging ones. The color red apparently primes people with an "avoidance" mindset—they avoid challenges and play it safe.

Just think of the real-world applications of this study. If you were a teacher preparing a test or an employer preparing a questionnaire for job candidates, you would now know that the color of paper and ink you use can make a difference. (Chapter 9 returns to this example and explains why Elliot and his colleagues' study stands up to interrogation.)

Four Scientific Cycles

As you learn about psychological research, you will also need to understand four fundamental scientific cycles. The first cycle is a give-and-take between theory and data: Scientists test theories through research and, in turn, adapt their theories based on the data that result from that research. Second, there is a give-and-take between applied research, which directly targets real-world problems, and basic research, which is intended to contribute to the general body of knowledge. Third, psychologists write up the results of their research for other scientists, submit them to journals for review, and respond to the opinions of other scientists. Fourth, the findings of psychological research are sometimes reported in the popular media, while a scientist might be inspired by current events to begin a new line of research. Through each of these cycles, scientists become inspired to refine their ideas and create new studies. Don't let the term *cycles* mislead you into thinking that science just goes around in circles, however. The opposite is true: These cycles of feedback, application, inspiration, communication, and publication move science forward, as researchers respond to a number of forces.

The Theory-Data Cycle

The most important cycle in science is the theory-data cycle, in which scientists collect data to test, change, or update their theories. Even if you have never been in a formal research situation, you have probably tested ideas and hunches of your own by asking specific questions that are grounded in theory, making predictions, and reflecting on data.

For example, imagine you pick up your cell phone to make a call. You hit the "on" button, but nothing happens. Something is obviously wrong, but what? Of course, the battery might have died, so you plug in the phone to charge it. If your phone still is not working an hour later, you might guess that something is wrong inside the phone. At the cell phone store, the customer service representative opens the back plate, takes out your SIM card, and puts it back in. But the phone still doesn't work, so he tries to see if your SIM card works in another, brand-new phone. If that works, then the representative (and you) can conclude that your phone itself is broken. (Let's hope your phone is under warranty.)

Note the series of steps in this process. First, you asked a particular series of questions, all of which were guided by your theory about how cell phones work. The questions you asked (Is it the battery? Is it the SIM card?) reflected your theory that cell phones operate by using electrical current, which is stored in batteries, as well as by using information that is stored in SIM cards. Because you were operating under this theory, you chose not to ask other kinds of questions, such as "Has a gremlin possessed my phone?" or "Does my phone have a bacterial infection?" Your theory set up the kinds of questions you asked.

Next, your questions led you to specific predictions, which you tested by collecting data. You tested your first idea about the problem (my battery is dead) by posing a specific prediction (if I charge it, it will work again). Then you set up a situation to test your prediction (you charged the battery for a while). The data (the phone is still not working) told you that your initial prediction was wrong. You used that outcome to change your idea about the problem (it's not the battery, so maybe it's the SIM card). And so on. When you take systematic steps to solve a problem, you are doing something similar to what scientists do in the theory-data cycle.

The Contact Comfort Theory Versus the Cupboard Theory

A classic example from the psychological study of attachment can illustrate the way researchers similarly use data to test their theories. You have probably observed that animals form strong attachments to their caregivers. If you have a dog, it probably is extremely happy to see you when you come home, wagging its tail and jumping all over you. And human babies, once they are able to crawl, may follow their parents or caregivers around, keeping close to them. Baby monkeys exhibit similar behavior, spending hours clinging tightly to the mother's fur. Why do animals form such strong attachments to their caregivers?

One theory, called the "cupboard theory" of mother-infant attachment, is that a mother is valuable to a baby mammal because she is a source of food. The baby animal gets hungry, gets food from the mother by nursing, and experiences a pleasant feeling (reduced hunger). Over time, the sight of the mother is associated with pleasure. In other words, the mother acquires positive value for the baby because she is the "cupboard" from which food comes. If you have ever assumed that your dog loves you just because you feed it, your beliefs are consistent with the cupboard theory.

An alternative theory, proposed by Harry Harlow (1958), is that hunger has little to do with why a baby monkey likes to cling to the warm, fuzzy fur of its mother. Instead, babies are attached to their mothers because of the comfort of cozy touch. This theory is called the "contact comfort theory." (And it offers a less cynical view of why your dog is so happy to see you!)

In the natural world, a mother offers both food and contact comfort at once, so when the baby clings to her, it is impossible to tell why. To test the alternative theories, Harlow had to separate the two influences—food and contact comfort. And the only way he could do so was to create "mothers" of his

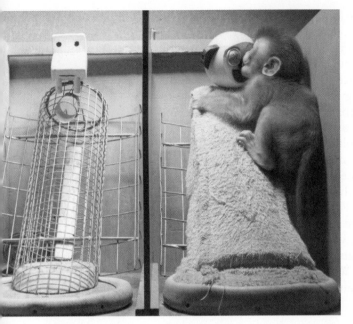

own. He built two monkey foster "mothers"—the only mothers his lab-reared baby monkeys ever had. One of the mothers was made of bare wire mesh but had a bottle of milk built in. This wire mother offered food but not comfort. The other mother was covered with fuzzy terrycloth and was warmed by a lightbulb suspended inside, but she had no milk. This cloth mother offered comfort but not food.

Note that this experiment offers three possible outcomes. The contact comfort theory would be supported if the babies spent most of their time clinging to the cloth mother. The cupboard theory would be supported if the babies spent most of their time clinging to the wire mother. And neither theory would be supported if monkeys divided their time equally between the two mothers.

FIGURE 1.3 The contact-comfort theory. Harlow's baby monkeys spent most of their time on the warm, cozy cloth mother, even though she did not provide any food.

When Harlow put the baby monkeys in the cages with the two mothers, the evidence in favor of the contact comfort theory was overwhelming. Harlow's data showed that the little monkeys would cling to the cloth mother for 12 to 18 hours a day (as shown in **Figure 1.3**). When they were hungry, they would climb down, nurse from the wire mother, and then at once go back to the warm, cozy cloth mother. In short, Harlow used the two theories to make two specific predictions about how the monkeys would interact with each mother. Then he used the data he recorded (how much time the monkeys spent on each mother) to support only one of the theories. The theory-data cycle in action!

Theory, Prediction, and Data

A **theory** is a statement, or a set of statements, that describes general principles about how variables relate to one another. For example, Harlow's theory, which he developed in light of extensive observations of primate babies and mothers, was about the overwhelming importance of bodily contact (as opposed to simple nourishment) in forming attachments. Contact comfort, not food, provided the primary basis for a baby's attachment to its mother. This theory led Harlow to investigate particular kinds of questions—he chose to pit contact comfort against food in his research. The theory meant that Harlow also chose *not* to study unrelated questions, such as the babies' food preferences or sleeping habits.

The theory not only led to the questions—it also led to specific **hypotheses**, or *predictions*, about the answers. A prediction, or hypothesis, is a way of stating the specific outcome that the researcher expects to observe if the theory is accurate. Harlow's predictions related to the way the baby monkeys would interact with two kinds of mothers. He predicted that the babies would spend more time on the cozy mother than the wire mother. Notably, a single theory can lead to a large number of predictions, because a single prediction, or hypothesis, is usually not sufficient to test the entire theory—it is intended to test only part of it. Most researchers test their theories with a series of empirical studies, each designed to test an individual hypothesis.

Finally, **data** are a set of observations. (Harlow's data were the amount of time the baby monkeys stayed with each "mother.") Depending on whether or not the data are consistent with predictions based on a theory, the data may either support or challenge the theory. Data that match the theory's predictions strengthen our confidence in the theory. But when the data do not match the theory's predictions, those results indicate that the theory needs to be revised. **Figure 1.4** shows how these steps work as a cycle.

Empiricism, also called the *empirical method* or *empirical research*, is the approach of collecting data and using it to develop, support, or challenge a theory. Empiricism involves using evidence from our senses (sight, hearing, touch) or from instruments that assist our senses (such as thermometers, timers, photographs, weight scales, questionnaires, and so on) as the basis for our conclusions. Empirical evidence is also independently verifiable by other observers or scientists. In Chapter 2, you will learn more about why empiricism is considered the most reliable basis for conclusions when compared with other forms of reasoning, such as experience or intuition.

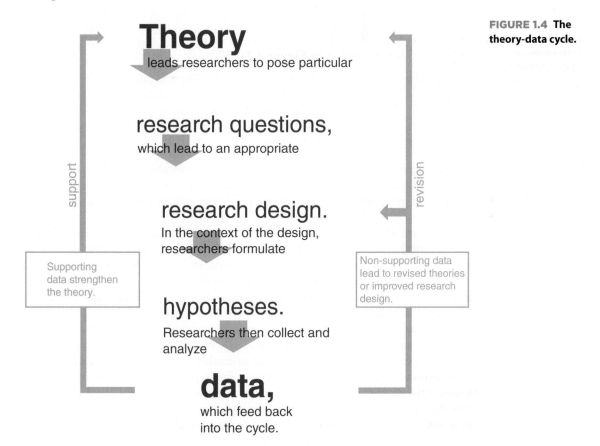

FIGURE 1.4 **The theory-data cycle.**

Theory
leads researchers to pose particular

research questions,
which lead to an appropriate

research design.
In the context of the design, researchers formulate

support

revision

Supporting data strengthen the theory.

Non-supporting data lead to revised theories or improved research design.

hypotheses.
Researchers then collect and analyze

data,
which feed back into the cycle.

What Makes a Good Theory?

In scientific practice, some theories are better than others. The best theories are supported by the data, are falsifiable, and are parsimonious.

Good Theories Are Supported by Data. The most important feature of a good theory is that it is supported by data. In this respect, the contact comfort theory of infant attachment turned out to be better than the cupboard theory, because it was supported by the data. Clearly, primate babies need food, but food is not the source of their emotional attachments to their mothers. In this way, good theories, like Harlow's, are consistent with our observations of the world. More important, scientists need to conduct multiple studies, using a variety of methods, to address different aspects of their theories. A theory that is supported by a large quantity and variety of evidence is a good theory.

Good Theories Are Falsifiable. A second important feature of a good theory is that it is **falsifiable**. That is, a theory needs to lead to predictions that, when tested, could prove to be wrong and thus challenge the theory itself. Remember that theories have to be supported by the data, but data are only useful if they can convince us that the theory is either correct or incorrect. The following unique theory may help illustrate this concept:

> I have discovered the underlying brain mechanism that controls behavior. You will soon be reading about this discovery (in the *National Enquirer*, available at your local supermarket). In the left hemisphere of the brain near the language area, reside two tiny green men. . . . [T]o make a long story short, they basically control everything. There is one difficulty, however. The green men have the ability to detect any intrusion into the brain (surgery, X-rays, etc.) and when they do sense such an intrusion, they tend to disappear (I forgot to mention that they have the power to become invisible). (Stanovich, 2010, p. 25)

Can we falsify this theory? If so, how? If we could see the little green men, that would support the theory. But if we look and we do not see the little green men, that would support the theory, too. The theory would seem to be supported either way.

Of course, the little green men example is ridiculous. Stanovich himself does not believe this theory—he invented it to make a point about falsifiability—but would anybody actually reason this way? Unfortunately, yes. In fact, some of the proponents of facilitated communication, discussed earlier in this chapter, have argued that the technique cannot be empirically tested because empirical tests introduce skepticism, which breaks down the necessary trust between the facilitator and client. Furthermore, some FC proponents assert that expressing doubt (for example, doubting that previously illiterate clients can write surprisingly complex sentences) shows a lack of faith in people with disabilities (see Twachtman-Cullen, 1997). This trust and faith, they claim, are key ingredients to FC and make FC much more difficult to test scientifically. If these claims are true, the theory behind facilitated communication is not falsifiable. In contrast, in developing a truly scientific theory, researchers must take risks. With every prediction they make, they must take the risk that their theory might not be supported.

Good Theories Are Parsimonious. A last feature of good theories is that they show **parsimony**: *All other things being equal, the simplest solution is the best* (sometimes referred to as "Occam's razor"). If two theories explain the data equally well but one is simpler, most scientists will opt for the simpler, more parsimonious theory. Stanovich's disappearing green men theory is not parsimonious, because its creatures, with their special abilities, require us to make several complex assumptions that happen to contradict most principles of physics and biology.

Parsimony sets a standard for the theory-data cycle. As long as a simple theory predicts the data well, there should be no need to make the theory more complex. Harlow's theory was parsimonious because it posed a simple explanation for infant attachment: Contact comfort drives attachment more than food does. As long as the data continue to support the simple theory, the simple theory stands. However, when the data contradict the theory, the theory has to change in order to accommodate the data. For example, over the years, psychologists have collected data showing that baby monkeys do not always form an attachment to a soft, cozy mother: If monkeys are reared in complete social isolation during their first, critical months, they seem to have problems forming attachments to anyone or anything. Thus, the contact comfort theory had to change a bit, so that it would emphasize the importance of contact comfort for attachment *in the early months of life*. The theory is slightly less parsimonious now, but it does a better job of accommodating the data.

"But That Doesn't Prove Anything"

The word *prove* is an important one. In psychology—indeed, in all of the modern sciences that rely on empiricism—researchers never say they have proved their theories. At most, they will say that some data *support* or *are consistent with* a theory, or they might say that some data *are inconsistent with* or *complicate* a theory. But no single confirming finding can prove a theory. New information might require researchers, tomorrow or the next day, to change and improve their ideas. Similarly, a single, disconfirming finding does not lead researchers to scrap a theory entirely. The disconfirming study may itself have been designed poorly. Or perhaps the theory needs to be modified, not discarded. Rather than thinking of a theory as proved or disproved by a single study, scientists evaluate their theories based on the **weight of the evidence**, for and against. Again, knowledge in psychology is intimately tied to studies: The data show what psychologists know for now, but future studies could change the weight of the empirical evidence.

The Basic-Applied Research Cycle

A second important cycle in psychological research is the reciprocity between applied research and basic research.

Applied research is done with a practical problem in mind; the researchers hope that their findings will be directly *applied* to the solution of that problem in a particular real-world context. In psychology, applied research can be about the treatment of mental disorders: The researchers may explore new treatments for depression, autism, or eating disorders. But applied psychologists might also experiment with new methods for teaching math or for evaluating teachers. Or they might be looking for better ways to identify those most at risk for depression, failing in school, or cheating. They might want to predict who is likely to do well in college or at a particular job.

Basic research, in contrast, is not intended to address a specific, practical problem. The goal of basic research is simply to enhance the general body of knowledge. Basic researchers might want to understand the structure of the visual system, the capacity of the human memory, the motivations of a depressed person, or the limitations of the infant attachment system. Because basic research does not always address real-world problems directly, it might not seem as important as applied research. But basic researchers do not just gather facts at random, and the knowledge they generate may be applied to real-world issues later on. A better understanding of the unimpaired human memory system could translate into treatments for memory disorders such as Alzheimer's disease or into techniques to improve the memory of children with ADHD. In most cases, solid basic research is an important basis for later, applied studies.

Applied and basic research can be difficult to distinguish. Elliot and his colleagues' studies on how the color red affects people's performance is one example of the blurry line between applied and basic research. Is this an example of an applied or a basic study? On the one hand, this research was an extension of the finding that avoidance goals (such as trying not to fail) usually inhibit people's achievement, whereas approach goals (trying to succeed) usually enhance people's achievement. In this respect, Elliot's study was basic research on this principle, because it merely found that the color red stimulates an avoidance goal. On the other hand, these studies are quite easy to apply to any real-world situation in which achievement is being tested.

Applied and basic research questions not only overlap but often influence each other as well: Basic research inspires applied research, and vice versa (see **Figure 1.5**). Elliot's basic research on approach and avoidance goals has also shown that approach and avoidance orientations can lead to different kinds of moods. Other researchers have applied this knowledge by developing a therapy that teaches depressed people to reframe their avoidance goals into approach goals (Strauman et al., 2006), which seems to work well for some depressed people. When researchers conduct studies in which they are intentionally using lessons from basic research to develop and test applications to health care, psychotherapy, or other interventions, they are doing **translational research**. Translational research represents a dynamic bridge from basic to applied research.

Applied research can also inform and inspire basic research. For example, more than a century ago, the education researcher Alfred Binet faced the applied problem of predicting which children needed extra help in school. He developed a test that would measure each child's abilities, relative to his or her classmates'—the first IQ (intelligence quotient) test (Gould, 1981). Although Binet's test was developed to solve an applied, real-world problem, it spawned decades of basic

FIGURE 1.5 **The basic-applied cycle.** Basic research on the visual system expands general knowledge, which might later be used in applied settings, for example, to improve vision.

research (and much debate) on the measurement and nature of intelligence. For example, because this early test focused on school-related behaviors, later IQ researchers tended to neglect other aspects of intelligence, such as social skills or creativity.

The Peer-Review Cycle

When scientists want to tell the scientific world about the results of their research, whether basic or applied, they write a paper and submit it to a scientific **journal**. Scientific journals are like magazines—they usually come out every month and contain articles written by various contributors. But unlike popular newsstand magazines, the articles in a scientific journal are *peer-reviewed*. That is, when an editor receives a manuscript, the editor sends it to three or four experts on the subject. The experts tell the editor about the manuscript's virtues and flaws, and the editor decides whether the paper deserves to be published in the journal.

The peer-review process is usually extremely rigorous in psychology. Peer reviewers are kept anonymous, so even if they know the author professionally or personally, they can feel free to give an honest assessment of the research. They comment on how interesting the work is, how novel it is, how well the research was done, and how clear the results are. Ultimately, peer reviewers are the gatekeepers for quality science. They ensure that the articles that are published in scientific journals contain novel, well-done studies. If the peer-review process works, research with major flaws does not get published. And even if the work is acceptable, peer reviewers point out minor flaws so that the author can correct them before the journal publishes the paper.

In some cases, the peer-review cycle ends after one rotation: A scientist writes a manuscript, the peer reviewers find irreconcilable flaws, and the paper is never published. In most cases, however, it is a true cycle: Peer reviewers ask for revisions, and the scientist responds, revises the paper, perhaps collects more data, and submits it again. If the paper has improved enough, the editor will decide to publish it.

The Journal-to-Journalism Cycle

One goal of this textbook is to teach you how to interrogate information about psychological science that you find not only in journals but also in more mainstream sources that you encounter in daily life. The fourth cycle, the journal-to-journalism cycle, is especially important in this context.

Scientific journals are read primarily by other scientists and by psychology students; the general public almost never reads them. **Journalism**, in contrast, includes the kinds of news and commentary that most of us read or hear on television, in magazines and newspapers, and on Internet sites—articles in *Psychology Today* and *Men's Health*, topical blogs, relationship advice columns, and so on. These sources are usually written by journalists or laypeople, not scientists, and they are meant to reach the general public; they are easy to access and do not require specialized education to read.

Of course, part of the journal-to-journalism cycle occurs when scientists find inspiration or ideas for a new topic of study in current events that they read about in the media. But it is more important to focus here on the other end of the journal-to-journalism cycle—how the news media cover the latest scientific findings. A journalist might become interested in a scientific study by reading the latest issue of a scientific journal or by hearing scientists talk about their work at a scientific conference. The journalist turns the research into a news story by summarizing it for a popular audience, giving it an interesting headline, and writing about it using nontechnical terms. For example, Elliot and his colleagues' article on the color red and achievement was summarized in an online magazine called *World Science* ("Seeing red affects achievement," 2007) and on a science blog ("Seeing red," 2007).

Benefits and Risks of the Journal-to-Journalism Cycle

It can be beneficial for psychologists when journalists publicize their research. By reading about psychological research in the newspaper, the general public can learn what psychologists really do. Those who read or hear the story might also pick up important tips for living: They might understand their children or themselves better; they might set different goals or change their habits. These important benefits of science writing depend on two things, however. First, journalists need to report on the most important scientific stories, and second, journalists need to describe the research accurately (see **Figure 1.6**).

Is the Story Important? When journalists report on a study, have they chosen research that has been conducted rigorously, that tests an important question, and that has been peer-reviewed? Or have they chosen a study simply because it is vivid and eye-catching? Sometimes journalists do select the important stories, especially when they cover research that has already been published in a selective, peer-reviewed journal. But sometimes journalists choose the sensational story over the important one. For example, a few years ago, a story about whether parents buckled their children into shopping carts hit the science headlines (Bakalar, 2005). The study found that "cute" children were more likely to be buckled into shopping carts than "ugly" children. Of course, this story was ripe for

FIGURE 1.6 The journal-to-journalism cycle. Cartoonist Jorge Cham parodies what can happen when journalists report on scientific research. An original study reported a relationship between two variables. Although the University Public Relations Office reports the story accurately, the story is exaggerated over time. Both the strength of the relationship and its implications become distorted with multiple retellings, much like a game of "telephone."

public consumption—it was shocking, easy to understand, and even a little funny. The original newspaper story was picked up by many other science columns on the Internet, and no doubt many people read it and discussed it around the watercooler that day. However, the original study had been presented only at a local conference and had not been peer-reviewed. Its importance, methods, and conclusions had not yet been assessed by scientists in the field. Indeed, years later, this study has yet to be published in a scientific journal.

Is the Story Accurate? Even when journalists report on reliable, important research, they do not always get the story right. Some science writers do an excellent, accurate job of summarizing the research, but not all of them do. Perhaps the journalist does not have the scientific training, the motivation, or the time before deadline to understand the original science very well. Perhaps the journalist dumbs down the details of a study to make it more accessible to a general audience.

Media coverage of a phenomenon called the "Mozart effect" provides an example of how journalists might misrepresent science when they write for a popular audience (Spiegel, 2010). In 1993, researcher Frances Rauscher found that when students heard Mozart music played for 10 minutes, they performed better on a subsequent spatial intelligence test when compared with students who had listened to silence or to a monotone speaking voice (Rauscher, Shaw, & Ky, 1993). Rauscher said in a radio interview, "What we found was that the students who had listened to the Mozart Sonata scored significantly higher on the spatial temporal task." However, Rauscher added, "It's very important to note that we did not find effects for general intelligence . . . just for this one aspect of intelligence. It's a small gain and it doesn't last very long" (Spiegel, 2010). But despite the careful way the scientist described the results, the media that reported on the story exaggerated its importance:

> The headlines in the papers were less subtle than her findings: "Mozart makes you smart" was the general idea. . . . But worse, says Rauscher, was that her very modest finding started to be wildly distorted. "Generalizing these results to children is one of the first things that went wrong. Somehow or another the myth started exploding that children that listen to classical music from a young age will do better on the SAT, they'll score better on intelligence tests in general, and so forth." (Spiegel, 2010)

FIGURE 1.7

The Mozart effect. Journalists sometimes misrepresent or exaggerate research findings. Exaggerated reports of the "Mozart effect" even inspired a line of consumer products for children.

Perhaps because the media distorted the effects of that first study, a small industry sprang up, recording child-friendly sonatas for parents and teachers (such as those shown in **Figure 1.7**). However, according to research conducted since that first study, the effect of listening to Mozart on people's intelligence test scores is not very strong and applies to most music, not just Mozart (Pietschnig, Voracek, & Formann, 2010).

The journalist Ben Goldacre has cataloged many examples of how his fellow journalists misrepresent science when they write about it for a popular audience. One example comes from a happiness survey of 5,000 people in the United Kingdom. Local journalists picked up on tiny city-to-city differences, creating headlines about how the city of Edinburgh is the "most miserable place in the country" or writing stories about the unhappy citizens of Basingstoke. But none of the journalists mentioned one important detail in their stories: The differences the survey found between the various places were not statistically significant (Goldacre, 2008). That is, even though there were slight differences in happiness from Edinburgh to London, the differences were small enough to be caused by random variation. Goldacre spoke to the researcher who conducted the study, who said, "I tried to explain issues of [statistical] significance to the journalists who interviewed me. Most did not want to know."

Check Your Understanding

1. What happens to a theory when the data do not support the theory's predictions? What happens to a theory when the data do support the theory's predictions?
2. Explain the difference between basic research and applied research, and describe how the two interact.
3. Describe the peer-review cycle in your own words.
4. What are two ways that journalists might distort the science they attempt to publicize?

1. See the discussion of Harlow's monkey experiment on pp. 9–10 and p. 11. 2. See pp. 13–14. 3. See p. 15. 4. See pp. 16–19.

Summary

Thinking like a psychologist means thinking like a scientist, and thinking like a scientist involves thinking about empirical data. Whether you plan to be a research producer or a research consumer, you will benefit from learning to ask good questions about what you encounter and learning to evaluate what the research has to say in response.

Psychological researchers participate in four cycles. The most important is the theory-data cycle, in which researchers posit theories, make predictions, and collect data. In turn, data lead scientists to change, challenge, and even reject their theories. A good theory must be supported by the data, must be parsimonious, and must be falsifiable—that is, the data could either support or challenge the theory. Because science is progressive, incremental, and evidence based, the word *prove* is not generally used in scientific discourse. Instead, a researcher might say that a theory is *well supported* or *well established*, meaning that most of the data have confirmed the theory and very little have disconfirmed it.

In the basic-applied research cycle, some researchers work on applied, real-world questions, and others work for basic understanding. Not only do basic and applied research sometimes overlap, but applied questions inspire basic research and basic research can lead to applied solutions for real-world problems.

The peer-review cycle is part of the process of scientific communication. Scientists publish their research in journals, but first their papers are reviewed by experts in the field. Often the peer-review process leads scientists to sharpen their thinking and improve their communication.

Finally, in the journal-to-journalism cycle, writers for the popular media try to translate scientific studies into everyday language. It takes time, training, and effort to get the story straight, and journalists do not always pull it off. Think critically about what you read in the papers, and when in doubt, go right to the original source—peer-reviewed research.

Key Terms

applied research, p. 13
basic research, p. 14
data, p. 11
empiricism, p. 11
falsifiable, p. 12
hypotheses, p. 10

journal, p. 15
journalism, p. 16
parsimony, p. 13
theory, p. 10
translational research, p. 14
weight of the evidence, p. 13

 **NEED HELP STUDYING?**
wwnorton.com/studyspace

Visit StudySpace to access free review materials such as:

- Diagnostic Review Quizzes
- Study Outlines

Learning Actively

1. Interview a teacher, social worker, or businessperson about the role of educational, psychological, or marketing research in their careers. Does this practitioner read research as part of his or her job? If so, what kind of research? Does he or she read the research online, in a journal, or in the popular press? Ask the person to give an example of a way that research has changed the way he or she works. Does this practitioner ever follow the empirical process as part of his or her job? (Be ready to explain the empirical process for your interviewee.) Ask for an example of a time when he or she collected and used data for work. (Later, you could share the stories with classmates.)

2. Ask a professor or graduate student in your department about a recent experience with peer review. What critiques did the peer reviewers make? Was the paper accepted or rejected? How did the peer-review process affect the content or format of the original paper?

3. Look for some articles about psychology in a popular newspaper or magazine. You might check Internet sources such as msnbc.com or *Science News Daily*, or magazines such as *Psychology Today* or *Scientific American Mind*. Are the stories you find there important ones? Do they appear to report on peer-reviewed research or on "hot" topics that may be less accepted scientifically? Give an example from the journalist's article that demonstrates what the journalist used to write the story: Did the journalist read the original source (perhaps quoting from the article)? Did the journalist interview the author of the paper (perhaps quoting from a conversation with the author)? Did the journalist copy the story from another journalist (the journalist quotes only from other popular media sources)?

4. Develop a theory about people's behavior in a domain that you know a lot about (Examples of domains might include soccer, reality television, lifeguards, fraternity or sorority life, Asian American cultures, restaurants, or babysitting.) Then, develop a theory about people's behavior in a domain that you do not know a lot about. Notice what guides your theory development: Which theory was guided most by data you have observed? Which theory was more guided by intuitions? Use the theory–data cycle to reflect on how data inform theory development. Which theory—the one you developed in your area of expertise, or the one you developed in an area you don't know much about—do you think is more likely to be supported by empirical research?

5. Harlow's study of attachment in baby monkeys is an example of basic research. Brainstorm some applied research questions that this basic research study might generate. Start by identifying some of the domains to which you might apply these findings (such as education, parenting, or health care), and then give a specific (applied) research question for each domain.

Does Venting Anger Feed or Extinguish the Flame?

(Personality and Social Psychology Bulletin, 2002)

The Case for Bottling Up Rage

(Psychology Today, 1973)

2

Sources of Information: Evaluating, Finding, and Reading Information

Learning Objectives

A year from now, you should still be able to:

1. Understand why psychologists value research-based information over information based on experience, intuition, or authority.
2. Know where to find research-based information and how to read it.

When the question "How can a person release built-up tension, anger, and stress in a healthy way?" was posted on the website Answerbag.com, users chimed in with advice. A few people suggested channeling anger by attacking household cleaning and chores. Many suggested exercising. Others mentioned "tackling the problem at its source" by talking through, accepting, or modifying the problem. A few recommended screaming, breaking dishes, hitting a punching bag, or even playing violent video games like Grand Theft Auto: "The senseless killing on the game makes you feel much better" (Answerbag.com, 2005).

You might be thinking that different people handle anger in their own way, so all of these answers can be right and all of them can be wrong, depending on the person. In fact, all of the answers posted on this website are based on the individual writers' personal experiences. But is it accurate to base your conclusions on your own personal experience or on the personal experience of others?

This chapter discusses three sources of evidence for people's beliefs—experience, intuition, and authority—and compares them to a superior source of evidence: *empirical research*. The chapter focuses on a particular type of response to the

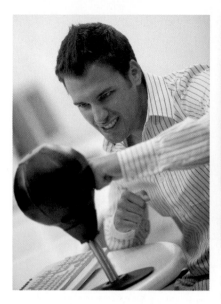

FIGURE 2.1 **Anger management.** Some people believe that venting physically or playing violent video games is the best way to work through anger, but what does the research suggest?

question about handling anger: the idea of cathartically releasing pent-up anger and tension by hitting a punching bag, screaming, or playing a violent video game (see **Figure 2.1**). Is catharsis a healthy way to deal with feelings of anger and frustration? Does hitting a punching bag make your anger go away? How could you find credible research on this subject if you wanted to read about it? And why should you trust the conclusions of the research instead of those based on your own experience and intuition?

The Research Versus Your Experience

When we need to decide what to believe, our own experiences are powerful sources of information. "Who says tanning beds are bad for you? I've used them for 10 years. No skin cancer yet!" "This energy drink really works! My attention span is much better after I have one." "When I'm mad, I feel so much better after I hit the punching bag." Often, too, we base our opinions on the experiences of friends and family. For instance, imagine you are considering buying a new car. You want the best repair record you can get, so after consulting *Consumer Reports*, you decide on a Honda Accord, because the reports of 1,000 Accord owners indicate that the repair history for that car is excellent. But then your father reminds you that the worst car he ever owned was a Honda Accord.

Why *shouldn't* we trust our own experience—or that of someone we know and trust—as a source of information? After all, who knows us better than we know ourselves?

Compared to What?

There are many reasons not to base beliefs solely on personal experience, but perhaps the most important is that when we do so, we usually do not take a **comparison group** into account. A comparison group enables you to compare what would happen both with *and without* the thing you are interested in—both with and without tanning beds, energy drinks, or punching bags. Here's a disturbing example of why a comparison group is so important: Centuries ago, Dr. Benjamin Rush drained blood from people's wrists or ankles as part of a "bleeding," or bloodletting, cure for illness (Eisenberg, 1977; see also **Figure 2.2**). The practice emerged from the belief that too much blood was the cause of illness, particularly yellow fever. To restore an "appropriate" balance, a doctor might remove up to 100 ounces of blood from a patient over the course of a week. Of course, we now know that draining blood is one of the last things a doctor would want to do to a sick patient. Why did Dr. Rush keep on using such a practice? Why did he believe that bleeding was a cure?

In those days, a doctor who used the bleeding cure would have noticed that some of his patients recovered and some died. That was the doctor's personal experience. Indeed, every time a patient recovered from yellow fever after bleeding, it *seemed* to support Rush's theory that bleeding worked. And what if a patient died after being bled? The death of the patient was regrettable, but it posed no problem for Rush's theory: The patient was too sick to recover and would have died anyway. Part of the problem here is that the doctor's theory was not *falsifiable*. (He was right if the patient recovered and still right if the patient died.) But another problem was that Dr. Rush never set up a systematic comparison.

To test the bleeding cure, doctors would have to systematically count death rates among patients who were bled versus those who received some comparison treatment (or no treatment). How many people were bled and how many were not? Of each group, how many died and how many recovered? Putting all the records together, the doctors could have come to an empirically derived conclusion about the effectiveness of bloodletting.

For example, what if Dr. Rush had kept records and found that 20 patients who were bled recovered, and 10 patients who refused the bleeding treatment recovered? At first, it might look like the bleeding cure worked; after all, twice as many bled patients as

FIGURE 2.2 Bloodletting in the eighteenth century. Describe how Dr. Rush's faulty attention to information led him to believe that bloodletting therapy was effective.

TABLE 2.1

	Bled	Not bled
Number of patients who recovered	20	10
Number of patients who died	80	40
(Number recovered divided by total number of patients)	20/100	10/50
Percentage recovered	20%	20%

TABLE 2.2

	Bled	Not bled
Number of patients who recovered	20	10
Number of patients who died	80	1
(Number recovered divided by total number of patients)	20/100	10/11
Percentage recovered	20%	91%

TABLE 2.3

	Bled	Not bled
Number of patients who recovered	20	10
Number of patients who died	80	490
(Number recovered divided by total number of patients)	20/100	10/500
Percentage recovered	20%	2%

untreated patients improved. But you need to know all of the numbers—the numbers of bled patients who died and the number of untreated patients who died, in addition to the number of patients in each group who recovered. In order to compare all of these numbers, you might find it helpful to create a table, or matrix, that looks something like **Table 2.1**. If you consider all four cells (or boxes) in Table 2.1, you will see that there is no relationship at all between treatment and improvement. Although twice as many bled patients as untreated patients recovered, twice as many bled patients as untreated patients died, too. If we calculate the percentages, the recovery rate among people who were bled was 20%, and the recovery rate among people who were not treated was also 20%: The proportions are identical. (Keep in mind that all of these data are invented for the purposes of illustration; doctors did not make systematic comparisons like this back in the 1700s.)

To make this comparison, we needed to know the values in all four cells of the table, including the number of untreated patients who died. **Table 2.2** shows an example of what might happen if the value in only that cell changes. In this case, the number of untreated patients who died is much lower, so the treatment is shown to have a *negative* effect. Only 20% of the treated patients recovered, compared with 91% of the untreated patients. In contrast, if the number in the fourth cell were increased drastically, as in **Table 2.3**, the treatment would be shown to have a *positive* effect. The recovery rate among bled patients is still 20%, but the recovery rate among untreated patients is a mere 2%.

Notice that in all these tables, we changed the number in only one cell and came up with dramatically different results. To draw conclusions about a treatment—whether the bleeding treatment, ways of venting anger, or a new energy drink—we need to compare data systematically from all four cells: the treated/improved cell, the treated/unimproved cell, the untreated/improved cell, and the untreated/unimproved cell. These comparison cells give us the relative rate of improvement of using the treatment, compared with no treatment.

Personal Experience Has No Comparison Group

Because Dr. Rush bled every yellow fever patient, he never had the chance to see how many patients would recover without the bleeding treatment. Similarly, when we rely on personal experience to decide what is true, we usually do not have a systematic comparison group because we are observing only one "patient": ourselves. The energy drink you have been using may seem to be working, but what would have happened to your attention *without* the drink? Perhaps your attention would have improved anyway, as you became a better student. Or you might think that playing the video game Grand Theft Auto makes you feel better when you're angry, but would you have felt better anyway, even if you had played a nonviolent game? What if you had done nothing and just let a little time pass?

Basing conclusions on personal experience is problematic because life often does not offer a comparison experience. In contrast, basing conclusions on systematic data collection has the simple but tremendous advantage of providing a comparison group. Only a systematic comparison can show you whether your attention improves when you have a special energy drink (compared with when you do not), or whether your anger goes away when you play violent games (compared with doing nothing).

Experience Is Confounded

Another problem with basing conclusions on personal experience is that in everyday life, too much is going on at once. That is, even if a change has occurred, we often cannot be sure what caused it. When a patient bled by Dr. Rush got better, that patient might also have been trying other treatments—eating special foods, drinking more fluids. Which one caused the improvement? When you notice a difference in your attention span after trying a new energy drink, you might also have had a good night's sleep or tried some new study strategies at the same time. Which one caused your attention to improve? If you play Grand Theft Auto, it certainly provides violent content, but you might also be distracting yourself from your anger or increasing your heart rate. Is it these factors or the game's violence that causes you to feel better after playing it?

In the real world, there are often several possible explanations for any outcome. In research, these alternative explanations are called **confounds**. Essentially, a confound occurs when you think one thing caused an outcome but in fact other things changed, too, so it is not clear what the cause really was. You might think that the energy drink improved your attention span, but since you were also getting extra rest and using better study strategies, you do not know which of these factors (or which combination of factors) caused the improvement.

What can we do about confounds like these? In the real world, it is hard to isolate variables. Think about the last time you were sick to your stomach—which of the many things you ate that day made you sick? Or those allergies you have in the spring—which of the blossoming spring plants are you allergic to? However, in a research setting, scientists can use careful controls to be sure they are changing only one factor at a time. Chapter 9 goes into more detail about confounds and about how to avoid them in research design.

Controlled Research Is Better Than Experience

What happens when scientists do set up a systematic comparison that controls for potential confounds? For example, by using controlled, systematic comparisons, several groups of researchers have tested the hypothesis that venting anger is beneficial. (See, for example, Berkowitz, 1973; Bushman, Baumeister, & Phillips, 2001; Feshbach, 1956; Lohr, Olatunji, Baumeister, & Bushman, 2007.) One such study was conducted by researcher Brad Bushman (2002). To examine the effect of venting, or *catharsis*, Bushman systematically compared what happened if angry people were allowed to vent their anger with what happened if angry people did not vent their anger. First, Bushman needed to make people angry. He invited 600 undergraduate students to arrive, one by one, to a laboratory setting, where each student wrote a political essay. Next, each essay was shown to another person, called Steve (actually a **confederate**, an actor playing a specific role for the experimenter), who insulted the essay calling it "the worst essay I've ever read" and delivering other unflattering comments. (Bushman knew that this technique made students angry because he had used it in previous studies, in which students whose essays were insulted had reported feeling angrier than students whose essays were not insulted.) Next, Bushman randomly divided the angry students into three groups, designed to systematically compare the effect of venting anger to not venting it. Group 1 was instructed to sit quietly in the room for 2 minutes. Group 2 was instructed to punch a punching bag for 2 minutes, having been told it was a form of exercise. Group 3 was instructed to punch a punching bag for 2 minutes while imagining Steve's face on it. (This was the important catharsis group.) Finally, all three groups of students were given a chance to get back at Steve. In the course of playing a quiz game with him, students had the chance to blast Steve's ears with a loud noise. (However, they only thought they were blasting Steve's ears; since Steve was a confederate, he did not actually experience these noise blasts.)

Which group gave Steve the loudest, longest blasts of noise? The catharsis hypothesis predicts that Group 3 should have calmed down the most, and as a result, this group should not have blasted Steve with very much noise. But in fact, this group gave Steve the loudest noise blasts of all! Compared with the other two groups, those who expressed their anger at Steve through the punching bag continued to punish him when they had the chance. (**Figure 2.3** shows the results in the form of a graph.) In contrast, Group 2, those who hit the punching bag for exercise, subjected him to less noise (it was not as loud and did not last as long). And those who sat quietly for 2 minutes punished Steve the least of all. So much for the cathar-sis hypothesis. When the scientists set up the comparison groups, they found that the opposite was true: People's an-ger will subside more quickly if they just sit in a room quietly than if they try to vent it.

Notice the power of systematic comparison here. In a controlled study scientists can set up the condi-tions such that they include at least one comparison group and avoid con-founds. Compare the scientist's larger view with more subjective views, in which each person consults only his or her own experience. That is, if you had asked some of the students in Group 3 whether using the punching bag helped their anger subside, these participants could only consider their own, idiosyncratic experiences. But when Bushman looked at the pattern overall—taking into account all three groups—the results indicated that Group 3 still felt the angriest.

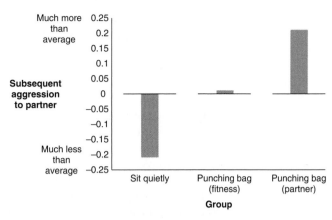

FIGURE 2.3 The results of Bushman's (2002) study on catharsis. After Steve insulted all the students, those in Group 1 sat quietly for two minutes, those in Group 2 hit a punching bag while think-ing about exercise, and those in Group 3 hit a punching bag while imagining Steve's face on it. Later, students in all three groups had the chance to blast Steve with loud noise. *Source*: Adapted from Bushman (2002, Table 1).

Scientists can also control for potential confounds. In Bushman's study, all three groups felt equally angry at first. Bushman even separated the effects of ag-gression only (using the punching bag for exercise) from the effects of aggression toward the person who made you mad (using the punching bag as a stand-in for Steve). In real life, these two effects—exercise and the expression of anger—would usually occur at the same time.

Of course, Bushman's study is only one example of research on catharsis. In other studies, researchers have made people angry, presented those people with an opportunity to vent their anger (or not), and then watched their be-havior. Over and over again, researchers have found that people who physi-cally express their anger at a target actually become *more* angry than when they started—practicing aggression just seems to teach people how to be aggressive (Berkowitz, 1973; Bushman et al., 2001; Feshbach, 1956; Geen & Quanty, 1977; Lohr et al., 2007; Tavris, 1989). The important point is that the results of a single study, such as Bushman's, are certainly better evidence than experience. And consistent results from several similar studies mean that scientists will feel confident in the findings. Furthermore, as more and more studies amass evidence on the subject, *theories* about how people can effectively regulate their anger will gain more and more support.

For more on the importance of replication, see Chapter 13, pp. 377–385.

"But My Experience Is Different"

Although research is usually more reliable than individual experience, sometimes our personal stories contradict the research results. Personal experience is powerful, and we often let a single experience distract us from the lessons of more rigorous research. But should you disagree with a study when your own experience is different? Should you continue to play Grand Theft Auto when you are angry because you believe it works for you? Should you disregard *Consumer Reports* when your father's experience with a Honda Accord was terrible?

At times, your experience (or your aunt's, or your father's) may be an exception to what the research finds. The question is, should that exception undermine the general research results? Not at all. Behavioral research is **probabilistic**, which means that inferences are not expected to explain all cases all of the time. Instead, the conclusions of research are meant to explain a certain proportion (preferably a high proportion) of the possible cases. In practice, this means that scientific conclusions are based on patterns that emerge only when researchers set up comparison groups and test many people. Your own experience is only one point in that overall pattern. So even though bleeding does not cure yellow fever, some sick patients did recover after being bled. However, those exceptional patients who recovered do not change the conclusion derived from all of the data. And even though your father's Honda did not run well, his case becomes only one of 1,001 Honda owners, so it does not invalidate the general trend. Similarly, just because there is a strong general trend (that Hondas are generally reliable), it does not mean that your Honda will be reliable too. The research may suggest that there is a *strong probability* that your Honda will be reliable, but the prediction is not perfect.

Check Your Understanding

1. What are two general problems with basing belief on experience? How does empirical research work to correct these problems?

1. See pp. 25–29.

The Research Versus Your Intuition

Personal experience is one way that we often reach conclusions. Another is intuition. People certainly think that intuition is a good source of information, but intuition can lead us to make less effective decisions. Why? The answer is simple: We are biased. (You will probably agree that other people are biased. But you? No way!) When we do not pay attention, certain biases of intuition can sneak up on us and we do not even notice. Other times, we might be aware that we have the potential to be biased, but we are too busy or not motivated enough to correct and control for these biases.

Biases of intuition fall roughly into two categories: thinking the easy way and thinking what we want to think. The more you practice applying scientific principles, the more you can guard against the pull of these biases and the better decisions you will make.

Thinking the Easy Way

At times, intuition is biased because some ideas are simply easier to believe than others, and some information comes to mind more readily than other information. It is easier to believe a "good story" than a more complicated or unfamiliar one, and it is easier to pay more attention to memorable events and harder to attend to everyday events.

The Good Story

One basic example of thinking the easy way is when we accept a conclusion just because it "makes sense." For example, to many people, bottling up negative emotions seems unhealthy, so expressing anger makes better sense. As with a skin abscess or a boiling kettle of water, it might seem better to release the pressure. In fact, one of the early proponents of catharsis was the neurologist Sigmund Freud, whose models of mental distress focused on the harmful effects of suppressing one's feelings and the benefits of releasing them. Some biographers (e.g., Gay, 1989) have speculated that Freud's ideas were influenced by the steam engines and the industrial technology of his day. Engines back then used the power of steam to create vast amounts of energy. If the steam was too compressed, it could have devastating effects on a machine. Freud seems to have reasoned that the human psyche functions the same way. Catharsis makes sense as a process, because it draws on a metaphor (steam) that was, and still is, familiar to most people.

Here's another "good story" that turned out to be wrong. Stomach ulcers were once thought to be caused by stress and excess stomach acid. Doctors treated ulcers with antacid medications and counseled patients with ulcers to avoid acidic foods such as hot sauce or carbonated drinks. Their intuition makes sense, doesn't it? Ulcers feel "hot" and they look a lot like burns. Ulcers seem to get worse when people are under stress. So it seems right to treat them with calming, antacid treatments. However, this intuition about "hot" ulcers was wrong. In fact, this approach to treatment probably delayed the discovery of the true cause of many ulcers: a bacterium called *H. pylori* (Marshall & Warren, 1983, 1984). As it turns out, common antibiotics can cure a stomach ulcer. So much for that hot story. (The real story was so important that the doctors who discovered it were awarded the Nobel Prize in Medicine in 2005.)

Sometimes a "good story" will turn out to be accurate, of course. But you should be aware of the limitations of common sense. When empirical evidence contradicts what your common sense tells you, be ready to adjust your beliefs on the basis of what you learn. Thinking the easy way is not necessarily the most accurate way.

The Present/Present Bias

In the story "Silver Blaze," the fictional detective Sherlock Holmes investigates the theft of a prize racehorse. The horse was stolen at night while two stable hands and their dog slept, undisturbed, nearby. Holmes reflects on the dog's "curious" behavior that night. When the other inspectors protest that "the dog did nothing in the night-time," Holmes replies, "That was the curious incident." Because the dog did *not* bark, Holmes deduces that the horse was stolen by someone familiar to the dog at the stable (Doyle, 1892/2002, p. 149; see Gilbert, 2005). Holmes solves the crime because he notices the *absence* of something.

For most of us, though, it is very hard to look for absences; in contrast, it is easy to notice what is present. This tendency, which can be called the **present/present bias**, is related to the need for comparison groups discussed earlier in the chapter. Dr. Rush may have fallen prey to the present/present bias when he was observing the effects of bleeding on his patients. He focused on patients who did receive the treatment and did recover (the cell in which treatment was "present" and the recovery was also "present"). He did not fully take into effect the *un*treated patients or those who did *not* recover (for example, the cell in which treatment was "absent" and recovery was also "absent").

Similarly, regarding the best way to handle anger, the present/present bias means that we will easily notice the times we did express frustrations at the gym, at the dog, or in traffic and subsequently felt better. That is, we notice the times when both the treatment (catharsis) and the desired outcome (feeling better) are present. But we are less likely to notice the times when we did not express our anger and still felt better—when the treatment was absent but the outcome was still present. **Table 2.4** shows the various possibilities. If we think the easy way and focus only on experiences that fall in the present/present cell, we would notice the five instances in which catharsis seemed to work. But if we think harder and look at the whole picture, we would conclude that catharsis does not work well at all.

The Pop-Up Principle

Another example of thinking the easy way is the **pop-up principle**, formally known as the *availability heuristic* (Tversky & Kahneman, 1974), which states that things that easily come to mind tend to guide our thinking. When events or memories are vivid, recent, or memorable, they seem more correct and therefore bias our thinking.

TABLE 2.4 The Present/Present Bias

	Expressed frustration (treatment present)	Did nothing (treatment absent)
Felt better (outcome present)	5 Present/present	10 Absent/present
Felt worse (outcome absent)	10 Present/absent	5 Absent/absent

Note: The number in each cell represents the number of times the two events coincided. We are more likely to focus on the times when two factors were both present or two events occurred at the same time (the shaded present/present cell), rather than on the full pattern of our experiences.

For example, give a quick, intuitive answer to this question before reading on: Which is more frequent—death by falling or death by fire? Most people think death by fire is more common, but death by falling is far more frequent (6 per 100,000 deaths by falling versus 1.5 per 100,000 deaths by fire; Ropeik & Gray, 2002). Why do people make this mistake? Deaths by fire are quite memorable and are more likely to be reported in the news, so they come to mind more easily and we inflate the risk associated with them. In contrast, deaths by falling seldom get much press. But if we think harder about the difference between falls and fires, we would realize that a large number of falling deaths probably occur among elderly people. Often we are too busy (or too lazy) to think beyond the easy answer. We decide that the answer that came to mind easily must be the correct one.

The psychologist Dan Gilbert (2005) describes another example of the pop-up principle: getting stuck in the slow line at the grocery store. Does it seem to you, as it does to me, that you always end up in the line with the slowest cashier, or behind the shopper with all the coupons or the one writing a check? We draw this conclusion because it is easy to notice the times when we are in the slow line, but we never seem to think, "Wow, this line is moving so quickly today!" Because the negative events pop into mind more easily than times when things have gone smoothly, we might conclude that we are exceptionally unlucky shoppers. Thinking the easy way can mean taking our first thoughts as the most correct thoughts.

Thinking What We Want

When we think the easy way, we draw the wrong conclusions because it is easier to notice things that make a good story, that are salient, or that come easily to mind. Sometimes, however, we do not *want* to challenge our preconceived ideas: We simply think what we want to think.

Cherry-Picking the Evidence

Most of us like to feel as if we understand things, but we do not like to rethink our ideas once we have them. Sometimes we are biased information gatherers because we simply do not want to let go of our beliefs. We therefore tend to "cherry-pick" the information we take in—seeking and accepting only the evidence that supports what we already think and what we want to think.

One study specifically showed how people cherry-pick the evidence. The participants took an IQ test and then were told that their IQ was either high or low. Shortly afterward, all the participants had a chance to look at some magazine articles about IQ tests. The participants who were told that their IQ was low spent more time looking at articles that *criticized* the validity of IQ tests, whereas those who were told that their IQ was high spent more time looking at articles that *supported* IQ tests as valid measures of intelligence (Frey & Stahlberg, 1986). They all wanted to think they were smart, so they analyzed the available information in biased ways that supported this belief. People keep their beliefs intact (in this case, the motivated belief that they are smart) by selecting only the kinds of evidence they want to see.

Asking Biased Questions

Another way we enable ourselves to think what we want is by asking questions that are likely to give the desired or expected answers. Take, for example, a study by Snyder and Swann (1978), who asked students to interview fellow undergraduates. Half of the students were given the goal of deciding whether their target person was extraverted, and the other half were given the goal of deciding whether their target person was introverted.

Before the interview, the students selected their interview questions from a prepared list. As it turned out, when the students were trying to find out whether their target was extraverted, they chose to ask questions such as "What would you do if you wanted to liven things up at a party?" and "What kind of situations do you seek out if you want to meet new people?" You can see the problem here: Even introverts will look like extraverts when they answer questions like these. The students were asking questions that would tend to confirm that their targets were extraverted. The same thing happened with the group of students who were trying to find out if their target was introverted: They chose to ask questions such as "In what situations do you wish you could be more outgoing?" and "What factors make it hard for you to really open up to people?" Again, in responding to these questions, wouldn't just about anybody seem introverted? Indeed, when the students asked these questions, targets gave answers that supported the interviewers' expectations. Snyder and Swann asked some judges to listen in on what the targets said during the interviews. Regardless of the targets' actual personality, the targets who were being tested for extraversion acted extraverted, and the targets who were being tested for introversion acted introverted.

Overall, then, the students selected questions that would lead them to a particular, expected answer. This phenomenon is formally called **confirmatory hypothesis testing**. However, unlike the hypothesis testing process in the theory-data cycle (Chapter 1), this process is conducted in a way that is decidedly not scientific. If interviewers were testing the hypothesis that their target was an extravert, they asked the questions that would confirm that hypothesis and did not ask questions that might disconfirm that hypothesis. Indeed, even though the students could have chosen neutral questions (such as "What do you think the good and bad points of acting friendly and open are?"), they hardly ever did. In follow-up studies, Snyder and Swann found that student interviewers chose hypothesis-confirming questions even if they were offered a big cash prize for being the most objective interviewer, suggesting that even when people are motivated to be objective, they cannot always be.

Left to our own devices, we are not very rigorous in gathering evidence to test our ideas. Over and over again, psychological research has found that when people are asked to test a hypothesis, they tend to ask only the questions that support their expectations (Copeland & Snyder, 1995; Snyder & Campbell, 1980; Snyder & White, 1981; see also **Figure 2.4**). People seek out confirmation—the information they want or expect—and fail to seek out the information that would disconfirm their ideas—the information they do not want (Klayman & Ha, 1987). As a result, they tend to gather only a certain kind of information, and then they conclude that their hypotheses are supported.

Being Overconfident

Once we decide what we think, we tend to be overconfident in our ideas—we want to think we are right. Therefore, overconfidence is another reason not to trust intuition. We may be confident in our reasoning, but being confident is not the same as being correct.

Sometimes our most confidently held beliefs are accurate. I am confident that I know my own name, my age, and what I ate for lunch yesterday. But confidence is not always the same as accuracy. Take eyewitnesses to a crime: Contrary to what you (and many judges and juries) might think, controlled studies of eyewitness memory show that very confident eyewitnesses are not much more accurate in their identifications than hesitant witnesses (Bothwell, Deffenbacher, & Brigham, 1987). For example, in one controlled study, people watched a video of a person stealing a credit card in a restaurant and then were asked to identify the perpetrator. People who said much later, "I'm sure that's who I saw" were not much more accurate than people who said, "I think that's him, but I'm not positive" (Brewer & Wells, 2006). Confident eyewitnesses may seem more credible, but their self-assurance can be misleading, especially as time passes.

FIGURE 2.4 Confirmatory hypothesis testing. This therapist suspects her client has an anxiety disorder. What kinds of questions should she be asking that would both potentially confirm and potentially disconfirm her hypothesis?

People can be overconfident in other domains, too. Students may be confident that they can complete a term paper in 3 hours—and then find that they needed much more time. Investors confidently predict that their investments will pay off well—and then are surprised when they lose money. A person who reports full confidence that he or she can prepare a meal in less than 30 minutes might actually need an hour to put dinner on the table.

Overconfidence might be the sneakiest of all of the biases of human thinking. For one, it makes us trust our (often faulty) reasoning all the more. Second, overconfidence makes it difficult for us to initiate the theory-data cycle. We might say, "I don't need to test this belief—I already know it is correct." Part of learning to be a scientist is learning not to use feelings of confidence as evidence for the truth of our beliefs. Rather than thinking what they want to, careful scientists use data.

The Intuitive Thinker Versus the Scientific Reasoner

When we think intuitively rather than scientifically, we make mistakes. We think the easy way and think what we want, tending to both notice and actively seek information that confirms our ideas.

Instead, you should try to adopt the empirical mindset of a researcher. In Chapter 1, you read that empiricism involves basing beliefs on information from the senses. Now we have added an additional nuance to what it means to reason empirically: To be a good empiricist, you must also strive to interpret the data that you collect in an objective way—by guarding against these common biases.

Researchers create comparison groups and look at all the data. Rather than accept the first evidence that pops up, researchers need to dig deeper and generate data through rigorous studies. Researchers know that they should not just go along with the story that everybody believes; instead, they train themselves to test their hunches with systematic, empirical observations. They strive to ask questions objectively and collect potentially disconfirming evidence, not just evidence that confirms their hypotheses. Researchers try harder to accept data provisionally (rather than be overconfident), and they change their theories when the data do not support them. They understand that the data lead to the best conclusions for now, not to absolute truths. In short, while researchers are not perfect reasoners themselves, they have trained themselves to guard against the many pitfalls of intuition—and they make smarter decisions as a result.

Trusting Authorities on the Subject

You should be cautious about basing your conclusions on your own personal experiences and on those of people you know. But what about advice that is given by someone who is (or claims to be) an authority? How reliable is television personality Ellen DeGeneres' advice on anger management? How reliable is the advice of Dr. Phil—a former clinical psychologist who now has a television talk show? How reliable is the advice of a psychology professor who is a specialist in emotion regulation? All of these people have some authority—as cultural messengers, as people with advanced degrees, as people with significant life experience. Should you trust them?

How about this example of anger management advice from John Lee, a person with a master's degree in psychology, several published books on anger management, a thriving workshop business, and his own website. He's certainly an authority on the subject, right? Here's his advice:

> Punch a pillow or a punching bag. Yell and curse and moan and holler.... If you are angry at a particular person, imagine his or her face on the pillow or punching bag, and vent your rage.... You are not hitting a person, you

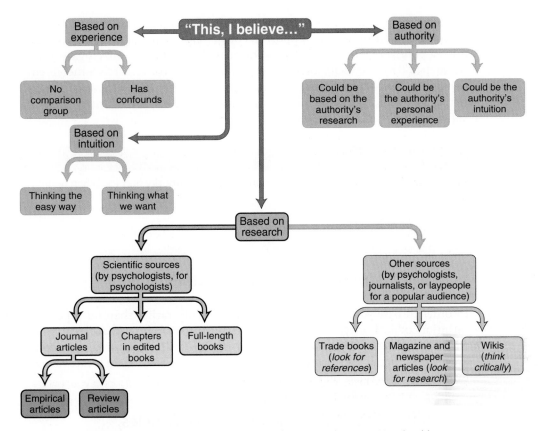

FIGURE 2.5 Concept map. People's beliefs can come from several sources. You should base your beliefs about psychological phenomena on research, rather than experience, intuition, or authority. Research can be found in a variety of sources, some more dependable than others.

are hitting the ghost of that person . . . a ghost alive in you that must be exorcised in a concrete, physical way. (Lee, 1993, p. 96)

Knowing what you know now, you probably do not trust John Lee's advice. In fact, this is a clear example of how a self-proclaimed "expert" might be wrong.

It is generally best to take the advice of "authorities" with a grain of salt. They might have systematically and objectively compared different conditions, as a researcher would do. Or maybe they have read the research and are interpreting it for you—that is, they may be practitioners who are basing their conclusions on empirical evidence. If you know that this is the case—that is, if they refer to research that supports their view—their advice might be worth attending to. However, authorities can also base their advice on their own experience or intuition, just like the rest of us. And they, too, might cherry-pick the evidence and present only the studies that support their own side. If you do not know whether the advice is based on a balanced assessment of the research, you should treat it with the same skepticism you would use with your own ideas based on experience and intuition.

Keep in mind, too, that not all research is equally reliable. The research that an authority figure uses to support his or her argument might have been conducted poorly. In the rest of this book, you will learn how to interrogate others' research and form conclusions about its quality. Also, the research someone cites to support an argument may not accurately and appropriately support that particular argument. In Chapter 3, you will learn more about what kinds of research support which kinds of claims.

Check Your Understanding

1. When might it be wise to accept the conclusions of authority figures? When might it not?

1. See pp. 36–37.

Finding and Reading the Research

In order to base your beliefs on empirical evidence rather than on experience, intuition, or authority, you will, of course, need to read about that research. But where do you find it? What if you wanted to read Bushman's studies on venting anger? How would you locate those studies? And how would you locate research by other psychologists on the same topic?

Consulting Scientific Sources: Journal Articles, Chapters, and Books

Psychological scientists usually publish their research in one of three places: journal articles, book chapters, or full-length books.

Journal Articles

Most commonly, psychological scientists publish their results in journal articles. Most journals come out monthly or quarterly, like magazines do. But unlike popular magazines, scientific journals usually do not have glossy, colorful covers or advertisements. You are most likely to find a scientific journal in academic, university libraries or in online academic databases, which you can usually access through your university's library. For example, the study by Bushman described earlier in this chapter was published in a journal called *Personality and Social Psychology Bulletin* (as shown in **Figure 2.6**). **Table 2.5** shows you a list of some of the most widely read journals in psychology. Journal articles are written for an audience of other psychological scientists and psychology students.

Journal articles can be either empirical articles or review articles. **Empirical journal articles** report, for the first time, the results of an (empirical) research study. Empirical articles contain details about the study's method, the statistical tests used, and the numerical results of the study. Bushman's article is an example of an empirical journal article.

Does Venting Anger Feed or Extinguish the Flame? Catharsis, Rumination, Distraction, Anger, and Aggressive Responding

Brad J. Bushman
Iowa State University

Does distraction or rumination work better to diffuse anger? Catharsis theory predicts that rumination works best, but empirical evidence is lacking. In this study, angered participants hit a punching bag and thought about the person who had angered them (rumination group) or thought about becoming physically fit (distraction group). After hitting the punching bag, they reported how angry they felt. Next, they were given the chance to administer loud blasts of noise to the person who had angered them. There also was a no punching bag control group. People in the rumination group felt angrier than did people in the distraction or control groups. People in the rumination group were also most aggressive, followed respectively by people in the distraction and control groups. Rumination increased rather than decreased anger and aggression. Doing nothing at all was more effective than venting anger. These results directly contradict catharsis theory.

The belief in the value of venting anger has become widespread in our culture. In movies, magazine articles, and even on billboards, people are encouraged to vent their anger and "blow off steam." For example, in the movie *Analyze This*, a psychiatrist (played by Billy Crystal) tells his New York gangster client (played by Robert De Niro), "You know what I do when I'm angry? I hit a pillow. Try that." The client promptly pulls out his gun, points it at the couch, and fires several bullets into the pillow. "Feel better?" asks the psychiatrist. "Yeah, I do," says the gunman. In a *Vogue* magazine article, female model Shalom concludes that boxing helps her release pent-up anger. She said,

> I found myself looking forward to the chance to pound out the frustrations of the week against Carlos's (her trainer) mitts. Let's face it: A personal boxing trainer has advantages over a husband or lover. He won't look at you accusingly and say, "I don't know where this irritation is

coming from." ... Your boxing trainer knows it's in there. And he wants you to give it to him. ("Fighting Fit," 1993, p. 179)

In a *New York Times Magazine* article about hate crimes, Andrew Sullivan writes, "Some expression of prejudice serves a useful purpose. It lets off steam; it allows natural tensions to express themselves incrementally; it can siphon off conflict through words, rather than actions" (Sullivan, 1999, p. 113). A large billboard in Missouri states, "Hit a Pillow, Hit a Wall, But Don't Hit Your Kids!"

Catharsis Theory

The theory of catharsis is one popular and authoritative statement that venting one's anger will produce a positive improvement in one's psychological state. The word *catharsis* comes from the Greek word *katharsis*, which literally translated means a cleansing or purging. According to catharsis theory, acting aggressively or even viewing aggression is an effective way to purge angry and aggressive feelings.

Sigmund Freud believed that repressed negative emotions could build up inside an individual and cause psychological symptoms, such as hysteria (nervous outbursts). Breuer and Freud (1893-1895/1955) proposed that the treatment of hysteria required the discharge of the emotional state previously associated with trauma. They claimed that for interpersonal traumas, such as

Author's Note: I would like to thank Remy Reinier for her help scanning photo IDs of students and photographs from health magazines. I also would like to thank Angelica Bonacci for her helpful comments on an early draft of this article. Correspondence concerning this article should be addressed to Brad J. Bushman, Department of Psychology, Iowa State University, Ames, IA 50011-3180; e-mail: bushman@iastate.edu.

PSPB, Vol. 28 No. 6, June 2002 724-731

724

FIGURE 2.6 Bushman's (2002) empirical article on catharsis. The first page is shown here, as it appeared in *Personality and Social Psychology Bulletin*.

Review journal articles provide a summary of all the research that has been done in one research area. For example, a review article by Anderson and colleagues (2003) gives a narrative summary of several studies on the effects of playing violent video games on children's aggression. Sometimes a review article uses a quantitative technique called *meta-analysis*, which combines the results of many studies and gives a number that summarizes the magnitude of a relationship

TABLE 2.5 Selected Journals in Psychology

Selected Clinical Psychology Journals

Behavior Therapy

Cognitive Therapy and Research

Counseling Psychologist

Journal of Abnormal Psychology

Journal of Consulting and Clinical Psychology

Psychological Assessment

Selected Applied Psychology Journals

Applied Developmental Psychology

Consulting Psychology Journal: Practice and Research

Journal of Applied Psychology

Journal of Educational Psychology

Journal of Experimental Psychology: Applied

School Psychology Quarterly

Selected Cognitive Psychology Journals

Acta Psychologica

Cognition

Journal of Experimental Psychology: Human Perception and Performance

Journal of Experimental Psychology: Learning, Memory, and Cognition

Selected Social and Personality Psychology Journals

Journal of Experimental Social Psychology

Journal of Personality and Social Psychology

Journal of Research in Personality

Personality and Social Psychology Bulletin

Personality and Social Psychology Review

Social Cognition

Selected Developmental Psychology Journals

Adolescence

Child Development

Developmental Psychology

Psychology and Aging

Selected Neuroscience Journals

Behavioral Neuroscience

Brain and Cognition

Developmental Psychobiology

Nature: Neuroscience

Physiological Psychology

Psychophysiology

Selected Journals Containing Review Articles

American Psychologist

Behavioral and Brain Sciences

Psychological Bulletin

Psychological Review

Review of General Psychology

Selected Psychology Journals Spanning Several Topics

Current Directions in Psychological Science

Emotion

Health Psychology

Journal of Social Issues

Psychological Methods

Psychological Science

Note: There are hundreds of journals in psychology; this is only a partial list of some of the most prominent journals in selected categories. In addition, some subfields of psychology—language, cultural psychology, child clinical psychology, and others—are not included here.

(called the *effect size*). For example, a recent study by Anderson and colleagues (2010) reviewed all of the 130 studies that had measured video game use and child aggression; the authors computed the average effect size across all of the studies. This technique is valued by psychologists because it weighs each study proportionately (it does not allow cherry-picking of only certain studies).

Before being published in a journal, both empirical articles and review articles must be peer-reviewed (see Chapter 1). Both types of article are prestigious forms of publication by psychological scientists.

For a full discussion of meta-analysis, see Chapter 13, pp. 381–385.

Chapters in Edited Books

In addition to publishing articles in journals, psychologists may describe their research in a chapter in an edited book. An edited book is a collection of chapters on a common topic, in which each chapter is written by a different contributor. For example, James Gross and Oliver John published a chapter called "Wise Emotion Regulation" in an edited book called *The Wisdom in Feeling: Psychological Processes in Emotional Intelligence* (2002). Seventeen other chapters appeared in this book, all written by different authors. The editors (Lisa Feldman Barrett and Peter Salovey) invited the authors to contribute. Generally, a book chapter is not the first place a study is reported; instead, the scientist is summarizing his or her research and the big picture behind it. Edited book chapters can therefore be a good place to find a summary of a set of research that a particular psychologist has done and the theory behind it (in this sense, book chapters are similar to review articles in journals). Chapters are not peer-reviewed as rigorously as empirical journal articles or review articles are. However, the editor of the book is careful to invite only experts—researchers who are intimately familiar with the empirical evidence on a topic—to write the chapters. Again, the audience for these chapters is usually other psychologists and psychology students.

Books

A psychologist might also describe his or her research in a full-length book. In some other disciplines (such as anthropology, art history, or English), full-length books are a common way for scholars to publish their work. Psychologists do not write many full-length scientific books for other psychologists, but those books that have been published are most likely to be found in a university library. (Psychologists may also write full-length books for a general audience—called *trade books*—as discussed later in this chapter.)

Finding Scientific Sources

When you have been in your university's library (or visited the library's website), you have undoubtedly observed one thing: Your library contains a lot of books and journals! The list of online or electronic journals, especially, in your library's collection might be immense. How can you find the articles or chapters you want? And how can you find trustworthy sources on a topic if you do not know any specific titles or authors?

PsycINFO

The best, most comprehensive tool for sorting through the vast number of psychological research articles is a search engine called PsycINFO, which is maintained and updated weekly by the American Psychological Association (APA). PsycINFO is like the Internet search engine Google, but instead of searching the Internet, it searches only sources in psychology, plus a few sources from related disciplines such as communication, marketing, and education. PsycINFO's database includes more than 2.5 million records, mostly peer-reviewed articles.

You cannot use PsycINFO from just any computer—you must have access to a college or university library that subscribes to it.

The best way to learn to use PsycINFO is to simply try it yourself. Depending on how your library subscribes, PsycINFO's search screens and search results will be presented differently. However, most setups are intuitive to learn and use, once you have an initial introduction. A reference librarian can teach you or your class the basics in a few minutes, and an online tutorial can also be helpful. (Online tutorials sponsored by the APA can be accessed at http://www.apa.org/pubs/databases/training/tutorials.aspx.)

Alternatives to PsycINFO

What if you want to find empirical research but you do not have access to PsycINFO? First, if you happen to know the author of the research you are looking for, and if that author is a college or university professor, you can try visiting that professor's home page. Most psychology researchers maintain a home page that includes a summary of their research interests and a list of their publications or even PDFs of the original articles. Going to a scientist's home page has limitations, however: You must know the professor's name in order to find the information, and the page will list only the articles by that person. Also, you may not be able to find older research this way, especially if a professor is no longer living, is not actively researching, or does not maintain a website. However, visiting a professor's website has the advantage of being a fast way to find specific information. This is also one of the only ways you can find an article that is "in press"—that has been accepted for publication but has not appeared in the journal yet. Sometimes it takes several months for an article to get into print, and articles in press are the freshest research from a professor's laboratory.

Second, you can use the tool Google Scholar (scholar.google.com). This site works just like the regular Google search engine, but it indexes only empirical journal articles and scholarly books. Google Scholar is easy to use: You just type a name or subject heading in the search box. The hits sometimes send you directly to a PDF version of the article. Google Scholar is an acceptable alternative if you do not have access to PsycINFO through a university library, but unlike PsycINFO, Google Scholar does not provide abstracts. Also, it does not allow you to search as easily in specific fields (such as restricting your search to key words in an abstract); it does not categorize the articles it finds, for example, as peer-reviewed or not, whereas PsycINFO does. And whereas PsycINFO indexes only psychology articles, Google Scholar contains articles from all scholarly disciplines. It may take more time for you to sort through the articles it returns, because the output of a Google scholar search is less organized.

Also, although you can easily find citation information in Google Scholar, you might not be able to read the articles for free. Many journals charge you or your library for online access. If you cannot access the articles for free, see whether your library subscribes to the paper version of that journal or offers online access to that journal. If not, you can request a copy of the article through your college's interlibrary loan office (sometimes for a fee).

Reading the Research

Once you have found an empirical journal article or chapter, now what? What is the best way to go about reading this material? At first glance, some journal articles may seem impenetrable. They often contain an array of statistical symbols. They may be full of unfamiliar terminology, and even the titles of journal articles and chapters are not always written in friendly terms. (Take this one for example: "Object Substitution Masking Interferes with Semantic Processing: Evidence from Event-Related Potentials," Reiss & Hoffman, 2006). How is a student supposed to read this sort of thing? It helps to know what you will find in an article, and to read with a purpose.

What You Will Find in an Empirical Journal Article

Most empirical journal articles (those that report the results of a study for the first time) are written in a standard format, as recommended by the *Publication Manual of the American Psychological Association*. Most empirical journal articles include certain sections in the same order: abstract, introduction, method, results, discussion. Each section contains a specific kind of information.

Abstract. The abstract provides a concise summary of the article. An abstract is about 120 words long, and in this brief space it tells you the study's hypotheses, method, and major results. When you are collecting articles for a project, the abstracts can help you quickly decide whether each article describes the kind of research you are interested in reading about or whether you should move on to the next article.

Introduction. The introduction is the first section of regular text. The first paragraphs of the introduction typically explain the topic of the study. The middle paragraphs lay out the theoretical and empirical background for the research. What theory or theories provide the background for the present study? What past studies have tested this theory? What makes the present study important, in light of past research? The final paragraph of the introduction states the specific research questions, goals, or hypotheses for the current study. These research questions and hypotheses provide tests of the theory.

Method. The Method section explains in detail how the researchers conducted their study. It usually contains subsections, such as Participants, Materials, Procedure, and Apparatus. An ideal Method section gives enough detail that if you wanted to repeat the study, you could do so without having to ask the authors.

Results. The Results section describes the quantitative and, as relevant, qualitative results of the study, including the statistical tests the authors used to analyze the data. It usually provides tables and figures to summarize key results. Although you may not understand all the statistics used in the article (especially early in your psychology education), you might still be able to understand the basic findings by looking at the tables and figures.

Discussion. The opening paragraph of the Discussion section generally summarizes the study's research question and methods and indicates how well the data supported the hypotheses. After this summary, the authors usually promote their study's contributions. They discuss the study's significance: Perhaps their hypothesis was new, or the method they used was a creative and unusual way to test a familiar hypothesis, or the participants were unlike others who had been studied before. In addition, the authors may discuss alternative explanations for their data and pose interesting questions raised by the research.

Reference List. The reference list contains a full bibliographic listing of all of the articles the authors cited in writing their article, acknowledging previous work in the field and enabling interested readers to locate these studies. Most reference lists in psychology articles conform to the guidelines provided in the *Publication Manual of the American Psychological Association*. When you are conducting a literature search, reference lists are excellent places to look for additional articles on a given topic. Once you find one relevant article, you can use the reference list of that article to find many more.

Reading with a Purpose: Empirical Journal Articles

Here's some revolutionary advice: Don't read every word of every article, from beginning to end. Instead, *read with a purpose*. In most cases, reading with a purpose means asking two questions as you read: (1) What is the argument? and (2) What is the evidence to support the argument? The obvious first step toward answering these questions is to read the abstract, which provides an overview of the study. What should you read next?

Empirical articles are stories from the trenches of the theory-data cycle, which you learned about in Chapter 1 (see Figure 1.4). Therefore, an empirical article reports on data that are generated to test a hypothesis, and the hypothesis is framed as a test of a particular theory. Therefore, after reading the abstract, you should skip to the end of the introduction, where you should find the primary goals and hypotheses of the study. After reading the goals and hypotheses, you can read the rest of the introduction to learn more about the theory that the hypotheses are testing. Another place to find information about the argument of the paper is the first paragraph of the Discussion section, where most authors summarize the key results of their study and state whether the results supported their hypotheses.

Once you have a sense of what the argument is, you can look for the evidence. In an empirical article, the evidence is contained in the Method and Results sections. What did the researchers do, and what results did they find? How well do these results support their argument (that is, their hypotheses)?

Reading with a Purpose: Chapters and Review Articles

Empirical journal articles tend to follow the format described above, but chapters and review articles often do not have an introduction and Method, Results, and Discussion sections. They do tend to have headings, but usually the authors create headings that make sense for their topics—there are no predetermined headings, as in empirical articles.

You can still read these sources with a purpose, asking, What is the argument? What is the evidence? The argument will be the purpose of the chapter or review article—the author's stance on the issue. In a review article or chapter, the argument often presents an entire theory (whereas an empirical journal article usually tests only one part of a theory). Here are some examples of arguments you might find in chapters or review articles:

Playing violent video games causes children to be more aggressive. (Anderson et al., 2010)

In East Asian cultural contexts, the self is construed as more interdependent with others, compared with North American cultural contexts. (Markus & Kitayama, 1991)

Suicidal behavior is a result of the combination of two constructs: the feeling of being alone, and the feeling of being a burden on others. (Van Orden et al., 2010)

In a chapter or review article, the evidence is the research that the author reviews. How much previous research has been done? What have the results been? How strong are the results? For example, to support the first argument above, "Playing violent video games causes children to be more aggressive," Anderson and his colleagues (2010) summarize the results of more than 100 studies on this topic.

With practice, you will get better at reading efficiently. You will learn to categorize what you read as argument or evidence, and you will learn how to evaluate how well the evidence supports the argument.

Finding Research in Other Places

Reading about research in its original form is the best way to get a thorough, accurate, and peer-reviewed report of scientific evidence, but there are other sources for reading about psychological research, too, such as trade books, websites, and popular newspapers and magazines. These can be good places to read about psychological research, as long as you choose and read your sources carefully.

Finding Research on the Retail Bookshelf

If you browse through the psychology section in a regular bookstore (or the popular book section of your college bookstore), you will mostly find trade books about psychology written for a popular audience. Unlike the scientific sources discussed so far, these books are written for people who do not have a psychology degree. They are written to help people, to inform, to entertain, and to make money for their authors.

The language in trade books is much more readable than the language in most journal articles. These books can also show how psychology applies to your everyday life, and in this way they can be useful. But how well do trade books reflect current research in psychology? Do they help you apply the best research to your real-life problems? Or do they simply present an uncritical summary of common sense, intuition, or the author's own experience? The best way to tell is to look at the end of the book, where you may find footnotes or references that tell you the research studies on which the argument is based. For example, *Stumbling on Happiness*, by psychologist Daniel Gilbert (2005), contains 35 pages of notes—mostly citations to research discussed in the rest of the book. Daniel Goleman's book *Social Intelligence: The New Science of Human Relationships* (2007) contains 53 pages of citations and notes. Sonja Ljubomirsky's *The How of Happiness* (2008) contains 44 pages of references. A book related to this chapter's theme, *Anger: The Misunderstood Emotion* (Tavris, 1989), contains 25 pages of references. These are excellent examples of trade books based on research that are written by psychologists for a popular audience.

In contrast, if you flip to the end of some other trade books, you may not find any references or notes. For example, the book *What Men Won't Tell You but Women Need to Know* (by Bob Berkowitz and Roger Gittines, 2008) cites no research, nor does *The Ultimate Secrets to Total Self-Confidence* (by Robert Anthony, 1986). The book *Why Mars and Venus Collide: Improving Relationships by Understanding How Men and Women Cope Differently with Stress* (by John Gray, 2008) has four pages of references. Four pages is better than nothing but seems a little light, given that literally thousands of journal articles have been devoted to the scientific study of gender differences. In addition, many of the references cited in such books are not to empirical journal articles at all but rather to opinion pieces or simple news articles.

If you find a book that claims to be about psychology but does not have any references, you should consider the book light entertainment (at best) or irresponsible (at worst). Vast, well-conducted literatures exist on such topics as self-esteem, gender differences, mental illnesses, and coping with stress, but some authors ignore this scientific literature and instead rely on hand-selected anecdotes from their own clinical practice. By now, you know that you can do better. If a psychology trade book does not contain references to research, keep looking until you find a book that does.

Finding Research on Wikis

Wikis can provide quick, easy-to-read facts about almost any topic. What does an ibex look like? Which of the Harry Potter books is not about Voldemort? How many albums has Lady Gaga released? What languages are spoken in South Africa? Wikis are democratic encyclopedias. Anybody can create a new entry, anybody can contribute to the content of a page, and anybody can log in and add details to an entry. Theoretically, wikis are self-correcting: If one user posts an incorrect fact, another user would come along and correct it.

Can we rely on wikis to tell us about psychology research? Yes and no. The most popular wiki, Wikipedia (www.wikipedia.org), is not yet used extensively by psychologists. Sometimes you will find a full review of a psychological phenomenon; sometimes you will not. And when you search Wikipedia for psychological terms, you may pull up something very different from what you wanted. Searching for the term *catharsis* is a good example: If you look up that term on Wikipedia, the first article you will find is not related to psychology at all; instead, it is about the role of catharsis in classical drama.

As an alternative to Wikipedia, two psychologists started a new wiki just for psychology, www.psychwiki.com. This wiki may be a better starting point for psychological information. For example, the search term *catharsis* on Psych-Wiki pulls up a page on the psychological meaning of the term, not the theatrical one (see **Figure 2.7**).

Of course, there are many downsides to using a wiki. First, wikis are not comprehensive in their coverage: You cannot read about a topic if no one has created a page for it. Second, wiki pages might not include references—or they might not include the most relevant or the most recent references. Third, the details on the pages might be incorrect, and they will stay incorrect until somebody else fixes them. Some Internet journalists and bloggers have intentionally inserted errors into wiki pages and then watched to see how long it took for them to be corrected. In one such attempt, all of 13 changed facts were corrected within hours (Halavis, 2004), perhaps because the person who found the first error was able to easily track and correct the other 12 facts. But in another attempt, an author added five plausible facts to five different websites—and *none* were corrected (Leppik, 2005).

If wikis gain in popularity, they might become more comprehensive, more accurate, and more likely to include references to relevant journal articles. But for now, wikis seem to be written only by a small, enthusiastic, and not necessarily

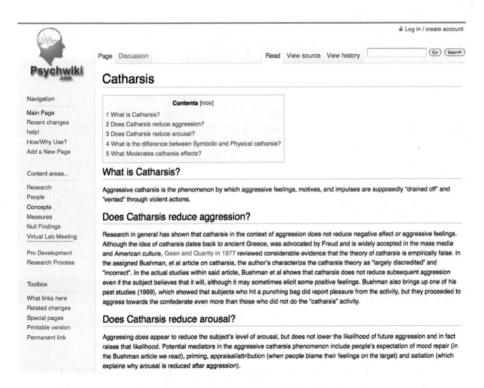

FIGURE 2.7 A page on PsychWiki. PsychWiki is a publicly edited, online source for psychological information. What are some of the downsides to using wikis as a source of research information?

Psychology Today (magazine and website)

Science News Daily (website; mind and brain section)

Current Directions in Psychological Science (journal)

American Psychological Association website (www.apa.org)

Scientific American Mind (magazine)

Science sections of major newspapers (print and web)

expert group of contributors. You should always double-check the information found there. And because of these weaknesses, most psychology professors do not accept wikis as sources in academic assignments.

Finding Research in the Popular Press

Overall, popular press coverage is good for psychology. Journalists play an important role in telling the public about exciting findings in psychological science. Psychological research is covered in magazines (such as *Time* and *Newsweek*), in daily newspapers, on television news programs, on radio news shows, in web-based magazines (such as msnbc.com), and in blogs. Some magazines, such as *Psychology Today* and *Scientific American Mind*, are devoted exclusively to covering psychology research for a popular audience (see **Table 2.6**).

Recall the discussion in Chapter 1 on the journal-to-journalism cycle. Journalists who specialize in science writing are trained to faithfully represent journal articles for a popular audience, but journalists who are not trained in science writing might not correctly summarize a journal article. Therefore, keep in mind that popular press stories are meant to tell you about a new research area or an interesting study. They can pique your interest and keep you somewhat informed. But plan to use your developing skills as a consumer of information to read the journalism critically. And if you really want to delve into the issue that the journalist is covering, use PsycINFO to locate the original article and read the research at its source.

Check Your Understanding

1. How are empirical journal articles different from review journal articles? How is each type of article different from a chapter in an edited book?
2. What two guiding questions can help you read any academic source?
3. What are the differences between PsycINFO, Google Scholar, and PsychWiki?
4. If you encounter a psychological trade book, what signals that it is research based?

1. See pp. 38–41. 2. See p. 44. 3. See pp. 41–42. 4. See p. 46.

Summary

These days, advice comes at you from all angles. Whom should you believe? Decisions that are based on your personal experience may not be accurate. Personal experience usually does not involve a comparison group, and often it is confounded.

Basing beliefs on intuition is not ideal, either. We can be lulled into the wrong conclusions if we consider only the thoughts that come to mind most easily. We find it easy to accept the explanation provided by a good story. We also find it easier to notice what is present than what is absent, and examples that are vivid or memorable are easier to pull up than mundane ones. Intuition is also subject to the bias of thinking what we want: We do not like to challenge our ideas, so we tend to focus on the data that support our ideas and to discount and criticize data that disagree. When gathering information, we may ask biased questions that tend to confirm our initial impressions. We also tend to confuse confidence for accuracy.

Scientific research may not be perfect, but researchers are aware of their potential for biased reasoning, so they create special situations in which they can systematically observe behavior. They create comparison groups, consider all the data, and allow the data to change their beliefs.

Sometimes, authorities attempt to convince us to accept their claims. If authorities' claims are based on their own experience or intuition, we should probably not accept them. But if authorities use empirical evidence to support their claims, we can be more confident about taking their advice.

Several tools are available to help you find research in psychology. Your university library probably provides access to PsycINFO, but if you do not have access to a university library, you can use Google Scholar or look for a researcher's website. Read journal articles, chapters, and books with a purpose, asking, What is the theoretical argument? and What is the evidence—what do the data say? Trade books, wikis, and popular press articles can be good sources of information about psychology research, but they can also miss the mark. Evaluate these sources by asking whether they are based on research and whether the coverage is comprehensive, accurate, and responsible.

Key Terms

comparison group, p. 25
confederate, p. 28
confirmatory hypothesis
  testing, p. 34
confounds, p. 27

empirical journal articles, p. 38
pop-up principle, p. 32
present/present bias, p. 32
probabilistic, p. 30
review journal articles, p. 39

NEED HELP STUDYING?

wwnorton.com/studyspace

Visit StudySpace to access free review materials such as:

- Diagnostic Review Quizzes
- Study Outlines

Learning Actively

1. Each of the examples below is a statement, based on experience, that does not take a comparison group into account:

   A. Texting makes me feel emotionally closer to my friends.
   B. Yoga has made me feel more peaceful.
   C. Younger teachers are better with kids.

   For each statement,

   a. ask one or more comparison group questions that would help you evaluate the conclusion,
   b. draw a 2 × 2 matrix for systematically comparing outcomes, and
   c. write down as many possible confounds as you can think of.

   Example: "Since I cut sugar from their diets, I've noticed that the campers in my cabin are much more cooperative!"

   a. Comparison group question: Would the campers have improved anyway, without the change in diet?
   b. A systematic comparison should be set up as follows:

	Reduce sugar in diet (treatment)	No change in diet (no treatment)
Kids are cooperative (outcome present)		
Kids are not cooperative (outcome absent)		

   c. Possible confounds: What else might have changed besides the sugar? Could the campers simply have gotten used to camp and settled down? Is it possible that the new swimming teacher made a difference? Might the weather have improved during the same time?

   ---

2. Using what you have learned in this chapter, write a sentence or two explaining why the reasoning reflected in each of the following statements is or is not sound. What further information might you need to determine the accuracy of the speaker's conclusions? For questions with * attached: Try to find literature on this topic in a PsycINFO search.

   a. "I'm positive my cousin has an eating disorder! I hardly ever see her eat anything other than diet bars."

b. A friend asks you, "Did you hear about the study conducted by RAND? It showed that the more sexually explicit TV a teenage girl watches, the greater her risk of teen pregnancy."*

c. "It's so clear that my favorite candidate won that debate! Did you hear all the zingers he delivered?"

d. "I read online that many cases of autism are caused by the MMR vaccine children get when they are two."

e. "There are way more dogs than cats in this city. That's all you see in the parks—dogs dogs dogs!"

f. "Tanning beds cause skin cancer? Maybe in rats—but I'm a person, and I've been using tanning beds for about 2 years. I don't even have any new freckles."

g. "I'm afraid of flying—planes are so dangerous!"

h. "I read in the newspaper's Science section that people who multitask with computers, cell phones, and other people actually have more trouble focusing and shutting out information they don't need."

3. If your library has PsycINFO access, do a basic search for the word "depression" and write down how many records this search finds. Then try restricting the fields by searching "depression" in the "Abstract" field. Did this search reduce the number of records you found? Now try combining terms (such as "depression" and "gender"). Do several searches, writing down how many records each search finds. What have you learned about restricting searches in PsycINFO? Why might you want to broaden a search? Why might you want to narrow a search?

4. Focus on one PsycINFO record from your "depression" search. For the purposes of this exercise, pick one that was published at least 3 years ago.

a. Does this source appear to be a journal article? If so, is it an empirical article or a review article? Or is it a chapter or a book?

b. How many other articles have cited this source since it was published?

c. Search for the personal website of the source's authors and write down their web addresses.

d. Now go to Google Scholar (scholar.google.com) and search for this same source. Are you able to locate it easily? What differences do you notice between Google Scholar and PsycINFO?

More Than 2 Million U.S. Youths Depressed

(Reuters, 2008)

Debt Stress Causing Health Problems, Poll Finds

(MSNBC.com, 2008)

Belly Fat Linked to Dementia, Study Shows

(MSNBC.com, 2010)

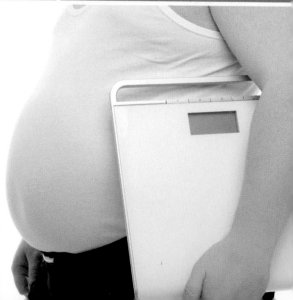

3

Three Claims, Four Validities: Interrogation Tools for Consumers of Research

Learning Objectives

A year from now, you should still be able to:

1. Differentiate among three kinds of claims: frequency, association, and causal.
2. Ask appropriate questions that would help you interrogate each of the four big validities: construct validity, statistical validity, external validity, and internal validity.
3. Understand which validities are most relevant for each of the three types of claims.

Increasingly, articles about psychology research, written for a general audience, appear in the popular press. Headlines about psychology can attract readers, because many people are interested in topics such as depression, ADHD (attention-deficit/hyperactivity disorder), and debt stress. As a psychology student, you are probably interested in these concepts too. But to what extent should you believe the information you read in the newspaper or online? Journalists who write about psychological science should simply report what the researchers did and why the study was important, but sometimes they end up misrepresenting or overstating the research findings. They may do so unintentionally, because they do not have the appropriate training to properly critique the findings, or intentionally, to draw readers' attention.

And what about the research reported directly, in an empirical journal article? How well does the study support the claims that a researcher might make? Your research methods course will help you understand both popular and research-based articles at a more sophisticated level. It will teach you how to raise the appropriate questions for interrogating the information behind a writer's claims about human behavior. And by extension, the skills you use to evaluate information behind the research you read will also help you plan your own studies if you intend to become a producer of information.

Think of this chapter as a scaffold; all of the information in later chapters will have a place on this framework of three claims and four validities.

This chapter introduces three kinds of claims: frequency claims, association claims, and causal claims. Each of these claims makes a statement about variables or about relationships between variables. Therefore, before learning about these types of claims, you need to learn some basics about variables.

Variables

Variables are the core unit of psychological research. A **variable**, as the word implies, is something that varies, so it must have at least two *levels*, or **values**.

Take the headline "More Than 2 Million U.S. Youths Depressed." Here, depression is the variable, and its levels are "not depressed and depressed." Similarly, the study that inspired the headline "ADHD Drugs Not Linked to Future Drug Abuse" has two variables: ADHD medications (whose levels are "medicated for ADHD" and "not medicated for ADHD") and drug abuse (whose levels are "abuses drugs" and "does not abuse drugs"). In contrast, in research on fathers, sex would not be a variable, because it only has one level in this study—every participant in the study would be male. Sex therefore would be a **constant** in this study, not a variable. A constant is something that could potentially vary but that has only one level in the study in question.

In many studies, variables have more than two levels. People's debt stress might have two levels, present and absent, but depending on how debt stress is measured, it might have three levels (high, medium, and low) or even 10 levels, if it is measured on a 10-point scale from low to high debt stress.

Measured Versus Manipulated Variables

In any study, the researchers either measure or manipulate each variable. The distinction is important because some claims involve **measured variables**, while other claims involve both measured and **manipulated variables**. When researchers measure a variable, they observe and record its levels. Some variables, such as height, IQ, or blood pressure, are typically measured in the everyday sense of the word (using scales, rulers, or devices). But other variables, such as sex and hair color, are also said to be "measured." And to measure abstract variables, such as depression or stress, researchers might devise a set of questions to represent the various levels. In each case, measuring a variable is a matter of recording an observation, a statement, or a value.

In contrast, when researchers manipulate a variable, they are controlling its levels by assigning participants to the different levels of that variable. For example, a researcher might give some participants 10 milligrams of a medication, other participants 20 milligrams, and still others 30 milligrams. Or a researcher might assign some people to take a test in a room with many other people and assign other people to take the test alone. The participants do not choose—the researchers do the manipulating, assigning people to be at one level of the variable or another.

Some variables cannot be manipulated—they can only be measured. Sex cannot be manipulated because researchers cannot assign people to be male or female; they can only measure what sex they already are. IQ cannot be manipulated because researchers cannot assign some people to have a high IQ and others to have a low IQ; they can only measure each person's IQ. Traits such as depression or ADHD cannot be manipulated, either. Such qualities are difficult or impossible to change for the purposes of a study. Other variables cannot be manipulated in an experiment because it would be unethical to do so. For example, in a study on the long-term effects of elementary education, you could not ethically assign children to "high-quality school" and "low-quality school" conditions. Nor could you ethically assign people to conditions that put their physical or emotional well-being at risk.

Some variables, however, can be either manipulated or measured, depending on the goals of a study. If childhood extracurricular activities were the variable of interest, you could *measure* whether children already do take music lessons or drama lessons, or you could *manipulate* this variable if you assigned some children to take music lessons and others to take drama lessons. If you wanted to study hair color, you could *measure* hair color by recording whether people are blonds or brunettes. But you could also *manipulate* this variable if you assigned some willing people to dye their hair blond and others to dye their hair brown.

For more on ethical choices in research, see Chapter 4.

From Conceptual Variable to Operational Definition

Each variable in a study can be described in two ways. When researchers are discussing their theories and when journalists write about research, they work with **conceptual definitions** of variables: abstract concepts such as "depression" or "debt stress." But to test hypotheses, researchers have to do something specific in order to gather data. When they are testing their hypotheses with empirical research, they use **operational definitions**, or *operationalizations*, of variables. Operationalization is the process of turning a concept of interest into a measured or manipulated variable.

For example, a researcher's interest in the conceptual variable "debt stress" might be operationalized as a structured set of questions used by a trained therapist to diagnose each person as "not stressed" or "mildly stressed" or "severely stressed." Alternatively, the same concept might be operationalized by asking people to answer a single Internet survey question, rating their own level of debt stress from 1 ("low") to 10 ("high").

Sometimes this operationalization step is simple and straightforward. For example, a researcher interested in a conceptual variable such as "weight gain" in

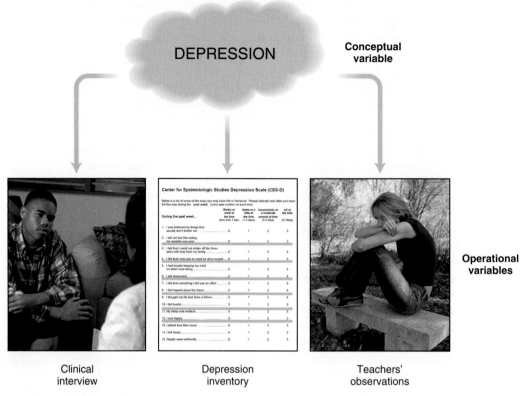

DEPRESSION

Conceptual variable

Operational variables

Clinical interview

Depression inventory

Teachers' observations

FIGURE 3.1 Operationalizing "depression." A single conceptual variable can be operationalized in a number of ways.

laboratory rats would probably just weigh them. Or a researcher who was interested in the conceptual variable "ADHD medications" might operationalize this variable by asking a patient's doctor about the medications the person takes. In these two cases, the researcher is able to operationalize the conceptual variable of interest quite easily.

Often, however, psychological concepts are difficult to see, touch, or feel, so they are also harder to operationalize. Examples are concepts such as personality traits, states such as "debt stress," or behavior judgments such as "drug abuse." The more abstract nature of these constructs does not stop psychologists from operationalizing them; it just makes studying them a little more difficult. In such cases, researchers spend extra time clarifying and defining the conceptual variables they plan to study. They might develop creative or elegant operational definitions to capture the construct of interest.

Most often, variables are stated at the conceptual level (such as *depression* or *intellectual abilities*). To discover how the variable was operationalized, you need to ask, "How did the researchers measure *depression* in this study?" (see **Figure 3.1**) or "What do they mean by *intellectual abilities* in this research?"

1. What is the difference between a variable and its levels?
2. Explain why some variables can only be measured, not manipulated.
3. What is the difference between the conceptual definition and the operational definition of a variable? How might the conceptual variables *affection* or *intelligence* or *stress* be operationalized by a researcher?

1. See p. 54. 2. See p. 54 3. See p. 55.

Three Claims

A **claim** is the argument someone is trying to make. Internet bloggers might make claims based on personal experience or observation ("The media coverage of congressional candidates has been sexist"). Politicians might make claims based on rhetoric ("I am the candidate of change!"). Literature scholars make claims based on textual evidence ("Based on my reading of the text, I argue that *Frankenstein* is an antifeminist novel"). But psychological scientists make their claims based on empirical research. Recall from Chapters 1 and 2 that psychological scientists use systematic observations, or data, to test and refine theories and claims. A psychologist might claim, based on data he or she has collected, that a certain percentage of Americans took antidepressant medications last year, or that people with poorer health tend to have lower incomes, or that music lessons can increase a child's IQ.

Notice the different wording in the claims in the previous section. In particular, the first claim merely gives a percentage of people who used a type of medication; this is a *frequency claim*. The second claim, about health and income, is an *association claim*: It suggests that the two variables are related, but does not claim that poor health causes low income or that low income causes poor health. The third claim, however, is a *causal claim*: The verb *increases* indicates that the music lessons actually cause the increase in IQ. The kind of claim a psychological scientist is able to make depends on the particular kind of study he or she conducts. How can you identify the types of claims researchers make, and how can you evaluate whether their studies accurately support each type of claim? And if you conduct research yourself, how will you know what kinds of study will support the type of claim you wish to make? (**Table 3.1** gives more examples of each type of claim, taken from actual science news headlines.)

TABLE 3.1 Examples of Each Kind of Claim

Claim type	Sample headlines
Frequency claims	8 Million Americans Consider Suicide Each Year
	At Times, Children Play with the Impossible
	Deadliest Day for Suicides: Wednesday
Association claims	Eating Disorder Risk Higher in Educated Families
	Sweet or Dry? Wine Choice Tied to Personality
	Sexual Orientation Linked to Handedness
Causal claims	Summer Sun May Trigger Suicidal Thoughts
	Loneliness "Makes You Cold"
	Collaboration Gives Recall Lift to Elderly

Frequency Claims

More Than 2 Million U.S. Teens Depressed

Half of Americans Struggle to Stay Happy

Williamsburg Charter School Outscores Other Schools on State Tests

Frequency claims describe a particular rate or level of something. In the first example above, "2 million" is the frequency, or count, of depression diagnoses among teens in the United States. In the second example, "half" is the rate (the proportion) of U.S. adults who are not always happy. These headlines claim how frequent or common something is. A frequency claim might also state the level of a variable—the charter school claim states the average score, or average level, of test scores across a set of students. Claims that mention the percentage of a variable, the number of people who fit a description, or some group's level on a variable can all be called frequency claims.

The best way to distinguish frequency claims from the other two types of claims (association and causal claims) is that they focus on only one variable—such as depression, happiness, or standardized test scores. Another distinguishing feature is that in frequency claims, the variables are always measured, not manipulated. In the examples above, the researchers have measured levels of happiness or depression using some kind of scale, interview, or metric and have reported the results.

Some reports give a list of single-variable results, all of which count as frequency claims. Take, for example, a report by the U.S. Centers for Disease Control (2008) on risky behaviors in U.S. residents ages 10–24. This report noted that 35.4% of teens watched television for more than 3 hours per school day. It also reported that 13.0% of teens were obese. These are two separate frequency claims—they measure single variables at a time. The researchers were not trying to show associations between these single variables. That is, the report did not claim that the teens who watched more than 3 hours of television per school day were more likely to be obese. Instead, these scientists simply reported that a certain percentage of teens watch a lot of television and a certain percentage of teens are obese.

Anecdotal Claims Are Not Frequency Claims

Besides the kinds of frequency claims mentioned above, you may also encounter stories in the popular press that are not based on research, even if they are related to psychology, such as:

Some Psych Patients Wait Days in ERs

She Turned Daughter's Bulimia Fight into Film

Such headlines do not argue for a particular percentage or level in a population. They may report a problem, a person's solution to a problem, or just an interesting story, but they do not say anything about the frequency or rate. The author of the story about the psychiatric patients is arguing that many emergency rooms need better resources so they can treat psychiatric patients quickly. But this article is not reporting a systematic study of how long patients wait for care in emergency rooms; the headline merely reports something that people have noticed.

These kinds of headlines could be called *anecdotal*: They do not report the results of a social science study; instead, they just tell an illustrative story—an anecdote. These stories may be interesting, and they might be related to psychology, but they are not frequency claims, in which a writer summarizes the results of a poll, survey, or large-scale study. Anecdotal stories are about isolated experiences, not about empirical studies. And as you read in Chapter 2, experience is not as good a source of information as empirical research.

Association Claims

Belly Fat Linked to Dementia, Study Shows
Heavy Cell Phone Use Tied to Poor Sperm Quality
ADHD Drugs Not Linked to Future Drug Abuse

These headlines are all examples of association claims. An **association claim** argues that one level of a variable is likely to be associated with a particular level of another variable. Variables that are associated are sometimes said to **correlate**, or *covary*, meaning that when one variable changes, the other variable tends to change, too. More simply, they may be said to be *related*. Notice that there are two variables in each example. In the first, the variables are amount of abdominal fat and diagnosis of dementia: Having more abdominal fat is associated with a greater risk of having dementia. (And therefore having less abdominal fat is associated with having less dementia.) In the second example, the variables are cell phone use and sperm quality: More frequent cell phone use is associated with poorer sperm quality.

An association claim must involve at least two variables, and the variables are measured, not manipulated. (This is one feature that distinguishes an association claim from a causal claim.) To make an association claim, the researcher measures the variables and then uses descriptive statistics to see whether the two variables are related. There are four basic types of associations among variables: positive associations, negative associations, zero associations, and curvilinear associations.

For more on correlation patterns, see Chapter 7.

Positive Associations

The headline "Belly Fat Linked to Dementia, Study Shows" suggests that, on average, the more abdominal fat people have, the more dementia symptoms they are likely to exhibit. The kind of association in this example, in which high goes with high and low goes with low, is called a **positive association**, or a *positive correlation*. That is, high scores on abdominal fat go with more symptoms of dementia, and low scores on abdominal fat go with fewer symptoms of dementia.

One way to represent an association is to use a **scatterplot**, in which one variable is plotted on the y-axis and the other variable is plotted on the x-axis; each dot represents one participant in the study, measured on two variables.

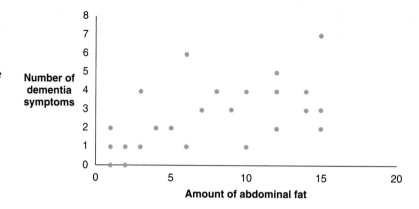

FIGURE 3.2 A positive relationship: "Belly fat linked to dementia, study shows." (Data are fabricated for the purpose of illustration.)

Figure 3.2 shows what a scatterplot of the association between abdominal fat and number of dementia symptoms might look like. Notice that the dots in the scatterplot form a cloud of points, as opposed to a straight line. If you were to draw a straight line that best fit through that cloud of points, however, the line would incline upward. In other words, the mathematical slope of the line would be positive.

Negative Associations

The second headline example, "Heavy Cell Phone Use Tied to Poor Sperm Quality," could be restated as "Men who spend more time using a cell phone have lower quality of sperm." This type of association, in which high goes with low and low goes with high, is called a **negative association**, or a *negative correlation*. That is, high rates of cell phone usage go with low sperm quality, and low rates of cell phone usage go with high sperm quality.

If we were to draw a scatterplot to represent this relationship, it might look something like the one in **Figure 3.3**. Again, in this scatterplot, each dot represents a person who has been measured on two variables. However, in this example, a line drawn through the cloud of points would slope downward—it would have a negative slope.

Keep in mind that the term *negative* refers only to the slope; it does not mean that the relationship is somehow bad. In this example, the reverse of the association—that men who use cell phones less tend to have better sperm quality—is another way to phrase this negative association. In other words, a negative association does not necessarily indicate negative news. To avoid this kind of confusion, some people prefer the term *inverse association*.

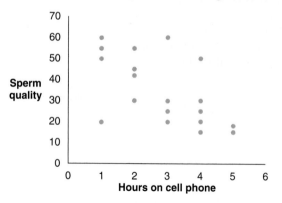

FIGURE 3.3 A negative (inverse) relationship: "Heavy cell phone use tied to poor sperm quality." (Data are fabricated for the purpose of illustration.)

Zero Association or Zero Correlation

The headline "ADHD Drugs Not Linked to Future Drug Abuse" is an example of **zero association**, or no association between the variables. In a scatterplot of

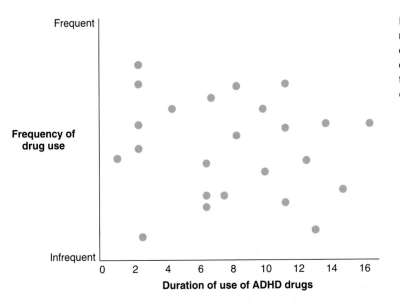

FIGURE 3.4 **A zero relationship: "ADHD drugs not linked to future drug abuse."** (Data are fabricated for the purpose of illustration.)

this association, both using and not using ADHD drugs would be associated with all levels of future drug abuse, as in **Figure 3.4**. This cloud of points has no slope—or more specifically, a line drawn through it would be nearly horizontal, and a horizontal line has a slope of zero.

Curvilinear Association

In some cases, associations can be curvilinear, meaning that the level of one variable changes its pattern as the other variable increases. An example of a **curvilinear association** is the relationship between age and frequency of health care visits, as depicted in **Figure 3.5**. The very young and the very old both have higher levels of health care use than those who are in their teens and middle adulthood.

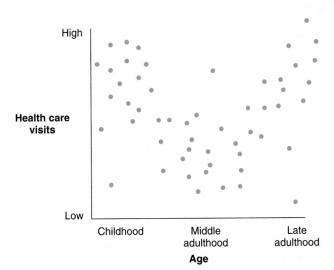

FIGURE 3.5 **A curvilinear relationship between age and use of health services.** High and low values on age are associated with high use of health services. A medium value on age is associated with lower use of health services. (Data are fabricated for the purpose of illustration.)

Making Predictions Based on Associations

Some association claims are useful because they help us make predictions. With a positive or negative association, if we know the level of one variable, we can more accurately guess, or predict, the level of the other variable. Note that the term *predict*, as used here, does not necessarily mean predicting into the future. It means predicting in a mathematical sense—using the association to make our estimates more accurate.

To return to the headlines, according to the positive relationship described in the first example, if you know how much abdominal fat a person has, you can predict certain brain changes related to dementia that the person might have. According to the negative relationship in the second example, if you know how many hours a man spends on his cell phone, you can predict his sperm quality. Are these predictions going to be perfect? No—they will usually be off by a certain margin. The stronger the relationship between the two variables, the more accurate your prediction will be; the weaker the relationship between the two variables, the less accurate your prediction will be. But if two variables are even somewhat associated, or correlated, it helps us make much better predictions than we would if we did not know about this association.

For instance, people's height at age 2 is positively associated with their height at age eighteen. If we know a tall 2-year-old, we can predict that the child will be a tall adult. Similarly, if an 18-year-old is relatively short, we can predict that he or she was a relatively short 2-year-old. (Note that in this second example we would be "predicting" into the past.)

To understand how an association can help us make more accurate predictions, imagine that we want to guess how tall an 18-year-old (we will call him Hugo) was as a 2-year-old. If we know absolutely nothing about Hugo's adult height, our best bet would be to guess that Hugo's 2-year-old height is exactly average. Hugo might have been taller than average or shorter than average, so we would do best to split the difference. In the United States, the average height (or 50th percentile) for a 2-year-old boy is 58 centimeters (see **Figure 3.6**)—so we would guess that Hugo was 58 centimeters tall as a 2-year-old.

But imagine that we learn that Hugo is a relatively short 18-year-old—that his height is 171 centimeters, in the 25th percentile of adult males in height. In that case, we would lower the prediction of Hugo's 2-year-old height accordingly, because we know that 2-year-old height is positively correlated with 18-year-old height. If Hugo is in the 25th percentile of adult males in height, we should guess that his 2-year-old height was 54 centimeters, the height of the 25th percentile among 2-year-olds.

Are our predictions of Hugo's childhood height likely to be perfect? Of course not—they will probably be off by a centimeter or two. But the error of prediction will be smaller if we use his adult height to guess his 2-year-old height, as opposed to estimating his 2-year-old height based on the average height of 2-year-olds. Let's say we find out that Hugo was actually 55 centimeters tall at age 2. If we had guessed that Hugo's 2-year-old height was average (58 centimeters), we would have been off by 3 centimeters. But using Hugo's adult height as a guide, we would have guessed lower (54 centimeters)—so we would have been off by only 1 centimeter. Associations help us make predictions by reducing the

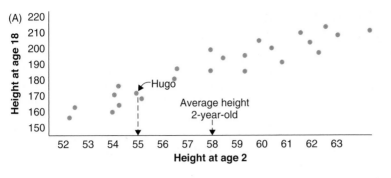

(A)

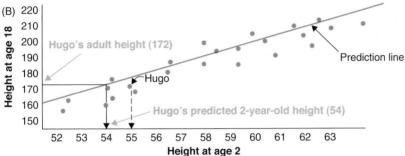

(B)

FIGURE 3.6 **(a)** If we used only the average 2-year-old height to predict Hugo, we would be off by 3 cm; **(b)** If we know that Hugo's adult height is in the 25th percentile (172 cm), the best estimation of his height at 2 years is that it was also in the 25th percentile (54 cm). If we used the correlation between 2-year-old and 18-year-old height to predict Hugo, we would be off by only 1cm. *Source*: Centers for Disease Control (2000).

size of our prediction errors. And the stronger the association is, the more accurate our predictions are (see **Figure 3.7**).

Both positive and negative associations can help us make predictions. In contrast, zero associations cannot. If we wanted to predict the chances that a teenager will use recreational drugs (say, marijuana) in a particular month, what information would we use? According to the CDC, 19.7% of teens in their survey reported using marijuana in the last 30 days, so we might predict that a particular teenager would have a 19.7% chance of using marijuana in a particular month, too. But what if this teenager has taken ADHD medications in the past? Could we use that information to predict his current marijuana use? No, we cannot. The study showed that use of ADHD medication is not correlated with drug use, so we cannot predict drug use any better by knowing whether a teenager took ADHD medication as a child. With a zero correlation, we cannot predict the level of one variable from the level of the other, so our best bet is simply to guess the mean, or average.

Causal Claims

Music Lessons Enhance IQ

Debt Stress Causing Health Problems, Poll Finds

Family Meals Curb Teen Eating Disorders

Whereas an association claim merely notes a relationship between two variables, a **causal claim** goes even further, arguing that one of these

FIGURE 3.7 **Houston Rockets basketball player Yao Ming.** Yao Ming, at 7 feet, 5 inches (2.26 meters) tall, is at the 99th percentile for height among young men. How tall would you predict he was as a 2-year-old?

TABLE 3.2 Verb Phrases That Can Help You Decide Whether a Claim Is Association or Causal

Association claim verbs	Causal claim verbs	
is linked to	causes	promotes
goes with	affects	reduces
is associated with	curbs	prevents
is correlated with	exacerbates	distracts
prefers	changes	fights
are more/less likely to	leads to	worsens
predicts	makes	increases
is tied to	helps	trims
is at risk for	hurts	adds

variables is responsible for changing the other. Note that each of the causal claims above has two variables, just like association claims: music lessons and IQ, debt stress and health problems, family meals and eating disorders.

In addition, like association claims, the causal claims above suggest that the two variables in question covary—children who take music lessons have higher IQs. People with more debt stress have more health problems. Like associations, causal relationships can be positive, negative, or curvilinear. Music lessons are positively associated with IQ, and family meals are negatively associated with eating disorders (the more family meals, the fewer eating disorders).

But the causal claims do not simply draw an association between the two variables. They use causal language to suggest that one variable causes the other—verbs such as *cause*, *enhance*, and *curb*. In contrast, association claims use verbs such as *linked*, *associated*, *correlated*, *predicted*, *tied to*, and *is at risk for*. Do you notice the difference between these types of verbs? The causal verbs tend to be more exciting somehow: they are active and forceful, suggesting that one variable acts on the other. It is not surprising, then, that journalists may be tempted to describe family meals as *curbing* eating disorders, for example, because it makes a better story than family meals just *being associated with* eating disorders. (See **Table 3.2** for more causal verbs.)

Here's another important point: A causal claim that contains tentative language—*could*, *may*, *seem*, *suggest*, *possible*, *potential*—is still a causal claim. That is, if the first headline read "Music Lessons *May* Enhance IQ," it would be more tentative, but it still would be a causal claim. The causal verb *enhance* makes it a causal claim, regardless of any softening language used.

Therefore, causal claims are special—they are a step above association claims. And because they make a stronger statement, we hold them to higher standards. To move from the simple language of association to the language of causality, a study has to meet three criteria. First, it must establish that the two variables (the cause variable and the outcome variable) are correlated—the relationship cannot be zero. Second, it must show that the causal variable came first and the outcome variable came later. Third, it must establish that no other explanations exist for the relationship. (Later in this chapter, you will read about how researchers design special types of studies, called *experiments*, that enable them to support causal claims.)

1. How many variables are there in a frequency claim? In an association claim? In a causal claim?
2. How can the language used in a claim help you differentiate between association and causal claims?
3. How are causal claims special, compared with the other two claims?

1. See p. 58, 59, and 64. **2.** See p. 64 and Table 3.2. **3.** See p. 64.

Interrogating the Three Claims Using the Four Big Validities

You now have the tools to differentiate among the three major claims you will encounter in research journals and in the popular media. But your job is just getting started. Once you identify the kind of claim a writer is making, you need to ask targeted questions as a critically minded consumer of information. The rest of this chapter will sharpen your ability to evaluate the claims you come across using what might be called "the four big validities": construct validity, external validity, statistical validity, and internal validity. In general, a *valid* claim is reasonable, accurate, and justifiable. But in psychological research, we do not say that a claim is simply "valid." Instead, psychologists specify which of the validities they are applying. As a psychology student, you will learn to pause before you declare that a study is "valid" or "not valid." Instead, you will learn to specify which of the four big validities the study has achieved.

Although the focus for now is on how you can evaluate other people's claims based on the four big validities, you will also use this same framework if you plan to conduct your own research. Depending on whether you plan to test a frequency, an association, or a causal hypothesis, you will need to plan your research carefully, in order to emphasize the validities that are most important for your goals.

Interrogating Frequency Claims

To evaluate how well a study supports a frequency claim, you will usually need to ask about two of the big validities: construct validity and external validity.

Construct Validity of Frequency Claims

To ask about the construct validity of a frequency claim, the question to consider is how well the researchers measured their variables. Take the claim "2 million U.S. teens depressed," for example. There are probably dozens of ways to evaluate whether a person is depressed. You could ask trained therapists to clinically interview teenagers and assess which of them are depressed. You could ask study participants to complete a structured, self-report questionnaire, such as the Beck Depression Inventory (Beck, Ward, & Mendelson, 1961). You could ask teachers or parents to report their observations of teenagers' moods, sleep habits, and motivation. In short, there are a number of ways to operationalize depression as a variable, some of which are better than others.

When you ask how well a study measured or manipulated a variable, you are interrogating the **construct validity** of the operationalization. Construct validity concerns how accurately a researcher has operationalized each variable, be it depression, happiness, debt stress, gender, body mass index, or self-esteem. For example, you would expect a study on obesity rates to use an accurate scale to weigh participants. Similarly, you should expect a study about depression in teenagers to use an accurate measure of depression, and a clinical interview is probably a better measure than casually asking teenagers, "Do you think you're depressed?" To ensure construct validity, researchers must establish that each variable has been measured reliably (that is, be sure that the measure gives similar scores on repeated testings) and that different levels of a variable accurately correspond to true differences in, say, depression or happiness.

For more detail on construct validity, see Chapter 5.

External Validity of Frequency Claims

The second important question to ask about frequency claims concerns **generalizability**: How did the researchers choose the study's participants, and how well do those participants represent the population they are supposed to represent? Take the example "Half of Americans struggle to stay happy." Did the researchers survey every American to come up with this number? Of course not. They surveyed only a small proportion of Americans, so the next question is, which Americans did they ask? That is, how did they choose their participants? Did they ask a few friends? Did they ask 100 college students? Did they dial random numbers on the telephone? Did they stop shoppers in the mall?

Such questions address one aspect of the study's **external validity**—how well the results of the study generalize to, or represent, people and contexts besides those in the study itself. If one of the researchers asked 20 of his own friends how happy they were and 10 of them said they struggled to stay happy, this researcher cannot claim that half of Americans struggle to stay happy. The researcher cannot even argue that half of his friends struggle to stay happy, because the twenty people he happened to ask may not be a representative selection of his friends. Maybe he asked his 20 Alaskan friends—and asked them in the middle of December, when the sun rarely shines and people are typically less happy than usual. To claim that half of Americans struggle to stay happy, the researchers in this study needed to ensure that the participants adequately represented all Americans.

For more on the procedures that researchers use to ensure external validity, see Chapter 6, pp. 164–176.

Interrogating Association Claims

Construct Validity of Association Claims

As we've seen, association claims differ from frequency claims in that they measure two variables instead of just one, and they describe how these variables are related to each other. When you encounter an association claim, you should evaluate construct validity, just as you would with a frequency claim. Because an association claim measures two variables, however, you need to assess the construct validity of *each* variable. For the headline "Heavy Cell Phone Use Tied to Poor Sperm Quality," you should ask how well the researchers measured cell phone use and how well they measured sperm quality. For example, cell phone use could be measured quite accurately using phone bills; a much less accurate measure would be obtained by asking people to remember how much they use their cell phones.

In any study, measurement of variables is a fundamental strength or weakness—and construct-validity questions assess how well such measurement was conducted. If you gather information on construct validity and conclude that one of the variables was measured poorly, you would not be able to trust the conclusions related to that variable. However, if you conclude that the construct validity in the study was excellent, you can have more confidence in the association being reported.

External Validity of Association Claims

You might also interrogate the external validity of association claims—whether the association in question can generalize to other populations, as well as to other contexts, times, or places. For the association between cell phone use and sperm quality, you would ask whether the results from this study's participants (perhaps a group of 20- to 30-year-old volunteers from Cleveland) would generalize to other people and settings. For example, would these same results be obtained if all of the participants were 35- to 40-year-old men in Dallas? You can ask about generalization to other contexts by asking, for example, if sperm quality might also be linked to other electronic devices besides cell phones—such as portable video games or music players.

Statistical Validity of Association Claims: Avoiding Two Mistaken Conclusions

Another important set of questions to ask about association claims concerns the appropriateness of the study's statistical conclusions. Psychologists use statistics to describe their data and to estimate the probability that a pattern of results can or cannot be attributed to chance. **Statistical validity**, also called *statistical conclusion validity*, is the extent to which those statistical conclusions are accurate and reasonable.

Generally speaking, a study that has good statistical validity has been designed to minimize two kinds of mistakes. First, a study might mistakenly conclude, based on the results from a sample of people, that there is an association between two variables (say, abdominal fat and dementia risk), when there really is *no* association in the real population. Careful researchers try to minimize the chance that they will make this kind of mistake—a "false alarm." They want to increase the chances that they will find associations only when they are really there.

Second, a study might mistakenly conclude from a sample that there is no association between two variables (say, use of ADHD medication and later drug abuse) when there really *is* an association in the full population. Careful researchers try to minimize the chances of making this kind of mistake, too—to reduce the chances that they will miss associations that are really there. These kinds of

TABLE 3.3 The Four Big Validities

Type of Validity	Description
Construct validity	How well the variables in the study are measured or manipulated. Are the operational variables used in the study a good approximation of the constructs of interest?
External validity	The degree to which the results of the study generalize to some larger population (do the results from this sample of children apply to all U.S. school children?), as well as to other situations (do the results based on this type of music apply to other types of music?).
Statistical validity	How well a study minimizes the probabilities of two errors: concluding that there is an effect when in fact there is none (a "false alarm," or Type I error) or concluding that there is no effect when in fact there is one (a "miss," or Type II error); also addresses the strength of an association and its statistical significance (the probability that the results could have been obtained by chance if there really is no relationship).
Internal validity	In a relationship between one variable (A) and another (B), the degree to which we can say that A, rather than some other variable (such as C), is responsible for the effect on B.

mistakes (false alarms and misses) are referred to as Type I and Type II errors, respectively, and are fully explained in Appendix B.

Statistical Validity of Association Claims: Strength and Significance

You need to consider some additional questions as you examine the statistical validity of a study. For an association claim, one important question to ask is, How strong is the association? Some associations—such as the association between height and shoe size—are quite strong. People who are tall almost always have larger feet than people who are short, so if you predict shoe size from height, you will predict fairly accurately. But other associations—such as the association between height and income—might be very weak. For example, it turns out that because of a stereotype that favors tall people (tall people are more admired in North America), taller people do earn more money than short people. However, the relationship is not very strong. Though you can predict income from height, your prediction will be less accurate than when you predict height from shoe size. Another question worth interrogating is the statistical significance of a particular association. Some associations that are reported by researchers might simply be due to chance connections between the two variables—but if an association is statistically significant, it is probably not due to chance. For example, if the association between abdominal fat and dementia risk is statistically significant, it would mean that there is a low probability that the association is merely a chance result (when there is not true association).

As you might imagine, evaluating statistical validity can be complicated. Full training in how to interrogate statistical validity requires a separate, semester-long statistics class. This book introduces you to the basics: You will

For more about association strength and statistical significance, see Chapter 7, pp. 193–195.

learn what research designs can help avoid Type I and Type II errors, as well as what statistical significance means and how many participants are usually needed for a study.

In sum, when you come across an association claim, you should ask about three validities: construct, external, and statistical. You can ask how well the two variables were measured (construct validity). You can ask whether you can generalize the result to a population (external validity). And you can ask about whether the researchers might have made any statistical conclusion errors, as well as evaluating the strength and significance of the association (statistical validity).

Interrogating Causal Claims

Unlike an association claim, a causal claim says not only that two variables are simply related but also that one variable causes the other. Instead of using verbs such as *is associated with*, *is related to*, and *is linked to*, causal claims use directional verbs such as *affects*, *leads to*, or *reduces*. When you interrogate such a claim, your first step will be to ensure that the research backing it up fulfills the three rules for causation: covariance, temporal precedence, and internal validity.

Three Rules for Causation

Of course, one variable usually cannot be said to cause another variable unless the two covary. **Covariance** is the first rule a study must meet in order to establish a causal claim. But to justify using a causal verb, the data must do more than just show that two variables are associated. A study must meet two additional criteria to justify the use of causal language: temporal precedence and internal validity (see **Table 3.4**).

To say that one variable has **temporal precedence** means that it comes first in time, before the other variable. To make the claim "Music lessons enhance IQ," a study must show that the music lessons came first and the gains in IQ came later. Although this statement might seem obvious, it is not always so. In a simple association, it might be the case that music lessons made the children smart. But it is also possible that children who start out smart are more likely to want to take music lessons. It is not always clear which one came first. Similarly, to make the claim "Debt stress causes health problems," the study needs to show that debt stress came first and the health problems came later. Otherwise,

TABLE 3.4 The Three Rules for Establishing Causation Between Variable A and Variable B

Rule	Definition
Covariance	As A changes, B changes; for example, as A increases, B increases, and as A decreases, B decreases.
Temporal precedence	A comes first in time, before B.
Internal validity	There are no possible alternative explanations for the change in B; A is the only thing that changed.

it might be that people who have health problems are more likely to rack up debt—and more debt leads to more debt stress.

Another criterion, called **internal validity**, or the *third-variable rule*, means that a study should be able to rule out alternative explanations for the association. For example, to claim that "Music lessons enhance IQ" is to claim that the music lessons *cause* the increase in IQ. But an alternative explanation could be that children from better school districts might both have higher IQ scores *and* be more involved in lessons and activities. That is, there could be an internal validity problem—it is the school district, not the music lessons, that causes these children to score higher on IQ tests. In Chapter 2 you read about confounds in personal experience. Such confounds are also examples of internal validity problems.

Experiments Can Test Causal Claims

What kind of study can satisfy all three criteria for causal claims? Usually, to support a causal claim, researchers must conduct a well-designed **experiment**, in which one variable is manipulated and the other is measured.

Experiments are considered the gold standard of psychological research because of their potential to support causal claims. In everyday life people tend to use the term *experiment* rather loosely, to refer to any trial of something to see what happens ("Let's experiment and try making the popcorn with olive oil instead"). But the term has a specific meaning for psychologists and other scientists. When psychologists do an experiment, they *manipulate* the variable they think is the cause and *measure* the variable they think is the effect. (In the context of an experiment, the manipulated variable is called the **independent variable**, and the measured variable is called the **dependent variable**.) For example, to see whether music lessons enhance IQ, the researchers in that study had to manipulate the music lessons variable and measure the IQ variable.

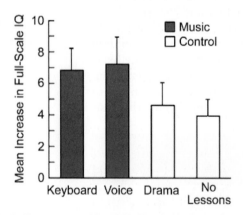

Fig. 1. Mean increase in full-scale IQ (Wechsler Intelligence Scale for Children–Third Edition) for each group of 6-year-olds who completed the study. Error bars show standard errors.

FIGURE 3.8 Results of Schellenberg's (2004) study of music lessons and IQ, including the original caption. What key features of Schellenberg's study made it possible for him to claim that music lessons increase children's IQ?

Remember—to *manipulate* a variable means to assign participants to be at one level or the other. In the music example, the researchers might assign some children to take music lessons, some children to take another kind of lesson, and a third group to take no lessons. In an actual study that tested this claim, researcher Glen Schellenberg (2004) of Toronto, Canada, manipulated the music lesson variable by assigning some children to take music lessons (either keyboard lessons or voice lessons), other children to take drama lessons, and still other children to take no lessons. After several months of lessons, he measured the IQs of all the children. At the conclusion of his study, Schellenberg found that the children who took keyboard and voice lessons gained an average of 3.7 IQ points more than the children who took drama lessons or no lessons. (**Figure 3.8** shows a graph of Schellenberg's results.) This was a statistically significant gain. Thus, he established the first part of a causal claim: covariance.

Experiments Provide Temporal Precedence and Internal Validity. Why does the process of manipulating one variable and measuring the other help scientists make causal claims? For one thing, manipulating the causal variable ensures that it comes first. By showing that the music lessons came before the increase in IQ, Schellenberg ensured temporal precedence in his study.

In addition, when researchers manipulate a variable, they can control for alternative explanations; that is, they can ensure internal validity. For example, when Schellenberg was investigating whether music lessons could enhance IQ, he did not want the children in the music lessons groups to have more involved parents than those in the drama lessons group or the no lessons group, because then the involvement of parents would have been a plausible alternative explanation for why the music lessons enhanced IQ. He did not want the children in the music lessons groups to come from a different school district than those in the drama lessons group or the no-lessons group, because then the schools' curricula or teacher quality might have been alternative explanations. Instead, Schellenberg used **random assignment** to ensure that the children in the four groups were as similar as possible. That is, he used a random method, such as drawing numbers out of hat, to decide whether each child in his study would take keyboard lessons, voice lessons, drama lessons, or no lessons. Only by randomly assigning children to one of the groups could Schellenberg ensure that the children who took music lessons were as similar as possible, in every other way, to those who took drama lessons or no lessons. Random assignment increased internal validity by allowing Schellenberg to control for potential alternative explanations.

For more on how random assignment helps ensure that the groups are similar, see Chapter 9, pp. 251–252.

Because Schellenberg's experiment met all three rules of causation—covariance, temporal precedence, and internal validity—he was justified in making a causal claim from his data. His study found that music lessons really do enhance (that is, *cause* an increase in) IQ.

When Causal Claims Are a Mistake

By now, you may have come to suspect that two of the causal claims used as examples in this chapter are problematic. Let's use them to illustrate how to interrogate causal claims by writers and journalists.

Does Debt Stress Really Cause Health Problems? To be convinced of the causal claim "Debt Stress Causing Health Problems, Poll Finds," we would first need to confirm that the study established the covariance of debt stress and health problems. And apparently it did: The article states that "among the people reporting high debt stress, 27% had ulcers or digestive tract problems, compared with 8 percent of those with low levels of debt stress," and "44% had migraines or headaches, compared with 15%." So far, so good—there is a positive association between debt stress and health problems.

Does the study described in the headline establish the temporal precedence of debt stress? That is, did the study establish that debt stress came before the health

FIGURE 3.9 Debt stress and health problems. When debt stress is associated with health problems, is it clear that the debt stress caused the health problems? Could the health problems lead to debt stress? Could some other variable cause both of these problems?

problems? The answer here is no. If the data came from a poll, the researchers measured health problems and debt stress at the same time. So we have no way of knowing whether the debt stress came first and caused the health problems (worries might take a toll on the human body) or whether the opposite is true: Perhaps people's health problems came first and contributed to their debt, and therefore their debt stress. After all, health problems can prevent people from working and can even put them into debt (see **Figure 3.9**). In short, a poll is ill-suited to establishing temporal precedence.

What about internal validity? Are there alternative explanations for the association? On this criterion too, this study comes up short. Some outside, third variable could be contributing to both the debt stress and the health problems. There may be some people—perhaps those who are not very conscientious—who are disorganized about their finances and who are not proactive about preventive health. In contrast, more conscientious people tend to lead healthier lives *and* be more responsible about financial obligations (Bogg & Roberts, 2004; Roberts & Robins, 2000). Or perhaps the debt-stressed, unhealthy people in this study happened to live in one type of community (such as suburban areas, where people get less exercise, leading to health problems, and buy houses that they cannot afford, leading to debt stress), and those who were less debt stressed and more healthy lived in another type of community (such as urban communities, where people rent apartments and are more likely to walk and get frequent exercise). Again, in a poll like this, both variables are simply measured, and such a study is not well suited for establishing internal validity.

Because it is not possible to set up an experiment about debt stress—researchers cannot practically or ethically assign people to have more debt or less debt—it is not possible to make a strong causal statement about debt stress and health problems. In this story, the journalist should have stuck with the less flashy (but still interesting) headline, "Debt Stress *Linked to* Health Problems, Poll Finds."

Do Family Meals Really Curb Eating Disorders? To interrogate the claim "Family meals curb teen eating disorders," we would again start by asking about covariance. Is there an association between family meals and eating disorders? Yes: The news report says that 26% of girls who ate with their families fewer than five times a week had eating-disordered behavior (such as the use of laxatives or diuretics or self-induced vomiting), whereas only 17% of girls who ate with their families five or more times a week engaged in these behaviors. The two variables are associated. But what about temporal precedence? Did the researchers make sure that family meals had increased before the eating disorders decreased? The best way to ensure temporal precedence is to assign some families to have more meals together than others. Sure, families who eat more meals together may have fewer daughters with disordered eating behavior, but the temporal precedence simply is not clear from this association. Indeed, one of the symptoms of an eating disorder is embarrassment about eating in front of others, so perhaps the eating disorder came first and the reduction in meals eaten together came second. Daughters with eating disorders may simply find excuses to avoid eating with their families.

Internal validity is a problem here, too. Without an experiment, we cannot rule out a wide variety of alternative, third-variable explanations. Perhaps girls from single-parent families are both less likely to eat with their families and to be vulnerable to eating disorders, whereas girls who live with both parents are not. Perhaps high-achieving girls are too busy to eat with their families and are also more susceptible to disordered dieting behavior. These are only two of many possible alternative explanations. Only a well-run experiment could have controlled for these internal validity problems (these alternative explanations), using random assignment to ensure that the girls who had frequent family dinners and those who had less-frequent family dinners were identical in all other ways: high versus low scholastic achievement, single- versus two-parent households, and so on. However, it would be impractical and probably unethical to do an experiment like this. Although the study's authors reported the findings appropriately, the journalist jumped to a causal conclusion by saying that family dinners *curb* eating disorders.

Other Validities to Interrogate in a Causal Claim

A study can support a causal claim only if it shows covariance, and only if the variables were collected in a way that ensures both temporal precedence and internal validity. Therefore, internal validity is only important for a causal claim. In addition, but it is one of the most important validities to evaluate for causal claims. Besides internal validity, the other three validities discussed in this chapter—construct validity, statistical validity, and to a lesser extent, external validity—can be interrogated, too.

Construct Validity of Causal Claims. Take the headline "Music Lessons Enhance IQ." First, we could ask about the construct validity of the measured variable in this study. How well was IQ measured? Was an established IQ test administered by trained testers? Then we would need to interrogate the construct validity of the manipulated variable, too. In operationalizing manipulated variables, researchers need to create a specific task or situation that will represent each level of the variable. In the current example, how well did the researchers manipulate music lessons? Did students take private lessons for several weeks or have one large group lesson, for example?

For more on how researchers use data to check the construct validity of their manipulations, see Chapter 9, pp. 265–267.

External Validity of Causal Claims. We could ask, as well, about external validity. If the study used children in Toronto, Canada, as participants, do the results generalize to Japanese children? Do the results generalize to rural Canadian children? That is, if Japanese students or rural students take music lessons, will their IQs go up, too? And what about generalization to other settings? Could the results generalize to other music lessons? Would flute lessons and violin lessons also work? In Chapters 9 and 13, you will learn more about how to evaluate the external validity of experiments and other studies.

Statistical Validity of Causal Claims. Finally, we can ask about statistical validity. To start, we would want to evaluate how well the design of the study allowed the researchers to minimize the probability of making the relevant conclusion mistake—a false alarm (concluding that music raises IQ when it really does not). We can also ask, as we did with association claims, how strong the association is. That is, how strong is the relationship between music lessons and IQ? In the study in question, the students who were assigned to take music lessons gained 7 points in IQ, whereas students who did not gained an average of 4.3 points in IQ—a net gain of about 3.7 IQ points. Is this a large gain? (In this case, the difference between these two groups is about 0.35 of a standard deviation, which is considered a moderate difference between the two groups.) Finally, asking whether the difference between the lessons groups was statistically significant helps ensure that the covariance rule was met—it helps us be surer that the difference is not just due to chance. You will learn more about interrogating the statistical validity of causal claims in Chapter 9.

For more on determining the strength of a relationship, see Appendix A, p. A13.

Producers of Information: Prioritizing Validities

Although the four validities discussed in this chapter are all important, no study can be perfect. In fact, when researchers plan studies to test hypotheses and support claims, they usually find it impossible to conduct a study that satisfies all four validities at once. Indeed, depending on their goals, sometimes researchers do not even try to satisfy all four validities. Why is that okay? Researchers decide what their priorities are—and so will you, when you participate in research as a producer.

For example, external validity is not always possible to achieve—and sometimes it may not even be relevant. As you will learn in Chapter 6, to be able to generalize results from a sample to a wide population requires a representative sample from that population. Consider the study by Schellenberg (2004) on music lessons and IQ. Because he was planning to test a causal claim, Schellenberg wanted to emphasize internal validity, so he focused on randomly assigning his group of participants to the music lessons groups or to the no-music groups. His focus was on internal validity, so Schellenberg was not prioritizing external validity. He did not randomly sample children from all over Canada. However, Schellenberg's study is still important and interesting because it used an internally valid experimental method—even though it did not have perfect external validity.

In contrast, if some researchers were conducting a telephone survey and did want to generalize its results to the entire Canadian population—to maximize external validity—they would have to randomly select Canadians from all 10 provinces. One way the researchers might do so would be to use a random-digit telephone dialing system to call people in their homes, but this technology is expensive. When researchers do use formal, randomly sampled polls, they often have to pay the polling company a fee to administer each question. So a researcher who wants to evaluate, say, the depression levels in a large population may be forced by economics to use a simple one- or two-question measure of depression, rather than a well-established, fifteen-question measure of depression, although the two-item measure of depression is not as good as the fifteen-item measure. In this example, the researcher might sacrifice some construct validity in order to achieve external validity.

You will learn more about these priorities in Chapter 13. The point, for now, is simply that in the course of planning and conducting a study, scientists weigh the pros and cons of research choices and decide which validities are most important.

Check Your Understanding

1. Which of the four big validities should you apply to a frequency claim? To an association claim?
2. What question(s) would you ask to interrogate a study's construct validity?
3. In your own words, describe at least three things that statistical validity addresses.
4. Define external validity, using the term *generalize* in your definition.
5. What is internal validity? Why is it mostly relevant for causal claims?
6. Why don't researchers usually aim to achieve all four of the big validities at once?

1. See pp. 65–66; see pp. 66–68. 2. See pp. 65–66. 3. See pp. 67–69. 4. See p. 66 and Table 3.3. 5. See p. 70. 6. See p. 74.

Review: Four Validities, Four Aspects of Quality

As a review, let's apply the four validities discussed in this chapter to another headline from a popular news source: "Social Isolation May Have a Negative Effect on Intellectual Abilities." The story appeared in *Medical News Today*, an online source that collects medical research stories from various sources. Should we consider this a well-designed study? How well does it hold up on each of the four validities? At this stage in the course, your focus should be on asking the right questions for each validity. In later chapters, you will also learn how to evaluate the answers to those questions.

Here is an excerpt from the online source, describing the study:

> In a[n] experiment, the researchers conducted a laboratory test to assess how social interactions and intellectual exercises affected memory and mental performance. Participants were 76 college students, ages 18 to 21. Each student was assigned to one of three groups. Those in the social interaction group engaged in a discussion of a social issue for 10 minutes before taking the tests. Those in the intellectual activities group completed three tasks before taking the tests. These tasks included a reading comprehension exercise and a crossword puzzle. Participants in a control group watched a 10-minute clip of *Seinfeld*.
>
> Then all participants completed two different tests of intellectual performance that measured their mental processing speed and working memory. "We found that short-term social interaction lasting for just 10 minutes boosted participants' intellectual performance as much as engaging in so-called 'intellectual' activities for the same amount of time," Ybarra said. ("Social Isolation," 2007)

Based on this short description, what questions might we pose about the study to assess each kind of validity? By asking questions and looking for answers, we begin to learn that some of the validities can be evaluated just from the web-based news source, but others can only be evaluated by reading the journal article itself (Ybarra et al., 2008).

Most important, the headline claims that social isolation negatively *affects* intellectual abilities. But does the study support a causal claim? That is, does the study show not just an association but also temporal precedence and internal validity? In fact, you can tell from the story that the researchers *did* run an experiment, because they manipulated the social interaction variable and measured the intellectual performance variable. Because they manipulated one variable and measured another, we can be much more certain that the researchers can support a causal statement. As you interrogate internal validity further, you might ask how the researchers ensured that the three experimental groups were the same. The article says that all three groups performed their respective activities for 10 minutes, but were the participants randomly assigned, in order to control for other possible third variables? The researchers probably did use random assignment, but you would need to access the journal article's Method section to be sure.

We might also interrogate the study's construct validity—asking, for example, how well the researchers measured the variable of intellectual ability. The story reports that the intellectual abilities measured were mental processing speed and working memory, but it does not say how they were measured. Because the journalist does not say, we know that we need to follow up by reading the original study in the journal—using the authors' names provided—to find out what kinds of measures were used. We can also ask about the construct validity of the manipulation: Is talking with others a good manipulation of "social inclusion"? Is watching *Seinfeld* a good manipulation of "social isolation" (**Figure 3.10**)?

You could also ask questions about the external validity of this study. The article says that the participants in the study were college students between the ages of 18 and 21. Can the study's findings be generalized to other U.S. populations? To children? How about generalizing to other forms of social interaction, such as sharing thoughts and feelings? Such questions address the study's external

For more on external validity, see Chapter 7, pp. 201–204; Chapter 9, pp. 267–269; and Chapter 13, pp. 385–399.

FIGURE 3.10 Construct validity in Ybarra and colleagues' (2008) study. In this study, social isolation was operationalized as watching television versus participating in a discussion group. What other ways could psychologists have studied the effects of social isolation?

validity. (Remember, however, that external validity is usually not researchers' first priority when they are conducting an experiment.) (See **Table 3.5** for a summary of the three types of claims and the validities that are relevant for each type.)

Finally, we might also ask questions about the statistical validity of this study. We could ask, What are the chances that this finding on social isolation is a false alarm? We could also ask about the size of the effect: *How much* better was the intellectual performance of those in the social interaction group? We could also ask, Was the difference statistically significant (not due to chance)? Some of the answers to these questions might be included in the story: For example,

TABLE 3.5 Interrogating the Three Types of Claims Using the Four Big Validities

	Frequency claims (e.g., "Half of Americans struggle to stay happy")	Association claims (e.g., "Cell phone use linked to poor sperm quality")	Causal claims (e.g, "Music lessons enhance IQ")
Construct validity	How well have you measured the variable in question?	How well have you measured each of the two variables in the association?	How well have you measured or manipulated the variables in the study?
Statistical validity	What is the margin of error of the estimate?	If the study finds a relationship, what is the probability the researcher's conclusion is a false alarm? If the study finds no relationship, what is the probability the researchers are missing a true relationship? What is the effect size? How strong is the association? Is the association statistically significant?	If the study finds a difference, what is the probability that the researcher's conclusion is a false alarm? If the study finds no difference, what is the probability the researchers are missing a true relationship? What is the effect size? Is there a difference, and how large is it? Is the difference between groups statistically significant?
Internal validity	Frequency claims are usually not asserting causality, so internal validity is not relevant.	People who make association claims are not asserting causality, so internal validity is not relevant to interrogate. However, you should avoid making a causal claim from a simple association (see Chapter 7).	Was the study an experiment? Does the study achieve temporal precedence? Does the study control for alternative explanations by limiting confounds and by randomly assigning participants to groups? Does the study avoid several internal validity threats (see Chapters 9 and 10)?
External validity	To what populations, settings, and times can we generalize this estimate? How representative is the sample—was it a random sample?	To what populations, settings, and times can we generalize this association claim? How representative is the sample? To what other settings or problems might the association be generalized?	To what populations, settings, and times can we generalize this causal claim? How representative is the sample? How representative are the manipulations and measures?

journalists sometimes write that one group scored "significantly" higher than the others. Most of the time, however, journalists do not report the technical details, so again we would need to turn to the original journal article to find answers to statistical validity questions.

Indeed, each validity addresses a different aspect of a study: the evidence it provides for a causal statement, the measurements used, the study's generalizability, and the statistical accuracy of its conclusions. Asking questions about each form of validity in turn is a good way to make sure you have considered all of the important questions about the study's quality.

Summary

Variables form the core of the research enterprise. Variables are things of interest that vary—that is, they must have at least two levels. They can be manipulated or measured. Variables in a study can be expressed at two levels: at the conceptual level (as elements of a theory) or at the operational level (as specific measures or manipulations in order to study the variables).

In your role as a consumer of information, you will need to identify three types of claims that researchers, journalists, and other writers make: frequency, association, and causal claims. Frequency claims make arguments about the level of a single, measured variable in a group of people (such as the level of happiness among U.S. adults or the level of depression among Canadian teens).

Association claims argue that two measured variables are related to each other. An association can be positive, negative, zero, or curvilinear; when you know how two variables are associated, you can use one to predict the other.

Causal claims go beyond mere association, stating that one variable comes first and is responsible for changes in the other variable. To make a causal claim, a study must meet three criteria: covariance (the two variables must show an association), temporal precedence (the causal variable has to come before the effect variable in time), and internal validity (the study must rule out alternative explanations for the relationship). Experiments, in which researchers manipulate one variable and measure the other, are necessary to satisfy these three criteria in a single study.

To interrogate a frequency claim, you can ask questions about the study's construct validity (the quality of the measurements) and external validity (its generalizability to a larger population).

To interrogate an association claim, you can ask questions not only about its construct and external validity, just as you would with a frequency claim, but also about its statistical validity. Statistical validity is the degree to which a study can minimize the probability of making a false alarm conclusion or of missing a true effect. It also addresses the strength of a research finding, and whether or not a finding is statistically significant.

To interrogate a causal claim, ask first and foremost whether the study conducted was an experiment—which is the only way to establish internal validity and temporal precedence. If the study was an experiment, you can further assess internal validity by asking whether the study was designed with any confounds and if the researchers used random assignment to place participants into groups. You can also ask about the study's construct, external, and conclusion validity.

Researchers cannot usually achieve all four validities at once in an experiment, so they need to prioritize among the validities. This situation is most common when researchers who want to make a causal claim emphasize internal validity: Their interest in making a causal statement means that they may trade off internal validity for some loss of external validity.

Key Terms

association claim, p. 59
causal claim, p. 63
claim, p. 57
conceptual definitions, p. 55
constant, p. 54
construct validity, p. 66
correlate, p. 59
covariance, p. 69
curvilinear association, p. 61
dependent variable, p. 70
experiment, p. 70
external validity, p. 66
frequency claim, p. 58
generalizability, p. 66

independent variable, p. 70
internal validity, p. 70
manipulated variables, p. 54
measured variables, p. 54
negative association, p. 60
operational definitions, p. 55
positive association, p. 59
random assignment, p. 71
scatterplot, p. 59
statistical validity, p. 67
temporal precedence, p. 69
value, p. 54
variable, p. 54
zero association, p. 60

 **NEED HELP STUDYING?**
wwnorton.com/studyspace

Visit StudySpace to access free review materials such as:

- Diagnostic Review Quizzes
- Study Outlines

Learning Actively

1. For each bolded variable below, indicate the variable's levels, whether it is measured or manipulated, and how you might describe the study at a conceptual and operational level.

Variable	Conceptual variable name	Levels of this variable	Measured or manipulated?	Operational definition of the variable
A questionnaire study asks for various demographic information, including participants' **sex**.	*Participant's sex*	*Male Female*	*Measured*	*Asking participants to circle "male" or "female" on a form*
A questionnaire study asks about **self-esteem**, measured on a 10-item Rosenberg self-esteem scale.				
A study of readability gives people a passage of text. The passage to be read is printed in one of three **colors** of text (black, red, or blue).				
A study of **school achievement** requests each participant to report his or her SAT score, as a measure of college readiness.				
A professor who wants to know more about **study habits** among his students asks students to report the number of minutes they studied for the midterm exam.				
A researcher studying self-control and **blood glucose levels** asks participants to come to an experiment at 1:00 PM. Some of the students are asked not to eat anything before the experiment; others are told to eat lunch before arriving.				

Variable	Conceptual variable name	Levels of this variable	Measured or manipulated?	Operational definition of the variable
In a study on **self-esteem**'s association with self-control, the researchers give a group of students a self-esteem inventory. Then they invite participants who score in the top 10% and the bottom 10% of the self-esteem scale to participate in the next step.				

2. The following headlines appeared in online news sources. For each, identify the claim as frequency/level, association, or causal. Identify the variable(s) in each claim.
   a. Fasting May Fend Off Jet Lag
   b. Reliving Trauma May Help Ward Off PTSD (Posttraumatic Stress Disorder)
   c. Long-Term 9/11 Stress Seen in Lower Manhattan
   d. Want a Higher GPA? Go to a Private College
   e. Those with ADHD Do 1 Month's Less Work a Year
   f. When Moms Criticize, Dads Back Off Baby Care
   g. Troubling Rise in Underweight Babies in U.S.
   h. MMR Shot Does Not Cause Autism, Large Study Says
   i. Breastfeeding May Boost Children's IQ
   j. Breastfeeding Rates Hit New High in U.S.
   k. Heavy Kids May Face Heart Risks as They Age
   l. OMG! Texting and IM-ing Doesn't Affect Spelling!
   m. Facebook Users Get Worse Grades in College

3. Imagine you encounter each of the following headlines. What questions would you ask if you wanted to understand more about the quality of the study behind the headline? For each of your questions, indicate which of the four validities your question is addressing.
   a. Kids with ADHD More Likely to Bully
   b. Breastfeeding May Boost Children's IQ
   c. Long-Term 9/11 Stress Seen in Lower Manhattan

4. You may have heard that spreading out your studying over several sessions (distributed studying) helps you retain the information longer than if you cram your studying into a single session. How could you design an experiment to test this claim? What would the variables be? Would each be manipulated or measured? Would your experiment fulfill the three criteria for supporting a causal statement? What limitations might it have?

PART 2

Research Foundations
for Any Claim

Respect for Persons

Beneficence

Justice

IF YOU'RE HERE FOR A PSYCH STUDY GO RIGHT TO LOBBY...

4

Ethical Guidelines for Psychology Research

No matter what type of claim researchers are investigating, they are obligated—by law, by morality, and by today's social norms—to treat subjects of their research with kindness, respect, and fairness. In the twenty-first century, researchers are bound to follow basic ethical principles in the treatment of humans and other animals.

Some Historical Examples

Times change. Indeed, in the past, researchers had different ideas about the ethical treatment of study participants. Two examples of research, one from medicine and one from psychology, follow. The first example clearly illustrates several ethical violations. The second example illustrates the difficult balance of priorities that researchers might face when they evaluate a study's ethicality.

The Tuskegee Syphilis Study: An Example of Three Major Ethics Violations

In 1932, people working with poor men in the southern United States were concerned that up to 35% of Black men living in the South were infected with syphilis. The disease was largely untreatable at the time, and it interfered with men's ability to work, contribute to society, and work their way out of poverty. The only treatment available at the time involved infusions of toxic metals, a treatment that had serious—even fatal—side effects. In 1932, the U.S. Public Health Service, cooperating with the Tuskegee (Alabama) Institute, began a study of 600 Black men. About 400 of them were already infected with syphilis, and about 200 were not. The researchers wanted to study the effects of untreated syphilis on the men's health over the long term. At the time, not treating the men was a reasonable choice, because the risky treatments that were available in 1932 were unlikely to work (Jones, 1993). The men were recruited in their community churches and schools, and many of them were enthusiastic about participating in a project that would allow them access to medical care for the first time in their lives (Reverby, 2009).

Early in the study, the researchers decided to study the men infected with syphilis until each had died, to obtain valuable data on how the disease progresses when untreated. The study lasted 40 years, during which the researchers made a long series of ethically questionable choices (see **Figure 4.1**). At the beginning, the researchers told the men they were being treated when in fact they were not treated at all. The researchers also withheld information. Men who had contracted syphilis were not informed that they had the disease; instead, they were told they had "bad blood." All the men in the study were required to come to the Tuskegee clinic for evaluation and testing, but they were never given any beneficial treatment. At one point, in fact, the researchers needed to conduct a painful, potentially dangerous spinal tap procedure on each man in the study, in order to follow the progression of the disease. To ensure that each man would come in for the procedure, the researchers lied, telling the men that the procedure was a "special free treatment" for their illness (Jones, 1993).

As the study continued, 250 of the men registered for the U.S. Armed Forces, which were then engaged in World War II. As part of the draft process, the men were diagnosed (again) with syphilis and told to reenlist after they had been treated. But instead of following these instructions, the study's researchers interfered by preventing the men from being treated. As a result, the men could not serve in the Armed Forces or benefit from subsequent G.I. Bills and benefits.

FIGURE 4.1 The Tuskegee Syphilis Study. What ethically questionable decisions were made by the researchers who conducted the Tuskegee Syphilis Study?

In 1947, penicillin was discovered to be a cure for syphilis. But the Tuskegee Institute did not provide information about the cure to the patients in their study. In 1969, in part because of concerns raised by Public Health Service employee Peter Buxtun, officials at the Centers for Disease Control met to discuss the continuation of the study. However, the researchers decided to proceed with the study as before. The study continued until 1972, when Buxtun told the story to the Associated Press (Gray, 1998; Heller, 1972). Over the years, many men got sicker, and dozens died. Several men inadvertently infected their wives and, through pregnancy, infected their children with congenital syphilis (Jones, 1993; Reverby, 2009).

FIGURE 4.2 In 1997 the U.S. government issued an apology to survivors of the Tuskegee Syphilis Study.

In 1974, the families in the study reached a settlement in a lawsuit against the U.S. government, and in 1997, President Bill Clinton formally apologized to the survivors on behalf of the nation (see **Figure 4.2**). Nonetheless, the Tuskegee study has contributed to an unfortunate legacy: Many African Americans believe the study was racist and, as a result, are more suspicious of government health services and research participation (McCallum, Arekere, Green, Katz, & Rivers, 2007).

Three Kinds of Ethical Violations

The researchers conducting this infamous study made a number of choices that are ethically questionable from today's perspective. Later writers have identified these choices as falling into three distinct categories (described, in part, in Childress, Meslin, & Shapiro, 2005; Gray, 1998). First, the men in the study were *harmed*: They were not told about treatment for a disease that, in the later years of the study, could be easily cured. (Many of the men were illiterate and thus were prevented from learning about the penicillin cure on their own.) They were also subjected to painful and dangerous tests. Second, the men were *not treated respectfully*: The researchers lied to them about the nature of their participation, withheld information from them (such as the information that there was a cure for the disease), and in so doing, did not give the men a chance to provide full, informed consent to the study. If the men had known in advance the true nature of the study, some might still have consented to participate, but some might not have. Third, the researchers *targeted a disadvantaged social group* in this study: Syphilis affects people from all ethnicities and social backgrounds, yet all of the men in this study were poor and African American (Gray, 1998; Jones, 1993).

The Milgram Studies: An Example of the Ethical Balance

The Tuskegee Syphilis Study provides several clear examples of ethical violations. But decisions regarding ethics are not always so clear. Another example, social psychologist Stanley Milgram's series of studies on obedience to authority, conducted in the early 1960s, illustrates some of the difficulties of ethical decision-making.

Imagine yourself as a participant in one of these studies. You are told that there will be two participants: you, the "teacher," and another participant, the "learner." As teacher, your job is to punish the learner when he makes mistakes in a learning task. The learner slips into a cubicle where you cannot see him, and the session begins (Milgram, 1974).

As the study goes on, you are told to punish the learner for errors by administering electric shocks at higher and higher intensity, as indicated on an imposing piece of equipment in front of you: the "shock generator." At first, while receiving the low-voltage shocks, the learner does not complain. But he keeps making mistakes on a test of word associations that he is supposed to be learning, and you are required by the rules of the study to deliver shocks that are 15 volts higher after each mistake (see **Figure 4.3**). As the voltage is increased, the learner begins to grunt with pain. At about 120 volts, you hear the learner shout that the shocks are very painful and say he wants to quit the experiment. At 300 volts, the learner screams that he will no longer respond to the memory task; he stops responding. But the experimenter, sitting behind you in a white lab coat, tells you to keep delivering shocks to the man—15 volts more each time, until the machine indicates that you are delivering 450-volt shocks. Whereas before the learner screamed in pain with each new shock, after 300 volts you now hear nothing from him. You cannot tell whether he is even conscious in his cubicle.

If you protest (and you probably do), the experimenter behind you says calmly, "Continue." If you protest again, the experimenter says, again calmly, "The experiment requires that you continue," or even, "You have no choice, you must go on." What would you do now?

You may believe that you would have refused to obey the demands of this inhumane experimenter. However, in the original study, about 65% of the participants followed the experimenter's demands and delivered the 450-volt shock to the learner. Only two or three participants (out of hundreds) refused to give even the first, 15-volt shock. Virtually all participants subjected another person to one or more electric shocks—or at least, they thought they did. Fortunately, the learner was actually a confederate of the experimenter—he was a paid actor playing a role, and he did not in fact receive any shocks. But participants did not know that: They thought the learner was an innocent, friendly man.

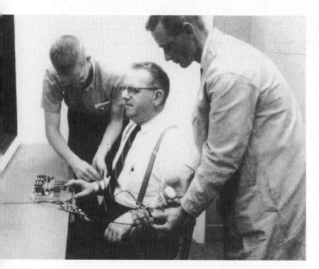

FIGURE 4.3 **Milgram's obedience study.**

Milgram conducted at least 18 variations of this study. In one variation, the learner mentioned that he had a heart condition; this made no difference— the level of obedience remained at about 65%. In another variation, Milgram changed laboratory locations, from his original Yale University laboratory to a seedy storefront in Bridgeport, Connecticut; this change also made no differ- ence—obedience for the full study stayed at about 65%. In another variation, the "learner" sat right in the room with the teacher-participant; in this condition, obedience dropped to 40%. In another variation, the experimenter supervised the situation from down the hall, giving his instructions ("Continue," "The ex- periment requires that you continue") over the phone; obedience in this condi- tion also dropped, and only 20% of participants delivered all of the shocks. In each variation, 40 new participants were asked to deliver painful shocks to the learner.

Ethical Questions

Was Milgram acting ethically when he conducted this study? Many later analy- ses point to two sources of ethical concern. First, the study itself was extremely stressful to the participant "teachers" (Baumrind, 1964). Milgram relayed an ob- servation by one of his research assistants:

> I observed a mature and initially poised businessman enter the laboratory smiling and confident. Within 20 minutes he was reduced to a twitching, nervous wreck, who was rapidly approaching a point of nervous collapse. He constantly pulled on his earlobe, and twisted his hands. At one point he pushed his fist into his forehead and muttered, "Oh, God, let's stop it." And yet he continued to respond to every word of the experimenter, and obeyed to the very end. (Milgram, 1963, p. 377)

Was it ethical of Milgram to put unsuspecting vol- unteers through such a stressful experience?

The second ethical question concerns the lasting effects of the study (Baumrind, 1964). Af- terward, each participant was **debriefed**: In an interview after the study, the participants were carefully informed about the study's true nature, details, and hypotheses, and they were introduced to the (unharmed) learner. However, despite the careful debriefing process, participants might have been dramatically affected by learning that they were willing to harm another human being, simply because someone in authority told them to. That is, even though the debriefing probably lessened people's initial feelings of stress, the sense that they were capable of harm may have stuck with them for a long time (see **Figure 4.4**).

According to Milgram, most of his partici- pants reported that they felt they had learned

FIGURE 4.4 Balancing ethical concerns. How do you balance the harm to participants with the benefits of knowledge in the Milgram obedience study?

something important and valuable about themselves. In some cases, Milgram and his research associates even called their participants at home, months later, to inquire after their current well-being. Most participants told Milgram that they were not suffering from their participation, and some still felt they had learned something important. For example, one participant reported, "What appalled me was that I could possess this capacity for obedience and compliance. . . . I hope I can deal more effectively with future conflicts of values I encounter" (Milgram, 1974, p. 54).

Balancing Risk and Benefit, Participants and Knowledge

At first, the results of Milgram's study—65% obedience—surprised even Milgram himself (Milgram, 1974). Experts at the time predicted that only 1% or 2% of people would obey the experimenter up to 450 volts. But after the first study, Milgram knew what kind of behavior to expect, and he had already seen first-hand the stress that his participants were going through. Once he knew that many of the people in the study would suffer anxiety and stress, Milgram might have taken steps to stop, or modify, the study. But he did not. Some psychologists, both at the time and today, have found Milgram's choices unethical (e.g., Baumrind, 1964). Other psychologists, in contrast, have pointed out that Milgram's studies contributed crucial lessons on obedience to authority and the "power of the situation"—lessons that we would not have learned without his research (Blass, 2002). Thus, we are faced with a fundamental conundrum in deciding whether this research is ethical; we try to balance the potential *risks to participants* against *the value of the knowledge* we can gain. In cases like Milgram's study, it is not easy to decide.

Check Your Understanding

1. What three categories of ethical problems were illustrated by the Tuskegee Syphillis Study?
2. What are two primary concerns that have been raised against Milgram's study of obedience? How did Milgram and his supporters counter these concerns?

1. See p. 87. 2. See pp. 89–90.

The Belmont Report: Principles and Applications

In 1976, a commission of physicians, ethicists, philosophers, scientists, and other citizens gathered at the Belmont Conference Center in Eldridge, Maryland, at the request of the U.S. Congress. They had been called together for an intensive discussion of basic ethical principles that researchers should follow as they conduct research with human participants. The commission was called partly in response to the egregious ethical example of the Tuskegee Syphilis Study and partly in response to the details of medical experiments conducted on concentration camp victims in Nazi-occupied Europe, which were revealed during the Nuremburg Trials (Jonsen, 2005).

The 4-day conference and the months of collaboration that followed produced a short document called the Belmont Report, which outlines three guiding principles for conducting research with human participants: respect for persons, beneficence, and justice. The Belmont Report is intended to guide ethical decision making in many disciplines, including medicine, sociology, anthropology, and basic biological research, as well as psychology.

In practice, researchers conduct their studies in the context of overlapping layers of guidance. They consider abstract ethical guidelines, as well as local institutional policies and federal laws. In the United States, for example, any institution (for example, a university, college, research hospital, or institute) that receives federal money must develop a set of procedures to ensure the ethical treatment of research participants. Often, such institutional procedures are grounded in the original Belmont Report.

The Principle of Respect for Persons

In the Belmont Report, **respect for persons** includes two provisions. First, individuals participating in research should be treated as autonomous agents: They should be free to make up their own minds about whether they wish to participate in a research study. Applying this principle means that each participant is entitled to give **informed consent** to participate. That is, each person learns about the research project, knows the risks and benefits, and decides whether to participate. In obtaining informed consent, researchers are not allowed to mislead people about the study's risks and benefits. Nor may they coerce or unduly influence a person into participating in a research study; doing so would violate the principle of respect for persons. Coercion occurs when researchers explicitly or implicitly suggest that participants who do not participate will suffer a negative consequence (such as a professor implying that students' grades will be lower if they do not participate in the professor's study). Undue influence would occur if researchers offered an incentive too attractive to refuse (for example, by offering people an irresistible amount of money in exchange for participating). The report notes that financially poor individuals may be more easily swayed into participating if a research study provides a large payment.

A provision of the respect-for-persons principle is that some people are entitled to special protection. For example, children, people with intellectual or developmental disabilities, and prisoners should be protected, according to the Belmont Report. Children and some other individuals may not be able to give informed consent to participate in research because they may not understand the procedures well enough to make informed choices (see **Figure 4.5**). Prisoners are especially susceptible to coercion, according to the Belmont Report, because they may perceive requests to participate in research as demands, rather than as invitations. All of these populations should be treated with special consideration.

FIGURE 4.5 Vulnerable populations in research.
Why might children be considered a vulnerable population that requires special ethical consideration?

In sum, the Belmont Report suggests that people should have the autonomy to decide freely whether they wish to participate in research, after receiving adequate information about the risks and benefits of the study.

The Principle of Beneficence

To conform to the principle of **beneficence**, researchers must take precautions to protect research participants from harm and to ensure participants' well-being. Applying the principle of beneficence requires researchers to carefully assess the risks and benefits of the research they plan to conduct. They must, of course, consider the risks and potential benefits to the individuals who are participating in the research, but they must also consider other people who might benefit from the research: Will a community benefit from the knowledge this research is producing? Will there be costs to a community if this research is not conducted?

The Tuskegee Syphilis Study failed to treat its participants in accordance with the principle of beneficence. The researchers harmed participants through risky and invasive medical tests, and they harmed the participants' families by exposing them to untreated syphilis. The researchers also withheld benefits from the men in the study. Today, researchers may not withhold treatments that are known to be beneficial to study participants. For example, if a researcher discovers halfway through a study that a treatment is proving to be very beneficial for an experimental group, the researcher must then give the participants in the control group the opportunity to receive the beneficial treatment, too.

Harm and benefit are usually straightforward to weigh when it comes to physical health, the type measured in medical research. Is a person sicker, or healthier? Is the community going to be healthier because of this research, or not? In contrast, some psychological studies can expose participants to psychological harm, such as anxiety, stress, depression, or cognitive strain, which may be harder to assess. Consider the participants in Milgram's study, who were clearly experiencing stress. How might you quantify the harm done in this situation? Would you measure the way participants felt at that time? Or would you ask how they felt about it a year later? Would you measure what they say about their own stress, or what an observer would say? It is difficult to quantify potential psychological harm, so it is difficult to evaluate how harmful a study like Milgram's might be. However, the principle of beneficence demands that researchers consider such stresses (and benefits) before beginning each study. As a point of reference, some institutions ask researchers to estimate how stressful a study's situation is compared with the normal stresses of everyday life. The other side of the equation—the benefits of psychological research to the community—may not be simple to evaluate, either. One could argue that Milgram's results are valuable, but their value is impossible to quantify in terms of lives or dollars saved. Nevertheless, to apply the principle of beneficence, researchers must attempt to predict the risks and benefits of their research, both to participants and to the larger community.

The Principle of Justice

The principle of **justice** calls for a fair balance between the people who participate in research and the people who benefit from it. For example, if a research study discovers that a procedure is risky or harmful, the participants in the study, unfortunately, "bear the burden" of that risk, while other people—those not in the study—are able to benefit from the study's results (Kimmel, 2007). The Tuskegee Syphilis Study illustrates a violation of this principle of justice: Anybody, regardless of race or income, can contract syphilis, but the participants in the study—who bore the burden of untreated syphilis—were all poor, African American men. Therefore, even though the researchers originally intended to help this population, the participants bore an undue burden of risk.

When the principle of justice is applied, it means that researchers might first ensure that the participants involved in a study are representative of the types of people who would also benefit from its results. If researchers decide to study a sample from only one ethnic group, or only a sample of institutionalized individuals, they must demonstrate that the problem they are studying is especially prevalent in that ethnic group or in that type of institution. For example, it might violate the justice principle if researchers studied a group of prisoners mainly because they were convenient. However, it might be perfectly acceptable to study only institutionalized people for a study on tuberculosis, for example, because tuberculosis is particularly prevalent in institutions, where people live together in a somewhat confined area.

Check Your Understanding

1. Name and define each principle of the Belmont Report.
2. Each principle in the Belmont Report has a particular application. For example, the principle of respect for persons has its application in the informed consent process. What are the applications of the other two principles?

1. See p. 91 for principles and pp. 91–93 for definitions. 2. See pp. 92–93.

Guidelines for Psychologists: The APA Ethical Principles

In addition to consulting the Belmont Report, policies of the local institution, and federal laws, psychologists may also consult another layer of ethical principles and standards written specifically for them by the American Psychological Association (APA; see **Figure 4.6**), called the Ethical Principles of Psychologists and Code of Conduct (2002).

FIGURE 4.6
The APA website.
The APA's website provides the full text of its ethics policies.

The APA chose to develop its own ethical principles and standards so psychologists would have a set of guidelines for three of their common roles: as research scientists, as professors and educators, and as practitioners (most commonly, as therapists). Other disciplines have their own codes of ethics as well (Kimmel, 2007).

Five General Ethical Principles

The APA outlines five general ethical standards that are meant to guide individual aspects of ethical behavior. In **Table 4.1**, you can see that three of the standards are identical to the three basic principles of the Belmont Report (beneficence, justice, and respect for persons). The other two are integrity (for example, your professors are obligated to teach you accurately, and therapists are obligated to stay up-to-date on the empirical evidence for therapeutic techniques) and fidelity and responsibility (for example, a clinical psychologist who teaches in a university may not serve as a therapist to one of his or her classroom students, and psychologists are obligated to avoid sexual relationships with their students or clients). These standards are meant to protect not only research participants but also students in psychology classes and clients of professional psychologists.

Ten Specific Ethical Standards

In addition to the five general principles, the APA also lists ten specific ethical standards. These standards are similar to enforceable rules or laws. Psychologist members of the APA who violate one of these standards can lose their professional licenses or may be disciplined in some other way by the association.

TABLE 4.1 Comparison of the Belmont Report's Basic Principles and the APA's Five General Principles

Belmont Report (1979)	APA Ethical Principles (2002)	Definition
Beneficence	**A. Beneficence and nonmaleficence**	Treat people in ways that benefit them. Do not cause suffering. Conduct research that will benefit society.
	B. Fidelity and responsibility	Establish relationships of trust; accept responsibility for professional behavior (in research, teaching, and clinical practice).
	C. Integrity	Strive to be accurate, truthful, and honest in one's role as researcher, teacher, or practitioner.
Justice	**D. Justice**	Strive to treat all groups of people fairly. Sample research participants from the same populations that will benefit from the research. Be aware of biases.
Respect for persons	**E. Respect for people's rights and dignity**	Recognize that people are autonomous agents. Protect people's rights, including the right to privacy, the right to give consent for treatment or research, and the right to have participation treated confidentially. Understand that some populations may be less able to give autonomous consent, and take precautions against coercing such people.

Note: The principles in boldface are shared by both documents and specifically involve the treatment of human participants in research. The APA guidelines are broader; they apply not only to how psychologists conduct research but also to how they teach and conduct clinical practice.

Of the 10 ethical standards, Ethical Standard 8 is the one most relevant in a research methods book; it is written specifically for psychologists in their roles as researchers. (The other standards are more relevant to the psychologists' roles as therapists, consultants, or teachers.) Ethical Standard 8 is reprinted on pages 108–110. You will notice that several of the details are familiar (e.g., informed consent, Standard 8.02, and protection of vulnerable groups, Standard 8.04), but some details deserve more explanation. The next sections outline the details of the APA's Ethical Standard 8, noting how they work together with the other layers of guidance that a researcher must follow.

The website of the APA Ethics Office provides the full text of the APA's ethics documents. If you are considering becoming a therapist or counselor someday, you may find it interesting to read the other ethical standards that are written specifically for practitioners (www.apa.org/ethics).

Institutional Review Boards (Standard 8.01)

The APA requires that psychologists comply with their local **institutional review board** (**IRB**). An IRB is a committee responsible for ensuring that research on humans is conducted ethically. Most colleges and universities, as well as hospitals and other institutions that conduct research, have IRBs. In the United States, IRBs are mandated by federal laws. If an institution conducts research using federal money (such as research grants from the government), then it must have a designated IRB.

In the United States, IRB panels must include at least five people, some of whom must come from specified backgrounds. At least one must be a scientist; one must have academic interests outside of the sciences; at least one member must be a community member who has no ties to the institution (perhaps a local pastor, a community leader, or an interested citizen). In addition, when the IRB discusses a proposal to use prison participants, one member must be recruited as a designated prisoner advocate. The IRB must consider particular questions for any research involving children. Most other countries' IRBs follow similar mandates for their composition.

At regular meetings, the IRB reviews proposals from individual scientists. Before conducting a study, researchers must fill out a detailed application, describing their study, its risks and benefits (both to participants and to society), its procedures for informed consent, and its provisions for protecting people's privacy—even describing how and for how long the data will be stored. Researchers must demonstrate to the IRB that they have taken all appropriate safeguards for their participants' welfare. The IRB then reviews each application. Different IRBs have different procedures. In some universities, when a study is judged to be of little or no risk (such as a completely anonymous questionnaire), the IRB might not meet to discuss it in person. In most institutions, though, any study that poses risks to humans or that involves vulnerable populations must be reviewed by an in-person IRB meeting.

In many cases, the IRB's oversight offers a neutral, multiperspective judgment on each study's ethicality. An effective IRB will not permit research that violates people's rights or research that poses unreasonable risk, and it will not permit research that lacks a sound rationale. However, an effective IRB should not obstruct valuable research, either. It should not prevent controversial—but still ethical—research questions from being investigated. In the ideal case, the IRB attempts to balance the welfare of research participants against the researcher's goal of contributing important knowledge to the field.

Informed Consent (Standard 8.02)

Informed consent, as defined by the APA, is the researcher's obligation to explain the study to potential participants in everyday language and to give them a chance to decide whether to participate. In most studies, informed consent is obtained by providing a written document that outlines the procedures, risks, and benefits of the research—including a statement about any treatments that are experimental (see **Figure 4.7**). Everyone who wishes to participate signs two

Certificate of Informed Consent

Title of Study: Rating Situations
Investigators: Beth Morling, Yukiko Uchida, Yuri Yano

Thank you for volunteering for this study today. In this study you will be reading short social support situations provided by previous research participants. There will be several short questions following each situation, and there is a final questionnaire at the end.

Risks and Benefits: There are no known risks of participating in this research. Your responses will be anonymous; no link is maintained between your name and your data. The data will be kept for a minimum of five years. One benefit that you may gain by participating in this research is an increased knowledge of the way research is conducted in psychology. You will be paid 1000 yen for participating.

Contacts: If you have any questions about the procedures used in this experiment, please contact Yukiko Uchida at yukikou@educ.kyoto-u.ac.jp.

Participation: Your participation is completely voluntary. You may choose to stop participating at any time and may refuse to answer any individual question. However, as long as you do not object, it is best if you answer all the items.

Age Requirement: You need to be at least 18 years of age to participate in this study. By signing below you are indicating that you meet this age requirement. By signing below, you are also indicating that the project for which you have appeared has been explained to you and that you agree to participate.

Date: ____/____/____

Name (print):_____
       Signature:_____
       Age:_____

FIGURE 4.7 An informed consent form for an anonymous, low-risk questionnaire study conducted by the author and her colleagues. In this particular study, the participants read and signed the informed consent form in Japanese.

copies of the document—one for the researcher to store and one for the participant to take home.

In some limited cases, the APA standards (and other federal laws that govern research) suggest that informed consent procedures are not necessary (see Standard 8.05, Dispensing with Informed Consent for Research). Specifically, researchers may not need to have participants sign informed consent forms if the study is not likely to cause harm and if it takes place in an educational setting. Written informed consent also may not be needed when participants answer a completely anonymous questionnaire, in which their answers are not linked to their names in any way. Written informed consent may not be required when the study involves naturalistic observation of participants in low-risk public settings, such as museums, classrooms, or malls—where people can reasonably expect to be observed by others anyway. The individual institution's regulations determine whether written informed consent is necessary in such situations. Such studies still must be approved by an IRB; however, the IRB will allow the researcher to proceed with the study without obtaining a formal, written consent form. Nevertheless, researchers are always ethically obligated to inform participants of their rights and of their participation in a research study.

According to Ethical Standard 8 (and most other ethical guidelines), obtaining informed consent also involves informing people whether the data they provide in a research study will be treated as private and confidential. Nonconfidential data might put participants at some risk. For example, in the course of research people might report on their health status, political attitudes, test scores, or study habits—information they might not want others to know. Therefore, informed consent procedures ordinarily outline which parts of the data are confidential and which, if any, are not. If data are to be treated as confidential, researchers agree to remove names and identifiers from the data that people provide. Handwriting, birthdays, or photographs might allow an individual's data to be identified, so researchers must take special care to protect such data if they have promised to do so. At many institutions, confidentiality procedures are not optional. Many institutions require researchers to store any identifiable data in a locked area or on secure computers.

Deception (Standard 8.07)

It is a difficult truth: Psychological researchers sometimes lie to participants. Consider some of the studies you may have learned about in your psychology courses. For example, in one study (Greenberg, Spangenberg, Pratkanis, & Eskanazi, 1991), researchers investigated the efficacy of "subliminal" messages on commercially available tapes that could supposedly help people improve their memory or raise their self-esteem. In the study, people were asked to listen to tapes containing subliminal messages for about 2 weeks. But at the start of the study, the experimenters lied to half of the participants by telling them they were listening to a memory tape when it was really the self-esteem tape and by telling others they were listening to a self-esteem tape when it was really a memory tape (see **Figure 4.8**). In another study, an experimental confederate posed as a thief, stealing money from another person's bag while an unsuspecting library patron sat reading at a table. In some versions of this study, the "thief," the "victim," and a third person who sat calmly nearby, pretending to read, were all experimental confederates. That makes three confederates and a fake crime—all in one study (Shaffer, Rogel, & Hendrick, 1975).

Even in the most straightforward study, participants may not be told about all the comparison conditions. For example, participants might be aware that they are writing in a booklet with a red cover, but they do not know that the covers of other participants' booklets are green or gray (Elliot et al., 2007). All of these studies contained an element of **deception**: Researchers withheld some details of the study from participants (deception through *omission*), and in some cases they actively lied to them (deception through *commission*).

Consider how these studies might have turned out if there had been no such deception. Suppose the researchers had said, "You will be listening to subliminal messages in a CD that's supposed to improve your memory, but pretend that it's *really* written to improve your self-esteem. Ready?" Or "We're going to see whether you're willing to help prevent a theft. Wait here—in a few moments, we will stage a theft and see what you do." Or "We want to know whether you make more mistakes because your test booklet has a scary red cover. Go!" Obviously, the data would be useless. Deceiving research participants by lying to them or by withholding information is, in many cases, necessary in order to obtain meaningful data.

Is deception ethical? Of course, lying to people seems to violate the principle of respect for persons. But we should also apply the principle of beneficence: What are the ethical costs and benefits of doing the study this way, compared with the ethical costs of not doing it this way? It is important, for example, to study whether subliminal educational CDs are effective for learning or whether they are a fraud. It is important to find out what kinds of situational factors influence people's willingness to report a theft. And in achievement contexts, it is important to understand incidental factors that might affect performance. Because most people consider these questions important, some researchers argue that the gain in knowledge seems worth the cost of lying (temporarily) to the participants (Kimmel, 1998). Even then, the APA principles and federal guidelines require researchers to use deceptive research designs only as a last resort and to debrief participants after the study.

FIGURE 4.8 **Deception in research.** In a study on the efficacy of subliminal recordings like these, Greenberg and colleagues (1991) lied to some participants about the true content of the recordings they listened to. When would it be ethical to deceive people about the procedures and purposes of a study?

Despite such arguments, some psychologists believe that deception undermines people's trust in the research process and should never be used in a study's design (Ortmann & Hertwig, 1997). Still others suggest that deception is acceptable under constrained circumstances (Bröder, 1998; Kimmel, 1998; Pittenger, 2002). Some researchers have studied how undergraduate students respond to participating in a study that uses deception. Such studies have concluded that students usually tolerate minor deception and even some discomfort or stress, considering them necessary parts of research. When students do find deception to be stressful, these negative effects are diminished when the researchers fully explain the deception in a debriefing session (Bröder, 1998; Sharpe, Adair, & Roese, 1992; Smith & Richardson, 1983).

Debriefing (Standard 8.08)

When researchers have used deception, they must spend time after the study is over *debriefing* each research participant in a structured conversation. In a debriefing, researchers describe the nature of the deception and explain why it was necessary. They explain the importance of their research and attempt to restore an honest relationship between the researcher and the participant. In the debriefing process, the scientist explains the design of the study and gives the participant some insight into the nature of psychological science.

Although debriefing is considered essential for studies in which deception is used, even nondeceptive studies normally include a debriefing session, too. At many universities, all student participants in research receive a written description of the study's goals and hypotheses, along with references for further reading. The goal is to make participation in research a worthwhile educational experience, so that the students can learn more about the research process in general, understand how their participation fits into the larger context of theory testing, and learn how their participation might benefit others. In debriefing sessions, researchers might also offer to share results with the participants. Even months after their participation, people can request a summary of the study's results.

Animal Research (Standard 8.09)

Psychologists do not study only human participants. Indeed, in some branches of psychology, research is conducted almost entirely on animal subjects: rats, mice, cockroaches, sea snails, dogs, rabbits, cats, chimpanzees, and others. The ethical debates surrounding animal research can be just as complex as those for human participants. Many people have a profound respect for animals and compassion for their well-being. Most people—psychologists and nonpsychologists alike—want to protect animals from undue suffering.

Legal Protections for Laboratory Animals. In Standard 8.09, the APA lists ethical points for the care of animals in research laboratories. Psychologists who use animals in research must care for them humanely, must use as few animals as possible, and must be sure their research is valuable enough to justify the use of animals.

In addition to these APA standards, psychologists must follow federal and local laws for the animals' care and protection. In the United States, for example, animals in research are also protected by government oversight. The Animal Welfare Act (AWA; 1966 and later) outlines standards and guidelines for the treatment of animals. (The AWA applies not only to many species of animals in laboratories but also to animals in pet stores, agriculture, and even zoos and circuses.) The AWA mandates that each institution at which animal research takes place must have a local board called the Institutional Animal Care and Use Committee (IACUC—pronounced EYE-a-kuk). Similar to an IRB, the IACUC must approve any animal research project before it can begin (AWA, 2005, Title 9, Chapter 1, Subchapter A—Animal Welfare, Section 2.31). Also like an IRB, the IACUC must comply with federal guidelines. It must contain at least three members: a veterinarian, a practicing scientist who is familiar with the goals and procedures of animal research, and a member of the community at large who is unconnected with the institution. The IACUC requires researchers to submit an extensive protocol that specifies how animals will be used, what will happen to each one, what precautions researchers plan to take to minimize the animals' distress (such as anesthetics or analgesics), and if and how the animals will be euthanized at the end of the study. The IACUC application also includes the scientific justification for the research: Applicants must demonstrate that the proposed study has not already been done and explain why the research is important. Curiosity is not enough.

After approving a research project, the IACUC monitors the care and treatment of animals throughout the research process. It inspects the labs every 6 months. If a laboratory violates a procedure outlined in the proposal, the IACUC or a government agency can stop the experiment, shut down the laboratory, or discontinue any government funding for the laboratory. If violations are severe enough, the government can choose to withdraw all federal funds from the entire university or institution. In short, in the United States, animal care and treatment are enforced quite rigorously by clear guidelines and by federal and local oversight. In European countries and in Canada, similar, if not stricter, laws apply.

Animal Care Guidelines and the Three R's. American animal researchers and IACUC committees use the resources provided by the *Guide for the Care and Use of Laboratory Animals* (National Research Council, 2011). The guide provides the "three R's"—replacement, refinement, and reduction—as a practical guide for animal researchers. *Replacement* means that researchers should find alternatives to animals in research when necessary. For example, some research can use computer simulations instead of animal subjects. *Refinement* means that researchers must modify experimental procedures and other aspects of animal care to minimize or eliminate animal distress. *Reduction* means that researchers should adopt experimental designs and procedures that require the fewest animal subjects possible.

In addition, the manual provides guidelines for housing facilities, diet, and other specifics of animal care in research. For example, the guide specifies that nonhuman primates be housed in enclosures that are wide enough and tall enough to accommodate these species' normal activities, and requires that primates be housed in social groups, as many species do not thrive when socially isolated. The guide also specifies cage sizes, temperature and humidity ranges, air quality, lighting and noise conditions, diet, and sanitation and makes suggestions for toys, bedding, and other enrichments.

Attitudes of Scientists and Students Toward Animal Research. In surveys, the majority of students and psychologists support the use of animals in research (Plous, 1996a). However, many students report being unsure of whether laboratory animals are treated humanely. For the most part, student and psychologist samples say they support monitoring the pain of animals in research and support the federal regulations that protect the well-being of primates used in studies (Plous, 1996b, p. 354). In addition, having taken a survey of 494 active animal researchers, Plous and Herzog (2000) reported that the vast majority of them supported extending the AWA's protections to laboratory mice, rats, and birds. (Current versions of the AWA protect primates, dogs, cats, hamsters, guinea pigs, and rabbits.) Although somewhat dated, these surveys suggest that animal researchers are in favor of protecting their animals from pain. They support the promotion of animal *welfare*.

Attitudes of Animal Rights Groups. Since the mid-1970s in the United States, some groups have increased in their visibility and have assumed a more extreme position—arguing for animal rights, rather than animal welfare (see **Figure 4.9**). Groups such as People for the Ethical Treatment of Animals (PETA), as well as other groups, both mainstream and marginal, violent and nonviolent, have tried to discover and expose cruelty to animals in research laboratories. Animal rights groups generally base their activities on one of two arguments (Kimmel, 2007). First, animal rights groups may believe that animals are just as likely as humans to experience suffering. They believe that humans should not be elevated above other animals: Because all kinds of animals can suffer, all of them should be protected from painful research procedures. In this view, some research with animals could be allowed, but only if it might also be permitted with human subjects. Some activists also believe that animals have inherent value and rights, equal to those of humans. These activists argue that most researchers do not treat animals as creatures with rights; instead, animals are treated as resources to be used and discarded (Kimmel, 2007). In a way, this argument draws on the principle of justice, as outlined in the Belmont Report and in the APA's Ethical Principles: Animal rights activists do not believe that animals should unduly bear the burden of research that benefits a different species (humans). Both arguments lead animal rights activists to conclude that many research practices using animals are morally wrong. Some groups' members accuse researchers who study animals of conducting cruel and unethical experiments (Kimmel, 2007).

The members of these groups may be politically active, vociferous, and sincerely devoted to the protection of animals. But in a survey of one group of animal rights activists, Herzog (1993) concluded that the members of these organizations are "intelligent, articulate, and sincere." He added that they were "eager to discuss their views about the treatment of animals" with a scientist (p. 118, cited in Kimmel, 2007). Consistent with this view, Plous (1998) polled animal rights activists and found most in his sample to be open to compromise—to a respectful dialogue with animal researchers.

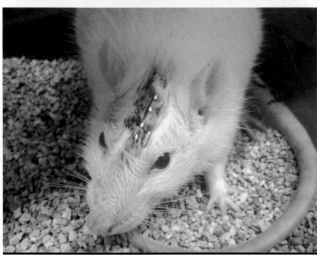

THIS IS ANIMAL EXPERIMENTATION

Don't let anyone tell you different.

PeTA

FIGURE 4.9 **A poster protesting against animal research.**

Ethically Balancing Animal Welfare, Animal Rights, and Animal Research. Given the careful laws governing animal welfare, and given widespread awareness (if not universal endorsement) of animal rights arguments, you can be sure that research with animals in psychology is not conducted lightly in the twenty-first century. On the contrary, though research with animals is widespread, animal researchers are generally careful, thoughtful, and respectful of animal welfare.

Animal researchers defend their use of animals with three primary arguments. The central argument is that animal research has resulted in numerous benefits to humans and animals alike (see **Figure 4.10**). Animal research has contributed countless valuable lessons about psychology, biology, and neuroscience: discoveries about basic processes of vision, the organization of the brain, the course of infection, disease prevention, and therapeutic drugs. Animal research has made fundamental contributions to both basic and applied science, for both humans and animals. Therefore, as outlined in the Belmont Report and APA Ethical Principles, ethical thinking means that researchers and the public must evaluate the costs and benefits of the research—in terms of both the subjects and the potential outcome of the research.

Best Supporting Role in a Medical Drama.
FOUNDATION FOR BIOMEDICAL RESEARCH

FIGURE 4.10 A poster in support of animal research.
How do researchers achieve an ethical balance between concern for animal welfare and the benefits to society from research on animals?

Second, supporters of animal research argue that researchers are sensitive to animal welfare. They think about the pain and suffering of animals in their studies and take steps to avoid or reduce it. The IACUC oversight process and the *Guide for the Care and Use of Laboratory Animals* help ensure that animals are treated with care. Third, researchers have successfully reduced the number of animals they need to use, because they have developed new procedures that do not require animal testing (Kimmel, 2007). Indeed, some animal researchers believe that animal rights groups have exaggerated (or even fabricated, in some cases) the cruelty of animal research (Coile & Miller, 1984) and that some animal rights groups have largely ignored the scientific and medical discoveries that have resulted from animal research.

Research Misconduct

Most discussions of ethical research focus on protection and respect for research participants, and rightly so. But in the research enterprise, psychologists are also expected to treat one another, and the research process, with respect.

Data Fabrication (APA Standard 8.10) and Data Falsification. Two forms of research misconduct are data fabrication and data falsification. **Data fabrication** occurs when, instead of recording what really happened in a study (or sometimes instead of running a study at all), researchers invent data that fit their hypotheses. **Data falsification** occurs when researchers influence the study's results, perhaps by deleting observations from a data set or by influencing their research subjects to act in the hypothesized way. It is difficult to determine how common fabrication of data is in psychology research because it is not always discovered, but it does happen. For example, two articles (published in 1999 and 2001) in social psychology were retracted after an investigation into their author, a Harvard professor. The professor's graduate student reported being suspicious when the professor refused to share her notes and raw data with him. Later, the author admitted that she had, in fact, fabricated the results for the two studies. She was directed to retract the papers from the journals and acknowledge that her co-authors did not participate in the fabrication. She was banned for 5 years from applying for federal funding, and she subsequently resigned from her faculty position (*Federal Register*, 2001).

Creating fabricated or falsified data not only is unethical but also impedes the progress of science. Scientists use data to test their theories, and they can do so only if they know that previously reported data are true and accurate. When scientists fabricate data, they mislead others about the true state of support for a theory. Fabricated data might inspire other researchers to spend time following a promising (but false) research lead. Or they might lead researchers to be more confident in theories than they should be.

For more on the theory-data cycle, see Chapter 1, pp 8–13.

Why might researchers fabricate or falsify data? In many universities, professors' reputations, income, and promotions are based on their publications and impact on the field. In such high-pressure circumstances, the temptation might be great to delete the contradictory data or create supporting data. In addition, some scientists may simply be convinced of their own hypotheses and believe that any data that do not support their predictions must be inaccurate. One biochemist who admitted to fabricating data said, "I published my hypotheses rather than experimentally determined results. The reason was that I was so convinced of my ideas that I simply put them down on paper" (cited in Kimmel, 2007, p. 306). This scientist was basing his views on his intuition rather than on formal observations, as a true empiricist would.

For a review of ways of knowing, see Chapter 2.

When a U.S. scientist's colleagues or students suspect such misconduct, they may report it to the scientist's institution. If the research is federally funded, suspected misconduct can be reported to the Office of Research Integrity, a branch of the Department of Health and Human Services, which then has the obligation to investigate.

Plagiarism (Standard 8.11). APA Standard 8.11 refers to **plagiarism**, another form of research misconduct that is usually defined as representing the ideas or words of others as one's own. A formal definition, provided by the U.S. Office of Science and Technology Policy, states that plagiarism is "the appropriation of another person's ideas, processes, results, or words without giving appropriate credit" (Federal Register, 2000). Academics and researchers consider plagiarism a violation of ethics because it is unfair for a researcher to take credit for another person's intellectual property: It is a form of stealing.

To avoid plagiarism, a writer must cite the sources of all ideas that are not his or her own, to give appropriate credit to other writers. There are many acceptable formats for giving appropriate credit. Psychologists usually follow the *Publication Manual of the American Psychological Association* (2010), which outlines a particular format for citations. Specifically, when a writer describes or paraphrases another person's ideas, the writer must cite the original author's last name and the year of publication. When quoting (or very closely paraphrasing) another person's ideas, the writer must put quotation marks around the quoted text and indicate the page number where the quotation appeared in the original. The writer then provides a full citation in the References section of the publication for every work quoted or paraphrased. (An abbreviated version of the APA guidelines is presented in Appendix C; see also **Figure 4.11** for an example.)

Plagiarism is a serious offense not only in published work by professional researchers but also in papers that students submit for college courses. Your university or college almost certainly has guidelines for plagiarism that prohibit students from copying the words or ideas of others without proper credit. Students who plagiarize in their academic work are subject to disciplinary action—even expulsion from their universities.

something important and valuable about themselves. In some cases, Milgram and his research associates even called their participants at home, months later, to inquire after their current well-being. Most participants told Milgram that they were not suffering from their participation, and some still felt they had learned something important. For example, one participant reported, "What appalled me was that I could possess this capacity for obedience and compliance. . . . I hope I can deal more effectively with future conflicts of values I encounter" (Milgram, 1974, p. 54).

Balancing Risk and Benefit, Participants and Knowledge

At first, the results of Milgram's study—65% obedience—surprised even Milgram himself (Milgram, 1974). Experts at the time predicted that only 1% or 2% of people would obey the experimenter up to 450 volts. But after the first study, Milgram knew what kind of behavior to expect, and he had already seen first-

References

Milgram, S. (1974). *Obedience to Authority*. New York: Harper & Row.

FIGURE 4.11
Acknowledging sources. This textbook cites sources in APA style. Within the text, the sources of ideas are acknowledged with the authors' last names and year of publication. Direct quotations are marked with quotation marks and page numbers. Full bibliographic information is presented in the reference list.

1. What are the five ethical principles outlined by the APA? Which two are not included in the three principles of the Belmont Report?

2. The APA has 10 ethical standards. Ethical Standard 8 outlines ethical practices in research for psychologists. Name and define each of the separate points included in Ethical Standard 8.

1. See p. 94 and Table 4.1. 2. See Ethical Standard 8 on pp. 108–112 and the discussion on pp. 96–105.

Ethical Decision Making: A Thoughtful Balance

Ethical decision making, as you have learned, does not involve simple yes-or-no decisions; it requires a balance of priorities. When faced with a study that poses potential harm to human participants or animals, researchers (and their IRBs) consider the potential benefits of the research: Will it contribute something important to society? Many people believe that research with some degree of risk is justified if the benefit from the knowledge is great. In contrast, if the risk to participants becomes too high, the knowledge to be gained may not be valuable enough to justify the harm.

Another example of this careful balance comes from the way researchers implement the informed consent process. On the one hand, researchers may wish to show gratitude and respect to their participants by compensating them with money or some other form of credit. Paying participants might help ensure that the samples represent a variety of populations, as the principle of justice requires, because some people might not participate in research without some incentive. On the other hand, if the rewards researchers offer are too great, they could tip the balance: Participants may no longer be able to give free consent because the rewards have become unduly influential.

Although in some cases it is easy to conduct important research that presents low risk to participants, other ethical decisions are extremely difficult. Researchers attempt to balance respect for animal subjects and human participants, protections from harm, benefits to society, and awareness of justice. As this chapter has emphasized, researchers do not weigh the factors in this balance alone: They are influenced by IRBs, IACUCs, peers, and sociocultural norms as they strive to conduct important research in an ethical manner.

In practice, ethics in research is not a set of permanent rules. Instead, it is an evolving and dynamic process that takes place in a historical and cultural context. Researchers refine their ethical decision making in response to good and bad experiences, changing social norms, and scientific discovery. By following ethical principles, researchers make it more likely that their work will benefit, and be appreciated by, the general public.

1. Give some examples from the text of how the ethical practice of research is conducted as a thoughtful balance of priorities.

1. Answers will vary.

Summary

Psychologists must balance various ethical principles and priorities, no matters what type of claim they are investigating. Achieving an ethical balance in research is guided by ethical standards and laws outlined by the Belmont Report and the American Psychological Association, as well as federal and local policies. The Belmont Report outlines three basic principles for research—respect for persons, beneficence, and justice—that have specific applications in the research setting. Respect for persons involves the process of informed consent. Beneficence involves the evaluation of risks and benefits, both to participants in the study and to society as a whole. Justice involves the way participants are selected for the research.

The APA attempts to guide psychologists by providing a set of principles and standards that psychologists are expected to follow in their research, teaching, and professional roles. The APA's Five General Principles include the three Belmont principles, plus two more: the principle of integrity and the principle of fidelity and responsibility. In addition, the APA's Ethical Standard 8 provides enforceable guidelines for researchers to follow. It includes specific information for informed consent, institutional review boards, deception, debriefing, animal research, and research misconduct.

Key Terms

beneficence, p. 92
data fabrication, p. 103
data falsification, p. 103
debriefed, p. 89
deception, p. 98
informed consent, p. 91

institutional review
   board (IRB), p. 96
justice, p. 93
plagiarism, p. 104
respect for persons, p. 91

NEED HELP STUDYING?

wwnorton.com/studyspace

Visit StudySpace to access free review materials such as:

- Diagnostic Review Quizzes
- Study Outlines

Ethical Standard 8 of the American Psychological Association

This set of standards, one of 10 ethical standards published by the APA, is the one most relevant to psychologists in their roles as researchers. The APA standards are practiced in concert with federal laws and local procedures required by the researchers' university or institution.

8.01 Institutional Approval

When institutional approval is required, psychologists provide accurate information about their research proposals and obtain approval prior to conducting the research. They conduct the research in accordance with the approved research protocol.

8.02 Informed Consent to Research

(a) When obtaining informed consent as required in Standard 3.10, Informed Consent, psychologists inform participants about (1) the purpose of the research, expected duration, and procedures; (2) their right to decline to participate and to withdraw from the research once participation has begun; (3) the foreseeable consequences of declining or withdrawing; (4) reasonably foreseeable factors that may be expected to influence their willingness to participate such as potential risks, discomfort, or adverse effects; (5) any prospective research benefits; (6) limits of confidentiality; (7) incentives for participation; and (8) whom to contact for questions about the research and research participants' rights. They provide opportunity for the prospective participants to ask questions and receive answers.

(b) Psychologists conducting intervention research involving the use of experimental treatments clarify to participants at the outset of the research (1) the experimental nature of the treatment; (2) the services that will or will not be available to the control group(s) if appropriate; (3) the means by which assign-ment to treatment and control groups will be made; (4) available treatment alternatives if an individual does not wish to participate in the research or wishes to withdraw once a study has begun; and (5) compensation for or monetary costs of participating including, if appropriate, whether reimbursement from the participant or a third-party payor will be sought.

8.03 Informed Consent for Recording Voices and Images in Research

Psychologists obtain informed consent from research participants prior to recording their voices or images for data collection unless (1) the research consists solely of naturalistic observations in public places, and it is not anticipated that the recording will be used in a manner that could cause personal identification or harm, or (2) the research design includes deception, and consent for the use of the recording is obtained during debriefing.

8.04 Client/Patient, Student, and Subordinate Research Participants

(a) When psychologists conduct research with clients/patients, students, or subordinates as participants, psychologists take steps to protect the prospective participants from adverse consequences of declining or withdrawing from participation.

(b) When research participation is a course requirement or an opportunity for extra credit, the prospective participant is given the choice of equitable alternative activities.

8.05 Dispensing with Informed Consent for Research

Psychologists may dispense with informed consent only (1) where research would not reasonably be assumed to create distress or harm and involves

(a) the study of normal educational practices, curricula, or classroom management methods conducted in educational settings; (b) only anonymous questionnaires, naturalistic observations, or archival research for which disclosure of responses would not place participants at risk of criminal or civil liability or damage their financial standing, employability, or reputation, and confidentiality is protected; or (c) the study of factors related to job or organization effectiveness conducted in organizational settings for which there is no risk to participants' employability, and confidentiality is protected or (2) where otherwise permitted by law or federal or institutional regulations.

8.06 Offering Inducements for Research Participation

(a) Psychologists make reasonable efforts to avoid offering excessive or inappropriate financial or other inducements for research participation when such inducements are likely to coerce participation.

(b) When offering professional services as an inducement for research participation, psychologists clarify the nature of the services, as well as the risks, obligations, and limitations.

8.07 Deception in Research

(a) Psychologists do not conduct a study involving deception unless they have determined that the use of deceptive techniques is justified by the study's significant prospective scientific, educational, or applied value and that effective non-deceptive alternative procedures are not feasible.

(b) Psychologists do not deceive prospective participants about research that is reasonably expected to cause physical pain or severe emotional distress.

(c) Psychologists explain any deception that is an integral feature of the design and conduct of an experiment to participants as early as is feasible, preferably at the conclusion of their participation, but no later than at the conclusion of the data collection, and permit participants to withdraw their data.

8.08 Debriefing

(a) Psychologists provide a prompt opportunity for participants to obtain appropriate information about the nature, results, and conclusions of the research, and they take reasonable steps to correct any misconceptions that participants may have of which the psychologists are aware.

(b) If scientific or humane values justify delaying or withholding this information, psychologists take reasonable measures to reduce the risk of harm.

(c) When psychologists become aware that research procedures have harmed a participant, they take reasonable steps to minimize the harm.

8.09 Humane Care and Use of Animals in Research

(a) Psychologists acquire, care for, use, and dispose of animals in compliance with current federal, state, and local laws and regulations, and with professional standards.

(b) Psychologists trained in research methods and experienced in the care of laboratory animals supervise all procedures involving animals and are responsible for ensuring appropriate consideration of their comfort, health, and humane treatment.

(c) Psychologists ensure that all individuals under their supervision who are using animals have received instruction in research methods and in the care, maintenance, and handling of the species being used, to the extent appropriate to their role.

(d) Psychologists make reasonable efforts to minimize the discomfort, infection, illness, and pain of animal subjects.

(e) Psychologists use a procedure subjecting animals to pain, stress, or privation only when an alternative procedure is unavailable and the goal is justified by its prospective scientific, educational, or applied value.

(f) Psychologists perform surgical procedures under appropriate anesthesia and follow techniques to avoid infection and minimize pain during and after surgery.

(g) When it is appropriate that an animal's life be terminated, psychologists proceed rapidly, with an effort to minimize pain and in accordance with accepted procedures.

8.10 Reporting Research Results

(a) Psychologists do not fabricate data.
(b) If psychologists discover significant errors in their published data, they take reasonable steps to correct such errors in a correction, retraction, erratum, or other appropriate publication means.

8.11 Plagiarism

Psychologists do not present portions of another's work or data as their own, even if the other work or data source is cited occasionally.

8.12 Publication Credit

(a) Psychologists take responsibility and credit, including authorship credit, only for work they have actually performed or to which they have substantially contributed.
(b) Principal authorship and other publication credits accurately reflect the relative scientific or professional contributions of the individuals involved, regardless of their relative status. Mere possession of an institutional position, such as department chair, does not justify authorship credit. Minor contributions to the research or to the writing for publications are acknowledged appropriately, such as in footnotes or in an introductory statement.
(c) Except under exceptional circumstances, a student is listed as principal author on any multiple-authored article that is substantially based on the student's doctoral dissertation. Faculty advisors discuss publication credit with students as early as feasible and throughout the research and publication process as appropriate.

8.13 Duplicate Publication of Data

Psychologists do not publish, as original data, data that have been previously published. This does not preclude republishing data when they are accompanied by proper acknowledgment.

8.14 Sharing Research Data for Verification

(a) After research results are published, psychologists do not withhold the data on which their conclusions are based from other competent professionals who seek to verify the substantive claims through reanalysis and who intend to use such data only for that purpose, provided that the confidentiality of the participants can be protected and unless legal rights concerning proprietary data preclude their release. This does not preclude psychologists from requiring that such individuals or groups be responsible for costs associated with the provision of such information.
(b) Psychologists who request data from other psychologists to verify the substantive claims through reanalysis may use shared data only for the declared purpose. Requesting psychologists obtain prior written agreement for all other uses of the data.

8.15 Reviewers

Psychologists who review material submitted for presentation, publication, grant, or research proposal review respect the confidentiality of and the proprietary rights in such information of those who submitted it.

Learning Actively

1. A developmental researcher applies to an IRB, proposing to observe children ages 2 to 10 playing in the local McDonald's play area. Because the area is public, the researcher does not plan to ask for informed consent from the children's parents. What ethical concerns exist for this study? What questions might an IRB ask?

2. A social psychologist plans to hand out surveys in her 300-level undergraduate class. The survey asks about student study habits. The psychologist does not ask the students to put their names on the survey; instead, students will put completed surveys into a large box at the back of the room. Because of the low risk involved in participation and the anonymous nature of the survey, the researcher requests to be exempted from formal informed consent procedures. What ethical concerns exist for this study? What questions might an IRB ask?

3. Consider the use of deception in psychological research. Does participation in a study involving deception (such as the study by Stanley Milgram described in this chapter) necessarily cause harm? Recall that when we evaluate the risks and benefits of a study, we consider both the participants in the study and society as a whole—anyone who might be affected by the research. What might be some of the costs and benefits to participants who are deceived? What might be some of the costs and benefits to society of studies involving deception?

4. Prisoners are considered a vulnerable population, according to both the Belmont Report and the APA Ethical Principles. First, apply the principle of respect for persons: Why do you think prisoners are considered a vulnerable population in this context? Second, apply the principle of justice: Might it be appropriate for some studies to study only prisoners?

5. Use the Internet to look up your college's definition of plagiarism. Does your college's definition match the one given in APA Ethical Standard 8.11? If not, what does it exclude or add? What behaviors count as plagiarism at your university? What are the consequences for plagiarism at your college or university?

Half of Americans Struggle to Stay Happy

(MSNBC.com, 2008)

Most People Are Happy

(Psychological Science, 1996)

5

Identifying Good Measurement

Learning Objectives

A year from now, you should still be able to:

1. Interrogate the construct validity of a study's variables.
2. Describe what kinds of evidence support the construct validity of a measured variable.

Whether studying the speed of a chemical reaction, the number of polar bears left in the Arctic Circle, the strength of a bar of steel, or the level of human happiness, every scientist faces the challenge of measurement. When researchers test theories or pursue empirical questions, they have to systematically observe the phenomena by collecting data. Such systematic observations require measurements, and these measurements must be good ones—or else they are useless.

Measurement in psychological research can be particularly challenging. Many of the phenomena psychologists are interested in—motivation, emotion, thinking, reasoning—are difficult to measure directly. Happiness, the topic of the two contradictory headlines on the opposite page, is a good example of a construct that could be difficult to measure. Could it be that these two headlines disagree because they used different measures of happiness? If so, which measure is the better one?

Of course, one reason for the different levels of happiness described in each headline may be that the studies were published 15 years apart; people may have been much less happy in 2008 (at the start of a recession) than they were in 1993. Another reason for the different headlines could be the quality of the research. You might trust the second article, since it was published in a scientific journal, more than the first one, which is from the popular press. But even though the first headline appeared in the popular press, it, too, is based on research—large-scale survey data collected by the Gallup polling organization. To decide which research is more credible (Gallup's or a university professor's), you need to interrogate the research behind the two claims. This chapter teaches you how to ask questions about the quality of the two studies' measures—the construct validity of their measures of happiness. Construct validity, remember, refers to how well a study's variables are measured or manipulated.

The two happiness claims in the headlines above are frequency claims—claims about a single, measured variable. Construct validity is a crucial piece of any psychological research study—for frequency, association, or causal claims. This chapter focuses on the construct validity of *measured variables*. The construct validity of *manipulated variables* is covered in Chapter 9. In this chapter you will learn, first, about different ways that researchers measure variables. Then you will learn how you can assess the reliability and validity of those measurements.

For a review of measured and manipulated variables, see Chapter 3, pp. 54–55.

Ways to Measure Variables

The process of measuring variables involves some key decisions. As researchers decide how they should operationalize each variable, they choose among common types of measures, including self-report, observational, and physiological measures. They also decide on the most appropriate scale of measurement for each variable they plan to measure.

More About Conceptual and Operational Variables

In Chapter 3, you read about operationalization, the process of turning a concept of interest into a measured or manipulated variable (see especially Figure 3.1). That is, any variable can be expressed in two ways: as a *conceptual variable* (also called a conceptual definition or construct) and as an *operational variable* (an operational definition). The conceptual definition, or construct, is the researcher's definition of the variable in question at an abstract level. The operational definition of a variable represents a researcher's specific decision about how to measure or manipulate the conceptual variable.

Operationalizing "Happiness"

To study the variable *happiness*, for example, researcher Ed Diener began by developing a precise conceptual definition. Specifically, Diener reasoned that the word *happiness* might have a variety of meanings, so he explicitly limited his interest to "subjective well-being" (that is, well-being from a person's own perspective).

After defining happiness at the conceptual level, Diener and his colleagues developed its operational definition. Because Diener was interested in people's perspectives on their own well-being, he chose to operationalize subjective well-being, in part, by asking people to report on their own happiness with their life in a questionnaire format. Furthermore, Diener and his colleagues decided that people should use their own criteria to define what a "good life" is (Pavot & Diener, 1993). They worded the questions such that people could think about the definition of life satisfaction that was appropriate for them. Ultimately, Diener and his colleagues operationally defined (that is, measured) subjective well-being by asking people to respond to five items about their life satisfaction, using a 7-point scale. On the scale, 1 corresponded to "strongly disagree" and 7 corresponded to "strongly agree":

____ 1. In most ways my life is close to my ideal.
____ 2. The conditions of my life are excellent.
____ 3. I am satisfied with my life.
____ 4. So far I have gotten the important things I want in life.
____ 5. If I could live my life over, I would change almost nothing.

The unhappiest people would get a total score of 5 on this self-report scale, because they would answer "strongly disagree," or 1, to all five items ($1 + 1 + 1 + 1 + 1 = 5$). The happiest people would get a total score of 35 on this scale, because they would answer "strongly agree," or 7, to all five items ($7 + 7 + 7 + 7 + 7 = 35$). Those at the neutral point would score 20—right in between satisfied and dissatisfied ($4 + 4 + 4 + 4 + 4 = 20$). When Diener and Diener (1996) concluded that "Most people are happy," they meant that most people scored above 20 on this well-being scale. For example, 63% of high school and college students scored above 20 in one study, and 72% of disabled adults scored above 20 in another study.

Notice that in choosing this operationalization of subjective well-being, Diener selected only one possible measure, even though there are many other ways to study this concept. (In fact, the Gallup organization chose a different one: a well-being "ladder" numbered from 0 to 10, as discussed later in this chapter.)

Operationalizing Other Conceptual Variables

Other researchers follow a similar process: They start by developing careful definitions of their constructs (the conceptual variables) and then create operational definitions. Intelligence is another example of a variable that has been carefully defined at the conceptual level. Many researchers have agreed to define intelligence as a mental ability that involves the capacity to "reason, plan, solve problems, think abstractly, comprehend complex ideas, learn quickly and learn from experience" (Gottfredsen, 1997, p. 13). Because intelligence is both a general mental capability and one with many subcomponents, researchers have often operationalized it by creating graded intelligence tests that measure a variety of skills, such as people's vocabulary, reasoning, and ability to detect patterns, assemble objects, match symbols, and so on (see **Figure 5.1**).

It is important to remember that any conceptual variable can be operationalized in a wide variety of ways. In fact, operationalizations are one place where creativity comes into the research process, as researchers work to develop new and better measures of their constructs.

FIGURE 5.1 Some of the subtests and examples from the Wechsler Intelligence Scale for Children.

Source: From *Intelligence and How to Get It* by Richard Nisbett. Copyright © 2009 by Richard E. Nisbett. Used by permission of W. W. Norton & Company, Inc. This selection may not be reproduced, stored in a retrieval system, or transmitted in any form or by any means without the prior written permission of the publisher.

Vocabulary:	What is the meaning of derogatory?
Comprehension:	Why are streets usually numbered in order?
Similarities:	How are trees and flowers alike?
Arithmetic:	If six oranges cost two dollars, how much do nine oranges cost?
Picture Completion:	Indicate the missing part from the incomplete picture.
Block Design:	Use blocks to replicate a two-color design.

Three Common Types of Measures

Psychologists' operationalizations of measured variables typically fall into three categories: self-report, observational, and physiological.

Self-Report Measures

A **self-report measure** operationalizes a variable by recording people's answers to verbal questions about themselves in a questionnaire or interview. Diener's five-item scale is an example of a self-report measure, in which people answer questions about their own life satisfaction. Similarly, a self-report measure of intelligence could ask, "How intelligent are you?" If stress was the variable being studied, a self-report measure might ask, "In the last month, how often have you felt nervous and stressed?" (Cohen, Kamarck, & Mermelstein, 1983). A somewhat different type of measure, such as a measure of stressful events in a person's life, might ask people to report on the frequency of specific events they might have experienced in the past year, such as marriage, divorce, or moving (e.g., Holmes and Rahe, 1967). In research on children, self-reports may be replaced with parent reports or teacher reports. Similar to self-reports, these reports ask parents or teachers to respond to a series of questions about the child. For example, the parent or teacher might be asked to describe the child's recent life events, the words a child knows, or the child's typical classroom behaviors. (Chapter 6 discusses situations when self-report measures are likely to be accurate and when they might be biased.)

Observational Measures

An **observational measure** (sometimes called a *behavioral measure*) operationalizes a variable by recording observable behaviors or physical traces of behaviors. For example, you could operationalize happiness by observing how many times a day a person smiles. Intelligence tests can be considered observational measures, because the people who administer the tests in person are observing people's intelligent behaviors (such as being able to correctly solve a puzzle or quickly detect a pattern). An observational measure of stress might involve recording a behavioral signs of stress, such as a person's negative facial expressions (frowning or grimacing) or bodily agitation (tapping toes or tense body language). Observational measures may record physical traces of behavior: You could measure stress behaviors by counting the number of tooth marks left on a person's pencil, or you could measure stressful events by using public legal records to record whether people have recently married, divorced, or moved. (Chapter 6 addresses how an observer's ratings of behavior might be accurate and how they might be biased.)

Physiological Measures

A **physiological measure** operationalizes a variable by recording biological data such as brain activity, hormone levels, or heart rate. Physiological measures usually require the use of equipment to amplify, record, and analyze biological activity. For example, moment-to-moment happiness has been measured using facial electromyography (EMG)—a way of electronically recording tiny movements in the muscles in the face. Facial EMG can detect a happy facial expression, because people who are smiling show particular patterns of muscle movement around the eyes and cheeks.

Other constructs might be measured using a brain scan technique called functional magnetic resonance imaging, or fMRI. In a typical fMRI study, people engage in a carefully designed series of psychological tasks (such as looking at three types of photos or solving two types of test problems) while they are lying in an MRI machine. The MRI apparatus (and computers associated with it) record and code the relative change in blood flow in particular regions of the brain, as shown in **Figure 5.2**. When more blood flows to a brain region during certain tasks, researchers conclude that that area of the brain is working harder during that task. Some research points to a way fMRI might be used to measure intelligence in the future. Specifically, the brains of more-intelligent people are more efficient at solving complex problems—that is, more-intelligent people show relatively less brain activity for complex problems (Deary, Penke, & Johnson, 2010). Therefore, future researchers may be able to use efficiency of brain activity as a physiological measure of intelligence. Another physiological measure, one that turned out to be flawed, comes from a century ago, when people used head circumference to measure intelligence, under the mistaken impression that smarter brains would be stored inside larger skulls (Gould, 1996).

A physiological way to operationalize people's level of stress might be to measure the degree of the hormone cortisol that is released in their saliva, because people under stress show higher rates of cortisol (Carlson, 2009). Skin conductance—an electronic way of measuring the activity in the sweat glands of a person's hands or feet—is another way to measure stress physiologically. People under more stress have more activity in these glands.

Other physiological measures used in psychology include the detection of hormones such as testosterone, oxytocin, or catecholamine, or the detection of electrical patterns in the brain (using electroencephalograph, or EEG).

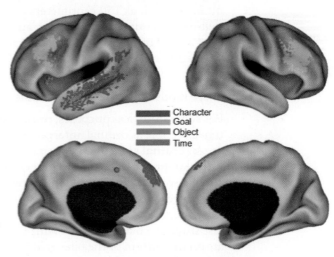

Character
Goal
Object
Time

FIGURE 5.2 Images from an fMRI. In this study, Speer, Reynolds, Swallows, and Zacks (2009) tracked changes in blood flow to different regions of the brain while participants read a story.

One Construct, Many Possible Operationalizations

A single construct can be operationalized in several ways, from self-report to behavioral observation to physiological measures. Many people erroneously believe that physiological measures are bound to be the most accurate. But even these measures must be validated by using other measures. For instance, researchers used fMRI to learn that the brain works more efficiently in intelligent people, but only because they gave participants an observational measure—an IQ test—first. No matter what mode a measure is in, it must have good construct validity—it must measure its construct well.

Scales of Measurement

All variables must have at least two levels (see Chapter 3). But the levels of operational variables may be coded using different scales of measurement.

Categorical Versus Quantitative Variables

First, we can classify operational variables as categorical or quantitative. The levels of **categorical variables**, as the term suggests, are categories. (Categorical variables are sometimes called *nominal variables*.) Examples are sex, whose levels are male and female, or species, whose levels in a study might be rhesus macaque, chimpanzee, and bonobo. A researcher might decide to assign numbers to the levels of a categorical variable (for example, using a 1 to represent rhesus macaques, 2 for chimps, and 3 for bonobos) during the data-entry process. However, the numbers do not have numerical meaning—a bonobo is different from a chimpanzee, but being a bonobo (a "3") is not quantitatively "higher" than being a chimpanzee (a "2").

In contrast, the levels of **quantitative variables** are coded with *meaningful* numbers. Height and weight are quantitative because they are measured in numbers, such as 150 centimeters or 45 kilograms. Diener's scale of subjective well-being is quantitative too, because a score of 35 represents more happiness than a score of 7. IQ score, level of brain efficiency, and amount of salivary cortisol are also quantitative variables.

Three Kinds of Quantitative Variables

For some statistical purposes, researchers may need to further classify a quantitative variable as ordinal, interval, or ratio.

An **ordinal scale** of measurement applies when the numerals of a quantitative variable represent a rank order. For example, a travel website might classify a set of beach resorts as two, three, or four stars. We know that four-star resorts are better than three- or two-star resorts, but we do not know *how much* better they are. A professor might use the order in which exams were turned in to operationalize how fast students completed the exam. This is ordinal data because the fastest exams are on the bottom of the pile—ranked 1. However, this variable has not quantified *how much* faster each exam was turned in, compared with the others.

An **interval scale** of measurement applies to the numerals of a quantitative variable that meet two conditions: First, the numerals represent equal intervals (distances) between levels, and second, there is no "true zero" (a score of 0 does not mean "nothing"). An IQ test is an interval scale—the distance between IQ scores of 100 and 105 represents the same as the distance between IQ scores of 110 and 115. However, a score of zero on an IQ test does not mean a person has "no intelligence." Temperature in degrees Celsius is another example of an interval scale—the intervals between levels are equal; however, a temperature of 0 degrees does not mean that some entity has "no temperature." Most researchers assume that questionnaire scales like Diener's (scored from 1 = "strongly disagree" to 7 = "strongly agree") are interval scales. They do not have a true zero but assume that the distances between numerals, from 1 to 7, are equivalent. Because they do not have a true zero, interval scales cannot allow us to say things like "twice as hot" or "three times happier."

Finally, a **ratio scale** of measurement applies when the numerals of a quantitative variable have equal intervals and when the value of zero truly means "nothing." Examples are weight or income: Something that has no weight will have a true value of 0, and a value of 0 on income means that a person has literally no income. Brain activity is also measured on ratio scales—a value of zero will mean that some area of the brain has not increased in activity. Because ratio scales do have a true zero, one can meaningfully say something like "Miguel ran twice as fast as Diogo."

Check Your Understanding

1. Explain why a variable will usually have only one conceptual definition but can have multiple operational definitions.
2. Name the three common ways in which researchers operationalize their variables.
3. In your own words, describe the difference between categorical and quantitative variables. Describe the differences between ordinal, interval, and ratio scales.

1. See pp. 114–115. 2. See pp. 116–117. 3. See pp. 118–119.

Reliability of Measurement

How do you know if a study's measures are good ones? That is, how do you know if the study's measures have construct validity? The construct validity of a measure has two aspects: **reliability** of measurement and validity of measurement. Reliability concerns how consistent a measure is; validity concerns whether the operationalization is measuring what it is supposed to measure. Both are important, but the first step is reliability.

Three Types of Reliability

Researchers collect data to be sure that their measures are reliable. That is, establishing the reliability of a measure is an empirical question. The reliability of a measure is just what the word suggests: whether or not you can rely on a particular score. If your measurement is reliable, you get a consistent pattern of scores every time. Reliability can be assessed in three ways, depending on how a variable was operationalized, and all three involve consistency in measurement. With **test-retest reliability**, the researcher gets consistent results every time he or she uses the measure. With **interrater reliability**, consistent results are obtained no matter who measures or observes. With **internal reliability**, a study participant gives a consistent pattern of answers, no matter how the researcher has phrased the question.

Test-Retest Reliability

To illustrate test-retest reliability, suppose a sample of people took an IQ test today. When they take it again 1 month later, the scores should be consistent. That is, the pattern should be the same—people who scored the highest at Time 1 should also score the highest at Time 2. Even if all the scores from Time 2 are higher than all the scores from Time 1 (perhaps because of practice), the pattern should be consistent. Test-retest reliability can be relevant no matter whether the operationalization is self-report, observational, or physiological. However, it is primarily relevant when researchers are measuring constructs (such as intelligence) that they expect to be stable over time. Subjective well-being, for example, may fluctuate from month to month or from year to year for a particular person, so we might not expect to see as much consistency in this variable.

Interrater Reliability

With interrater reliability, two or more independent observers will come up with the same (or very similar) findings. Interrater reliability is most relevant for observational measures. For example, say you are assigned to observe the number of times each child smiles in 1 hour on a daycare playground. Your lab partner is assigned to sit on the other side of the playground and make his own count of the same children's smiles. If, for one child, you record 12 smiles during the first hour, and your lab partner also records 12 smiles in that hour for the same child, there is interrater reliability. Any two observers watching the same children at the same time should agree about which child has smiled the most and which child has smiled the least.

Internal Reliability

As an example of the third kind of reliability, internal reliability, suppose a sample of people take Diener's five-item well-being scale. The questions on his scale are worded differently, but each item is intended to be a measure of the same construct. Therefore, people who agree with the first item on the scale should also agree with the second item (as well as with Items 3, 4, and 5). Similarly, people who disagree with the first item should also disagree with Items 2, 3, 4, and 5. If the pattern is consistent across items in this way, the scale has internal reliability.

To show that a measure is reliable most of the time, researchers collect data from samples of people and evaluate the results. Specifically, researchers often use two statistical devices: scatterplots, which were introduced in Chapter 3 to discuss association claims, and the correlation coefficient r. In fact, evidence for reliability is a special example of an association claim—the association between one version of the measure and another, between one coder and another, or between an earlier time and a later time.

Using a Scatterplot to Evaluate Reliability

Years ago, when people thought that smarter people had larger heads, they may have tried to use head circumference as an operationalization of intelligence. Would this measure be reliable? Probably. Suppose you record the head circumference, in centimeters, for everyone in a classroom, using an ordinary tape measure. To see if the measurements were reliable, you could measure all of the heads twice (test-retest) or you could measure them first, and then have someone else measure them (interrater).

Figure 5.3 shows what the results of such a measurement might look like, in the form of a data table and a graph. In the graph, the first measurements of head circumference for four students are plotted on the y-axis. The circumferences as measured the second time—whether by you again (test-retest) or by a second observer (interrater)—are plotted on the x-axis. In this scatterplot, each dot represents a person measured twice.

We would expect the two measures of head circumference to be about the same for each person. They are, so the dots on the scatterplot all fall almost

(A)

	Measurement	
	1	2
Taylor	50	52
Kendra	61	59
Mateo	65	64
Kurt	75	80

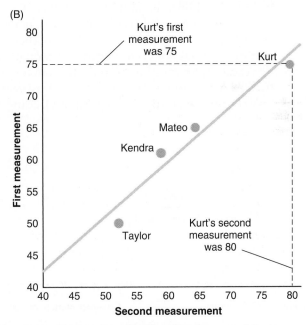

FIGURE 5.3 Two measurements of head circumference in each of four imaginary participants. Panel A shows the data in table form; Panel B presents the data as a scatterplot.

exactly on the sloping line that would indicate perfect agreement. The two measures will not always be exactly the same because there is likely to be some measurement error (maybe from variations in exactly where the tape measure was placed in each trial) that will lead to slightly different scores even for the same person.

Scatterplots Can Show Interrater Agreement or Disagreement

In a different scenario, suppose 10 young children are being observed on a playground. Two independent observers, Mark and Matt, rate how happy each child appears to be, on a scale of 1 to 10. They later compare notes to see how well their ratings agree. From these notes, they create a scatterplot, plotting Observer Mark's ratings on the x-axis and Observer Matt's ratings on the y-axis.

If the data looked like those in **Figure 5.4A**, the ratings would have high interrater reliability. Both Observer Mark and Observer Matt rate Jay's happiness as 9. Observer Mark rates Jackie a 2; Observer Matt rates her 3, and so on. The two observers do not show perfect agreement, but there are no great disagreements either. Again, the points are scattered around the plot a bit, but they hover close to the sloping line that would indicate perfect agreement.

In contrast, suppose the data looked like **Figure 5.4B**, which shows much less agreement. Here, the two observers are Mark and Peter, and they are watching the same children at the same time, but Mark gives Jay a rating of 9 and Peter thinks he rates only a 6. Mark considers Jackie's behavior to be shy and withdrawn and rates her a 2, but Peter thinks she seems calm and content and rates her a 7. Here the interrater reliability is low—in fact, for most purposes, it would be considered unacceptably low. One reason it is low could be that the way the researchers operationalized "happiness" is poor, so the observers did not have a clear enough definition to work with. Another reason could be that one or both of the coders has not been trained well enough yet.

A scatterplot can thus be a helpful tool for assessing the agreement between two administrations of the same measurement (test-retest reliability) or between two coders (interrater reliability). Using a scatterplot, you can see whether the two ratings agree (if the individual dots are close to a straight line drawn through them) or whether they disagree (if the individual dots scatter widely from a straight line drawn through them).

Scatterplots are an important first step in evaluating reliability. But a more common and efficient way to evaluate reliability relationships is to use the correlation coefficient.

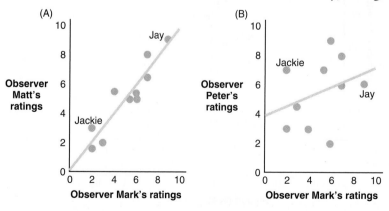

FIGURE 5.4 Interrater reliability. In Panel A, interrater reliability is high; in Panel B, interrater reliability is low.

Using the Correlation Coefficient *r* to Evaluate Reliability

Researchers can use a single number to indicate how close the dots on a scatterplot are to a line drawn through them: the **correlation coefficient *r***. Notice that the scatterplots in **Figure 5.5** differ in two important ways. One difference is that the scattered clouds of points slope in different directions. In Figure 5.5A and Figure 5.5B the points slope upward from left to right, in Figure 5.5C they slope downward, and in Figure 5.5D they do not slope up or down at all. This slope is referred to as the direction of the relationship, and the **slope direction** can be positive, negative, or zero—that is, sloping up, sloping down, or not sloping at all.

The other way the scatterplots differ is that in some, the dots are close to a straight, sloping line; in others, the dots are more spread out. This spread

For more on the slope of a scatterplot, see Chapter 3, pp. 59–61.

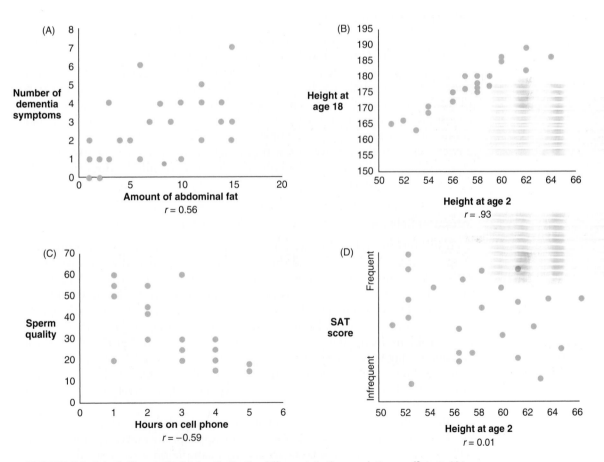

FIGURE 5.5 Correlation coefficients. Notice the differences in the correlation coefficients (*r*) in these scatterplots. The correlation coefficient describes the direction and strength of the association between the two variables. (Data are fabricated for the purpose of illustration.)

corresponds to the **strength** of the relationship. In general, the relationship is strong when dots are close to the line; it is weak when dots are spread out.

The numbers below the scatterplots are the correlation coefficients, or r. The r tells you the same two things that the scatterplot does—the direction of the relationship and the strength of the relationship, both of which are used by psychologists in evaluating reliability evidence. Notice that when the scatterplot's slope is positive, r is positive; when the slope is negative, r is negative. The value of r can only fall between 1.0 and -1.0. When the relationship is strong, r is close to either 1 or -1; when the relationship is weak, r is closer to zero. An r of 1.0 represents the strongest possible positive relationship, and an r of -1.0 represents the strongest possible negative relationship. If there is no relationship between two variables, r will be 0.0 or close to 0.0 (such as 0.02 or -0.04).

Those are the basics. How do psychologists use the strength and direction of r to evaluate reliability evidence?

For more on how to compute r, see Appendix A, pp. A14–A15.

Test-Retest Reliability

To assess test-retest reliability, we would measure the same set of participants at least twice—at Time 1 and Time 2. Then we could compute r. If r is positive and strong (for test-retest, we might expect 0.5 or above), we would have very good test-retest reliability. If r is positive but weak, we would know that participants' scores on the test changed from Time 1 to Time 2. This result would be a sign of poor measurement reliability if we are measuring something that should stay the same over time. For example, a trait like intelligence is not usually expected to change over a few months, so if we assess the test-retest reliability of an intelligence test and obtain a low r, we would be doubtful about the reliability of this test.

Interrater Reliability

To test interrater reliability, we might ask two observers to rate the same participants at the same time, and then we would compute r. If r is positive and strong (according to many researchers, $r = 0.70$ or higher), we would have very good interrater reliability. If r is positive but weak, we probably would not trust the observers' ratings. We would retrain the coders or refine our operational definition so it can be more reliably coded. A negative r would indicate a big problem: In the daycare example, that would mean that Observer Mark considered Jay very happy but Observer Peter considered Jay very unhappy; Observer Mark considered Jackie unhappy but Peter considered Jackie happy, and so on. When you are assessing reliability, a negative correlation is rare and undesirable.

Although r can be used to evaluate interrater reliability when the observers are rating a quantitative variable, a more appropriate statistic, called *kappa*, will be used when the observers are rating a sample on a categorical variable. Although the computations are beyond the scope of this book, kappa measures the extent to which two raters place participants into the same categories.

Internal Reliability

Internal reliability is relevant mainly for self-report measures that contain more than one question to measure the same construct. Researchers who use self-report scales often ask the same question in multiple phrasings, such as the questions on Diener's five-item well-being scale, because each wording of the question might leave room for some measurement error. When researchers assess the internal reliability of a multi-item scale, they are evaluating whether people's responses to the different wordings are consistent. That is, researchers want to be sure that they are getting the same score every time, no matter how they ask the question.

A set of items like this has internal reliability if its items correlate strongly with one another. And if they correlate strongly, the researcher can reasonably take an average of all of the items to create a single score for each person.

As an example, take Diener's well-being scale: Would a group of people show a similar pattern of responses to all of his items? Imagine that Diener had asked the following five items instead:

____ 1. In most ways my life is close to my ideal.
____ 2. The conditions of my life are excellent.
____ 3. I am fond of polka dots.
____ 4. I am a good swimmer.
____ 5. If I could live my life over, I would change almost nothing.

Obviously, these items would probably not be correlated in a sample, so we could not average them together for a meaningful well-being score. Item 1 and item 2 are probably correlated, since they are similar to each other, but item 3 and item 1 are probably not correlated, since people can prefer polka dots whether or not they are living their ideal lives. Item 4 is probably not correlated with any other item, either. But how could we quantify these intuitions? How do we know that this subjective well-being scale, or any other measure, has internal reliability?

Most commonly, researchers will run a correlation-based statistic called **Cronbach's alpha** to see if their measurement scales have internal reliability. First, they collect data on the scale from a large sample of participants, and then they compute all possible correlations among the items. (Does item 1 correlate with item 2? Does item 1 correlate with item 3? Does item 2 correlate with item 3? And so on.) The formula for Cronbach's alpha returns one number, computed from the average of the inter-item correlations and the number of items in the scale. The closer the Cronbach's alpha is to 1, the better the scale's reliability. (For self-report measures, researchers are looking for Cronbach's alpha of 0.70 or higher.) If the internal reliability is good, the researchers can average all the items together. If the internal reliability is low, the researchers are not justified in combining all the items into one scale. They have to go back and revise the items—or average together only those items that correlate strongly with one another.

Why Ask So Many Similar Questions? But if the items in the scale are correlated, why ask five questions in the first place? Why not ask just one question?

It helps to consider the following analogy: Imagine that you ask 12 people to measure the length of a hallway using a meter stick. Each person measures the hallway and reports the measurement. Do you expect these 12 measurements to all be the same? Probably not. Each of the 12 people will probably measure the hallway a little bit differently, and a little bit wrong. But if you assume that the twelve people's errors are *random*, then half of their measurements will come up too short, and half will come up too long. In fact, if you average all 12 of these measurements, you are likely to get a measure that is very close to the true length of the hallway. All the random errors in measurement will cancel each other out.

Of course, the example above has to do with interrater reliability, but the same principle applies to the internal reliability of a self-report questionnaire. Diener assumed that each of his five questions had some error in it: Some items might underestimate well-being for a particular respondent, and some might overestimate it for the same respondent. But in averaging all five items, he hoped to cancel out these random errors and get a fairly accurate measure of each person's well-being. Psychologists will often ask the same (or similar) questions in many different ways. Then they average all of the responses into one score, thus canceling out random errors.

Check Your Understanding

1. Reliability is about consistency. Define the three kinds of reliability, noting what kind of consistency each is designed to show.
2. For each of the three common types of operationalizations—self-report, observational, and physiological—indicate which type(s) of reliability would be relevant.
3. Which of the following correlations is the strongest: $r = 0.25$, $r = -0.65$, $r = -0.01$, or $r = 0.43$?

1. See pp. 119–120. **2.** Self-report: test-retest and internal may be relevant; observational: interrater would be relevant; physiological: interrater may be relevant. **3.** $r = -0.65$.

Validity of Measurement

Once we know that a study's measures are reliable, we must evaluate how well the operationalization is measuring what it is supposed to be measuring. Have the researchers done a good job of operationalizing their conceptual variables—that is, their constructs? Construct validity is generally more challenging for measures of abstract constructs such as intelligence or happiness (Cronbach & Meehl, 1955; Smith, 2005b) than for measures of concrete constructs such as weight or school dropout rates. In the case of a concrete measure, researchers just need to be sure to weigh or count things accurately. But when the constructs are more abstract, the question is whether the exact operational measures that the researchers used really represent the construct the researchers are interested in. So you might ask of Deiner's study whether the five-item measure really reflects how subjectively happy people are.

Measurement reliability and measurement validity are separate steps. To demonstrate the difference between them, consider the example of head circumference as an operationalization of intelligence. Although head circumference measurements may be very reliable, almost all studies have shown that head circumference is not strongly related to intelligence (Gould, 1996). Therefore, the head-circumference test may be reliable, but it is not valid as an intelligence test: It does not measure what it is supposed to measure.

Measurement reliability and measurement validity are both important pieces in establishing a measure's construct validity.

Measurement Validity of Abstract Constructs

Did you know that the U.S. National Institute of Standards and Technology (NIST) has a platinum-iridium bar, kept in a special case at a constant temperature, that represents the international standard for measuring a meter? (Several governments around the world have identical meter sticks in their measurement collections.) Now suppose that I have a cheap, wooden meter stick, received as a promotional gift from my local garden store, that I have been using to measure the height of my tomato plant. I always take the daily measurement twice and always get the same result both times, so I know it is a reliable meter stick. But I don't know whether it is an accurate meter. Maybe it warped over the years, or it was made from a bad batch of wood, or the ends have worn down. If I took my meter stick to NIST and compared it to theirs, would mine match this platinum-iridium standard? If so, then my wooden meter stick is a valid measure of a meter: It measures what it is supposed to measure.

Physical scientists are fortunate to have this kind of standard measurement so they can make sure they are measuring things reliably and precisely. But psychological scientists often want to measure abstract constructs, such as happiness, intelligence, stress, or self-esteem, for which there is no national "meter stick" (Smith, 2005a, 2005b).

Construct validity is therefore important in psychological research, especially when a construct is not directly observable. Take happiness: We have no means of directly measuring how happy a person is. We could estimate it in a number of ways, such as scores on a well-being inventory, daily smile rate, blood pressure, stress hormones, or even the level of activity in certain brain regions. But each of these measures of happiness is indirect.

Even technologically sophisticated measures are not necessarily "direct" measures of an abstract concept. Of course, many people suspect that an fMRI might be a "direct" measure of happiness or intelligence—much better than a self-report. After all, an fMRI can tell us exactly which parts of the brain are active, so if a person's orbitofrontal, insula, or medial prefrontal cortices (specific regions of the brain's neocortex) are showing a lot of activity, we can use that as a direct, unbiased measure of the person's level of happiness, right? But in fact, the only reason we know that activity in these regions indicates happiness in the first place is that people have told researchers (through self-reports) that they were feeling happy at the same time these brain areas were active (Kringelbach &

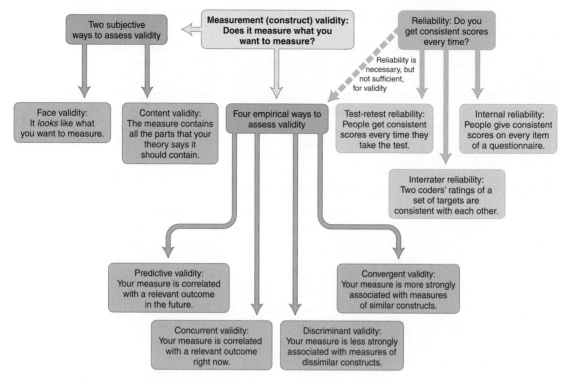

FIGURE 5.6 Summary of reliability and validity concepts.

Berridge, 2009; see also Gilbert, 2005, Chapters 2 and 3). For some abstract constructs, there really is no single, direct measure. And that is the challenge: How can we know if these indirect operational measures of our construct are really measuring happiness and not something else?

We know by looking at data—at the weight of the evidence. The evidence for construct validity is always a matter of degree. Psychologists do not say that a particular measure is or is not valid. Instead, they ask, What is the weight of evidence in favor of this measure's validity? And as with reliability, there are a number of ways to estimate measurement validity. Most are based on data, although researchers might begin by assessing face validity and content validity, which depend on experts' judgments. (See **Figure 5.6** for a map of these concepts.)

Face Validity and Content Validity

A measure has **face validity** to the extent that it is a plausible measure of the variable in question. In other words, if it looks as if it should be a good measure, it has face validity. Nowadays, a measure of head circumference has high face validity as a measure of people's hat size, but it has low face validity as a measure of intelligence. In contrast, rapidity of problem solving, vocabulary size, or creativity would have higher face validity than head circumference as measures of intelligence. Normally, researchers will check face validity by consulting experts. For example, we might assess the face validity of Diener's well-being scale by asking a panel of judges (say, personality psychologists) how reasonable they think the scale is as a way of estimating happiness.

Content validity also involves subjective judgment about a measure. To ensure content validity, a measure must capture all parts of a defined construct. For example, consider the conceptual definition of intelligence quoted earlier in the chapter (Gottfredson, 1997), which contains elements such as the ability to reason, plan, think abstractly, comprehend complex ideas, learn quickly, and so on. To have adequate content validity, any operationalization of intelligence should include questions or items to assess each of these components.

Predictive and Concurrent Validity

To evaluate the validity of a measure, face and content validity are a good place to start, but most psychologists prefer to rely on more than a subjective judgment: They prefer data from a sample of potential participants. There are several ways to do so, but in all cases, the point is to make sure the measurement is associated with something it *should* be associated with. In some cases, such relationships can be illustrated by using scatterplots and correlation coefficients. But they can be illustrated with other kinds of evidence too, such as comparisons of groups with known properties.

Correlational Evidence for Predictive and Concurrent Validity

Predictive validity and **concurrent validity** evaluate whether the measure under consideration is related to a concrete *outcome* that it should be related to, according to the theory being tested. For example, suppose you worked for a company that wanted to predict how well job applicants would do as salespeople. And suppose that for a few years the company has been using IQ to predict sales aptitude but wanted to establish a better measure. So the company hires a consultant to develop a paper-and-pencil scale to measure sales aptitude. How valid is the consultant's measure? The items might look good on a face-validity level, but do the employee test scores correlate with success in selling? This is an empirical question—meaning that it can be settled only via direct, unbiased observations. In this case, you would collect unbiased observations about whether the new sales aptitude test is correlated with success in selling.

You could conduct a study to look at that correlation in two ways. You could give the sales test to each current sales representative and, at the same time, measure each representative's sales figures. Or you could give the sales test to all of the current sales representatives and then measure their sales figures sometime later—say, 3 months from now. In both cases, you would be testing the correlation between the new measure and some relevant outcome. In the first case, you would be testing the correlation with the outcome at the same time (concurrent validity); in the second case, you would be testing the correlation with the outcome in the future (predictive validity). The difference can be subtle (in fact, many researchers call both of them predictive validity). In both cases, you have evaluated the association of the measure (the sales test) with a measure of actual selling behavior.

We can use scatterplots or *r* to assess the validity of the sales measure. **Figure 5.7A** shows results for the predictive validity scenario, in which the representatives' actual sales figures were measured 3 months after the self-report scale. The score on the sales test is plotted on the x-axis, and actual sales performance is plotted on the y-axis. (For example, in Figure 5.7A, Alex scored 39 on the test and brought in $38,000 in sales, whereas Irina scored 98 and brought in $100,000.) **Figure 5.7B**, in contrast, shows the association of sales performance with IQ, the measure the company formerly used.

Looking at these two scatterplots, we can see that the relationship depicted in Figure 5.7A is much stronger than the one in Figure 5.7B. In other words, future sales performance is correlated more highly with scores on the sales test than with scores on the IQ test. If the data looked like this, the company would conclude that the new test has high predictive validity as a measure of sales aptitude. In contrast, the results in Figure 5.7B show that scores on an IQ test are a poorer indicator of future sales performance. The IQ test has low predictive validity as a measure of sales aptitude.

The behavioral criteria provided by predictive and concurrent validity provide excellent evidence for construct validity. No matter what type of operationalization is used, if it is a good measure of its construct, it should correlate with a behavior or outcome that is related to that construct.

For example, most colleges in the United States use standardized tests such as the SAT or ACT to measure the construct "aptitude for college-level work." To demonstrate that these tests have predictive validity, an educational psychologist might want to show that scores on these measures are correlated with college grades (an outcome that represents "college-level work").

FIGURE 5.7
Predictive validity. On the left, predictive validity is high. On the right, predictive validity is lower.

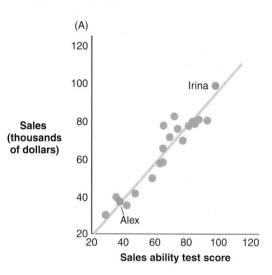

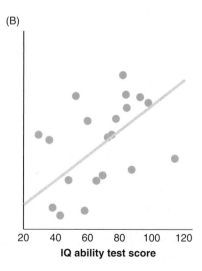

(A)

In a different context, a health psychologist might use the physiological measure of salivary cortisol to measure people's stress. To show that this observational measure has concurrent validity, the health psychologist could demonstrate that salivary cortisol levels in a particular situation are correlated with observers' ratings of behaviors that indicate stress (such as tense expressions or agitated movements).

If an intelligence (IQ) test has predictive validity, it should be correlated with behaviors that capture the construct of intelligence, such as how fast people can learn a complex set of symbols (an outcome that represents the conceptual definition of intelligence). Of course, the ability to learn quickly is only part of the conceptual definition of intelligence. Further validity evidence could show that IQ scores are correlated with other outcomes that are theoretically related to intelligence, such as ability to solve problems or life success (graduating from college, being employed in a high-level job, or earning a large income).

Known-Groups Evidence for Predictive and Concurrent Validity

Although evidence for predictive and concurrent validity is commonly represented with correlation coefficients, it does not have to be. Another way to gather evidence for predictive or concurrent validity is to use a *known-groups paradigm*, in which researchers see whether scores on the measure can discriminate among a set of groups whose behavior is already well understood.

For example, to validate the use of salivary cortisol as a measure of stress, a researcher could compare the salivary cortisol rates of two groups of people: those who are about to give a speech in front of a classroom, and those who are merely in the audience. Public speaking is well understood to be a stressful situation for almost everybody. Therefore, if salivary cortisol is a valid measure of stress, people in the speech group should have higher levels of cortisol than those in the audience group.

Lie detectors are another good example. These instruments record a set of physiological measures (such as skin conductance and heart rate) whose levels are supposed to indicate which of a person's statements are truthful and which are lies. If skin conductance and heart rate are valid measures of lying, we could conduct a known-groups test in which we know which of a person's statements are true and which are false. The physiological measures should be elevated only for the lies, not for the true statements. (For a review of the evidence on lie detection, read Saxe, 1991.)

Known groups can also be used to validate self-report measures. Many years ago, psychiatrist Aaron Beck and his colleagues developed the Beck Depression Inventory (BDI), a 21-item self-report scale with items that ask about major symptoms of depression (Beck, Ward, Mendelson, Mock, & Erbaugh, 1961). People are asked to circle one of four choices, such as the following:

0 I do not feel sad.
1 I feel sad.
2 I am sad all the time and I can't snap out of it.
3 I am so sad or unhappy that I can't stand it.

0 I have not lost interest in other people.
1 I am less interested in other people than I used to be.
2 I have lost most of my interest in other people.
3 I have lost all of my interest in other people.

A clinical scientist adds up the scores on each of the 21 items for a total BDI score, which can range from a low of 0 (not at all depressed) to a high of 36 (very depressed).

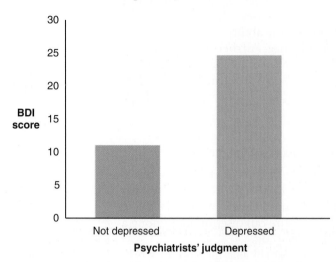

FIGURE 5.8 **Beck Depression Inventory (BDI) scores of different depressed groups.** Patients judged to be more depressed by psychiatrists also scored higher on the BDI. *Source*: Adapted from Beck and colleagues (1961).

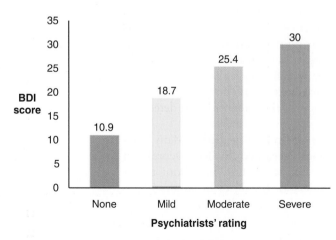

FIGURE 5.9 **Beck Depression Inventory (BDI) scores of different depressed groups—broken down by severity of depression.** *Source*: Adapted from Beck and colleagues (1961).

To test the validity of the BDI, Beck and his colleagues gave this self-report scale to two known groups of people. Some were suffering from clinical depression and some were not, as determined by four psychiatrists who conducted clinical interviews and diagnosed the individuals. The researchers computed the mean BDI scores of the two groups and created a bar graph, shown in **Figure 5.8**. The evidence supports the concurrent validity of the BDI: As you can see from the graph, the BDI scores of the depressed people were higher, supporting the concurrent validity of this measure of depression. The BDI is still widely used today when researchers need a quick and valid way to identify people who are vulnerable to depression.

Beck also used a known-groups technique to calibrate scores on the BDI. After the psychiatrists interviewed the people in the sample, they indicated not only whether the people were depressed but also the level of depression in each person: none, mild, moderate, or severe. As expected, the BDI scores of the groups rose as their level of depression (as assessed by a psychiatrist) was more severe. (The findings are shown in a bar graph in **Figure 5.9**.) This result was even clearer evidence that the BDI was a valid measure of depression. It also means that researchers can use specific ranges of BDI scores to categorize how severe a person's depression might be (for example, "mild" "moderate," or "severe").

Convergent and Discriminant Validity

Besides concurrent and predictive validities, another criterion for validity is whether the test shows a meaningful pattern of associations with other measures. That is, the measure should correlate more strongly with other measures of the same constructs, showing **convergent validity**, and it should correlate less strongly with measures of other, distinct constructs, showing **discriminant validity**, or *divergent validity*.

Convergent Validity

As an example of convergent validity, consider Beck's test of depression, the BDI, again. One set of researchers wanted to test the convergent and discriminant validity of the BDI (Segal, Coolidge, Cahill, & O'Riley, 2008). If the BDI really measures depression, the researchers reasoned, it should be correlated with (that is, it should converge with) other measures of depression. They therefore asked a sample of 376 adults to fill out the BDI as well as a number of other questionnaires, including a self-report instrument called the Center for Epidemiologic Studies Depression scale (CES-D).

As expected, the BDI was positively correlated with the CES-D ($r = 0.68$, a fairly strong correlation). That is, people who scored as depressed on the BDI measure of depression also scored as depressed on the CES-D measure of depression, and people who scored as not depressed on the BDI measure of depression also scored as not depressed on the CES-D measure of depression. **Figure 5.10** provides a scatterplot of the results. (Notice that most of the points fall in the lower left-hand portion of the scatterplot, because most people in the sample are not depressed: They score low on both the BDI and the CES-D.) This correlation between similar measures of the same construct (depression) provided good evidence for the convergent validity of the BDI.

For more on the strength of correlations, see Chapter 7 and Appendix A.

You might notice that testing for convergent validity can be a circular process. That is, even if researchers validate the BDI with the CES-D, there is no assurance that the CES-D measure is the perfect gold standard. Indeed, its validity would need to be established, too! So then the researchers might try to validate the CES-D with a third measure, but that measure's validity would also need to be supported with evidence. Eventually, however, we may be satisfied that a measure is valid after we evaluate the *weight* and *pattern* of the evidence. Many researchers are most convinced when measures have been associated with a variety of behaviors (using predictive or concurrent validity). However, remember that no single definitive test will establish validity (Smith, 2005a).

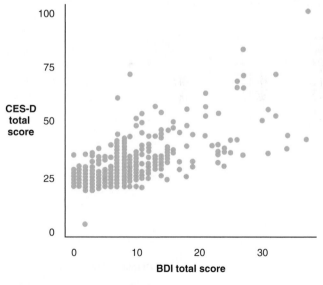

FIGURE 5.10 Evidence supporting the convergent validity of the BDI. The BDI is strongly correlated with another measure of depression, the CES-D ($r = 0.68$), providing evidence for convergent validity.

Discriminant Validity

Whereas the BDI should correlate with another measure of depression, it should not correlate strongly with other measures; in other words, it should show discriminant validity with those measures. It is most important to demonstrate a measure's discriminant validity for other traits that might reasonably be mistaken for the trait being measured. For example, depression is not the same as a person's perception of his or her overall physical health. Although mental health and physical health probably do overlap somewhat, we would not expect a measure of depression to be strongly correlated with a measure of perceived physical health. In fact, Segal and his colleagues found a correlation of only $r = -0.17$ between the BDI and a measure of perceived physical health. This weak correlation shows that the BDI is different from people's perceptions of their physical health, so we can say that the BDI has discriminant validity, or divergent validity, with physical health. **Figure 5.11** shows a scatterplot of the results. Notice something important: What matters is that this correlation is weak, not that it is negative. To provide evidence for discriminant validity, we care mostly that the (discriminant) correlation of the BDI with physical health is not as strong as its (convergent) correlation with CES-D. (Notice also that most of the points fall in the upper left-hand portion of the scatterplot, because most people in the sample are both physically healthy and not depressed: They score low on the BDI and high on the physical health scale.)

It is usually not necessary to establish the discriminant validity between a measure and something that is completely unrelated. Because depression is unlikely to be associated with the movies you like or the amount of coffee you drink per day, we would not need to examine its discriminant validity with these variables. Instead, researchers worry about discriminant validity when they want to be sure that their measure is not accidentally capturing a similar but different construct. Does the BDI measure depression or perceived health? Does Diener's subjective well-being measure capture enduring happiness or just temporary mood? Does a measure of social skills capture social skills or just extraversion?

Convergent validity and discriminant validity are usually evaluated together. A measurement should correlate more strongly with similar traits (convergent validity) and less strongly with dissimilar traits (discriminant validity). There are no hard-and-fast rules for what the correlations should be. Instead, the overall pattern of convergent and discriminant validity helps researchers decide whether their operationalization really measures the construct they want it to measure—as opposed to other constructs.

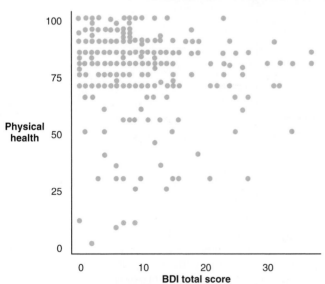

FIGURE 5.11 Evidence supporting the discriminant validity of the BDI. As expected, the BDI is only weakly, negatively correlated with physical health ($r = -0.17$), providing evidence for discriminant validity.

Relationship Between Reliability and Validity

One point is worth reiterating: The validity of a measure is not the same as its reliability. A journalist might boast that some measure of behavior is "a very reliable test," but to say that a measure is "reliable" is only half of the story. A measure (such as a measure of head circumference) can be extremely reliable but still may not be valid for an intended use (as a measure of intelligence).

Although a measure may be less valid than it is reliable, it cannot be more valid than it is reliable. Intuitively, this statement makes sense. Reliability has to do with how well a measure correlates with itself. For example, an IQ test is reliable if it is correlated with itself over time. But validity has to do with how well a measure is associated with some other similar, but not identical, measure. For example, an IQ test is valid if it is associated with another variable, such as school grades or life success. If a test does not even correlate with itself, then how can it be more strongly associated with a measure of some other variable? Therefore, reliability is necessary (but not sufficient) for validity.

An Applied Review: Interrogating Construct Validity as a Consumer

After learning about reliability and construct validity, you are ready to return to the contradictory headlines from the beginning of the chapter: "Most People Are Happy" and "Half of Americans Struggle to Stay Happy." Do these claims differ so much because of the different measures of happiness used in the two studies? And if so, which measure is better?

Interrogating Diener's Measure of Happiness

Diener made the frequency claim "Most people are happy." Imagine that we are going to interrogate the construct validity of the operationalization on which this claim is based. Our first step is to ask how the researchers operationalized the variable, happiness. Then we should think about the operationalization's face and content validity. Does common sense suggest that the operationalization fits the construct mentioned in the claim?

We also need information about data-oriented (empirically established) reliability and validity. Such information tends to be detailed and technical, so it is usually not presented in popular press coverage of research. However, when you read empirical journal articles, construct validity information should be presented in some detail. Usually, these details will appear in the Method section of the journal article. Take, for example, this quotation from one of Ed Diener's papers:

> The [scale] has shown strong internal reliability and moderate temporal stability. Diener et al. (1985) reported a coefficient alpha of .87 for the scale and a 2-month test-retest stability coefficient of .82. . . . Since that time a number of other investigators have reported both internal consistency and temporal reliability data. (Pavot & Diener, 1993, p. 165)

The sentences above describe a table, reproduced in **Figure 5.12**, in which Pavot and Diener present a list of six studies that used their scale. Across the table, the test-retest reliability (which they refer to as "stability") correlations range from 0.50 to 0.84; the Cronbach's alpha ranges from 0.79 to 0.89, showing good internal reliability. (They did not test interrater reliability because their scale is a self-report measure, and interrater reliability is relevant only when two or more observers are doing the ratings.)

Next, we need to assess *validity*. Here, what matters most is the pattern from the entire body of evidence. Pavot and Diener therefore present a variety of evidence for the construct validity of their scale. For example, they used a known-groups paradigm to show concurrent validity. Male prison inmates—a group that would be expected to have low subjective well-being—have lower scores on the scale, averaging 12.3, compared with older American adults, who averaged 24.2. Selected data from Pavot and Diener's original table providing this evidence is reproduced in **Table 5.1**. For convergent validity, the scale correlated with expected measures of well-being; for example, one study showed a correlation of $r = 0.43$ between scores on the scale and an interviewer's rating of each person's well-being. There is no absolute correlation or result that will indicate convergent validity. What is important, however, is that the researchers expected to find a correlation between two measures of the same construct, and they found one.

FIGURE 5.12
Reliability of the well-being scale. Pavot and Diener (1993) created this table to show how six studies supported the reliability of their scale. (Reproduced from original journal.)

Table 2

Estimates of Internal Consistency and Temporal Reliability for the Satisfaction with Life Scale

Sample	Coefficient alpha	Test–retest	Temporal interval
Alfonso & Allison (1992a)	.89	.83	2 weeks
Pavot et al. (1991)	.85	.84	1 month
Blais et al. (1989)	.79–.84	.64	2 months
Diener et al. (1985)	.87	.82	2 months
Yardley & Rice (1991)	.80, .86	.50	10 weeks
Magnus, Diener, Fujita, & Pavot (1992)	.87	.54	4 years

TABLE 5.1 Selected Data for the Satisfaction with Life Scale

Study reference	Sample characteristics	N	M	SD
Pavot & Diener (1993)	American college students	244	23.7	6.4
Blais et al. (1989)	French Canadian college students (male)	355	23.8	6.1
Balatsky & Diener (1993)	Moscow State University students	61	18.9	4.5
Suh (1993)	Korean university students	413	19.8	5.8
Pavot et al. (1991)	Older American adults	39	24.2	6.9
George (1991)	Printing trade workers	304	24.2	6.0
Frisch (1991)	Veterans Affairs hospital inpatients	52	11.8	5.6
Fisher (1991)	Abused women	70	20.7	7.4
Joy (1990)	Male prison inmates	75	12.3	7.0

Source: Pavot & Diener (1993), Table 1.

As further evidence of convergent validity, the scale also correlates negatively with psychological distress ($r = -0.55$). Happy people are less distressed, and unhappy people are more distressed. Notice something important here: A negative correlation is providing evidence for convergent validity. It is the strength, not the direction, of the correlations, that matters for convergent and discriminant validity. Researchers expect to see stronger correlations (in the predicted direction) with measures of related constructs and weaker correlations with measures of unrelated constructs. For example, Diener's scale also shows discriminant validity because it does not correlate with a construct it should not correlate with: the intensity of emotional experience. Feeling emotions intensely is different from general well-being, so it should not be correlated with the well-being scale, and Diener showed that the two are not correlated. In short, if we were to read about the measurement and construct validity information of Diener's scale in an empirical journal article, we would come away with a favorable impression. His scale has acceptably high reliability and good construct validity.

Interrogating the Gallup Poll's Measure of Happiness

What if we interrogated the construct validity of the measure of happiness used in the Gallup poll, which led to the frequency claim "Half of Americans struggle to stay happy"? Gallup operationalized happiness by conducting phone interviews in which they asked people to rate their well being:

[T]he Gallup-Healthways Well-Being Index asks Americans to evaluate their lives today as well as their lives five years from now by imagining a "ladder" with steps numbered from 0 to 10, where "0" represents the worst possible life and "10" represents the best possible life. (Gallup-Healthways, 2009, p. 9)

People who are on the seventh step or above are categorized by the researchers as "thriving." Those on the fourth step or below are "suffering," and anyone in between (step five or six) is categorized as "struggling." The headline "Half of Americans Struggle to Stay Happy" indicates that 47% of people who took the poll scored either 5 or 6 on this ladder.

In a publicly available methodology statement, the Gallup-Healthways organization provides a bit of information about the ladder's validity (but not its reliability). For example, it mentions that across U.S. states, those with higher incomes, less poverty, less disease, and higher life expectancies also have people who report higher scores on the ladder (Gallup-Healthways, 2009).

Therefore, the organization provides some state-level evidence for concurrent validity. However, there is no information given in the report about the reliability of the ladder scores over time. In addition, it is important to ask about the method of assigning certain scores on the ladder to "suffering," "struggling," and "thriving." The online methodology report does not present evidence that, say, a person who scores a 7 is thriving and a person who scores a 6 is struggling. Unlike Beck and his colleagues, who used psychiatrists' ratings to calibrate what a "mildly," "moderately," or "severely" depressed person's score would be on the BDI, Gallup-Healthways does not present such evidence for the well-being ladder.

A number of possible explanations could account for the lack of detailed construct evidence in the article. As private organizations, Gallup and Healthways are in the business of designing survey instruments, so they might not want to provide too much background information for free. Or perhaps they simply do not expect that their general readers are trained or motivated to ask such questions. (If this is the case, Gallup may be willing to share additional reliability and validity details on request.) However, until you have clearer evidence for this measure's reliability and validity, you might want to take the claim about "struggling" Americans with a grain of salt.

Summary

This chapter has focused on something that you will interrogate for any type of claim: the construct validity of the study's measured variables. Psychological scientists measure variables in every study they conduct. Three common forms of variable operationalizations include self-report, in which a person reports on his or her own behaviors, beliefs, or attitudes; observational, in which raters record the visible behaviors of people or animals; and physiological, in which researchers measure biological data such as heart rate, brain activity, or hormone levels.

Depending on how they are operationalized, variables may be categorical or quantitative. The levels of categorical variables are categories. The levels of quantitative variables are meaningful numbers, in which higher numbers represent more of some variable. Quantitative variables can be further classified as ordinal, interval, or ratio scales.

Both measurement reliability and measurement validity are important for establishing a measure's construct validity. Researchers use scatterplots and correlation coeffients (among other methods) to evaluate evidence for a measure's reliability and validity.

To establish a measure's reliability, researchers collect data to see whether the measure works consistently. There are three types of measurement reliability. Test-retest reliability establishes whether a sample gives a consistent pattern of scores at more than one testing. Interrater reliability establishes whether two observers give consistent ratings of a sample of targets. Internal reliability is established when a sample of people answer a set of similarly worded items in a consistent way. Measurement reliability is necessary but not sufficient for measurement validity.

Measurement validity can be established with subjective judgments (face and content validity) or with empirical data. Empirically derived (or criterion) validities include predictive, concurrent, discriminant, and convergent validity. Predictive and concurrent validity require showing that an operationalization is correlated with outcomes that it should correlate with, according to the understanding of the construct. Convergent and discriminant validity require showing that a measure is correlated more strongly with measures of similar constructs than it is with measures of dissimilar constructs. You can read about a measure's reliability and validity by looking at the details reported in the Method and Results sections of empirical journal articles.

Key Terms

categorical variable, p. 118
concurrent validity, p. 129
content validity, p. 129
convergent validity, p. 133
correlation coefficient *r*, p. 123
Cronbach's alpha, p. 125
discriminant validity, p. 133
face validity, p. 128
internal reliability, p. 120
interrater reliability, p. 120
interval scale, p. 118

observational measure, p. 116
ordinal scale, p. 118
physiological measure, p. 117
predictive validity, p. 129
quantitative variable, p. 118
ratio scale, p. 119
reliability, p. 119
self-report measure, p. 116
slope direction, p. 123
strength, p. 124
test-retest reliability, p. 120

 **NEED HELP STUDYING?**
wwnorton.com/studyspace

Visit StudySpace to access free review materials such as:

- Diagnostic Review Quizzes
- Study Outlines

Learning Actively

1. Classify each operational variable below as categorical or quantitative. If the variable is quantitative, further classify it as ordinal, interval, or ratio.

   a. Degree of pupil dilation in a person's eyes in a study of romantic couples
   b. Number of books a person owns
   c. A book's sales rank on amazon.com
   d. Location of a person's hometown (urban, rural, or suburban)
   e. Nationality of the participants in a cross-cultural study of Canadian, Ghanaian, and French students
   f. A student's grade in school

2. Match each scatterplot below to the r that it is most likely to represent.

   a. $r = 0.775$
   b. $r = -0.959$
   c. $r = 0.032$
   d. $r = 0.458$

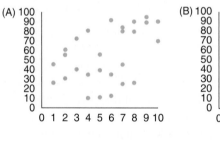
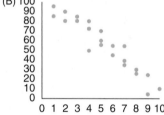
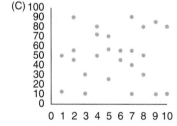
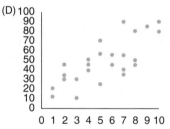

3. For each measure below, indicate which kinds of reliability would need to be evaluated. Then, draw a scatterplot that would indicate that the measure has good reliability and one that would indicate that the measure has poor reliability. (Pay special attention to how you label the axes of your scatterplots.)

   a. Researchers place unobtrusive video recording devices in the living rooms of 20 children. Later, coders view tapes of the living areas and code how many minutes each child spends playing video games.

b. Clinical psychologists have developed a seven-item self-report measure to quickly identify people who are at risk for panic disorder.

c. Psychologists measure how long it takes a mouse to learn an eye-blink response. For 60 trials, they present a mouse with a distinctive blue light followed immediately by a puff of air. The 5th, 10th, and 15th trials are test trials, in which they present the blue light alone (without the air puff). The mouse is said to have learned the eyeblink response if observers record that it blinked its eyes in response to a blue light test trial. The earlier in the 60 trials the mouse shows the eye-blink response, the faster it has learned the response.

d. A restaurant owner uses a response card with four items in order to evaluate how satisfied customers are with the food, service, ambience, and overall experience. Each item is scaled from one to four stars.

e. Educational psychologists use teacher ratings of classroom shyness (on a nine-point scale, where 1 = "not at all shy in class" and 9 = "very shy in class") to measure children's temperament.

4. Consider how you might validate the nine-point classroom shyness rating example in Question 3e. First, what behaviors might be relevant to use to test this rating's concurrent and predictive validity? Why did you choose those behaviors? Draw a scatterplot that would show results of a study in which the classroom shyness rating has good predictive or concurrent validity (pay careful attention to how you label your axes). Second, come up with ways to evaluate the convergent and discriminant validity of this rating system: What traits should correlate strongly with shyness? What traits should correlate only weakly or not at all? Explain why you chose those traits. Draw a scatterplot that would show results of a study in which the shyness rating has good convergent or discriminant validity (pay careful attention to how you label your axes).

5. Pop-psychology tests are a common form of entertainment online. Find a personality or relationship quiz (try the relationship tests on www.marsvenus.com or the personality tests at www.cosmomag.com). Can you find any evidence for the reliability and validity of the quizzes on the websites? Choose one of these pop psychology tests and explain how you would test its reliability and validity. That is, explain the data that you would collect and state the results you would predict. You might frame your predictions in this form: "If this pop-psychology scale is valid, I would expect it to be correlated with . . ." or "If this scale is reliable, I would expect . . ."

PART 3

Tools for Evaluating Frequency Claims

"**Should I buy these boots? They got four out of five stars on Zappos.**"

"*I'm not taking that class. The professor has a frowny face on ratemyprofessor .com.*"

"**What's the difference between a pit bull and a hockey dad? There is no difference.**"

(*Star Tribune*, 2008)

6

Describing What People Do: Surveys, Observations, and Sampling

Learning Objectives

A year from now, you should still be able to:

1. Explain how carefully prepared questions improve the construct validity of a poll or survey.
2. Describe how researchers can make observations with good construct validity.
3. Understand why external validity often matters for a frequency claim, and describe the relationship between sampling techniques and external validity.

By now you can easily identify the three statements that open this chapter as one-variable frequency (or level) claims. They are each about one variable—the rated quality of a pair of boots, opinions about a professor, or beliefs about the aggression of hockey fans. You might also encounter claims about people's understanding of history or their political leanings. This chapter focuses on frequency claims that come from surveys and polls, in which researchers ask people questions, as well as frequency claims that come from observational studies, in which researchers watch the behavior of people or other animals, often without asking any questions at all. You will apply what you have learned about construct validity to each kind of study, and you will learn more about interrogating the external validity of a frequency claim.

Construct Validity of Surveys and Polls

Researchers use surveys and polls to ask people questions over the phone, in door-to-door personal interviews, through the mail, or over the Internet. You may have been asked to take surveys in various situations. Perhaps when you called to check your credit card balance you were asked to take a survey about the customer service agent. Or maybe a survey popped up while you were reading an online newspaper. Or a polling organization, such as Gallup or Pew Research Center, may have called you at home.

Often, the term *survey* is used when people are asked about a consumer product, whereas the term *poll* is used when people are asked about their opinions. However, the terms are used interchangeably, and in this book *survey* and *poll* are both used to mean the same thing: a sample of people being asked to answer questions on the phone, in personal interviews, on a paper-and-pencil questionnaire, or over the Internet. Psychologists might conduct national polls as part of their research, or they may use the polling information they read (as consumers of information) to inspire further research.

How much can you learn about a phenomenon just by asking people questions? It depends on how, and whom, you ask. As you will learn, researchers who develop their questions carefully can draw frequency claims that have excellent construct validity.

Choosing Question Formats

Survey questions can follow many formats. Researchers may ask **open-ended questions** that allow respondents to answer in any way they see fit. For example, they might ask people to name the public figure they admire the most. They might ask a sample of people to describe their views on affirmative action. They might ask students, "What are your comments about this professor?" People's responses to open-ended questions can provide spontaneous, rich information to researchers. The downside is that the responses must be coded and categorized, a process that can often be difficult and time-consuming.

Because coding open-ended responses takes time, researchers in psychology often restrict the answers people can give, in the interest of efficiency. There are many options for doing so.

One specific type of survey question is the **forced-choice format**, in which people give their opinion by picking the best of two or more options. This type of question is frequently used in political polls, which might ask which of two or three candidates the respondent is most likely to vote for. Or respondents might be asked about their opinions on current issues or their preference between two options.

An example of a psychology measure that uses forced-choice format is the Narcissistic Personality Inventory (NPI; Raskin & Terry, 1988), which asks people to choose one statement from each of 40 pairs of items, such as the following:

1. ___ I really like to be the center of attention.
   ___ It makes me uncomfortable to be the center of attention.
2. ___ I am going to be a great person.
   ___ I hope I am going to be successful.

To score a survey like this, the researchers add up the number of times people choose the "narcissistic" response over the "non-narcissistic" one (in the example items above, the narcissistic response is the first option).

In another question format, people are presented with a statement and are asked to use a rating scale to indicate their degree of agreement. When such a scale contains more than one item and is anchored by the terms *strongly agree, agree, neither agree nor disagree, disagree, and strongly disagree*, it is often called a **Likert scale** (the name is pronounced "lick-urt"; Likert, 1932). If it does not follow this format exactly, it may be called a *Likert-type scale*. A commonly used measure of self-esteem, the Rosenberg self-esteem inventory (Rosenberg, 1965), is an example of a Likert-type format. Here is one of its ten items:

I am able to do things as well as most other people.

1	2	3	4	5
Strongly disagree				Strongly agree

In addition to degree of agreement, respondents might be asked to rate a target object using a numeric scale that is anchored with adjectives (a **semantic differential format**). For example, on the Internet site ratemyprofessors.com, students give their opinions about a professor using the following adjectives:

Easiness:

Easy	1	2	3	4	5	Hard

Helpfulness:

Useless	1	2	3	4	5	Extremely helpful

Clarity:

Incomprehensible	1	2	3	4	5	Crystal clear

The five-star rating format that many Internet shopping sites use, similar to the one shown in **Figure 6.1**, is another example of this technique. Often one star means "poor" or "I hate it," and five stars means "outstanding" or "I love it."

There are other question types, of course, and researchers might even combine formats on a single survey. But the format of a question (such as open-ended, forced choice, or Likert-type) does not make or break its construct validity. The way a question is worded and the order of survey questions is much more important.

FIGURE 6.1 A five-star product rating on the Internet. The ratings of products people might buy online are examples of frequency claims. Are such "five-star" ratings valid indicators of a product's quality?

CUSTOMER FEEDBACK

This product currently has 14 reviews
Overall Rating:

36%
14%
29%
7%
14%

Customer Fit Survey:

Customers surveying this product said...

55% "Felt a half size larger than marked"
75% "Felt true to width"
61% "No arch support"

Writing Well-Worded Questions

As with other research findings, when we interrogate a survey result, the first question is, How well was that variable measured? The way a question is worded and presented in a survey can make a tremendous difference in how people answer it. In a survey, it is crucial that each question be clear and straightforward to answer. The creators of the survey work to ensure that the wording and order of the questions do not influence respondents' answers.

Leading Questions

An example of the way question wording can affect survey responses comes from a study in which the researcher asked people about their views on U.S. race relations in a Gallup Poll (Wilson, 2006). Half of the participants heard this (forced choice) version of the question:

> Do you think that relations between Blacks and Whites
> —Will always be a problem?
> —Or that a solution will eventually be worked out?

The other half heard this version:

> Do you think that relations between Blacks and Whites
> —Are as good as they're going to get?
> —Or will they eventually get better?

On the surface, these two questions seem to measure the same thing—how optimistic respondents felt about race relations. However, the results of the study showed that the two questions elicited very different responses. Only 45% of respondents who heard the first version of the question reported being optimistic about race relations—that is, only 45% said that relations "will eventually work out." But among those who heard the second version, a full 73% reported being optimistic about race relations, saying that relations "will eventually get better." Why would the responses be so different when the questions seem to be asking the same thing? Clearly, there is a difference in meaning in the two versions: Framing of race relations as a "problem" that needs to be "worked out" is more negative than the framing of relations as "good" and possibly getting "better." But from this study, we cannot tell if the negative version primed people to be negative or if the positive version primed people to be positive—or whether both happened. We have learned, however, that question wording matters!

In general, if the intention of a survey is to capture respondents' true opinions, the survey writers might attempt to word every question as neutrally as possible. When researchers want to measure the extent to which question wording matters for their topic, the best way is to word the questions more than one way. If the results are the same no matter what, they can conclude that question wording does not affect people's responses to that topic. But if the results are different, they may need to report the results separately for each wording of the question.

Double-Barreled Questions

Sometimes, too, the question wording becomes so complicated that respondents have trouble answering in a way that accurately reflects their opinions. In a survey, it is always best to ask a simple question. When people can understand the question, they can give a clear, direct, and meaningful answer. But sometimes, survey writers forget this rule. For example, one online survey on students' study habits asked this question:

I look for main ideas as I read, and I formulate answers to questions I have as I read an assignment.

1	2	3	4	5
Disagree				Agree

This kind of question is called *double-barreled*, meaning that it asks two questions in one. Double-barreled questions have poor construct validity, because people might be responding to the first half of the question, the second half, or both. So the question could be measuring the first construct, the second construct, or both. Careful researchers would have asked each question separately:

I look for main ideas as I read.

1	2	3	4	5
Disagree				Agree

I formulate answers to questions I have as I read an assignment.

1	2	3	4	5
Disagree				Agree

Double Negatives

Double negatives can also make the wording of survey questions unnecessarily complicated. Because double-negative responses are cognitively difficult for people, they can cause confusion and thus reduce the construct validity of a survey.

An example comes from a survey on Holocaust denial, which found that 20% of Americans denied that the Nazi Holocaust ever happened. In the months that followed the publication of this survey's results, writers and journalists decried and analyzed the "intensely disturbing" news (Kagay, 1994).

Upon further investigation, the Roper polling organization reported that the people in the original telephone poll were asked, "Does it seem possible or does it seem impossible to you that the Nazi extermination of the Jews never happened?" Think for a minute about how you would answer that question. Would you find it awkward to answer? If you wanted to convey the opinion that the Holocaust happened, you would have to say, "It's impossible that it never happened." That is, the question, containing the words *impossible* and *never*, requires you to think in the double negative. In order to give your opinion about the Holocaust accurately, you must also be able to unpack this double negative and respond to it appropriately. So instead of measuring people's beliefs, the question may be measuring people's working memory or their motivation to pay attention.

We know that the awkward question wording may have affected people's responses because the same polling organization repeated the survey less than a year later, asking the question more clearly: "Does it seem possible to you that the Nazi extermination of the Jews never happened, or do you feel certain that it happened?" This time, only 1% responded that the Holocaust might not have happened; 8% did not know, and 91% said they were certain that it happened (Kagay, 1994). This new result, followed by other polls reflecting similarly low levels of Holocaust denial, indicate that the original wording of the question had poor construct validity: It probably did not measure people's true beliefs.

Sometimes even one negative word can make a question difficult to answer. For example, consider the following question:

Guns should never be controlled.

1	2	3	4	5
Disagree				Agree

To answer this question, those who support gun control must think in the double negative ("I *dis*agree that guns should *never* be controlled"), while those who do not support it would be able to answer more easily ("I agree— guns should never be controlled"). When possible, a double-negative wording should be avoided. But sometimes, researchers ask questions both ways, like this:

Guns should never be controlled.

1	2	3	4	5
Disagree				Agree

Gun control is a good idea.

1	2	3	4	5
Disagree				Agree

After asking the question the both ways, you can study the items' internal consistency (using Cronbach's alpha) to see whether people respond similarly to both questions (in this case, agreement with the first item should covary with disagreement with the second item). Like double-barreled questions, double-negative questions can lead to low construct validity because they might capture people's ability or motivation to do the cognitive work, rather than their true opinions.

Question Order

The order in which questions are asked can also affect the responses to a survey. The earlier questions can change the way respondents understand and answer the later questions. For example, a question on a parenting survey such as "How often do your children play?" would have different meanings if the previous questions had been about sports versus music versus daily activities. Consider this example: Political opinion researcher David Wilson and his colleagues asked people whether they supported affirmative action for different groups (Wilson, Moore, McKay, & Avery, 2008). Half of the people he surveyed were asked two forced-choice questions in this order:

1. Do you generally favor or oppose affirmative action programs for women?
2. Do you generally favor or oppose affirmative action for racial minorities?

The other half of the people were asked the same two questions, but in the opposite order:

1. Do you generally favor or oppose affirmative action for racial minorities?
2. Do you generally favor or oppose affirmative action programs for women?

Wilson found that white respondents to this survey reported more support for affirmative action for minorities when they had first been asked about affirmative action for women. Presumably, most white people support affirmative action for women more than they do for minorities. And to be consistent, they might feel obligated to express support for affirmative action for racial minorities if they have just indicated their support for affirmative action for women.

The most direct way to control for order effects is to prepare different versions of a survey, with the questions in different orders. That way, researchers can look for order effects. If the results for the first order differ from the results for the second order, researchers can report the results for the two orders separately. In addition, they might be safe in assuming that people's endorsement of the first question on a survey is unaffected by previous questions.

Encouraging Accurate Responses

Careful researchers pay attention to how they word and order their survey questions. But what about the people who answer them? People do not, or cannot, always give truthful or accurate responses. Most people do not intend to be dishonest. However, they might give inaccurate answers because they do not make an effort to think about each question, because they want to give the "right" answer, or because they think they know the correct answer when they actually do not.

Using Shortcuts

Response sets are a type of shortcut respondents can take when answering a survey. They do not cause many problems for answering a single, stand-alone survey question. But when answering a set of related questions, some people might adopt a consistent way of answering all the questions that has little to do with their sincere opinions. Essentially, when people use response sets, they tend to answer all questions positively, negatively, or right in the middle. Response sets hurt construct validity, because these survey respondents are not saying what they really think.

Yea-Saying and Nay-Saying. **Acquiescence**, or *yea-saying*, occurs when people say "yes" or "strongly agree" to every item instead of thinking carefully about each one. For example, a respondent might answer "5" to every item on Diener's scale of subjective well-being from Chapter 5—not because she is a happy person, but because she is using the yea-saying shortcut. The opposite type of response, **nay-saying**, occurs when the respondent disagrees with every item (see **Figure 6.2**). This type of response set would threaten construct validity, because instead of measuring the construct of people's true feelings of well-being, the survey would be measuring the construct of people's laziness or agreeableness.

How can researchers tell the difference between somebody who is yea-saying and somebody who really intends to agree with all of the items? The most common way is by including reverse-worded items. (For example, Diener might have asked, "If I had my life to live over, I'd change almost *everything*.") One benefit is that reverse-worded items can slow people down so that they answer questions more carefully. In addition, reverse-worded items can help distinguish yea-sayers from true believers. Before computing a scale average for each person, the researchers rescore only the reverse-worded items so that, for example, "strongly disagree" becomes a 5 and "strongly agree" becomes a 1. That way, the person

FIGURE 6.2

Diener's Satisfaction with Life Scale. If people use a response set, they might agree with every item, disagree with every item, or answer every item right in the middle. *Source*: Diener, Emmons, Larsen, and Griffin (1985).

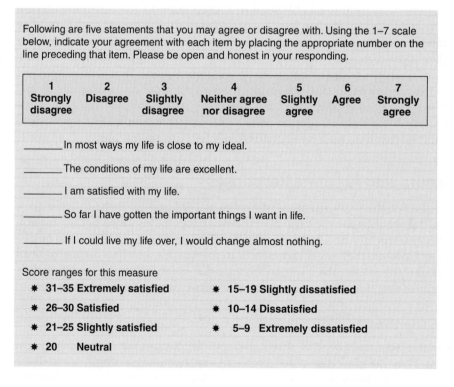

Following are five statements that you may agree or disagree with. Using the 1–7 scale below, indicate your agreement with each item by placing the appropriate number on the line preceding that item. Please be open and honest in your responding.

1 Strongly disagree	2 Disagree	3 Slightly disagree	4 Neither agree nor disagree	5 Slightly agree	6 Agree	7 Strongly agree

_____ In most ways my life is close to my ideal.

_____ The conditions of my life are excellent.

_____ I am satisfied with my life.

_____ So far I have gotten the important things I want in life.

_____ If I could live my life over, I would change almost nothing.

Score ranges for this measure

* 31–35 Extremely satisfied
* 26–30 Satisfied
* 21–25 Slightly satisfied
* 20 Neutral
* 15–19 Slightly dissatisfied
* 10–14 Dissatisfied
* 5–9 Extremely dissatisfied

with a tendency to circle only 5's will end up scoring closer to the middle of the scale and will not be mistaken for a truly happy person. The scale with reverse-worded items would have more construct validity because high or low averages would be measuring true happiness or unhappiness, instead of response laziness. (A drawback of reverse-worded items is that sometimes they are more difficult to answer because they might contain double negatives.)

Fence Sitting. Another specific way people might use response sets is by **fence sitting**. Especially when a survey asks controversial questions, some respondents will play it safe by answering in the middle of the scale. People might also answer in the middle when a question is confusing or unclear. Fence sitters may threaten a survey's construct validity when people's middle-of-the-road scores suggest that they do not have an opinion, when they actually do. Of course, some people honestly may have no opinion on the questions; in that case, they choose the middle option for a valid reason. It can be difficult to distinguish people who are unwilling to take a side from those who are truly ambivalent.

Researchers may try to jostle people out of this tendency. One approach is to take away the neutral option. Compare these two formats:

My life is close to ideal.

1	2	3	4	5

Strongly disagree   Strongly agree

My life is close to ideal.

1	2	3	4

Strongly disagree   Strongly agree

When a scale contains an even number of response options, the person has to choose one side or the other, because there is no neutral choice. The downside to this approach is that sometimes people really do not have an opinion, so for them, having to choose a side is an invalid representation of their truly neutral stance. Therefore, researchers carefully consider which format is best.

Another common way to get people off the fence is to use a forced-choice format, discussed earlier, in which people must pick one of the two answers. This type of question reduces fence sitting, but again, it can frustrate people who feel that their own opinion is somewhere in the middle of the two options. In a telephone survey, interviewers will write down a response of "I don't know" or "No opinion" if people volunteer that response. This way, more people get off the fence, but truly ambivalent people can also validly report their neutral opinions.

Trying to Look Good

Most of us want to look good in the eyes of others, but when survey respondents give answers that make them look better than they really are, these responses decrease the survey's construct validity. This phenomenon is called **socially**

desirable responding, or sometimes *faking good*. (The opposite phenomenon is called **faking bad**.) In some cases, certainly, these respondents know what they really think, but they are too embarrassed, shy, or worried about giving an unpopular opinion to give that answer on a survey. To avoid this type of inaccurate response, a researcher might ensure that the participants know their responses are anonymous—perhaps by conducting the survey online, or by having people put their unsigned responses into a large, closed box.

More often, however, people are not consciously being dishonest; they believe that what they are saying is the truth. In such cases, of course, the survey's anonymity will not prevent people from giving socially desirable responses. A better way to test whether respondents are responding in a socially desirable way is to include questions like these:

My table manners at home are as good as when I eat out in a restaurant.
I am always a good listener, no matter who I am talking to.
I never hesitate to go out of my way to help someone in trouble.

People who agree with many such items are assumed to be high in socially desirable responding (Crowne & Marlowe, 1960). Their reported behavior is probably too good to be true. When a respondent agrees with too many of these kinds of items, the researchers will discard that person's data from the final set, under suspicion that they are exaggerating on the other survey items, too.

Another way to control for socially desirable responding is to include "filler" items. Some surveys mask the true purpose of a sensitive survey by including several unrelated filler items. For example, they might ask three or four questions about racial attitudes, the true focus of the study, within a 20-item scale that includes several other questions about politics, gender roles, and education.

Finally, researchers increasingly use special, computerized measures to evaluate people's implicit opinions about sensitive topics. One widely used test, the Implicit Association Test (e.g., Greenwald, Nosek, & Banaji, 2003) asks people to respond quickly to positive and negative words on the right and left of a computer screen. Intermixed with the positive and negative words may be faces from different social groups, such as Black and White faces. People respond to all possible combinations, including positive words with Black faces, negative words with White faces, negative words with Black faces, and positive words with White faces. When people respond more efficiently to the White-positive/Black-negative combination than to the White-negative/Black-positive combination, researchers infer that the person may hold negative attitudes at an implicit, or unconscious, level (Greenwald et al., 2003). (You can try different versions of the test yourself, at implicit.harvard.edu.)

Self-Reporting "More Than They Can Know"

A final question is whether people are *able* to accurately self-report on their own feelings, thoughts, and actions. Each person knows his or her opinions better than anyone else does, right? Only *I* know my level of support for a political candidate. Only *you* know how much you liked a professor. Only *the shopper* knows how much she liked those boots.

Indeed, data from self-reports are often the best and most meaningful information we can get. Ed Diener and his colleagues, in their studies of well-being (discussed in Chapter 5), were specifically interested in participants' own perspectives on their happiness, so it made sense for them to ask participants to self-report on their life satisfaction. In other cases, self-reports might be the only option. For example, researchers who study dreaming can monitor brain activity to identify *when* someone is dreaming, but they need to use self-reports to find out the *content* of the person's dreams, because only the dreamer experiences the dream.

But in some cases, self-reports can be inaccurate, especially when people are asked to describe *why* they are thinking, behaving, or feeling the way they do. When asked, most people willingly provide an explanation or an opinion to a researcher, but sometimes they unintentionally give inaccurate responses.

Self-Reporting Reasons for Behavior. Psychologists Richard Nisbett and Timothy Wilson (1977) conducted a set of studies to demonstrate this phenomenon. In one study, they put six pairs of nylon stockings on a table and asked female shoppers in a store to tell them which of the stockings they preferred. As it turned out, almost everyone selected the last pair on the right. The reason for this preference was something of a mystery—especially since all of the stockings were exactly the same! Then, Nisbett and Wilson asked each woman why she selected the pair she did. Every participant reported that she selected the pair on the right for its excellent *quality*. Even when Nisbett and Wilson suggested to the women that they might have chosen the pair because it was on the far right side of the table, the women insisted that they made their choices based on the quality of the stockings. In other words, the women easily formulated answers for

the researchers, but their answers had nothing to do with the real reason they selected the one pair of stockings (see **Figure 6.3**). And the women did not seem to be aware that they were inventing a justification for their preference. They gave a sincere, reasonable response—one that just happened to be wrong. Therefore, without a cross-check on what people say, researchers treat with skepticism people's self-reports of the reasons for their own behavior.

Self-Reporting Memories of Events. Even if people cannot always self-report reasons behind their behaviors, surely they know what those behaviors were, right? In fact, psychological research has shown that people's memories for their own behaviors are not very accurate. For example, many Americans can say exactly where they were when they heard the news that two planes

FIGURE 6.3 **The accuracy of self-reports.** If you ask this consumer why she chooses one of these items, she will probably give you a reasonable answer. But does her answer represent the true reason she made her choice?

had crashed into New York's World Trade Center on September 11, 2001, and their memories are often startlingly vivid. But cognitive psychologists have taken the opportunity to check the accuracy of such "flashbulb memories." To conduct such a study, researchers might administer a short questionnaire to their students on the day after a dramatic event, asking them to recall where they were, whom they were with, and so forth. A few years later, the researchers ask the same students the same questions as before, and also ask them to rate their confidence in their memories. Such studies have shown that overall accuracy is very low: For example, about 73% of students recalling their memories of the 9/11 attacks recalled seeing the first plane hit the World Trade Center, when in fact no such television footage existed (Pezdek, 2004).

However, the other important finding from these studies is that people's confidence in the accuracy of their memories is virtually unrelated to how accurate the memories actually are. Three years later, people who are extremely confident in their memories are about as likely to be wrong as people who report their memories with little or no confidence. Even after people are told that their memories are wrong, they may retain their inaccurate memories. One study participant said, "I still remember everything happening the way I told you. I can't help it." Studies like these remind us to question the construct validity of even the most vivid "memories" of the past. That is, asking people what they remember is probably not the best operationalization for studying what really happened to them.

Self-reports therefore are not appropriate for evaluating all research questions. Surveys and polls can be excellent measures of what people *think* they are doing and of what people *think* is influencing their behavior. But if you want to know what people are *really* doing or what *really* influences people's behavior, you should probably watch them. If you want to know how hot a person feels, you can ask him or her to tell you, but if you want to know how hot it actually is, you should check a thermometer. Indeed, many researchers prefer to observe behavior directly, rather than rely on self-reports. (You will read about observational studies in the next section.)

Check Your Understanding

1. What are three potential issues with question wording? Can they be avoided?
2. What are three potential issues with people's ability to respond to surveys? Can they be avoided?

1. See pp. 148-151. 2. See pp. 151-156.

Construct Validity of Behavioral Observations

Surveys and polls are probably the most common types of data used to support a frequency or level claim—the kind you read most often in newspapers or on websites. But researchers also study people (or other animals) simply by watching them in action. When a researcher watches people or animals and systematically records what they are doing, it is called **observational research**. Many scientists believe that observing behavior is better than self-reports collected through surveys, because people cannot always state the true reasons for their behavior or report on past events accurately. Given the potential for question order effects, response sets, socially desirable responding, and other problems, many psychologists trust behavioral data more than survey data.

Observational research can be the basis for frequency claims. Researchers might record how much people eat in fast-food restaurants. They might observe drivers on the road and count how many are wearing seat belts or how many are talking on cell phones. They might count how many words people say or might listen in on the comments of fans watching a hockey game. Observational research is not just for frequency claims: Observations can also be used to operationalize variables in association claims and causal claims. Regardless of the type of claim, it is important that observational measures have good construct validity.

Some Examples of Frequency Claims Based on Observational Data

Many researchers use data from direct observations to make frequency claims about what people do. In many cases, these observations provide much richer, more accurate information than survey and poll data can.

Observing How Much People Talk

One example of how observational methods have been used in psychology comes from researcher Matthias Mehl, who has observed what people say in everyday contexts. He recruited several samples of students and asked them to wear an electronically activated recorder (EAR) for 2 to 10 days (depending on the sample). This device contains a small, clip-on microphone and a digital sound recorder, as shown in **Figure 6.4A**. At 12.5-minute intervals throughout the day, the EAR records 30 seconds of ambient sound. Later, research assistants transcribe

(A)

(B)

Table 1. Estimated number of words spoken per day for female and male study participants across six samples. $N = 396$. Year refers to the year when the data collection started; duration refers to the approximate number of days participants wore the EAR; the weighted average weighs the respective sample group mean by the sample size of the group.

Sample	Year	Location	Duration	Age range (years)	Sample size (N) Women	Sample size (N) Men	Estimated average number (SD) of words spoken per day Women	Estimated average number (SD) of words spoken per day Men
1	2004	USA	7 days	18–29	56	56	18,443 (7460)	16,576 (7871)
2	2003	USA	4 days	17–23	42	37	14,297 (6441)	14,060 (9065)
3	2003	Mexico	4 days	17–25	31	20	14,704 (6215)	15,022 (7864)
4	2001	USA	2 days	17–22	47	49	16,177 (7520)	16,569 (9108)
5	2001	USA	10 days	18–26	7	4	15,761 (8985)	24,051 (10,211)
6	1998	USA	4 days	17–23	27	20	16,496 (7914)	12,867 (8343)
				Weighted average			16,215 (7301)	15,669 (8633)

FIGURE 6.4 Mehl and collegues' (2007) EAR studies. Panel A shows a participant wearing the EAR. Panel B shows the study's results, as they were reported in the original article.

everything the person says during the recorded time periods. A table of data from these samples, copied from one of the empirical journal articles Mehl and his colleagues have published, is shown in **Figure 6.4B**. The data demonstrate that on average, women speak 16,215 words per day, while men speak 15,669 words per day. This difference is not statistically significant. Therefore, despite stereotypes of women being the chattier sex, women and men showed the same level of speaking (Mehl, Vazire, Ramirez-Esparza, Slatcher, & Pennebaker, 2007).

For more detail on statistical significance, see Chapter 3, pp. 68–69, and Appendix B.

Observing Hockey Moms and Dads

Another example of observational research comes from Canadian researchers who decided to look into popular press stories about parents who had acted violently at youth ice hockey games (Bowker et al., 2009). To see how widespread this "problem" was, the researchers decided to observe a sample of hockey games and to record the frequency of violent, negative behavior (as well as positive, supportive behavior) by parents. Although the press had reported dramatic stories about fights among parents at youth soccer games, these few instances seem to have been an exception. After sitting in the stands at 69 boys' and girls' hockey games in one Canadian city, the researchers found that 64% of the parents' comments were positive, and only 4% were negative. The authors concluded that their results were "in stark contrast to media reports, which paint a grim picture of aggressive spectators and out-of-control parents" (Bowker et al., 2009, p. 311).

Observing Parent and Child Reunions

A final example comes from a study of dual-earner families (families in which both parents work). A set of researchers recruited 30 such families and placed video cameras in strategic locations around each family's home (Campos, Graesch, Repetti, Bradbury, & Ochs, 2009). They were interested in observing the quality of home-based social interaction between the two parents and between the parents and their children. One of the variables the researchers studied was the quality of reunions—how did the children greet their parents when they returned home? After coding the quality of 44 reunion episodes across the families, the researchers found that greetings were generally positive: Children greeted mothers positively about 59% of the time and greeted fathers positively 44% of the time. The family was coded as "distracted" when the returning parent was not greeted at all (usually because the family members were engaged in something else, such as a phone call or video game). Distracted greetings happened more for fathers' return from work (38%) than for mothers' (22%).

Are Observations Better Than Self-Reports?

The three examples above illustrate a variety of ways that researchers have conducted observations, either through direct means (such as sitting in the stands during a hockey game) or with the use of technology, such as an EAR or a video camera. In addition, you can reflect on the benefits of behavioral observation in these studies. What might have happened if the researchers had asked the participants in these studies to self-report? The college students most certainly would not have been able to report how many words they spoke per day. The hockey parents might have reported that their own comments at the rink were mostly positive—but they might have exaggerated their reports of other parents' degree of negativity. And would parents want to admit that sometimes their children are too distracted to greet them when they return home? People cannot (or will not) always tell you what they are doing or have done, so observations can tell a more accurate story than self-reporting.

Just like self-reports, observational research is a way to operationalize a key variable, so when interrogating a study we need to ask about the construct validity of any observation. What is the variable of interest, and did the observations accurately measure that variable? Although observational research may seem straightforward—someone does something, and the observer writes down what that person did—researchers actually work quite diligently to be sure their observations are reliable and valid.

Such diligence is necessary because untrained observers can be biased when they observe another person's behavior. You may have noticed that sports fans tend to see the opposing team's fouls more often than their own team's fouls (Hastorf & Cantril, 1954). People watching a political debate are more likely to notice the flaws and foibles of the candidate they do not support and to ignore the flaws and foibles of their own candidate. These examples demonstrate what you probably already suspect: Without training, most people are biased observers. In a research setting, **observer bias** is a potential threat to construct validity, in which observers record what they want to see or expect to see, rather than what is really happening.

Observer bias can affect how observers interpret the behaviors they are watching; in other cases observer bias can affect what behaviors actually happen.

Observers Might See What They Expect to See

In one study, panels of mental health professionals were shown a videotape of a younger man talking to an older man about his feelings and experiences. Some of the clinicians were told the young man was a patient, while others were told he was a job applicant. After seeing the videotape, the clinicians were asked for their observations. What kind of person was this young man?

Although all of the viewers saw the same videotape, their reactions were not the same. Those who thought the young man was a job applicant described him with terms such as "attractive," "candid," and "innovative." Those who saw the videotape thinking the young man was a patient described him as a "tight, defensive person" "frightened of his own aggressive impulses" (Langer & Abelson, 1974). Since everyone saw the same tape, these striking differences can only have reflected the judges' biases in interpreting what they saw.

Observers Can Affect What They See

It is problematic when observers' biases affect their interpretation of what they see; it is even more problematic when the observers' biases actually change the behavior of those they are observing. This phenomenon can occur even in the most basic, seemingly objective observations.

Bright and Dull Rats. In a classic study, Rosenthal and Fode (1963) gave each student in an advanced psychology course five rats to test as part of a final lab experience in the course. Each of twelve student experimenters timed how long it took for their five rats to learn a simple maze, timing the rats every day for five days. Although each of the student assistants actually received a randomly selected group of five rats, Rosenthal and Fode told six of the students that their rats were bred to be "maze-bright" and told the other six students that their rats were bred to be "maze-dull."

Even though the rats in each group were genetically the same, the rats that were believed to be maze-bright completed the maze a little faster each day and with fewer mistakes. In contrast, the rats that were believed to be maze-dull did not improve their performances over the five testing days. This study showed that observers not only see what they expect to see; sometimes they even cause the behavior of those they are observing to conform to their expectations.

The Example of Clever Hans. A horse nicknamed Clever Hans provides another classic example of how observers' subtle behavior changed a target's behavior—and how blind observers corrected the problem. More than 100 years ago, a schoolteacher named William von Osten tutored his horse, Hans, in mathematics (see **Figure 6.5**). If he asked Hans to add 3 and 2, for example, Hans would tap his hoof five times and then stop. The horse was gifted at subtraction, multiplication, and division—at least as good at math as your average fifth grader. Von Osten allowed many scientists to test Clever Hans's abilities, and they were satisfied that von Osten was not feeding the horse cues on the sly, because Hans could do math even when his owner was not in the room.

Just when other scientists had concluded that Hans was truly capable of simple math, an experimental psychologist, Oskar Pfungst, came up with a more rigorous set of checks. Suspecting that Hans was reading subtle cues from his human questioners, Pfungst set up situations in which the questioners did not know what question the horse heard. For example, one of the onlookers would whisper into Hans's ear, "Seven." Then another observer would whisper into the horse's ear, "Plus four." That way, the horse got the question, but each questioner was blind to the correct answer.

Under these conditions, Hans was helpless. He would go on tapping and tapping indefinitely. As it turned out, the horse *was* extremely clever—but not at math. He was very good at detecting the subtle changes in breathing and posture that his questioners would make as his taps approached the right answer. A raised eyebrow, a subtle intake of breath—Hans had learned that signs like these were cues to stop tapping.

FIGURE 6.5 William von Osten and Clever Hans.

"Masked" Research Designs. Both Rosenthal and Fode's study and the "Clever Hans effect" demonstrate that observers can give unintentional cues that affect how their subjects act. Whenever researchers use observations to record a variable, they attempt to control for biases and for any influence observers might have on the behavior of those being observed. Careful researchers train their research assistants to observe and code behaviors objectively, but in addition, they may use a **masked**, or *blind*, study design, in which the observers are unaware of ("blind" to) the conditions to which participants have been assigned, and sometimes are even unaware of what the study was about.

The Observed Might React to Being Watched

Sometimes the mere presence of an outsider is enough to change the behavior of those being observed. Imagine that you visit a first-grade classroom to observe the children's behavior. You walk quietly to the back of the room and sit down to observe what the children do. What will you see? A roomful of little heads swiveled around to look at you! Do first-graders usually spend most of their time staring at the back of the room? Of course not. What you are witnessing is an observer effect. **Observer effects**, also known as *reactivity*, occur when people change their behavior (react) when they know another person is watching. They might be on their best behavior—or in some cases, their worst behavior—rather than display their typical behavior. Observer effects occur not only with human participants but also with other animals. The psychologist Robert Zajonc once demonstrated that even cockroaches perform differently in front of an audience of other cockroaches (Zajonc, Heingartner, & Herman, 1969). If people and animals can change their behavior just because they are being watched, what should a careful researcher do?

Solution 1: Hide. One way to avoid observer effects is to make **unobtrusive observations**—that is, hide. Developmental researchers might hide behind a one-way mirror, like the one shown in **Figure 6.6**, so they can observe how children interact in a classroom without letting the children know. In a public setting, a researcher might pretend to be a casual onlooker—another face in the crowd—to observe the behavior of other people. In Bowker and colleagues' hockey fan study, observers hid in plain sight—they posed as fans in the stands. Across the 69 hockey games they observed, only two parents ever asked the observer what he or she was doing, suggesting that the observer's presence was unobtrusive.

Solution 2: Wait It Out. Another solution is to wait it out. A researcher who plans to observe at a school might let the children get used to his or her presence until they forget about being observed. Jane Goodall, in her studies of chimpanzees in the wild, used a similar tactic. When she began introducing herself to the chimps in the Gombe National Park in Africa, they fled, or at best dropped whatever else they were doing to focus on her. After several months, the chimps got used to having her around and were no longer afraid to go about their usual activities in

FIGURE 6.6 Unobtrusive observations. This one-way mirror allows researchers to unobtrusively record the behaviors of children in a preschool classroom.

her presence. Similarly, participants in Mehl and colleagues' EAR study reported that after a couple of days of wearing the EAR, they did not find the device to be invasive (Mehl & Pennebaker, 2003).

Solution 3: Measure the Behavior's Results. Another way to avoid observer effects is to use unobtrusive data. Instead of measuring behavior, researchers measure the traces that a behavior leaves behind. For example, in a museum, wear-and-tear on the floor tiles can tell you which areas of the museum are the most popular. Or the number of empty liquor bottles in residential garbage cans can indicate how much alcohol is being consumed in a community (Webb, Campbell, Schwartz, & Sechrest, 1966).

Observing People Ethically

Is it ethical for researchers to observe the behaviors of others? That depends. Most psychologists believe that it is ethical to observe the behavior of people behaving in museums, classrooms, hockey games, or even at the sinks of public bathrooms, because in those settings people can reasonably expect their behavior to be public, not private. Of course, when psychologists report the results of such an observational study, they do not specifically identify any of the people they observe. More secretive ways to observe—such as one-way mirrors or covert videotaping—are also considered ethical in some conditions. In most cases, psychologists must obtain permission in advance to watch or to videotape people's private behavior. And if researchers videotape people covertly, they must explain the taping at the conclusion of the study. If people object to having been taped, the psychologist must erase the tape without watching it. However, ethical decisions may also be influenced by the policies of a university where a study is conducted. As discussed in Chapter 4, institutional review boards (IRBs) assess each study to decide whether it can be conducted ethically.

Positive, General (Pg). These comments were defined as positive in tone and as directed at the team in general, with no instructional content (e.g., "Go Crusaders"; 'Nice try"; "Good work").

Positive, Specific (Ps). These comments were defined as being positive, but directed at a specific player (e.g., "Nice play JD"; "Way to go LJ").

Corrective/Instructional (Cor). These comments were defined as including a specific action or play that the player was instructed to do. They included comments which were positive in nature (e.g., "Go after it"), and those with a more negative tone (e.g., "Get back"; "You've got to cover him").

Negative (Neg). These comments were defined as those meant to criticize the target in some way (usually directed toward the referee). Much of the time, the negativity of the comment was due to a sarcastic tone (e.g., "What kind of call is that?"; "Come on ref, you call that a penalty?").

Neutral (Neu). These comments were defined as those not fitting into any of the other categories, and/or were unrelated to the game (e.g., "Did you book your hotel room for the tournament?").

Each remark was coded for intensity, based on a three-point scale: 1 = spoken relatively quietly, with little to no emotion; 2 = louder, more intense speech, stronger emotion, but controlled; 3 = loud, intense speech, extreme emotional content.

FIGURE 6.7 Excerpt from Bowker and colleagues' (2009) description of coding hockey fan comments. This information was included in the empirical journal article's Method section.

Good Observations Are Both Reliable and Valid

Because of potential problems in gathering observational data, researchers need to take steps to ensure the construct validity of observational measures. First and foremost, careful researchers train their observers well. They create clear rating scales—often called *codebooks*—so that observers can make reliable judgments with less bias. For example, **Figure 6.7** gives an example of how the parents' comments were coded in the hockey fan study.

Table 1

Examples and Coder Reliabilities for Behaviors Displayed by Family Members Upon Mother and Father Return Home From Work

Coded behaviors	Behavior examples	κ	Description of agreements[a]
Positive behaviors	"Hello, how are you?" in warm voice tone "Daddy!" in warm voice tone Hugs, physical approach toward parent	.84	62 agreements of 77 instances
Information reports	"Guess who lost a tooth today?" "I got an A on my test today!"	.79	16 agreements of 21 instances
Logistic behaviors	"Could you pick up Child X from soccer?" "The bill came in the mail"	.65	6 agreements of 11 instances
Distraction	Not acknowledging returning adult, otherwise engaged in activity (e.g., watching TV, playing video game, phone)	.57	10 agreements of 19 instances
Negative behaviors	"You're home late AGAIN"	.49	1 agreement of 3 instances
All behaviors together		.78	95 agreements out of 131 instances

[a] Number of times coders agreed out of all instances when either judge coded a behavior occurrence.

FIGURE 6.8 Table 1 from Campos and colleagues' (2009) study of family interactions. The table depicts the degree of interrater reliability for each of the behaviors coded.

Researchers can also enhance the construct validity of a measure by using multiple observers. Doing so allows the researchers to assess the interrater reliability of their measures. Using multiple observers does not eliminate anyone's biases, of course, but if two observers of the same event agree on what happened, the researcher can be more certain that it really happened that way. If observers do not agree, the researcher may need to train the observers better or develop a clearer coding system for rating behaviors. **Figure 6.8** shows an example of how interrater reliability information was presented in Campos and colleagues' family interaction study. The table shows that for some of the coded behaviors, interrater reliability (measured with a statistic called kappa) was above 0.70. For other categories (such as negative behaviors), however, interrater reliability was not very high, so the researchers appropriately cautioned readers of the study to interpret results from those categories with less confidence.

Even when an operationalization has good interrater reliability, it still might not be valid. Even if two observers agree with each other, they might share the same biases, so their common observations are not necessarily valid. Think about the participants in Langer and Abelson's study. The psychologists who were told that the man in the videotape was a patient might have showed interrater reliability in their descriptions of how defensive or frightened he appeared. But because they shared similar biases, their reliable ratings were not valid descriptions of the man's behavior.

For more on interrater reliability, see Chapter 5.

Check Your Understanding

1. What are two ways that observers might make biased observations in a research study?
2. What are three approaches researchers can take to be sure that respondents do not react to being observed?

1. See pp. 159–160. 2. See pp. 161–162.

Generalizing to Others: Sampling Participants

When we interrogate external validity, we ask whether the results of a particular study can be generalized, either to other people in a population or to other kinds of settings we might be interested in (such as to other days of the week, to other sports besides hockey, or to other boots from the same manufacturer). External validity is often extremely important for frequency claims. To interrogate the external validity of a frequency claims, for example, we might ask the following types of questions:

> "Do the students who rated the professor on this website adequately represent all of the professor's former students?"
>
> "Can we predict the results of the presidential election from the results of this poll if the sample consisted of 1,500 people?"
>
> "Can we generalize this result about the number of words people speak to other college students? How about to other people who are not in college?"

Such questions address external validity.

Populations and Samples

Have you ever been offered a free sample in the grocery store or a cost-saving warehouse store? Say you tried a sample spinach mini-quiche and you loved it. You probably assumed that all 50 in the box would taste just the same. Or, if you liked one baked pita chip, you assumed that all the chips in the bag would be good, too. The single bite you tried is the **sample**. The box or bag it came from is the **population**. You do not need to eat the whole box (that is, the whole population) to know whether you like that food; you only need to test a small sample. (If you did taste every chip in the population, you would be conducting a **census**.)

Researchers usually do not need to study a whole population either—that is, they do not need to do a census. Instead, they study a sample of people, assuming that if the sample does something, the population will act the same. The external validity of a study involves whether the sample used in the study is adequate to represent the unstudied population. If the sample can generalize to the population, there is good external validity. If the sample is biased in some way, there is not.

What Is "the Population"?

Although the world's population is almost 7 billion human beings, researchers do not usually have that entire population in mind when they conduct a study. Before researchers can decide whether a sample is biased or unbiased, they have to specify the population to which they want to generalize. There is no such thing as "the population" pure and simple; a study's population is whatever the researchers say it is. When you are sampling food at the grocery store, you can specify that the population is the 50 quiches in the box, or the 200 pita chips in the bag.

Similarly, if we evaluated the sample of people who rated a pair of boots on a five-star scale, we would care only about the population of people who have bought those boots. If we investigated online ratings of a professor, we would care only about the population of students who have taken a class with this professor. When we are interrogating the results of a national election poll, we care about the population of people who will vote in the next election in the country.

When Is a Sample Biased?

Once we have defined the population of interest, we can better assess how good the sample is. Let's return to the food samples to illustrate. If you happened to sample the one burnt pita chip in the whole bag, that sample would be *biased*. The sample is biased because it is unrepresentative of the population—it would cause you to draw the wrong conclusions about the quality of that bag of chips. Similarly, suppose the box of 50 quiches were a variety pack, containing various flavors of quiche. In that case, a sample spinach quiche would be unrepresentative, too. If the other types of quiche are not as good as the spinach, you would draw incorrect conclusions about the varied population.

In a consumer survey or an online opinion poll, a biased sample could be like a burnt pita chip. That is, a researcher's sample might contain too many of the most *unusual* people. For instance, the students who rate a professor on a website might tend to be the ones who are angry or disgruntled, so they may not represent the rest of the professor's students very well. A biased study sample could also be like an unrepresentative spinach quiche. A researcher's sample might include only one kind of people, when the sample of interest is more like a variety pack. Imagine a poll that sampled only Republicans when the population of interest contains Republicans, Democrats, and people with other political views (see **Figure 6.9**). Or imagine a study that sampled only men when the

FIGURE 6.9
Unrepresentative samples. If your population of interest includes members of all political parties, a sample from a political convention would not provide a representative sample to study.

population of interest contains both men and women. But always remember that the population is what the researchers say it is, so if the population is only male Republicans, it is appropriate to use only men who are registered Republicans in your sample.

What Causes Biased Samples?

A sample could be biased in at least three ways: Researchers might study only those cases they can contact easily, study the cases they can contact at all, or study the people who are most eager to respond. All of these biases can threaten the external validity of a study.

Sampling Only Those Who Are Easy to Contact. Even if a sample contains the same kinds of people as the population—that is, even if only men are sampled to learn about a population of men—the sample might still be biased. Many psychology studies (such as Mehl and colleagues' study on how much people talk) are conducted by psychology professors who find it easy to study a sample of college students. But those convenient college students may not be representative of some population that is more educated, less educated, older, or younger (e.g., Connor, Snibbe, & Markus, 2005). In another example, imagine you are conducting an exit poll during a presidential election and you have hired interviewers to ask voters, as they are leaving the polling station, whom they voted for. (Exit polls are widely used in the United States to help the media predict the results of an election before the votes are completely counted.) The sample for your exit poll might be biased in a couple of ways. For one, maybe you did not have enough money to send pollsters to every precinct, so you sent them only to polling stations that were close to you—easy to reach. The resulting sample might be biased, because some local polling precincts are more liberal, others more conservative. So it would be important to send interviewers to a sample of precincts that represent the population of precincts as a whole.

In addition, at a particular precinct, the exit pollsters might approach the population of exiting voters in a biased way. Exit poll workers may feel most comfortable approaching voters who look friendly, look similar to themselves, or look as if they are not in a hurry. For example, younger pollsters might find it easiest to approach younger voters. But because younger voters tend to be more liberal, that sample's result might lead the researcher to conclude that the voters at a station are more liberal than they really are. In this case, sampling only the people who are convenient would lead to a biased sample.

Sampling Only Those One Is *Able* to Contact. A sample can also be biased because the sample the researchers *can* contact is different from the population to which they want to generalize. For example, during past election cycles, U.S. opinion polls have almost always selected their samples from landline telephone numbers. Until recently, this approach made sense, because almost all U.S. voters had telephones in their homes. But in recent years, a growing proportion of U.S. voters used only cell phones. If cell phone-only users are excluded from opinion poll samples, would it matter?

It could matter—but only if the cell phone-only group is different from the group of people who have landlines. And, in fact, a study by the Pew Research Center concluded that in the United States, people who only have cell phones are more likely to be young, less affluent, unmarried, and more liberal on political questions. For example, in 2010, 25% of U.S. households had cell phones only (no landlines), and a full 49% of U.S. adults ages 25–29 had cell phones only (Christian, Keeter, Purcell, & Smith, 2010). These differences did translate into somewhat biased polling results. In the 2008 U.S. presidential election, polls that included both cell phone-only and landline voters showed slightly more support for the Democratic candidate, Barack Obama, and less for the Republican candidate, John McCain, than polls that sampled only landlines (Pew Research Center, 2008).

Sampling Only Those Who Invite Themselves. Another way a sample might be biased is through **self-selection**, a form of sampling bias that emerges when a sample is known to contain only people who volunteer to participate. Self-selection is a ubiquitous problem in polls on the Internet, and it can cause serious problems for external validity. For example, one Internet poll asked parents, "Was your child an early reader?" The poll found, surprisingly, that 27% of children learn to read before age three (see **Figure 6.10**). In truth, however, most children in the United States are taught to read in kindergarten, when they are about five or six years old. The reason the web poll had such different results is that its respondents were self-selected: The parents who would be most likely to respond to a poll like this would be those who wanted to brag about their children. Parents whose children read at a later age might not be as motivated to share this information, so the poll ended up with a skewed estimate.

In addition, this poll appeared in a forum for parents of "gifted" children, and gifted children are more likely to start reading early. Therefore, there are two selection biases at work: This poll result may apply only to the populations of parents who think their children are gifted and to those who want to brag about when their child learned to read.

Self-selection occurs on most other Internet polls, too. Whenever Internet users rate anything—a book on Amazon.com, a story on msnbc.com, a professor on ratemyprofessors.com—they are self-selecting to do so. This self-selection may lead to biased samples, because the people who rate the items are not

FIGURE 6.10 Online polls. Can you trust the Internet poll's finding that 27% of children learn to read by age 3?

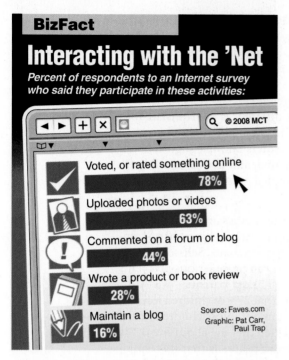

Interacting with the 'Net

Percent of respondents to an Internet survey who said they participate in these activities:

© 2008 MCT

Voted, or rated something online
78%

Uploaded photos or videos
63%

Commented on a forum or blog
44%

Wrote a product or book review
28%

Maintain a blog
16%

Source: Faves.com
Graphic: Pat Carr,
Paul Trap

FIGURE 6.11 Internet usage survey. Can we conclude from this poll that 16% of Americans maintain a blog? Why or why not?

necessarily representative of the population of all people who have bought the book, read the story, or taken the class. All these ratings are made by people who care enough to take a survey. Researchers do not know much yet about how Internet "raters" differ from "non-raters," but they speculate that the people who take the time to rate things on the Internet might have stronger opinions, might be more willing to share ideas with others, and are perhaps more engaged with Internet content in general (see **Figure 6.11**).

How to Get a Representative Sample

When external validity is vital and researchers need a representative sample from a population, **probability sampling**—drawing the sample at random from that population—is the best option. In a probability sample, every member in the population has an equal chance of being in the sample. True probability samples have external validity, at least to people in that population, because all members of the population—no matter whether they are close, easy to contact, or motivated— are equally likely to be represented.

Here's an easy way to visualize **simple random sampling**—the most basic form of probability sampling. Imagine that each member of the population has his or her name written on a ticket. The tickets are tossed into a hat and stirred, and someone reaches in blindly and selects a number of tickets equal to the size of the desired sample. The people whose names are on the selected tickets will make up the sample.

Another way to create a simple random sample would be to assign a number to each population member's name and then use a table of random numbers (such as the one in Appendix D, pp. A91–A93) to select a sample from the population. These days, the work of randomizing is done by computer programs (such as www.randomizer.org) that generate numbers that are random, or very nearly so. Similarly, professional pollsters use a computer program that randomly selects telephone numbers from a database of eligible cell phone and landline telephone numbers.

The goal of probability sampling is to create a sample that, as closely as possible, represents all kinds of people in the population. Because each person has an equal chance of being selected, a probability sample does not systematically omit key constituents or subgroups. Even people who are far away, hard to reach, or unmotivated have an equal chance of being in the sample.

Variants of Probability Sampling

Although simple random sampling works well in theory, it can be surprisingly difficult and time consuming, so researchers usually use variants of simple random sampling that are equally externally valid. For example, even dialing telephone numbers at random can result in a biased sample because of who is most likely to answer the phone. Consider the technique used by the Pew Research Center. This organization calls telephone numbers at random but then first asks to speak to the "youngest male, 18 years of age or older, who is now at home." If no eligible male is at home, they ask to speak to the "youngest female, 18 years of age or older, who is now at home" (Pew Research Center, n.d.). Why? If the interviewer talked only to the person who first picked up the phone, the resulting sample would have too many older women and not enough young people or men. (Presumably, Pew has found that in most U.S. homes, Mom is most likely to answer the phone.)

Cluster Sampling and Multistage Sampling. Researchers can also use shortcuts that lead to the same, representative results as simple random sampling. One example is **cluster sampling**. For example, if you wanted to randomly sample college students in the state of Pennsylvania, you could start with a list of colleges (clusters) in that state, take a random sample of five of those colleges (clusters), and then include every student from each of those five colleges in your sample. Bowker and colleagues' hockey game study used a version of cluster sampling. They selected 69 games at random, out of 630 possible hockey games in Ottawa, Canada, that they could have attended during the season. After the games were chosen, the research assistants sampled every single comment at each game.

Another version of this technique is **multistage sampling**. As with cluster sampling, you would start with a list of colleges (clusters) in the state and take a random sample of five of those colleges. Then, in the second stage, you would take a random sample of students from within each of the five colleges. In multistage sampling, you therefore select two random samples: a random sample of clusters and then a random sample of people within clusters. Both cluster and multistage sampling are easier than sampling from all Pennsylvania colleges, and both should still produce a representative sample.

Stratified Random Sampling. Another multistage technique is **stratified random sampling**. Here, the researcher selects particular demographic categories on purpose and then randomly selects individuals within each of the categories. For example, a group of researchers might want to be sure that their sample of 1,000 Canadians includes people of South Asian descent in the same proportion as in the Canadian population (which is 4%). They could stratify the population on ethnicity and sample separately from South Asians and other Canadians to ensure that the sample includes at least 40 members of the category of interest (South Asian Canadians). Similarly, some U.S. telephone polls use stratified random samples to ensure that they are including respondents from all geographic areas. They stratify their sample on the basis of area code (the first three digits), telephone exchange (the next three digits), and "bank" (the next two digits). The final two digits are dialed at random by the computer, but the categories themselves are chosen more purposefully, so that they represent the population of the phone numbers in a county, state, or country.

Oversampling. A variation of stratified random sampling is called **oversampling**. Imagine that a researcher wants to sample 1,000 people, making sure to include South Asians in the sample. Imagine further that the researcher's population of interest has a low percentage of South Asians (say, 4%). Because 40 individuals may not be enough to accurately detect trends in the data, the researcher decides that of the 1,000 people she samples, a full 100 will be sampled at random from the Canadian South Asian community. In this example, the ethnicities of the participants are still the categories, but the researcher is oversampling the South Asian population: The South Asian group will constitute 10% of the sample, even though it represents only 4% of the population. A survey that includes an oversample adjusts the final results so that members in the oversampled group are weighed to their actual proportion in the population. However, this is still a random sample, because those South Asians in the final sample were sampled randomly from the population of South Asians.

In **systematic sampling**, the researcher starts by selecting two random numbers using a computer or a random number table—say, 4 and 7. If the population is a roomful of students, the researcher would start with the fourth person in the room and then count off, choosing every seventh person until the sample was the desired size. Mehl and colleagues (2007) used the EAR to sample conversations every 12.5 minutes; although they did not choose this value (12.5 minutes) at random, the effect is essentially the same as being a random sample of participants' conversations. (Note here that although external validity often involves generalizing to populations of *people*, researchers may also generalize to settings—in this case, to a population of conversations.)

In sum, there are many acceptable ways to obtain a representative sample. Because all these techniques involve a component of randomness, they all ensure that each individual, cluster, or systematic interval has an equal chance of being selected. In other words, people are not excluded from the sample for any of the reasons that might lead to bias.

Random Sampling Versus Random Assignment

Be careful not to confuse random sampling and random assignment. With *random sampling* (that is, probability sampling), researchers draw a sample using some random method—drawing names from a hat or using a random-digit phone dialer, perhaps—so that each member of the population has an equal chance of being in the sample. Random sampling enhances *external validity*.

Random assignment is used only in experimental designs. When researchers want to assign participants into different groups (often a treatment group and a comparison group), they usually assign them at random to the groups—for example, by flipping a coin. Random assignment enhances *internal validity*

For more detail on random assignment, see Chapters 3 and 9.

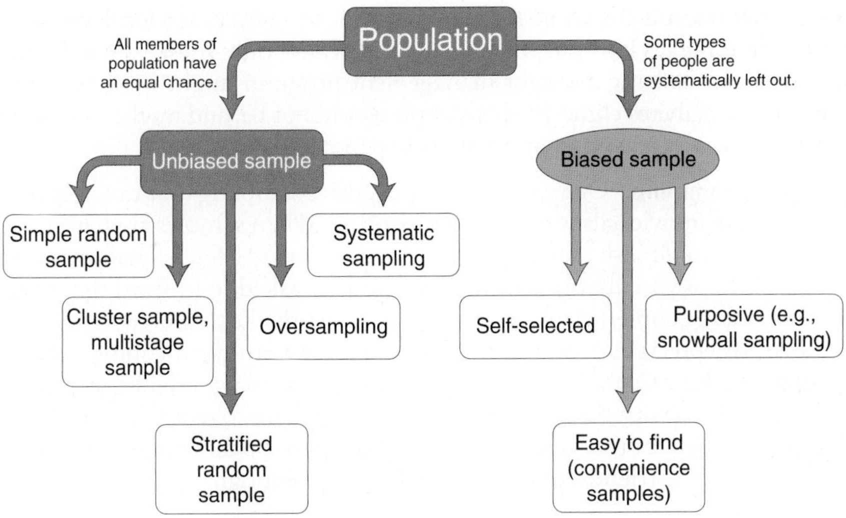

FIGURE 6.12

Populations and samples.

by helping ensure that the comparison group and the treatment group have the same kinds of people in them—and it thus controls for alternative explanations. For example, in a study of a treatment's effect on overall health, random assignment would make it likely that the people in the treatment and comparison groups are about equally healthy to start with.

Nonrepresentative Sampling Methods

In cases where external validity is not vital to a study's goals, the researchers might be content with a nonrepresentative kind of sampling. Depending on the type of study they are conducting, researchers can choose among a number of methods for gathering such a sample. (See **Figure 6.12** for a diagram of the various types of random and nonrandom sampling methods.)

Convenience Sampling. By far the most common in behavioral research is **convenience sampling**, in which samples are chosen merely on the basis of who is easy to access. Many psychologists study students on their own campuses because these students are the easiest subjects to reach. The researchers may ask for volunteers among students in an introductory psychology class or among residents of a dormitory. In the study on hockey fans, the researchers sampled hockey games in their own city, instead of randomly sampling games from all over the province.

Purposive Sampling. When researchers want to study only certain kinds of people, it makes sense to seek out only those kinds of people. When researchers do so, it is called **purposive sampling**. Researchers who wanted to study, for example, the effectiveness of a particular intervention for smoking would probably only include smokers in the sample. Notice that limiting a population to only one type of person does not make a sample purposive—for instance, if researchers recruit smokers by phoning a random sample of community members to find the smokers, that sample would not be called "purposive," because it is a random sample. However, if researchers recruit the sample of smokers by posting flyers at a local tobacco store, that action makes it a "purposive" sample, because only smokers will participate. Researchers studying a weight management program might want to study only people in a diabetes clinic. Such a sample would not be, and might not need to be, representative of the population of obese people in some area.

Snowball Sampling.   One variation on purposive sampling that can help researchers find rare individuals is **snowball sampling**. When samples are hard to obtain, a researcher might ask each participant to recommend a few acquaintances for the study. Perhaps you take an online survey and are asked to forward the survey link to a few more people. (Many Facebook quizzes work like this, even though they are created for entertainment, not for research.) For a study on coping behaviors in people who have Crohn's disease, for example, a researcher might start with one or two individuals with the diagnosis, and then ask them to recruit people from their support groups for that disease. Each of those participants might, in turn, recruit one or two more friends, until the sample is large enough.

When Does External Validity Matter?

Remember that frequency claims are claims about how often or how much something happens in a population. When you read headlines such as "More Than 2 Million U.S. Teens Depressed" or "Polling Predicts Republican Candidate Will Receive 55% of the State Vote" or "1% of Americans Are Holocaust Deniers," it might be obvious to you that external validity is important. If the depression researchers used sampling methods that made them less likely to reach depressed teens (perhaps they asked for volunteers in high schools, and depressed teens are less likely to volunteer), the estimate of 2 million depressed teenagers is too low. If the election poll's sampling methods did not include cell phone numbers, the estimate of 55% might be too high. In such studies, external validity, which relies on random sampling methods, is crucial.

On some occasions, the external validity of surveys based on random samples can actually be confirmed. The best example is in political races, where the results of opinion polling can be compared with the final voting results. During U.S. elections, polling websites and blogs compete to make the most accurate predictions, usually combining polls from several sources to come up with their estimates. For instance, the Pew Research Center poll estimated that Barack Obama would get 52% of the vote in the 2008 presidential election. This estimate was off by half a percent: Obama received 52.5% of the national vote. Apparently, the Pew survey's sampling was quite successful. (Incidentally, its construct validity was also responsible for this poll's accuracy; the way the question was worded was a valid measure of people's intent to vote.)

On most occasions, however, researchers are not able to check the accuracy of their samples' estimates, because they hardly ever take a full census of a population. For example, a psychologist could never evaluate all of the teenagers in the United States to find out how many are depressed. And because you usually cannot directly check accuracy when you interrogate a frequency claim, the best you can do is interrogate the sampling techniques used, asking how the researchers

For more on when external validity may not be a priority, see Chapter 7, p. 202; Chapter 9, pp. 267–269; and Chapter 13.

obtained the sample. As long as the researchers used a random sampling technique, you can be more confident in the external validity of the result.

When a Representative Sample Is Not the Top Priority

Although external validity is crucial for many frequency claims, external validity may not be a priority when researchers study association or causal relationships. Many associations and causes can still be accurately detected even in a convenient or haphazard sample. However, what should you think if you encounter a *frequency* claim that is not based on a random sample? If a frequency claim is not based on a probability sample, it might matter a lot—or not. You will need to carefully consider whether the cause of the sample's bias is relevant to the claim.

Nonrandom Samples in the Real World

Consider, for a moment, whether self-selection affects the results of a five-star shopping rating like the one on those boots you might buy. You can be pretty sure that the people who rated the boots are self-selected and therefore are not representative of all the people who own those boots. The raters obviously have Internet access, whereas some of the boot owners might not. They probably do more Internet shopping, whereas some of the boot owners bought their pairs in bricks-and-mortar stores. But more important, the raters cared enough to rate the boots online. Some people probably responded because they either loved or hated the boots. That is, people who think the boots are fine, but not great, simply are not motivated enough to log in and report a three-star rating. (However, if that were the case for all product raters, the ratings for most items on the Internet would be extreme—either one star or five stars—and Internet ratings do not typically show this kind of pattern.)

Another reason people care enough to respond might be that they are conscientious. They like to keep others informed, so they tend to rate everything they buy. In this case, the shopping rating sample is self-selected to include people who are more helpful than average.

The question is, do the opinions of these nonrandom shoppers apply to other shoppers, such as you, and to how much you will like the boots? Suppose that the ratings are based on a number of factors: comfort, style, quality. In terms of comfort, are the feet of opinionated or conscientious raters likely to be very different from those of the general population? Probably not, so their opinions about the comfortableness of the boots is likely to generalize. And the raters' fashion sense might even be the same as yours, too. (After all, they were attracted to the same image online.) If you believe that on the relevant dimensions the members of this self-selected sample are roughly the same as the population, it might be safe to trust them.

In an analogous situation, let's say a driver calls the radio station to report bad traffic near Exit 9 on Highway 35. This driver is not a randomly selected sample of drivers on that stretch of road; he is just more conscientious than the other drivers there, and probably more willing to place calls to the radio station. But of course, the personality traits of this sample are not that relevant to the report of traffic. Traffic is the same for everybody, conscientious or not, so even though this driver is a nonrandom sample, the report of the traffic can probably generalize to the other drivers on that road. The feature that has biased the sample (being conscientious) is not relevant to what is being measured (being in traffic).

In short, when you know that a sample is not representative, you should think carefully about how much it matters. Are the characteristics that make the sample unrepresentative actually relevant to what you are measuring? On some occasions, you will be perfectly fine in trusting the reports of an unrepresentative sample.

Nonrandom Samples in Research Studies

Let's use this reasoning to work through a couple of other examples. What about the 30 dual-earner families who allowed the researchers to videotape their social interactions (Campos et al., 2009)? It is probably a special kind of family that will allow researchers to plant video cameras in their homes and let research assistants walk around the house with laptops, recording the positions of each member of the family. What does this mean for the conclusions of the study? Here, it seems possible that a family that is open to such intrusion could also show a different overall level of greeting—perhaps the larger population of dual-earning families is less likely to greet each other positively than the sample of dual-earning families that participated. Without more data on families who do not readily agree to be taped, we cannot know for sure. The researchers may have to live with some uncertainty about the generalizability of their data. (However, they might reasonably expect that the gender difference they observed—that children greeted mothers positively than fathers—would be observed in any sample.)

Or what about Mehl and colleagues' (2007) study on how many words people say in a day? Their sample of participants was not drawn randomly from a population of college students; instead, it was a convenience sample who participated because they were trying to earn class credit or a few extra dollars. Could the qualities that make these students likely to volunteer for the study also be qualities that affect how many words they would say? Probably not, but it is possible. Again, we live with some uncertainty about whether Mehl and colleagues' findings would generalize—not only to other college students, but to other populations outside of the college setting as well. We know that Mehl found the same results among college students in Mexico, but we do not know if the results for these college samples will apply to samples of middle-aged or elderly adults. However, just because we do not know whether the finding generalizes to other populations does not mean that Mehl's results from college students are wrong or even uninteresting. Indeed, future research by Mehl and his colleagues could investigate this question in new populations.

Are Bigger Samples Better Samples?

In research, is a bigger sample always a better sample? The answer may surprise you: Not necessarily. Of course, when a phenomenon is rare, we do need a large sample in order to locate enough instances of that phenomenon for analysis. For example, we might need to sample 10,000 children to locate enough of them with a diagnosis of autism or ADHD. But when researchers are striving to generalize a frequency claim from a sample to a population, the size of a sample is in fact much less important than *how* that sample was selected.

Suppose you try to predict the outcome of a national presidential election by polling 4,000 people at the Republican National Convention. You would have a grand old sample, but it would not tell you anything about the opinions of the entire country's voting population because everyone you sampled would be a member of one party. Similarly, some Internet polls are so popular that thousands of people choose to vote in them. But even so, 10,000 self-selected people are not likely to be representative of the population. Remember the poll about children reading early? More than 1,300 parents voted, yet the results are ungeneralizable.

When researchers conduct public opinion polls, it turns out that 1,000 people are all they usually need—even for populations as large as the U.S. population of 300 million. For reasons of statistical accuracy, many polls shoot for, at most, a sample of 2,000. A researcher will choose a sample size for the poll in order to optimize the "margin of error" of the estimate. Margin of error is a statistical term that quantifies the degree of sampling error in a study's results. For instance, you might read that 28% of Canadians in some polls support the Liberal Party, plus or minus 3%. In this example, the margin of error ("plus or minus 3%") means that if the researchers conducted the same poll many, many times, 95% of those times they would get results between 25% and 31%. In other words, it would mean that the true percentage of Canadians who support the Liberal Party is probably between 25% and 31%.

Table 6.1 shows the margin of error for samples of different sizes. You can see in the table that the larger the sample size, the smaller the margin of error—that is, the more accurately the sample's results reflect the views of the population. However, after a sample size of 1,000, it takes many more people to gain just a little more accuracy in the margin of error. That is why many researchers consider 1,000 to be an optimal balance between accuracy and effort. A sample of 1,000 people, *as long as it is random*, allows them to generalize to the population (even a population of 300 million) quite accurately.

TABLE 6.1 Margins of Error Associated with Different Survey Sample Sizes

If your percentage is estimated on a survey sample of size	The margin of error on your percentage is
2,000	Plus or minus 2%
1,500	Plus or minus 3%
1,000	Plus or minus 3%
500	Plus or minus 4%
200	Plus or minus 7%
100	Plus or minus 10%
50	Plus or minus 14%

1. How do each of the forms of random sampling ensure that each member of the population has an equal chance of being in the sample?

2. In your own words, describe the difference between random sampling and random assignment.

3. Why are purposive, convenience, and snowball sampling *not* examples of random sampling?

4. Why do you think researchers might decide to use an unrepresentative sample, when a random sample might be better for external validity?

5. Which of these samples is more likely to be representative of a population of 100,000?
   a. A snowball sample of 10,000 people
   b. A randomly selected sample of 100 people

1. See pp. 168–170. 2. See p. 170. 3. See pp. 171–172. 4. Answers will vary; see pp. 173–174. 5. b.

Summary

When you interrogate a claim based on a survey, you should evaluate its construct validity: How clearly were the survey's questions phrased, and were they asked in ways that controlled for order effects and response biases? Good survey questions should assess people's beliefs and opinions, not their tendencies to agree, their desire to look good, or their understanding of the questions.

Similarly, you need to evaluate construct validity when you interrogate a frequency claim that is based on observational data. Good observations record people's true behavior, rather than what the observer wanted to see, what the observer caused to happen, or how people act when they are conscious of being watched. Did the observers take care to avoid biasing their participants' behavior?

You also need to interrogate the external validity of frequency claims based on both surveys and observational studies. Most of the time, the quality of a frequency claim hinges on the ability to generalize from the sample to a given population. When generalization is the goal, random sampling techniques—rather than sample size—are vital, because they give nonbiased estimates of a population. Probability samples are the gold standard for opinion polls, for estimating the frequency of mental and physical disorders, or for estimating the frequency of behaviors such as talking, greeting, or praising in some population. In contrast, nonrandom and self-selected samples do not represent the population; they may be biased toward people who are easy to reach or more willing to answer. However, nonrandom samples can occasionally be appropriate when the cause of the bias is not relevant to the survey topic. Random samples are crucial primarily when researchers are estimating the frequency of a particular opinion, condition, or behavior in a population.

Key Terms

acquiescence, p. 152
census, p. 164
cluster sampling, p. 169
convenience sampling, p. 171
faking bad, p. 154
fence sitting, p. 153
forced-choice format, p. 146
Likert scale, p. 147
masked study, p. 161
multistage sampling, p. 169
nay-saying, p. 152
observational research, p. 156
observer bias, p. 159
observer effects, p. 161
open-ended questions, p. 146

oversampling, p. 170
population, p. 164
probability sampling, p. 168
purposive sampling, p. 171
random assignment, p. 170
response sets, p. 151
sample, p. 164
self-selection, p. 167
semantic differential format, p. 147
simple random sampling, p. 168
snowball sampling, p. 172
socially desirable responding, p. 153
stratified random sampling, p. 169
systematic sampling, p. 170
unobtrusive observations, p. 161

 **NEED HELP STUDYING?**

wwnorton.com/studyspace

Visit StudySpace to access free review materials such as:

- Diagnostic Review Quizzes
- Study Outlines

Learning Actively

1. Consider the various question formats: open-ended, forced-choice, Likert-type, and semantic differential. For each of the following research questions, write a question in each format, keeping in mind some of the pitfalls in question writing. Which of the questions you wrote would have the best construct validity, and why?

    a. A study that measures attitudes about gays and lesbians working in the military
    b. A customer service survey that asks people about their satisfaction with their most recent online shopping experience
    c. A poll that asks people which political party they have supported in the past

2. During a recent U.S. election, the news media interviewed a group of women in Florida. Although opinion polls strongly supported the liberal candidate, these conservative women were still optimistic that their own side would win. One woman said, "I don't think those polls are very good—after all, they've never called *me*. Have they called any of you ladies?"

    Is this woman's critique of polling techniques appropriate? Why or why not?

3. Imagine that you are planning to estimate the price of the average book at your college bookstore. The bookstore carries 13,000 titles, but you plan to sample only 200 books. You will select a sample of 200 books, record the price of each book, and use the average of the 200 books to estimate the average price of the 13,000 books in the bookstore. (Example adapted from Cozby [2007].)

    Based on this information, answer the following questions:

    a. What is the sample in this study, and what is the population?
    b. How might you collect a simple random sample of books?
    c. How might you collect a stratified random sample?
    d. How might you collect a convenience sample?
    e. How might you collect a systematic random sample?
    f. How might you collect a cluster sample of 200 books?

4. For which of the following claims is a representative sample, rather than a biased sample, likely to be essential? For which would a biased sample be acceptable?

    a. A political poll predicting who will win a governor's race
    b. Online readers' ratings of a recently released film
    c. Estimating school achievement from a sample of test scores from 10 district schools, in order to evaluate which of the 10 is the highest achieving.

5. Evaluate the situations below and indicate whether you think the variable is better measured as self-report or with an observation. Propose an exact operationalization of how you would measure the variable. (Either write a self-report question, or describe how you would observe the behavior.)

   a. A political psychologist wishes to measure the percentage of people who vote in elections in a certain rural area.
   b. A psychology student wants to measure how often people send text messages while driving in a local neighborhood.
   c. A relationships researcher wants to measure how much jealousy women feel in their relationships with their partners.

6. Plan an observational study to see who is more likely to hold open a door for another person, men or women. Think about how to maximize your construct validity. Will observers be biased about what they record? How might they influence the people they observe, if at all? How will you evaluate the interrater reliability of your observers? Write a two- to three-sentence operational definition of what it means to "hold the door" for somebody. Your operational definition should be clear enough that if you asked two friends to use it to code "holding the door" behavior, it would have good reliability and validity.

   Consider, as well, how you will sample men and women for this study. What will be your population? People on your campus? People at a shopping center? Do you plan to ensure that each person in the population is equally likely to be included in your sample? Why or why not?

PART 4

Tools for Evaluating Association Claims

People Who Are Extroverted Like Upbeat, Conventional Music

(*Journal of Personality and Social Psychology*, 2003)

Maternal Employment Is Not Associated with Children's Academic Achievement

(*Developmental Psychology*, 1999)

7

Bivariate Correlational Research

Learning Objectives

A year from now, you should still be able to:

1. Explain what types of studies support association claims: Measured variables, not any particular statistic, make a study correlational.

2. Explain why you should prioritize construct validity and statistical validity (and, to a lesser extent, external validity) for interrogating association claims.

3. Recognize and guard against the temptation to make a causal inference from an association claim.

The statements on the opposite page are examples of association claims that are supported by data. Each of these statements is an association claim because it describes a relationship between two measured variables: extraversion and musical preference, maternal employment and academic achievement. Because there are two variables involved, these are called **bivariate associations**, or *bivariate correlations*.

Even without reading the full details of each study, we can be pretty sure the variables in these claims were measured, because it would be difficult to manipulate them. That is, researchers can measure people's music preferences and their level of extraversion, but they cannot reasonably make people like one kind of music or another, and they cannot assign people to have certain personality traits. Researchers can measure whether a mother works, but they cannot reasonably assign a mother to work or not to work. They can measure children's achievement, but they cannot assign children to do well or poorly in school. Because it's a plausible assumption that the two variables in both claims were measured, we can infer that they are association claims. You might also notice that the verbs in each case are not strong, causal verbs. Instead, they use less ambitious language to indicate association. The first one simply notes that that people who exhibit one personality trait also exhibit a particular peference. And the second statement clearly uses the language of an association claim. Neither of the statements argues that X *causes* Y, or X *makes* Y *happen*, or X *increases rates of* Y. (If they did, they would be causal claims instead of association claims.)

This chapter describes the kinds of studies that lead to association claims, explains what kinds of graphs and statistics are used to describe the associations, and shows how you can systematically interrogate an association claim using the four big validities framework. What kinds of questions should you ask when you encounter an association claim? And what should you keep in mind if you plan to conduct a study to test such a claim?

Introduction to Bivariate Correlations

An association claim describes the relationship found between two measured variables. Chapter 3 introduced the main types of associations—positive, negative, zero, and curvilinear. To investigate associations, researchers need to measure the first variable and then measure the second variable—in the same group of people. Then they use graphs and simple statistics to describe the type of relationship between the variables.

Matthias Mehl and his colleagues (2010) wanted to know whether people's level of happiness affects how much small talk they engage in. To find out, they measured people's happiness by combining two measures: Pavot and Diener's (1993) satisfaction with life scale (introduced in Chapter 5) and a measure of overall happiness. Then they measured people's level of "chit-chat" by having them wear an electronically activated recorder (EAR) for 4 days. (The EAR, introduced in Chapter 6, is an observational measurement device—an unobtrusive microphone worn by a participant that records 30 seconds of ambient sound every 12.5 minutes.) After people's daily conversations were recorded and transcribed, research assistants coded the extent to which the recorded snippets of each person's conversations represented "small talk" or "substantive conversation." Each person was assigned a value representing the percentage of their conversation time spent on small talk and on substantive conversation.

To investigate the association between extraversion and musical preference, Peter Rentfrow and Sam Gosling (2003) asked a set of undergraduate students about their favorite types of music, using a self-report questionnaire they called the STOMP (short test of music preferences). They also measured the same students' personality traits using a self-report measure that assesses people's extraversion, agreeableness, conscientiousness, and other traits.

To test the relationship between maternal employment and children's achievement, researcher Elizabeth Harvey (1999) used data from a large probability sample of American children called the National Longitudinal Study of Youth (NLSY). The NLSY included several measures of school achievement in a set of children, such as a picture-based vocabulary test and a set of academic tests measuring mathematics and reading skills. The NLSY also recorded data about the employment history of each child's mother. It asked, for example, how soon she returned to work after the child's birth and how many hours she typically worked per week. From these data, Harvey created a categorical variable: whether the mother did or did not work during the child's first 3 years of life.

An example of how the data points for each of the opening statements might have looked appears in **Tables 7.1**, **7.2**, and **7.3**. In the three sets of data, notice that each row shows one person's scores on two measured variables of interest. In addition, notice that even though each study measured more than two variables, an analysis of bivariate correlations looks at only two variables at a time. Therefore, a correlational study might have measured multiple variables, but the authors present the bivariate correlations between different pairs of variables separately.

Review: Describing Associations Between Two Quantitative Variables

After recording the data, the next step in testing an association claim is to describe the relationship between the two measured variables using scatterplots and the correlation coefficient, *r*. We could create a scatterplot for the relationship between small talk and well-being, for example, by placing scores on the well-being measure on the x-axis and

TABLE 7.1 Representative Data from Mehl and Colleagues' (2010) Study on Well-Being and Small Talk

Person	Score on well-being index	Percentage of conversations rated as "small talk"
A	4.5	15%
B	3.0	25
C	3.2	22
D	4.1	13
E	4.9	14
...	...	...
ZZ	2.8	21

TABLE 7.2 Excerpt of Data from Rentfrow and Gosling's (2003) Study on Music Preference and Personality

Student	Liking for upbeat, conventional music (STOMP)	Extraversion score from personality questionnaire
Alek	4.00	3.75
Juniper	3.00	2.75
Sofia	2.43	5.00
Clark	3.57	4.00
Max	4.29	5.75
...		...
Yuri	2.29	3.50

TABLE 7.3 Representative Data from Harvey's (1999) Study on Maternal Employment and Achievement

Child	Did mother work in the first 3 years?	Achievement test score (PPVT)
a	Yes	85
b	No	90
c	Yes	75
d	Yes	91
e	No	86
...	...	...
yy	Yes	88

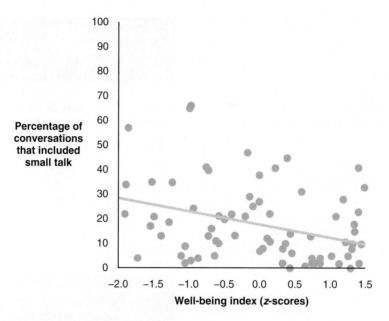

FIGURE 7.1 Scatterplot of the association between small talk and well-being.

Source: Adapted from Mehl and colleagues (2010).

Percentage of conversations that included small talk

Well-being index (*z*-scores)

percentage of conversations that include small talk on the y-axis, then placing a mark on the graph to represent each person, as shown in **Figure 7.1**.

In addition creating the scatterplot, Mehl and colleagues computed the correlation coefficient for their data and came up with an *r* of −0.33. As discussed in Chapter 3, the negative *r* means that the relationship is negative: High scores on one variable go with low scores on the other. In other words, high percentages of small talk go with low levels of well-being, and low percentages of small talk go with high levels of well-being. Second, the magnitude of *r* is about 0.33, which indicates a relationship that is moderate in strength.

How do we know that this relationship is moderate? We know because psychological scientists typically follow a set of guidelines provided by the psychological statistician Jacob Cohen (1992). Recall that *r* has two qualities: direction and strength. The direction refers to whether the association is positive, negative, or zero; the strength refers to how closely related the two variables are—how close *r* is to 1 or −1. To help researchers label the strength of their associations as small, medium, or large, Cohen provided a set of benchmarks, shown in **Table 7.4**. According to these conventions, the magnitude of the small talk/well-being association is *medium*. (Later in this chapter you will read about these conventions in more detail.)

TABLE 7.4 Cohen's (1992) Guidelines for Evaluating Strengths of Association (based on *r*)

An *r* of approximately	Would be considered to have an effect size that is
0.10 (or −0.10)	Small, or weak
0.30 (or −0.30)	Medium, or moderate
0.50 (or −0.50)	Large, or strong

Figure 7.2 shows a scatterplot for the study on music and extraversion. When Rentfrow and Gosling computed the correlation coefficient between liking for upbeat, popular music and extraversion, they found an *r* of 0.24. The positive *r* means that more extraversion is associated with more liking for upbeat popular music, and less extraversion is associated with less liking for upbeat, popular music.

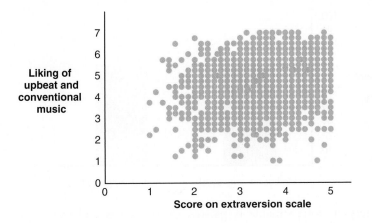

FIGURE 7.2 **Scatterplot of the association between extraversion and liking for upbeat, popular music.** This scatterplot was created from data provided by Rentfrow and Gosling (2003). Does this cloud of points slope up or down? Is it a strong or a weak relationship?

According to Cohen's conventions, the size of the correlation, 0.24, means that this association is small to medium in strength.

Describing Associations with Categorical Data

In the two examples we have discussed so far, the nature of the association can be described with scatterplots and the correlation coefficient, *r*. But in the association between maternal employment and child achievement, the maternal employment variable is a yes-or-no variable. Recall that this kind of variable is considered a *categorical variable*; that is, its values fall in either one category or another. A child's mother was either employed or not employed. The second variable in this association, child achievement, is not categorical; it is a *quantitative variable*—80 means more achievement than 70, 70 means more than 55, and so on.

When both variables in an association are measured on quantitative scales (as were extraversion and liking for popular music), a scatterplot is usually the best way to represent the data. But is a scatterplot the best representation of an association in which one of the variables is measured categorically? **Figure 7.3** shows what a scatterplot for the association between maternal employment and child achievement would look like.

For more on categorical and quantitative variables, see Chapter 5, p. 118.

FIGURE 7.3 **Scatterplot of maternal employment and child achievement.** Do you see an association here between maternal employment and child achievement? (Data are fabricated for the purpose of illustration; pattern based on Harvey [1999].)

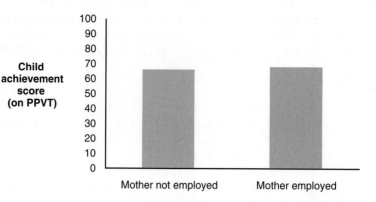

FIGURE 7.4 **Bar graph of maternal employment and child achievement.**

These are the same data as in Figure 7.3, only graphed differently. Do you see an association here between maternal employment and child achievement?

As in all scatterplots, one variable is plotted on the x-axis and the other on the y-axis, and one dot represents one person. You can even look for an association in this graph: Do the scattered points slope up from right to left, do they slope down, or is the slope flat? If you answered that you see no slope—a flat slope—you would be right. So you would conclude from this scatterplot that there is *no association* between maternal employment and child achievement, just as Harvey (1999) found when she conducted her study. If you computed the correlation between these two variables, you would get an *r* very close to zero: *r* = 0.0012. Far more often, however, when one of the measured variables is categorical, the researchers will plot the results of the association as a bar graph, as in **Figure 7.4**. In this bar graph, each individual child is not represented by one data point; instead, the graph shows the average achievement score for all the children whose mothers did work in the first 3 years and the average achievement score for the children whose mothers did not work.

In a bar graph, you would examine the difference between the average scores to see whether there is an association. In the graph of maternal employment and child achievement in Figure 7.4, you can see that the average achievement score is virtually the same in the two groups (mother not employed and mother employed), indicating that this study found *no* association between maternal employment and achievement in the sample of 3- to 4-year-olds.

In contrast, consider the relationship between maternal employment and another variable in Harvey's study: behavioral problems. In one subsample, Harvey found that maternal employment was associated with slightly greater incidence of behavioral problems. In a graph, this association would show up as a *difference*. Look at the data depicted in **Figure 7.5**. Because there is a difference between the two averages, we would conclude that there is an

FIGURE 7.5 **Bar graph of maternal employment data and behavior problems.** Do you see an association between maternal employment and behavior problems? (This result comes from one subsample consisting of 7- to 9-year-olds from high-income families. There was no relationship between maternal employment and behavior problems in other subsamples.) *Source*: Harvey (1999).

association between maternal employment and behavioral problems in this subsample. Specifically, the association shown in Figure 7.5 is that in this subsample at least, employed mothers had children with more behavioral problems.

Analyzing Associations When One Variable Is Categorical

When at least one of the variables in an association claim is categorical, as in the maternal employment example, researchers may use different statistics to analyze the data. Although they occasionally use r, it is more common to test whether the difference between means is statistically significant (usually by using a statistic called the **t test**). Alternatively, they might describe the relationship by using a statistic called a **point-biserial correlation**. The point-biserial correlation is a correlation coefficient similar to r, but it is especially intended for evaluating the association between one categorical variable and one quantitative variable. In addition, you might encounter a study that evaluates the association between two categorical variables (perhaps between maternal employment and whether the child graduated from high school). Frequently, researchers in this situation will use a **phi coefficient**, a statistic designed to evaluate the association between two categorical variables. In a full-semester statistics course, you will learn more about how to compute and apply these tests.

For more detail about the *t* test, see Appendix B, pp. A35–A38.

Two Measured Variables Make a Study Correlational

It might seem confusing that association claims can be depicted by either scatterplots or bar graphs, or that association claims can be described using a variety of statistics, such as r or difference scores. So it is important to remember that no matter what kind of graph you make, no matter what kind of statistic you use, when both variables are measured, the claim being tested is an association claim. (In contrast, recall from Chapter 3 that if one of the variables is *manipulated*, you have an experiment, which is more appropriate for testing a causal claim.) An association claim is not characterized by a particular kind of statistic or a particular kind of graph; it is characterized by a study design in which both of the variables are measured.

Check Your Understanding

1. At minimum, how many variables are there in an association claim?
2. What characteristic of a study's variables makes a study correlational?
3. Sketch three scatterplots: one that would show a positive correlation, one that would show a negative correlation, and one that would show a zero correlation.
4. Sketch three bar graphs: one that would show a positive correlation, one that would show a negative correlation, and one that would show a zero correlation.
5. When do researchers typically use a bar graph, as opposed to a scatterplot, to display correlational data?

1. Two. **2.** See p. 189. **3.** Answers may vary; see Figures 7.1–7.3. **4.** Answers may vary; see Figures 7.4–7.5. **5.** See pp. 187–188.

Interrogating Association Claims

When you are interrogating an association claim, the two most important validities to interrogate are construct validity and statistical validity. You might also ask about the external validity of the association. And although internal validity is not usually relevant to an association claim, keep in mind why it is not relevant. The next section details the questions you will use to interrogate each of the four big validities specifically in the context of association claims.

Construct Validity: How Well Was Each Variable Measured?

An association claim describes the relationship between two measured variables, so it is relevant to ask about the construct validity of *each* variable. That is, how well was each of the two variables measured?

To interrogate Mehl and colleagues' study, for example, you would ask questions about their operationalizations of—the way they measured—small talk and well-being. As you read earlier, small talk in this study was observed via the EAR recordings and coded later by research assistants, while well-being was measured using the satisfaction with life scale. Once you know what kind of measure was used for each variable, you can ask questions to assess the construct validity of each: Does the measure have good reliability? Is it measuring what it is intended to measure? That is, what is the evidence for its face validity, its concurrent validity, its discriminant and convergent validity? **Table 7.5** gives a specific example of how you might interrogate the construct validity of Harvey's claim that maternal employment is not associated with child achievement.

Statistical Validity: How Well Do the Data Support the Conclusion?

When you ask about the statistical validity of an association claim, you are asking about factors that might have affected the scatterplot, correlation coefficient (r), bar graph, or difference score that led to your association claim. You need to consider the effect size and statistical significance of the relationship, any subgroups or outliers that might have affected the overall findings, and whether a seemingly zero relationship might actually be curvilinear.

Statistical Validity Question 1: What Is the Effect Size?

All associations are not equal—some associations are stronger than others. *Effect size* describes the strength of an association. For example, **Figure 7.6** depicts two correlations: Both are positive, but the one in Panel B is stronger (its r is closer to 1). That is, Panel B depicts a stronger effect size.

Earlier, this chapter introduced Cohen's conventions for labeling correlations as small, medium, or large in strength. In Mehl and colleagues' study, the association between small talk and well-being was $r = 0.33$, a relationship of medium strength. In Rentfrow and Gosling's study, the size of the

TABLE 7.5 Interrogating the Construct Validity of an Association Claim: Harvey's (1999) Study on Maternal Employment and Child Achievement

	Variable 1: maternal employment	Variable 2: achievement
Operationalization (How was the construct measured?)	Mother's report of whether she was employed during the child's first 3 years of life	Peabody Picture Vocabulary Test (PPVT; Dunn & Dunn, 1981), individually administered test of child's language skill; child is shown a set of pictures and asked to name them or point to a picture that represents a spoken word
Reliability Questions		
Test-Retest Reliability	Does the mother give the same answer to this question each time she completes this survey?	Do children get consistent scores on the PPVT each time they take it?
Internal Reliability	[Not relevant, since this was a one-item measure]	Do children score the same on PPVT items of similar difficulty?
Interrater Reliability	[Not relevant for self-report measures]	Do two testers agree on a set of children's PPVT scores?
Measurement Validity Questions		
Face Validity/ Content Validity	Does the survey question clearly seem to ask about employment history?	Is the PPVT accepted by educational specialists as a good test of achievement?
Predictive/Concurrent Validity	Do mothers' answers to this question correlate with their actual employment history?	Does the PPVT predict school achievement in children?
Convergent Validity	If there is more than one measure of mother's employment history, do they correlate with each other?	Does the PPVT correlate with other, similar measures of child achievement?
Discriminant Validity	Is this yes/no question getting at a mother's employment status or something else, such as her ability to remember accurately?	Does the PPVT not correlate with dissimilar measures of a child's ability, such as social skills or physical ability?

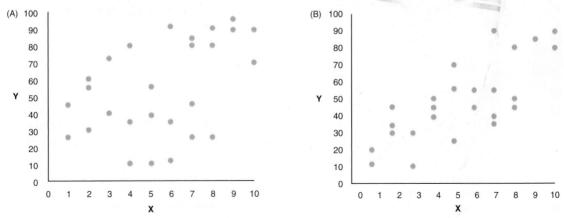

FIGURE 7.6 Two scatterplots depicting different association strengths. Both of these are positive relationships. Which scatterplot shows the stronger relationship?

association between extraversion and liking for popular, upbeat music was 0.24—a relationship of small to medium strength. The size of the association between maternal employment and achievement in Harvey's study was $r = 0.013$—that is, virtually *no* relationship. Therefore, of the three relationships, the strongest one is the small talk/well-being relationship. (Note that this relationship is the strongest, even though it is a negative relationship.) But how strong is -0.33 compared with 0.24? What is the logic behind these conventions?

One thing that a stronger effect size means is that we can make more accurate predictions of one variable from another. Recall from Chapter 3 that if we know height at age 2 is strongly correlated with adult height (that is, if the r is strong), you can use people's 2-year-old height to make fairly accurate predictions of their adult height. If two variables are weakly correlated, the predictions will be less accurate. For example, the correlation between people's newborn length and their adult height is much weaker than the correlation between 2-year-old height and adult height. Therefore, if you guess someone's height from newborn length, your guess is likely to be off by more than if you had guessed from 2-year-old height.

In addition, in some cases, effect sizes indicate how *important* the result is—that is, when all else is equal, a larger effect size is often considered more important than a small one. However, there are exceptions to this rule. Depending on the context, even a small effect size can be important. A medical study on heart disease provides one famous example in which a small r was considered extremely important. The study (reported in McCartney & Rosenthal, 2000) found that taking an aspirin a day was associated with a lower rate of heart attacks, though the size of the association was only $r = 0.03$. According to the guidelines in Table 7.4, this is a very weak association, but in terms of the number of lives saved, even this small association was substantial. The full sample in the study consisted of about 22,000 people. Comparing the 11,000 in the aspirin group to the 11,000 in the placebo group, the study showed 85 fewer heart attacks in the aspirin group. An r of only 0.03 therefore represented 85 heart attacks avoided. This outcome was considered so dramatic that the doctors ended the study early and told everyone in the nonaspirin group to start taking aspirin (**Figure 7.7**). In such cases, even a tiny effect size, by Cohen's standards, can be considered important, especially when it has life-or-death implications.

When the outcome is not as extreme as life or death, however, an effect size of 0.03 might indeed be negligible in importance. For instance, the effect size of the association between maternal employment and child achievement (in Harvey's data) was $r = 0.012$ (almost zero). This effect size translates into a difference of less than half a point on the test they used to measure child achievement. So maternal employment has only a tiny practical impact on children's achievement, at least according to Harvey's study.

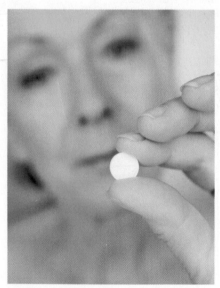

FIGURE 7.7 Effect size and importance. In some studies, such as those showing that an aspirin a day can reduce heart attack risk, even a very small effect size can be an important result.

Statistical Validity Question 2: Is the Correlation Statistically Significant?

Whenever researchers obtain a correlation coefficient, r, they not only establish the direction and the strength (effect size) of the relationship but also determine whether the correlation is **statistically significant**, as explained in this section. (Appendix B provides more detailed information about statistical significance.)

The Logic of Statistical Inference. Determining statistical significance is a process of inference. Researchers usually cannot study everybody in a population, so they study only one sample at a time and make an inference from the sample about the population. The sample's result usually mimics what is happening in the population, but not always. That is, if there is an association between two variables in a population, we will probably observe an association between those two variables in the sample, too. And if there is no association between two variables in a population, we will probably observe no association between those two variables in the sample.

Sometimes, however, even if there is *zero* association between two variables in a population, just by chance a study happens to use a sample in which an association shows up. The correlation from that particular sample would have been caused by mere chance. Because such chance results sometimes occur, when we find an association in a sample we can never know for sure whether there really is an association in the larger population or whether there is not.

For example, a researcher conducts a study on a sample of 100 college students and finds that extraversion correlates with liking for upbeat music at $r = 0.24$. That correlation might really exist in the whole population of college students. But it could also be a fluke, a result of mere chance from that particular sample. Even if there is no correlation between extraversion and liking that kind of music, once in a while a sample may, for reasons of chance alone, find such a correlation.

Statistical significance calculations help researchers evaluate the probability that the result (such as $r = 0.24$) came from a population in which the association is really zero. That is, even though we can never know for sure whether our sample's result mimics the population, we can nevertheless estimate the probability that our sample's result is a fluke. The calculations estimate the following: What kinds of r results would we typically get from a zero-correlation population if we conducted the same study many, many times with samples of the same size? How often would we get an r of 0.24 just by chance, even if there is no association in the population?

What Does a Statistically Significant Result Mean? Statistical significance calculations provide a probability estimate (p, sometimes abbreviated as *sig*). The p value helps researchers evaluate the probability that the sample's association came from a population in which the association is zero. If the probability (p) associated with the result is very small—that is, less than 5%—we know that the result is very *unlikely* to have come from a "zero-association" population. The correlation is considered statistically significant.

What Does a Nonsignificant Result Mean? By contrast, if the probability (p) of getting some correlation just by chance is relatively *high* (that is, higher than $p = 0.05$), the result is usually considered to be "nonsignificant" or "not statistically significant." It means we cannot rule out the possibility that the result came from a population in which the association is zero.

Effect Size, Sample Size, and Significance. Statistical significance is related to effect size; usually, the stronger a correlation (and the larger its effect size), the more likely the correlation will be statistically significant. That's because the larger an association is, the less likely it could have been sampled, just by chance, from a population in which the association is zero. But you cannot tell whether a particular correlation is statistically significant by looking at its effect size alone. You will also need to look for the significance calculations—the p values— associated with it.

Statistical significance calculations depend not only on effect size but also on sample size. A very small correlation (say, $r = 0.08$) will be statistically significant if it is identified in a very large sample (say, a sample of 1,000 or more). But that same small correlation of $r = 0.08$ would not be statistically significant if the study used a small sample (say, a sample of 30). A small sample is more easily affected by chance events than a large sample is. In other words, in a population in which the association is zero, studies with small samples might show weak correlations relatively frequently. Therefore, a weak correlation based on a small sample is more likely to be the result of chance variation and is more likely to be judged "not significant."

For more detail on effect size, sample size, and significance, see Appendix B.

Reading About Significance in Journal Articles. In an empirical journal article, you can recognize statistically significant associations by their p values. Significance information may also be indicated by an asterisk (*), which usually means that an association is significant, with the word *sig*, or with a notation such as $p < 0.05$ or $p < 0.01$. See, for example, the table in **Figure 7.8**, which appeared in

Table I. Daily Interaction Variables: Reliabilities and Correlations With Well-Being

Interaction variable	Intercoder reliability	Overall correlation with well-being			Correlation with well-being on weekdays	Correlation with well-being on weekends[b]	Correlation with well-being after accounting for personality differences
		Well-being index	Satisfaction with life	Happiness			
Alone[a]	.97	−.35**	−.36**	−.27*	−.29**	−.35**	−.40**
Talking to others[a]	.95	.31**	.31**	.26*	.30**	.30**	.39**
Small talk[a]	.76	−.07	−.03	−.10	−.01	−.09	.08
Small talk as a percentage of all conversations	—[c]	−.33**	−.25*	−.35**	−.30**	−.34**	−.17
Substantive conversations[a]	.84	.31**	.26*	.30**	.27*	.31**	.36**
Substantive conversations as a percentage of all conversations	—[c]	.28**	.20	.31**	.28**	.27*	.22*

Note: N = 79. Intercoder reliabilities were computed as intraclass correlations, ICC(2, k), from a training set of 221 Electronically Activated Recorder (EAR) sound files that were independently coded by all coders. Satisfaction with life was assessed using participants' responses on the Satisfaction With Life Scale (Diener, Emmons, Larsen, & Griffin, 1985); happiness was assessed using self-reports and informant reports on a single item. The happiness and life-satisfaction measures were combined to create the well-being index. Personality was measured using self-reports and informant reports on the Big Five Inventory (John & Srivastava, 1999).
[a]These variables were calculated as the proportion of the total number of sampled sound files in which the indicated activity occurred. [b]The weekend was defined as beginning Friday at 6:00 p.m. and ending Sunday at midnight. [c]No reliability is reported because the variable is a quotient of two coded variables.
*$p \leq .05$ (two-tailed). **$p < .01$ (two-tailed).

FIGURE 7.8 **Statistical significance as indicated In Mehl and colleagues' (2010) article.** This table presents a variety of bivariate correlations. It also presents interrater reliability information for the variables that were coded from the EAR. (The last column shows a multiple-regression analysis, described in Chapter 8.)

Mehl and colleagues' (2010) journal article. In this table, some of the correlations have asterisks next to them; the footnote explains that one asterisk indicates a p value less than 0.05, and two asterisks indicate a p value less than 0.01. Therefore, the probability is low that these starred correlations came from a population in which the correlation is zero, so they are statistically significant. In contrast, a popular press article usually will not specify whether a correlation is significant or not. The only way to know for sure is to track down the original study.

Statistical Validity Question 3: Are There Subgroups?

Imagine that you have a large sample of college students and you measure the number of times each student skips class per semester, along with his or her GPA for that semester. You make a scatterplot, which looks something like the one in **Figure 7.9**.

Most people would be surprised by this outcome: More absences are associated with higher grades? But notice that this scatterplot lumps all students together, whereas there are four subgroups being studied: freshmen, sophomores, juniors, and seniors. Now consider that the seniors, because they are taking classes in their own major, tend to get higher grades overall. The freshmen, because they are taking many required classes and are still trying to find a major that matches their talents, get lower grades overall. In addition to getting higher grades, the seniors are skipping more classes than the conscientious freshmen (exhibiting what is often called "senioritis").

Now imagine that *within* each of these subgroups, the association between skipping class and grades is actually negative, as most people would expect. **Figure 7.10** shows how the scatterplot might be drawn to distinguish the four subgroups. This dramatic (and hypothetical) example illustrates the potential problems subgroups can cause. Sometimes, when you have an association between two variables, the apparent overall association is **spurious**, meaning that the overall

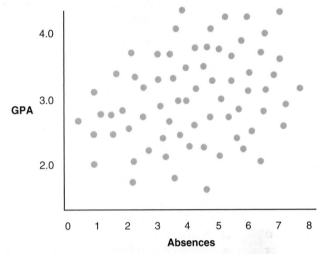

FIGURE 7.9 A scatterplot of the semester grades and number of absences per semester in a sample of college students. (Data are fabricated for the purpose of illustration.)

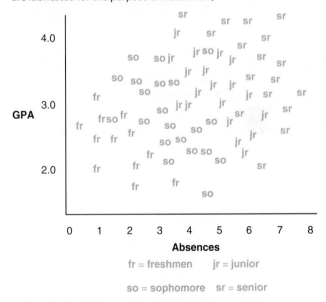

fr = freshmen   jr = junior

so = sophomore   sr = senior

FIGURE 7.10 The positive association between absences and semester grades. The association is actually negative within each of the four subgroups. (Data are fabricated for the purpose of illustration.)

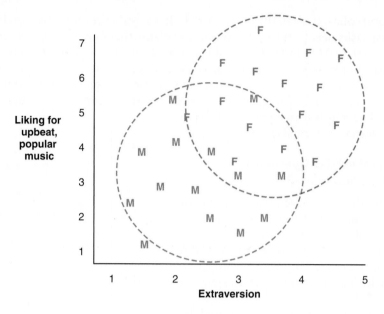

FIGURE 7.11 Possible subgroups in the extraversion/music example. Perhaps women are both more extraverted and more likely to prefer upbeat, popular music. Within each sex, however, there is no relationship between these two variables. (Data are fabricated for the purpose of illustration.)

relationship is attributable only to systematic mean differences on subgroups within the sample. In this case, the overall relationship between absences and grades is attributable only to the fact that seniors score higher than freshmen on both variables. When you consider the subgroups separately, there is no association (and indeed, in this case, the *opposite* association appears). When you are interrogating an association claim, it is important to think about subgroups. Sometimes the subgroup problems are hard to detect, and it might look like there is an overall association when there actually is none.

Going back to the association between extraversion and liking for upbeat, popular music, recall that the association was positive (see Figure 7.2). Subgroups might be relevant here: It could be that women are more extraverted than men and that women like upbeat, popular music more than men do. If so, the overall association might be attributable to gender, as shown in **Figure 7.11**. In this example, among women there actually is no relationship between extraversion and liking for upbeat, popular music, and the same is true among men. In this case, the subgroups—and the fact that women are higher on both variables—explains the overall correlation. It would therefore be wrong to say that extraversion is associated with liking for upbeat, popular music. That association would be considered spurious, because it is attributable only to systematic mean differences on the two variables (women are higher than men on both variables).

Of course, subgroups within a sample do not necessarily change the original association. Consider the scatterplot in **Figure 7.12**. In this example, there are two subgroups, and again, the only way to determine whether there is an overall association is to consider the subgroups separately. As before, one of the groups is generally higher than the other on both variables, but this time the subgroups do not change the original correlation. The original correlation still exists within each subgroup, so the original correlation is not spurious.

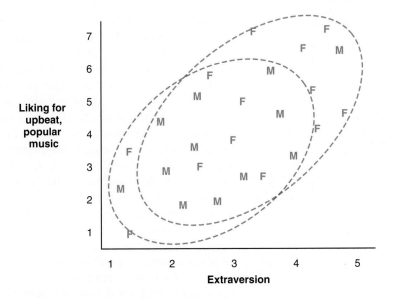

It is possible that women are both more extraverted and more likely to prefer upbeat, popular music, but within each sex there is still a positive relationship between these two variables. (Data are fabricated for the purpose of illustration.)

Statistical Validity Question 4: Could Outliers Be Affecting the Relationship?

An **outlier** is an extreme score—a single case (or sometimes a few) that stands out far away from the pack. Depending on where it sits in relation to the rest of the sample, a single outlier can have a strong effect on the correlation coefficient, r. The two scatterplots in **Figure 7.13** show the potential effect of an outlier, a single person who happened to score high on both x and y. Why would a single outlier be a problem? As it turns out, adding that one data point changes the correlation depicted in the scatterplot from $r = 0.26$ to $r = 0.37$! Depending on where the outlier is, it can make a medium-sized correlation appear stronger, or a strong correlation appear weaker, than it really is.

Outliers can be problematic for an association claim, because even though they are only one or two data points, they may exert disproportionate influence. Think of an association as a teeter-totter. If you sit close to the center of the teeter-totter, you do not have much power to make the teeter-totter move, but if you sit way out on one end, you can have

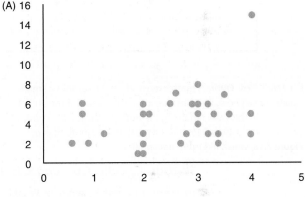

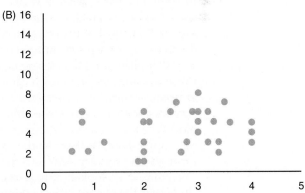

FIGURE 7.13 The effects of an outlier. These two scatterplots are identical, except for the outlier in the upper right-hand corner of Panel A. In Panel A, $r = 0.37$. In Panel B, $r = 0.26$.

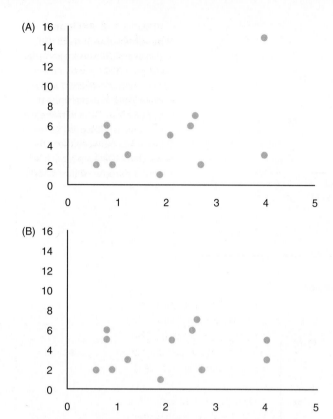

FIGURE 7.14 **Outliers matter most when the sample is small.** Again, these two scatterplots are identical except for the outlier. However, in this case, removing the outlier changed the correlation from $r = 0.49$ to 0.15; this is a much bigger jump than in Figure 7.13, which has more data points.

a much larger influence on whether it moves. Outliers are like people on the far ends of a teeter-totter: They can have a large impact on the direction or strength of the correlation. In a bivariate correlation, outliers are mainly problematic when they involve extreme scores on *both* of the variables. In evaluating the correlation between height and weight, for example, a person who is both extremely tall and extremely heavy would make the r appear stronger; a person who is both extremely short and extremely heavy would make the r appear weaker. When interrogating an association claim, it is therefore important to ask whether a sample has any outliers. The best way to find them is to look at the scatterplots and see if one or a few data points stand out.

Outliers matter the most when a sample is small. If you have 500 points in a scatterplot (a whole bunch of people sitting in the middle of the teeter-totter), one outlier is not going to have as much impact. But if you have only 12 points in a scatterplot (only a few people in the middle of the teeter-totter), an outlier has much more influence on the pattern. (See **Figure 7.14**.)

Statistical Validity Question 5: Is the Relationship Curvilinear?

In some rare cases, when a study reports that there is no relationship between two variables, the relationship between the variables is actually curvilinear, as in **Figure 7.15**. In this example, as people's age increases, their use of health care decreases up to a point. But then, as people's age approches 60 or more, their use of health care increases again. A curvilinear relationship clearly exists between age and use of a health care system. However, when we compute a simple bivariate correlation coefficient, r, on this data, we get only $r = -0.01$, because r is designed to describe the slope of the best *straight line* through the scatterplot. When the slope of the scatterplot goes up and then down (or down and then up), r does not describe the pattern very well. The straight line that fits best through this set of points is a flat, horizontal line, which has a slope of zero. Therefore, if we looked only at the r and not at the scatterplot, we might conclude that there is no relationship between age and use of health care. When researchers suspect a curvilinear relationship, the statistically valid way to analyze it is to use a quadratic model—specifically by testing the correlation between one variable and the square of the other.

For more on curvilinear relationships, see Chapter 3, p. 61.

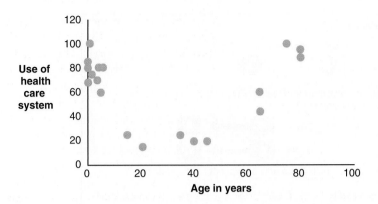

FIGURE 7.15 A curvilinear relationship. As age increases, use of the health care system decreases and then increases again. A curvilinear relationship is not captured adequately by the simple bivariate correlation coefficient, r. In these data, $r = 0.01$, a value that does not describe the relationship. (Data are fabricated for the purpose of illustration.)

Internal Validity: Can We Make a Causal Inference from an Association?

Even though we do not have to formally interrogate internal validity for an association claim, we still need to think about internal validity every time we read one of these claims. Why? Because we always need to guard against the *causal temptation*—the powerful automatic tendency to make a causal inference from any association claim we read. Perhaps we can't help ourselves. We hear that small talk is associated with worse well-being and assume that the small talk causes people to become unhappy. We hear that extraversion is associated with liking for upbeat, popular music and assume that happy music makes people more outgoing. Recently, someone e-mailed me a story saying that boys with unusual names are more likely to break the law. Of course, this is only an association claim, but the person who sent it to me added, "Your boys are in trouble!"—meaning, of course, that my boys' unusual names will *cause* them to become delinquent.

Because the causal temptation is so strong, you need to remind yourself repeatedly that correlation is not causation. Why is a simple association insufficient to establish causality? As discussed in Chapter 3, to establish causation, a study has to fulfill three criteria:

1. *Covariation of the cause variable and the effect variable*. There must be correlation, or association, between the cause and the effect.
2. *Temporal precedence*. The causal variable has to come first in time, before the effect variable.
3. *Internal validity*. There must be no plausible alternative explanations for the relationship.

The temporal precedence rule is sometimes called the **directionality problem** because we do not know which variable came first. The internal validity rule is often called the **third-variable problem**: When you can come up with an alternative explanation for the association between two variables, that alternative explanation is the third variable. **Figure 7.16** provides a shorthand description of these three rules.

FIGURE 7.16
The three rules for establishing causation.
When A is correlated with B, does that mean that A causes B? To decide, apply the three rules.

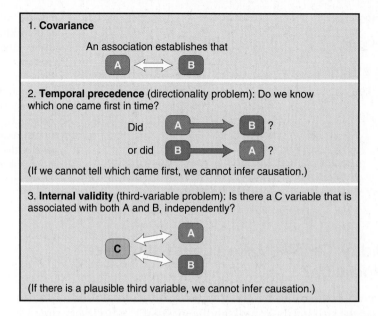

Let's apply these rules to the small talk and well-being association, to determine whether we can conclude from this association that small talk *causes* a decrease in well-being:

1. *Covariance of cause and effect*: We already know that small talk is associated negatively with well-being. As the percentage of small talk goes up, well-being goes down, thus showing covariance of the proposed cause and the proposed effect.

2. *Temporal precedence:* The study measured small talk and well-being during the same, short time period, so we cannot be sure whether an increase in small talk came first, followed by a decrease in well-being, or whether people were unhappy first and then engaged in more small talk.

3. *Internal validity*: The negative association between small talk and well-being could be attributable to some third variable that is connected to both small talk and well-being. For instance, a busy, stressful life might lead people both to report lower well-being and to have less time for substantive conversations. Or perhaps in this college sample, having a strong college-preparatory background is associated with both avoiding small talk and having higher levels of well-being (because those students are more prepared for college). But be careful—not any third variable will do. The third variable, to be plausible, must correlate logically with *both* of the measured variables in the original association. (For example, you might propose that the third variable is income, arguing that people with higher incomes will have higher well-being. But for income to work as a plausible third variable, you would have to explain how higher income is related to less small talk, too.)

As you can see, the bivariate relationship between well-being and small talk does not allow us to make a causal claim that high levels of small talk cause low levels of well-being. It also does not allow us to make a causal claim the other way around—that low levels of well-being cause people to engage in more small talk. Although the two variables are associated, the study has established only one of the three causal rules: covariance. Further research using a different kind of study would be needed to establish temporal precedence and internal validity before we would accept this relationship as causal.

What about the article claiming that boys with unusual names are more likely to commit crimes? Should I worry about my own boys and their unusual names? Let's see how this study stands up to the three causal rules:

1. *Covariation of cause and effect:* The study reported an association between unusual names and the risk for committing a crime.
2. *Temporal precedence:* We can be pretty sure that the unusual names came first (when the boys were born) and the crimes came later (when the boys were adolescents).
3. *Internal validity:* This rule is not met by the study. It is possible that people of some backgrounds are more at risk for committing crimes and tend to have statistically unusual names. Or adolescents from certain geographical regions may commit more crimes, and in those regions parents tend to give their children unusual names, too, so we could explain this association with the third variable of geographic region. (Again, to be plausible, the proposed third variable must correlate with both of the original variables—the names and the criminal behavior.)

In this case, the two variables are associated, so the study has established covariance, and the temporal precedence requirement has also been satisfied. However, the study does not establish internal validity, so we cannot make a causal inference.

When you are interrogating a simple association claim, you may not need to interrogate its internal validity, but you do need to keep reminding yourself that covariance fulfills only one of the three rules for causation. Before you assume that an *association* suggests a *cause*, you need to apply what you know about temporal precedence and internal validity.

External Validity: To Whom Can the Association Be Generalized?

When you interrogate the external validity of an association, you ask whether the association can generalize to other people, places, and times. Consider again the association between liking upbeat, popular music and being extraverted. If you wanted to interrogate the external validity of this association, one of your first questions would be who the participants were and how they were selected. If you check Rentfrow and Gosling's original article, you will find that the sample contained about 3,000 college students.

When you interrogate external validity, the size of the sample does not matter as much as the way the sample was selected from its population. So next you would ask whether the 3,000 students in Rentfrow and Gosling's sample were selected using random sampling. If so, you could then generalize from these 3,000 students to their population—in this case, college students in Austin, Texas. If the

For more on sample size, see Chapter 6, p. 175.

students were not chosen by a random sample of the population in question, you could not be sure that the sample's results would generalize to that population.

As it turns out, Rentfrow and Gosling do not say in their article whether these 3,000 students were a random sample of Austin, Texas, students or not. And of course, because the college students in this sample were only from Austin, the study results may not generalize to other college students in other areas of the country. And because the sample consisted entirely of college students, the association may not generalize to nonstudents and older people. Rentfrow and Gosling's study seems to come up short when we interrogate its external validity.

Just How Important Is External Validity?

What should we conclude when a study does not use a random sample? Is it fair to disregard the entire study? In the case of Rentfrow and Gosling's study, the construct validity is excellent; the measures of extraversion and music preference were reliable and valid. In terms of statistical validity, the correlation is statistically significant, and the effect size is moderately strong. The sample was large enough to avoid the influence of outliers, and there did not seem to be subgroups. Rentfrow and Gosling did not make any causal claims that would make internal validity relevant. In most respects, this association claim stands up; it lacks only external validity.

An association study like this may not have used a random sample, but we should not automatically reject the association for that reason. Instead, we can accept the study's results and leave the question of generalization to the next study, which might test the association between these two variables in some other population.

In addition, many associations do generalize—even to samples that are very different from the original one. You might think that the music/extraversion association would not generalize to people who are 70 to 80 years old, because you might assume that older people are less extraverted in general than college students and that they do not like upbeat, popular music as much. You would probably be right about these mean differences between the samples. However, *within* a sample of people ages 70 to 80, those who do like upbeat, popular music may also be the more extraverted people in that sample. The new sample of people might score lower, on average, on both of the variables in your association, but even so, the association might still hold true within that new sample. A scatterplot that included both of these samples, such as the one in **Figure 7.17**, would look similar to the example of subgroups shown in Figure 7.12, where the association holds true both within each subgroup and when both groups are studied together.

Moderating Variables

In association research, when the relationship between two variables changes depending on the level of a third variable, that third variable is called a **moderator**. In the study about maternal employment and child achievement, Harvey (1999) measured not only those two variables but also whether the mother was married or single. The results are given in **Table 7.6**, which shows that the relationship between maternal employment and child vocabulary (as measured by the PPVT) depends on whether the mother was married or single. Notice that the association

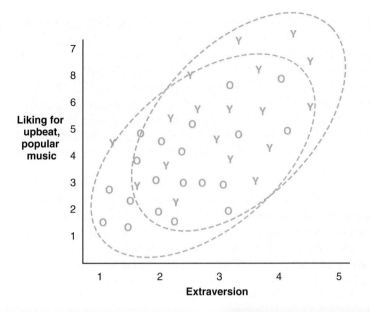

FIGURE 7.17 An association in two different samples. Older people might be less extraverted than college students, and they might like upbeat, popular music less. But there may still be the same association between the two variables *within* each sample of people. (In the graph, *Y* represents a college-aged participant, and *O* represents an older participant. Data are fabricated for the purpose of illustration.)

between maternal employment and child achievement is zero when the mothers are married (meaning that working married mothers and nonworking married mothers have children who achieve the same), but it is positive when the mothers are single (meaning that working, single mothers actually have higher-achieving children than nonworking, single mothers). The researchers concluded that marital status *moderates* the association between maternal employment and child achievement (Harvey, 1999). That is, the association between maternal employment and child outcomes depends on marital status.

Mehl and colleagues also looked for moderators in the relationship they found between small talk and well-being. They wondered if the relationship would differ depending on whether conversations took place on a weekend or a weekday. However, the results suggested that weekend/weekday status did not moderate the relationship between small talk and well-being: The relationship was positive and of equal strength in both time periods (see **Table 7.7**).

TABLE 7.6 Marital Status Moderates the Relationship Between Maternal Employment and Child Achievement

Mother's marital status	Association (*r*) between maternal employment and child's vocabulary at age 3 and 4
Single	0.07*
Married	−0.03

*$p < 0.05$
Maternal employment and child achievement are significantly associated when mothers are single; there is no relationship when mothers are married.

TABLE 7.7 Weekend/Weekday Status Does Not Moderate the Relationship Between Small Talk and Well-Being

Day of the week	Association (*r*) between percentage of small talk and well-being
Weekday	−0.30*
Weekend	−0.34**

*$p < 0.01$

In correlation research, moderators can inform external validity. When an association is moderated by day of the week, marital status, gender, or some other variable, we know that the association may not generalize from one of these situations to the others. For example, in asking whether the association between extraversion and liking for upbeat, popular music would generalize to a group of 70- to 80-year-olds, we were asking whether that association would be moderated by age. Similarly, Mehl and colleagues found that the association between small talk and well-being does generalize well from the weekends to weekdays: The strength of the association is almost the same in the two contexts.

In some ways, the process of looking for moderators is similar to the process of asking whether the association is attributable to subgroups. However, when we are asking about moderators, our goal is to ask whether the association between the two variables is *different* within the levels of some third variable (the moderator). When we are asking about subgroups, however, our goal is to make sure that the overall association between the two variables is the *same* within the two subgroups.

Check Your Understanding

1. In one or two brief sentences, explain how you would interrogate the construct validity of a bivariate correlation.
2. What are five questions you can ask about the statistical validity of a bivariate correlation? Do all of the statistical validity questions apply the same way when bivariate correlations are represented as bar graphs?
3. Which of the three rules of causation is almost always met by a bivariate correlation? Which two rules might not be met by a correlational study?
4. Give examples of some questions you can ask to evaluate the external validity of a correlational study.

1. See p. 190. 2. See pp. 190–198; questions about outliers and curvilinear relationships may not be relevant for correlations represented as bar graphs. 3. See pp. 200–201. 4. See pp. 201–204.

Summary

Association claims involve two variables, both of which are measured in a set of people. (If either of the variables is manipulated, the study is an experiment, which could potentially test a causal claim.) Depending on the types of variables being measured, researchers will use different types of graphs to depict the data and different statistics to describe the relationship. The variables can be either quantitative or categorical. If both variables are quantitative, the data are usually depicted in a scatterplot; if one variable is categorical, the data are usually depicted in a bar graph. For a scatterplot, the correlation coefficient, or r, can be used to describe the relationship. For a bar graph, the difference between the two averages can be used to describe the relationship.

Construct validity refers to how well a variable has been measured or manipulated. Because an association claim involves two measured variables, it is relevant to interrogate the construct validity of *each* measure in a bivariate correlation study.

When you ask about the statistical validity of an association claim, you are asking about the appropriateness of its statistical conclusions. First, you should ask about the effect size: How strong is r? Second, you should ask whether a correlation is statistically significant: What is the probability that the association in this sample came from a population in which the association is zero? Third, are any subgroups influencing the direction or magnitude of the overall correlation? Fourth, are there any outliers that might be affecting the size of r? Fifth, if $r = 0$, might it be hiding a curvilinear relationship?

You do not need to ask about internal validity for an association claim, but remember to guard against the temptation to assume causality. You would need to apply the three rules—covariance, temporal precedence, and internal validity—to determine whether a causal claim is justified. Finally, an association claim can generalize to some population as long as its samples are drawn at random from that population. However, if a correlational study does not use a random sample of people or contexts, you cannot necessarily generalize the results to the population the sample was taken from. But a lack of external validity should not lead you to disregard the entire study. If the study fulfills the other three kinds of validity, you can accept its results and leave the question of generalization for a future investigation.

Key Terms

bivariate associations, p. 183
directionality problem, p. 199
moderator, p. 202
outlier, p. 197
phi coefficient, p. 189

point-biserial correlation, p. 189
spurious, p. 195
statistically significant, p. 193
t test, p. 189
third-variable problem, p. 199

NEED HELP STUDYING?

wwnorton.com/studyspace

Visit StudySpace to access free review materials such as:

- Diagnostic Review Quizzes
- Study Outlines

Learning Actively

1. For each association claim below, identify the two measured variables. Then, for each claim, indicate whether the association would be best plotted with a bar graph or a scatterplot.

   a. Conscientious people are more likely to take health precautions (such as getting vaccinated and getting regular checkups) (Bogg & Roberts, 2004).
   b. People who are depressed eat more chocolate than people who are not depressed (Steenhuysen, 2010).
   c. Students at private colleges are getting higher GPAs than those at public colleges (Rampell, 2010).

2. Interrogate the construct validity, the statistical validity, and the external validity of the following association claims. What questions would you ask? What answers would you expect?

   a. On the playground, children's physical activity is associated with the objects the children are playing with. Preschool children engage in more vigorous physical activity when they play with balls and similar toys, and they are more sedentary when they play with fixed equipment (Brown, Pfeiffer, McIver, Dowda, Addy, & Pate, 2009).
   b. "Kids with ADHD May Be More Likely to Bully": "The study followed 577 children—the entire population of fourth graders from a municipality near Stockholm—for a year. The researchers interviewed parents, teachers and children to determine which kids were likely to have ADHD. Children showing signs of the disorder were then seen by a child neurologist for diagnosis. The researchers also asked the kids about bullying. [The study found that] children with attention deficit hyperactivity disorder are almost four times as likely as others to be bullies."(Carroll, 2008)

3. Could a causal claim be made from either of the two examples in Question 2? Imagine a possible causal claim that you might be tempted to make for one of the association claims, and apply the three causal rules to evaluate it.

4. A researcher conducted a study of 34 scientists (Grim, 2008). He reported a correlation between the amount of beer each scientist drank per year and the likelihood of that scientist publishing a scientific paper. The correlation was reported as $r = -0.55, p < 0.01$.

   a. What does a negative correlation mean in this example? Is this relationship strong or weak?
   b. What does $p < 0.01$ mean in this result?
   c. What might happen to this correlation if you added one person in the sample who drank much more beer than other scientists and also published far fewer papers than other scientists?

d. Draw a scatterplot of this association. Then think about whether the association might be attributable to subgroups. Redraw the overall scatterplot, marking two different subgroups (such as male and female, or different branches of science, such as biology, psychology, and physics). In the drawing you made, is the overall association between beer consumption and scientific publication spurious, or not?

e. A popular press report about this article was headlined, "Suds seem to skew scientific success" (*San Diego Union-Tribune*, 2008). Is such a causal claim justified?

The Three R's? A Fourth Is Crucial, Too: Recess

(*New York Times*, 2009)

Does Television Violence Cause Aggression?

(*American Psychologist*, 1972)

8

Multivariate Correlational Research

Studies that support association claims can provide interesting new information in their own right—it might be interesting, for instance, to note that children who watch violent TV also act aggressively, or that schoolrooms with longer recesses also have fewer behavior problems. But more often, an association claim is merely an early step down the path to establishing a causal relationship between two variables. Psychological researchers—and the rest of us—often want to know about causes and effects, not just correlations. When we read that watching violence on television *is associated with* imitating aggressive behavior, we often want to know whether the violent television shows *cause* the aggression. Similarly, when we read that recess is associated with fewer behavior problems, we might wonder: Does the recess cause the drop in bad behavior? Or is it the case that a certain type of classroom (perhaps a private school classroom) both allows more recess and has better-behaved kids? Knowing about causes enables applied researchers to make interventions. If violent TV causes aggression, advocacy groups could try to persuade parents to limit their children's exposure to violent shows. If recess causes children to do better in school, schools should require recesses. But unless these relationships are causal, such interventions would not work.

So what can we do? Because correlation is not causation, what are the options? Researchers have developed some techniques that allow them to test for cause. One of these is experimentation: Instead of measuring both variables, researchers manipulate one variable and measure the other. Even without setting up an experiment, however, researchers can use some advanced correlational techniques to get closer to making a causal statement. This chapter outlines three such techniques: longitudinal designs, which allow researchers to evaluate temporal precedence in their data; multiple-regression designs, which help researchers rule out certain third-variable explanations; and the "pattern and parsimony" approach, in which the results of a variety of correlational studies all support a single, causal theory. In all three techniques, as in all association studies, the variables are measured—that is, none are manipulated. But unlike the bivariate examples covered in Chapter 7, which involved only two measured variables, these designs are **multivariate designs**, which involve more than two measured variables. While these techniques are not perfect solutions to the causality conundrum, they are extremely useful and widely used tools, especially when experiments are impossible to run.

Experimental designs are covered in Chapters 9, 10, and 11.

Review of the Three Causal Rules

Remember that the three causal rules for establishing causation are covariance, temporal precedence, and internal validity. You might apply these rules to the association between violent TV and aggressive behavior as follows:

- *Is there covariance?* Yes—many studies have shown that the correlation between watching violent TV and acting aggressively is moderately strong, around $r = 0.35$ (Paik & Comstock, 1994). These two variables are clearly related.

- *Is there temporal precedence?* A typical correlational study cannot establish temporal precedence. In some early studies on TV viewing and aggressive behavior, researchers measured aggressive behavior at the same time as TV preferences. Such a study does not show which one comes first. It is possible that watching violent TV shows comes first and causes people to be more aggressive. It is also possible, however, that a person's aggressiveness comes first and affects his or her TV viewing habits. (That is, aggressive people choose to watch more violent TV shows, and less aggressive people choose to watch less violent ones.) So perhaps the violent TV comes first and causes the aggression.

- *Are there third variables that could explain the relationship?* The association between TV and aggressiveness could be explained by a personality trait. Perhaps people who seek extreme emotional situations (known as "sensation seekers") are more likely both to act aggressively *and* to prefer violent television shows. In this explanation, sensation seeking comes first and causes both aggressive behavior and preference for violent shows. Or perhaps the third variable is gender: Men are both more likely to watch violent shows and more likely to act aggressively than women.

Check Your Understanding

1. Why can't a simple bivariate correlational study meet all three rules for establishing causation?

1. See pp. 209–210.

Establishing Temporal Precedence with Longitudinal Designs

A **longitudinal design** can provide evidence for temporal precedence by measuring the same variables in the same people at different points in time. Often, longitudinal research is used in developmental psychology to study change in a trait or ability over time. But in other cases, this design is adapted to test causal claims. For example, in a classic study that evaluated TV violence and aggression (Eron, Huesmann, Lefkowitz, & Walder, 1972), the researchers collected data on 875 children in 1960—the entire third-grade population of a small town in New York State. Ten years later, the researchers tracked down 427 of these original children, who were now teenagers. (As shorthand, they called the second study time "thirteenth grade.") At each of the two times, the researchers measured two important variables. First, they measured children's aggression by asking their peers which students in the class were most likely to hit, push, say mean things, or start fights. Second, they measured children's interest in violent television programs by asking what their four favorite TV shows were. The children's parents reported the TV information when the children were in the third grade; in thirteenth grade, the teenagers self-reported the TV information.

Eron and colleagues' study was longitudinal because the researchers measured the *same* variables in the *same* group of people across time—10 years apart. The study is also a multivariate correlational study because four variables were measured: preference for TV violence at Time 1, preference for TV violence at Time 2, aggression at Time 1, and aggression at Time 2.

Interpreting Results from Longitudinal Designs

Because there are more than two variables involved, a multivariate design gives several individual correlations. The results for the various correlations in Eron and colleagues' study are given in the following sections. (Note that the researchers in this study conducted their analysis on boys and girls separately so that they could investigate the causal paths for each gender separately. Only the results for the boys are presented in this section.)

Cross-Sectional Correlations

The first two correlations are **cross-sectional correlations**; that is, they test to see whether two variables, measured at the same point in time, are correlated. For example, the study reports that the correlation between a preference for TV violence in third grade and aggression in third grade was $r = 0.21$. That correlation was not surprising, since the researchers already knew from several previous studies that TV violence was associated with aggression. There was also a correlation between preference for TV violence in thirteenth grade and aggression in thirteenth grade, but it was only $r = -0.05$ (not significantly different from zero). Because most studies on this topic do show a correlation, Eron and colleagues' zero result was an exception to an otherwise strong empirical pattern (Paik & Comstock, 1994). That is, even when the weight of the evidence shows a strong pattern (such as a relationship between TV preferences and aggression), occasional exceptions can occur, like this one. **Figure 8.1** shows a graphic of how this study was designed, with the two cross-sectional correlations labeled. These first two correlations are simple cross-sectional associations; they could have been obtained from any sample that measured TV violence and aggression at the same time.

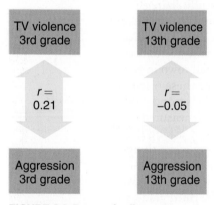

FIGURE 8.1 Eron and colleagues' (1972) longitudinal study design. In this longitudinal study, we would first look at the correlations of the variables when measured at the same time. In third grade, a preference for TV violence is correlated with aggression; in thirteenth grade, these two variables do not appear to be correlated. Notice that the arrows point in both directions, because in these cross-sectional correlations there is no way to know which of the variables came first in time.

Autocorrelations

Eron and colleagues' next step was to evaluate the associations of each variable with itself across time. For example, they asked whether preference for TV violence in third grade is associated with preference for TV violence in thirteenth grade, and whether aggression in third grade is associated with aggression in thirteenth grade. Such correlations are sometimes called **autocorrelations**, because they determine the correlation of one variable with itself, measured on two different occasions. The results in **Figure 8.2** suggest that TV viewing is not stable over time (the correlation is low), but that aggressive habits are stable over time (the correlation is moderate).

Cross-Lag Correlations

So far so good, but these cross-sectional correlations and autocorrelations usually are not the researchers' primary interest. Rather, the researchers usually are most interested in the **cross-lag correlations**, which show whether the earlier measure of one variable is associated with the later measure of the other variable. The two cross-lag correlations thus address the directionality problem and help establish temporal precedence. In Eron and colleagues' study, the cross-lag correlations would show whether TV violence in third grade is correlated with aggression later on, or whether aggression in third grade is correlated with preference for TV violence later on.

By inspecting the cross-lag correlations in a longitudinal design, we can investigate how people change over time—and therefore establish temporal precedence. In this example, only one of the cross-lag correlations is statistically significant. That is, children who prefer more violent TV in third grade are more aggressive in thirteenth grade, but children who are aggressive in third grade do not prefer more violent TV later on. This pattern of results suggests that the preference for TV violence, not the aggression, came first.

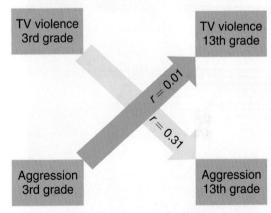

| TV violence 3rd grade | $r = 0.05$ → | TV violence 13th grade |
| Aggression 3rd grade | $r = 0.38$ → | Aggression 13th grade |

FIGURE 8.2 **Autocorrelation in Eron and colleagues' study.** In a longitudinal study, researchers also investigate the autocorrelations. Although TV violence preferences are not stable over time, aggression levels appear to be somewhat stable. Notice that the arrows point in only one direction, because the third-grade measurements came before the thirteenth-grade measurements.

The results of Eron and colleagues' study (1972) were replicated several years later in another sample of 707 families (Johnson, Cohen, Smailes, Kasen, & Brook, 2002). Both studies found similar results: Watching violent TV at younger ages was associated with aggression at older ages, but aggression at younger ages was not as strongly related to watching violent TV at older ages.

Three Possible Patterns from a Cross-Lag Study. In Eron and colleagues' study, the results of the cross-lag correlation could have followed one of three patterns. As depicted in **Figure 8.3**, the study did show that TV at Time 1 predicts aggression at Time 2; such a pattern indicates that TV preferences lead to aggression over time. However, the study could have shown the opposite results—that aggression at Time 1 was correlated with TV preferences at Time 2 but that TV preferences at Time 1 were not correlated with aggression at Time 2. Such a pattern would have indicated that the children's aggressive traits came first, leading to preferences for violent TV later.

Finally, a study might show that *both* correlations are significant—for example, if Eron and colleagues' study had shown both that aggression at Time 1 predicted TV preference at Time 2 *and* that TV preference at Time 1 predicted aggression at Time 2. Occasionally, cross-lag studies on TV and aggression have shown such a pattern, indicating that TV preferences and aggression are mutually reinforcing—that there is a cyclical, reinforcing relationship in which a preference for violent TV leads to aggression and aggression also leads to a preference for violent TV shows (Johnson et al., 2002).

TV violence 3rd grade		TV violence 13th grade
	$r = 0.01$ / $r = 0.31$	
Aggression 3rd grade		Aggression 13th grade

FIGURE 8.3 **Results of Eron and colleagues' cross-lag study.** The cross-lag correlations in this study suggest that TV violence causes aggression, because a preference for TV violence in third grade predicts later aggression, but aggression in third grade does not predict later preferences for TV violence. (In this figure, the arrows point in only one direction, because in each case we know which variable came first in time—third grade comes before thirteenth grade.)

Longitudinal Studies and the Three Rules for Causation

Longitudinal designs can provide some evidence for a causal relationship by means of the three rules for causation:

1. *Covariance*: Significant relationships in longitudinal designs help establish covariance. When two variables are significantly correlated (as in the cross-sectional correlations in Figure 8.1), there is covariance.

2. *Temporal precedence*: A longitudinal design can help researchers make inferences about temporal precedence. By comparing the relative strength of the two cross-lag correlations, the researchers can see which path is stronger. If one of them is stronger (as in the TV/aggression example), the researchers move a little closer to determining which variable comes first, causing the other.

3. *Internal validity*: When conducted simply—that is, by measuring only the four key variables (for example, Time 1 and Time 2 of the two key variables)—longitudinal studies do not help us rule out third variables. For example, Eron's study on TV and aggression cannot clearly rule out the possible third variable of "sensation seeking," a trait that describes people's desire to engage in risky or dangerous activities. Kids who are higher in sensation seeking would probably have preferred violent TV shows as third graders and might also have acted more aggressively in thirteenth grade. The study design that Eron and his colleagues used does not allow us to rule out this possibility.

FIGURE 8.4 Television violence and aggressive behavior. In Eron and colleagues' study, it appeared that gender moderates the association between preference for TV violence and aggressive behavior.

However, careful researchers may be able to design their studies or conduct the subsequent analyses in ways that address some third variables. For example, in the study of TV and aggression, one possible third variable is gender. Boys usually show higher levels of aggression than girls, and boys are more likely to prefer violent TV than girls are. So, like sensation seeking, gender is undoubtedly associated with both variables. However, participant gender does not threaten internal validity here, because, as mentioned above, Eron and his colleagues studied boys and girls separately. They found that a preference for violent TV predicts aggression for boys but not for girls. Girls showed no strong associations between the two variables (see **Figure 8.4**). Therefore, in the case of TV preferences and aggression, gender is a potential third variable. But by studying the longitudinal patterns of boys and girls separately, Eron and his colleagues were able to rule it out. (And in the process, they happened to discover that gender moderated the relationship between TV preferences and aggression.)

Why Not Just Do an Experiment?

Why would Eron and colleagues go to all the trouble of finding the same children after ten years? Why didn't they just do an experiment? After all, an experiment is the best way to confirm or disconfirm causal claims. The problem is that in many cases people cannot be randomly assigned to a variable. One reason is that they cannot be assigned to preferences—people either prefer violent TV shows or they do not, and it is hard to manipulate this variable. A second reason is that it could be unethical to assign some people—especially children—to a condition in which they are forced to watch certain violent television shows for ten years. Similarly, if researchers suspect that smoking causes lung cancer, it would be unethical (and difficult) to assign some people to smoke cigarettes for several years. When an experiment is not practical or ethical, a longitudinal correlational design is a good option.

Nevertheless, researchers in the area of TV and aggression have not relied solely on correlational data. They have developed ethical experiments to study the TV/aggression relationship in both adults and children, at least over a short-term study. By randomly assigning children and adults to watch violent or nonviolent shows and then measuring their aggressive responses, researchers have produced some solid evidence that watching violent media does, in fact, cause aggression (Bushman & Anderson, 2001). Because the ethicality of assigning children to watch violent videos is questionable, these studies had to pass strict ethical standards before they were conducted, and the exposure was short term (about one hour or less of violent media exposure, followed by a test of aggression). It would be much more challenging to do an ethical experimental study of the effects of long-term exposure to violent media, though, so longitudinal correlational designs become an attractive alternative.

Check Your Understanding

1. Why is a longitudinal design called a multivariate design?
2. What three kinds of correlations are obtained from a longitudinal design?
3. Describe which patterns of temporal precedence are indicated by different cross-lag correlational results.

1. See p. 211. 2. See p. 212. 3. See p. 213.

Ruling Out Third Variables with Multiple-Regression Designs

A study published this month in the journal *Pediatrics* studied the links between recess and classroom behavior among about 11,000 children age 8 and 9. Those who had more than 15 minutes of recess a day showed better behavior in class than those who had little or none. (Pope, 2009)

The newspaper article quoted here, on recess and children's behavior, reports a simple association between amount of recess and behavior in class. But is there a causal link? Does the recess *cause* the good behavior? Certainly there is covariance: More recess is associated with fewer behavior problems. What about temporal precedence? Did recess come before the behavior, or did the behavior come before the recess? This study is not a longitudinal design, so we do not know whether the recess policy came before the good behavior or whether the good behavior led to the recess policy. You might reason that a classroom of badly behaved children might be punished by being denied recess. In many schools, however, the recess structure was probably in place already, before any good or bad behavior was observed.

What about internal validity? Several third variables could explain the recess/behavior relationship. Perhaps recess and behavior problems are correlated because of school type—public versus private. That is, perhaps private schools both have better-behaved students and have more flexibility to offer recess. Or perhaps class size is a third variable: Children may be better behaved in smaller classes, and smaller classes may be more likely to have recess. Or perhaps income is a third variable: Children from disadvantaged groups may have more behavior problems, and they also go to schools that do not have the resources or time for a long recess.

So how do we know whether one of these variables—or another one—is the true explanation for the association? The study in question used a statistical technique called **multiple regression**, which can help rule out third variables. Multiple regression can address questions of internal validity.

Correlational Studies and the Third-Variable Problem

To obtain the important correlation in the recess study, the researchers measured a sample of classrooms on the two key variables: how much recess time the class had daily (they asked the teacher how many minutes of recess the students got each day) and the level of behavior problems in the class (they used a standardized measure of classroom behavior, in which each teacher rated how well-behaved his or her students were). These two variables were negatively correlated (as time for recess increased, behavior problems decreased), as **Figure 8.5** shows.

If the researchers had stopped there and measured only these two variables, they would have conducted a bivariate correlational study. However, besides measuring length of recess and level of behavior problems, the researchers also measured several other variables. For instance, they measured the proportion of children in each classroom who were eligible for free lunch—a signal of how economically disadvantaged the children were. They measured whether the classroom was public or private, the number of students in each classroom, and so on. By measuring all these variables (with the goal of testing the interrelationships among them all), they conducted a multivariate (more than two variables) correlational study.

Introduction to Statistical Control of Third Variables

By conducting a multivariate design, researchers are able to evaluate whether a relationship between two key variables still holds when they **control for** another variable. To understand what "controlling for" means, let's focus on only

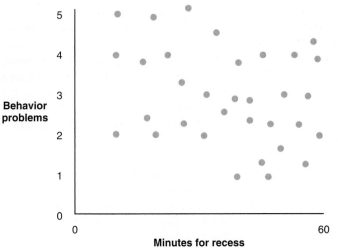

FIGURE 8.5 **Scatterplot of recess and behavior problems.** Because of the way this study was conducted, each dot here represents a classroom rather than a person. In this case, we would say that the classroom is the unit of analysis—meaning that each classroom was measured on the number of behavior problems and the minutes of recess the students were allowed per day. (Data are fabricated for the purpose of illustration.)

one potential third variable—the measure of how economically disadvantaged the children were. Perhaps recess and behavior problems are correlated only because poorer children both are more likely to have behavior problems and are more likely to be in schools that have less time for recess. If this is the case, all three variables are correlated with one another—recess and behavior are correlated, as we knew, but recess and income are also correlated with each other, and income and behavior are correlated, too. The researchers want to know whether economic disadvantage, as a third variable correlated with both recess and behavior, can account for the relationship between recess and behavior problems. To answer the question, they will see what happens to the relationship between recess and behavior when they *control for* income.

The most statistically accurate way to describe the phrase *control for income* is to talk about proportions of variability. Researchers are asking whether, after they take the relationship between income and behavior into account, there is still a portion of variability in classroom behavior that is attributable to recess. But this is extremely abstract language. The meaning is a bit like asking about the overall movement (the variance) of your wiggling, happy dog when you return home. You can ask, "What portion of the variability in my dog's overall movement is attributable to his tail moving? To his shoulders moving? To his back legs moving?" You can ask, "Will the dog still be moving when he greets me, even if I were to hold his tail constant—hold it still?"

An easier way to understand the phrase "controlling for" is to recognize that testing a third variable with multiple regression is similar to identifying subgroups (see Chapter 7). We can think of the process of controlling for income like this: We start by looking only at the highest level of income and see whether recess and behavior are still correlated. Then we move to next highest level of income, then the next highest, and so on, until we have analyzed the relationship at the lowest level of income. We ask whether the bivariate relationship still holds at each level of income.

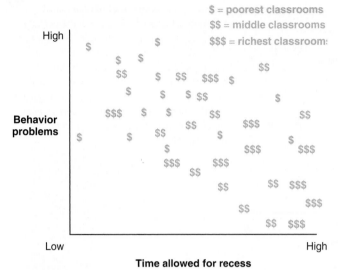

$ = poorest classrooms
$$ = middle classrooms
$$$ = richest classrooms

High

Behavior problems

Low

Time allowed for recess

High

FIGURE 8.6 The association between recess and behavior problems, accounting for family income. In this example, the overall relationship is negative, and this negative relationship holds even when you look only at the poorest classrooms, the middle-income classrooms, or the richest classrooms.

For example, in the scatterplot in **Figure 8.6**, the overall relationship is negative—the more time for recess, the fewer behavior problems. In addition, the classrooms with the poorest children (the $ symbols) have, overall, more behavior problems and shorter recess. The classrooms with the wealthiest children (the $$$ symbols) have, overall, fewer behavior problems and longer recess. But if we look *only* at the poorer classrooms, or *only* at the middle-income classrooms, or *only* at the wealthier classrooms, we still find the key relationship between behavior problems and recess: It is still negative even within these income subgroups. Therefore, the relationship is still there, even when we control for income.

In contrast, in **Figure 8.7**, the *overall* relationship is still negative, just as before—the more time for recess, the fewer behavior problems. In addition, just as before, the classrooms with the poorest children (the $ symbols) have, overall, more behavior problems and shorter recess, and the classrooms with the wealthiest children (the $$$ symbols) have, overall, fewer behavior problems and longer recess. However, this time, when we look *only* at the children from poorer classrooms or *only* at the children from the wealthier classrooms, the relationship between behavior problems and recess (the key relationship) is absent. The scatterplots *within* the individual income groups do not show the relationship anymore. Therefore, the relationship between recess and behavior goes away when we control for income. In this case, income was, indeed, the third variable that was responsible for the relationship.

FIGURE 8.7

Family income as a third variable in the association between recess and behavior problems. In this example, the overall relationship is negative, but when you look *only* at the poorest classrooms, the middle-income classrooms, or the richest classrooms, there is no relationship between the two variables.

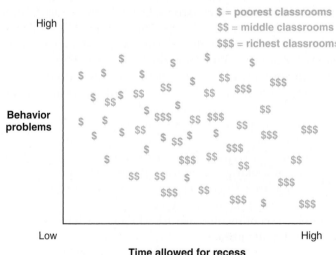

$ = poorest classrooms
$$ = middle classrooms
$$$ = richest classrooms

High

Behavior problems

Low

Time allowed for recess

High

Multiple Regression Helps with the Third-Variable Problem

Which one of the two scatterplots, Figure 8.6 or 8.7, best describes the relationship between recess and behavior? Multiple regression can tell us. When researchers use regression, they are testing whether some key relationship holds true even when a suspected third variable is statistically controlled for.

You are most likely to work with the end result of this process, when you encounter regression results in tables of empirical journal articles. Imagine you are reading a journal article and you come across **Table 8.1**, which shows what the

TABLE 8.1 Sample Multiple Regression Results for the Study Predicting Behavior Problems from School Recess and Poverty		
Dependent variable: behavior problems in a classroom	Beta	Sig
Predictor variables (independent variables)		
Number of minutes of recess for the classroom	−0.05	**
Proportion of students in the classroom eligible for free lunch	0.10	**

** $p < 0.001$

Note: These data are based on what the results in Barros and colleagues (2009) might have shown if the researchers had used only two predictor variables.

regression results would look like for the recess/behavior example. What do these numbers mean? What steps did the researchers follow to come up with them?

Dependent Variables and Predictor Variables

When researchers use multiple regression, they are studying three or more variables, so their first step is to choose a *dependent variable* (sometimes referred to as the **criterion variable**)—the variable they are most interested in understanding or predicting. In the case of recess and behavior problems, the researchers decided they were most interested in understanding behavior problems, so they chose that as their dependent variable. The dependent variable is almost always specified either in the top row or in the title of a regression table.

The rest of the variables measured in a regression analysis are called **predictor variables** (sometimes referred to as *independent variables*). For instance, in the recess study, the predictor variables are the amount of recess each classroom had and the proportion of students eligible for free lunch. In Table 8.1, the two predictor variables are listed below the dependent variable.

Use of Beta to Test for Third Variables

The point of the multiple regression illustrated in Table 8.1 is to see whether the relationship between recess and behavior problems might be explained by a third variable—economic disadvantage (measured by free lunch eligibility). Does the relationship between recess and behavior problems remain, even within each level of income (as in Figure 8.6)? Or does the relationship between recess and behavior problems go away within different levels of income (as in Figure 8.7)? The betas in Table 8.1 help answer this central question.

Beta Basics. When you see a regression table like Table 8.1, you will often see a column labeled *beta*, β, or even *standardized beta*. There will be one beta value for each predictor variable. Beta is similar to r, but it reveals more than r does. A positive beta, like a positive r, indicates a positive relationship between that predictor variable and the dependent variable, when the other predictor variables are statistically controlled for. A negative beta, like a negative r, indicates a negative relationship between two variables (when the other predictors are controlled for). A beta that is zero, or not significantly different from zero, means that there is no relationship (when the other predictors are controlled for). Therefore, betas are similar to correlations in that they denote direction and strength of some relationship. The higher beta is, the stronger the relationship is between that predictor variable and the dependent variable. The smaller beta is, the weaker the relationship is. Within a single regression table, you can usually compare predictor variables that show larger betas to predictor variables with smaller betas—the larger the beta, the stronger the relationship. (However, it is not appropriate to compare the strengths of betas from one regression table to the strengths of betas from some other regression table.)

Unlike r, however, there are no quick guidelines for beta to indicate effect sizes that are weak, moderate, or strong. That's because betas change, depending on what other predictor variables are being used—being controlled for—in the regression.

Finally, sometimes a table will present the symbol b instead of beta. The coefficient b is also called an unstandardized coefficient. A b is similar to beta in that the sign of b—positive or negative—still denotes a positive or negative association (when the other predictors are controlled for). But unlike two betas, you cannot compare two b values within the same table to each other. The reason is that b values are computed from the original measurements of the predictor variables (such as dollars, centimeters, percentages, or inches), whereas betas are computed from predictor variables that have been changed to standardized units. A predictor variable that shows a large b may not actually denote a stronger relationship to the dependent variable than a predictor variable with a smaller b.

Interpretation of Beta. In Table 8.1, notice that the predictor variable "number of minutes for recess" has a beta of -0.05. This negative beta, just like a negative r, means that as recess minutes go up, behavior problems go down. But it also means that as minutes for recess go up, behavior problems go down, even while we statistically control for the other predictor variable in this table—the free lunch variable. In other words, it means that even when we hold the free lunch variable constant statistically, the relationship between recess and behavior problems is still there. This result is consistent with the relationship depicted in Figure 8.6, not the one in Figure 8.7.

The other beta in this table—the one associated with the school lunch predictor variable—is positive. This beta means that as the proportion of students on free lunch goes up, the behavior problems go up, too, *when the number of minutes of recess is controlled for*. In other words, it means that when we hold the number of minutes of recess constant, poverty levels predict behavior problems, too. In summary, the beta that is associated with a predictor variable represents the relationship between that predictor variable and the dependent variable, when the other predictor variables in the table are controlled for.

TABLE 8.2 Different Ways to Describe the Significant Beta of −0.05 in Table 8.1

Each of these sentences is an appropriate description of the relationship.

The relationship between recess and behavior problems is negative (as recess minutes go up, behavior problems go down), even when the proportion of students eligible for school lunch **is controlled for**.

The relationship between recess and behavior problems is negative (as recess minutes go up, behavior problems go down), **independent of** the proportion of students eligible for school lunch.

The relationship between recess and behavior problems is negative (as recess minutes go up, behavior problems go down), even when the proportion of students eligible for school lunch **is held constant**.

The relationship between recess and behavior problems is negative (as recess minutes go up, behavior problems go down), and is **not attributable to the third variable of poverty**, because it holds even when the proportion of students eligible for school lunch is held constant.

Statistical Significance of Beta. The regression tables in empirical journal articles often have a column labeled *sig* or *p*, or they may have footnotes, marked with asterisks, giving the *p* value for each beta. Whether in a column or in footnotes, these data indicate whether each beta is statistically significantly different from zero. As discussed in Chapter 7 (see also Appendix B), the *p* value gives the probability that the beta came from a population in which the relationship is zero. When *p* is less than 0.05, the beta (that is, the relationship between that predictor variable and the dependent variable, when the other predictor variables are controlled for) is considered statistically significant. When *p* is greater than 0.05, the beta is considered not significant, meaning that we cannot conclude that beta is different from zero.

In Table 8.1, both of the betas reported are statistically significant, so we can interpret them as describing true, replicable relationships. **Table 8.2** shows several appropriate ways to explain what these significant betas mean.

What If Beta Is Not Significant? The original study by Barros, Silver, and Stein (2009) found that the relationship between recess and behavior problems is not explained by the third variable of poverty. The regression analysis showed that the beta for this relationship was still significant when the proportion of students in the classroom eligible for free lunch was held constant statistically. The relationship Barros and colleagues found is similar to the one shown in Figure 8.6. But imagine that the results were different, as shown in **Table 8.3**. What would this pattern of results have meant?

TABLE 8.3 Fabricated Multiple-Regression Results for a Study Predicting Behavior Problems from Recess and Poverty

Dependent variable: behavior problems in a classroom	Beta	Sig
Predictor variables		
Number of minutes of recess for the classroom	−0.01	n.s.
Proportion of students in classroom eligible for free lunch	0.09	**

** $p < 0.001$

Note: These data were fabricated and do not follow the true pattern reported by Barros and colleagues (2009).

Notice that in this new pattern of results (which are fabricated—the real data did not look like this), the beta for the recess predictor variable is no longer significant. This result means that recess is not significantly associated with behavior problems in a classroom when the proportion of students eligible for free lunch is controlled for. In other words, although recess and behavior problems seemed significantly related in their bivariate relationship, that relationship goes away when the potential third variable, free lunch, is controlled for. Indeed, the results would mean that the situation is like the one shown in Figure 8.7, rather than the one in Figure 8.6. When you look at the different income groups separately, there is no relationship between recess and behavior problems.

Adding More Predictors to a Regression

Up to now, we have focused on only one third variable—socioeconomic status. But remember that there are many other potential third variables for the recess/behavior relationship. What about class size? What about private versus public schools? In fact, Barros and colleagues measured each of those third variables and even added a few more—such as the proportion of boys in the classroom and the proportion of students in each classroom reading above grade level. **Table 8.4** shows every variable that Barros and her colleagues tested—as well as the multiple regression results for all of these other variables.

Even when there are so many more predictor variables in the table, beta still means the same thing. The beta for the recess variable is negative: The more time for recess, the fewer behavior problems, when the researchers controlled for

TABLE 8.4 Multiple-Regression Results for the Study Predicting Behavior Problems from Recess and Other Variables

Dependent variable: behavior problems in a classroom	Beta	Sig
Predictor variables		
Availability of recess for the classroom	−0.042	**
Proportion of students in classroom eligible for free lunch	0.097	**
Proportion of boys in class	0.154	**
Proportion of students above grade in math	−0.108	**
Proportion of students above grade in reading	−0.045	**
Number of students in the class	0.062	**
Proportion of minorities in class	0.091	**
Parental education	−0.031	**
Private school[a]	0.041	**

** $p \leq 0.001$

[a]Private school is coded so that a higher value means private school. *Source*: Data from Barros and colleagues (2009).

all of the other predictors (the proportion of the class receiving free lunch, the proportion of boys, the proportion of students reading above grade level, and so on). Even after controlling for all of the variables listed in Table 8.4, Barros and colleagues found that recess predicts fewer behavior problems.

Adding several predictors to a regression analysis can help answer two kinds of questions. First, it helps control for several "third" variables at the same time. Indeed, in Barros and colleagues' study, even after all of the other variables were controlled for, recess still predicted fewer behavior problems. A result like that gets the researchers closer to making a causal statement, because the relationship between the suspected cause (recess) and the suspected effect (behavior problems) does not appear to be attributable to any of the other variables that were measured.

Second, by looking at the betas for all of the other predictor variables, we can get a sense of which factors most strongly affect classroom behavior problems. One strong predictor is the proportion of boys in the classroom. The more boys, the more behavior problems, even when availability of recess, free lunch, reading level, and every other variable in the table is controlled for. In fact, we know that the effect of boys is *larger* than the effect for recess, because the beta for the "boys" predictor is larger than the beta for the "recess" predictor. Even though the authors of this study were most interested in describing the benefits of recess, they were also able to evaluate which other variables are important in predicting behavior problems. (Recall, however, that when a table presents *b* values, or unstandardized coefficients, it is not appropriate to compare their *relative* strength. We can only do so with beta, and even then, remember that betas change depending on what other predictor variables are used.)

Regression in Popular Press Articles

When you encounter association claims in popular press sources, such as magazines, newspapers, or websites, the journalists will rarely discuss betas, *p* values, or predictor variables. After all, journalists write for a general audience, so they assume that most of their readers will not be familiar with these concepts. However, if you read carefully, you can detect the telltale signs that a multiple regression has been used. For example, you should keep an eye out for the following terminology.

"Controlled for"

When the recess/behavior study was reported in an online newspaper, the journalist mentioned the simple relationship between recess and behavior, and then wrote:

> Although disadvantaged children were more likely to be denied recess, the association between better behavior and recess time held up *even after researchers controlled for a number of variables*, including sex, ethnicity, public or private school and class size. (Pope, 2009; emphasis added)

The term *controlled for* is a clue that the study used multiple regression. (In an empirical article, the things that the study controlled for would be listed as the predictor variables.)

"Taking into Account"

Here is another example from a popular press story about a study of veterans with the headline, "Perk of a Good Job: Aging Mind Is Sharp":

> Mentally demanding jobs come with a hidden benefit: less mental decline with age. Work that requires decision making, negotiating with others, analysis, and making judgments may not necessarily pad your bank account. But it does build up your "cognitive reserve"—a level of mental function that helps you avoid or compensate for age-related mental decline. (DeNoon, 2008)

In this story, the central association is between how mentally demanding a man's job is and his cognitive functioning as he ages. The more demanding the job, the less cognitive decline he suffers. But could there be a third variable, such as intelligence or level of education? Perhaps the veterans in the study who were better educated were more likely both to have a cognitively demanding job and to suffer less cognitive decline. However, the story goes on to say,

> *After taking into account both intelligence and education,* Potter and colleagues found that men with more complex jobs—in terms of general intellectual demands and human interaction and communication—performed significantly better on tests of mental function. (DeNoon, 2008; emphasis added)

The phrase *taking into account* means that the researchers conducted regression analyses. When they controlled for education and intelligence, they still found a relationship between job complexity and cognitive decline.

"Correcting for"

The following excerpt is from a story reporting an association between birth order and IQ. The study found that firstborn children are smarter than later-born siblings:

> In the study, Norwegian epidemiologists analyzed data on birth order, health status and IQ scores of 241,310 18- and 19-year-old men born from 1967 to 1976, using military records. *After correcting for factors that may affect scores,* including parents' education level, maternal age at birth and family size, the researchers found that eldest children scored an average of 103.2, about 3 percent higher than second children (100.3) and 4 percent higher than thirdborns (99.0). (Carey, 2007; emphasis added)

Again, the phrase *after correcting for* indicates that the researchers used multiple regression.

You might also come across other terminology, such as "this relationship was above and beyond the effect of . . ." or "holding [some variable] constant." Being able to recognize these key phrases will help you interrogate the association claims you read about in popular sources. When you encounter an association claim, one of your questions should be whether the researchers controlled for possible third variables. If you cannot tell from the news story what the researchers controlled for, then it is reasonable to suspect that some third variables may be responsible for the association.

Regression Does Not Establish Causation

Multiple regression might seem to be a foolproof way to rule out all kinds of third variables. If you look at the recess and behavior problems data in Table 8.4, for example, you might think you can safely make a causal statement now, since the researchers controlled for so many third variables. They seem to have thought of everything! However, there are still two problems with concluding that longer recess causes children to behave better. One is that even though multivariate designs analyzed with regression statistics can control for third variables, they cannot establish temporal precedence. Recess could cause behavior problems to decline, but it is still possible that the behavior problems in certain classrooms came first and caused teachers to restrict their classes' recess times.

The second problem is that researchers cannot control for variables that they do not measure. Even though multiple regression controls for any third variables that the researchers measure in the study, there could be an important third variable—one that they did not consider—that accounts for the relationship. In the recess example, some unmeasured variable—maybe the number of windows in the classroom, the teacher's level of experience, the quality of the food in the school—is really accounting for the relationship between recess and behavior. But since those variables were not measured (or even considered), we have no way of knowing (see **Figure 8.8**).

This unknown third-variable problem is one reason that a well-run experimental study is ultimately more convincing than a correlational study. An experimental study on recess, for example, would randomly assign a large sample of classrooms to a "recess condition" and a "no recess condition." The power

FIGURE 8.8 Possible third variables in the association between recess and behavior. What possible third variables might explain why classrooms with more time for recess have fewer behavior problems?

of random assignment would make the two groups likely to be equal on any possible third variable—even the third variables the researchers did not happen to measure. The classrooms with the smartest students would be divided at random between the two experimental groups. The classrooms with the most experienced teachers and the fewest boys would also be divided at random between the two experimental groups. A randomized experiment is still the gold standard for determining causation. Multiple regression, in contrast, allows researchers to control for potential third variables, but only for the variables that the researchers choose to measure.

Getting at Causality with Pattern and Parsimony

So far this chapter has focused on two techniques that help researchers investigate causation, even when they are working with correlations among measured variables. Longitudinal correlational designs help meet the temporal precedence rule. Multiple-regression designs help meet the internal validity rule by statistically controlling for potential third variables.

This section explores how researchers can investigate causality by using a variety of correlational studies that all point in a single, causal direction. This approach might be called "pattern and parsimony" because there is a pattern of results that is best explained by a parsimonious causal explanation. *Parsimony*, as discussed in Chapter 1, means the simplest explanation of a pattern of data—the best explanation that requires making the fewest exceptions or qualifications.

The Power of Pattern and Parsimony

A great example of pattern and parsimony is the case of smoking and lung cancer. (The example was first articulated by methodologist Robert Abelson [1995]). Decades ago, it started becoming clear that smokers had higher rates of lung cancer than nonsmokers (the correlation has been estimated at about $r = 0.4$). But did the smoking *cause* the cancer? Cigarette manufacturers certainly did not want people to think so. If somebody were to argue that this correlation was causal, a critic might counter that the cigarettes were not the cause; perhaps people who smoked generally had more nervous tension, which predisposed them to lung cancer. Or perhaps smokers also drank a lot of coffee, and it was the coffee, not the cigarettes, that caused cancer. The list of third-variable explanations could go and on—and even though regression designs could control for these third variables, critics could always argue that regression cannot control for every possible third variable.

Another problem, of course, is that even though an experiment could rule out these third-variable explanations, a smoking experiment would not be ethical or practical. A researcher could not reasonably assign a sample of volunteers to become lifetime smokers or nonsmokers. The only data that researchers had to work with were correlational.

Abelson explains that the way out of such a conundrum is to specify a mechanism for the causal path. Specifically, in the case of cigarettes, researchers proposed that cigarette smoke contains chemicals that are toxic when they come into contact with human tissue. The more contact human tissue has with these chemicals, the more toxicity people are exposed to. This simple theory leads to a set of predictions, all of which could be explained by the single, parsimonious theory that chemicals in cigarettes cause cancer (Abelson, 1995, p. 184):

1. The longer a person has smoked cigarettes, the greater his or her chances of getting cancer.
2. People who stop smoking have lower cancer rates than people who keep smoking.
3. Smokers' cancers tend to be in the lungs and of a particular type.
4. Smokers who use filtered cigarettes have a somewhat lower rate of cancer than those who use unfiltered cigarettes.
5. People who live with smokers would have higher rates of cancer, too, because of their passive exposure to the same chemicals.

Incidentally, this process exemplifies the theory-data cycle explained in Chapter 1. A theory—cigarette toxicity—led to a particular set of research questions. The theory also led researchers to frame hypotheses about what the data should show.

Indeed, converging evidence from several individual studies, conducted by medical researchers, has supported each of these separate predictions (their evidence became part of the U.S. Surgeon General's warning in 1964), and that's where parsimony comes in. Because all five of these diverse predictions are tied back to one central principle (the toxicity of the chemicals in cigarette smoke), there is a strong case for parsimony (see **Figure 8.9**).

FIGURE 8.9 Pattern and parsimony. A variety of studies, using a variety of methods, provide converging evidence to support the argument that cigarettes contain toxic chemicals that are harmful to humans.

For a discussion of the weight of the evidence, see Chapter 1, p. 13.

Notice, also, that the diversity of these five empirical findings makes it much harder to raise third-variable explanations. Suppose a critic argued that coffee drinking was a third variable. Coffee drinking could certainly explain the first result (the longer one smokes—and presumably drinks coffee, too—the higher the rates of cancer). But it cannot explain the effect of filtered cigarettes or the cancer rates among secondhand smokers. The most parsimonious explanation of this entire pattern of data—and the weight of the evidence—is the toxicity of cigarettes.

It is hard to overstate the strength of the pattern and parsimony technique. In psychology, researchers commonly use a variety of methodologies and a variety of studies as they explore the strength and limits of some research question. The TV and violence connection is another good example of how a single, parsimonious causal statement (violence on TV leads to violent behavior) explains a wide body of evidence (Anderson et al., 2003).

Many psychologists build their careers by doing study after study devoted to one research question. They use a variety of methods, combining results to develop their causal theories and support them with converging evidence.

Pattern, Parsimony, and the Popular Press

When journalists write about science, they do not always fairly represent pattern and parsimony in research. Instead, they may report only the results of the latest study. For example, they might present a news story on the latest nutrition research—without describing the other studies done in that area. They might report that children with ADHD are more likely to be bullies—but fail to cover the full pattern of studies on bullying. They might report on a single study that showed an association between red wine and cardiovascular health—without mentioning the rest of the studies on that same topic, and without tying the results to the theory they are supporting. When journalists report only one study at a time, they selectively present only a part of the scientific process. They might not describe the context of the research, such as what previous studies have revealed, or what theory the study was testing. Reporting on the latest study, without giving the full context, can make it seem as though scientists conduct single, unconnected studies on a whim. It might even give the impression that a single study can reverse decades of previous research. In addition, skeptics who read such science stories might find it easy to deride the results of a single, correlational study. But in fact, science accumulates incrementally. Ideally, journalists should report on the entire body of evidence, as well as the theoretical background, for a particular claim.

Check Your Understanding

1. Why do many researchers find pattern and parsimony an effective way to support a causal claim?

1. See pp. 226–227.

Mediation

So far, we have discussed the research designs and statistical tools that researchers use to get closer to making causal statements. But once a causal relationship between two variables has been proposed, we often want to explore it further, by thinking about *why*. For example, we might ask *why* recess apparently leads to a drop in behavior problems. Many times, these explanations about the reasons behind a causal relationship involve a **mediating variable**, or *mediator*. That is, researchers propose a mediating step between two of the variables (the root of the word *mediate* means "middle"). A study does not have to be correlational to include a mediator—even experimental studies can test them. But mediation analyses often rely on multivariate tools such as regression analyses.

Here's an example: We know that conscientious people live longer than less conscientious people. But why? The mediator of this relationship might be that conscientious people engage in more healthy behaviors—that is why they live longer. Engaging in healthy behaviors would then be the mediator of the relationship between the trait, conscientiousness, and the outcome, a long life (Bogg & Roberts, 2004). Similarly, we know that there is an association between recess and behavior problems, as shown in Figure 8.5. Researchers might next propose a reason for the association; that is, they may propose a mediator of this relationship. One likely mediator could be physical activity—recess gives children a chance for physical activity, and the more tired they get from the physical activity, the fewer behavior problems they show. The researchers could draw this mediation hypothesis as shown in **Figure 8.10**. That is, they would propose that there is an overall relationship, *c*, between recess and behavior problems. But this overall relationship exists only because there are two other relationships—*a* (between recess and physical activity) and *b* (between physical activity and behavior problems). In other words, physical activity mediates the relationship between recess and behavior problems. (Of course, there are other possible mediators, such as exposure to fresh air or experience in natural settings. Those mediators could be tested, too, in another study.)

The researchers could test this mediation hypothesis by conducting four tests (Kenny, 2008):

1. Test for relationship *c*. Is recess associated with behavior problems? (If it is not, there is no relationship to mediate.)

2. Test for relationship *a*. Is recess associated with the proposed mediator, physical activity? Do children who have recess engage in more physical activity than children who do not? (If physical activity is the aspect of recess that explains why recess

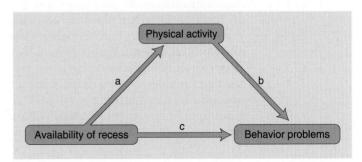

FIGURE 8.10 **Testing for a mediating variable.** More recess might lead to more physical activity, which leads to fewer behavior problems.

leads to fewer behavior problems, then logically, classes that have more recess must also show higher levels of physical activity.)

3. Test for relationship *b*. Do children who engage in more physical activity have fewer behavior problems? (Again, if physical activity explains behavior problems, then logically, classes with more physical activity must also have lower levels of behavior problems.)

4. Finally, run a regression test, using both physical activity and recess as predictor variables to predict behavior problems, to see whether relationship *c* goes away. (If physical activity is the mediator of relationship *c*, the relationship between recess and behavior problems should drop when physical activity is controlled for. Here we would be using regression to show that recess was associated with classroom behavior in the first place only because physical activity was responsible.)

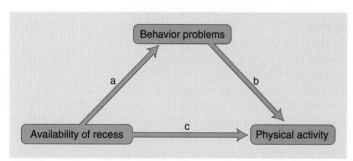

FIGURE 8.11 Reverse-mediation model. Mediation tests often involve testing the opposite pattern as well and comparing how well each pattern fits the data. Is it likely that behavior problems could moderate an association between recess and physical activity?

If all four of these conditions are met, the data would be consistent with the proposed mediation model.

In addition, to be sure that their own model is the best one, most researchers would also test the reverse model, such as the one in **Figure 8.11**, even if they do not believe that this reverse model explains the relationship. Using special statistics (such as a technique called structural equation modeling), researchers can compare the two mediational models—the one they prefer and its opposite—to see which model fits the data best. If you encounter such terms as you read journal articles, remember that these complex analyses are simply one more technique that researchers use to try to infer causation from their data.

Mediators Versus Third Variables

Mediators are similar to third-variable explanations. Both involve multivariate research designs, and researchers can use the same statistical tool (multiple regression) to detect both mediators and third variables. However, mediators and third variables function differently with respect to some bivariate correlation. In a third-variable explanation, the proposed third variable is external to the two variables in the original bivariate relationship—it might even be seen as a problematic "lurking variable" that potentially distracts from the relationship of interest. For example, if economic disadvantage is a third variable that is responsible for the recess/behavior relationship, recess and behavior are correlated with each other only because they are each correlated separately with economic disadvantage, as shown in **Figure 8.12**. In other words, the relationship between recess and behavior is there only because both of those variables happen to vary with the external third variable, economic disadvantage. The third variable may seem like a nuisance—it may not be of central interest to the researchers. (For example, if the researchers are really interested in recess and behavior, they have to control for income before they can study this relationship.)

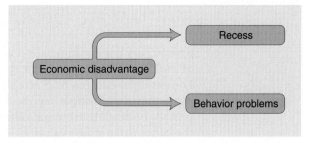

FIGURE 8.12 A third variable. In a third-variable scenario, the third variable is seen as external to the original two variables. Here, economic disadvantage might lead to both less than for recess and more behavior problems.

In contrast, when researchers propose a mediator, they are interested in isolating which aspect of the causal variable is responsible for that relationship. A mediator variable is *internal* to the causal variable and often of direct interest to the researchers, rather than a nuisance. In the recess example, the researchers believed that that physical activity was the important aspect of recess, the one responsible for reducing behavior problems.

Mediators Versus Moderators

How is mediation different from moderation, introduced in Chapter 7? The similar-sounding names of these two research questions can make them confusing at first (Baron & Kenny, 1986). However, testing for mediation versus moderation involves asking different questions. When researchers test for mediating variables, they ask, "Why are these two variables linked?" When they test for moderating variables, they ask, "Are these two variables linked the same way for everyone, or in every situation?" For example, a mediation hypothesis could propose that healthy behaviors are the reason that conscientiousness is related to longevity. In contrast, a moderation hypothesis could propose that the link between conscientiousness and longevity is strongest among wealthy people (because they can afford quality health care and can choose to use or not use these services) and weakest among poorer people (because they have less access to health care overall).

Check Your Understanding

1. Explain why each of the four steps in a mediation test is important to establishing evidence for a mediator.

1. See pp. 229–230.

Multivariate Designs and the Four Validities

Researchers use multivariate designs, such as longitudinal correlation studies or multiple regression, so that they can get closer to making causal statements. Longitudinal designs help establish temporal precedence, and multivariate designs that use multiple regression help rule out third variables and therefore provide evidence for internal validity. But remember that you should interrogate the other three major validities—construct, external, and statistical conclusion validity—as well.

For any multivariate design, as for any bivariate design, it is appropriate to interrogate the *construct validity* of the variables in the study, by asking how well each variable was measured. In Eron and colleagues' television/aggression study, what do you think of the measure of TV viewing? Is asking children or their parents what TV shows they like to watch a reliable and valid way to measure their preference for media violence? What do you think of the measure of aggression? Is asking peers a reliable and valid way to measure a child's levels of aggression? Similarly, in Barros and colleagues' study, what do you think of the measures of recess and classroom behavior problems? Is it reliable and valid to ask teachers to rate their own students' behavior problems? Why or why not?

You can also interrogate the *external validity* of a multivariate design. In Eron and colleagues' TV and aggression study, the researchers studied every third grader in a single small town in New York. Because they used a census, not a sample, it is irrelevant to ask whether the sample was random. However, it might be appropriate to question whether the results of Eron's study would generalize to urban children, to children from different regions of the United States, or to children from different countries. You might also wonder if the link generalizes to other kinds of media, such as video games. Remember, however, that even when associations are established in a restricted sample, those associations might very well still generalize to other groups or to other media.

To interrogate the external validity of the recess and school behavior study, you would ask whether the classrooms were sampled randomly, and from what kind of population. But even before you ask about sampling, recall that the researchers measured each classroom's poverty level, proportion of boys, private versus public status, and proportion of minorities. These controls give you confidence that the sample of classrooms in the study did in fact represent a variety of class types.

Finally, you can interrogate a multivariate study's *statistical validity*. Some of the statistical validity issues discussed in Chapter 7 may be applied here. You can ask about the effect size and statistical significance. Take, for instance, the effect of recess on classroom behavior. We know that the beta was statistically significant, so we know that the result would probably be replicated in a future study. However, compared with the other predictors, the effect size was smaller—beta was just -0.04 (see Table 8.4). Although there are no guidelines for what constitutes a "small" beta, we can compare it with other betas in the regression,

TABLE 5 Bivariate Comparison of TRCB Scores According to Level of Exposure to Recess

Level of Exposure	*N*	TRCB Score, Mean ± SD (95% Confidence Interval)
None/minimal break	3369	3.44 ± 0.900(3.41–3.47)
Little recess[a]	595	3.62 ± 0.811(3.55–3.68)
More recess[a]	2132	3.57 ± 0.900(3.53–3.60)
A lot of recess[a]	2299	3.61 ± 0.829(3.58–3.64)
Minimal recess/lunch[a]	3027	3.60 ± 0.845(3.57–3.63)
Recess/lunch of >30 min[a]	107	3.74 ± 0.925(3.56–3.92)

[a] $P < .001$ for none/minimal break versus all other groups.

FIGURE 8.13 Statistical validity in Barros and colleagues' (2009) study. To illustrate the magnitude of the effect of recess on behavior, Barros and colleagues indicated exactly what the behavior rating was at each level of the recess variable. Do you think the impact of recess is strong or weak? TRCB = Teachers Rating of Classroom Behavior, ranging from 1 (*misbehaves very frequently and almost always difficult to handle*) to 5 (*behaves exceptionally well*). A confidence interval is a statistical estimate of where the means would probably lie if the study were run again many times.

noting, for example, that the effect of the proportion of boys on a classroom's behavior problems was larger: beta = 0.154. But even though the beta is small, the importance of a small effect size depends on the researchers' perspective. On the one hand, it is both interesting and important that recess is significantly associated with better classroom behavior, even after a large number of third variables are controlled for. On the other hand, the effect of recess is small, so in practical terms, providing longer recess may amount to only a small decrease in classroom behavior problems. The authors of the paper presented a helpful table, presented here as **Figure 8.13**, of the true level of classroom behavior at each level of the recess variable. See for yourself: Do you think that the effect of recess on behavior is strong? Is it important?

Other statistical validity questions apply to multivariate designs, too. When researchers use multivariate designs, they need to take precautions to look for subgroups, outliers, and curvilinear relationships, all of which can be more complicated to detect when there are more than two variables.

Check Your Understanding

1. Give an example of a question you would ask to interrogate each of the four validities for a multivariate study.

1. See pp. 232–233.

Summary

Research often begins with a simple bivariate relationship, such as the relationship between recess and behavior, TV violence and aggression, or smoking and lung cancer. A simple, bivariate correlation indicates that there is covariance, but it does not indicate temporal precedence or internal validity, so it cannot establish causation. But researchers have developed certain techniques that help them get closer to making a causal claim.

All of the techniques in this chapter started with a simple bivariate relationship. For example, longitudinal correlational designs start with the two key variables but then measure the same group of people on those two variables at multiple points in time. By inspecting the cross-lag correlations, researchers can see which of the variables probably came first in time, before the other (or if they are mutually reinforcing each other). Longitudinal designs show researchers which variable came first in time, to help establish temporal precedence.

In a regression design, researchers start with a bivariate relationship and then measure other potential third variables that might affect it. Using multiple-regression analysis, they can see whether the basic relationship is still present, even when they statistically control for one or more third variables. If the beta is still significant for the key variable, even when the researchers control for the third variables, then the key relationship is not explained by those third variables. If the beta becomes nonsignificant when the researchers control for any of the other variables, then the original relationship is attributable to the third variable.

Researchers can also approach causal certainty through pattern and parsimony—by specifying a mechanism for the causal relationship and combining the results of diverse studies. When a single causal theory explains all of the disparate results, researchers are closer to making a causal statement.

In a mediation hypothesis, researchers specify a variable that comes between the two variables of interest. The researchers collect data on all three variables (the original two, plus the mediator) and follow specific steps to evaluate how well the mediation hypothesis fits the data.

When you interrogate multivariate correlational designs, you can interrogate not only internal validity and temporal precedence but also construct validity, external validity, and statistical validity. No single study is ever perfect, but by exploring each validity in turn, you can more easily assess a study's strengths and weaknesses.

Key Terms

autocorrelations, p. 212
control for, p. 216
criterion variable, p. 219
cross-lag correlations, p. 212
cross-sectional correlations, p. 212

longitudinal design, p. 211
mediating variable, p. 229
multiple regression, p. 216
multivariate design, p. 210
predictor variable, p. 219

NEED HELP STUDYING?

wwnorton.com/studyspace

Visit StudySpace to access free review materials such as:

- Diagnostic Review Quizzes
- Study Outlines

1. A headline in Yahoo! News made the following (bivariate) association claim: "Facebook Users Get Worse Grades in College" (Hsu, 2009).

   a. What are the two variables in this claim, and how do you think they might have been measured?
   b. Graph what this association might look like, using a scatterplot or a bar graph.
   c. Can you infer that using Facebook causes students' grades to drop? Apply the three causal rules. Is there covariance? Is there temporal precedence? Are there third variables that could explain the association?

2. In the Facebook/grades example, imagine that the story read, "People who use Facebook got worse grades in college, even when the researchers controlled for the SAT scores of the students." What would this sentence mean?

3. The following regression table comes from a study on adolescents' perceptions of how risky it is to use marijuana (Fleary, Heffer, McKyer, & Newman, 2010). The researchers measured adolsecents' risk perceptions as well as a few other variables.

Hierarchical Regression Analyses Predicting Adolescents' Perceptions of the Risk of Using Marijuana

Predictor	Dependent variable: perceived risk of using marijuana
	Beta
Age	−0.17***
Gender	0.16
Impulse control	0.001
Body and self-image	0.06
Mastery of the external world	0.04

*** $p < 0.01$

Source: Adapted from Fleary and colleagues (2010).

   a. What is the dependent variable in this analysis, and where do you find it?
   b. How many predictor variables are there in this study?
   c. Write a sentence that describes what the beta for the *Age* predictor means. (Use the sentences in Table 8.2 as a model.)
   d. Write a sentence that describes what the beta for the *Body and self-image* predictor variable means. (Note: higher scores on this variable mean that adolescents have a more positive body image.)

e. If in this study, males were coded as 0 and females were coded as 1, who estimates the risk of using marijuana to be higher—males or females?

4. Studies have shown that maternal responsiveness (that is, how quickly a mother responds to her infant's cries) is associated with the fussiness of the baby (Hubbard & van Ijzendoorn, 1991). Specifically, more responsive mothers have less fussy babies. But which variable comes first? Consider how you might design a longitudinal correlational study to test this question.

a. Map out the different pairs of correlations you might find—cross-sectional correlations, autocorrelations, and cross-lag correlations.
b. Which pattern of cross-lag correlations would suggest that responsiveness causes less fussiness? Which pattern of cross-lag correlations would suggest that infant fussiness causes less responsiveness? Which pattern would suggest that these two variables are in a mutually reinforcing relationship?

5. Indicate whether each statement below is describing a mediation hypothesis, a third-variable argument, or a moderator result. First, identify the key bivariate relationship. Then decide whether the extra variable comes between the two key variables or is causing the two key variables simultaneously. (It helps to sketch the various explanations to see the difference.)

a. Viewing violent television is associated with aggressive behavior because children model what they see on TV.
b. Viewing violent television is associated with aggressive behavior because people who watch more violent TV have more lenient parents, and these lenient parents also do not care if their children are violent.
c. Viewing violent television is associated with aggressive behavior very strongly among teenagers, but less strongly among young adults.
d. Having a cognitively demanding job is associated with cognitive benefits in later years because people who are highly educated take cognitively demanding jobs, and people who are highly educated have better cognitive skills.
e. Having a cognitively demanding job is associated with cognitive benefits in later years, but only among men, not among women.
f. Having a cognitively demanding job is associated with cognitive benefits in later years because cognitive challenge builds lasting connections in the brain.
g. Children with unusual names are more likely to have delinquency records as adolescents, but the link is especially strong in the United States; the link is weaker in Canada.
h. Children with unusual names are more likely to have delinquency records as adolescents because they got teased more, and the teasing makes them act out.
i. Children with unusual names are more likely to have delinquency records as adolescents because middle-class children have more typical names than children in other socioeconomic groups, and middle-class children are less likely to be identified as delinquent than children in other socioeconomic groups.

PART 5

Tools for Evaluating Causal Claims

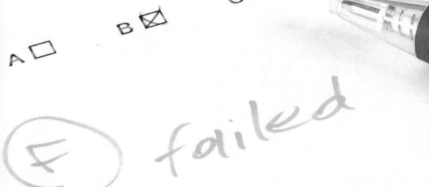

Seeing Red Affects Achievement

(World Science, 2007)

Feeling Cold? Maybe You're Lonely

(CBS News, 2008)

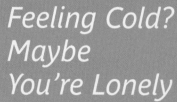

Introduction to Simple Experiments

A causal claim is the boldest kind of claim a scientist can make. A causal claim replaces verbs such as *related to* or *is associated with* or *linked to* with such powerful verbs as *causes, influences, affects,* or *makes*. Causal claims are special—when researchers make a causal claim, they are also stating something about interventions and treatments. If seeing the color red affects achievement, then changing a color may improve people's achievement. If social isolation makes people feel colder, then we can make people feel warmer by making them feel socially included. Interventions are often the ultimate goal of scientific studies—but they must be based on sound research. For example, if the treatment is difficult to implement (or if it comes at the cost of other therapies), we would want to be sure that it works in the causal way we think it does.

Experiments: Two Examples

Let's begin with two examples of experiments that supported valid causal claims. As you read about the two studies, consider how each differs from the bivariate correlational studies you read about in Chapter 7. What makes each of these studies an experiment? How does the experimental design allow the researchers to make a causal claim rather than an association claim?

Example 1: Seeing Red

What do you think about when you see the color red? You might think of fire trucks, fast cars, or valentines, since red is associated with heat, speed, and passion. But in many North American contexts, red is also associated with caution. Teachers may use a red pen to correct papers. The stop signs you see in traffic are red—and so are the signals for biohazards and hot stoves. Red means danger—"Be careful!"—in many contexts (**Figure 9.1**).

A few years ago, Andrew Elliot, a psychologist who studies academic achievement, wanted to know whether the color red could affect people's performance on academic tasks. On the face of it, this idea may seem ridiculous. How could a single color affect people's ability to solve a math problem or finish a puzzle?

However, in the context of his broader theory of academic achievement, the color red was important. Through his research and theory over the years, Elliot learned something important about school achievement: Students in school tend to do better when they have an "approach" orientation rather than an "avoidance" orientation. When students adopt an *approach* orientation toward an academic task, they try to succeed. That is, they focus on getting questions right, learning something new, seeking challenge, and doing their best—and generally they do well. In contrast, when students adopt an *avoidance* orientation toward an academic task, they try not to fail. In the avoidance mode, students address the task of learning with anxiety and awareness of inferiority. They may withdraw effort or choose easy problems to protect themselves from failure. As a result, students in an avoidance mode typically do not perform as well in academic situations.

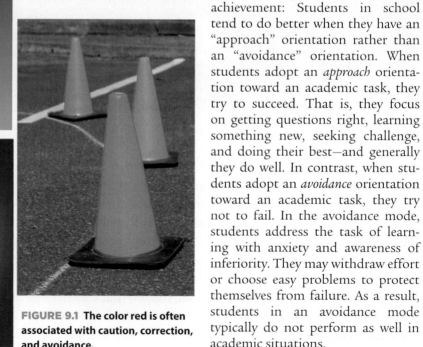

FIGURE 9.1 The color red is often associated with caution, correction, and avoidance.

Enter the dangerous, cautious color red. Because American contexts tend to pair red with danger and avoidance, Elliot's theory led to a specific hypothesis: Exposing students to something red on a test booklet would cause them to withdraw effort and perform worse on an academic test.

Elliot and his colleagues (2007) conducted an experiment to test their hypothesis. They recruited 71 students into a laboratory setting, one at a time. During the study, all students took a 5-minute test in which they unscrambled anagrams (for example, unscrambling the letters KRNID to form the word DRINK). The test booklets looked identical on the front, but inside, each student's participant number had been written in ink on the top corner of the first page. For some participants, the ID number was written in red ink; for others, the number was in green; and for still others, the number was in black. Behind the scenes, one experimenter rolled a die to decide which group each participant would be placed in (black, green, or red), but another experimenter—the one who was in the room with the participant—never saw which color the participant was working with. Other than the color of the ID number, all other things about the test books were the same. The booklets had the same problems inside, students had the same amount of time to work on the problems, and the experimenter who handed it to the student was always the same person.

The results Elliot and his colleagues obtained are depicted in **Figure 9.2**. Students in the red ink group solved fewer anagrams than those in the two comparison groups. The color of the ID number apparently *caused* a difference in students' achievement on an academic test.

Perhaps because he was surprised by the results, or perhaps because he is a good scientist, Elliot ran the study again. This time, he manipulated the color in a slightly different way: by using a red, green, or white cover page for the test. The results were the same (see **Figure 9.3**). In fact, Elliot and his colleagues ran the study several more times in somewhat different ways, and each time they concluded that an ID number written in red ink or a red exam cover caused

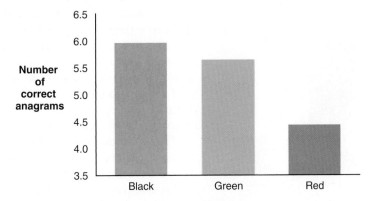

FIGURE 9.2 The results of Elliot and colleagues' (2007) study.
Students whose participant numbers were written in red ink solved fewer anagrams than students whose participant numbers were written in green or black ink.

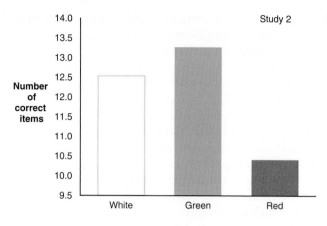

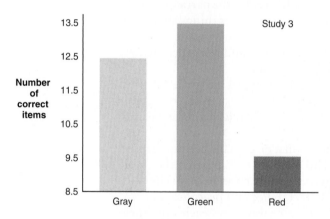

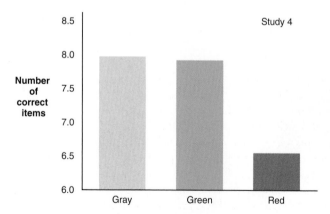

FIGURE 9.3 The results of Elliot and colleagues' (2007) further studies. In each study, the experimenters manipulated the color of a test booklet cover. They measured how many anagrams (Study 2), vocabulary analogies (Study 3), or math problems (Study 4) people in each group solved.

performance to worsen. You read that right—they concluded that red *caused* performance to get worse.

The results are interesting in their own right, but also because they support Elliot's longstanding theory about the ways approach and avoidance modes work in school achievement. Now, think carefully about the choices that Elliot and his colleagues made. Do you think their study supports this causal claim?

Example 2: Feeling Cold

The article "Feeling Cold? Maybe You're Lonely" appeared on websites for CBS News and WebMD. It summarized research originally published in the journal *Psychological Science*. Two researchers, Chen-Bo Zhong and Geoffrey Leonardelli (2008), asked 65 participants to come, one-by-one, into their laboratory and write down a memory from their lives. Behind the scenes, the researchers assigned participants to groups by flipping a coin: Half of the participants were asked to recall and write about a time they were socially excluded; the other half were asked to recall and write about a time they were socially included. A few minutes after writing about one of these two memories, the participants were asked to estimate the temperature in the lab room. It was an unusual question, but the experimenters made it seem natural by explaining that the lab maintenance staff wanted to collect some data on the facilities. Each participant wrote down a temperature estimate.

The results are shown in **Figure 9.4**. On average, the participants who remembered feeling excluded estimated the room to be colder, compared with those in the comparison group, who remembered feeling included. On the basis of this study, the authors Zhong and Leonardelli concluded that "being rejected by others induces an actual feeling of coldness" (p. 840).

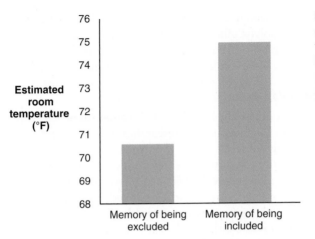

FIGURE 9.4 **The results of Zhong and Leonardelli's (2008) study.** Participants who remembered a time they were socially excluded estimated the temperature in the experimental room to be lower than did participants who remembered a time they were socially included.

Experiments: The Basics

You have probably heard the word *experiment* in everyday speech. Colloquially, *to experiment* means to try something out. People might say they have experimented with drugs. They might say they experimented with a recipe by replacing the eggs with applesauce. Or they might say they experimented with a different driving route to the beach. But in a scientific context, the word *experiment* means something more specific: It means that the researchers *manipulated* at least one variable and *measured* another. But this definition does not imply that experiments always involve scientists wearing white lab coats and carrying clipboards. Of course, experiments *can* take place in a laboratory setting, as Elliot's study did, but they can also take place just about anywhere else: in movie theaters, zoos, classrooms, or daycare centers—anywhere a researcher can manipulate one variable and measure another.

Experimental Variables

As you learned in Chapter 3, a variable is *manipulated* when the researchers assign participants to one level or another of the variable. So, for example, Elliot and his colleagues manipulated ink color by rolling a die to determine whether each participant's number would be written in red ink, green ink, or black ink. (In other words, the participants did not choose which color was used.) Ink color was a variable because it had more than one level (red, green, or black), and it was a manipulated variable because the experimenter assigned each participant to a particular level. Zhong and Leonardelli similarly manipulated social inclusion and rejection by having some participants recall memories of being included and other participants recall memories of being excluded. (Participants did not choose what they were going to remember.)

Measured variables take the form of records of behavior or attitudes—such as self-report, behavioral observations, or physiological measures. After an experimental situation is set up, the researchers simply record what happens. In their first study, Elliot and his colleagues measured performance on anagram tests.

After manipulating ink color, they watched and recorded—that is, they measured—how many anagrams each person solved. Zhong and Leonardelli measured feelings of coldness in their study. After manipulating social exclusion or inclusion, they recorded each person's self-report of how cold he or she believed the room to be.

Independent and Dependent Variables

In an experiment, the manipulated variable is called the **independent variable**. The term *independent* comes from the fact that the researcher has some "independence" in assigning people to different levels of this variable. As you label a study's independent variable, remember not to confuse the independent variable with its levels. The independent variable in Elliot's study was not "the red pen." It was "pen color," which had three levels (also called three **conditions**): red, green, and black.

The measured variable is called the **dependent variable**. How a participant acts on the measured variable *depends* on the level of the independent variable. Researchers have less control over the dependent variable—they manipulate the independent variable and then watch what happens to people's self-reports, behaviors, or physiological responses. A dependent variable is not the same as its levels, either. The dependent variable in Elliot's study was not "solving eight anagrams." It was "how many anagrams each person solved."

How can you tell the two kinds of variables apart? For one thing, when researchers graph their results, the independent variable is almost always on the x-axis, and the dependent variable is almost always on the y-axis (see Figures 9.2 and 9.3 for examples). A mnemonic for remembering the two types of variables is that the independent variable comes first in time (and the letter *I* looks like the number *1*), and the dependent variable is measured afterward (or second).

Control Variables

When researchers are manipulating an independent variable, they need to make sure they are varying only one thing at a time—the potential causal force, or treatment (for example, only color, or only feelings of social rejection or inclusion). Therefore, besides the independent variable, researchers also control potential third variables (or nuisance variables) in their studies by holding all other factors constant between the levels of the independent variable. For example, Elliot and his colleagues manipulated (that is, purposely varied) the color of the pen, but they held constant a number of other potential variables: The colored ID numbers were all the same size, the participants took the exact same anagram tests, the same experimenters ran each session, and so on. Any variable that an experimenter holds constant on purpose is called a **control variable**.

In Zhong and Leonardelli's study, one control variable was the actual temperature of the room: It was always the same. The researchers also controlled how long participants spent recalling each memory and how long they sat in the laboratory. If one of the independent variable groups had more time to get used to the temperature in the room, the difference in temperature estimates might have been due to that group's habituation to the temperature, rather than the intended independent variable.

Control variables are not really variables at all, because they do not vary: Experimenters keep levels the same for all participants. And, as you might imagine, control variables are essential in experiments. They allow researchers to separate one potential cause from another and thus eliminate alternative explanations for results. Control variables are therefore important for establishing internal validity.

How Do Experiments Support Causal Statements?

In both of the examples above, the researchers manipulated one variable and measured another, so both studies can be considered experiments. But are these researchers really justified in making causal claims on the basis of these experiments? Yes. To understand how experiments support causal claims, you can first apply the three rules for causation to Elliot's study. The three rules should be familiar to you by now:

1. *Covariance*: Is the causal variable related to the effect variable? That is, are the levels of the independent variable associated with distinct levels of the dependent variable?
2. *Temporal precedence*: Does the causal variable come before the effect variable in time?
3. *Internal validity*: Are there alternative explanations for the results?

Experiments Are Able to Establish Covariance

The experiment by Elliot and his colleagues did show covariance between the causal variable (color of ID number) and the effect variable (performance on the anagram test). As shown in Figure 9.2, on average, students whose ID numbers were written in red had lower scores, and students whose ID numbers were written in green or black had higher scores. In this case, covariance is indicated by a *difference* in the group means: The red ink group had lower performance scores than the other two groups. Zhong and Leonardelli's study also showed covariance: The levels of social exclusion and inclusion were associated with different average temperature estimates.

Independent Variables Can Show "Compared to What?" The covariance rule might seem obvious. But remember that in our everyday reasoning, we tend to ignore its importance. Most of our personal experiences, for example, do not have the benefit of a comparison group. For instance, you might suspect that a teacher's red pen is making you anxious about a class, but without at least one comparison color, you cannot know for sure. Elliot's experiment, in contrast, gives the comparison group you need. Therefore, an experiment is a better source of information than your own experience, because an experiment allows you to ask, "Compared to what?"

For a review of experience versus empiricism, see Chapter 2.

If independent variables did not vary, a study could not establish covariance. Suppose Elliot had tested only one group, whose ID numbers were written in red ink, and found that they scored only 57% on the anagram test. This study would not tell us anything: Because we would have nothing to compare that 57% to, the study would not show evidence for covariance. Instead, Elliot included two other levels of the variable, green and black, which provided data to compare with the red ink group's data. Because experiments manipulate an independent variable, and because every independent variable has at least two levels, true experiments are always set up to look for covariance.

Covariance: It Takes Two. Manipulating the independent (causal) variable is only part of establishing covariance, however. The outcome matters, too. Imagine that Elliot had found no difference in performance on the anagram tests among the three color groups. In that case, the study would have found no covariance, and Elliot would have had to conclude that ink color does not cause performance to worsen. After all, if performance does not vary with ink color, there is no causal impact to explain.

Comparison Groups, Treatment Groups, and Control Groups. There are a couple of ways that an independent variable might be designed to show covariance. Your elementary science classes may have emphasized the importance of a **control group** in an experiment. A control group is a level of an independent variable that is intended to represent "no treatment" or a neutral condition. When a study has a control group, the other level or levels of the independent variable are usually called the **treatment group(s)**. For example, if an experiment is testing the effectiveness of a new medication, the researchers might assign some participants to take the medication (the treatment group) and other participants to take an inert sugar pill (the control group). When the control group is exposed to an inert treatment such as a sugar pill, it is called a **placebo group**, or a *placebo control group*.

For more details on the placebo effect and how researchers control for it, see Chapter 10, pp. 289–291.

But not all experiments have—or need—a control group. Often, in fact, a clear control group does not even exist. Elliot's study had two *comparison groups* (or *comparison conditions*)—the green and the black—but neither was a control group, in the sense that neither of them clearly establishes an "absence of red." Consider also Harry Harlow's (1958) experiment, discussed in Chapter 1, in which baby monkeys were put in cages with artificial "mothers" made of either cold wire or warm cloth. Harlow's study did not have a control group, either—just a carefully designed comparison condition. When a study uses comparison groups, the levels of the independent variable differ in some intended and meaningful way. All experiments need a comparison group, so that the researchers can compare one condition to another. However, the comparison group does not need to be a control group.

Experiments Establish Temporal Precedence

Elliot's experiment also established temporal precedence: The experimenters manipulated the causal variable (the color of the ID number) to ensure that it came first in time. Then the students took the anagram test and their performance was measured. The "cause" variable clearly did come before the "effect" variable. This ability to establish temporal precedence, by controlling which variable comes first, is a strong advantage of experimental designs. By manipulating the causal variable, the experimenter virtually ensures that the cause comes before the effect.

Establishing temporal precedence is a feature that makes experiments superior to correlational designs. A simple correlational study is a snapshot—all variables are measured at the same time, so when two variables covary (such as recess and school behavior, or small talk and well-being), we cannot tell which variable came first. In contrast, experiments unfold over time, and the experimenter makes sure that the independent variable comes first.

Well-Designed Experiments Establish Internal Validity

Did Elliot and his colleagues' study establish internal validity? That is, are there any alternative explanations for why the red ink group scored lower than the other groups?

A well-designed experiment establishes internal validity, which is one of the most important validities to interrogate when we encounter causal claims. To be internally valid, a study must ensure that the proposed causal variable, and not other factors, is responsible for the change in the effect variable. We can interrogate internal validity by exploring potential alternative explanations. For example, you might ask whether the participants in the red ink group were given harder anagrams to solve than those in the other color groups. If so, the harder anagrams would be an alternative explanation for their lower scores. However, Elliot gave all of the participants the same anagram test. In fact, the test itself was a *control variable*: It was held constant for all participants, for just this reason.

Or perhaps you wonder whether the experimenters treated the red ink group differently than the other groups. Maybe the experimenters were sterner with participants in the red ink group and made them more nervous than those in the other groups. That would have been another threat to internal validity, but remember that the people who handed out the tests did not know which color of ink each participant's number was written in. In fact, these experimenters were undergraduate research assistants who were kept in the dark about the study's hypothesis, so you can rule out that alternative explanation, too. Elliot and his colleagues were careful to control for internal validity threats like these.

Chapter 10, pp. 288–289, discusses how researchers use blind and double-blind designs to control internal validity.

For any given research question, there may be several potential alternative explanations. Most generally, these alternative explanations are called **confounds**, or *threats to internal validity*. The word *confound* can mean "confuse": When a study has a confound, we are confused about what is causing the change in the dependent variable. Is it the causal variable we intended (such as pen color)? Or is it some alternative explanation (such as the stern experimenter)? Internal validity is subject to a number of distinct threats, three of which are introduced in this chapter; the rest are covered in Chapter 10. As experimenters design and interpret studies, they keep these threats to internal validity in mind and try to avoid them.

Design Confounds. A **design confound** (often just called a *confound*) refers to a second variable that happens to vary systematically along with the intended independent variable and therefore is an alternative explanation for the results. As such, a design confound is a classic threat to internal validity. If Elliot had given the red ink group more difficult anagrams than the other groups, the difficulty of the test would have been a design confound, because the second variable, "anagram difficulty," would have systematically varied along with the independent variable (see **Figure 9.5**). If Elliot's research assistants had treated the red ink group more severely, the treatment of each participant would have been a confound, too.

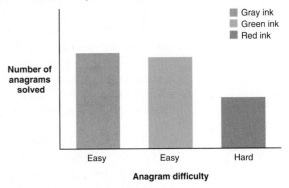

FIGURE 9.5 Design confounds. If the anagrams in the red ink group had been more difficult than those in the other two groups, there would have been a confound in Elliot and colleagues' study.

Consider Zhong and Leonardelli's study on social exclusion. If all of the students in the social exclusion memory group were studied in the beginning of the spring semester, when the outdoor temperature was cold, and all of the students in the social inclusion memory group were studied at the end of the spring semester, when the temperature was warmer, that would be a design confound. We would not know whether the difference in temperature estimates was caused by the season or by the experimental manipulation. However, the researchers did not make this error—instead, they alternated the two memory conditions so that there would not be any systematic difference in the outside weather across groups.

When an experiment has a design confound, it has poor internal validity and cannot support a causal claim. Because Elliot's study did not have any apparent design confounds, its internal validity is sound. Elliot and his colleagues took care to think about confounds in advance and turned them into control variables instead. And Zhong and Leonardelli's approach was to distribute variable weather conditions across different experimental conditions. In both cases, the care that the researchers took means that they can justify making a causal claim.

Systematic and Unsystematic Variability. We need to be careful before we accuse a study of having a design confound. Not every potentially problematic variable is a confound. Consider the example of Elliot's experimenters. It might be the case that some of the research assistants were sweet and others were surly. But the temperament of the research assistants is a problem for internal validity only if it shows **systematic variability** with the independent variable. That is, did the surly experimenters work only with the red ink group and the sweet ones only with the green and black ink groups? Then it would be a design confound. However, if the experimenters' temperaments showed **unsystematic** (random or haphazard) **variability** across all three ink color groups, then temperament would not be a confound.

Consider another example. Perhaps some of the participants in Zhong and Leonardelli's study were wearing coats during the study, and others were not. This variability in clothing in the study would not be a confound unless it varied systematically with the memory condition students were exposed to. If the students in the social inclusion memory group were all wearing coats and the students in the social exclusion memory group were not, that would be systematic variability in the clothing conditions—and would be a confound. But if some students in each memory condition wore coats and some did not, that would be unsystematic variability and would not be a confound.

Unsystematic variability can lead to other problems in an experiment—specifically, it can obscure (make it difficult to detect differences in) the dependent variable, as discussed fully in Chapter 10. However, unsystematic variability should not be called a design confound.

Selection Effects. A **selection effect** occurs in an experiment when the kinds of participants at one level of the independent variable are systematically different from the kinds of participants at the other level of the independent variable. A selection effect is another example of a confound, in which the alternative explanation is related to the types of participants placed in each level of the independent variable. Selection effects can occur when the experimenters allow participants to choose which level of the independent variable they want to be in. They might also occur if experimenters assign one type of person (such as all the women, or all who sign up early in the semester) to one condition, and another type of person (such as all the men, or all those who wait until later in the semester) to another condition.

In a real-world example, a study was designed to test a new intensive therapy for autism, involving one-on-one sessions with a therapist for 40 hours per week (example cited in Gernsbacher, 2003). To determine whether this therapy would cause a significant improvement in children's autistic symptoms, the researchers recruited a large number of families that had children with autism. Then, in an experiment, the researchers arranged for some children to receive the intensive treatment while others received their treatment as usual. To be accommodating, the researchers asked each family whether they would be interested in trying the intensive treatment or whether they preferred to continue their usual treatment. Some of the families might have lived far away from the treatment center and the parents did not want to drive in every day; other families might not have been ready to commit 40 hours per week to an untested treatment. Other families, however, were willing and able to try it.

At the end of the study, the researchers found that the autistic symptoms of the children in the intensive-treatment group had improved more than the symptoms of those who received their usual treatment. However, this study suffered from a clear selection effect: The families in the intensive-treatment group were systematically different from the treatment-as-usual group, because each group "self-selected." Because of their willingness to try an intensive, 40-hour-per-week treatment regimen, parents in that group may have been more motivated to help their autistic children, so there was a clear threat to internal validity. The confound here means that we do not know: Did the children in that group improve because of the intensive treatment? Or did they improve because the families who selected the new therapy were simply more motivated and engaged in their children's treatment? (See **Figure 9.6**.) Of course, in any therapy study, some participants will be more motivated than others. This variability in motivation becomes a confound only when the more motivated folks are all in one group—that is, when the variability is systematic.

True Experiments Avoid Selection Effects. Good experiments use **random assignment** to avoid selection effects. In Elliot and colleagues' study, an experimenter rolled a die to decide which participants would be in each group, so each participant had an *equal chance* of being in the red, green, or black ink group. What does this mean? Imagine that out of the 71 participants who volunteered for the study there were 12 exceptionally clever people. Probabilistically speaking, the rolls of the die would have placed about 4 of them in the red group, about 4 in the green group, and about 4 in the black group. Similarly, if 15 of the participants were having a bad day on the day of the study, random assignment would place about 5 of them in each group. In other words, since Elliot used random assignment, it is very unlikely, given the random (that is, deliberately unsystematic) way

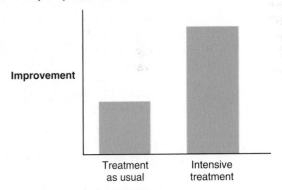

Improvement

Treatment as usual   Intensive treatment

FIGURE 9.6 **Selection effects.** In a study critiqued in Gernsbacher (2003), parents could choose to enroll their children in either the new, intensive-treatment group or the treatment-as-usual group. Because they had this choice, we do not know whether the improvement in the intensive group was caused by the treatment itself or by the fact that the more motivated parents chose it.

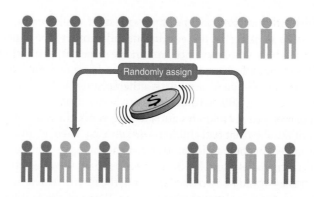

people were assigned to each group, that all the clever, lazy, or unlucky people would have been clustered in the same group. Assigning participants at random to different levels of the independent variable—by flipping a coin, rolling a die, or using a random number generator—controls for all sorts of potential selection effects. In practice, random assignment does not usually create numbers that are perfectly even (for instance, the 12 exceptionally smart people may not be distributed exactly as 4, 4, and 4). But it can often result in fairly even distributions.

Random assignment is a tool to desystematize the types of participants who end up in each level of the independent variable. Sure, some people are more motivated than others; some are more educated than others; some are more extraverted. But successful random assignment spreads these differences out more evenly. It creates a situation in which the experimental groups will become virtually equal, on average, before the independent variable is applied (see **Figure 9.7**). After random assignment (and before manipulating the independent variable), you should be able to test the experimental groups for intelligence, extraversion, motivation—whatever—and averages of each group should be comparable on these traits.

Matched-Groups Designs Also Take Care of Selection Effects. In the simplest type of random assignment, researchers assign participants at random to one condition or another of their experiment. But in some situations, random assignment does not work perfectly. For example, imagine a sample of 30 people who vary on their ability to do anagrams. They are randomly assigned to three groups. Now imagine that there are 6 exceptionally clever people in the original sample. Theoretically, when assigned at random into three groups, 2 of these talented people should end up in each group.

In practice, however, random assignment does not always work perfectly, especially when the samples are on the small side. For example, when you randomly assign your sample of 30 to three groups, you could reasonably end up with 4 of those clever people in one group, and 1 in each of the other groups. You might even end up with 5 clever people in one group and none in another. Such unevenness is more likely when researchers are dealing with smaller numbers. In contrast, over a very large sample, the unevenness is less noticeable. A subset of 60 clever people might be distributed as 23, 18, and 19, but that is not as imbalanced as when a subset of 6 is distributed as 4, 1, and 1.

For this reason, some researchers choose to use a **matched-groups design**—especially when they are assigning small numbers of participants to groups. For a group of 30 participants, the researchers first would measure the participants on a particular variable that might matter to the dependent variable—IQ, perhaps, might matter to anagram ability. Then they match participants up set by set; that is, they would take the three participants with the highest IQ scores and then *within that matched set*, randomly assign one of them to each of the three groups. They would then take the participants with the three next-highest IQ scores and within that set again assign randomly to the three groups. They would continue this process until they reach the participants with the lowest three IQ scores and assign them at random, too (see **Figure 9.8**).

The matched-groups technique has the advantage of randomness. Because each member of the matched set is randomly assigned, the technique prevents selection effects. But this method also ensures that the groups are equal on some important variable, such as IQ, before the manipulation of the independent variable. The downside, of course, is that the matching process requires an extra step—in this case, administering an IQ test to everyone in the sample before assigning them to groups.

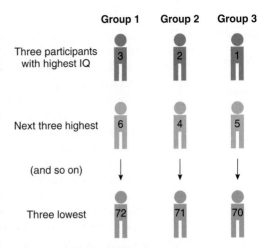

FIGURE 9.8 Matched-groups designs. In a matched-groups design with three groups, participants are sorted from lowest to highest on some trait. They are then assigned at random to experimental groups.

Check Your Understanding

1. What are the minimum requirements for a study to be an experiment?
2. How do experiments satisfy the three causal rules?
3. In your own words, define the terms *independent variable*, *dependent variable*, and *control variable*.
4. How are design confounds and control variables related?
5. How does random assignment address confounds caused by selection effects? How does a matched-groups design address selection effects?

1. See p. 245. 2. See pp. 247–249. 3. See p. 246. 4. See pp. 249–250; control variables are used to eliminate potential design confounds. 5. See pp. 251–253.

Simple Experiments: Independent-Groups Designs

Although the minimum requirement for an experiment is that researchers manipulate one variable and measure another, experiments come in many forms and sizes. One of the most basic distinctions among the designs is between independent-groups designs and within-groups designs.

Independent-Groups Versus Within-Groups Designs

In Elliot and colleagues' and Zhong and Leonardelli's studies, there were different participants at each level of the independent variable. In Elliot's study, some participants saw a number written in red ink, but other participants saw a number written in green, and still other participants saw a number written in black. In Zhong and Leonardelli's study, some participants remembered being socially included, while others remembered being socially excluded. In both of these examples, the design used was an **independent-groups design**, in which different groups of participants are placed into different levels of the independent variable. These designs are also called **between-subjects designs**, or *between-groups designs.*

Another way to manipulate an independent variable is to use a **within-groups design**, also known as a *within-subjects design.* In a within-groups design, there is only one group of participants, and each participant is presented with *all* levels of the independent variable. For example, Elliot and his colleagues might have run their study as a within-groups design if they had asked each person in the study to solve three sets of anagrams—one with numbers in red pen, one with numbers in green pen, and with numbers in black pen.

Two Possible Independent-Groups Designs

Two basic forms of independent-groups designs are the posttest-only design and the pretest/posttest design. The two types of designs are used in different situations.

Posttest-Only Designs

One of the simplest independent-groups experimental designs is the **posttest-only design**. (Formally, it is known as an *equivalent groups, posttest-only design*). In this design, participants are randomly assigned to independent variable groups and are tested on the dependent variable once. **Figure 9.9** shows a schematic drawing of a posttest-only design.

Elliot and colleagues' study of the color red and Zhong and Leonardelli's social inclusion study are both examples of posttest-only designs. In the social exclusion study, for example, participants were randomly assigned to recall either social exclusion (Group 1) or social inclusion (Group 2). Participants in both groups were then measured on the dependent variable of perceived room temperature, as shown in **Figure 9.10**. Elliot and colleagues' study was also a posttest-only design, but it had three independent variable levels, as shown in **Figure 9.11**.

Posttest-only designs meet each of the three rules for causation. They allow researchers to test for covariance by detecting differences in the dependent variable. (Having at least two groups makes it possible to do so.) They establish temporal precedence because the independent variable comes first in time. And

FIGURE 9.9
A posttest-only design.

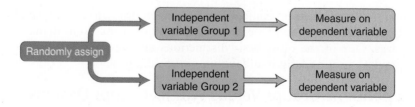

CHAPTER 9 Introduction to Simple Experiments

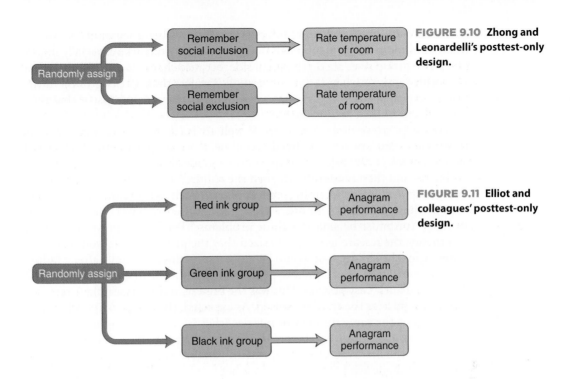

FIGURE 9.10 **Zhong and Leonardelli's posttest-only design.**

FIGURE 9.11 **Elliot and colleagues' posttest-only design.**

when they are conducted well, they establish internal validity: When researchers use appropriate control variables, there should be no design confounds, and random assignment takes care of selection effects.

Pretest/Posttest Designs

At other times, researchers conduct **pretest/posttest designs** (formally known as *equivalent groups, pretest/posttest designs*). In such designs, participants are randomly assigned to at least two groups and are tested on the key dependent variable twice—once before and once after exposure to the independent variable. If Zhong and Leonardelli had included a pretest, the experiment would have been a pretest/posttest design, as shown in **Figure 9.12**.

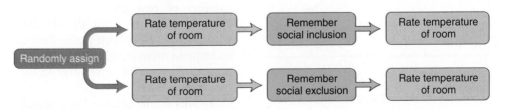

FIGURE 9.12 **Zhong and Leonardelli's study as pretest/posttest design.**

Researchers might use a pretest/posttest design when they want to evaluate whether random assignment made the groups equal. It may be especially important when group sizes are on the small side, because chance is more likely to lead to lopsided groups when samples are small (say, less than 10 per group). In this case, a pretest/posttest design allows researchers to be absolutely sure that there is no selection effect in a study.

Pretest/posttest designs also work well to track how participants in the experimental groups have changed over time. For example, in one study, Mueller and Dweck (1998) asked a sample of fifth-grade children to complete a set of problems, and then randomly assigned the children to hear two kinds of praise. One group of children received "process praise," such as "You must have worked hard at these problems." Another group of children received "person praise," such as "You must be smart at these problems." Because of previous research and theory, the researchers hypothesized that the process praise would be more adaptive for the children—it would be more motivating, especially after a failure.

The researchers used a pretest/posttest design. In the first stage, all the children solved fairly easy puzzles. This was the pretest, and the researchers recorded how many puzzles the children solved. As expected, the children in both groups solved about the same number of puzzles (that is, random assignment worked by making the groups equal before the independent variable was manipulated). Right after the first stage, the independent variable was administered: The children received one kind of praise or the other.

All the children were then asked to solve a second set of problems—but these problems were intended for tenth graders, and most of the fifth-grade children did not do well. (However, no data were collected at this stage. The researchers wanted all children to have a failure experience, which acted as a control variable.) Finally, all of the children were given a third set of puzzles—these were easy ones again, the same level of difficulty as the first set. This was the posttest. The researchers recorded how many of the second, easy puzzles children in the two groups could solve.

As Mueller and Dweck's theory predicted, the children who received person praise showed a decline in the number of easy puzzles they could solve after failure, while the children who received the process praise showed an improvement in the number of easy puzzles they could solve after failure (see **Figure 9.13**).

In this study, because the researchers used a pretest/posttest design, they could easily track the increase and decrease in performance in the two

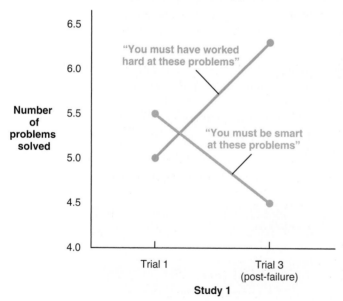

FIGURE 9.13 The results of Mueller and Dweck's (1998) study. Mueller and Dweck used a pretest/posttest design to study person and process praise.

groups: Although the two groups started out, as expected, solving about the same number of problems, after different kinds of praise followed by a failure experience, the two groups diverged dramatically.

Which Design Is Better?

Why might Zhong and Leonardelli have chosen to do a posttest-only experiment? Shouldn't they have tested how warm or cold people felt in the room *before* they recalled the social memory? That way, at least the researchers would know how warm or cold people in each group already felt before they arrived.

In fact, Zhong and Leonardelli probably made the right choice by not pretesting. By using a posttest-only design with 65 participants, they trusted in random assignment to create equivalent groups. Participants who already felt cold at the start (or were wearing coats, or were tested in the winter) had an equal chance of being in either one of the memory groups, and if they were distributed evenly across both groups, their effect canceled out. Therefore, any observed difference in overall, perceived temperature between these two groups should be attributable only to the different memories they recalled. To put it in other words, being "already cold" could have been a selection effect, but random assignment helped control for selection effects. In addition, it would have been problematic to run a pretest for Zhong and Leonardelli's study. As discussed later in this chapter, participants might have become suspicious if they were asked to guess the temperature of the room more than once, and they might have begun to guess the researchers' hypothesis. Or participants might have simply stated the same temperature the second time they were tested—after all, indoor temperatures do not normally change, and they would easily remember the estimate they wrote the first time. Therefore, pretest/posttest designs might give some assurance that the groups were equal, but there can be costs, too.

In contrast, Mueller and Dweck could justify giving their sample of children multiple sets of problems, because the situation was quite similar to other classroom situations, and it was unlikely to arouse suspicion.

In short, the posttest-only design may be the most basic independent-groups experiment, but its combination of random assignment plus a manipulated variable can lead to powerful causal conclusions. The pretest/posttest design adds a pretesting step to the most basic independent-groups design. Researchers might use a pretest/posttest design if they want to be extra sure that two groups were equivalent at pretesting—as long as the pretest does not make the participants change their more spontaneous behavior.

Check Your Understanding

1. What is the difference between independent-groups and within-groups designs?
2. Describe how posttest-only and pretest/postest designs are both independent-groups designs. Explain how they differ.

1. See p. 254. 2. See pp. 254–256.

Simple Experiments: Within-Groups Designs

There are two basic types of within-groups designs. When researchers expose participants to all levels of the independent variable, they might do so concurrently, or they might do so by repeatedly exposing the participants, over time, to different levels of the independent variable.

Concurrent-Measures Designs

One simple within-groups design is a **concurrent-measures design**, in which participants are exposed to all the levels of an independent variable at roughly the same time, and a single attitudinal or behavioral preference is the dependent measure.

An everyday example of a concurrent measures design would be a taste test in which participants sample two options, such as Coke and Pepsi, and indicate the one they prefer. Here, the independent variable is the brand of cola, and participants taste both of the levels, manipulated within groups. Each participant's soda preference (indicated only once) would be the dependent variable. **Figure 9.14** shows how such a taste test would be conducted.

Another example of a concurrent-measures design comes from Chapter 1. Harry Harlow presented baby monkeys with two "mothers": a wire mother that gave milk and a cloth mother that was warm and cozy but did not provide milk. The monkeys indicated their preference between the two by spending time with one mother or the other. In Harlow's study, the type of mother was the independent variable (manipulated as within-groups), and each baby monkey's clinging behavior was the dependent variable.

Repeated-Measures Designs

Repeated-measures designs are a type of within-groups design in which participants are measured on a dependent variable more than once—that is, after exposure to each level of the independent variable. In an example of a repeated-measures design, developmental researchers Bick and Dozier (2008) were interested in the hormone oxytocin, which is believed to be involved in social bonding. The participants were mothers whose toddlers were 2 or 3 years old. In one phase of the study, the women's oxytocin levels were monitored as they interacted closely with their own toddlers. In the other phase, at the same time of day, the mothers' oxytocin levels were monitored as they interacted closely with a different toddler they did not previously know. (The mothers traded toddlers with each other for this part of the study.) The study found that

FIGURE 9.14

A concurrent-measures design for a cola taste test.

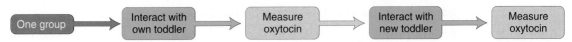

FIGURE 9.15 **Bick and Dozier's (2008) repeated-measures design.**

oxytocin levels were higher when women were interacting with the new child than with their own. In this experiment, the independent variable was the interaction partner and had two levels: own toddler and new toddler. The dependent variable was oxytocin levels: Oxytocin levels *depended* on the interaction partner. Because women were tested on the dependent variable (oxytocin levels) after each toddler, this was a repeated-measures design. **Figure 9.15** gives a visual representation of Bick and Dozier's experimental design.

Advantages of Within-Groups Designs

The principal advantage of a within-groups design is that it ensures that the participants in the two treatment groups will be equivalent—after all, they are the same participants. For example, Bick and Dozier knew that oxytocin levels were variable across women: Some women have normally high levels of this hormone; others have low levels. If the researchers had randomly assigned women to interact with either their own toddler or a new toddler, they would have run the risk that, by chance, a few extra women with high oxytocin levels would be assigned to one group, and the groups would not be perfectly equivalent.

In Bick and Dozier's repeated-measures design, however, a woman with a naturally high or low level of oxytocin, or even a naturally high or low interest in toddlers, would bring that same baseline to her interactions with both toddlers. As a result, the only difference between the two groups should be attributable to the independent variable (which toddler a woman was with), not to individual or personal variables. We say that each woman "acted as her own control," because by exposing all participants to both independent variable conditions, Bick and Dozier controlled for—kept constant—a number of individual difference variables (oxytocin levels, parenting style, personality, and so on) across conditions.

Similarly, if researchers ran a taste test between Coke and Pepsi as a within-groups design, they would not have to worry that all the habitual Coke drinkers might be in one group or the other, or that more people who like soda are in one group or the other. Every participant tastes both kinds of soda, so the two taste groups are identical to each other on any extraneous personal variables.

In fact, the idea of "treating each participant as his or her own control" also means that matched-groups designs (discussed on pp. 252–253) can be treated as within-groups designs. In a matched design, researchers carefully match sets of participants on some key control variable (such as IQ) and assign each member of a set to a different group. The matched participants in the groups are assumed to be more similar to each other than in a more traditional independent-groups design, which uses random assignment.

Additional Reasons to Use Within-Groups Designs

Besides providing the ability to use each participant as his or her control, within-groups designs also give researchers more **power** to notice differences between conditions. Statistically speaking, when extraneous differences (unsystematic variability) in personality, sex, ability, and so on are held constant across all conditions, researchers will be more likely to detect an effect of the independent variable manipulation if there is one. *Power* is the ability of a sample to show a statistically significant result when something is truly going on in the population. For example, if seeing an ID number written in red really does make a difference in achievement, will the study show a difference? Maybe not: If extraneous differences exist between groups, too much unsystematic variability may be obscuring the true difference. It's like being at a noisy party—your ability to detect somebody's words is hampered when many other conversations are going on around you.

For more on variability between groups, see Chapter 10, pp. 299–304, and Appendix B.

Within-groups designs can also be attractive options because they generally require fewer participants overall. Imagine that a group of researchers is running a study with three conditions. If they want 12 participants in each condition, they will need a total of 36 people for an independent-groups design. However, if they run the same study as a within-groups design, they will need only 12 participants, because each participant experiences all levels of the independent variable (see **Figure 9.16**). In this way, repeated-measures designs can be much more efficient.

Covariance, Temporal Precedence, and Internal Validity in Within-Groups Designs

Do within-groups designs allow researchers to make causal claims? In other words, do they stand up to the three causal rules?

Because within-groups designs enable researchers to manipulate an independent variable and incorporate comparison conditions, they provide an opportunity for establishing *covariance*. For example, Bick and Dozier observed that oxytocin levels covaried with the toddler with whom each woman was

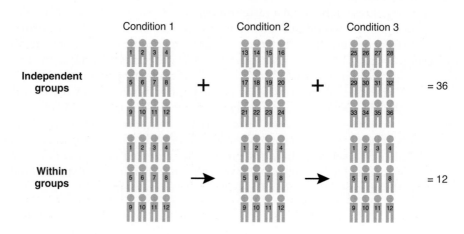

FIGURE 9.16
Within-groups designs. If you want to use 12 people in each of three experimental conditions, a within-groups experiment is more efficient.

interacting. Repeated-measures designs also establish *temporal precedence*, because the experimenter controls the independent variable and can ensure that it comes first. In Bick and Dozier's study, the toddler interaction came before the oxytocin measurement.

So far so good. But within-groups designs have the potential for a particular threat to internal validity: Sometimes, being exposed to one condition changes how people react to the other condition. Such problems are called **carryover effects**, **practice effects**, or, generally, **order effects**. An order effect in a within-groups design is a confound—meaning that participants' performance at later levels of the independent variable might be caused not by the experimental manipulation but rather by the sequence in which the conditions were experienced. Such a sequence might lead to practice, fatigue, boredom, or some other contamination that carries over from one condition to the next.

As an example, imagine what would have happened if Elliot and his colleagues had conducted their study as a repeated-measures design, in which participants took the quiz three times—first with an ID number written in red pen, then with the number in green pen, and finally with the number in black pen. We would wonder, then, if the higher scores in the later green and black pen conditions were simply due to practice—not to the color of the pen. Such a practice effect would be an internal validity threat: We are not sure whether the higher scores in the green and black pen conditions are due to color (the real independent variable) or to practice (the alternative explanation). And indeed, the practice could have also obscured the true effect of a red pen, too: If the order had been green, black, red, the practice effect might have canceled out the avoidance effect of the red color. Similarly, Bick and Dozier might have wondered whether women who interacted with the unfamiliar toddler showed an increase in oxytocin simply as a carryover effect, too. Maybe the oxytocin increased only because the women were contrasting the new toddler with their own, familiar one.

Order effects can apply to the taste test example as well. What if people always tasted the Pepsi product after the Coke product? There might be a particular carryover effect of tasting Coke first—perhaps its aftertaste affects the way the Pepsi tastes. (Think, for example, how sour orange juice tastes if you drink it right after brushing your teeth.)

Counterbalancing Controls for Order Effects

If effects such as practice, fatigue, aftertaste, or boredom are potential alternative explanations in a within-groups design, experimenters may use **counterbalancing** to avoid these effects. That is, they present the levels of the independent variable to participants in different orders. When counterbalancing is used, any order effects should cancel each other out when all of the data are collected.

Bick and Dozier used counterbalancing in their experiment: Half of the women interacted with their own toddler first, followed by the new toddler, and the other half interacted with the new toddler first, followed by their own toddler. If oxytocin had risen over time just because of experience in the study, the increase should have occurred in the new-toddler condition for half of the women and in the own-toddler condition for the other half of the women.

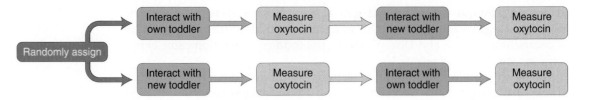

FIGURE 9.17 Counterbalanced designs. Counterbalanced designs help control order effects in a repeated-measures design.

(**Figure 9.17** gives a visual representation of Bick and Dozier's counterbalanced experiment.) When all the data were combined from these two orders, any order effect dropped out of the comparison between the own-toddler and new-toddler conditions. As a result, Bick and Dozier knew that the difference they noticed was attributable only to the different toddlers—and not to fatigue, practice, or some other order effect.

Procedures Behind Counterbalancing. When researchers counterbalance conditions (or levels) in a within-groups design, they must split their participants into groups; each group receives one of the condition orders. How do the experimenters decide which participants receive the first order of presentation and which receive the second order? Through random assignment, of course! They might recruit, say, 30 participants to a study and randomly assign 15 of them to receive the order A then B, and assign the remaining 15 the order B then A.

There are two methods for counterbalancing an experiment. When a within-groups experiment has only two or three levels of an independent variable, experimenters can use full counterbalancing, in which all possible condition orders are represented. For example, a repeated-measures experiment with two conditions is easy to counterbalance—there are two orders (A → B and B → A). In a repeated-measures experiment with three conditions—A, B, and C—each group of participants would be randomly assigned to one of the six following orders:

$$A \rightarrow B \rightarrow C \qquad B \rightarrow C \rightarrow A$$
$$A \rightarrow C \rightarrow B \qquad C \rightarrow A \rightarrow B$$
$$B \rightarrow A \rightarrow C \qquad C \rightarrow B \rightarrow A$$

As the number of conditions increases, however, the number of possible orders needed for full counterbalancing increases dramatically. For example, a study with four conditions requires 24 possible orders! If experimenters want to put at least a few participants in each order, the need for participants can quickly increase, counteracting the typical efficiency of a repeated-measures design. Therefore, experimenters might use **partial counterbalancing**, in which only some of the possible condition orders are represented. One way to partially counterbalance is to present the conditions in a randomized order for each subject. (This is easy to do when an experiment is administered by a computer; the computer delivers conditions in a new random order for each participant.) Another technique for partial counterbalancing is to use a **Latin square**—a formal system of partial counterbalancing that ensures that each condition appears in each position at least once. A Latin square for five conditions might look like this:

A	B	E	C	D
B	C	A	D	E
C	D	B	E	A
D	E	C	A	B
E	A	D	B	C

The first row is set up according to a formula, and then the conditions simply go in alphabetical order down each column. (You can find formulas for setting up the first row of a Latin square online, at sites such as this one: http://rintintin.colorado.edu/~chathach/balancedlatinsquares.html.)

Disadvantages of Within-Groups Designs

Within-groups designs are true experiments because they involve a manipulated variable and a measured variable. They potentially establish covariance, they ensure temporal precedence, and when experimenters control for order effects, they can establish internal validity, too. So why wouldn't a researcher choose a within-groups design all the time?

Within-groups designs have three main drawbacks. As noted earlier, repeated-measures designs have the potential for order effects, which can threaten internal validity. But a researcher can usually control for order effects by using counterbalancing, so such effects may not be much of a concern.

A more serious problem occurs when people see all levels of the independent variable and then change the way they would normally act. For instance, imagine what would have happened if Zhong and Leonardelli had run their study as a within-groups design. Participants would have recalled a memory of social inclusion, and then estimated the temperature of the room. They would then have recalled a memory of social exclusion and would have estimated the temperature of the room—again! In such a study, many people would become suspicious and would wonder why they were asked twice about the room's temperature—especially after exposure to each level of the independent variable. Many participants might have guessed what the experimenters were testing and might have altered their answers. That is, to try to be "good participants," they would change their temperature estimates in the direction they thought the experimenters wanted. When an experiment contains cues that lead participants to guess its hypotheses, the experiment is said to have **demand characteristics**, or *experimental demand*. When demand characteristics of an experiment are high, they may create an alternative explanation for a study's results. We would have to ask, "Did the manipulation work? Or did the participants simply guess what the researchers expected them to do, and act accordingly?"

In still other cases, a within-groups design might be impossible. Suppose someone has devised a new way of teaching children how to ride a bike, called Method A. She wants to compare Method A with the older method, Method B. Obviously, she cannot teach a group of children to ride a bike with Method A and then return them to baseline and teach them again with Method B. Once

Pretest/posttest design

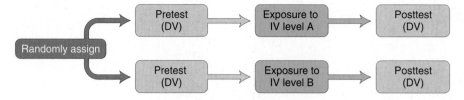

Within-groups design

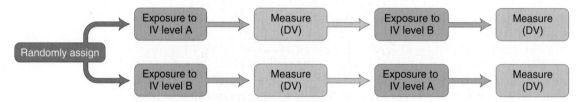

FIGURE 9.18 Pretest/posttest designs versus within-groups designs. In a pretest/posttest design, participants see only one level of the independent variable, but in a within-groups design, they see all the levels.

taught, the children are permanently changed. In such a case, a within-groups design, with or without counterbalancing, would make no sense at all.

Is the Pretest/Posttest Design a Within-Groups Design?

Finally, you might wonder whether pretest/posttest independent-groups designs should be considered within-groups designs. In one sense, this design is within-groups: Participants are tested twice—at pretest and posttest.

However, in a true within-groups design, participants are exposed to all levels of a meaningful independent variable, such as which toddler they are working with, or which soda they are tasting. The levels of such independent variables can also be counterbalanced. In contrast, the difference between pretest and posttest levels of an independent variable is not normally the central independent variable of a study, and pretest and posttest cannot be counterbalanced (see **Figure 9.18**).

Check Your Understanding

1. What are the two simple forms of within-groups designs?
2. Describe how counterbalancing improves the internal validity of a within-groups design.
3. In your own words, summarize all of the advantages and disadvantages of within-groups designs (the text mentions three of each).

1. See p. 258. **2.** See pp. 261–263. **3.** See pp. 259–260, 263–264.

Interrogating Causal Claims with the Four Validities

Let's use Zhong and Leonardelli's study on social exclusion to illustrate how we might interrogate a causal claim or an experimental design using the four big validities as a framework. What questions should you ask, and what do the answers mean?

Construct Validity: How Well Were the Variables Measured and Manipulated?

In an experiment, researchers operationalize *two* constructs: The independent variable and the dependent variable. When you interrogate the construct validity of an experiment, you should ask about the construct validity of each of these variables.

Construct Validity of Dependent Variables: How Well Were They Measured?

Chapters 5 and 7 explained in detail how to interrogate the construct validity of a dependent, measured variable. To interrogate construct validity in Zhong and Leonardelli's study, for example, you could ask how well the researchers measured their dependent variable: perceived temperature. In the study, the researchers measured how cold people felt by asking them to estimate the temperature in the experimental room. Is this a good measure of how cold people feel? Is it reliable—do people give the same answer every time they are asked (provided that the room temperature has not changed)? Is it valid—are people's estimates of room temperature meaningfully associated with how warm or cold they are actually feeling, and not with some other variable, such as feeling annoyed?

Zhong and Leonardelli do not present any empirical evidence for the reliability and validity of their measure of perceived temperature, but it does have face validity: Asking people to estimate the temperature of a room is a straightforward measure of how warm or cold they feel. It is also a meaningful use of a subjective measure: Zhong and Leonardelli did not want to know what temperature the room really *was*; they wanted to know how warm or cold the room *felt* to participants in each group. Finally, the fact that people's estimates of room temperature did vary in a predicted way (the room felt colder to those who remembered being rejected) is also some evidence for this measure's construct validity.

Construct Validity of Independent Variables: How Well Were They Manipulated?

To interrogate the independent variables, you would ask how well the researchers manipulated (or operationalized) them. In Zhong and Leonardelli's study, for example, the independent variable was social inclusion versus social exclusion. The researchers manipulated this variable by having participants recall an instance of either social inclusion or social exclusion. To evaluate this manipulation, we can simply assess its face validity. Does the manipulation (the operationalization) fit the researchers' definition of the construct? For example, is reliving a memory of social exclusion a good manipulation of the construct of social exclusion? Another way we might evaluate the manipulation's construct validity is to see whether and how other researchers have used this manipulation before. Have other scientists reviewed the manipulation and decided it was a meaningful one?

Manipulation Checks Help Test the Construct Validity of an Independent Variable. In some cases, researchers use **manipulation checks** to collect empirical data on the construct validity of their independent variables. A manipulation check is an extra dependent variable that researchers can insert into an experiment to help them quantify how well an experimental manipulation worked. For example, after each participant recalled one memory or the other, Zhong and Leonardelli might have asked each participant to report how socially included or popular they felt right after writing about the social memory. If they found that people in the social inclusion group felt more popular and included than the people in the social exclusion group, the researchers would have some evidence that their memory manipulation worked. The same procedure—exposing people to the manipulation and then asking them if they felt socially excluded—might also be used in a **pilot study**. A pilot study is a simple study, using a separate group of participants, that is completed before (or sometimes after) the study of primary interest is conducted. Researchers may use pilot study data to confirm the effectiveness of their manipulations.

Manipulation checks and pilot studies are not always necessary, but careful experimenters often use them. For instance, Elliot and his colleagues believed that the pen colors they used would be perceived by their participants as red, green, and black. But just to be sure, they conducted a pilot study to ask participants to describe the pen colors they used. The pilot group confirmed that, indeed, the red, green, and black pens the researchers planned to use were "conventional" and "typical" examples of these three colors. When researchers have taken such a step, you can feel more confident in the construct validity of the independent variable.

Construct Validity and Theory Testing

When we evaluate the construct validity of an experiment, we assess the quality of two operationalizations: the one for the independent variable and the one for the dependent variable. The standard for evaluating these operational variables is provided by the theory the study is testing. That is, construct validity also allows researchers to say that the results of the study support their theory. Recall that Elliot and colleagues conducted the pen study in the first place because they wanted to test a theory about avoidance orientation in academic tasks. Therefore, they should be able to show that the results came out the way they did because the red pen led people to have an avoidance orientation—and not for some other reason.

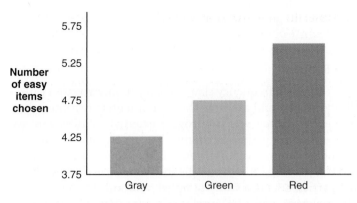

FIGURE 9.19 Construct validity of Elliot and colleagues' color manipulation. Elliot and colleagues showed that exposure to the color red made students more likely to select easy problems on a test—evidence that the color red was activating the motivation to avoid challenge. This study helped support the construct validity of Elliot's color manipulation.

For example, the key independent variable condition, red, in Elliot's study is not just an avoidance color—it is also a "warm" color, compared with green and black. Therefore, a critic could argue that the results do not support Elliot's theory, since we cannot be sure whether the key color, red, was working because it suggested avoidance or because it was a warm color. To improve construct validity, Elliot could have added a fourth condition to his study—a warm color such as an orange or a pink pen. If the results showed that only the red pen, not the other warm colors, led to poor performance, Elliot would have stronger support for the avoidance aspect of his theory. That is, the operationalization of his manipulation (pen color) would have been more clearly tied to the construct (avoidance) it was meant to represent.

Another way that researchers can show that results support their theory is by collecting additional data. In fact, Elliot and his colleagues conducted two additional experiments. One showed that viewing a red test booklet (versus a green or gray one) caused people to select easy, rather than hard, items on a puzzle. Because people in an avoidance mode are known to prefer easy problems and avoid difficult ones, this study showed that the color red was probably working in the previous study because it prompted avoidance (and not something else). That supports the construct validity of the independent variable (see **Figure 9.19**). In still another experiment, Elliot and his colleagues evaluated the brain activity of participants who received a red, green, or gray test booklet. They found that the pattern of right- and left-brain activity of participants with the red test booklet was consistent with an avoidance orientation, too. (Past studies have shown that when people are motivated to avoid something, they have more activity in the right than in the left frontal cortex.)

Therefore, when you are interrogating the construct validity of an experiment, you can ask what evidence exists to determine that these manipulations and measures actually represent the intended constructs in the theory.

External Validity: To Whom or to What Can You Generalize the Causal Claim?

Chapters 6 and 7 discussed external validity in the context of frequency claims and association claims. Interrogating external validity in the context of causal claims is similar: When you interrogate the external validity of a causal claim, you ask whether the causal relationship can generalize to other people, places, and times. (Chapter 13 goes into even more detail about external validity questions.)

Generalizing to Other People

As with an association claim or a frequency claim, when you interrogate a causal claim's external validity, you should ask how the experimenters recruited their participants. Remember that when you interrogate external validity, you ask about *random sampling*—randomly gathering a sample from a population. (In contrast, when you interrogate internal validity, you ask about *random assignment*—randomly assigning each participant in a sample into one experimental group or another.) Were the participants in a study sampled randomly from the population of interest? If they were, you can be relatively sure that the results can be generalized, at least to the population of participants that the sample came from. In Zhong and Leonardelli's study, the 65 participants were a convenience sample (rather than a random sample) of undergraduates at the professors' own institution, the University of Toronto, so the results may not be generalizable to that university's student body—or to people from other regions, people of other ages, and so on.

Generalizing to Other Situations

External validity also applies to the types of *situations* to which an experiment might generalize. For example, Zhong and Leonardelli's study can generalize to other situations in which people recall their memories of social exclusion. But how well does their memory manipulation represent other situations in which people feel socially excluded? To find out, the experimenters would manipulate social exclusion in other ways. In fact, Zhong and Leonardelli (2008) conducted a second study, in which they manipulated social exclusion differently: Participants played an online computer game that involved tossing virtual balls back and forth. Participants were told that they would be playing with three other people, but in fact the three other players were not real; instead, participants were playing the game with a computer that had been programmed in advance. With one group of participants (assigned by a coin flip), the computer was programmed to play the game normally. With the other group of participants, the computer was rigged to toss the participant the ball only twice at the beginning of the game; for the next 30 throws, the computer did not toss the ball to the participant at all. Presumably, being left out of the game in this way would make participants feel excluded. Incidentally, this second study operationalized "feeling cold" in a different way, too. After playing the computer game, participants were asked to rate how much they desired several foods, including hot coffee, hot soup, and Coke. In this second study, the results were similar to the first: Socially excluded participants rated hot coffee higher than socially included ones did (see **Figure 9.20**).

Zhong and Leonardelli's two different manipulations of their independent variable suggest that the effect of social exclusion on feeling cold is not limited to situations in which people remember being excluded, since it also occurred in a situation involving current feelings of exclusion (being rejected in a game). And the two different operational definitions of the dependent variable suggest that the effects of social exclusion include both rated temperature and desire for a warm drink. This second study thus boosts the external validity of Zhong and Leonardelli's causal claim. (And because the different operationalizations concur with the theory, this also supports the construct validity of the manipulations and measures.)

What If External Validity Is Poor?

Should we be concerned that Zhong and Leonardelli did not select their participants at random from a population? And should we be concerned that their study was conducted in a contrived, laboratory situation that might not generalize well to the real world? Remember from Chapter 3 that in an experiment, researchers usually prioritize experimental control—that is, internal validity. To get a clean manipulation, they may have to conduct their study in a contrived environment such as a university laboratory. Often, such environments—and the people who participate in the studies conducted there—are not cleanly representative of people in the real world. Although it is possible to achieve both internal and external validity in a single study, doing so can often be difficult. Therefore, many experimenters decide to sacrifice real-world representativeness for internal validity. Teasing out the causal variable from potential confounds is the step most experimenters take care of first. In addition, running an experiment on a relatively homogenous sample (such as college students) means that the unsystematic variability is less likely to obscure the effect of the independent variable. Replicating the study using a variety of samples and in a variety of contexts is a step saved for later. In Zhong and Leonardelli's research, other studies might test to see whether social exclusion also affects temperature perception among elderly people in Milwaukee, Latino children in Los Angeles, or high school students in Kyoto. According to the theory, there is no reason to expect that social exclusion would affect those groups any differently than it does university students in Toronto, but it is worth doing the studies to be sure.

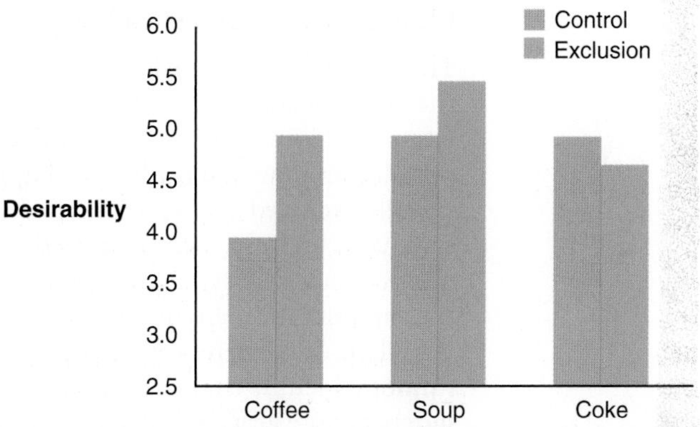

FIGURE 9.20 Zhong and Leonardelli's manipulation of social exclusion. Socially excluded people rated warm foods as more desirable than did people in the control condition. Zhong and Leonardelli manipulated social exclusion two ways—with a memory task in their first study and with a computer game in their second study. They also measured feelings of coldness in two ways—by asking people to estimate the temperature and by asking them to rate warm and cold foods. The variety of manipulations and measures helps support external validity.

For more on prioritizing validities, see Chapter 13.

Statistical Validity: How Well Do Your Data Support Your Causal Conclusion?

In your statistics class, you will learn how to ask specific questions about experimental designs, such as whether the researchers did the right statistical tests. For now, you should know to ask two basic questions about the statistical validity of an experiment.

Is the Difference Statistically Significant?

The first question to ask is whether the difference between means obtained in the study is statistically significant. Recall from Chapter 7 that when a result is statistically significant, it is unlikely to have been obtained by chance from a population in which nothing is happening. When the difference (say between a socially excluded and a socially included group) in a study is statistically significant, you can be reasonably sure that the difference is not a fluke result. In other words, a statistically significant result suggests that covariance exists between the variables in the population the sample was drawn from.

When the difference between conditions is not statistically significant, you cannot conclude that there is covariance—that is, you cannot conclude that the independent variable had a detectable effect on the dependent variable. In other words, any observed difference between the groups found in the study is similar to the kinds of differences you would find just by chance when there is no covariance. And if there is no covariance, the study does not support a causal claim.

How Large Is the Effect?

For more detail on effect size and standard deviation, see Appendix A.

Knowing that a result is statistically significant assures you that the result probably was not drawn by chance from a population in which there is no difference. But depending on the study, even tiny differences might be statistically significant. Therefore, asking about effect size can help you evaluate the strength of the covariance (that is, the difference). In general, the larger the effect size, the more important, and the stronger, the causal effect probably is.

As discussed in Chapter 7, psychologists often use the correlation coefficient (r) to help evaluate the strength of an association. In experiments, researchers often use a different indicator of standardized effect size, called d. In general, this measure represents how far apart two experimental groups are on the dependent variable. It represents not only how far apart the means are but also how much scores within the groups overlap—that is, d takes into account not just the difference between means but also the spread of scores within each group (the standard deviation). When d is larger, it usually means that the independent variable caused the dependent variable to change for more of the participants in the study. When d is smaller, it usually means that the scores of participants in the two experimental groups overlap more. **Figure 9.21** provides examples of what two d values might look like when a study's results are graphed showing all participants. Even though the difference between means is the same in the two graphs, the effect sizes reflect the degrees of overlap between the group participants.

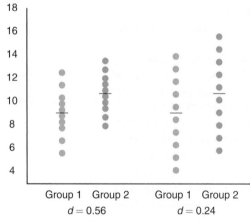

FIGURE 9.21 Effect size and overlap between groups. Effect sizes are larger when the scores in the two groups overlap less. Overlap is a function of how far apart the group means are, as well as how variable the scores are within each group. On both sides of the graph, the two group means are the same distance apart (about 2 units), but the overlap of the scores between groups is greater in the pair of means on the right. Because there is more overlap between groups, the effect size is smaller.

TABLE 9.1 Cohen's Conventions for Effect Size *d*. Is the Effect Size Weak, Moderate, or Strong?		
An effect size in which $d =$	Can be described as	Is comparable to an *r* of
0.20	Weak/small	0.10
0.50	Moderate/medium	0.30
0.80	Strong/large	0.50

In Zhong and Leonardelli's study, the effect size for the difference in perceived temperature between the social exclusion group and the social inclusion group was $d = 0.53$. According to statistical conventions, a *d* of 0.50 is considered a medium, or moderate, effect size (see **Table 9.1**). Therefore, if you were interrogating the statistical validity of Zhong and Leonardelli's causal claim, you would conclude that social exclusion's effects on perceived temperature are moderate. As a comparison, the effect size for the difference between the red and green groups in Elliot and colleagues' study was about $d = 0.64$. According to Cohen's conventions, this *d* represents a moderate to large effect of pen color on performance. (See also Appendix B for more questions to ask about statistical validity, such as whether the researchers used the appropriate tests or whether they made any inferential errors.)

Internal Validity: Are There Alternative Explanations for the Outcome?

When we interrogate causal claims, internal validity is often the priority. Experimenters isolate and manipulate a key causal variable, while controlling for all possible other variables, precisely so they can achieve internal validity. If the internal validity of an experiment is sound, you know that a causal claim is almost certainly appropriate. But if the internal validity is flawed—if there is some confound—a causal claim would be inappropriate. It should instead be demoted to an association claim.

Some common threats to internal validity have already been discussed in this chapter. Recall that three fundamental internal validity questions are worth asking of any experiment:

1. Did the design of the experiment ensure that there were no design confounds? Or did some other variable accidentally covary along with the intended independent variable?
2. If the experimenters used an independent-groups design, did they control for selection effects by using random assignment or matching?
3. If the experimenters used a within-groups design, did they control for order effects by counterbalancing?

Chapter 10 goes into further detail on these threats to internal validity plus nine other threats.

1. How do manipulation checks provide evidence for the construct validity of an experiment? Why does theory matter as you evaluate construct validity?

2. Besides generalization to other participants, what other aspect of generalization is external validity concerned with?

3. What does it mean when an effect size is large (as opposed to small) in an experiment?

4. Summarize the three threats to internal validity that this chapter has covered.

1. See p. 266; see pp. 266–267. 2. See p. 268; generalization to other settings.
3. See pp. 270–271. 4. See p. 271.

Summary

Experiments study the effect of an independent (manipulated) variable on a dependent (measured) variable, while purposefully keeping all extraneous variables constant as control variables. Experiments enable causal claims because they potentially allow researchers to establish covariance, temporal precedence, and internal validity.

Experimenters can manipulate the independent variable in an independent-groups design, in which different participants are exposed to each level of the independent variable, or in a within-groups design, in which the same participants are exposed to all levels of the independent variable. One simple independent-groups design is the posttest-only design, in which participants are randomly assigned to one of at least two levels of an independent variable and then measured once on the dependent variable. Another simple independent-groups design is the prettest/posttest design, in which participants are randomly assigned to one of at least two levels of an independent variable, and are then measured on a dependent variable twice—once before and once after they experience the independent variable. Random assignment or matching helps establish internal validity in such independent-groups designs by minimizing selection effects.

One simple within-groups design is a concurrent-measures design, in which participants are exposed to at least two levels of an independent variable at the same time and then indicate a preference for one level (the dependent variable). Another simple example is a repeated-measures design, in which participants are tested on the dependent variable after each exposure to an independent variable condition. Within-groups designs offer distinct advantages over independent-groups designs, but they also present some pitfalls.

When you interrogate a causal claim, you will apply all of the four big validities. You will ask about construct validity by assessing whether the variables were manipulated and measured in ways consistent with the theory behind the experiment. You will ask about external validity by asking whether the experiment's results can be generalized to other people or to other situations. You can begin to interrogate an experiment's statistical validity by asking how strongly the independent variable affects the dependent variable and whether the effect is statistically significant. Finally, you will ask about the internal validity by looking for design confounds and seeing whether the researchers used techniques such as random assignment and counterbalancing.

Key Terms

between-subjects designs, p. 254
carryover effects, p. 261
concurrent-measures design, p. 258
conditions, p. 246
confounds, p. 249
control group, p. 248
control variable, p. 246
counterbalancing, p. 261
demand characteristics, p. 263
dependent variable, p. 246
design confound, p. 249
independent variable, p. 246
independent-groups design, p. 254
Latin square, p. 262
manipulation checks, p. 266
matched-groups design, p. 252

order effects, p. 261
partial counterbalancing, p. 262
pilot study, p. 266
placebo group, p. 248
posttest-only design, p. 254
power, p. 260
practice effects, p. 261
pretest/posttest design, p. 255
random assignment, p. 251
repeated-measures designs, p. 258
selection effect, p. 250
systematic variability, p. 250
treatment group, p. 248
unsystematic variability, p. 250
within-groups designs, p. 254

NEED HELP STUDYING?

wwnorton.com/studyspace

Visit StudySpace to access free review materials such as:

- Diagnostic Review Quizzes
- Study Outlines

Learning Actively

1. Indicate whether each variable below is manipulated or measured.

   a. participant's age
   b. number of siblings each participant has
   c. how long a participant is given to complete a task: 30 minutes, 20 minutes, or 10 minutes
   d. how long a participant takes to complete a task
   e. dose of a drug a participant is given: 1 milligram or 5 milligrams
   f. participant's height
   g. participant's score on an anagram test
   h. level of test participants receive: easy or difficult
   i. level of test participants choose to take: easy or difficult
   j. whether or not a participant has worn braces
   k. personality of the experimenter: friendly or stern

2. Design a posttest-only experiment that would test each of the following causal claims. For each one, identify the study's independent variable(s), identify its dependent variable(s), and suggest some important control variables. Then, sketch a bar graph of the results you would predict (remember to put the dependent variable on the y-axis). Finally, apply the three causal rules to each study.

   a. Having a friendly (versus a stern) teacher causes children to score better on a school achievement test.
   b. Shaking hands with a stranger who has warm hands (versus cold hands) causes people to perceive the stranger more positively.
   c. Practicing the piano for 30 minutes a day (compared with 10 minutes a day) causes new neural connections in the temporal region of the brain.

3. What kind of procedure would you use to study each of the following independent variables with an independent-groups design? What if you wanted to use a repeated-measures design? Explain each of your answers in terms of the advantages and disadvantages of the different kinds of manipulations.

   a. Shaking a stranger's cold hand versus a stranger's warm hand
   b. Listening to a lecture from a nice teacher versus a nasty teacher
   c. Practicing the piano for 30 minutes a day versus 10 minutes a day

4. To study people's willingness to help others, social psychologists Bibb Latané and John Darley (1968) invited people to work on questionnaires in a lab room. After handing out the questionnaires, the female experimenter

went next door and staged a loud accident: She pretended to fall off a chair and get hurt, although she actually played a tape recording of this accident. Then the experimenters observed whether each participant stopped filling out the questionnaire and went to try to help the "victim."

Behind the scenes, the experimenters had flipped a coin to assign participants randomly to either an "alone" group, in which they were in the questionnaire room by themselves, or a "passive confederate" group, in which they were in the questionnaire room with a confederate (an actor) who sat impassively during the "accident" and did not attempt to help the "victim."

In the end, Latané and Darley found that when participants were alone, 70% reacted, but when participants were with a passive confederate, only 7% reacted. This experiment supported Latané and Darley's theory that during an accident, people take cues from others—looking to others to decide how to interpret the situation.

a. What are the independent, dependent, and control variables in this study?
b. Sketch a graph of the results of this study.
c. Is the independent variable in this study manipulated as independent groups or as repeated measures? How do you know?
d. For this study, ask at least one question for each of the four validities.

5. Your friend reads about Latané and Darley's helping behavior study described in Question 4 and says, "Maybe the people who were doing the questionnaires by themselves were just more helpful people, and that's why they helped more." What kind of validity would your friend be addressing? Is her criticism appropriate?

How should we interpret a null result?

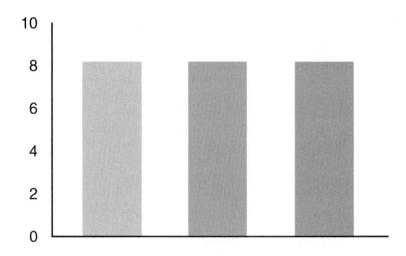

Was it really the therapy, or something else, that caused symptoms to improve?

10

More on Experiments: Confounding and Obscuring Variables

Learning Objectives

A year from now, you should still be able to:

1. Interrogate an experiment to identify signs of 12 potential threats to internal validity.
2. Describe how researchers can design studies to prevent internal validity threats.
3. Interrogate an experiment with a null result, identifying possible obscuring factors.
4. Describe how researchers can design studies to minimize possible obscuring factors.

Chapter 9 covered the basic structure of an experiment; this chapter addresses a number of questions about why experiments are designed the way they are. Why is it so important to use a comparison group? Why do so many experimenters create a standardized, controlled, seemingly artificial environment? Why do they use so many (or so few) participants? Why do researchers often use computers to measure their variables? Why do they insist on double-blind designs? To create the best possible studies, good researchers specifically design their experiments with many factors in mind. They want to detect differences that are really there, and they want to determine conclusively when their predictions are wrong.

The first major section in this chapter describes potential internal validity problems and how researchers usually avoid them. The second section discusses some of the reasons that experiments sometimes give null results.

Threats to Internal Validity: Did the Independent Variable Really Cause the Difference?

When you interrogate an experiment, internal validity is the most important of the big validities to focus on. As discussed in Chapter 9, three of the most common threats to internal validity are design confounds, selection effects, and order effects. All three of these threats involve an *alternative explanation* for the results.

For example, with a design confound, there is an alternative explanation because another variable happened to vary systematically along with the intended independent variable. Chapter 9 gave the hypothetical example of the study on ink color. If the problems given to the red ink group had been more difficult than the problems given to the green and gray ink groups, that would have been a confound (see Figure 9.5). It would not be clear whether the ink color or the problem difficulty caused the red ink group to perform more poorly.

With a selection effect, a confound exists because the different independent variable groups have different types of participants. In Chapter 9, the example used was a study of an intensive therapy for autism, in which children who received the intensive experimental therapy did, indeed, improve over time. However, their improvement may have been caused by the therapy, or it may have been caused by greater overall involvement on the part of the parents who elected to be in the intensive therapy group. Those parents' greater motivation to treat their children could have been an alternative explanation for the improvement of children in the intensive therapy group.

With an order effect (in a within-groups design), there is an alternative explanation because the outcome might be caused by the independent variable, but it also might be caused by the order in which the levels of the variable are presented. When there is an order effect, we do not know whether the independent variable is really having an effect or whether the participants are just getting tired, bored, or well-practiced.

But these types of threats are just the start. There are other ways—about one dozen total—that an experiment might be at risk for a confound. Experimenters try to think about all of them, and they plan studies accordingly. Good researchers will creatively apply common design strategies to work around threats and make strong causal statements.

The Really Bad Experiment (A Cautionary Tale)

Previous chapters have used examples of real studies to illustrate the material. In contrast, this chapter opens with three fictional experiments. They have to be fictional, because responsible scientists would never conduct studies like these.

> Nikhil, a summer camp counselor and psychology major, has noticed that his current cabin of 15 boys is an especially rambunctious bunch. He has heard that a change in diet might help them calm down, so he eliminates the sugary snacks and desserts from the boys' meals for 2 days.

As he expected, the boys are much quieter and calmer by the end of the week, after refined sugar has been eliminated from their diets.

Dr. Yuki has recruited a sample of 40 depressed women, all of whom are interested in receiving psychotherapy for their depression. She measures their level of depression using a standard depression inventory at the start of therapy. For 12 weeks, all the women participate in Dr. Yuki's style of cognitive therapy. At the end of the 12-week session, she measures the women again and finds that on the whole their levels of depression have significantly decreased.

A dorm on a university campus has started a "Go Green" Facebook campaign, focused on persuading students to turn out the lights in their dormitory rooms. Dorm residents receive e-mails and messages on Facebook that encourage energy-saving behaviors. At the start of the campaign, the head resident assistant noted how many kilowatt hours the dorm was using by checking the electric meters on the building. At the end of the 2-month campaign, the head resident checks the kilowatt hours again and finds that the number of kilowatt hours used has dropped. He tests the two measures (pretest and posttest) and finds that they are significantly different.

Note that all three of these examples fit the same template, which we might diagram as in **Figure 10.1**. If you graphed the data of the first two studies, they would look something like **Figure 10.2A** and **Figure 10.2B**. Before going on, reflect on the three examples: What alternative explanations can you think of for the results of each?

The formal name for this kind of design is the **one-group, pretest/posttest design**. A researcher recruits one group of participants, measures them on a pretest, exposes them to a treatment, intervention, or change, and then measures them on a posttest. However, a better name for this design might be "the really bad experiment." Understanding why this design is so problematic can help you learn about threats to internal validity—and appreciate how researchers can avoid them by applying better research designs.

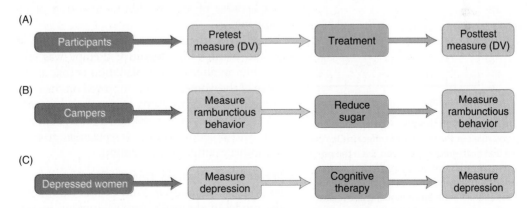

FIGURE 10.1 The "really bad experiment." Panel A presents a general diagram of the really bad experiment. Panels B and C show how you might diagram two of the examples given in the text. Using these as a model, can you sketch a diagram of the "Go Green" example?

Threats to Internal Validity: Did the Independent Variable Really Cause the Difference?　　**279**

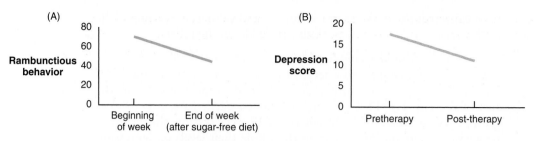

FIGURE 10.2 **Graphing the "really bad experiment."** The first two examples in the chapter can be graphed this way. Using these as a model, can you sketch a graph of the "Go Green" example, too?

Six Threats to Internal Validity That Especially Apply to One-Group, Pretest/Posttest Designs

The really bad experiment lends itself to a variety of alternative explanations. They include maturation threats, history threats, regression threats, attrition threats, testing threats, and instrumentation threats. In many cases (but not all) these six threats can be avoided simply by changing the design.

Maturation Threats to Internal Validity

Why did the boys in Nikhil's cabin start acting better? Was it because they had eaten less sugar? Perhaps. But an alternative explanation is that the boys just settled in ("matured" to) the camp setting after they had time to get used to the place. The boys' behavior improved on its own; the sugar-free diet may have had nothing to do with it. Such an effect is called **maturation**, because it is a change in behavior that emerges more or less spontaneously over time. People slowly adapt to strange environments; children get better at walking and talking; plants grow taller—but not because of any outside intervention. It just happens.

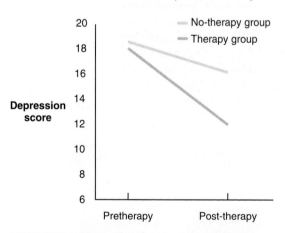

Similarly, the depressed women may have improved because the cognitive therapy was effective, but an alternative explanation is that at least some of the women simply improved on their own. Sometimes the symptoms of depression or other disorders get better, for no known cause, with time. This phenomenon, known as *spontaneous remission*, is another example of maturation.

FIGURE 10.3 **Maturation threats.** A comparison group would help you rule out the maturation effect in Dr. Yuki's study. Notice that both groups improved: Even the no-treatment group showed a maturation effect. However, the treatment group showed an even larger effect, indicating that the cognitive therapy is working above and beyond the effect of maturation. The new study controls for the effect of maturation, since both groups experience some maturation.

Preventing Maturation Threats. Because the studies both Nikhil and Dr. Yuki conducted followed the model of the really bad experiment, we have no way of knowing whether the improvements they noticed were caused by maturation or by the treatments they administered. In contrast, if the two researchers had conducted true experiments, they would also have included an appropriate comparison group. Nikhil would have observed a comparison group of equally rambunctious campers who did not switch to a low-sugar diet. Dr. Yuki would have studied a comparison group of women who started out equally depressed but did not receive the cognitive therapy. If the treatment groups improved and the comparison groups did not, each researcher could rule out the effect of maturation. **Figure 10.3** shows the benefits of a comparison group.

History Threats to Internal Validity

Sometimes a threat to internal validity occurs not just because time has passed, but because something specific has happened between the pretest and posttest. In our third example, why did the dorm residents use less electricity? Was it the Go Green campaign? Perhaps. But a plausible alternative explanation is that the weather got cooler and the residents did not use the air conditioning as much.

Why did the campers' behavior improve? It could have been the low-sugar diet, but perhaps they all started a difficult swimming course in the middle of the week, and the exercise tired them out.

These alternative explanations are examples of **history threats**—threats to internal validity that occur when a "historical" or external event occurs to *everyone* in the treatment group at the same time as the treatment, so it is unclear whether the change in the experimental group is caused by the treatment received or by the historical event. To be a history threat, the event must affect everyone or almost everyone in the group (that is, systematically), not just a few people (that is, unsystematically).

Preventing History Threats. As with maturation threats, a comparison group can help control for history threats. In the Go Green study, the students would need to measure the kilowatt usage in another, comparable dormitory during the same 2 months but not give the students in the second dorm the Go Green campaign materials. (Note that this would be a pretest/posttest design, covered in Chapter 9.) If both groups decreased their kilowatt usage about the same over time, as shown in **Figure 10.4A**, the decrease probably resulted from the change

For more on pretest/ posttest designs, see Chapter 9, pp. 255–257.

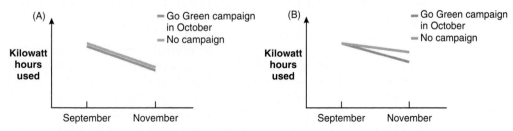

FIGURE 10.4 History threats. A comparison group would help rule out the history threat of seasonal differences in electrical usage. If both dorms reduced their kilowatt hours equally, as shown in Panel A, we would conclude that the Go Green campaign did not work—that all dorms reduced their energy usage over the fall months. In Panel B, both dorms show a decreased in kilowatt usage in November; however, the Go Green campaign dorm's usage decreased even more, indicating that the campaign worked.

of seasons, not from the Go Green campaign. However, if the treatment group decreased its usage more than the comparison group did, as shown in **Figure 10.4B**, we can rule out the history threat. Both the comparison group and the treatment group should experience the same seasonal "historical" changes; therefore, including the comparison group controls for this threat.

In some cases, history threats can occur even in a pretest/posttest design if some outside event systematically affects one level of the independent variable, but not the other (such as a construction crew that uses electric tools from the power supply—but in only one dorm).

Regression Threats to Internal Validity

For more detail on arithmetic means, see Appendix A.

A **regression threat** refers to a statistical concept called *regression toward the mean*: When a performance is extreme at Time 1, the next time that performance is measured (Time 2), it is likely to be less extreme—that is, closer to a typical, or average performance. The "mean" here refers to the arithmetic average of all the performances (or scores) of a particular group.

Everyday Regression to the Mean. Everyday situations help illustrate regression to the mean. For example, during the baseball season of 2009, the Philadelphia Phillies beat the Cincinnati Reds 22–1. That's a blowout: Baseball scores are hardly ever that high. Without knowing a thing about these two teams, people who know anything about baseball would predict that in their next game, the Phillies would score fewer runs. Why? Simply because most people have an intuitive understanding of regression to the mean.

Here's the statistical explanation: The Phillies' score in the first game was exceptionally high partly because of the team's talent, but partly because of a unique combination of random factors that came out in the Phillies' favor. The team's injury level was, just by chance, much lower than usual. Just by chance, Ryan Howard (a strong hitter) was up to bat just when the Reds' pitching weakened. Just by chance, the Phillies were playing at home and thus had a slight advantage. Just by chance, the Reds' defense was off in four of the innings. So despite the Phillies' legitimate talent, they also benefited from randomness—a chance combination of lucky events that is unlikely to occur in the same combination again. So overall, the team's score in the next game would almost necessarily be worse than in this game. And indeed, the team regressed: The very next night, they scored only 3 runs against the Reds. That is, the Phillies finished closer to their average level of performance.

In another example, suppose you are normally cheerful and happy. On any particular day, however, your mood is attributable to your normal, cheerful state plus other factors that are determined at random, such as the weather, your friends' moods, and even parking problems. Every once in a while, just by chance, a large number of these random factors will affect you negatively: It will pour rain, your friends will be grumpy, and you will not be able find a parking spot. Your day is terrible! But the good news is that tomorrow will almost certainly be better, because those random factors are unlikely to occur in that same, unlucky combination again. It might still be raining, but your friends will not be grumpy, and you will quickly find a good parking spot. If even one of these factors is better, your day will go better, and you will regress back toward your average, happy mean.

Regression works at both extremes. An unusually good performance or outcome is likely to regress downward (toward its mean) the next time. And an unusually bad performance or outcome is likely to regress upward (toward its mean) the next time. Either extreme is explainable by an unusually lucky, or an unusually unlucky, combination of random events.

Regression and Internal Validity. When the people measured in a pretest condition are extreme on the dependent variable, regression is likely to be a threat to internal validity. That is, if the group is unusually high or low at pretest, you can expect them to regress toward the mean somewhat when it comes time for the posttest. For example, the 40 depressed women Dr. Yuki studied were, on average, quite depressed. Their pretest average may have been, in part, due to their true, baseline level of depression. But because the 40 women had just volunteered for treatment, it is likely that at least some of them were feeling especially bad at the time of the pretest, in part because of random events (perhaps the winter blues, a recent illness, parenting troubles, job loss, or divorce). They were therefore especially interested in getting therapy just at that time. At the posttest, the random effects on their moods probably would not be the same as they were at pretest (maybe the season changed or their job situation improved), so the overall depression score would go down. The change would not occur because of the treatment, but simply because of regression toward the mean, so in this case there would be an internal validity threat.

Preventing Regression Threats. What can a researcher do to prevent regression threats? Once again, comparison groups can help, along with a careful inspection of the pattern of results. If the comparison group and the experimental group are equally extreme at pretest, the researchers can account for any regression effects in their results.

In **Figure 10.5A**, you can rule out regression and conclude that the therapy really does work: Even though both groups started out equally extreme, their depression decreases at different rates. Both groups become less depressed over time, but the levels of depression in the therapy group decrease even more. If regression played a role, it would have done so for both groups, because they were equally at risk for regression at the start. In contrast, if you saw the pattern of results shown in **Figure 10.5B**, you would suspect that regression had occurred. The therapy group did improve more than the no-therapy group, but this group also started out more depressed—more extreme—than the comparison group. Regression is a particular threat in exactly this situation—when one group starts out more extreme. Even though those in the therapy group were less depressed at posttest than at pretest, the drop could be attributed to a regression effect, rather than to the therapy. In short, the results from Figure 10.5B should not convince you that the therapy works.

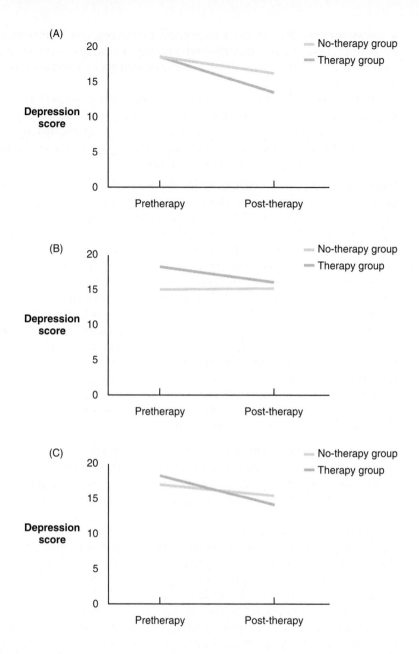

FIGURE 10.5 Regression to the mean. Regression to the mean can be analyzed by inspecting different patterns of results. Regression effects can be ruled out as an internal validity threat in Panel A because both groups started out equally extreme at pretest. Regression can be ruled out in Panel C, too, because regression effects alone do not make an extreme group cross over the mean to the other side. In Panel B, however, regression is a possibility, because the therapy group started out more extreme than the no-therapy group—extreme pretest scores are at the most risk for regression.

In **Figure 10.5C**, in contrast, the therapy group started out more extreme on depression—and therefore probably experienced some regression to the mean. However, this pattern shows a clear effect of therapy, too. If we can assume that both the therapy and comparison samples are drawn from the same population (that is, both samples have the same usual mean), then it would be implausible for the therapy group to surpass the mean of the comparison group through regression alone. Regression pulls an extreme group closer to the mean, but regression alone will not cause a group to cross back over the mean in the opposite direction, as depicted here. Therefore, these results suggest that the therapy probably did have an effect (in addition to a little help from regression effects).

Attrition Threats to Internal Validity

Why did the average level of rambunctiousness in Nikhil's campers decrease over the course of the week? It could have decreased because of the low-sugar diet, but maybe it decreased because the most obnoxious camper had to leave camp early.

Similarly, the level of depression among Dr. Yuki's patients might have decreased because of the cognitive therapy. But it could also have decreased because three of the most depressed women in the study had symptoms so severe that they could not maintain the therapy regimen and dropped out of the study: The posttest average is lower only because these extra-high scores are not included.

In many studies that have a pretest and a posttest, **attrition** (sometimes called "mortality") occurs when people drop out of the study before it ends. Attrition sometimes happens when a pretest and posttest are administered on separate days, but it becomes a threat to internal validity when it is systematic—that is, when only a certain kind of participant drops out. If just any camper leaves midweek, it might not be a problem for Nikhil's research, but it is a problem when the most rambunctious camper leaves early. His departure creates an alternative explanation for Nikhil's results: We do not know if the posttest average is lower because the low-sugar diet worked, or whether the average is lower just because that one extreme score is gone.

Similarly, as depicted in **Figure 10.6**, it would not be unusual if 3 of 40 women in the depression therapy study dropped out. However, if the 3 most depressed women *systematically* drop out, the mean for the posttest is going to be lower, only because it does not include these three extreme scores (not because of the therapy). So if the depression score goes down from pretest to posttest, we would not know whether the decrease occurred because of the therapy or because of the alternative explanation—that the highest-scoring women had dropped out.

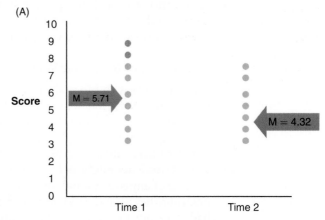

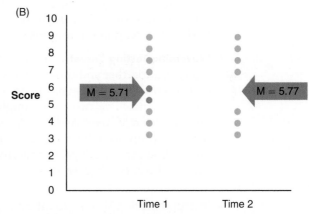

FIGURE 10.6 Attrition threats. If two people drop out of a study, both of whom scored at the high end of the distribution on the pretest, the group mean changes substantially when their scores are omitted—even if all the other scores stay the same. But when the dropouts' scores on the pretest are close to the group's mean, removing their scores does not change the group mean so much.

A comparison group is not always a cure-all for attrition, unfortunately. In a two-group experiment (such as a pretest/posttest design), if both groups experience the same pattern of dropouts, then attrition is not an internal validity threat. But attrition can be a threat when only one group experiences attrition. For example, if a treatment is rigorous or time-consuming, the unmotivated people in the treatment group might drop out over time; however, unmotivated people would not drop out of the less arduous control group.

Preventing Attrition Threats. Attrition is fairly easy for researchers to identify and correct. When participants drop out of a study, most researchers will remove those participants' original scores from the pretest average, too. That way, they look only at the scores of participants who completed both parts of the study. Another approach is to check the pretest scores of the dropouts. If they have extreme scores on the pretest, their attrition is more of a threat to internal validity than if their scores are closer to the group average.

Testing Threats to Internal Validity

A **testing threat** to internal validity is a kind of order effect. Specifically, a testing threat means that scores have changed over time just because participants have taken the test more than once. People might have become more practiced at taking the test, leading to improved scores, or they may become fatigued or bored, which could lead to worse scores over time. For example, in an educational setting, students might perform better on a posttest than on a pretest, but not because of any educational intervention. Instead, perhaps they had the jitters the first time they took the test, so they did better on the posttest simply because they had more practice the second time around. Taking a pretest might also sensitize people to particular issues—for example, the questions on a depression pretest might have made the women in Dr. Yuki's study more sensitive to subtle symptoms of depression. They might have changed their posttest answers in response to this sensitivity, not in response to the treatment.

Preventing Testing Threats. To avoid testing threats, researchers might abandon a pretest altogether and use a posttest-only design (see Chapter 9). If researchers do use a pretest, they might opt to use alternative forms of the test for the two measurements. The two forms might both measure depression, for example, but use different items to do so. A comparison group can also help. If the comparison group takes both the pretest and the posttest, too, but the treatment group shows an even larger change, testing effects can be ruled out as an internal validity threat (see **Figure 10.7**).

Instrumentation Threats to Internal Validity

Instrumentation threats to internal validity (also called *instrument decay*) occur when a measuring instrument changes over time from having been used before. (In contrast, a testing threat occurs when a *participant* changes over time from having been tested before.) One example of instrumentation comes from observational research: Over time, the people who are coding behaviors

Treatment group
Comparison group

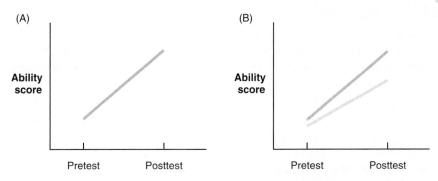

(A)

Ability score

Pretest   Posttest

(B)

Ability score

Pretest   Posttest

FIGURE 10.7 Testing threats. If there is no comparison group, it is hard to know if the improvement from pretest to posttest is caused by the treatment, or simply by practice (Panel A). However, the results from a comparison group can help rule out testing effects. Both groups might improve, but the treatment group improves even more—suggesting that both practice and a true effect of the treatment are causing the improvement.

(that is, the coders are the measuring instrument) might change their standards for judging behavior—they may become more tired, more strict, or more lenient. So perhaps Nikhil's campers did not really become less rambunctious; instead, the people judging the campers' behavior became more tolerant of shoving and hitting.

Another example of instrumentation might occur when a researcher uses different forms for the pretest and posttest, but the two forms are not sufficiently equivalent. For example, Dr. Yuki might have used a measure of depression at pretest that people tend to score a little higher on, and another measure of depression at posttest that people tend to score a little lower on. As a result, the pattern she observed was not a sign of how good the cognitive therapy is, but merely reflected the way the alternative forms of the test are calibrated.

Preventing Instrumentation Threats. One simple way to prevent an instrumentation threat is to use a posttest-only design (in which behavior is measured only once). But if a pretest/posttest design is required for other reasons, researchers should take steps to ensure that the pretest and posttest measures are equivalent. To do so, a researcher might collect data from each instrument to be sure that the two are calibrated the same. Or, to avoid shifting standards of behavioral coders, researchers might take care to train their coders multiple times throughout the experiment, establishing their reliability and validity at both pretest and posttest. Using clear coding manuals would be an important part of this process.

Finally, to control for the problem of different forms, Dr Yuki could also counterbalance the versions of the test, giving some participants version A at pretest and version B at posttest, and giving other participants version B, and then version A.

Three Threats to Internal Validity That Can Apply to Any Experiment

Many internal validity threats are likely to occur in the really bad experiment, these threats can often be corrected for simply by adding a comparison group. Doing so would result in a two-group, pretest/posttest design. The posttest-only design, explained in Chapter 9, is another option. However, three more threats to internal validity—observer bias, demand characteristics, and placebo effects—might apply even for designs with a clear comparison group.

Observer Bias

Observer bias can be a threat to internal validity in almost any study in which there is a behavioral dependent variable. Observer bias occurs when researchers' expectations influence their interpretation of the results—or even influence the outcome of the study. For example, Dr. Yuki might be a biased observer of her patients' depression: She expects to see her patients improve, whether they do or do not. Nikhil may be a biased observer of his own campers: He may expect his low-sugar diet to work, so he views the campers' posttest behavior more positively.

For more on observer bias, see Chapter 6, pp. 159–161.

Although comparison groups can prevent many threats to internal validity, they do not necessarily control for observer bias. Even if Dr. Yuki used a no-therapy comparison group, observer bias could still occur: If she knew which participants were in which group, her biases could lead her to see more improvement in the therapy group than in the comparison group.

Observer bias can threaten two kinds of validity in an experiment. It threatens internal validity, because an alternative explanation exists for the results. (Did the therapy work, or was Dr. Yuki biased?). But observer bias also can threaten the construct validity of the dependent variable, because it means that the depression ratings given by Dr. Yuki do not represent the true levels of depression of her participants.

Demand Characteristics

Demand characteristics (introduced in Chapter 9) are a problem when participants guess what the study is supposed to be about and change their behavior in the expected direction. For example, Dr. Yuki's patients know they are getting therapy. If they think that Dr. Yuki expects them to get better, they might change their self-reports of their symptoms in the expected direction. Nikhil's campers, too, might realize that something fishy is going on when they are not given their usual snacks. The campers' awareness of a change in their diet could certainly change the way they act.

Blind Studies Can Control for Observer Effects and Demand Characteristics. To avoid observer effects and demand characteristics, researchers need to do more than add a comparison group to their studies. One way to avoid such problems is to conduct a **double-blind study**, in which neither the participants nor the researchers who evaluate them know who is in the treatment group and who is in the comparison group.

We could imagine conducting a study of Nikhil's hypothesis as a double-blind study. Nikhil could arrange to have two cabins of equally rambunctious boys and for only one group of them, replace their sugary snacks with low-sugar versions. The boys would not know which kind of snacks they were eating, and the people observing the boys' behavior would also be blind to which boys were in which group.

When a double-blind study is not possible, a variation might be an acceptable alternative. For example, in some studies, participants know which group they are in, but the observers do not. The students exposed to the Go Green campaign would certainly be aware that someone was trying to influence their behavior. But ideally, the raters who were recording their electric usage should not know which dorm was exposed to the campaign and which was not. Of course, keeping observers blind to condition is even more important when they are rating behaviors that are more difficult to code, such as symptoms of depression or behavior problems at camp.

Chapter 9 discussed Elliot and colleagues' (2007) study, in which the color red affected test-takers' performance. The research assistants in that study were blind to the ink colors that each participant received, presumably so they could not subtly influence the test-takers' behavior. The participants themselves were not blind to the color of their materials (in fact, seeing the color was central to Elliot's manipulation). But since the test-takers participated in only one condition, they were not aware that color was an important feature of the experiment. Therefore, they were blind to the *reason* their numbers were written in a particular color.

Placebo Effects

Perhaps the women who received Dr. Yuki's therapy improved because the cognitive therapy really works. But an alternative explanation is that there was a placebo effect: The women improved simply because they *believed* that they were receiving an effective treatment.

A **placebo effect** occurs when people receive a treatment and really improve—but only because they believe they are receiving a valid treatment. In most drug studies, one group receives a pill or injection with the real drug, while another group receives a pill or injection with nothing active in it—a sugar pill or a saline injection. People can even receive placebo psychotherapies, in which they simply talk to a friendly listener about their problems; these placebo conversations have no therapeutic structure. The inert pill, injection, or therapy is the placebo. Often, the people who receive the placebo see their symptoms improve simply because they believe that the treatment they are receiving is effective.

Placebo effects are not imaginary. Placebos have been shown to reduce real symptoms such as depression (Kirsch & Sapirstein, 1998), postoperative pain or anxiety (Benedetti, Amanzio, Vighetti, & Asteggiano, 2006), terminal cancer pain, and epilepsy (Beecher, 1955). Placebo effects are not only psychological—

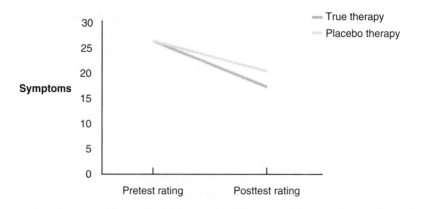

FIGURE 10.8

Placebo control studies. Adding a placebo comparison group can help you subtract out a potential placebo effect from the true effect of a therapy.

they can also be physical. Nor are they always beneficial or harmless: Physical side effects such as skin rashes or headaches can be produced by placebos, too. People's symptoms appear to respond not just to the active ingredients in drugs and therapies, but also to their belief in those therapies.

A placebo can be strong medicine. Kirsch and Sapirstein reviewed studies that gave either antidepressant drugs, such as Prozac, or placebos to depressed patients and concluded that the placebo groups improved almost as much as groups that received real medicine. In fact, up to 75% of the depression improvement in the Prozac groups was also achieved in placebo groups.

Designing Studies to Rule Out the Placebo Effect. To determine whether an effect is caused by a therapeutic treatment or by placebo effects, the standard approach is to include a special kind of comparison group. Specifically, one group receives the real drug or real therapy, and the second group receives the placebo drug or placebo therapy. Crucially, neither the person treating the patients nor the patients themselves know whether they are in the real group or the placebo group. These designs are called **double-blind placebo control studies**.

The results of such a placebo study might look like the graph in **Figure 10.8**. Notice that both groups improved, but the group receiving the real drug improved even more, showing placebo effects *plus* the effects of the real drug. If the results turn out like this, the researchers can conclude that the treatment they are testing does cause improvement. Once again, an internal validity threat—a placebo effect—can be controlled for with a careful research design.

Is That Really a Placebo Effect? If you thought about it carefully, you probably noticed that the results shown in Figure 10.8 do not definitively show a placebo effect pattern. Both the group receiving the real drug and the group receiving the placebo improved over time. However, some of the improvement in both groups could have been caused by maturation, testing, instrumentation, history, or regression effects (Kienle & Kiene, 1997). If you were interested in showing a placebo effect specifically, you would need to include a no-treatment comparison group—one that receives neither drug nor placebo. Imagine that

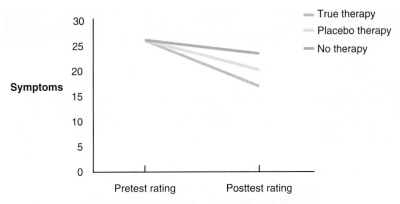

FIGURE 10.9 **Ruling out a placebo threat.** To definitively show a placebo threat requires three groups: one that receives the true treatment, one that receives placebo treatment, and one that receives no treatment. If there is a placebo effect, the pattern of results will show that the "no treatment" group does not improve as much as the placebo group.

your results looked something like those in **Figure 10.9**. Because the placebo group improved over time—even more than the no-therapy/no-placebo group did—we can attribute its improvement to some effect of placebo and not just to maturation, history, attrition, testing, or instrumentation.

With So Many Threats, Are Experiments Useless?

After reading about the dozen ways a good experiment can go wrong (see **Table 10.1**, pp. 292–293, for a summary), you might be tempted to assume that most experiments you read about are faulty. However, good researchers consciously avoid internal validity threats when they design and interpret their work. Many of the threats discussed in this chapter are a problem only in one-group pretest/posttest studies—those with no comparison group. A carefully designed comparison group will correct for many but not all of these threats. Researchers also use reliable coding procedures, double-blind designs, placebo conditions, and control variables to prevent these internal validity threats.

Check Your Understanding

1. What is a one-group, pretest/posttest design, and which threats to internal validity are especially applicable to this design?
2. Using Table 10.1 as a guide, indicate which of the threats to internal validity would be relevant even to a two-group, posttest-only design.

1. See pp. 278–280. 2. See pp. 292–293.

TABLE 10.1 A Dozen Possible Internal Validity Threats in Experiments

Internal validity threat	Definition	Example	Questions to ask
Design confound	When a second variable unintentionally varies systematically with the independent variable	If the group that received red test booklets also received harder problems than the group that received green test booklets (instead of keeping difficulty constant, as Elliot et al. did).	Did the researchers turn nuisance variables into control variables (e.g., keeping the problem difficulty constant—see Chapter 9, pp. 249–250)?
Selection effect	In an independent-groups design, when the two independent variable groups have systematically different kinds of participants in them	In the intensive therapy for autism study, parents chose whether they wanted their children to be in the intensive treatment group or the control group.	Did the researchers use random assignment (Chapter 9, pp. 251–252) or matched groups (Chapter 9, pp. 252–253) to equalize groups?
Order effect	In a within-groups design, when the effect of the independent variable is confounded with practice, fatigue, boredom, or carryover from one level to the other	Participants in a marketing study taste Coke first, taste Pepsi second, and then give their preference. Pepsi tastes sweeter than Coke, and the order effect exaggerates this sweetness (and preference).	Did the researchers counterbalance the orders of presentation (Chapter 9, pp. 261–263)?
Maturation	An experimental group improves over time only because of natural development or spontaneous improvement	Rambunctious boys settle down as they get used to the camp setting.	Did the researchers use a comparison group of boys who had an equal amount of time to mature but who did not receive the treatment?
History	An experimental group changes over time because of an external event that affects all or most of the people in the group	Dormitory residents use less power in November than in September because the weather is cooler.	Did the researchers include a comparison group that had an equal exposure to the external event but did not receive the treatment?
Regression to the mean	An experimental group whose score is extreme at pretest will get better (or worse) over time, because the many random events that caused the extreme pretest scores do not recur the same way at posttest	A group scores as extremely depressed at pretest, in part because some of the people volunteered for therapy when they were feeling much more depressed than usual.	Did the researchers include a comparison group that was equally extreme at pretest but did not receive the therapy?

Internal validity threat	Definition	Example	Questions to ask
Attrition	An experimental group changes over time, but only because the most extreme cases have systematically dropped out and their scores are not included in the posttest	Because the most rambunctious boy in the cabin leaves camp early, his rambunctiousness affects the pretest mean but not the posttest mean.	Did the researchers compute the pretest and posttest scores with only the final sample included, removing any dropouts' data from the pretest group average?
Testing	An experimental group changes over time because repeated testing has affected the participants	A classroom's math scores improve only because the students take the same version of the test both times and therefore are more practiced at posttest.	Did the researchers have a comparison group take the same two tests? Did they use a posttest-only design, or did they use alternative forms of the measure for the pretest and posttest?
Instrumentation	An experimental group changes over time, but only because the pretest and posttest are not measured equivalently. Repeated measurements have changed the quality of the measurement instrument	Behavior at pretest is rated more strictly than behavior at posttest.	Did the researchers train coders to use the same standards when coding? Are pretest and posttest measures demonstrably equivalent?
Observer bias	An experimental group's ratings differ from a comparison group's, but only because the researcher expects the groups' ratings to differ	Nikhil expects his low-sugar diet to decrease his campers' rambunctious behavior, so he notices only their calm behavior and ignores the wild behavior.	Were the observers of the dependent variable blind to the level of the independent variable? (A comparison group does not automatically get rid of the problem of observer bias.)
Demand characteristics	Participants guess what the study's purpose is and change their behavior in the expected direction	Campers guess that the low-sugar diet is supposed to make them calmer, so they change their behavior accordingly.	Were the participants blind to the purpose of the study? Was it an independent-groups design?
Placebo effects	Participants in an experimental group improve only because they believe in the efficacy of the therapy or drug they receive	Women receiving cognitive therapy improve simply because they believe the therapy will work for them.	Did a comparison group receive a placebo (inert) drug or a placebo therapy?

Interrogating Null Effects: What If the Independent Variable Does Not Make a Difference?

The first part of this chapter discussed cases in which a researcher needs to be sure that any covariance found in an experiment was caused by the independent variable, not by a threat to internal validity. But what happens when a study finds that the independent variable did not make a difference in the dependent variable—that there is no significant covariance between the two variables? In other words, what happens when a study finds a **null effect**?

You might not read about null effects very often. Journals, newspapers, and websites are much more likely to report the results of a study in which the independent variable does have an effect. But studies that show null effects are surprisingly common—something many students learn when they start to conduct their own studies. Often, researchers who get a null effect will say their study "didn't work." Why might null effects happen?

The following three hypothetical examples illustrate null effects:

Many people believe that having more money will make them happy. But will it? One researcher, Dr. Williams, designed an experiment in which he randomly assigned people to three groups. He gave one group nothing, gave the second group a little money, and gave the third group a lot of money. The next day, he asked each group to report on its mood. The group who received cash (either a little or a lot) was no more happy than the group who received nothing.

Do GRE test preparation courses really work? An educational psychologist recruited a sample of students, all of whom wanted to raise their GRE scores. She randomly assigned the students to two groups. One group received a one-day version of a GRE test prep course, and one group received a "pep talk" control session, in which the same instructor gave students a pep talk and encouragement but no actual instruction on how to improve their scores. Afterward, students took a real GRE test. There was no significant difference in the average GRE scores between the two groups.

Researchers have hypothesized that feeling anxious can cause people to reason less carefully and logically. To test this hypothesis, a group of researchers placed people in three groups: low, medium, and high anxiety. After a few minutes of being exposed to the anxiety manipulation, the researchers gave each participant reasoning problems, which required logic, rather than emotional reasoning, to solve. Although the researchers had predicted that the anxious people would do better on the problems, participants in the three groups scored roughly the same.

These three examples of null effects, depicted as graphs in **Figure 10.10**, are all posttest-only designs. However, a null effect can happen in a within-groups design or a pretest/posttest design, too (indeed, even in a correlational study). In all three

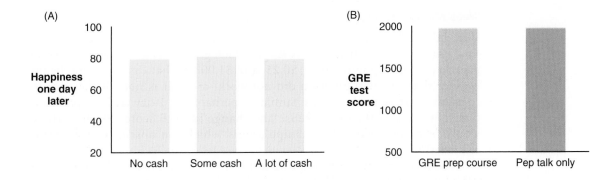

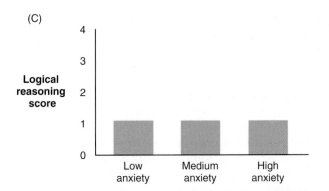

FIGURE 10.10 **The results of the three hypothetical experiments that show a null effect.** Why might cash not have made people happy, in Panel A? Why might the GRE prep course not have worked, in Panel B? Why might anxiety not have affected logical reasoning, in Panel C?

of these cases, the independent variable manipulated by the experimenters did not result in a change in the dependent variable. Why didn't these experiments show covariance between the independent variable and dependent variable?

In general, there are two possible answers to this question. Any time an experiment gives a null result, one possible explanation is simply that the independent variable really does not affect the dependent variable. In the real world, perhaps money does not make people happier, GRE prep courses do not work, and being anxious does not affect logical reasoning. In other words, the experiment gave an accurate result, showing that the manipulation the researchers used did not cause a change in the dependent variable.

A second possible explanation for a null result is that the study was not designed well enough. That is, the independent variable actually does cause a change in the dependent variable, but some obscuring factor in the study prevented the researchers from detecting the true difference. Such obscuring factors can take a number of forms.

Perhaps There Is Not Enough Between-Groups Difference

When a study returns a null result, sometimes the culprit is the design of the study. Weak manipulations, insensitive measures, and reverse confounds might prevent an experiment from detecting a true difference that exists between two or more experimental groups.

Weak Manipulations

Why did Dr. Williams's study show that money did not affect people's moods? You might ask how much money he gave each group. What if the amounts he gave to each group were $0.00, $0.25, and $1.00? In that case, it would be no wonder that the manipulation did not work—a dollar is not enough money to affect most people's moods. Similarly, perhaps the 1-day GRE preparation course was not sufficient to cause any change in GRE scores. Both of these would be examples of weak manipulations, which can obscure a true causal relationship.

When you interrogate a null result, it is therefore important to ask how the researchers operationalized the independent variable. In other words, you have to ask about construct validity. Dr. Williams might have obtained a very different pattern of results if he had given $0.00, $5.00, and $150.00 to different groups. The educational psychologist might have found that GRE courses work if they are provided daily for 3 weeks rather than for just 1 day.

Insensitive Measures

Sometimes a study finds a null result because the researchers have not used an operationalization of the dependent variable with enough sensitivity. If a medication brings a fever down by one-half a degree Celsius, you could not detect it with a thermometer that was calibrated only in one-degree increments—the thermometer would not be sensitive enough. Similarly, if a GRE course improves people's test scores about 15 points, you would not be able to detect the improvement if you used only a simple pass/fail test (where students either pass the test or fail it—nothing in between). When it comes to dependent measures, it is smart to use dependent measures that have detailed, quantitative increments—not just two or three levels.

For more on scales of measurement, see Chapter 5, pp. 118–119.

Ceiling and Floor Effects

Ceiling effects and **floor effects** are special cases of weak manipulations and insensitive measures. These effects cause independent variable groups to score almost the same on the dependent variable. All the scores are squeezed together, either at the high end (in the case of a ceiling effect) or at the low end (in the case of a floor effect).

Ceilings, Floors, and Independent Variables. Ceiling and floor effects can be the result of a problematic independent variable. For example, if Dr. Williams really did manipulate his independent variable by giving people $0.00, $0.25, or $1.00, that would be a floor effect because these three amounts are all low—that is, they are squeezed close to a "floor" of $0.00.

Or consider the example of the anxiety and reasoning study. Imagine that the researcher manipulated anxiety by telling the groups that they were about to receive an electric shock. The low-anxiety group was told to expect a 10-volt shock, the medium-anxiety group was told to expect a 50-volt shock, and the high-anxiety group was told to expect a 100-volt shock. This manipulation is likely to cause a ceiling effect on anxiety, because expecting any amount of shock is likely to lead to anxiety. It would not matter whether the expected intensity was 10 volts, 50 volts, or 100 volts. As a result, the various levels of the independent variable would appear to make no difference.

Ceilings, Floors, and Dependent Variables. Poorly designed dependent variables can also lead to ceiling and floor effects. Imagine if the logical reasoning test in the anxiety study was so difficult that nobody could solve the four problems. That would cause a floor effect: The three anxiety groups would score the same, but only because the measure for the dependent variable results in low scores in all groups.

Or imagine that in the money and happiness study, Dr. Williams asked participants to rate their happiness on the following scale:

1 = I feel horrible.
2 = I feel awful.
3 = I feel bad.
4 = I feel fine.

Because there is only one option on this measure to indicate feeling good (and because people usually tend to feel good, rather than bad), the majority of people would report the maximum, "4," on this measure. Money would appear to have no effect on happiness, but only because the dependent measure of happiness used was subject to a ceiling effect.

Here is an even better example of a ceiling effect: Imagine that we tried to show that women and men are equally good at mathematics by asking the men and women in a sample to solve the problem $7 \times 5 = ?$. Almost everyone would answer this question correctly. Could we then conclude that men and women are equally good at math? Again, this measure would result in a ceiling effect, because everybody would get a perfect score; there would be no room for between-group variability on this measure (see **Figure 10.11**).

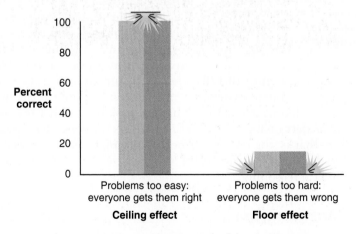

FIGURE 10.11 Ceiling and floor effects. A ceiling or floor effect on the dependent variable can obscure a true difference between groups. If problems on a math test are all too easy, everyone would get a perfect score. If the problems are too difficult, everyone will score low on the test.

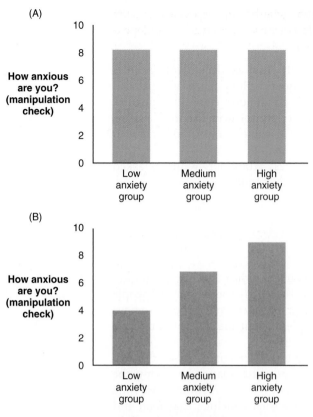

(A)

How anxious are you? (manipulation check)

Low anxiety group — Medium anxiety group — High anxiety group

(B)

How anxious are you? (manipulation check)

Low anxiety group — Medium anxiety group — High anxiety group

FIGURE 10.12 Possible results of a manipulation check. The results in Panel A would suggest that the anxiety manipulation did not work, because people at all three levels of the independent variable reported being equally anxious. The results in Panel B would suggest that the independent variable anxiety manipulation did work, because the anxiety of people in the three independent variable groups did vary in the expected way.

Manipulation Checks Help Detect Weak Manipulations, Ceilings, and Floors

When you interrogate a study with a null effect, it is important to ask how the independent and dependent variables were operationalized. Was the independent variable manipulation strong enough to cause a difference between groups? And was the dependent variable measure sensitive enough to detect that difference?

Manipulation checks can help you identify potential problems with independent variables: Recall from Chapter 9 that a manipulation check is a separate dependent variable that experimenters include in a study, just to make sure the manipulation worked. For example, in the anxiety study, the researchers might have asked, "How anxious are you right now, on a scale of 1 to 10?" after telling people that they were going to receive a 10-volt, 50-volt, or 100-volt shock. If the manipulation check showed that participants in all three groups felt nearly the same level of anxiety (as shown in **Figure 10.12A**), we would know that the researchers did not effectively manipulate what they intended to manipulate. If the manipulation check showed that the independent variable levels differed in an expected way—that the participants in the high-anxiety group really felt more anxious than those in the other two groups (as shown in **Figure 10.12B**)—then we would know that the researchers did effectively manipulate anxiety, the independent variable. If the manipulation check worked, researchers would have to look for another reason for the null effect of anxiety on logical reasoning. Perhaps the dependent measure has a floor effect—that is, the logical reasoning test might be too difficult, so everyone scores low (as in Figure 10.11). Or perhaps there really is no effect of anxiety on logical reasoning.

Confounds Acting in Reverse

Most of the time, we think of confounds as internal validity threats—alternative explanations for some observed difference in a study. However, they can apply to null effects, too. A study might be designed in such a way that a confound actually counteracts some true effect of an independent variable.

For example, in the GRE study, perhaps the group assigned to take the test preparation course was also put under extra pressure to do well, whereas the comparison group did not take a test-prep course and was not exposed to the extra pressure. In this case, the extra pressure applied to the test-prep group was a confound that might have worked against any real effect of the course. Or perhaps the students who received more money in Dr. Williams's study happened to be given the money by a grudging experimenter, while students who received less money were not exposed to such a person; this confound could also work against any true effect of money on mood.

Perhaps Within-Groups Variability Obscured the Group Differences

Another reason that a study might return a null effect is that there is too much unsystematic variability—too much **noise**—*within* each group. Noisy data can come from three sources: measurement error, individual differences, and situation noise. But no matter where it comes from, noisy within-group variability (also known as *error variance*) can get in the way of detecting a true difference between groups. Consider the sets of scores depicted in **Figure 10.13**. Both images depict the same data, just in two graphing formats. In each case, the

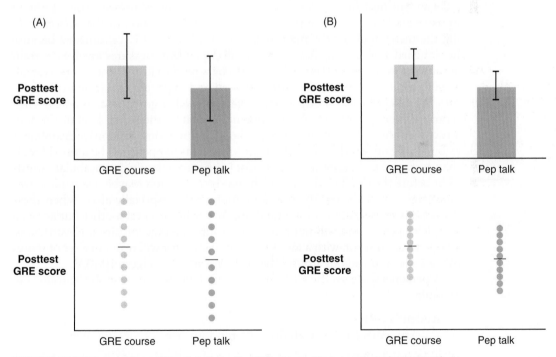

FIGURE 10.13 Two versions of the data from the GRE preparation course study. Notice that the group averages are the same in both versions, but the variability within each group is greater in Panel A than in Panel B. Panel B is the situation researchers prefer, because it allows them to better detect true differences in the independent variable.

difference *between* the two group averages is the same. However, the variability *within* each group is much larger in Figure 10.13A than in Figure 10.13B. You can see that when there is more variability within groups, it obscures the differences between the groups, because more overlap exists between the members of the two groups. The greater the overlap between groups, the smaller the effect size, and the less likely it is that the two group means will be statistically significant—that is, the less likely it is that the study will detect covariance. In turn, when the data show less variability within the groups, as in Figure 10.13B, the larger the effect size will be, and the more likely the mean difference will be statistically significant. Less within-group variability is less likely to obscure a true group difference.

The more unsystematic variability there is within each group, the more the scores in the two groups overlap with each other. And the more they overlap, the less apparent the average difference is. As described next, most researchers prefer to keep within-group variability to a minimum, so that they can more easily detect between-group differences. They keep in mind a few common culprits: measurement error, individual differences, and situation noise.

For more on statistical significance, see Chapter 9 and Appendix B.

Measurement Error

One reason for high within-group variability is measurement error. *Measurement error* is a term used for factors that can inflate or deflate a person's true score on a dependent measure. For example, a man who is 160 centimeters tall might be measured at 161 centimeters because of the angle of vision of the person reading the meter stick, or the man might be measured at 159 centimeters because he slouched a bit during measurement. All dependent measures involve a certain amount of measurement error, but researchers need to keep those errors as small as possible. For example, the GRE test used as a dependent variable in the educational psychologist's study is not perfect. Indeed, a group's score on the GRE represents the group's "true" GRE potential—that is, the actual level of the construct we want to measure in a group—plus or minus some random measurement error. Maybe one student's batch of GRE problems happened to be more difficult than average. Maybe another student just happened to study the vocabulary words right before the test, but the rest of the students did not. Maybe one student was especially drowsy during the test, and another was especially alert. When these distortions of measurement are random, they will cancel each other out across a sample of people and will not affect the group's average, or mean. Nevertheless, an operationalization with a lot of measurement error will result in a set of scores that are more spread out around the group mean (as in Figure 10.13A).

A person's score on the GRE measure can be represented with the following formula:

student's GRE score =
    student's true GRE ability $+/-$ random error of measurement

Or, more generally:

dependent variable score =
    participant's true score $+/-$ random error of measurement

The more sources of random error there are in a dependent variable's measurement, the more variability there will be within each group in an experiment (as in Figure 10.13A). In contrast, the more precisely and carefully a dependent variable is measured, the less variability there will be within each group (as in Figure 10.13B). And lower within-groups variability is better, making it easier to detect a difference between independent variable groups.

Solution 1: Reliable, Precise Measurements. When researchers use measurement tools that have excellent reliability (internal, interrater, and test-retest), they can reduce errors in measurement, as discussed in Chapter 5. And when measurement tools also have good construct validity, there will be less error in measurement as well.

Another factor to consider is precision. The more precisely an experimenter can measure the dependent variable, the less chance there is that measurement error will obscure results. For example, in timing how long people take to solve logical reasoning problems, experimenters would have less measurement error if the stopwatch read to the nearest tenth of a second than if it read only to the nearest second. In measuring how much food a person eats, researchers would have less measurement error if they weighed each plate of food before and after the participant eats than if an observer simply looked at the plate and reported whether the person ate "a lot" versus "a little." In fact, many researchers use computerized tools to get the most precise measurements they can and thus reduce this source of within-groups variability.

Solution 2: Measure More Instances. Sometimes, a precise, reliable measurement tool is impossible to find. What then? When an experimenter does not have access to a precise measurement tool, the best alternative is to measure a larger sample—more people, more animals, more books, more buildings. In other words, one solution to measuring badly is to take more measurements. When a measurement device contains a great deal of random measurement error, we can cancel out many errors simply by including more people in the sample. Is one person's score 10 points too high because of a random error in measurement? If so, it is not a problem, as long another participant's score is 10 points too low because of a random error in measurement. And the more participants there are, the better our chances of having a full representation of all the possible measurement errors. That way, the measurement errors cancel each other out, and we get a better estimate of the "true" average for that group. The reverse is true as well: When a measurement tool is known to have very little measurement error, researchers can get away with having fewer participants in their study.

Individual Differences

Individual differences are another source of within-group variability. Individual differences can be a problem in independent-groups designs. In Dr. Williams's experiment on money and mood, for example, participants' normal moods must have varied. Some people are more cheerful, others more sanguine; such individual differences have the effect of spreading out the scores of

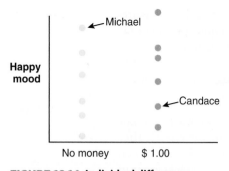

FIGURE 10.14 Individual differences.
Overall, students who received money were slightly more cheerful than students in the control condition, but the scores in the two conditions overlapped a great deal.

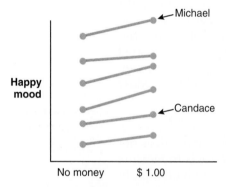

FIGURE 10.15 Within-groups designs control for individual differences. When each person participates in both levels of the independent variable, the individual differences are controlled for, and it is easier to see the effect of the independent variable.

the people within each group, as shown in **Figure 10.14**. In the $1.00 condition, you might have Candace, who is always grumpy. The gift of $1.00 might have made her happier, but her mood would still be relatively low because of her normal level of grumpiness. Michael, a cheerful guy, was in the no-money control condition, but he still scored high on the mood measure. Looking over the data, we might see that, on average, the participants in the experimental condition did score a little higher than those in the control condition. But the data are mixed and far from consistent—a lot of overlap exists between the scores in the money group and the control group. Because of this overlap caused by individual differences, the effect of a gift of money might not reach statistical significance; individual differences in overall mood would obscure it. The effect of the money gift would be small in comparison to the variability within each group.

Solution 1: Change the Design. One way to accommodate individual differences is to use a within-groups design instead of an independent-groups design. In **Figure 10.15**, each pair of points, connected by a line, represents a single person whose mood was measured under both conditions. Therefore, the top pair of points represents Michael's mood both after a cash gift and after no gift. Another pair of points represents Candace's mood both after a cash gift and after no gift. Do you see what happens? The individual data points are exactly where they were in Figure 10.14, but the pairing process has turned a scrambled set of data into a clear and very consistent finding: Every participant was happier after receiving a cash gift than after no gift. This included Michael, who is always cheerful, and Candace, who is usually grumpy, as well as others in between.

A within-groups design like this, which compares each participant with himself or herself, controls for individual differences. Finally, notice that the study required only half as many participants as the original independent-groups experiment did. You can see again the two strengths of within-groups designs (first identified in Chapter 9): They control for individual differences, and they require fewer participants than independent-groups comparisons.

Experimenters can achieve a similar effect with a matched-groups design. Before introducing the independent variable, Dr. Williams might measure the participants' usual daily mood. Then he might match the two most cheerful people and the two least cheerful people. The graphed results would look similar to Figure 10.15, but now the lines would connect matched pairs, as shown in **Figure 10.16**. Dr. Williams could then see the same reduction in individual difference variability as in the within-groups design.

Solution 2: Add More Participants. If within-groups or matched-pairs designs are inappropriate (and sometimes they are, because of order effects or demand characteristics), another solution to individual difference variability is to measure more people. The principle is the same as it is for measurement error: When a great deal of variability exists because of individual differences, one simple thing to do is to measure many people: The more people you measure, the less impact any one, extreme person will have on the group's average. Adding more participants to a study reduces the impact of individual differences *within* groups and will increase a study's ability to detect differences *between* groups.

The reason is mathematical. The number of people in a sample goes in the denominator of the statistical formula for "detecting a difference." As you will learn in your statistics class, the formula for the usual *t* test is

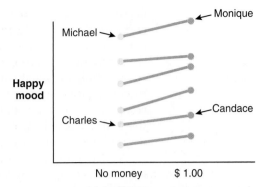

FIGURE 10.16 Graphing the results of a matched-groups design. When pairs are matched on some individual difference variable (such as baseline happiness), it is easier to see the effect of the independent variable.

$$\dfrac{\text{mean difference}}{\left(\dfrac{\text{standard deviation}}{\sqrt{n}}\right)}$$

The larger *n* (the number of participants) is, the smaller the denominator of *t* is. And the smaller that denominator is, the larger *t* can get, and the easier it is to find a significant *t*.

For more on *t* tests, see Appendix B, pp. A35–A38.

Situation Noise

Besides measurement error and individual differences, **situation noise** is a third factor that could cause variability within groups and obscure true group differences. Imagine if Dr. Williams had conducted his study on money and happiness in the middle of a campus's student union. The sheer number of potential distractions in this setting would make a mess of the data. The smell of the nearby coffee shop might make some participants feel peaceful, seeing friends at the next table might make some feel extra happy, and seeing the cute guy from sociology class might make some feel nervous or self-conscious. The kind and amount of distraction in the student union would vary from participant to participant and from moment to moment. The result, once again, would be variability within each group.

Therefore, variability in the external situation can create variability within each group in an experiment. And this variability, like that caused by random measurement error or individual differences, will obscure true differences between groups.

Researchers will often attempt to control this variability by carefully controlling the external situation. Dr. Williams might choose to distribute money and measure people's moods in a consistently undistracting laboratory room, far from coffee shops and classmates. Similarly, the researcher studying anxiety and logical reasoning might reduce situation noise by administering the logical reasoning test on a computer in a standardized classroom environment.

Sometimes the controls for situation noise need to be extreme. Consider one study on smell (cited in Mook, 2001), in which the researchers needed to control *all* extraneous odors that might reach the participants' noses. The researchers put participants in a steam-cleaned plastic enclosure and dressed them in steam-cleaned plastic parkas fastened tightly under the chin to trap odors from their clothes. They put a layer of Vaseline over participants' faces to trap odors from their skin. Only then did the researchers introduce the odors being studied by means of tubes placed directly in participants' nostrils.

Obviously, researchers do not usually go to these extremes. Dr. Williams would not need to put Vaseline on people's faces or put them in a steam-cleaned environment to adequately study the effect of money on happiness. However, researchers typically try to control the potential distractions that might affect the dependent variable. Dr. Williams would want to control the situation so that it does not induce variability in mood (his dependent variable), so, for example, he would not have a television set turned on in the laboratory. The educational psychologist would want to control the situation so that it does not induce unsystematic variability in her dependent variable, GRE performance, so she would control people's exposure to outside study guides or motivational posters. The researchers in the anxiety and reasoning study would want to control any kind of unsystematic situational factor that might distract people from doing their best on the logical reasoning test.

Perhaps There Really Is No Difference

When an experiment reveals that the independent variable conditions are not significantly different, what should you conclude? The study might be flawed in some way, so you might first ask whether the study was adequately designed to elicit and detect true between-group differences. Was the manipulation strong? Was the dependent measure sensitive enough to detect group differences? Could either variable be limited to a ceiling or floor effect? Are any confounds working against the independent variable?

You would then ask whether the study was designed to control within-group differences. Was the dependent variable measured as precisely as possible, to minimize measurement error? Could individual differences be obscuring the effect of the independent variable? Did the study include enough participants to counteract the effects of measurement error and individual differences? Was the study conducted with appropriate situational controls? Any of these factors, if problematic, could explain why an experiment showed a null effect. **Table 10.2** summarizes the possible reasons for a null effect in an experiment.

If, after interrogating these possible obscuring factors, you find that the study was conducted appropriately, you may conclude that the independent variable truly does not affect the dependent variable. A study with a strong

TABLE 10.2 Summary of Reasons That an Experiment Might Show a Null Result

Obscuring factor	Example	Questions to ask
Not enough variability between levels		
Ineffective manipulation of the independent variable	A 1-day GRE course might not improve scores (compared with a control group), but a 3-week GRE course might improve scores.	How did the researchers manipulate the independent variable? Was the manipulation strong? Do manipulation checks suggest that the manipulation did what it was intended to do?
Insufficiently sensitive measurement of the dependent variable	Researchers used a pass/fail measure, when the improvement was detectable only by using a finer-grained measurement scale.	How did the researchers measure the dependent variable? Was the measure sensitive enough to detect group differences?
Ceiling or floor effects on the independent variable	The researchers manipulated three levels of anxiety by threatening people with 10-volt, 50-volt, or 100-volt shocks (a ceiling effect on anxiety).	Are there meaningful differences between the levels of the independent variable? Do manipulation checks suggest that the manipulation did what it was intended to do?
Ceiling or floor effects on the dependent variable	The researchers measured logical reasoning ability with an extremely difficult test (a floor effect on logical reasoning ability).	How did the researchers measure the dependent variable? Do participants cluster near the top or near the bottom of the distribution?
Too much variability within levels		
Measurement error	GRE scores are affected by multiple sources of random error, such as item selection, participant's mood, fatigue, and so on.	Is the dependent variable measured precisely and reliably? Does the measure have good construct validity? If measurements are imprecise, did the experiment include enough participants to counteract this obscuring effect?
Individual differences	GRE scores are affected by individual differences in motivation and ability.	Did the researchers use a within-groups design to better control for individual differences? If an independent-groups design is used, then larger numbers of participants can reduce the impact of individual differences.
Situation variability	The money and happiness study was run in a distracting location, which introduced several external influences on the participants' mood.	Did the researchers attempt to control any situational influences on the dependent variable? Did they run the study in a standardized setting?
It's also possible that …		
The independent variable, in truth, has no effect on the dependent variable		Did the researchers take precautions to maximize between-group variability and minimize within-group variability? If they did, and they still do not find a group difference, it is reasonable to conclude that the independent variable does not affect the dependent variable.

independent variable manipulation, a sensitive and precise dependent variable measure, careful situational controls, and a large number of participants might still return a null result. The interpretation in that case is that the independent variable in question simply does not affect the dependent variable. Perhaps money really does not cause happiness. Perhaps that GRE prep course does not help students score higher. Or perhaps anxiety really does not affect people's logical reasoning.

Null Effects Can Be Hard to Find

When studies are well conducted, null results can be just as interesting and just as informative as experiments that show group differences. There are many examples of true null effects in psychology. Some therapies and some therapeutic drugs apparently do not work (such as facilitated communication therapy, discussed in Chapter 1). Some commonsense hypotheses do not hold true in research; for example, after a certain level of income, money does not appear to cause happiness (Diener, Horwitz, & Emmons, 1985; Lyubomirsky, King, & Diener, 2005; Myers, 2000). And, despite stereotypes to the contrary, women and men apparently do not differ in how much they talk (Mehl, Vazire, Ramirez-Esparza, Slatcher, & Pennebaker, 2007).

However, if you are looking for examples of studies that found null effects in the popular press, you are not going to find many. There is a bias, both in what gets published in scientific journals and in which stories are picked up by magazines and newspapers: We are more interested in independent variables that matter than in those that do not. We may be more likely to read that a vaccine puts children at risk for autism than to read that the same vaccine has no effect on risk for autism. We are more likely to read that chocolate affects our health than to read that chocolate has no effect on health. And we are much more likely to hear that women and men differ on some trait than to hear that women and men are the same. Differences seem more interesting than null effects, so a publication bias exists that favors differences.

Check Your Understanding

1. How can a study maximize variability between independent variable groups? (There are four ways.)

2. How can a study minimize variability within groups? (There are three ways.)

3. In your own words, describe how within-groups designs minimize unsystematic variability.

1. See pp. 295–299 or Table 10.2. **2.** See pp. 299–304 or Table 10.2. **3.** See p. 302.

Summary

When an experiment finds that an independent variable affected a dependent variable, you can interrogate the study for the possible internal validity threats summarized in Table 10.1 (pp. 292–293). If the study passes all of your internal validity queries, you can conclude with confidence that the study was a strong one: You can trust the result and make a causal claim.

If you encounter a study that suggested that the independent variable had no effect on the dependent variable (a null effect), you can review the possible obscuring factors covered in this chapter, as summarized in Table 10.2 (p. 305). If you can be reasonably sure that the study avoided all of the obscuring factors, then you can trust the result and conclude that the independent variable really does not cause a change in the dependent variable.

Key Terms

attrition, p. 285
ceiling effects, p. 296
demand characteristics, p. 288
double-blind placebo
   control studies, p. 290
double-blind study, p. 288
floor effects, p. 296
history threats, p. 281
instrumentation threats, p. 286

maturation, p. 280
noise, p. 299
null effect, p. 294
one-group, pretest/posttest design,
   p. 279
placebo effect, p. 289
regression threat, p. 282
situation noise, p. 303
testing threat, p. 286

NEED HELP STUDYING?

wwnorton.com/studyspace

Visit StudySpace to access free review materials such as:

- Diagnostic Review Quizzes
- Study Outlines

Learning Actively

Each of the scenarios described in Questions 1-3 might (or might not) contain threats to internal validity. For each scenario,

  a. identify the independent variable (IV) and dependent variable (DV).
  b. identify the design (posttest-only? one-group, pretest/posttest? within groups?).
  c. sketch a graph of the results. (Reminder: put the dependent variable on the y-axis.)
  d. decide whether the study is subject to any of the internal validity threats listed in Table 10.1.
  e. indicate whether you could redesign the study to correct or prevent any of the internal validity threats.

1. For his senior thesis, Jack was interested in whether viewing alcohol advertising would cause college students to drink more alcohol. He recruited 25 seniors for a weeklong study. On Monday and Tuesday, he asked them to log in to a secure website and record how many alcoholic beverages they had consumed the day before. On Wednesday, he invited them to a laboratory theater, where he showed them a 30-minute television show interspersed with entertaining alcohol advertising. Thursday and Friday were the follow-up measures: Students logged in to the secure website and recorded their alcoholic beverage consumption again. Jack found that students reported drinking more after seeing the alcohol advertising. He concluded that the advertising caused them to drink more.

2. In a cognitive psychology class, a group of student presenters wanted to demonstrate the power of retrieval cues. First, the student presenters asked the class to memorize a list of 20 words that they read in a random order. One minute later, members of the class wrote down as many words as they could remember. On average, the class recalled 6 words. Second, the student presenters told the class to try sorting the words into categories as the words were read. The categories to use were as follows: color words, vehicle words, and sports words. The student presenters read the words again, in a different random order. On the second test of recall, the class remembered, on average, 14 words. The student presenters told the students that this experiment demonstrated that categorizing helps people remember words because they are able to develop rich connections to the words.

3. Can we be "primed" to see someone's actions in either a good or a bad light? Solange believed so. Solange randomly assigned her participants to two groups. In Stage 1, the participants completed word-search puzzles that exposed them to different adjectives. For one group, the puzzles in Stage 1 contained adjectives with positive connotations (e.g., *adventurous*), while for the other group the connotations were negative (e.g., *reckless*). In Stage 2, all participants heard stories about people performing daring feats, such as hot-air ballooning and mountain climbing. In Stage 3, all participants were asked to write an essay in which they gave their impressions of these risk-takers. Solange asked two research assistants to help her run the experiment, neither of whom was aware of the purpose of her research. One colleague interacted with the subjects in both groups, and the other scored all of the essays. The daring feats of the imaginary people were rated more favorably by participants who had read the positive adjectives in Stage 1 than by participants who had read the negative adjectives in Stage 1. Solange concluded that the adjectives introduced in Stage 1 predisposed her participants to respond positively or negatively to the adventures of the fictional people.

---

4. Dr. Dove was interested in the effects of chocolate on well-being. She randomly assigned 20 participants to two groups. Both groups ate as they normally would, but one group was instructed to eat three 1-ounce squares of dark chocolate after both lunch and dinner. After the participants spent 4 weeks on this diet, Dr. Dove asked each one to complete a questionnaire measuring well-being (happiness, contentment). However, Dr. Dove was surprised to find that the chocolate had no effect: Both groups, on average, scored the same on the well-being measure. Help Dr. Dove troubleshoot her study. What should she do next time to improve her chances of finding a significant effect for the chocolate-enhanced diet?

5. Is it always necessary to use a large sample in a study? Reflect for a moment on when a study might need to use many participants, and when a study might not need to use many participants. Which of the four big validities does the number of participants address?

If You See It, You'll Eat It

(CNN, 2007)

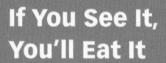

Should Cell Phone Use by Drivers Be Illegal?

(*New York Times*, 2009)

11

Experiments with More Than One Independent Variable

Chapters 9 and 10 introduced you to experiments with one independent variable and one dependent variable. This chapter moves on to discuss experiments with more than one independent variable. To start, consider the headlines on the facing page, on two commonplace activities: eating and driving. Both examples begin with one independent variable, but what happens when we add more independent variables to the mix?

Review: Experiments with One Independent Variable

Let's start with the eating example: What affects how much you eat?

In several studies, food and consumer psychologist Brian Wansink manipulated package size and measured how much people would eat from the package.

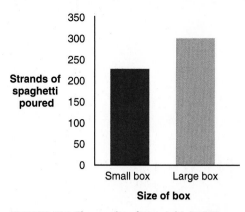

FIGURE 11.1 The results of Wansink's (1996) study. People poured more pasta from large boxes.

For example, in one study he asked people to pour out enough dry spaghetti to prepare dinner for two adults (Wansink, 1996). He had randomly assigned people to pour the spaghetti from a small box or from a large box. Regardless of the size of the box, the amount of the spaghetti inside was held constant.

The results showed that when the spaghetti was in a small package, people poured out 234 strands of spaghetti, on average, for two servings. But when the spaghetti was in a large package, people poured out 302 strands of spaghetti (29% more). Here was a simple, independent-groups study with one independent variable (package size) and one dependent variable (serving size). Wansink demonstrated the same phenomenon—people using more from large containers—with many other products as well, including popcorn, cooking oil, and bottled water. That shows good external validity: No matter what the product, Wansink found that when the same amount of food is in a large container, people use more of the product than when it is in a small container (Wansink's results are shown in **Figure 11.1**.) The studies thus showed a simple *difference*.

The second headline, from another popular press story, is about whether cell phone use makes a difference in people's driving ability. The study in question found that cell phone use during driving does seem to make a difference. The evidence comes from experiments by David Strayer and his colleagues, who asked people to talk on hands-free cell phones in a high-fidelity driving simulator (one that looked almost exactly like a real car). As they drove, he recorded several dependent variables, including driving speed, braking time, and following distance. In a repeated-measures (within-groups) design, Strayer and Drews (2004) had participants drive on several 10-mile segments of highway in the simulator. For two of the segments, the drivers carried on a conversation on a hands-free cell phone. For the other two segments, drivers were not on the phone (of course, their participation in the different segments was counterbalanced). The results showed that when drivers were talking on cell phones, their reactions to road hazards were 18% slower. Drivers on cell phones also took longer to regain their speed after slowing down and got into more (virtual) accidents. (The results are shown in **Figure 11.2**.)

For a review of counterbalancing, see Chapter 9, pp. 261–263.

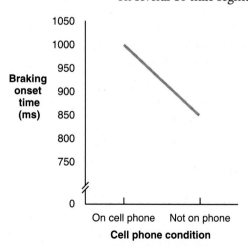

FIGURE 11.2 The results of Strayer and Drews's (2004) study. Drivers using cell phones were slower to hit the brakes in response to a road hazard.

Strayer and Drews's study, like Wansink's, had one independent variable (cell phone use, manipulated as a within-groups variable) and one dependent variable (driving quality). Their study also showed a *difference*: People drove more poorly while using cell phones. Studies with one independent variable are able to show a difference between conditions. The arithmetic in each of these results was a simple difference score: large package size minus small package size, or cell phone minus control.

Experiments with Two Independent Variables Can Show Interactions

Strayer and Drews's study found that cell phones cause people to drive badly. But these researchers also wondered whether that overall difference would apply in all situations and to all people. For example, might younger drivers be less distracted by using cell phones than older drivers? On the one hand, they might, because they grew up using cell phones and are more accustomed to them. On the other hand, older drivers might be less distracted, because they have more years of driving experience. If you are asking these questions, you would be thinking about adding another independent variable to Strayer and Drews's original study: driver age, whose levels could be old and young. Specifically, you would be asking whether a driver's age will change the effect of driving while using a cell phone.

When you ask about the effect of an additional independent variable, you are usually wondering about the **interaction** of two independent variables—whether the effect of the original independent variable (cell phone use) *depends on* another independent variable (driver age). Therefore, interactions of two independent variables allow researchers to establish whether or not "it depends." They can now ask: "Does the effect of cell phones depend on age?"

The mathematical way to describe an interaction of two independent variables is to say that there is a *difference in differences*. In the driving example, we are suggesting that the *difference* between the cell phone and control conditions (cell phone minus control) might be *different* for older drivers than younger drivers.

$$\text{Interaction} = \frac{\text{a difference}}{\text{in differences}} = \begin{array}{l}\text{the effect of one independent} \\ \text{variable depends on the level of} \\ \text{the other independent variable}\end{array}$$

Intuitive Interactions

Behaviors, thoughts, motivations, and emotions are rarely simple; they usually involve interactions between two or more influences. Therefore, much of the most important research in psychology explores interactions among multiple independent variables. How do researchers design studies to investigate interactions? How are these studies conducted, and what do their results mean?

Here's one example of an interaction: Do you like hot foods or cold foods? Your preference probably depends on what the food is. You probably like your ice cream cold, but you like your pancakes hot. In this example, there are two independent variables: which food you are judging (ice cream or pancakes) and the temperature of the food (cold or hot). The dependent variable is how much you like the food. We can graph the interaction as shown in **Figure 11.3**. Notice that

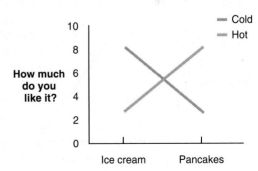

FIGURE 11.3 A crossover interaction. How much we like certain foods depends on the temperature at which they are served.

the lines cross each other—this kind of interaction is sometimes called a *crossover interaction* for this reason.

To describe this interaction, we could say that when people eat ice cream, they like their food cold more than hot; when people eat pancakes, they like their food hot more than cold. We could also apply the mathematical definition by saying that there is a *difference in differences*. You like ice cream cold more than you like it hot (cold minus hot is a positive value), but you like pancakes cold less than you like them hot (cold minus hot is a negative value).

Another example comes from the behavior of my dog, Fig. Does he sit on command? It depends on whether I say, "Sit," and on whether I have a treat in my hand. When I don't have a treat, Fig will not sit, even if I tell him to sit. But if I do have a treat, he will sit, but only when I say, "Sit." (In other words, my stubborn dog has to be bribed.) In this example, my dog's sitting behavior is the dependent variable, and the two independent variables are what I say ("Sit" or nothing) and what I am holding (a treat or nothing). The interaction could be graphed as in **Figure 11.4**. Notice that the lines are not parallel, and they do not cross over each other. This kind of interaction is sometimes called a *spreading interaction*.

We could describe this interaction by saying that when I say nothing, my dog's rate of sitting is the same at both the "treat" and the "no treat" conditions. But when I say, "Sit," my dog's rate of sitting is higher in the treat than the no-treat condition. We could also apply the mathematical definition to this interaction: When I say nothing, there is *zero* difference between the treat and no-treat conditions (treat minus no treat equals zero). When I say, "Sit," there is a *large* difference between the treat and no-treat conditions (treat minus no treat equals a positive value). There is a difference in differences.

When there is an interaction, you can describe it accurately from either direction. So it is equally accurate to say, "When I am not holding a treat, there is zero difference between the 'Sit' and say-nothing conditions," and "When I am holding a treat, there is a large difference between the 'Sit' and say-nothing conditions."

You can also graph the interaction accurately either way—by putting the "What I say" independent variable on the x-axis, as shown in Figure 10.4, or by putting the "What I'm holding" independent variable on the x-axis, as shown in **Figure 11.5**. The figure may look a little different each way, but each is still an accurate representation of the data.

As psychologists think about behavior, they might start with a simple link between an independent and a dependent variable,

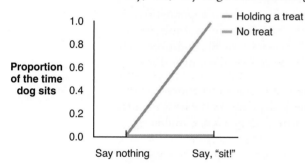

FIGURE 11.4 A spreading interaction. Whether or not my dog sits when I say, "Sit," depends on whether or not I am holding a treat.

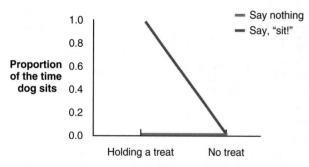

FIGURE 11.5 The same spreading interaction, graphed the other way. The data in Figure 11.4 can be graphed equally accurately with the other independent variable on the x-axis.

but often they find that they need a second independent variable to tell the full story. For example, in a romantic relationship, are positive attitudes such as forgiveness healthy? (In other words, does the independent variable of positive attitudes versus negative attitudes affect the dependent variable, relationship health?) The answer to that question turns out to depend on the how severe the problems are in the relationship. When problems are minor, positive attitudes are healthy for the relationship, but when problems are severe (for example, one partner is abusive to the other or abuses drugs), positive attitudes seem to prevent the couple from addressing the problems. So the severity of the relationship's problems (minor versus severe) is the second independent variable (McNulty, 2010).

Does going to day care hurt children's social and intellectual development? That might depend on the quality of care. When high-quality day care is provided, children's social and intellectual development might improve (compared with that of children given only parental care); when the quality of day care is poor, development might be impaired (Vandell, Henderson, & Wilson, 1988). Reflect for a moment: What would the dependent and independent variables be in this example?

Factorial Designs Study Two Independent Variables

When researchers want to test for interactions, they do so with factorial designs. A **factorial design** is one in which there are two or more independent variables (independent variables may also be called *factors*). In the most common factorial design, researchers *cross* the two independent variables; that is, they study *each possible combination* of the independent variables. Strayer and Drews, for example, created a **crossed factorial design** to test whether the effect of driving while talking on a cell phone depended on the driver's age. They manipulated two independent variables (cell phone use and driver age), creating a condition representing each possible combination of the two. As shown in **Figure 11.6**, to cross the two independent variables, Strayer and Drews essentially overlaid one independent variable on top of another. This overlay process created four conditions, or "**cells**": older people driving while using cell phones, older people driving without using cell phones, younger

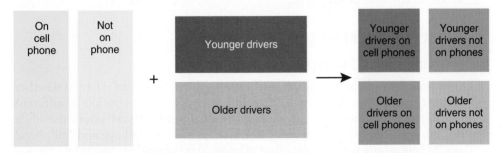

FIGURE 11.6 Strayer and Drews's factorial design. Strayer and Drews created a factorial design by overlaying a second independent variable on top of a first independent variable, creating (in this case) four new experimental conditions, or cells.

people driving while using cell phones, and younger people driving without using cell phones.

Figure 11.6 shows the simplest possible crossed factorial design. There are two independent variables (that is, two factors)—cell phone use and age—and each of these independent variables has two levels (driving while using a cell phone or not; older or younger driver). This particular design is called a 2×2 (two-by-two) factorial design, meaning that two levels of one independent variable are crossed with two levels of another independent variable. And since $2 \times 2 = 4$, there are four cells in this design.

Crossed Versus Nested Factorial Designs

Another variation on the factorial design is a **nested factorial design**, in which one independent variable is primary, and the other independent variable is nested under it. For example, a researcher might study two school districts and then study three schools within each district. The district is the first independent variable, and the three individual schools are the second, nested one. The levels of the nested variable (the schools) are not exactly the same within each school district—that's what makes this design "nested."

A detailed description of nested designs and their interpretation is beyond the scope of this book. For simplicity, when you read "factorial design" here, you should assume that it is a crossed, not a nested, factorial design.

Use of Factorial Designs to Study Manipulated Variables or Participant Variables

You might have noticed that one of Strayer and Drews's variables, the cell phone use condition, was truly manipulated—he had participants either talk or not talk on cell phones. The other variable, age, was not manipulated; it was a measured variable. That is, Strayer and Drews did not assign people to be older or younger; they simply selected participants who fit these levels. Age is an example of a **participant variable**—a variable whose levels are selected (that is, measured), not manipulated. Because the levels are not manipulated, variables such as age, sex, ethnicity, and culture are not truly "independent" variables. However, when they are studied in a factorial design, researchers often call them independent variables, for the sake of simplicity.

What Factorial Designs Can Do

Factorial Designs Can Test Limits

One reason researchers conduct studies with factorial designs is to test whether an independent variable affects different kinds of people, or people in different situations, in the same way. Strayer and Drews's research on cell phone use while driving is a good example of this purpose. When he crossed age and cell phone use, he was asking whether the effect of using a cell phone was limited to one age group only, or whether it would have the same effect on people of different ages.

Strayer and Drews conducted the study on a sample of 18- to 25-year-olds and a sample of 65- to 74-year-olds. Each participant drove in the simulator for a warm-up period and then drove 10-mile stretches of simulated traffic four times. During two of the four segments, drivers carried on a conversation on a hands-free phone, chatting with a research assistant about their day (see **Figure 11.7**). While the participants drove, the researchers collected data on a variety of dependent variables, including braking onset time (how long it takes for people to brake for an upcoming road hazard), accidents, and following distance. The results for braking onset time in Strayer and Drews's study are depicted in **Figure 11.8**. Notice that the same results are presented in two ways: as a table and as a graph.

The results might surprise you. In fact, the primary conclusion from this study is that the effect of talking on a cell phone did not depend on age. Older drivers did tend to brake more slowly than younger ones, overall; that finding is consistent with past research on aging drivers. However, Strayer and Drews wanted to know

FIGURE 11.7 A young driver in the simulator used in Strayer and colleagues' experiments.

whether the *difference* between the cell phone and control conditions would be *different* for older drivers. The answer was no. The effect of using a cell phone (that is, the simple difference between the cell phone condition and the control condition) was about the same in both age groups. In other words, cell phone use *did not interact with* (did not *depend on*) age. At least for these two groups, the harmful effect of cell phone use was the same.

A Form of External Validity. You might have recognized this goal of testing limits as related to external validity. When researchers test an independent variable in more than one group at once, they are testing whether the effect generalizes. Sometimes, as in the example of age and cell phone use, the independent variable affects the groups in the same way, suggesting that the effect of cell phone use generalizes to drivers of all ages.

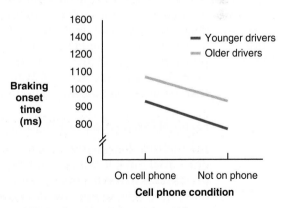

DV: Brake onset time (ms)	IV$_1$: Cell phone condition	
	On phone	Not on phone
IV$_2$: Driver age — Younger drivers	912	780
IV$_2$: Driver age — Older drivers	1086	912

FIGURE 11.8 Results for braking onset time presented in two formats. *Source*: Adapted from Strayer and Drews (2004).

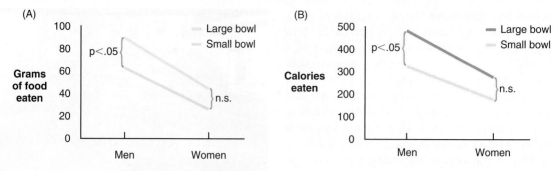

FIGURE 11.9 The results of Wansink and Cheney's (2005) Super Bowl study.

Other times, the groups might respond differently to an independent variable; in such cases, the effect may not generalize. For example, Wansink and a graduate student conducted one of their food studies on students they had invited to a Super Bowl party (Wansink & Cheney, 2005). They manipulated the size of the serving bowls for the snack foods at the party, so bowl size was one independent variable. They compared men and women, so gender was the second factor. The dependent variable was how much each person ate. The researchers found that men ate significantly more from large bowls than from small bowls, both in the number of grams they ate and the number of calories. Women ate more from large bowls too, but the difference was not statistically significant, as shown in **Figure 11.9**. The tendency to eat more from large bowls apparently may not generalize from men to women, at least in this study. (However, Wansink's other experiments show that with most other products, women do show significant results for the effect of package size.)

Interactions Show Moderators. The process of using a factorial design to test limits is sometimes called testing for moderators. A moderator is a variable that changes the relationship between two other variables (Kenny, 2009). In factorial design language, a moderator is an independent variable that changes the relationship between another independent variable and a dependent variable. In other words, a moderator results in an interaction, because we say that the effect of one independent variable depends on (is moderated by) the level of another independent variable. When Strayer and Drews studied whether driver age would interact with cell phone use, he found that driver age did not moderate the impact of cell phone use on brake onset time. However, Wansink and Cheney's Super Bowl party showed that gender might moderate the effect of larger serving bowls.

To read about how moderators work in correlational designs, see Chapter 7, pp. 202–204.

Factorial Designs Can Test Theories

Researchers can use crossed factorial designs not only to test the generalizability of a causal variable but also to test theories. The goal of most psychological experiments is to test hypotheses derived from theories. And indeed, many theories make statements about how variables interact with one another. The best way to study how variables interact is to combine them in a factorial design and measure whether the results are consistent with the theory.

For more on the theory-data cycle, see Chapter 1, pp. 8–13.

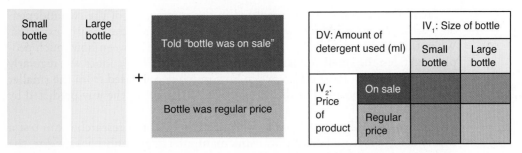

FIGURE 11.10 A crossed factorial design. This type of design creates all possible combinations of the independent variables. Here, one independent variable (package size) is crossed with another independent variable (product price) to create all four possible combinations.

Using an Interaction to Test the Low-Price Theory. To demonstrate that people use more of a product when it is presented in a larger package, Wansink (1996) started with a simple study with one independent variable (package size). But Wansink also wanted to know *why* people use more from a large package. He theorized that people use more from a large package because they perceive that the product in the large package costs less—that people feel freer to use the product from a large package because they know that products in large packages typically cost less per serving than products in smaller packages.

To test his theory, Wansink presented consumers with either a large or a small bottle of Mr. Clean cleanser. Again, the amount of cleanser in the two containers was exactly the same; only the size of the container was different. Then he added a second independent variable: Half of the people were told that their bottle of cleanser was on sale, and the other half were not. Wansink's factorial design is shown in **Figure 11.10**.

Wansink figured that if a lower perceived price was the reason that people used more from a large bottle, people should also pour more cleanser from the small bottle when they believed it was on sale. He predicted that people in all except one cell in his design would pour a lot of cleanser; only from the small, regularly priced bottle would people pour less. The results of Wansink's factorial study are shown in **Figure 11.11**.

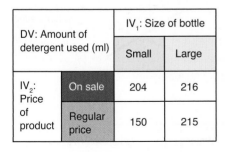

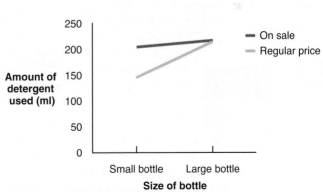

FIGURE 11.11 Results from Wansink's (1996) factorial study in table and graph form. The data are the actual results from the study.

Here, Wansink was most interested in the interaction of the two independent variables, price and package size. The interaction told the story he expected: When the product was on sale, there was no difference between how much people used from the small and large packages. But when the product was regularly priced, there was a large difference in how much people used from the smaller versus the larger bottle. The differences were different, in the way predicted by the theory.

Wansink's study is therefore a good example of how a researcher can test a theory using a factorial design. Wansink manipulated not only package size, the variable he knew would make a difference, but also product price, the variable he thought was responsible for the package size effect. The interaction was consistent with his theory: People seem to use more from large packages because they perceive the product to be cheaper.

Using an Interaction to Test a Memory Theory. In another example of theory testing with factorial designs, two cognitive psychologists wanted to test a theory about context-dependent memory. The theory predicted that when people study a list of words, they associate the words with the context around them—the desk they are sitting at, the notebook the words are written in, even the carpet on the floor. When people try to remember the list of words later, they may be able use the desk, notebook, and carpet as reminders of what the words were—if those same objects are present when the people are trying to recall the words.

Psychologists Godden and Baddeley (1975) came up with a creative way to test this theory of context-dependent learning. They asked a group of scuba divers to memorize a list of words and then tested them on the words later. One group memorized the material while sitting on the edge of the water, and the other group memorized the material while they were 20 feet below the surface (both groups were tested in their full scuba gear). That was one independent variable: where they memorized (on the edge or in the water). Then each group was divided in two; half of the participants in each group were tested for memory while at the edge of the water, and the other half were tested underwater. That was the second independent variable: where they were tested

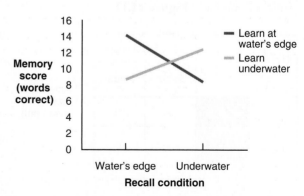

FIGURE 11.12 **Godden and Baddeley's (1975) study of context-dependent learning.**
Do people recall material better on land or underwater? It depends on where they learned the material. (The figure shows the actual results from Godden and Baddeley.)

(on the edge or in the water). Sure enough, participants who learned the material on the edge of the water remembered it best on the edge of the water; participants who learned it underwater remembered it best underwater. The results are shown in **Figure 11.12**.

In this example, the psychologists used a factorial design to test their theory about context-dependent learning. The study results supported the clear interaction predicted by the theory: Is memory better underwater or at the water's edge? It depends on where you learned the material: underwater or at the water's edge.

Interpreting Factorial Results: Main Effects and Interactions

So far this chapter has discussed what a factorial design is, what an interaction is, and why researchers might use a factorial design. After running a study with a factorial design with two independent variables, researchers need to analyze the results. In an analysis with two independent variables, there will be three results to inspect: two main effects and one interaction.

Main Effects: Is There an Overall Difference?

In a factorial design, researchers will test each independent variable to look for a **main effect**. A main effect is the overall effect of one independent variable on the dependent variable, averaging over the levels of the other independent variable. That is, a main effect is a simple difference. In a factorial design with two independent variables, there are two main effects.

Figure 11.13 shows the data from Wansink's study on cleanser package size. One independent variable, price, is highlighted in blue; the other, bottle size, is highlighted in yellow. First, to look for a main effect of bottle size, we would compute the amount poured from the small bottle, averaged across the two price conditions, and the serving size poured from the large bottle, also averaged across the two price conditions. These two **marginal means** are shown in the bottom row of the table. Marginal means are the means for each level of an independent variable, averaging over levels of the other independent variable. If the sample size in each cell is exactly equal, marginal means are a simple average—say, of the sale and regular price conditions. If the sample

DV: Amount of detergent used (ml)		IV$_1$: Size of bottle		
		Small	Large	Main effect for IV$_2$: price of product
IV$_2$: Price of product	On sale	204	216	210 (average of 204 and 216)
	Regular price	150	215	182.5 (average of 150 and 215)
Main effect for IV$_1$: Size of bottle		177 (average of 204 and 150)	215.5 (average of 216 and 215)	

FIGURE 11.13 Using marginal means to look for main effects. To find the main effect for an independent variable, we compute the overall score for each level of that independent variable, averaging over the levels of the other independent variable. (The example assumes equal numbers of participants in each cell.

sizes are unequal, the marginal means will be computed using the weighted average, counting the larger sample more. In Figure 11.13, notice that overall, there is a difference in the amount poured for this variable: Overall, people use more (215.5 milliliters) from large bottles and less (177 milliliters) from small bottles. So we can say that there appears to be a main effect for bottle size.

Second, to find the main effect for the other independent variable, we would compute the amount poured from the bottle that was on sale, averaged across the two size conditions, and the amout poured from the regular-priced bottle, also averaged across the two size conditions. These two marginal means are shown in the right-hand column of the table. Here again, there is an overall difference: On average, people pour more from bottles that are on sale (210 milliliters) than from bottles sold at regular price (182.5 milliliters). In technical terms, we would say that there appears to be a main effect for product price.

Main Effects May or May Not Be Statistically Significant. Researchers look at the marginal means to inspect the main effects in a factorial design, and they use statistics to see whether the difference in the marginal means is statistically significant. Just as Elliot asked, in his study on the color red (Chapter 9), whether the differences he observed between the red, green, and gray conditions were statistically significant, Wansink asked whether the overall difference in serving size between the large and the small bottle was statistically significant. He also asked whether the overall difference in serving size between the on-sale bottle and the regular-price bottle was statistically significant. (In Wansink's study, both main effects were statistically significant.)

Sometimes statistical significance tests tell you that the difference is not statistically significant. In that case, you would conclude that any observed difference in marginal means is no larger than what you would expect to see by chance if there were no difference in the population. It means that there is no main effect for that independent variable.

Main Effect = Overall Effect. The term *main effect* is usually misleading, because it seems to suggest that it is the most important effect in a study. It is not. In fact, when a study's results show an interaction, the interaction itself is the most important effect. Think of a main effect instead as an *overall effect*—the overall effect of one independent variable at a time.

Interactions: Is There a Difference in Differences?

In a factorial design with two independent variables, the first two results obtained are the main effects for each independent variable. The third result is the interaction. Whereas the main effects are simple differences, the interaction is the difference in differences.

Detecting Interactions from a Table. We can use a table to determine whether a study's results show an interaction. Because an interaction is a difference in differences, we would start by computing two differences. **Figure 11.14** illustrates how we would do this. We start with one level of the first independent variable: the small bottle. The difference between the sale and regular price conditions for the small bottle is $204 - 150 = 54$. Next we go to the second level of the first independent

For more on statistical significance, see Chapter 9 and Appendix B.

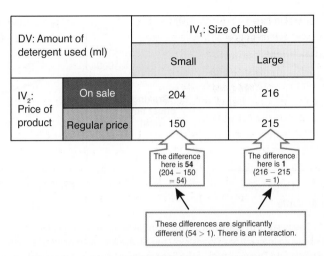

DV: Amount of detergent used (ml)		IV₁: Size of bottle	
		Small	Large
IV₂: Price of product	On sale	204	216
	Regular price	150	215

The difference here is **54** (204 − 150 = 54)

The difference here is **1** (216 − 215 = 1)

These differences are significantly different (54 > 1). There is an interaction.

FIGURE 11.14 Computing the interactions in Wansink's package size study from a table (the difference in differences).

variable: the large bottle. The difference between the sale and regular price conditions for the large bottle is 216 − 215 = 1. (Be sure that you compute the difference in the same direction both times—in this case, subtracting the results for the regular-priced bottle from those for the on-sale bottle.) We have come up with two differences: 54 and 1. These differences are different: One is large, and one is virtually zero. Indeed, Wansink's statistical tests told him that the difference of 54 is significantly larger than the difference of 1. Since the differences are significantly different, we can conclude that there is an interaction in this factorial study.

If you wanted to, you could estimate the difference in differences the other way instead. That is, you could compute the difference between the small and large bottle, first at the sale price (204 − 216 = −12) and then at the regular price (150 − 215 = −65). Although the values will be slightly different this time, you will reach the same conclusion—there is an interaction. The differences are different (−12 is different from −65).

Similarly, **Figure 11.15** shows how we would estimate the interaction for Strayer and Drews's cell phone study. Again, if we start with one level of one independent variable, the younger drivers, the difference in braking time between drivers using cell phones and drivers who are not using cell phones is 912 − 780 = 132. Next, among the older drivers, the difference in braking time between drivers using cell phones and drivers not using cell phones is 1086 − 912 = 174. Are the two differences, 132 and 174, different? They may look a little different, but this

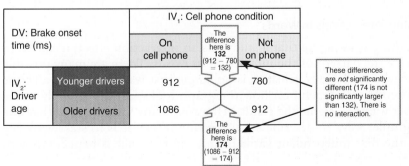

DV: Brake onset time (ms)		IV₁: Cell phone condition		
		On cell phone	The difference here is **132** (912 − 780 = 132)	Not on phone
IV₂: Driver age	Younger drivers	912		780
	Older drivers	1086	The difference here is **174** (1086 − 912 = 174)	912

These differences are *not* significantly different (174 is not significantly larger than 132). There is no interaction.

FIGURE 11.15 Computing the interactions in Strayer and Drews's study from a table (the difference in differences). Notice here that we are looking at the difference in column differences, whereas in the first example, we looked at the difference in row differences. You can look for the interaction either way.

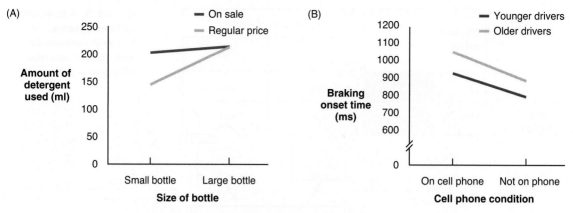

FIGURE 11.16 The results of Wansink's study and Strayer and Drews's study in line graph form. Panel A shows an interaction in Wansink's study—the lines are not parallel. Panel B shows no interaction in Strayer and Drews's study—the lines are almost perfectly parallel.

is where statistics come in. Just as with main effects, researchers use significance tests to tell them whether a difference in differences is significantly different from zero. Strayer and Drews's statistical significance tests told them that the two differences are not significantly different. So, in this case, there is not a significant difference in differences. In fact, at each age level, there is a 15% drop in brake onset time.

Detecting Interactions from a Graph. It is possible to look for interactions in a table, but it is much easier to detect interactions from a graph. When results from a factorial design are plotted as a line graph, we simply look to see whether the lines are parallel. If the lines are not parallel, as in **Figure 11.16A**, there probably *is* an interaction. If the lines are parallel, as in **Figure 11.16B**, there probably is *no* interaction. Of course, we would also need to confirm our observations with a significance test.

You can also detect interactions from a bar graph. As you inspect the bar graphs in **Figure 11.17**, imagine connecting the tops of each matching bar (the two dark blue bars and the two light blue bars) with straight lines. Would the resulting lines be parallel or not? Or you might look at the differences between the bars' heights on each side of the graph. Are the differences different, or are the differences the same?

Describing Interactions in Words

It's one thing to estimate that a study has an interaction effect; it's another to describe the pattern of the interaction in words. There are many possible patterns for interactions, so there is no single best way to describe any one interaction: It will depend on how the graph looks, as well as on how the researcher wants to frame the results. However, many students find that one of the simpler ways to describe an interaction in words is to start with one level of the first independent variable and explain what is happening with

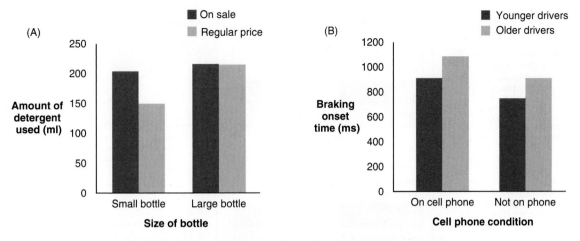

FIGURE 11.17 The Results of Wansink's and Strayer and Drews's studies in bar graph form.
Again, Panel A shows the results of Wansink's study and Panel B shows the results of Strayer and Drews's study. Is it easier to detect interactions in this format or in the line graphs shown in Figure 11.16?

the second independent variable at that level, and then move to the next level of the first independent variable and do the same thing. For example, to describe the interaction for Wansink's study shown in Figures 11.16 and 11.17, you could say, "When people poured from the *small bottle*, they poured more detergent when it was on sale than when it was regular price. When people poured from the *large bottle*, they poured the same amount of detergent when it was on sale as when it was regular price." As you move from level to level, you make it clear that the size of the effect of the other independent variable (product price) is changing. (More descriptions of different interactions are given in Figure 11.18.)

Interactions Are More Important Than Main Effects

When researchers analyze the results of a factorial design, they look at main effects for each independent variable, and they look for interactions. But when a study shows both a main effect and an interaction, *the interaction is almost always more important.*

Wansink's package-size study provides a good example of this principle. If you study the results, you will notice that this factorial design resulted in a main effect for package size (large packages led to larger servings), a main effect for price (cheaper products led to larger servings), and a significant interaction. However, the overall difference (main effect) for package size actually hides the fact that package size makes a difference *only* at a regular price. And the overall difference (main effect) for price actually hides the fact that price matters *only* for small packages. So there may be real differences in the marginal means, but the exciting—and most accurate—story in this study is the interaction.

Summary of effects	Cell means and marginal means	Line graph of the results
Main effect for cell phone: *No* Main effect for age: *No* Age x cell phone interaction: *Yes*—younger drivers on a cell phone cause more accidents; older drivers on a cell phone cause fewer accidents	**DV: Number of accidents** / On cell phone / Not on phone Younger drivers: 10, 4, 7 Older drivers: 4, 10, 7 (marginal): 7, 7	Graph with Younger driver, Older driver
Main effect for cell phone: *No* Main effect for Age: *Yes*—younger drivers have more accidents Age x cell phone interaction: *No*	**DV: Number of accidents** / On cell phone / Not on phone Younger drivers: 10, 10, 10 Older drivers: 4, 4, 4 (marginal): 7, 7	Graph with Younger drivers, Older drivers
Main effect for cell phone: *Yes*—cell phones cause more accidents Main effect for age: *No* Age x cell phone interaction: *No*	**DV: Number of accidents** / On cell phone / Not on phone Younger drivers: 10, 4, 7 Older drivers: 10, 4, 7 (marginal): 10, 4	Graph with Younger drivers, Older drivers
Main effect for cell phone: *Yes*—cell phones cause more accidents Main effect for age: *Yes*—younger drivers have more accidents Age x cell phone interaction: *Yes*—for younger drivers, phones do not make a difference, but for older drivers, phone use causes more accidents	**DV: Number of accidents** / On cell phone / Not on phone Younger drivers: 10, 10, 10 Older drivers: 10, 4, 7 (marginal): 10, 7	Graph with Younger drivers, Older drivers

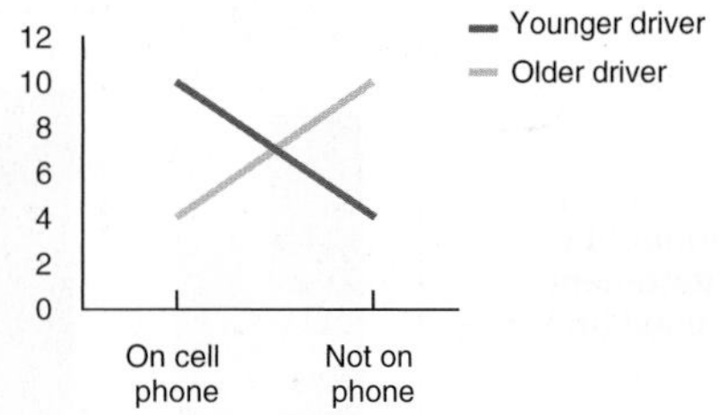

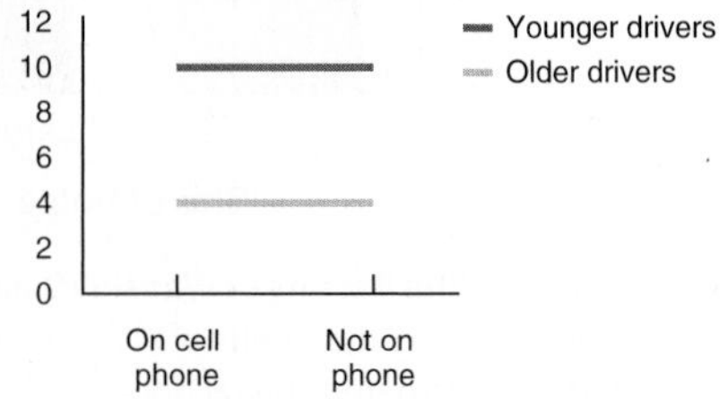

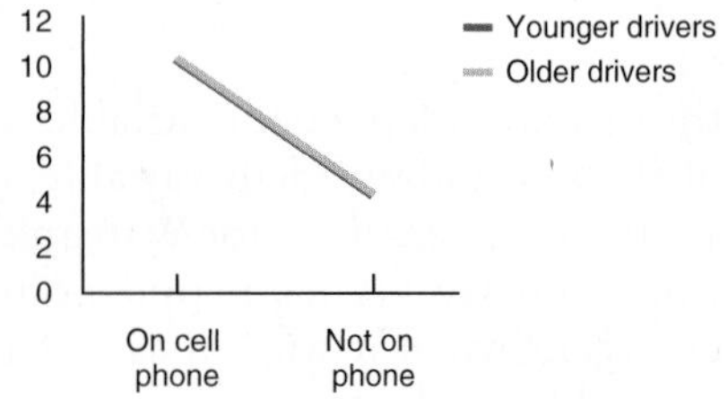

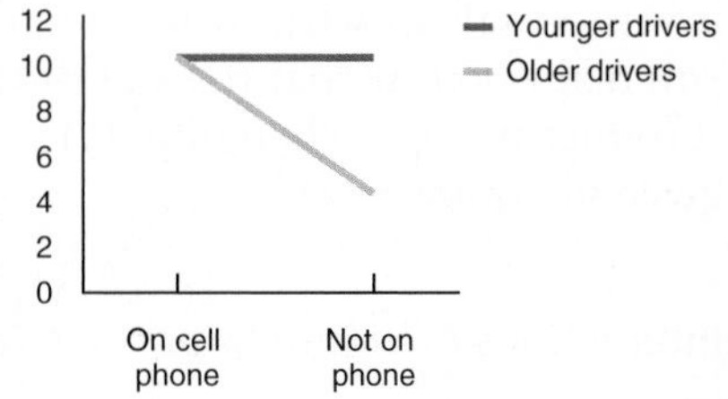

FIGURE 11.18 All of the possible outcomes from a single 2 × 2 factorial design.
(Data are fabricated for the purposes of illustration.)

Possible Main Effects and Interactions in a 2 × 2 Factorial

Figure 11.18 shows a variety of hypothetical outcomes from a single study. In all the examples, the independent variables are the same: a cell phone condition and an age condition. The dependent variable is the average number of accidents. This figure presents a variety of outcomes, all hypothetical, to show some possible combinations of main effects and interactions in a 2 × 2 factorial design. Note, too, how each main effect and interaction can be described in words.

Summary of effects	Cell means and marginal means	Line graph of the results
Main effect for cell phone: *Yes*—phones cause more accidents. Main effect for age: *Yes*—older drivers have more accidents. Age × cell phone interaction: *Yes*—impact of a cell phone is larger for older than for younger drivers	**DV: Number of accidents** / On cell phone / Not on phone — Younger drivers: 8, 2, 5; Older drivers: 12, 3, 7.5; marginal: 10, 2.5	
Main effect for cell phone: *No* Main effect for age: *No* Age × cell phone interaction: *No*	**DV: Number of accidents** / On cell phone / Not on phone — Younger drivers: 5, 5, 5; Older drivers: 5, 5, 5; marginal: 5, 5	
Main effect for cell phone: *Yes*—cell phones cause more accidents Main effect for age: *No* Age × cell phone interaction: *Yes*—for younger drivers, cell phones make no difference, but for older drivers, cell phones are associated with more accidents	**DV: Number of accidents** / On cell phone / Not on phone — Younger drivers: 5, 5, 5; Older drivers: 8, 2, 5; marginal: 6.5, 3.5	
Main effect for cell phone: *No* Main effect for age: *Yes*—younger drivers have more accidents Age × cell phone interaction: *Yes*—for younger drivers, cell phones use causes more accidents, but for older drivers phone use causes fewer accidents	**DV: Number of accidents** / On cell phone / Not on phone — Younger drivers: 8, 5, 6.5; Older drivers: 2, 5, 3.5; marginal: 5, 5	

(continued)

1. In your own words, describe why Wansink's study on price and package size was a factorial design.
2. What are two common reasons to use a factorial design?
3. How can you detect an interaction from a table of means? From a line graph?
4. Why is a main effect better called an "overall effect"?

1. See pp. 319–320. 2. See pp. 315–319. 3. See pp. 322–324. 4. See pp. 321–322.

Factorial Variations

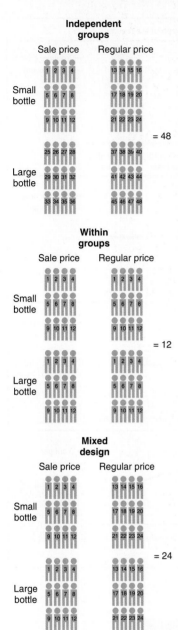

Independent groups

Sale price   Regular price

Small bottle

Large bottle

= 48

Within groups

Sale price   Regular price

Small bottle

Large bottle

= 12

Mixed design

Sale price   Regular price

Small bottle

Large bottle

= 24

FIGURE 11.19 Within-groups designs are more efficient. To achieve a goal of 12 observations per cell, an independent-groups factorial design would need 48 participants. A within-groups factorial design would require 12 participants, and a mixed design would require 24 participants.

Now that we have covered the basics of factorial designs, this next section discusses some advanced variations on the basic 2 × 2 design. What happens when an independent variable has more than two levels? What happens when one of the independent variables is manipulated within groups? What if we add a third independent variable?

Independent-Groups, Within-Groups, and Mixed Designs

Recall from Chapter 9 that in a simple experiment, the independent variable can be manipulated either as an independent-groups variable (different people participate at each level) or as a within-groups variable (the same people participate at each level, as in a repeated-measures design). The same is true for factorial designs. Researchers can choose whether to manipulate *each* independent variable as independent-groups or within-groups.

Independent-Groups Factorial Designs

In an independent-groups factorial design (also known as a between-subjects factorial), both independent variables are manipulated as independent groups. Therefore, if the design is a 2 × 2, there are four different groups of participants in the experiment. Wansink's portion-size study was designed this way: One group of participants poured cleanser from a regular-priced small bottle, another group poured cleanser from a regular-priced large bottle, a third group poured from a sale-priced small bottle, and a fourth group poured from a sale-priced large bottle.

Wansink used 50 participants in each cell of the design. Since he had four conditions, he needed 200 total participants in his study. He randomly assigned each of his 200 participants to one of the four groups.

Within-Groups Factorial Designs

In a within-groups factorial design (also called a repeated-measures factorial), both independent variables are manipulated as within groups. Therefore, if the design is 2 × 2, there is only one group of participants, but they participate in all four combinations, or cells, of the design. An example of such a design might be a study in which participants rate the honesty of people depicted in several photographs. The people in the photos might vary in whether they are attractive or unattractive (the first independent variable) and in whether they are male or female (the second independent variable).

In a within-groups factorial design, all participants are involved in each possible combination in the design. So if you wanted 50 people to rate each photograph, you would need a total of only 50 participants in this study—a distinct advantage of this type of design (see **Figure 11.19**).

In this example, each person would rate at least four photographs: attractive male, attractive female, unattractive male, and unattractive female. The researcher would counterbalance the order of presentation of the photos for each participant (randomly assigning them to different orders) to help protect against order effects and ensure internal validity.

Mixed Factorial Designs

In a mixed factorial design, one independent variable is manipulated as independent groups and the other is manipulated as within groups. Strayer and Drews's study on cell phone use and driving among different age groups is an example of a mixed factorial design. Age was an independent-groups participant variable: Participants in one group were old, and those in the other group were young. But the cell phone condition independent variable was manipulated as within groups. Each participant drove in both the cell phone and control conditions of the study.

If Strayer and Drews had wanted 50 people in each cell of their 2×2 mixed design, they would have needed a total of 100 people: 50 old drivers and 50 young drivers, each participating at both levels of the cell phone condition.

Increasing the Number of Levels of an Independent Variable

So far, we have focused on the simplest factorial design, the 2×2. This design has two independent variables, each with two levels, creating four conditions ($2 \times 2 = 4$). But researchers can add more levels to each independent variable. For example, Strayer and Drews might have manipulated their cell phone condition using three levels (handheld cell phone, hands-free cell phone, and no cell phone) and then crossed it with age (older and younger drivers). This design would be represented as shown in **Figure 11.20**. This design would be called a 2×3 factorial design. It still has two independent variables, but one independent variable has two levels, and the other independent variable has three levels, resulting in six cells ($2 \times 3 = 6$).

This is a good opportunity to discuss the notation for factorial designs. Factorials are notated in the form "__ × __." The quantity of numbers (a 2×3 design

DV: Brake onset time (ms)	IV$_1$: Cell phone condition		
	Hands-free cell phone	Handheld cell phone	No phone
IV$_2$: Driver age — Younger drivers	1100	1200	850
IV$_2$: Driver age — Older drivers	1450	1500	1050

FIGURE 11.20 A 2 × 3 factorial design. (Data are fabricated.)

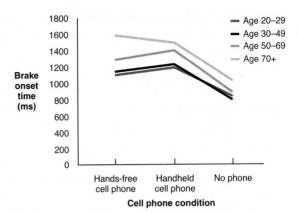

DV: Brake onset time (ms)		IV₁: Cell phone condition		
		Hands-free cell phone	Handheld cell phone	No phone
IV₂: Driver age	Age 20–29	1100	1200	850
	Age 30–49	1120	1225	820
	Age 50–69	1300	1400	900
	Age 70+	1600	1500	1050

FIGURE 11.21

A 3 × 4 factorial design. (Data are fabricated for the purpose of illustration.)

is represented with two numbers, 2 and 3) indicates the number of independent variables. The value of each of the numbers indicates how many levels there are for each independent variable (two levels for one and three levels for the other). When you multiply the two numbers, you get the total number of cells in the design.

What would happen if Strayer and Drews also increased the number of levels of the other independent variable, age? For example, what if they used four groups of drivers: drivers in their 20s, 30s, 50s, and 70s? If the cell phone condition had three levels and age had four levels, the new design could be represented as in **Figure 11.21**. This new design still has two independent variables, but one of them has three levels and the other has four levels. The new design is called a 3 × 4 factorial and results in 12 cells (3 × 4 = 12).

When independent variables have more than two levels, researchers can still investigate main effects and interactions by computing the marginal means and seeing whether they are different. The easiest way to look for interactions is to plot the results in a line graph and see whether the lines run parallel. As in a 2 × 2 factorial design, statistical tests would confirm whether any of the main effects or interactions are statistically significant.

Increasing the Number of Independent Variables

So far, we have discussed only factorial designs with two independent variables. But for some research questions, researchers find it necessary to have three (or even more) independent variables in a crossed factorial design. For instance, what would happen if Strayer and Drews wanted to study not only the cell phone independent variable and the age independent variable, but also two kinds of traffic conditions: dense traffic and light traffic? Would this third independent variable make a difference?

Such a design would be called a 2 × 2 × 2 factorial, sometimes called a *three-way design*. There are two levels of the first independent variable, two levels of the second, and two levels of the third. This design would create eight cells, or conditions, in the experiment (2 × 2 × 2 = 8). The best way to depict a three-way design is to draw the original 2 × 2 table twice, once for each level of the third independent variable, as shown in **Figure 11.22A**. To graph a three-way design, you create two side-by-side line graphs, as shown in **Figure 11.22B**.

means, we can investigate the difference in differences using the table, just as we did for a two-way design. Or it may be easier to look for the interaction by graphing it and checking for nonparallel lines. (Statistical tests will show whether each two-way interaction is statistically significant or not.)

Three-Way Interactions: Are the Two-Way Interactions Different? In a three-way design, the final result is a single three-way interaction. In the cell phone example, this would be the three-way interaction among driver age, cell phone condition, and traffic condition. A three-way interaction, if it is significant, means that the two-way interaction between two of the independent variables *depends on* the level of the third independent variable. In mathematical terms, a significant three-way interaction means that the "difference in differences ... is different." (You are allowed to smile when you say this.)

A three-way interaction is easiest to detect by looking at line graphs of the data. Look back at Figure 11.22B. Notice that in light traffic, there is a two-way interaction between driver age and cell phone condition, but in heavy traffic, there is no two-way interaction between these two independent variables. The two-way interaction of driver age × cell phone condition therefore depends on the level of traffic conditions. The interaction of driver age and cell phone is not the same on both sides of the graph. In other words, there is a difference in differences for the light traffic side of the graph, but there is no difference in differences for the heavy traffic side of the graph.

You would find a three-way interaction whenever there is a two-way interaction for one level of a third independent variable but not for the other (because the two-way interactions are different—there is a two-way interaction on one side but not on the other). You will also find a three-way interaction if a graph shows one pattern of two-way interaction on one side but a different pattern of two-way interaction on the other side—in other words, if there are different two-way interactions. However, if you found the same kind of two-way interaction for both levels of the third independent variable, there would not be a three-way interaction. **Figure 11.24** gives a visual representation of some of the possible outcomes of a three-way design.

Factorial designs are a useful way of testing theories and exploring outcomes that depend on multiple factors, and they provide researchers with a way of quantifying the interactions they want to study. Of course, a study can have more than three independent variables. Some studies may have four or five independent variables. With each additional independent variable (or factor), the researchers will be looking at more main effects and even more kinds of interactions.

Why Worry About All These Interactions?

Managing two-way and three-way interactions can be complicated, but both in studying psychology and in thinking about daily life, you will need to understand interaction effects. Why? Because we do not live in a main-effect world. Most outcomes in psychology (and, by extension, in life) are not main effects; they are interactions.

For example, consider the main-effect question, "Is it good to be forgiving in a relationship?" The answer would reflect an interaction: It depends on how severe the problems are in the relationship (McNulty, 2010).

FIGURE 11.24

Three-way interactions in a 2 × 2 × 2 design.
If there is a three-way interaction, it means that the two-way interactions are different, depending on the level of a third independent variable. This table shows different possible patterns of data in a 2 × 2 × 2 design. (Data are fabricated for purpose of illustration.)

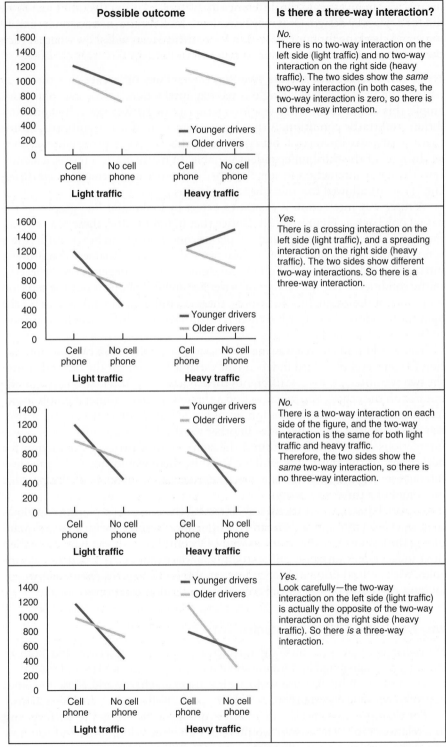

Possible outcome	Is there a three-way interaction?
	No. There is no two-way interaction on the left side (light traffic) and no two-way interaction on the right side (heavy traffic). The two sides show the *same* two-way interaction (in both cases, the two-way interaction is zero, so there is no three-way interaction.
	Yes. There is a crossing interaction on the left side (light traffic), and a spreading interaction on the right side (heavy traffic). The two sides show different two-way interactions. So there is a three-way interaction.
	No. There is a two-way interaction on each side of the figure, and the two-way interaction is the same for both light traffic and heavy traffic. Therefore, the two sides show the *same* two-way interaction, so there is no three-way interaction.
	Yes. Look carefully—the two-way interaction on the left side (light traffic) is actually the opposite of the two-way interaction on the right side (heavy traffic). So there *is* a three-way interaction.

The main-effect question, "Does day care lead to social and emotional problems in kids?" would probably have an interaction answer as well: It depends on the quality of the day care. We might even have a three-way interaction answer: It depends on quality of the care *and* the nature of the home environment.

1. Describe how the same 2 × 2 design might be conducted as an independent-groups factorial, a within-groups factorial, or a mixed factorial design. Indicate how the different designs change the number of participants required: Which design requires the most? Which requires the fewest?
2. How does the notation (e.g., 2 × 2, 3 × 4, 2 × 2 × 3) tell you about the number of independent variables in a study? How does the notation tell you about the number of cells in a study?
3. How many main effects and interactions are there in a 2 × 2 × 2 design?
4. In your own words, describe how you can tell whether a study has a three-way interaction.

1. See pp. 328–329; an independent-groups factorial requires the most participants, and a within-groups factorial requires the least. 2. See pp. 329–330. 3. See pp. 331–333; three two-way interactions and one three-way interaction. 4. See p. 333 and Table 11.1.

Identifying Factorial Designs in Your Reading

Whether you are reading original research published in a journal or secondhand reports of research published in the popular media, certain clues will alert you that the study had a factorial design.

Identifying Factorial Designs in Empirical Journal Articles

In an empirical journal article, researchers almost always describe the design they used in the Method section. You will know that the researchers used a factorial design if they refer to their study as a 2 × 2 design, a 3 × 2 design, a 2 × 2 × 2 design, or the like. Such descriptions also tell you the number of independent variables in the study and how many levels there were of each independent variable.

For example, Wansink describes the study with the cleaning products, depicted in Figure 11.10, as follows: "A 2 × 2 between-subjects design was specified that varied sales promotion (regular price, sale price) and package size (small package, large package)" (Wansink, 1996, p. 5). This sentence tells us that the study was a factorial design with two independent variables of two levels each. It tells us the levels of each variable and that both variables were manipulated as independent groups.

Strayer and Drews describe their design, in a subsection titled "Design and Statistical Analysis," as follows:

The design was a 2 (Age: Younger vs. Older adults) × 2 (Task: Single vs. Dual-task) factorial. Age was a between subjects factor and single- vs. dual-task condition was a within-subjects factor. (Strayer & Drews, 2004, p. 643)

(In their article, they called the driving while using a cell phone condition "dual task" and the driving without a cell phone "single task.") Notice, again, that Strayer and Drews use the notation 2 × 2, labeling each independent variable in parentheses. They also specified that the design was factorial. You can also infer that they used a mixed factorial design, because they mentioned that one independent variable was independent groups ("between subjects") and one was within groups (or "within-subjects").

Whereas the Method section outlines the study's design, independent variables, and dependent variables, the Results section of an empirical article discusses whether the main effects and interactions are significant. Authors may use the term *significant*, the notation $p < 0.05$, or even an asterisk in a table to indicate that a main effect or interaction is statistically significant. Here is an example of how Strayer and Drews described the main effects and interactions in their study:

> The MANOVA indicated significant main effects of age, $F(4, 35) = 8.74$, $p < .01$, and single versus dual task, $F(4, 35) = 11.44$, $p < .01$. However, the Age × Single- versus Dual-Task interaction was not significant, $F(4, 35) = 1.46$, $p > .23$. This latter finding suggests that older adults do not suffer a significantly greater penalty for talking on a cell phone while driving than do their younger counterparts. (Strayer & Drews, 2004, p. 644)

Although you might not know what "MANOVA" and "F" are in the quoted text above, you should now be able to recognize the terms "main effect," "interaction," and "significant."

Identifying Factorial Designs in Popular Press Articles

Whereas empirical journal articles must specify what kind of design was used in a study, popular press articles usually do not. These media outlets probably assume that most of their readers do not know what a 2 × 2 factorial design is. Indeed, most journalists gloss over the details of an experimental design to make their articles simpler. However, you can detect a factorial design from a popular press report if you know what to look for.

Here's an example of how a journalist described one of Wansink's food serving studies. See if you can figure out the design of his study from this journalist's description:

> [One] study gave people popcorn when they came into a movie theater. Some were given a medium bucket and some were given an extra large bucket. Another difference was that some were given fresh popcorn and some were given 5 day old popcorn. Results: People ate 45% more fresh popcorn from the extra large containers than the medium ones. Even when the popcorn was stale, they ate 34% more out of the extra large than the medium ones. Lesson learned: When we are given a larger container, we eat more . . . even if it doesn't even taste very good! (Gidus, 2008)

If you know about factorial designs, you can probably infer from this description that the researcher conducted a 2 × 2 factorial, with popcorn taste as one independent variable and bucket size as the other independent variable. You can also infer that there was no significant interaction between bucket size and taste: The writer gives you the two difference scores (45% and 34%). While they seem to differ, you can infer that there was no significant interaction from the phrase "even when the popcorn was stale," which implies that staleness did not significantly change the effect of bucket size.

In other cases, you may need to read between the lines in order to know that a study had a factorial design. There are certain clues you can look for to identify factorial designs in the popular media.

Look for "It Depends"

Journalists might gloss over the details of a factorial design, but sometimes they will use the phrase *it depends* to highlight an interaction in a report of a factorial design. Here are a few examples:

> [*From an article on gender differences in talking*]
> In her own and others' work, LaFrance noted, "the research is consistently showing either no sex differences in the amount that men and women talk, or if there *is* a difference, then it depends on the context. For example, in a professional context, men actually outspeak women by a long shot." (Mundell, 2007)

> [*From an article on whether religious people are more helpful*]
> Religion can spur goodness—but it depends. Belief in God encourages people to be helpful, honest and generous—but only when religious thoughts are fresh in their minds or when such behavior enhances reputation, researchers say. ("Religion Can Spur Goodness," 2008)

> [*From an article on whether spending money makes people happy*]
> Should I spend money on a vacation or a new computer? Will an experience or an object make me happier? A new study in the *Journal of Consumer Research* says it depends on different factors, including how materialistic you are. ("Do Experiences or Material Goods Make Us Happier?," 2009)

In these three examples, you can identify the dependent variable and then use the phrase *it depends* to identify the independent variables. Notice that each article first mentions how a dependent variable is affected by only one factor; then it complicates that basic difference with a second factor. The first example starts with the dependent variable of how much people talk. It mentions one factor (gender) and then adds a second factor (the context: work, nonwork) to describe the interaction. The effect of gender on how much people talk *depends on* the context in which they are talking.

The second example starts with the dependent variable "goodness." It mentions one factor (religiousness) and then adds the second factor (whether religious thoughts are fresh in one's mind). The effect of religiousness on good behavior *depends on* whether religious thoughts are fresh in one's mind.

The third example starts with the dependent variable "happiness" and first asks whether happiness is affected by one factor—what a person spends money on (experiences or possessions). Then it adds the second factor, saying that the effect of experiences (versus possessions) on happiness *depends on* a person's level of materialism. Thus, materialism is a second factor that interacts with what people spend their money on.

Look for Participant Variables

You can sometimes detect factorial designs when articles discuss a participant variable, such as sex, age, or ethnicity. In such stories, the participant variable often moderates another independent variable. And when there is a moderator, there is an interaction (as well as a factorial design to test it). For instance, the following article discusses how male and female monkeys respond to cocaine prenatally:

> Adult male monkeys exposed to cocaine while in the womb have poor impulse control and may be more vulnerable to drug abuse than female monkeys, even a decade or more after the exposure, according to a new study by researchers at Wake Forest University School of Medicine. The findings could lead to a better understanding of human drug abuse. . . .
>
> For the study, researchers compared adult monkeys—both male and female—prenatally exposed to cocaine more than 15 years ago, to monkeys who were raised under similar conditions, but not exposed to cocaine during gestation. To determine if the animals differed in impulse control, they performed four tests. For one of the tests, the researchers gave the animals the choice between pushing a lever that delivered a single banana pellet reward immediately or a lever that delivered several banana pellets, but required the animals to wait up to 5 minutes before the reward was delivered. ("Cocaine Exposure During Pregnancy," 2009)

In this excerpt, you should be able to identify that the dependent variable was impulsivity, as tested with the banana pellet lever. The excerpt specifies that one independent variable, cocaine exposure, made a difference for males, but not for females—a sign of an interaction. Sex (a participant variable) interacted with cocaine exposure (an independent variable) to determine how the monkeys responded to a self-control task.

In the following example of a factorial design with a participant variable, the author again does not mention the study's factors or design. How can you tell that there is an interaction?

> Joanne Wood of the University of Waterloo in Ontario and two colleagues conducted experiments in which they asked students to repeat statements to themselves such as "I am a lovable person"—then measured how it affected their mood. But in one of their studies involving 32 male and 36 female psychology students, the researchers found that repeating the phrase did not improve the mood of those who had low self-esteem, as measured by a standard test. They actually ended up feeling worse, and the gap between those with high and low self-esteem widened. (Stein, 2009)

The statement that "the gap between those with high and low self-esteem widened" is a sign that there was a difference in differences—an interaction (probably a spreading interaction). Reading between the lines, you can infer that the dependent variable was mood. One factor in this design was self-esteem (high or low); the other was the phrase that people repeated (they said "I am a lovable person" or did not).

Check Your Understanding

1. In an empirical journal article, in what section will you find the independent and dependent variables of the design? In what section will you find whether the main effects and interactions are statistically significant?
2. Describe at least two cues that tell you a popular press article is probably describing a factorial design.

1. See pp. 335–336. 2. See pp. 336–338.

Summary

Factorial designs enable researchers to test their theories, to generalize a simple effect to more than one type of person or situation, and to test and establish multiple influences on behavior. Factorial designs often cross two or more independent variables with one another, creating conditions, or cells, that represent every possible combination of the levels of each independent variable. The factors can be independent-groups or within-groups variables; the factors can be manipulated (independent) variables or measured, participant variables. To analyze the data from a factorial design, look for main effects for each independent variable by estimating marginal means. Then look for interaction effects by checking for a difference in differences. (If there is a line graph, you would look for nonparallel lines.) When a factorial design has three or more independent variables, the number of interactions increases to include all possible combinations of the independent variables. Factorial designs are straightforward to identify in empirical journal articles—the design is given in the Method section. In a popular press story, you can identify a factorial design by looking for language such as "it depends" or descriptions of both participant variables and independent variables.

Key Terms

cells, p. 315
crossed factorial design, p. 315
factorial design, p. 315
interaction, p. 313

main effect, p. 321
marginal means, p. 321
nested factorial design, p. 316
participant variable, p. 316

NEED HELP STUDYING?

wwnorton.com/studyspace

Visit StudySpace to access free review materials such as:

- Diagnostic Review Quizzes
- Study Outlines

Learning Actively

1. For practice, compute the marginal means in the studies shown in this figure. (Assume that each cell has an equal number of participants.) You would need significance tests to be sure, but does it look as if there will be significant main effects for both the cell phone condition and the driver age condition? Why or why not? Does it look as if there are main effects for the testing condition and the learning condition? Why or why not?

DV: Brake onset time (ms)		IV_1: Cell phone condition		
		Cell phone	Not on phone	Main effect for IV_2: Driver age
IV_2: Driver age	Younger drivers	912	780	
	Older drivers	1086	912	
Main effect for IV_1: Cell phone condition				

DV: Number of words memorized		IV_1: Testing condition		
		Water's edge	Underwater	Main effect for IV_2: Learning condition
IV_2: Learning condition	Water's edge	13.5	8.6	
	Underwater	8.4	11.4	
Main effect for IV_1: Testing condition				

2. In one of their studies, Strayer and his students tested whether people would get better at driving while talking on a cell phone if they practiced doing so (Cooper & Strayer, 2008). They asked people to drive in a simulator, both while talking on a hands-free cell phone and while not talking on a phone. In addition, the same people participated over several days, so that they had a chance to practice this multitasking. On the first day, they were considered to be least experienced. On the last day, they were considered to be most experienced. In addition, on the last day, they were tested both in a familiar environment and in a slightly different driving environment, to see if the first days of practice would transfer to a new context. Cooper and Strayer collected data on

how many collisions (accidents) the drivers got into on the simulator (trained in the "city" condition). See the following table for their data.

		Number of collisions	
	Day 1	Day 4 (driving in a familiar context)	Day 4 (driving in a new context)
Single-task (not using cell phone)	15	6	10
Dual-task (using cell phone)	20	7.5	24

Source: Cooper and Strayer (2008).

a. What kind of design is this? (Put your answer in the form "__ × __.")
b. What are the independent and dependent variables?
c. Indicate whether each independent variable was manipulated as independent groups or within groups.
d. Create a line graph depicting these results.
e. Estimate and describe any main effects and interactions in this study.
f. What might you conclude from the results of this study? Does experience affect cell phone use while driving?

3. For the following factorial designs, indicate how many cells would be created, and then indicate how many main effects and interactions you would look for.

a. 3 × 2 design
b. 3 × 4 × 2 design
c. 3 × 4 × 5 × 2 design

4. Practice applying the four big validities (construct, internal, external, and statistical) to Wansink's package size × product price experiment, depicted in Figure 11.10. For each of the validities, write at least one appropriate question and, based on what you know, evaluate what the answers to your questions might be. If you do not have enough information about an aspect of the study's validity, write what Wansink might say if his study had excellent validity in that category.

Pay special attention to the internal validity of Wansink's package size manipulation. What does it mean that Wansink kept the amount of product constant, while varying the package size from small to large?

5. Are participant variables independent-groups variables or within-groups variables? Why?

PART 6

Balancing Research Priorities

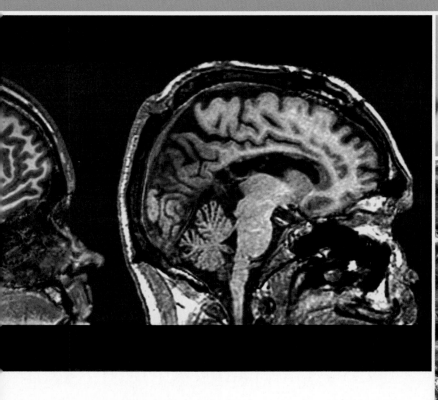

Can a study have internal validity without random assignment?

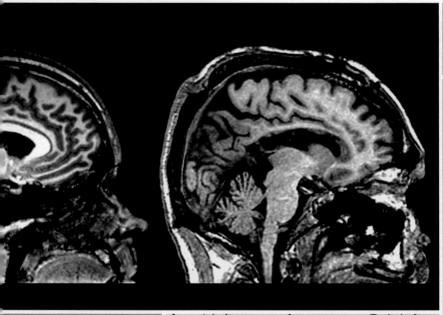

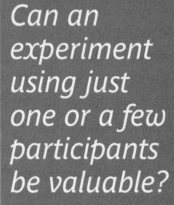

Can an experiment using just one or a few participants be valuable?

12

Quasi-Experiments and Small-*N* Designs

Learning Objectives

A year from now, you should still be able to:

1. Articulate how quasi-experiments differ from true experiments.
2. Analyze the design and results of quasi-experiments to evaluate the support they provide for causal claims.
3. Explain the major differences between small-*N* designs and large-*N* designs.
4. Analyze the design and results of small-*N* experiments to evaluate the support they provide for causal claims.

Previous chapters of this book have explained how to interrogate frequency claims (Chapter 6), association claims (Chapters 7 and 8), and causal claims (Chapters 9, 10, and 11). The last two chapters in this book focus on a more general issue: how researchers balance research priorities in conducting their studies. Of course, researchers always want to do the best research possible, but they are constrained by practical issues, and they must conduct their research ethically. How do researchers balance their ideal research goals with the practicalities of real-world research situations?

This chapter discusses situations in which researchers cannot conduct a true experiment. For example, they may not be able to randomly assign participants to different groups or counterbalance conditions in a within-groups experiment. What are the trade-offs of doing research in such situations? How do researchers achieve internal validity when full experimental control is impossible? In other instances, researchers may be able to collect data from only one case, such as a person who has a rare disorder or a rare behavioral condition. How might practitioners and researchers balance priorities for internal and external validity when they study a single case?

Quasi-Experiments

Quasi-experiments are similar to true experiments: As in a true experiment, researchers select an independent variable and a dependent variable; then they study participants who are exposed to each level of the independent variable. But in a quasi-experiment, the experimenters do not have full experimental control. For example, they may not be able to randomly assign participants to one level or the other. Instead, participants are assigned to the independent variable conditions by teachers, political regulations, acts of nature—or even by their own choice.

Two Examples of Independent-Groups Quasi-Experiments

The following two examples of quasi-experiments follow an independent-groups model. In these examples, there are different participants at each level of the independent variable. This type of quasi-experimental design is typically called a **nonequivalent control group design**: a quasi-experimental study that has at least one treatment group and one comparison group, but participants have not been randomly assigned to the two groups.

The Head Start Study

Head Start is a government-funded, early-childhood education program in the United States that gives a quality preschool experience to children from economically poor homes. Does the program really work? Does it improve the academic performance of the children it serves? To find out, early in the program's history education researchers compared the academic performance of children in the Head Start program with that of children who were not in the program (Cicirelli & Associates, 1969). However, they soon ran into a real-world policy that could harm the internal validity of their studies: Any child who qualifies for Head Start has a right to enroll. Therefore, children are assigned to Head Start by social workers and administrators; they cannot be randomly assigned to Head Start versus some comparison program.

Nevertheless, one early study attempted to assess the efficacy of Head Start by finding a comparison group of children who had not been enrolled in Head Start programs but who nevertheless seemed similar to Head Start children. Specifically, the comparison group's scores on an early childhood achievement test were about the same. (The researchers had attempted to match the children on their achievement test scores.) But even though the Head Start children and the comparison children had similar achievement scores, they were probably different in other ways. One important difference was their family incomes: The Head Start children were economically disadvantaged, while the comparison children were not. (After all, economic disadvantage was the main reason children were eligible for Head Start to begin with.) Therefore, although this study had an independent variable (being in Head Start or not) and a dependent variable (later school achievement), the study was a quasi-experiment. The children were not randomly assigned to the two groups, so the groups were not perfectly equivalent—hence the term *nonequivalent control group design*.

Administrators of Head Start hoped to show that this intensive preschool program would help at-risk children perform better in school when they got to grade school. However, the results of the study showed that the school achievement of the Head Start children was *worse* than that of the comparison group, as shown in **Figure 12.1**. As you read the rest of this chapter, consider what these results mean: Did the program simply fail to work? Did the Head Start program actually interfere with children's academic progress? Or was there something about the quasi-experiment that led to this result?

The StayWell Program

A group of health psychologists designed a program called StayWell to encourage elderly adults to become more independent and proactive about their health (Brice, Gorey, Hall, & Angelino, 1996). They administered this 8-week training program to 96 people. An additional 50 people were placed on a waiting list, so they were not enrolled in the StayWell program. The health psychologists used the waiting list group as the comparison group. Nine months later, the researchers found that the participants who experienced the StayWell intervention were living a healthier lifestyle than those on the waiting list.

This study looks like an experiment—there is an independent variable (receiving the StayWell treatment or not) and there are dependent variables (measures of healthy behaviors and need for medication). However, the participants were not randomly assigned to receive the training or be on the waiting list. Instead, members of four senior citizen centers participated in the StayWell program right away, and seniors at four other centers were put on the waiting list. As in the first example, the lack of random assignment made this a quasi-experiment. People were assigned to the two independent variable groups simply according to what senior center they attended. The StayWell study was therefore another example of a nonequivalent control group design, because the participants were in two groups but were not randomly assigned to them.

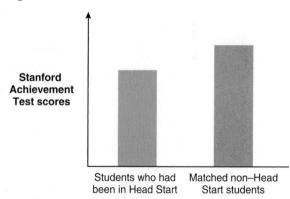

FIGURE 12.1 The Head Start study. Students who had been in Head Start programs scored lower than students who did not participate in Head Start. Is the Head Start program a failure, according to this quasi-experiment? *Sources*: Adapted from results reported by Cicirelli and Associates (1969); Shadish and Luellen (2006).

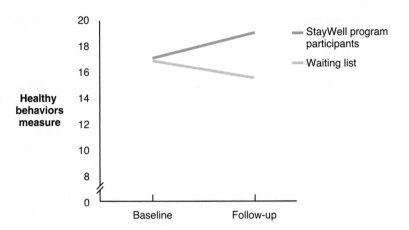

FIGURE 12.2 **The StayWell study.** Participants in the StayWell program for senior citizens reported more healthy behaviors after the program than senior citizens who were on the waiting list and did not participate in this program. According to the results of this quasi-experiment, does the StayWell program seem to work? That is, does it cause senior citizens to become healthier?

The results of the study are shown in **Figure 12.2**. Although both the Stay-Well group and the waiting list group started out the same on a standard index of healthy behaviors, only the members of the StayWell group had increased their healthy behaviors at posttest. Does this study allow us to say that the StayWell program *caused* healthy behaviors to improve?

Two Examples of Repeated-Measures Quasi-Experiments

Quasi-experiments can be repeated-measures designs, too, in which participants experience both levels of an independent variable. In a quasi-experimental version of this design, as opposed to a true repeated-measures experiment, the researcher takes advantage of an already-scheduled event, a new policy or regulation, or a chance occurrence to manipulate the independent variable. The following two studies are examples of repeated-measures quasi-experiments.

Vacations and Job Burnout

Do vacations reduce job burnout? To find out, an organizational psychologist gave a questionnaire measuring job burnout to 76 employees at an electronics company. The employees described their level of burnout three times: before the company closed for a 2-week vacation (which was already scheduled), in the middle of the vacation, and after the vacation. Because each employee was measured all three times, this study was similar to a repeated-measures experimental design. However, the researchers did not manipulate the levels of the independent variable; instead, the vacation was scheduled in advance by the company (Westman & Eden, 1997). The researchers simply took advantage of this "natural" manipulation and conducted their own surveys before, during, and after the break.

The results of this study are depicted in **Figure 12.3**, which shows the level of burnout at each of the time periods. Apparently, people feel less job burnout during and right after their vacations, but burnout rates eventually rise again.

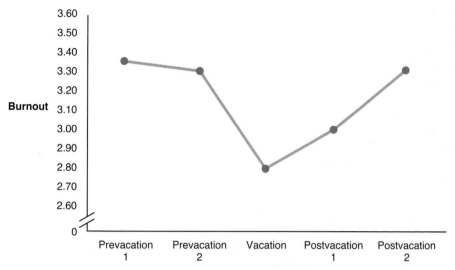

FIGURE 12.3
The vacation/burnout study.
Employees at an electronics firm reported their level of burnout before, during, and after their 2-week vacation period. Does this quasi-experiment show that vacations reduce employee burnout? *Source*: Adapted from Westman and Eden (1997).

The important question is whether the results of this study really show that vacations *cause* a decrease in job burnout.

The vacation study is an example of an **interrupted time-series design**—a quasi-experimental study that measures people repeatedly on a dependent variable (in this case, job burnout) before, during, and after the "interruption" caused by some event (in this case, a vacation).

TV and Larceny

Another quasi-experiment took advantage of a historical event. In the early days of television in the United States, individual cities had to apply for a license to transmit television signals. After issuing licenses up to 1949, the Federal Communications Commission (FCC) stopped issuing broadcasting licenses for 3 years (from 1949 to 1952); therefore, in the early 1950s, some U.S. cities had access to television, but others did not.

Years later, some clever researchers (Hennigan et al., 1982) took advantage of this situation to study crime rates in cities with and without television. Specifically, they measured whether rates of larceny rose in a city in the months after television became available. This quasi-experiment has an independent variable (television exposure) and a dependent variable (larceny rates). The researchers measured larceny rates both before and after the introduction of television. This independent variable (the introduction of television) was not controlled by the researchers but instead was a historical event. The lack of full experimenter control is what made the study a quasi-experiment.

In this study, the researchers also compared larceny rates in cities that had television with rates in cities that did not—an independent-groups comparison. This independent-groups manipulation of the independent variable was not controlled by the researchers, either: Cities were not randomly assigned to have access to television or not; instead, the FCC had inadvertently assigned cities to

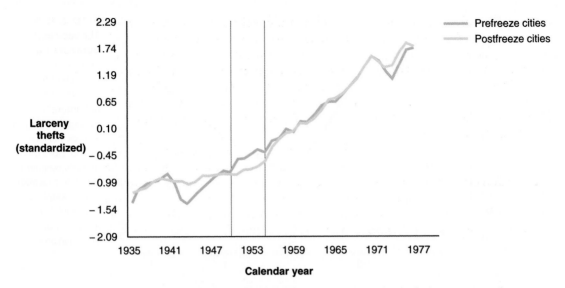

FIGURE 12.4 **The television/larceny study.** Among cities that had television access, larceny rates were higher between 1951 and 1955. After 1955, an FCC freeze on television licenses was lifted, and the cities with newly introduced television showed a rise in larceny rates. Does this quasi-experiment show that television caused larceny rates to increase? *Source*: Adapted from Hennigan and colleagues (1982).

these two groups by imposing the freeze on new television licenses. Therefore, the comparison groups in the independent-groups part of the study were also quasi-experimental.

The results of this analysis are shown in **Figure 12.4**. Notice that larceny rates rose right after 1951, but only in cities that had access to television. After 1955, however, larceny rates showed a similar increase only in those cities that had just acquired television. Do these results show that television *caused* these increases in crime?

The design used in this study is sometimes called a **nonequivalent groups interrupted time-series design**. It combines two of the previous designs (the nonequivalent control groups design and the interrupted time-series design). In this example, the independent variable was studied both as a repeated-measures variable (interrupted time-series) and as an independent-groups variable (nonequivalent groups). In both cases, however, the researchers did not have experimental control over the manipulation of the independent variable or the assignment of participants to conditions.

Internal Validity in Quasi-Experiments

Each of the four examples in the previous section *looks* like a true experiment: Each one has an independent variable and a dependent variable. What is missing in each is full experimenter control over the independent variable.

What did these researchers give up when they conducted studies in which they did not have full experimenter control? The main concern is internal validity—the researchers' ability to draw causal conclusions from the results. The degree to which a quasi-experiment supports a causal statement depends on two things: its design and its results. To interrogate internal validity, you ask about alternative explanations for an observed pattern of results. The internal validity threats for experiments discussed in Chapters 9 and 10 also apply to quasi-experiments. How well do these four examples of quasi-experiments hold up to an internal validity interrogation? Are they susceptible to these internal validity threats?

As you read this section, keep in mind that quasi-experiments can take a variety of designs, and the support that a quasi-experiment provides for a causal claim depends partly on its design and partly on the results a researcher obtains. Researchers do not have full control of the independent variable in a quasi-experiment (as they do in a true experiment), but they can choose better designs, and they can use the pattern of results to rule out some internal validity threats.

Selection Effects / Selection Threats

Selection effects are relevant only for independent-groups designs, not for repeated-measures designs. A selection threat to internal validity applies when the groups at the various levels of an independent variable contain different types of participants. In such cases, it is not clear whether it was the independent variable or the different types of participants in each group that led to a difference in the dependent variable between the groups.

Consider the Head Start study in the first example. The results showed that the Head Start group performed worse than the non–Head Start group on school achievement tests in grade school. Can we claim, on the basis of these results, that the Head Start program *caused* the children to do worse? That is one explanation—but we cannot rule out the alternative explanation of a selection effect. Even though the Head Start children's early childhood achievement scores were equivalent to those of the children in the comparison group (because the children were matched on this variable), the Head Start group was different in many other important ways. For example, the Head Start children were living in poverty, but the comparison children were not, and the Head Start children were more likely to come from single-parent homes than the children in the comparison group. The internal validity threat is that we do not know whether the Head Start children's test scores in grade school were lower because of the Head Start program or because this group had different kinds of children in it (**Figure 12.5**). These children might have performed more poorly over time because of their poverty or because they lived in single-parent homes, not because the Head Start program was detrimental.

In the Head Start study, the researchers could not use a wait-list design, because any child who was eligible for Head Start had a legal right to begin the program right away. In contrast, the StayWell study did use a wait-list design. Although people were not randomly assigned to the StayWell program or to the wait list, the researchers knew that all participants in both groups were at least eligible for the StayWell program. Thus, the seniors who participated in

the StayWell program did not seem to be different from those in the wait-list comparison group—indeed, health behaviors of the participants in both groups looked the same at the pretest (see Figure 12.2). In short, the StayWell study was less susceptible to selection threats to internal validity than the Head Start study. In the StayWell study, we can be more sure that it was the program (the intended cause), not the type of participant (an alternative explanation), that caused the treatment group to act healthier.

FIGURE 12.5 A Head Start classroom. In many studies, the children eligible for Head Start were different from children in comparison groups on several variables, including school achievement, parenting styles, family income, and cultural background.

Maturation Threat

Maturation threats occur when, in an experimental or quasi-experimental design that has a pretest and a posttest, a treatment group shows an improvement over time, but it is not clear whether the improvement was caused by the treatment or whether the group would have improved spontaneously, even without a treatment.

The StayWell study had a pretest and a posttest, so it was potentially susceptible to a maturation threat. Because the participants in the StayWell program did improve over time (see Figure 12.2), we might ask whether the StayWell program was effective, or whether these seniors' health habits would have improved anyway, through maturation (perhaps as people age, they naturally become more interested in maintaining their health). Fortunately, the design of this quasi-experiment included a comparison group—and the results indicated that the comparison group did not improve over time. Because of the design and the pattern of results, we can probably rule out maturation. If seniors generally improve their health habits over time, the seniors on the waiting list would have improved, too—but they did not. The design of the study provided a comparison group, and the results from that comparison group allow us to see that only the seniors in the targeted StayWell group improved.

What about the study on vacation and job burnout? The authors of that study were investigating whether vacation reduces job burnout, and their results supported an argument that it does. A skeptic might argue for maturation, saying that people's job burnout might just get better on its own, but the results of the study showed that job burnout changed systematically with the timing of the company's vacations. After all, when the vacation was over, burnout rates went back up, and maturation is unlikely to reverse itself spontaneously. Therefore, even though the vacation study was not designed to have a comparison group, the results of this study help us rule out maturation threats to internal validity.

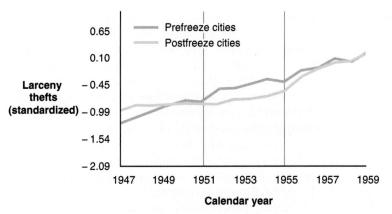

FIGURE 12.6 **Maturation (spontaneous change) in the television/larceny study.** Although larceny increased in all cities, rates rose especially quickly in cities with television, so spontaneous change is not a viable alternative explanation for increased crime.

In the fourth example, did access to television cause larceny rates to rise, or did larceny rates simply increase on their own? The overall trend in Figure 12.4, across all years, clearly shows that larceny rates went up over time. But this study's design allows us to rule out maturation as the sole explanation for the rise in larceny after the introduction of television. Because this study used a comparison group, we can compare the increases in crime rates in the two types of cities (those with television and those without). Larceny rates did rise between 1951 and 1955 in the cities without television (a sign of possible maturation), but the rates rose even faster in cities with television. In addition, right after 1955, larceny rates continued to rise everywhere, but they rose even faster in cities that had just received their television licenses. In short, the design and results of the study enable us to rule out the maturation threat to internal validity (as shown in **Figure 12.6**).

History Threat

A history threat occurs when an external, historical event happens for everyone in a study at the same time as the treatment variable. With a history threat, it is unclear whether the outcome is caused by the treatment or by the common, external event.

For example, we might suggest that crime rates rose between 1951 and 1955 not because of television but because of a political policy introduced during that time period, because of economic recession, or even because of feelings of Cold War alienation. As you might imagine, history threats can be especially relevant when a quasi-experimental design relies on historical events (like the FCC's television policies) to manipulate its key variable. Fortunately, the design of this particular study, which included a comparison group, helps rule out most history threats. Policies, recessions, and cold wars would have affected *all* cities, but according to the results, only the cities with television access showed the jump in larceny rates during this time period.

Of course, it is possible that the cities that had earlier access to television also experienced some local historical event (perhaps a local economic downturn) that would explain the rise in larceny in only those cities. Such a threat would be called a

selection-history threat, because the history threat applies to only one group, not the other. In a selection-history threat, the historical event systematically affects the subjects only in the treatment group or only in the comparison group—not in both. The group membership interacts with some historical event. Although a selection-history threat is a possibility in the study on television and larceny, it seems unlikely that only the cities that happened to receive FCC television licenses would also have some other historical event in common. In addition, it is unlikely that in 1952, when the remaining cities got their licenses, the same local historical event that had occurred in the cities licensed earlier just happened to occur again in the cities licensed later. Selection-history seems implausible in this case.

When quasi-experiments include a comparison group, we can often rule out history threats to internal validity. But quasi-experiments with only one group, such as the vacation and employee burnout study, are more susceptible. Recall that the vacation in the job burnout study was scheduled by the electronics company, not by the experimenters. Job burnout did, in fact, decrease during the vacation period, but it is also possible that people's job burnout decreased because the vacation occurred during the summer. Could the warm, sunny weather have been an external event that was responsible for people's decreased burnout? That would be a history threat, too: It could be the nice weather, not the vacation, that causes people to feel less burned out.

The lack of a comparison group in the vacation study makes it difficult to rule out a history threat. However, to see if the weather might be responsible, we could check the job burnout rates that were recorded a month or two after the vacation period. The weather probably had not changed much, yet job burnout rates were increasing again as soon as employees returned to the office. Again, the results of the quasi-experiment help us assess the likelihood of a history threat.

Regression to the Mean

Regression to the mean occurs when an extreme score is caused by a combination of random factors that are unlikely to happen in the same combination again, so the extreme score gets less extreme over time. Chapter 10 gave the example of the Phillies' lucky 22–1 win over the Reds. That extreme score was a lucky combination of random factors that did not repeat itself in the next game, so the next game's score regressed back toward the average.

Many educational researchers have suggested that regression to the mean was partly responsible for the surprising results of the 1969 Head Start study (Cicirelli & Associates, 1969; Shadish & Luellen, 2006). Recall that the researchers attempted to create equivalent groups of Head Start and non–Head Start children by matching them on their achievement scores at the beginning of the study. Because children who are eligible for Head Start typically have lower achievement scores than children who are not eligible, the researchers had to select special subsets of these two types of children to create their matched design. Specifically, they may have selected a relatively *high-scoring* group of Head Start children and a relatively *low-scoring* group of non–Head Start children.

Although that process created groups that were matched at pretest, it may have also introduced the potential for regression. The high-scoring group of Head Start children had a high pretest average for a combination of reasons.

They may have been smart, but they also benefited from a random combination of lucky factors. Some of the children may have happened to eat a great breakfast, others had an exceptionally good night's sleep, and a few others just happened to know some of the test questions perfectly. In short, this group's pretest average was partly a result of skill and partly a result of good luck. In turn, the comparison group of non–Head Start children may have had low scores, in part, because of an unlucky combination of random factors: Some had skipped breakfast, others had gone to bed late, and others had blanked on some of the easy questions. In short, this group's pretest average was partly a result of skill and partly a result of bad luck.

When the high-scoring Head Start children were tested again later, they would not have experienced the same lucky combination of random factors, so their score regressed down, closer to the mean of other Head Start children. In contrast, when the low-scoring non–Head Start children were tested again later, they would not have experienced the same unlucky combination of random factors, so their score regressed up—closer to the mean of other non–Head Start children (see **Figure 12.7**). The outcome was a disappointing difference: The Head Start program appeared to have hurt the children's academic progress. But after considering the details of the study, many researchers have come to suspect that the posttest difference was attributable to regression. Indeed, this study is only one in a large body of research on the efficacy of the Head Start program. In many other studies, children in this program show academic achievement gains; in addition, they show more positive social outcomes such as graduation from high school (Barnett, 1998; McKey et al., 1985).

Remember that regression effects are a threat to validity primarily when a group is selected because of its extremely high or low scores. Those scores may be extreme, in part, because of a combination of random factors that is unlikely to occur the same way twice. For example, in the other three examples of quasi-experiments in this chapter, the groups were not selected on purpose for their high or low scores, so regression was less likely to be

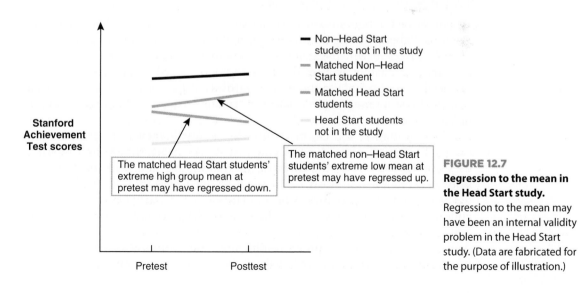

Stanford Achievement Test scores

— Non–Head Start students not in the study
— Matched Non–Head Start student
— Matched Head Start students
— Head Start students not in the study

The matched Head Start students' extreme high group mean at pretest may have regressed down.

The matched non–Head Start students' extreme low mean at pretest may have regressed up.

Pretest   Posttest

FIGURE 12.7

Regression to the mean in the Head Start study.
Regression to the mean may have been an internal validity problem in the Head Start study. (Data are fabricated for the purpose of illustration.)

a problem. And true experiments use random assignment to place subjects into groups, a practice that eliminates regression to the mean as an internal validity threat.

Attrition Threat

The attrition (or mortality) threat applies when people drop out of a study for some systematic reason. It occurs mainly in designs with pretests and posttests. In the job burnout study, for example, we might wonder whether job burnout rates appeared to decrease during vacation only because the most burned out people did not bother to fill out the questionnaire in the middle of their vacation. If only the happiest, least burned-out workers complied with the study during vacation, that would explain the apparent decline in the burnout rate during the vacation period. In this case, it would not be the vacation but the attrition of the most burned-out workers that caused the decrease.

Fortunately, attrition is easy to check for, and the researchers in the vacation study made sure that it was not an explanation for their results. The study's Method section specifies as follows:

> *Sample.* We collected data in an administrative department numbering 90 clerical employees at the headquarters of an electronics firm in Central Israel. Of the 90, 2 refused to participate because they thought the questions were too personal, and 12 did not complete the questionnaires on all five occasions due to illness, travel, or reserve duty. The final sample of 76 included 31 women (41%) and 45 men (59%). (Westman & Eden, p. 519)

Because Westman and Eden included in their final analysis only people who completed all five of the questionnaires, we can be sure that attrition is not a threat to their results.

Testing and Instrumentation Threats

Whenever researchers measure participants more than once, they need to be concerned about testing threats to internal validity. A testing threat is a kind of order effect in which participants—whether students, animals, or anyone else—tend to change as a result of having been tested before. Repeated testing might cause people to improve, regardless of the treatment they received. Repeated testing might also cause performance to decline because of fatigue or boredom.

Instrumentation, too, can be an internal validity threat when participants are tested or observed twice. A measuring instrument could change over repeated uses, and this change would threaten internal validity. If a study uses two versions of a test with different standards (say, one test is more difficult), or if a study uses coders who change their standards over time, then participants might appear to change, when in reality there is no change between one observation and the next.

Again, you can use a study's results and design to interrogate testing and instrumentation threats to internal validity. For example, the decline of job burnout in the vacation study might have been caused by a testing effect (such as practice answering the items), but since scores first declined and then rose again, it seems unlikely that repeated testing is the culprit. Instrumentation, as well, can be ruled out here because the instrument did not change: The study used the same questionnaire all five times.

Consider the design and results of the StayWell study. Participants in both the treatment group and the wait-list control group were tested twice on their level of healthy behaviors. Either a testing effect or an instrumentation effect would have caused both groups to improve or both to worsen, but the treatment group improved over time, while the control group declined. A comparison group like the one in this study almost always helps rule out a testing threat to validity.

Observer Bias, Experimental Demand, and Placebo Effects

Three final threats to internal validity are related to human subjectivity. Specifically, observer bias, in addition to being a threat to construct validity, can also threaten internal validity when the experimenters' expectations influence their interpretation of the results. Other threats include experimental demand (when participants guess what the study is about and change their behavior in the expected direction) and placebo effects (when the participants improve, but only because they believe they are receiving an effective treatment). Fortunately, these three threats are easy to interrogate. For observer bias, you simply ask who measured the behaviors. Was the design blind or double-blind? For experimental demand, you can think about whether the participants were able to detect the study's goals and responded accordingly. For placebo effects, you can ask whether the design of a study included a comparison group that received an inert, or placebo, treatment.

Consider the study that evaluated the StayWell program. This study was not double-blind because the experimenters knew who was in the program and who was not. The participants, too, knew whether they had or had not participated in the program. Therefore, the experimenters could have been biased when they measured the health behaviors of the participants at the posttest, but because they asked people to report on their own healthy behaviors, the chance of observer bias was low. However, the participants might have been susceptible to experimental demand. That is, all the participants in the StayWell program knew that the program was designed to improve their healthy behaviors (after all, they knew that the name of the program was *StayWell*). Therefore, the StayWell seniors might have changed their reports of their health behaviors just because they wanted to help the researchers (see **Figure 12.8**).

In addition, we cannot rule out a placebo effect in this study. Was the StayWell program really effective, or could a placebo program have resulted in the same improvement? Ideally, the researchers could have presented a placebo workshop (such as a set of engaging activities that were not meant to be therapeutic) to a comparison group to rule out a placebo effect. Because they did not include such a condition, we cannot be sure that the StayWell program, instead of a placebo effect, is the true cause of the seniors' health improvements.

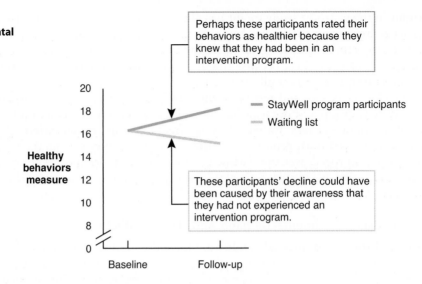

FIGURE 12.8
Interrogating experimental demand in the StayWell study.

Perhaps these participants rated their behaviors as healthier because they knew that they had been in an intervention program.

These participants' decline could have been caused by their awareness that they had not experienced an intervention program.

StayWell program participants

Waiting list

Healthy behaviors measure

Baseline   Follow-up

Balancing Priorities in Quasi-Experiments

What does an experimenter gain by conducting a quasi-experiment? In other words, if quasi-experimental studies can be vulnerable to internal validity threats, why would anybody do one?

Opportunity

One reason researchers conduct quasi-experiments is that these designs, such as those in the television and larceny study and the vacation and burnout study, enable them to take advantage of real-world opportunities to study interesting phenomena and events. Hennigan and his colleagues would never have been able to randomly assign towns to have television access (or not), but they took advantage of the research opportunity that the FCC inadvertently provided. Similarly, Westman and Eden capitalized on an opportunity to study vacations; they did not manipulate the vacation themselves, but the company's vacation policy offered them the next-best thing—and in a real-world setting.

External Validity

The real-world settings of many quasi-experiments can enhance external validity: the likelihood that the patterns observed in the quasi-experiment will generalize to other settings and to other individuals. We do not have to ask whether the vacation study applies to real-world settings, because the study occurred in a real-world setting. We do not have to ask whether television increases larceny in the real world, because the events in the study did take place in the real world. We might still ask whether the vacation study's results would generalize to other companies or whether the television study's results would generalize to world regions other than the United States. But in general, quasi-experiments capitalize on real-world situations, even as they give up some control over internal validity. (In contrast, as discussed in Chapter 13, many laboratory experiments seek to maximize internal validity while giving up some "realism.")

Ethics

Ethical concerns are another reason researchers might choose a quasi-experimental design. Many questions of interest to researchers would be unethical to study in a true experiment. The Head Start question is a good example: It would not be ethical to withhold free preschool education from a group of children by randomly assigning some children to be enrolled in the Head Start program and others not to be enrolled. Even a wait-list design would not be ethical here: By the time the wait-listed children started the program, they might be too old to benefit from it. Therefore, quasi-experiments are the only ethical way to study Head Start. Similarly, it probably would not be ethical to withhold vacations from some employees or to withhold television from residents of randomly assigned towns, but quasi-experiments can be an ethical option for studying these important questions.

Construct Validity and Statistical Validity in Quasi-Experiments

So far in this chapter, we have emphasized internal validity, because researchers usually conduct quasi-experiments in order to make causal statements. But the other big validities should be interrogated, too. For construct validity, you would interrogate how well the study manipulated or measured its variables. Often, quasi-experiments show excellent construct validity for the independent variable, as illustrated by the examples in this chapter. In the StayWell study, the seniors really were or were not in the StayWell program. In the job burnout study, the employees really were or were not on vacation. But we would also need to ask how well the dependent variables were measured in these studies: How well did the StayWell researchers measure healthy behaviors? How well did the vacation researchers measure job burnout? Were these measures reliable? Did they measure what they were intended to measure?

Finally, to assess a study's statistical validity, we would ask how large the group differences were (the effect size) and whether the results were statistically significant.

Are Quasi-Experiments the Same as Correlational Studies?

Some quasi-experiments seem similar in design to correlational studies, which were discussed in Chapters 7 and 8. When a quasi-experiment uses an independent-groups design (that is, when it compares two groups without using random assignment), the groups in the study can look similar to those in correlational studies.

Consider, for example, Harvey's (1999) research about maternal employment and child achievement (discussed in Chapter 7), which studied the school achievement of children whose mothers either worked or did not work. The categorical variable here—maternal employment—looks like a quasi-experimental independent variable. There are two categories (working mothers and nonworking mothers), and the children were not randomly assigned to one or the other category. It seems like a correlational study because there were two measured variables, but it also seems like a quasi-experiment, because it studied two groups of people who were not randomly assigned. Quasi-experiments and correlational designs also have similar internal validity concerns: Just as we might ask about third variables or unmeasured "lurking" variables in a correlational study, we might ask about selection effects in a quasi-experimental study.

Although the two are similar, in quasi-experiments the researchers tend to do a little more meddling than they do in most correlational designs. In correlational studies, researchers simply select a sample, measure two variables, and test the relationship between them. In quasi-experiments, however, the researchers might attempt to achieve internal validity by matching participants (as in the Head Start study), implementing a wait-list policy (as in the StayWell study), or seeking out comparison groups provided by nature or by public policy (as in the television and larceny study). Therefore, whereas correlational researchers primarily measure variables in a sample and analyze their relationships, quasi-experimental researchers more actively select groups for an independent variable so they can achieve a greater degree of internal validity. Ultimately, however, the distinction between quasi-experiments and correlational studies can be a blurry one, and some studies may be difficult to categorize. Rather than becoming too concerned about how to categorize a particular study as quasi-experimental versus correlational, focus instead on applying what you know about threats to internal validity and evaluating causal claims.

Check Your Understanding

1. How is a nonequivalent control groups design different from a true independent-groups experiment?
2. How are interrupted time-series designs and nonequivalent control groups interrupted time-series designs different from true within-subjects experiments?
3. Describe why both the design and the results of a study are important for assessing a quasi-experiment's internal validity.
4. What are three reasons that a researcher might conduct a quasi-experiment, rather than a true experiment, to study a research question?

1. See p. 346; only a true independent-groups experiment randomly assigns participants to the groups. 2. See p. 350; only a true within-subjects experiment can counterbalance the order of presentation of the levels of the independent variable. 3. See pp. 350–357. 4. See pp. 358–359.

Small-*N* Experiments: What Can We Learn from a Few Individuals?

Sometimes researchers have to conduct experiments and studies with only a few participants. As discussed in earlier chapters, having a very large sample (a large *N*) is not always necessary. For instance, for the purposes of external validity, how a sample is selected is more important than the sample's size (see Chapter 7). And even a small sample can detect a large effect size (see Chapter 9), meaning that statistical validity is not necessarily undermined by a small sample. So if small

TABLE 12.1 Three Differences Between Large-*N* and Small-*N* Designs

Large-*N* designs	Small-*N* designs
Participants are grouped. The data from an individual participant are not of interest in themselves; data from all participants in each group are combined and studied together.	*Each participant is treated as a separate experiment.* Small-*N* designs are almost always repeated-measures designs, in which researchers observe how the person or animal responds to several systematically designed conditions.
Data are represented as *group averages*.	*Individuals' data* are presented.
Researchers decide whether a result is replicable by doing a test of *statistical significance*.	Researchers decide whether a result is replicable by *repeating the experiment* on a new participant.

samples are often appropriate in research, how low can we go? Can we draw conclusions from a study that uses only one or two participants? What priorities are researchers balancing when they study only a few people or animals at a time?

When researchers use a **small-*N* design**, instead of gathering a little information from a larger sample, they obtain a lot of information from just a few cases. They may even restrict their study to only one animal or one person, using a **single-*N* design**. Large-*N* designs differ from small-*N* designs in three key ways. These major differences are summarized in **Table 12.1**.

Research on Split Brains

Neuroscientist Michael Gazzaniga (2005) and his colleagues worked with only a few very unrepresentative people, but their work has taught psychologists a great deal about how the human brain is organized—and even about the nature of human consciousness and the sense of self. Gazzaniga was a student of Nobel Laureate Roger Sperry, who pioneered techniques to study the brain's two hemispheres (e.g., Sperry, 1961). The people Gazzaniga studied all had a history of severe epilepsy (Gazzaniga, Bogen, & Sperry, 1962). Their seizures were both strong and intractable, such that doctors could not control the electrical "storms" that would surge through their brains. All patients also underwent an effective last-resort treatment: surgery to cut apart the *corpus callosum*, a large band of nerve fibers at the center of the brain that allows neural messages to travel from the right hemisphere to the left hemisphere and back again. When doctors sever the corpus callosum of a patient with severe seizures, they essentially cut a main highway for the electrical storms, and the seizures become less debilitating.

People with so-called split brains appear to function normally, even though the two hemispheres do not communicate directly with each other. But Gazzaniga and his colleagues wanted to create specially designed conditions in which they could study the two hemispheres separately—to try to send visual information to only one hemisphere of the brain at a time and observe what would happen.

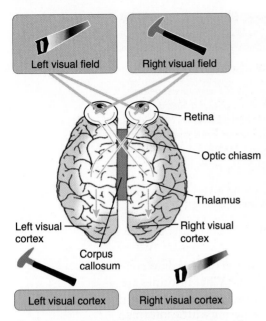

Left visual field

Right visual field

Retina

Optic chiasm

Thalamus

Left visual cortex

Right visual cortex

Corpus callosum

Left visual cortex

Right visual cortex

FIGURE 12.9 The human brain, dorsal view. The lens of the eye inverts the right and left visual fields, so that the right visual field projects images onto the left half of each retina and vice versa. Meanwhile, the left half of each retina sends information to the left visual cortex, and the right half of each retina sends information to the right visual cortex. If the image of a hammer is presented to the right visual field, it will be processed by the left hemisphere of the brain.

The researchers started with their existing understanding of how the visual system works. As **Figure 12.9** shows, an image from the left visual field goes to the right hemisphere, and an image from the right visual field goes to the left hemisphere. As a result, the normal human brain takes in a *full picture* of the visual field. Even with only one eye open, people can process the whole scene, because the corpus callosum sends the images to both sides of the brain. A split-brain patient can take in a full picture of the visual field, too, by quickly shifting his or her eyes from right to left—that way, both hemispheres typically get the whole picture. But Gazzaniga and his colleagues wanted to send a different picture to each hemisphere. To do so, they used a device that presented the images to the split-brain patients so quickly that they did not have time to shift their eyes. The researchers thus ensured that the image from the left visual field went only to the right hemisphere of the brain, and the image from the right visual field went only to the left hemisphere of the brain.

As it turned out, if Gazzaniga presented a picture of a hammer to the left hemisphere (by showing on the right side of the visual field) and asked the split-brain patients what they saw, the patients could easily say that they saw a hammer. But when a picture of a saw went only to the right hemisphere (it fell on the left side of the visual field), the patients would report that they did not see anything. This initial result supported what researchers had already learned—that, for most of us, speech is produced by the left hemisphere.

Even more interesting, when Gazzaniga placed a pen in the patients' left hand (the hand that the right hemisphere controls) and asked them to draw what they had seen, the split-brain patients could draw the tool that had been presented to the right hemisphere—the saw. The right brain knew what tool it had seen but could not articulate it. When the patients opened their eyes to look at the pictures they had drawn, the left hemisphere now got involved and could say verbally, "That's a saw." The patients could not say *why* they drew the saw, but they could recognize it just the same.

Based on research with people who have split brains, Gazzaniga and his colleagues (2005; Turk, Heatherton, Macrae, Kelley, & Gazzaniga, 2003) have also suggested that the left hemisphere may be responsible for making cause-and-effect judgments. For example, when shown an image with a chicken foot and a snow-covered farm, a person with a split brain chose two cards to represent what he saw. The left hand chose a picture of a chicken, to go with the chicken foot that the right brain had processed, while the right hand chose a picture of a shovel, to go with the snow that the left brain had processed. But when the experimenter asked why those two pictures had been chosen, the left hemisphere studied both selections (the shovel and the chicken foot) and concocted a plausible story: "Oh that's simple. The chicken claw goes with the chicken, and you need a shovel to clean out the chicken shed" (Turk et al., 2003, p. 71). The left hemisphere alone appears to be a "storyteller" that combines information into plausible cause-and-effect inferences—even if they are wrong.

Because the left hemisphere is apparently responsible for combining, interpreting, and telling a story about the many different inputs to the brain, Gazzaniga and colleagues have suggested that the left hemisphere may be a seat of the self-concept—responsible for the conscious "sense of self" that humans have (Turk et al., 2003). These are important conclusions from only a small sample of individuals.

Balancing Priorities in the Split-Brain Experiments

How convinced should we be by the results of split-brain research? These experiments, after all, were conducted with a very small number of participants. (Fortunately, only a small number of people require this kind of surgery.) Can we really conclude anything from research conducted on so few people?

Experimental Control, Manipulation, and Replication. Because of the empirical strengths of these studies, we can, in fact, make some conclusions on the basis of a small-N study. First, Gazzaniga and his colleagues used the power of experimental control: They controlled the eye movements of the participants, exposing images only briefly so that the right and left hemispheres would view completely different information. Second, they used strong manipulations: Tasks that would be easy for someone with an intact brain (such as identifying a picture flashed to the left visual field) were simply impossible for a split-brain patient. By ensuring that some stimuli went only to one hemisphere or the other, the researchers could infer that the left hemisphere of the brain (but not the right) can produce language, construct stories, and make cause-and-effect explanations. Therefore, the research took advantage of the split-brain surgery to manipulate the independent variable—which part of the brain received the input. Finally, researchers were able to replicate the results across five split-brain patients.

Studying Special Cases. One feature of these split-brain experiments is that they took advantage of a unique population. Just as quasi-experiments can take advantage of natural accidents, laws, or historical events, small-N studies often take advantage of special medical cases. For example, using the split-brain patients gave researchers the opportunity to send information to only one brain hemisphere at a time under controlled conditions.

Disadvantages of Small-N Studies. What are the downsides to small-N designs? One problem is that a few participants may not represent the human population very well. Although it is important that the team obtained the same findings in all five patients, the history of epilepsy they shared means that their brains may have been set up differently from those of nonepileptic people. That is a fair question about external validity: Can we generalize the results from these people, who all had severe epilepsy, to other people?

We cannot be sure, of course, whether Gazzaniga and his colleagues' results would apply to people without a history of epilepsy. Furthermore, it clearly would be unethical to sever the corpus callosum of a nonepileptic person's brain to create the necessary comparison. What could a researcher do to explore the generalizability of the findings from split-brain patients? One option would be to triangulate. For example, Gazzaniga's results were consistent with animal studies by Sperry (1961), as well as contemporary research using functional brain imagery on nonepileptic adults. The results from these studies of animals and nonepileptic people often confirm what has been observed behaviorally in people with split brains. In sum, this is another example of how the weight of a variety of evidence supports a parsimonious theory about how the human brain is organized.

For more on pattern and parsimony, see Chapter 8, pp. 226–228.

Behavior Change Studies in Clinical Settings: Three Small-*N* Designs

Split-brain research is only one example of the power of a small-*N* design. In clinical settings, practitioners can use small-*N* designs to learn whether their interventions work. For example, an occupational therapist might teach an elderly Alzheimer's patient a new memory strategy and then observe whether the patient's memory has improved. Or a special education teacher might try a behavioral correction technique to help a mentally handicapped student, and then observe whether the student's behavior has improved. In such clinical settings, practitioners, like researchers, need to think empirically: They develop theories about their clients' behaviors; make theory-based predictions about what treatments should help; and then implement changes, observe the results, and modify their treatments or understandings in response to these observations.

For a review of the theory-data cycle, see Chapter 1, pp. 8–13.

When practitioners notice an improvement after a treatment, they might wonder whether the improvement was caused by the intervention or by something else. Would the Alzheimer's patient's memory have improved anyway, or could the memory improvement have been caused by, say, a change in medication? Did the correction technique decrease the student's distracting behaviors in the classroom, or did the behaviors decrease simply because the teacher paid more attention to the student? Notice that all these questions are internal validity questions—questions about alternative explanations for the result.

Carefully designed small-*N* or single-*N* studies can help practitioners decide whether changes are caused by their interventions or by some other influence.

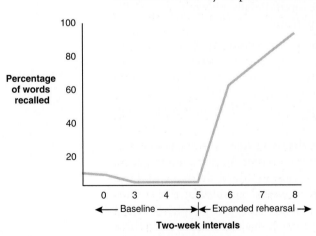

FIGURE 12.10 The results of a stable-baseline design. Miss S's memory was consistently low until the new expanded rehearsal technique was introduced. *Source*: Moffat (1989).

Stable-Baseline Designs

One example of a **stable-baseline design** comes from a study of a memory strategy called "expanded rehearsal" that was used with a real Alzheimer's patient, Miss S. Before teaching her the new strategy, the researcher spent several weeks recording baseline information, such as how many words Miss S could recall after hearing them only once. It was important that the baseline data were stable: Miss S remembered very few words, and there was no upward trend. Then she was taught the new strategy (Moffat, 1989), as researchers continued to monitor how many words she could remember. The researchers noticed a sudden improvement in her memory ability (see **Figure 12.10**).

Why should these results convince us that the patient's improvement was caused by the new extended rehearsal strategy? One reason is that the baseline was stable. If the researchers had done a single pretest before the new training and a single test afterward (a before-and-after comparison), the improvement could be explained by any number of factors, such as spontaneous recovery (maturation) or a regression effect. (In fact, a single baseline record

FIGURE 12.11 Speech therapist testing a patient at home for Alzheimer's disease. Alzheimer's disease is a disorder that causes the loss of brain cells and is the leading cause of dementia. It was first described by the German physician Dr. Alois Alzheimer in 1906.

followed by a single posttreatment measure would have been a small-N version of the "really bad experiment"; see Chapter 10.) Instead, the researcher recorded an extended, stable baseline, which made it unlikely that some sudden, spontaneous recovery just happened to occur right at the time the new therapy began. Furthermore, the stable baseline meant that there was not a single, extreme low point from which improvement would almost definitely occur (a regression effect). Performance began low and stayed low until the experimental strategy was introduced. The stable baseline gave this study internal validity, enabling the researcher to rule out some alternative explanations. In addition, the study was later repeated with a few other Alzheimer's patients (**Figure 12.11**). This replication provided further evidence that expanded rehearsal can help Alzheimer's patients.

Multiple-Baseline Designs

In a **multiple-baseline design**, research-practitioners stagger their introduction of an intervention across a variety of contexts, times, or situations. For example, teachers in a special education classroom were trying to teach a 12-year-old mentally handicapped girl to refrain from several distracting behaviors, such as repeatedly touching her face, touching her hair, and grabbing objects in the classroom. First they recorded baselines of each of the three behaviors for a few days. Then they started a treatment strategy, at first only targeting her face-touching behaviors. If the girl touched her face, she was placed in a special "overcorrection" period for 3 minutes, when she was made to sit quietly with the palms of her hands on a table. At first, the overcorrection was applied only when face touching occurred. A few days later, the overcorrection was extended to include hair touching, and later still, it was extended to grabbing objects.

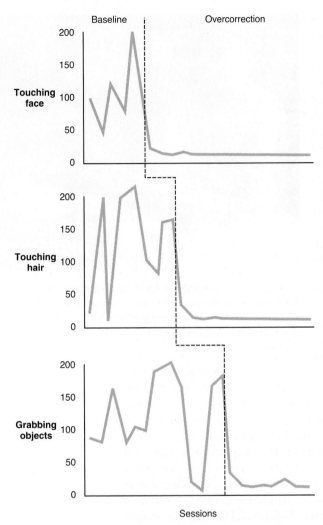

FIGURE 12.12 The results of a multiple-baseline design.
In a special education classroom, an overcorrection consequence was first applied when a girl touched her face. Later, the teachers used overcorrection when the girl touched her hair and, still later, when she grabbed objects in the classroom. The graphs show how the rate of each behavior changed when the overcorrection consequence was introduced.

As each behavior was followed by an overcorrection consequence, the behavior was promptly and dramatically reduced. (The results are shown in **Figure 12.12**.) Notice how the three behaviors served as controls for one another to improve internal validity in this study, making it clear that it was the overcorrection that improved this girl's behavior and not something else. It is unlikely that each of these three problem behaviors just happened to have improved spontaneously, right at the time the teachers started using overcorrection. In addition, we can be sure that face touching did not improve just because the extra attention put the girl on her best behavior; if it had been the extra attention that caused the improvement, then all of the behaviors would have decreased at the same time, and they did not. Therefore, by studying multiple behaviors and collecting multiple baselines, these special education teachers could conclude that their overcorrection strategy improved the girl's behavior. This multiple-baseline design had enough internal validity to support a causal conclusion.

In this example, the multiple baselines were represented by a set of behaviors within a single person. In other studies, the baselines might be represented by different situations for one person (for example, correcting a problem behavior at home, school, and work). The baselines might also be represented by three different people (for example, correcting the problem behaviors of three children in the same classroom, but starting at different times). In any format, the multiple baselines provide comparison conditions to which a treatment or intervention can be compared.

Reversal Designs

In a **reversal design**, as in the other two small-*n* designs, a researcher also observes a problem behavior both with and without treatment. But in a reversal design, the practitioner takes the treatment away for a while (the "reversal" phase) to see whether the problem behavior returns (reverses). By discontinuing a treatment that seems to be working, the researcher can test for internal validity and make a causal statement: If the treatment was really working, the behavior should worsen again when the treatment is discontinued.

In one example, a woman went into a severe depression following the death of her mother. Her family participated in treating her at home, under the guidance of a behavioral therapist, by modifying the consequences of her actions (Liberman & Raskin, 1971). Her behavior was typical of depression—low energy, weakness, and expressions of helplessness. Her husband and children originally responded with sympathy and consolation to her actions. Their compassion was understandable, but also short-sighted: What if their sympathetic attention was actually reinforcing the woman's depressive behaviors?

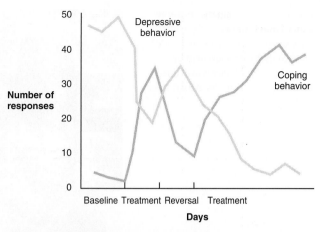

FIGURE 12.13 **The results of a reversal design.** Note how the patient's depressive behavior responded to periods of nontreatment (baseline and reversal) compared with periods of treatment. This pattern supports the idea that the treatment caused the decrease in the patient's depressive behavior and the increase in her coping behavior. *Source*: Adapted from Liberman and Raskin (1971).

On the advice of therapists, the family members forced themselves to change their reactions. They ignored her depressive behaviors and gave her attention and encouragement only when she coped in a positive way. **Figure 12.13** shows the results. Baselines were initially stable (depressive behaviors were high, and coping behaviors were low), but when the family's reaction changed (during the "treatment" period), the patient's actions changed as well: She coped better and acted depressed less frequently. Then (still on advice from the therapist), the family went back to its original ways of reacting; this was the reversal period. Sure enough, during reversal, the woman's depressive actions increased and her coping actions declined. Finally, the family resumed the treatment conditions once again. In response, the woman acted less depressed and coped more positively. It seemed clear that it was the family's actions, not a maturation or regression effect, that had influenced the woman's grieving versus coping behaviors in this situation.

Reversal designs like this one are appropriate mainly for situations in which the treatment would not cause lasting change. For example, it would not make sense to use a reversal design to test an educational intervention. Once a student has learned a new skill (such as Miss S's expanded rehearsal technique), it is unlikely that the skill will simply "reverse," or go away. In addition, while the reversal design in the example enables the clinical scientist to evaluate the efficacy of the treatment, some researchers would question the ethics of the choice to withdraw a treatment that appears to be working. In fact, two ethical priorities come into play here: On the one hand, it may be considered harmful to withdraw effective treatment from a patient; on the other hand, it also may be unethical to use a treatment that is not empirically supported as effective.

For a full discussion of ethics in psychological research, see Chapter 4.

FIGURE 12.14 Piaget's conservation of mass theory. Piaget (right) developed and tested his theories of child cognitive development by systematically testing his own three children on carefully developed tasks.

Other Examples of Small-*N* Studies

Research in psychology has boasted some influential and famous single-*N* and small-*N* studies. The Swiss scientist Jean Piaget (1923) developed a theory of child cognitive development through careful, systematic observations of his own three children: Jacqueline, Lucienne, and Laurent. He found, for example, that as children get older, they learn that when the shape of a lump of clay is changed (say, from a ball into a pancake), the amount of clay does not change (see **Figure 12.14**). (Younger children, in contrast, tend to think that there is more clay in the pancake, because it is wider and therefore appears larger.) Although Piaget observed only a few children, he designed systematic questions, made careful observations, and replicated his extensive interviews with each of them.

Another early-20th-century researcher, Hermann Ebbinghaus (1913), made himself memorize long lists of nonsense words such as *mip* or *pon*. In a long series of studies conducted over many years, Ebbinghaus systematically varied how many times and for how long he studied each list, and he carefully recorded how many syllables he remembered at different intervals of time. Ebbinghaus was the first to document several fundamental memory phenomena. One example is the "forgetting curve," shown in **Figure 12.15**, which describes how memory for a newly learned list of nonsense syllables declines most dramatically over the first hour, but then declines more slowly after that. Although he studied

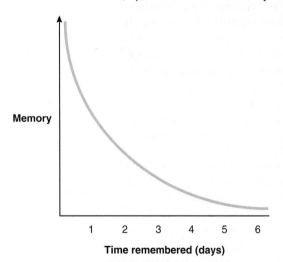

FIGURE 12.15 Ebbinghaus's forgetting curve. Herman Ebbinghaus's carefully designed experiments on memory processes contributed important knowledge to psychology, even though he used only one person—himself—as a subject.

only himself, Ebbinghaus created testing situations with experimental precision and, eventually, replicability.

Or consider the memory researchers who recruited a single, relatively ordinary college student (known as S.F.) and asked him to come to their laboratory three to five times a week for 1.5 years (Ericsson, Chase, & Faloon, 1980). Each day in the laboratory, researchers read S.F. random digits—one digit per second. Later, S.F. would try to recall the digits in the correct order. Ordinarily, a human memory span is about seven digits (Miller, 1956). But after practicing in the laboratory so regularly, S.F. developed the ability to recite back 79 random digits (such as those in **Figure 12.16**) at a time. S.F.'s remarkable performance was caused, in part, by his strategy of grouping clusters of numbers according to track and field times (for example, a string of 3392 might become 3:39.2, "a great time for the mile"). In fact, the researchers tested whether the "running time" strategy *caused* his improved performance by generating some number strings that purposefully did not correspond well to running times. S.F.'s memory span for those special strings dropped down to his beginning performance level. S.F.'s remarkable performance demonstrates what can happen with extensive training and motivation. And the researchers' clever manipulation also demonstrated *why* S.F. got so good at learning strings of numbers—supporting a causal conclusion.

2	7	1	2	5	8	2	3
7	0	8	7	5	0	9	9
9	2	5	4	1	6	1	8
7	9	6	1	0	0	5	6
7	8	0	0	1	1	5	6
6	2	6	2	5	3	4	8
2	1	1	9	1	8	4	3
1	1	3	9	5	4	9	2
3	9	9	9	5	6	5	8
7	8	0	5	6	8	5	5

FIGURE 12.16

Remembering random digits. Do you think you could recall up to 80 random digits like these, after hearing them only once? A college student known as S.F. learned to do so by practicing short-term memory skills for a year and a half.

Evaluating the Four Validities in Small-*N* Designs

The discussion of small-*N* designs has focused so far on how such designs can eliminate alternative explanations—how they can enhance *internal validity*. In all of the examples described in this chapter, researchers designed careful, within-subject experiments that allowed them to draw causal conclusions. Even if there was only one participant, the researchers usually measured behaviors repeatedly, both before and after some intervention or manipulation. Therefore, the internal validity of these single-*N* designs is high.

At first glance, it may seem easy to criticize the *external validity* of a small-*N* design; after all, how can one person represent a population? Even when researchers show that their manipulation, intervention, or procedure replicates in a second or third case, we might still have questions about generalizability. But remember that researchers can take steps to maximize the external validity of their findings. First, in relevant situations, researchers can triangulate by combining the results of single-*N* studies with other studies on animals or on larger groups, as Gazzaniga and colleagues did when they compared results from split-brain studies with the results of other research on animals and nonepileptic humans. Second, remember that researchers are able to specify the population to which they want to generalize, and they rarely intend to generalize to everyone who has ever lived. They may not care, for example, if a memory strategy for Alzheimer's patients applies to everybody in the world—but they do care whether it generalizes to other Alzheimer's patients. Therefore, researchers sometimes limit a study's external validity to a particular subset of possible participants.

Third, sometimes researchers do not care about generalizing at all. It may be important to a special education teacher to learn that the overcorrection technique works for one 12-year-old girl in the classroom. In such cases, even if the causal statement applies only to one person, it is still useful.

When you interrogate a small-*N* design, you should also evaluate *construct validity*. Of course, researchers want to be sure that their measurements are reliable and valid. The researchers in our examples recorded what people drew, what objects they picked up, or what they said. They recorded how many words or numbers people remembered. They observed whether a girl grabbed objects or touched her face and hair. Construct validity is fairly straightforward when researchers are recording whether a split-brain patient reports seeing a hammer or a saw, and for objective measures such as memory for a string of numbers. But when researchers are recording the number of times a girl grabs objects in a special education classroom, they should use multiple observers and check for interrater reliability, in case one observer is biased or the behavior is difficult to identify.

Regarding *statistical validity*, in single-*N* designs, researchers do not typically use traditional inferential statistics. However, they still draw conclusions from data, and they should treat data appropriately. In many cases a graph (such as those in Figures 12.10, 12.12, and 12.13) provides enough quantitative evidence. Instead of using statistical tests, in small-*N* designs the researchers can run the study again to see whether the result replicates. In addition, we might think about effect sizes more simply in small-*N* cases, by asking, for example, "By what margin did the client's behavior improve?"

Summary

Studies do not always take place in perfect conditions, with clean manipulations, large samples of participants, and perfect random assignment. When a quasi-experiment includes an appropriate comparison group and the right pattern of results, researchers can often support causal claims—even when participants cannot be randomly assigned to conditions and the researchers do not have complete experimental control of the independent variable. In quasi-experiments, researchers often need to balance the priority of complete confidence in internal validity with other priorities—opportunities to study in a real-world situation, to take advantage of a historical event, or to conduct an ethical investigation of a new program or some other intervention.

By examining the *results* and *design* of a quasi-experiment, you can interrogate whether it is vulnerable to alternative explanations such as selection, maturation, attrition, testing, instrumentation, observer biases, experimental demand, and placebo effects—the same kinds of internal validity threats that can occur in true experiments.

Small-*N* studies balance an intense, systematic investigation of one or a few people against psychology's more usual approach of studying groups of people. The trade-offs here are not as dramatic, because the internal validity of small-*N* studies can be just as high as that of repeated-measures experiments conducted on larger samples.

Overall, researchers need to be aware of the priorities and trade-offs of each research decision, making conscious choices about which validities are most important—and most possible—to prioritize as they study a particular scientific question.

Key Terms

interrupted time-series design, p. 349
multiple-baseline design, p. 365
nonequivalent control group
  design, p. 346
nonequivalent groups interrupted
  time-series design, p. 350

quasi-experiments, p. 346
reversal design, p. 366
selection-history threat, p. 354
single-*N* design, p. 361
small-*N* design, p. 361
stable-baseline design, p. 364

 **NEED HELP STUDYING?**
wwnorton.com/studyspace

Visit StudySpace to access free review materials such as:

- Diagnostic Review Quizzes
- Study Outlines

Learning Actively

For questions 1 and 2, read the study description and answer the following questions about each:

   a. Determine whether the study is a nonequivalent control group design, an interrupted time-series design, or a nonequivalent groups interrupted time-series design.
   b. Graph the results of the study, according to the results in the description. (You may not have exact values to plot, but you can indicate which groups are higher or lower.)
   c. What causal statement is the researcher trying to make, if any? Is it appropriate? If the researcher is making a causal statement, use the results and design to interrogate the study's internal validity.
   d. If you notice any internal validity flaws, can you redesign the study to remove the flaw?
   e. Ask one question to address construct validity and one to address external validity.

1. Researchers Dutton and Aron (1974) wanted to test a theory of romantic attraction. Specifically, they proposed that people can be fooled about their feelings of romantic attraction. The researchers proposed that feelings of anxiety can be similar to feelings of being in love. So they suggested that if a man who just happened to be feeling anxious met an attractive woman, the man might feel especially attracted to her. In effect, the man might mistake his feelings of anxiety for feelings of romantic attraction.

    To test their theory, Dutton and Aron studied male tourists who were walking across one of two pedestrian bridges. One bridge was a solid stable bridge, only 10 feet above a river. The other one (the Capilano Suspension Bridge) was 230 feet above the river and was made of wooden boards attached to wire cables, with a low wire handrail. Most people who cross this precarious bridge feel anxious. Dutton and Aron hired a female research assistant to approach male tourists, one by one, as they crossed one of the two bridges. After administering a short questionnaire, the woman handed each man her phone number, saying, "If you'd like to know the results, call me and I'll tell you about them." The researchers simply counted the number of calls the woman received—from men who had crossed the high bridge and from men who had crossed the low one. Of the men who crossed the high bridge, 50% phoned in for results, but of those on the safe bridge, only 12% did so.

2. Researchers Langer and Rodin (1976) were interested in improving the quality of life for nursing home residents. They reasoned that in many nursing homes, residents had very little say in how they spent their days. The researchers suspected that having more control over their daily schedules

would improve the quality of life for residents. They studied two floors of a nursing home: Floor 6 and Floor 3. Administrators at the nursing home assured them that people on the two floors had very similar levels of medical problems and were of similar ages.

For a baseline period, Langer and Rodin asked nurses and doctors to record the health and activity levels of the residents on both floors. Then they introduced an intervention: Residents on Floor 6 listened to a "pep talk" about all of the activities and services they could take advantage of if they chose to. In addition, residents on this floor were offered a potted plant and were told that they could take care of it however they wanted to. And they were offered a new movie night option—they could choose either Tuesday or Friday, or no movie, depending on their preference. In contrast, Residents on Floor 3 listened to a speech, too; while this speech was positive, it did not emphasize taking personal control. In addition, residents on this floor were offered a potted plant, but they were told that the nurses would take care of it. And residents on this floor were offered a new movie night as well, but they were told which night they would be watching the movie.

Eighteen months later, the doctors and nurses rated the residents' health again. Although residents of the two floors were equal at the baseline measurement, the residents of Floor 3 showed dramatic decreases in health and activity level at the follow-up. In addition, residents of Floor 6 actually showed an improvement in mental alertness and activity level. Twice as many residents of Floor 3 had died after 18 months, compared with the residents of Floor 6.

3. Design three quasi-experiments—a nonequivalent control group design, an interrupted time-series design, and a nonequivalent groups interrupted time-series design—to test the following statement: "Joining a fraternity or sorority causes students to become more concerned with their physical appearance." Explain how you would design each study, and create a hypothetical graph of each study's results. Finally, explain whether or not each study can support the causal statement.

4. Imagine that you are a dog owner and you are working with your 3-year-old Labrador retriever. When the dog goes for walks, he growls fiercely at other dogs. You want to reduce your dog's aggressive behavior, so you decide to try a technique you learned on television: pressing firmly on the dog's neck and saying forcefully, "Shhhhh!" when the dog begins to growl at other dogs. You decide to apply a small-N design to investigate the results of your training regimen.

   a. Which small-N design(s) would be appropriate for this situation?
   b. Choose one small-N design, and describe how you would conduct your study.
   c. Sketch a graph of the results you would predict from your design if your treatment plan worked.
   d. Explain whether you could conclude from your study that the treatment plan caused your dog's aggression to decrease.

Would we find these same results in other cultural contexts?

Should this study use a random sample of participants?

13

Replicability, Generalization, and the "Real World"

What makes a study important? Judging a study's importance will be one of your goals as a consumer of research. As you read about studies, either in the popular press or in your classes, you will want to know not only whether the study was conducted well but also whether the study is important.

For a psychologist, an important study helps advance scientific progress by supporting or shaping scientific theories (that is, by contributing to the theory-data cycle introduced in Chapter 1). In other words, an important study helps contribute a piece of knowledge to the body of scientific evidence.

This chapter outlines several dimensions to consider as you judge a study's importance. Some of the topics, such as replicability, have been discussed in previous chapters. Other topics, such as a study's applicability to "real-world" contexts, might challenge what you already think. To decide what makes a study important, you will keep in mind the researcher's priorities as well as the study's purpose.

To Be Important, a Study Must Be Replicable

Good researchers will always consider whether the results of a study could be a fluke or whether they will get the same result if they do the study again. In other words, they will ask whether the study is **replicable**.

It makes sense that a study must be replicable to be important. If a scientist claimed to have discovered evidence of life on Mars, but nobody else could find similar evidence, we would not believe there is life on Mars. If a study found that a certain therapy improved people's anxiety disorders, but a second study did not find that same result again, we would not trust the first result. Replicability gives a study credibility—it is crucial in science.

Psychological scientists use two strategies to determine whether a research result is likely to be replicable. One is to use inferential statistics; the other is to conduct the same study again.

Inferential Statistics: Estimating Whether a Study Is Replicable

When researchers use **inferential statistics**, they use theories of probability to decide whether or not a study's result is "statistically significant." Calling a result statistically significant is not the same as calling the result important—the meaning is more precise. Typically, in inferential statistical practice, a finding is evaluated as statistically significant when the result found in a sample is so extreme that it is unlikely to have happened by chance. That is, when researchers use inferential statistics, they compute a probability estimate (p), which predicts the likelihood that the result was sampled from a population in which there is no difference, no correlation, or no relationship. Suppose a researcher finds a correlation of $r = 0.31$ between two variables. What is the probability that a correlation of that size could happen by chance, if there really is no correlation in the population? To find out, the researcher would compute inferential statistics to get the p-value associated with this r and would assess the result as follows:

Chapter 7, Chapter 9, and especially Appendix B discuss statistical significance in detail.

- If p is less than 0.05, the researcher would conclude that the result is significant—that the relationship between the two variables probably did not come, just by chance, from a population in which there is no relationship.
- If p is larger than 0.05, the result is not statistically significant. The researcher cannot rule out the possibility that the result is a chance occurrence from a population in which there is no relationship.

A statistically significant result also leads researchers to infer that if they were to repeat the study exactly (with the same sample size and a similar set of participants), they would get similar results a high percentage of the time. That is why statistically significant results are sometimes referred to as "reliable." This use of the term *reliable* is different from that introduced in Chapter 5 (in which a measure was described as reliable). In the present case, it simply means that, according to our analysis, there is a strong chance that the result would be statistically significant again if the study were repeated.

Replication Studies: Making Replication an Empirical Question

Researchers can use inferential statistics to estimate the probability that a result will happen again if they do the study again. But when a researcher actually performs the study again, it is called a replication study. These days, in order to have their findings published, most researchers conduct replication studies, of which there are three major types: direct replication, conceptual replication, and replication-plus-extension.

Direct Replication

In **direct replication** (or *exact replication*), researchers repeat an original study as closely as they can, to see whether the original effect shows up in the newly collected data.

In one example, researchers Bargh, Chen, and Burrows (1996) wondered whether reading about a stereotype of a social group would change people's behavior. (Past research had demonstrated that reading about stereotypes of a social group can affect people's cognitions and emotions; the researchers were interested in whether this pattern extended to behaviors, too.) To test this question, they gave people puzzles to work on that had certain types of words embedded in them. The treatment group worked with words that evoked stereotypes of elderly people, such as *old*, *lonely*, *Florida*, *wrinkle*, and *retired*. The comparison group worked with neutral words such as *thirsty*, *clean*, and *private*. Bargh and colleagues then observed how long participants took to walk down a hall after the experiment. The researchers found that participants primed with the elderly stereotype walked about 1.1 seconds more slowly after the experiment than the neutrally primed participants did. Bargh and colleagues wanted to be sure that their result was replicable, so they conducted the study again using exactly the same methods as they did the first time. They obtained virtually the same results (for a graph of their results, see **Figure 13.1**).

Of course, a direct replication can never replicate the first study exactly. In Bargh and colleagues' studies, the two samples contained different sets of 30 participants. The two studies may have been conducted at different times of the year. The experimenters themselves might have been different people. Some other minor circumstances might have changed. Despite these small differences, however, in a direct replication the researchers try to replicate the original experiment as closely as possible.

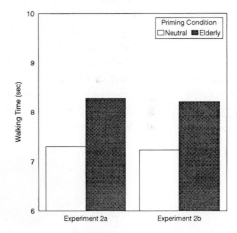

Figure 2. Mean time (in seconds) to walk down the hallway after the conclusion of the experiment, by stereotype priming condition, separately for participants in Experiment 2a and 2b.

FIGURE 13.1 The results of Bargh and colleagues' (1996) studies. The graph shows the results for the original study (Experiment 2a) and the direct replication study (Experiment 2b), as they appeared in the original journal article.

Direct replication makes good sense, but keep in mind that if there were any threats to internal validity or flaws in construct validity in the original study, such threats would be repeated in the direct replication, too. For this reason, researchers also value other forms of replication as a supplement or alternative to direct replication.

Conceptual Replication

In a **conceptual replication**, researchers study the same research question but use different procedures. At the abstract level, the variables in the study are the same, but the procedures for operationalizing the variables are different.

Elliot and colleagues' (2007) experimental study on the color red and school performance, discussed in Chapter 9, is a good example of a conceptual replication study. In the first study, Elliot and his colleagues manipulated the independent variable, exposure to the color red, by writing participating students' ID numbers in red ink, green ink, or black ink. They then measured the dependent variable, academic performance, by measuring how many anagrams students could solve correctly. They found that students whose names were written in red ink solved fewer anagrams.

Elliot and his colleagues also conducted some conceptual replication studies after this first study. For instance, in Study 2, they manipulated the same independent variable, exposure to the color red, by the color of the cover of the test booklet: red, green, or white. And this time, they measured the dependent variable, academic performance, by measuring how many correct analogy IQ test items students could solve. The researchers again found that exposure to red caused students to perform worse on the academic task. In still another conceptual replication study (Study 3), they manipulated the test cover color with the levels red, green, and gray, and this time they measured how many numeric IQ test items people could solve.

In all three studies, Elliot and colleagues obtained similar results, even though they used different methods and measures in each study. No matter whether they manipulated the independent variable using the ink or the test cover, and no matter whether they measured the academic performance variable with anagrams, analogies, or numeric problems, they found the same thing: Exposure to red caused people to perform worse on academic tasks. (See **Figure 13.2** for a visual representation of Elliot and colleagues' three

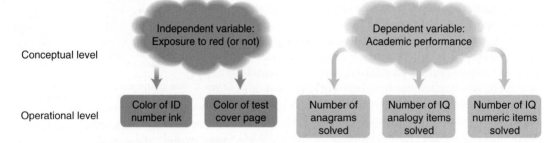

FIGURE 13.2 Elliot and colleagues' (2007) conceptual replications. In a conceptual replication, the abstract (conceptual) level of the variables is the same, but the operational level of the variables changes.

studies.) Because these researchers found the same result at least three times, we can have more confidence that the results of their study are not due simply to the particular manipulations and measures they used the first time. As the theory would predict, the same conceptual variables (avoidance color and achievement) show the same relationship, no matter how they are operationalized.

Replication-Plus-Extension

In a direct replication study, researchers use the same methods to study the same variables as they did in an original study. In a conceptual replication, researchers use different methods to study the same variables as in the original study. In a **replication-plus-extension** study, researchers replicate their original study but add variables to test additional questions.

One example of a replication-plus-extension study comes from Strayer's research on the effect of cell phones on driving performance, discussed in Chapter 11. As you might recall, Strayer and his colleagues first conducted experiments in which college students used a driving simulator. They found that talking on a hands-free cell phone caused the students to drive worse (Strayer, Drews, & Johnston, 2003). A later study extended this basic finding to a new population by using both college students and elderly participants (Strayer & Drews, 2004). The later study was a replication-plus-extension study, because it was an attempt to repeat the original study with college students (the replication) but also added a new population of elderly drivers (the extension).

Strayer's replication-plus-extension study was important for two reasons. First, it replicated a finding the researchers had noticed in their previous study: College students drove worse when they were talking on cell phones. Second, the study extended this original result into a new population: Elderly drivers also drove worse when they talked on cell phones. Strayer's research is a good example of introducing a *participant variable* (in this case, participant age) to conduct a replication-plus-extension study—that is, extending an original finding to a new population.

Another way to conduct a replication-plus-extension study is to introduce a new *situational variable*. For example, in one study, Strayer and his colleagues wanted to know whether the ability to drive and talk at the same time would improve with practice (Cooper & Strayer, 2008). Therefore, degree of practice became the new situational variable in this replication-plus-extension study. The researchers conducted a 4-day study in which people practiced driving in a simulator while talking on a hands-free cell phone. Cooper and Strayer compared the accident rates on Day 1 (when people had had no practice) with those on Day 4 (when people had had 4 days of practice). On Days 1 and 4, people drove part of the course without a cell phone and drove part of the course while talking on a cell phone.

In this study, Cooper and Strayer therefore had two independent variables: being on a cell phone or not, and having had practice or not (Day 1 versus Day 4). (You might recognize this as a 2×2 factorial design.) The results showed that while people got into fewer accidents overall on Day 4, the effect of a cell phone was the same: Talking on a cell phone made people get into more accidents on Day 4, by just as much as on Day 1; in other words, there was no interaction. This study was a replication-plus-extension because Cooper and Strayer extended the

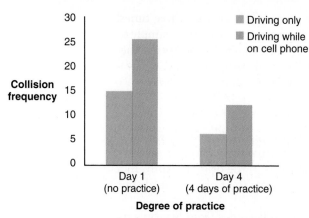

FIGURE 13.3 The results of Cooper and Strayer's (2008) replication-plus-extension study on cell phone use while driving. The figure displays the highway driving condition only. This study replicated Strayer's original finding that people get into more car accidents while talking on a cell phone and extended this original finding to investigate the effect of practice.

original finding—the effects of using a cell phone on driving—to a new situation (performance after a few days of practice). The results are shown in **Figure 13.3**.

Strayer, Drews, and Crouch (2006), in still another replication-plus-extension study, compared three driving conditions: driving alone, driving while talking on a cell phone, and driving drunk. (They actually had people drink enough vodka to reach a 0.08 blood alcohol level!) In this replication, the extension involved adding a drunk driving condition to the independent variable. The results of the study showed that both talking and drinking affected people's driving, but in different ways. Drunk drivers braked just as quickly but with more force than nonimpaired drivers (that is, those who were neither drunk nor on the phone). In contrast, drivers talking on cell phones were slower to hit the brakes, but they braked with the same amount of force as the nonimpaired drivers (see **Figure 13.4**).

This replication-plus-extension study first replicated the finding that driving while talking on a cell phone worsens people's driving performance. Second, the study directly compared the effect of driving drunk to the effect of driving while on a cell phone. By combining three conditions in the same study (talking on a cell phone, drinking, and baseline), the researchers learned more about the similarities and differences between different conditions that can impair driving ability.

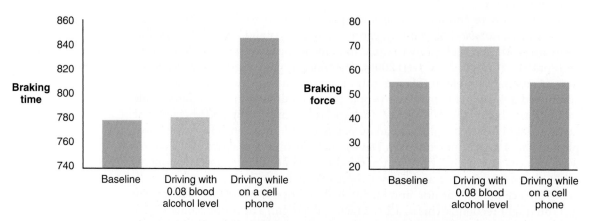

FIGURE 13.4 The results of Strayer, Drews, and Crouch's (2006) study. This study replicated previous research showing that talking on cell phones causes people to hit the brakes more slowly. Extending the study by adding the alcohol-impaired condition demonstrated that alcohol also impairs driving, but in different ways.

Replication, Importance, and the "Weight of the Evidence"

As the Chinese philosopher Lao Tzu is believed to have said, "The longest journey begins with a single step." Similarly, when researchers complete a single, well-conducted study, psychological science progresses a bit, but a single study is important only if it can be replicated. (After all, if we cannot be certain that the same result occurs consistently under the same conditions, how can that result be important?) If you read a result from a single study, you must at least ask whether the result is statistically significant—whether it has statistical validity. But even statistically significant results should be tested through replication studies. Psychological science progresses only as researchers conduct systematic sets of replications, conceptual replications, and replication-plus-extension studies.

Meta-analysis: What Does the Literature Say?

Because psychological science values replication, the most important conclusions in psychology are those based on a body of evidence—that is, on a large **scientific literature**. Scientific literatures (or simply *literatures*) consist of a series of related studies, conducted by various researchers, that have tested similar variables. Thus, literatures are composed of several studies on a particular topic, often conducted by many different researchers. For example, you might hear your instructors or other students talk about the literature on the effects of cell phone use while driving, or the literature on the effects of color on behavior.

Sometimes, researchers collect all the studies on a topic and consider them together—generating what is known as a review article, or a literature review (discussed in Chapter 2). One approach is simply to summarize the literature in a narrative way—to describe verbally what the studies typically show, explaining how the body of evidence supports a theory. But researchers may also use a quantitative technique known as meta-analysis to create a mathematical summary of a scientific literature.

What Is a Meta-analysis?

A **meta-analysis** is a way of mathematically averaging the results of all the studies that have tested the same variables, to see what conclusion that whole body of evidence supports. The following examples will help you understand the basic process involved in a meta-analysis.

Example: Religion and Depression. One group of researchers was interested in the relationship between degree of religious feeling (religiousness) and depressive symptoms. Smith, McCullough, and Poll (2003) scoured the literature (using PsycINFO databases and other tools) to locate every study that had measured religiousness and depression. For example, one study they located (Blaine & Crocker, 1995) found a correlation between religiousness and depression of $r = -0.06$ in 146 college students. Another study (Hertsgaard & Light, 1984), using 44 adults, found a correlation of $r = -0.13$. In total, Smith and his colleagues collected 147 studies. All of them used different samples, and many of them used slightly different operational measures of depression and religiousness (that is, they were conceptual replications), but they all investigated the

FIGURE 13.5 Religiousness and depression. People who report being religious are also less depressed. How do meta-analysis data contribute to our understanding of this relationship?

bivariate relationship between religiousness and depression, asking whether religiousness is correlated with depression.

Using a meta-analytic formula, Smith and colleagues found the average correlation across all 147 studies. (The formula is similar to that for a statistical mean, but it also weights studies with larger sample sizes more heavily.) Smith and colleagues found that the average correlation was $r = -0.09$. Because this relationship is negative, it means that as religiousness increases, depressive symptoms decrease. Furthermore, the size of this relationship (0.09) means that the strength of the association between depression and religiousness, while statistically significant, is small.

Meta-analysis, then, is the process of collecting all possible studies on a particular research question and combining them mathematically to study the overall trend in the data. Smith and colleagues used their meta-analysis to conclude that there is a small, negative relationship between depression and religiousness (see **Figure 13.5**). Religious people are slightly less likely to be depressed. (Of course, because this is a correlation, we cannot conclude from it whether being religiousness causes a decrease in depression, or whether being depressed causes a decrease in religiousness.)

Example: Effectiveness of Psychotherapy for Children and Adolescents. Another example of a meta-analysis, conducted by Weisz, McCarty, and Valeri (2006), collected all possible studies that investigated whether youths (children and adolescents) improve after psychotherapy for depression. The authors searched databases and contacted research colleagues to collect 35 experiments in which researchers had randomly assigned youths either to receive psychotherapy or to be in a nonpsychotherapy control group. To be included, each study had to have used depressed youths as participants, and each study had to have included an appropriate control group of youths who did not receive therapy.

For each study they collected, the researchers computed the effect size (d), comparing the psychotherapy group to the no-therapy comparison group. As explained in Chapter 9, the effect size measure d is a descriptive statistic that describes the difference between two means in standard deviation units. In these studies, the larger the d, the greater was the difference between the therapy and no-therapy group. In other words, the larger the d, the less the degree of overlap between the distributions of depression scores in the two groups.

Note that in the previous example, the meta-analysis on religiousness and depression, the meta-analysis computed the average of several correlations, or r values. But Weisz and colleagues computed the average of several d values for their meta-analysis, because the studies they collected had compared the difference between two groups (as described in Chapter 9), rather than the association between two quantitative variables (as described in Chapter 7). When two group means are compared, the effect size d evaluates how far apart the two group means are in standard deviation units—or how much the two group means overlap (see Figure 9.21). In contrast, the effect size r is most appropriate when a study evaluates the association between two numeric variables. Values of r closer to 1 or -1 indicate a stronger relationship between the two variables.

For more on the effect size r, see Chapter 7, pp. 190–192.

In their meta-analysis, Weisz and colleagues (2006) discovered that across these 35 studies on psychotherapy for youths the average effect size was $d = 0.34$, meaning that the therapy group scored 0.34 of a standard deviation higher than the comparison group. This effect size falls between "small" and "medium" in its magnitude (see **Table 13.1**). An effect size of $d = 0.34$ means that the mean of the psychotherapy group was 1/3 of a standard deviation lower in depression than no-therapy group. In other words, the average youth who received psychotherapy was better off than 63% of the youths who did not receive any therapy.

Weisz and his colleagues also conducted some follow-up analyses. They separated the studies into different categories depending on what kind of therapy was used. (Chapter 7 describes this technique as *testing for moderators*.) In some of the studies, the psychotherapy technique focused on identifying and changing the depressed youths' cognitions (a technique called cognitive therapy). Other studies did not emphasize cognitive change; instead, they taught relaxation training or some other behavioral change. When Weisz and colleagues separately computed the average effect sizes for these two categories, they found that the average effect size for cognitive therapies was $d = 0.35$, while the average effect size for noncognitive therapies was $d = 0.47$. These two effect sizes (0.35 and 0.47) were not significantly different from each other. Therefore, Weisz and colleagues learned that the type of therapy does not seem to moderate the effect of the therapy; there is no significant difference between the two kinds of therapies, cognitive and noncognitive (see **Table 13.2**).

TABLE 13.1 Cohen's Conventions for Effect Sizes

Effect size d	Strength of relationship	Effect size r
0.20	Weak/small	0.10
0.50	Moderate/medium	0.30
0.80	Strong/large	0.50

Cohen's (1992) conventions for effect sizes can be used in meta-analyses to describe the average effect size as weak, moderate, or strong.

TABLE 13.2 Weisz and Colleagues' (2006) Results for the Effectiveness of Psychotherapies That Emphasize Cognitive Change Versus Those That Do Not

Type of psychotherapy	Effect size d (psychotherapy group—comparison group)
Focused on cognitive change	0.35
Not focused on cognitive change	0.47

The two effect sizes are each significantly different from zero, but they are not significantly different from each other.

TABLE 13.3 Results for the Effectiveness of Psychotherapies for Children of Different Ages

Age of child	Effect size d (psychotherapy group—comparison group)
7 to 12	0.41
13 to 17	0.33

The two effect sizes are each significantly different from zero, but they are not significantly different from each other. *Source*: Weisz and colleagues (2006).

In another follow-up analysis, the researchers compared the effect sizes for children (aged 7 to 12) and for adolescents (aged 13 to 17). The effect size for psychotherapy with depressed children was $d = 0.41$, and the effect size for psychotherapy with depressed adolescents was $d = 0.33$. These two effect sizes also were not significantly different from each other, suggesting that psychotherapy might work equally well for both children and adolescents. In other words, child age is not a statistically significant moderator of the relationship between therapy and depression (see **Table 13.3**).

What Meta-analyses Can Do. The two examples just discussed illustrate several important features of meta-analysis. First, in a meta-analysis, researchers collect all possible examples of a particular kind of study. They then average all the effect sizes to find an overall effect size. The type of effect size used (r or d) depends on the research question—whether it is a correlation or a group difference. Using meta-analyses, researchers can also sort a group of studies into categories (that is, moderators), computing separate effect size averages for each category. From these follow-up analyses, researchers can detect new patterns in the literature as well as test new questions.

Because meta-analyses usually contain data that have been published in empirical journals, you can be more certain that the data included in them have been peer-reviewed, providing one check on their quality. However, there is a publication bias in psychology: Significant relationships are more likely to be published than null effects. This phenomenon leads to something called the **file drawer problem**. (That is, instead of being published, these studies sit forgotten in the researchers' filing cabinets.) The file drawer problem refers to the idea that a meta-analysis might be overestimating the true size of an effect because null effects have not been included. To combat the problem, researchers who are conducting a meta-analysis usually contact their colleagues (via e-mail groups and subscription lists) requesting both published and unpublished data for their project.

Meta-analyses are considered valuable by many psychologists because they combine the findings of a variety of studies—direct replications and conceptual replications—into a single average. Combining study results in this way means that small differences across studies are ignored, but the conceptual variables of interest remain. Therefore, a meta-analysis can be a valuable way to assess the weight of the evidence in a research literature. It tells us whether, across a number of studies, there is a relationship between two variables—and if so, how strong it is.

Replicability in the Popular Press

Journalists do not always consider replicability when they report on science stories. Sometimes journalists will report on a single, hot-off-the-press study because it makes a splashy headline. Responsible journalists, however, not only report on the *latest* studies but also give readers a sense of what the *entire literature* says on a particular topic. For example, rather than merely announcing the results of a recent study on chocolate and mood, a responsible journalist should talk about the context, too: How well does this latest study fit in with the entire literature on chocolate and mood? Does it contradict a study done last year on chocolate and mood? If journalists do not provide the context of the entire literature surrounding a study, then you would be right to reserve judgment about the study's importance.

Check Your Understanding

1. How do inferential statistics help researchers estimate whether their studies are replicable?
2. Describe how the three types of replication studies are similar and different.
3. Compare the value of a single study to that of a body of research, or a literature.
4. In your own words, describe the steps a researcher follows in a meta-analysis. What can a meta-analysis tell us?

1. See p. 376. 2. See pp. 377–380. 3. See p. 381. 4. See pp. 381–384.

To Be Important, Must a Study Have External Validity?

Asking about replicability is one way to judge a study's importance. Replicating a study's results is an essential step in the scientific process, allowing researchers to be far more confident in the accuracy of their results and more convinced of the results' importance.

But replication also helps you interrogate one of the four big validities: external validity. Although direct replication studies do not support external validity, conceptual replications and replication-plus-extension studies can. When researchers test their questions using slightly different methods, different kinds of participants, or different situations, or when they extend their research to study new variables, they are demonstrating how their results generalize to other populations and settings. The more settings and populations in which a study is conducted, the better we can assess the generalizability of the findings.

Review: External Validity

Remember that external validity, one of the four big validities, is the degree to which a study's results are generalizable, both to other participants and to other settings.

Generalizing to Other Participants

To assess a study's generalizability to other people, you would ask *how* the participants were obtained. Recall that if a study is intended to generalize to some population, the researchers must draw a probability sample from that population. If a study uses a convenience sample (for example, a haphazard sample of whoever is close by), we cannot be sure of the study's generalizability to the population that the researcher intends. So, for example, if a group of researchers wanted to generalize a study's results from a sample of U.S. soldiers to the population of all U.S. soldiers, they would have to draw the sample using random sampling techniques.

It's *A Population* Not *The Population*. Keep in mind, as well, that the population to which researchers want to generalize usually is not the population of every living person. Instead, when researchers are generalizing from a sample to a population, they will specify what that target population is. It might be all U.S. soldiers. It might be all of the college students in Toronto. It might be all of the third graders in a London elementary school. It might be a group of lab-reared rhesus monkeys. Researchers are at liberty to specify what their population of interest is, based on the variables they are interested in and the theories they are testing.

External Validity Comes from *How*, Not *How Many*. Finally, recall that when we are assessing the generalizability of a sample to a population, "how" matters more than "how many." That is, for the purposes of generalization, a randomly selected sample of 200 participants is much more valuable than a haphazardly selected sample of 2,000 participants.

For a review of sample size and generalizability, see Chapter 6, pp. 164–176.

Generalizing to Other Settings

The other aspect of external validity is a study's generalizability to other settings. Conceptual replications illustrate this aspect of external validity very well. In one study (described in Chapter 9), participants were made to feel socially excluded (versus included) and then were asked how cold they felt. The researchers conducted two studies in which they made people feel socially excluded in two different ways: In the first study, participants were asked to remember a time they felt excluded; in the second study, participants played a computer game with others, who seemed to ignore them (Zhong & Leonardelli, 2008). This study showed that the results of feeling socially excluded generalized from one setting (memories) to another setting (computer games).

Sometimes we want to know whether a laboratory situation created for a study generalizes to real-world settings. For example, we might ask whether Elliot's study on the color red and achievement, which took place in a laboratory, would generalize to "real-world" settings such as college examinations or achievement tests. A study's similarity to real-world contexts is sometimes called its **ecological validity**, or *mundane realism* (explained in detail later in this chapter). Many psychologists consider ecological validity to be one aspect of external validity. (Brewer, 2000).

To Be Important, Does a Study Need to Be Generalizable to Many People?

How is external validity related to a study's importance? First, read the following two statements and decide whether they are true or false:

1. The best research uses random samples from the population.
2. The best research studies people of both sexes and from all ethnicities, socioeconomic classes, ages, regions, countries, and so forth.

Of course, both of these statements address the **external validity** of a particular study. When the sample for a study has been selected from a population *at random* (using a *probability sample*), the results from that sample may be generalized to the population it was drawn from. It also makes sense that if a study's sample includes only men, we may not generalize its results to women; if a study's sample includes only college students from California, we may not generalize its results to elderly residents of Florida. Because most people have a strong intuitive understanding of external validity, they will agree with the two statements above.

However, the two statements are only *sometimes* right. The importance of external validity depends on a researcher's priorities. Whether a researcher strives for external validity in a study depends on what research mode he or she is operating in: theory-testing mode or generalization mode.

Theory-Testing Mode

When researchers work in **theory-testing mode**, they are usually testing association or causal claims to investigate support for a theory. As discussed in Chapter 1, the theory-data cycle is the process of designing studies to test a theory and using the data from the studies to reject, refine, or support the theory. In theory-testing mode, external validity matters much less than internal validity.

Example: Testing the Contact-Comfort Theory. Harlow's (1958) classic study of attachment in infant monkeys (described in Chapter 1) is a good example of theory-testing mode. Harlow created two artificial monkey "mothers" in order to test two competing theories of infant attachment: the cupboard theory (babies are attached to their mothers because their mothers feed them) and the contact-comfort theory (babies are attached to their mothers because their mothers are soft and cozy). In a real monkey mother, of course, the features of food and coziness are confounded. So Harlow separated the two features by creating one "mother" that was soft and cozy but did not provide food and one "mother" that was cold and uncomfortable but did provide food. By separating the two confounded variables, Harlow was prioritizing internal validity.

Harlow was clearly in theory-testing mode here, wondering which theory, the cupboard theory or the contact-comfort theory, was right. And the results from his study could not have been clearer: The baby monkeys in this study spent almost all of their time cuddling with the soft, cozy mother. The contact-comfort theory was overwhelmingly supported.

The monkeys in Harlow's study were hardly representative of monkeys in the wild. Harlow did not even use a random sample of monkeys from his laboratory. But Harlow did not care because he was in theory-testing mode: He created the artificial situation to test his *theory*—not to test the truth in some population of monkeys. In fact, according to the cupboard theory, *any* sample of monkeys—no matter how representative—should have been equally or more interested in the wire mother than they were in the cloth mother. But the data did not support the cupboard theory of attachment.

Example: Testing the "Parent-as-Grammar-Coach" Theory. Another example of a study conducted in theory-testing mode comes from studies of how children learn grammar. Psychologists used to believe that children learn correct grammar through reinforcement. That is, they believed that parents praise a child's grammatical sentences and correct a child's ungrammatical ones. They thought that children learned grammar through this constant correction process.

The reinforcement theory predicted that if a researcher were to observe a group of parents interacting with their children, the parents would praise the children's grammatical sentences and correct the children's ungrammatical sentences. But read the following interaction, audiotaped by Brown and Hanlon (1970, cited in Mook, 1989, p. 27):

Child: Mama isn't boy, he girl.
Parent: That's right.

Child: There's the animal farmhouse.
Parent: No, that's a lighthouse.

What Brown and Hanlon noticed—and you probably did, too—is that the parent accepted the child's first sentence, which was ungrammatical but factually true. (That's right—he girl!) But the parent corrected the child's second sentence, which was grammatical but factually wrong. (Not a farmhouse—a lighthouse!) This one incident illustrates the overall trend in the data. After coding hours of conversations between parents and children, Brown and Hanlon found that most of the time, parents corrected their children's sentences for factual accuracy but not for grammar. Furthermore, the reinforcement theory predicted that the children in this study would not learn to speak correctly without corrections to their grammar. But even though parents did not correct their children's grammar, the children did learn to speak grammatically. The reinforcement theory of speech development therefore appeared to be wrong.

Brown and Hanlon's study included only upper-middle-class Boston families, so the children and parents in this study were not representative of all children or even of all U.S. children. Further, the parents were willing to let a researcher record their interactions with their children on tape—they might have been especially eager to be involved in research and thus more educated than average. But the bias of this sample did not matter, because Brown and Hanlon were testing a theory: If the reinforcement theory of grammar were true, *any* sample of parents should have corrected ungrammatical sentences. But the parents in this study did not.

Of course, the reinforcement theory of grammar might apply to some other population in the world—and if Brown and Hanlon had studied a wider sample of people, they might have found evidence that some parents, somewhere, do correct their children's grammar. But keep two things in mind: First, Brown and Hanlon chose a strong test of their theory. If the reinforcement theory of grammar should apply anywhere, it would be among precisely the kinds of parents who volunteered for the study—upper-middle-class, well-educated, and interested in research. Such parents presumably use standard grammar themselves and are likely to be educated enough to explain grammar rules to their children. Second, if Brown and Hanlon had found some other cultural group of parents who did correct their children's grammar, the researchers would have to amend the reinforcement theory to fit this new data. They would need to change the theory to explain why reinforcement applies only in this population but not in others. In either case, the data from Brown and Hanlon's study mean that the original theory must be rejected or at least modified.

Other Examples. In your psychology studies, you have probably encountered many other examples of research conducted in theory-testing mode. In fact, the overwhelming majority of psychology studies are of the theory-testing type (Mook, 1989). Most researchers design variables that enable them to test competing explanations and confirm or disconfirm their hypotheses. For example, Elliot and his colleagues were testing the theory that red—a color associated with avoidance—would lead to avoidant behaviors and therefore would weaken academic performance. Zhong and Leonardelli, in their research on social exclusion and feeling cold, were testing the theory that the "cold shoulder" is more than a metaphor. Strayer's research on cell phones and driving tested the theory that cell phones are distracting to drivers. When researchers are in theory-testing mode, they are not very concerned (at least not yet) with the external validity of their samples or procedures (Berkowitz & Donnerstein, 1982).

Generalization Mode

Although much of the research in psychology is conducted in theory-testing mode, there are times when researchers work in **generalization mode**, in which they want to generalize the findings from the sample in their study to a larger population. They therefore are careful to use probability samples with appropriate diversity of sex, age, and ethnicity, and so on. In other words, researchers in generalization mode are concerned about external validity.

Applied research tends to be done in generalization mode, and basic research tends to be done in theory-testing mode. But this distinction is not absolute: Applied researchers often test theories, too, and basic researchers may extend their findings to larger populations.

For more on applied research versus basic research, see Chapter 1, pp. 13–15.

Frequency Claims: Always in Generalization Mode. Survey research that is intended to support frequency claims is done in generalization mode. To answer a question such as "How many U.S. teens are depressed?" or "What percentage of voters support gay marriage?" or "At what age do children learn to read?" a researcher must have a representative sample. It would not be acceptable to estimate U.S. teen depression rates from a haphazard sample of teens in an upper-middle-class high school in New York City. It would not be acceptable to estimate the percentage of voters who support gay marriage by interviewing only people living in San Francisco. And it would not be acceptable to estimate the age at which children learn to read by asking a self-selected sample on a webpage dedicated to gifted children. All of these samples would be biased.

As you have learned, representative samples are essential for supporting frequency claims. (For a review, see Chapters 3 and 6.) Therefore, when researchers are testing frequency claims, they are always in generalization mode.

Association and Causal Claims: Sometimes in Generalization Mode. What about association and causal claims? Most of the time, association and causal claims are conducted in theory-testing mode. But researchers sometimes conduct them in generalization mode, too.

Suppose a researcher tries out a new therapeutic technique on a limited sample of clients (say, on a sample of American women of European descent) and finds that it works. If the therapy is effective in this sample, the researcher would then want to learn whether it will also be effective more generally, in other samples: Will it work on Latino women? Will it work on men? To learn whether the therapy's effectiveness generalizes to other populations, the researcher will need to determine how representative the first study's sample is. In this case, the researcher cares about external validity—generalizability from sample to population.

Or consider a marketing researcher who finds that a sample of local teenagers prefers an advertising campaign that features tattoo artists over an advertising campaign that features a professional skateboarder. The researcher would hope to generalize the pattern from this particular sample of teenagers to the teenagers around the country who will eventually view the advertising campaign. Therefore, the marketing researcher would care very much that the sample used in the study resembles teenagers nationwide. Are they the same age? Are they of the same social class? Do they show the same distribution of ethnicities? Is the focus group sample unusually interested in tattoos, compared with the rest of the U.S. teenage population? Only if the external validity were sound would the preferences of this sample be generalizable to the preferences of the nation's teens.

Cultural Psychology: A Special Example of Generalization Mode

Cultural psychology is a subdiscipline of psychology that makes generalization mode its primary business. Cultural psychologists are interested in how cultural background and environment shapes the way a person thinks, feels, and behaves (Heine, 2012; Markus & Hamedani, 2007; Shweder, 1989).

Cultural psychologists have frequently challenged researchers who operate exclusively in theory-testing mode. While they understand why theory-testing mode focuses on internal validity, cultural psychologists point out that a theory that has been supported by a study in one human sample will not necessarily hold true for human beings in general. In contrast, cultural psychologists have shown that many theories may be supported in some cultural contexts but not in others. Indeed, cultural psychologists have collected dozens of examples of theories that were supported by data in one cultural context but not in any other cultural context.

Example 1: The Müller-Lyer Illusion. You may already be familiar with the Müller-Lyer illusion, illustrated in **Figure 13.6**. Does the vertical line B appear longer than the vertical line A? If you take out a ruler and measure the two vertical lines, you will find that they are exactly the same length.

Almost all North Americans fall for this illusion, but not all *people* do. Indeed, Segall and colleagues (1966) found that many people around the world, when tested, do not see line B as being longer than line A (see **Figure 13.7**).

Imagine that a group of North American researchers in theory-testing mode used the Müller-Lyer data from a single North American sample to formulate and test a theory about the human visual system and basic cognitive processes. Although they might briefly consider whether the results would generalize, they might discount the relevance of generalizability. After all, they might reason, culture would not affect such a basic cognitive process. But they would be wrong.

Indeed, Segall and colleagues used their data from around the world to conclude that people who grow up in a "carpentered world" have more experience with right angles as cues for depth perception than people who grow up in other societies. (Look at the angles formed where two walls and the ceiling meet in the

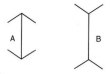

FIGURE 13.6
The Müller-Lyer illusion. The vertical lines labeled A and B are the same length, but many people perceive line B to be longer than line A.

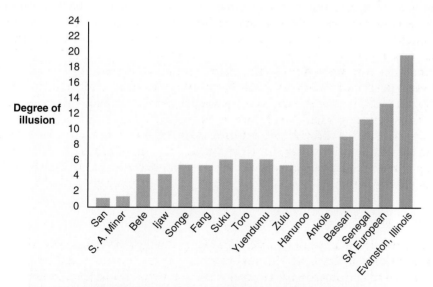

FIGURE 13.7 Cross-cultural results for the Müller-Lyer illusion. Segall and colleagues tested the Müller-Lyer illusion on adults in 16 societies and found that North Americans are most likely to perceive the illusion. The y-axis shows how much longer line B appears to participants compared with line A. The higher the value, the greater the degree of the illusion. *Source*: Adapted from Henrich and colleagues (2010).

farthest corner of the room you are in right now. Do you see the patterns of line B in the Müller—Lyer illusion?) In cultures with few square buildings, the child's developing visual system never learns that end-lines angling in suggest that a corner is close to you, while end-lines angling out suggest that the corner is farther away. These culturally learned cues are apparently responsible for the Müller-Lyer illusion.

Cultural psychologists such as Segall and his colleagues remind other researchers that they cannot take generalization for granted. Scientists cannot assume that any psychological processes—even those that seem most basic—are not influenced by culture.

Example 2: Figure and Ground. Research conducted by Masuda and Nisbett (2001) provides another example of cultural psychology in action. When you look at the scene illustrated in **Figure 13.8**, what do you notice first? Most North Americans will notice the largest fish swimming in the middle of the scene—the focal object. As you study the image, you may also notice the objects in the background, such as the plants, water, and smaller fish. This makes sense, right? Of course we focus on what seems to be the most important object—the large object in front.

When Masuda and Nisbett showed this image to a sample of Japanese college students, however, the students appeared to notice the background first. Apparently, Japanese participants attended to the background as much as, or even more than, the "focal" object. Later, Masuda and Nisbett quizzed participants from both groups on what they had seen. Sometimes the researchers showed people one of the original fish but changed the background (as

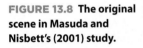

FIGURE 13.8 **The original scene in Masuda and Nisbett's (2001) study.**

Previously Seen Objects

with original background

with no background

with novel background

FIGURE 13.9 Stimuli from Masuda and Nisbett's memory test. To investigate how well people could recognize the fish they saw, the researchers manipulated the background.

shown in **Figure 13.9**). When the background was changed, North Americans could still recognize the fish, suggesting that the North Americans had processed the focal fish separately from the surrounding scene. In contrast, the Japanese students were less good at identifying the fish when it was removed from the surrounding scene. (The graph in **Figure 13.10** shows the results.) Their errors suggested, in fact, that the Japanese participants had processed the fish in context, and when the context changed, their memories were less accurate.

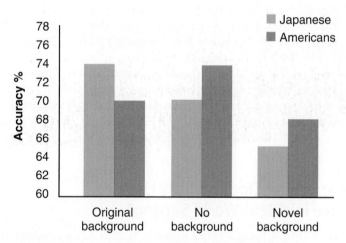

FIGURE 13.10 The results of Masuda and Nisbett's context-sensitivity study. Americans were more accurate than Japanese at recognizing the target fish when it was presented without its original background. But Japanese were more accurate than Americans when the fish were presented in their original backgrounds. These results suggest that the way Americans attend to "focal" and "ground" aspects of a scene does not generalize to an East Asian sample.

If Masuda and Nisbett had been in theory-testing mode rather than generalization mode and had studied only the North American sample, they might have formed and tested theories about how all humans perceive complex scenes. They might have theorized that human attention is drawn to "focal objects" first and foremost, whereas background objects receive much less visual attention. However, because Masuda and Nisbett were in generalization mode, they found that visual attention worked differently in different cultures. Thus, this study is another good example of how cultural psychologists challenge other researchers to combine generalization mode with theory-testing mode—to test a theory in multiple cultures before assuming that it applies to all humans.

Most Theory Testing in Psychology Is Done on WEIRD People

To understand the importance of cultural psychologists' work, consider that most psychology research has been conducted on North American college students. For example, one researcher recorded the samples used in the top six journals in psychology for the year 2007. In these core journals, 68% of the participants were American, and 96% of the participants were from North America, Europe, Australia, or Israel (Arnett, 2008). Of course, participants from these countries are from a unique subset of the world's population, which researchers refer to as *WEIRD*: Western, educated, industrialized, rich, and democratic (Henrich, Heine, & Norenzayan, 2010). And WEIRD samples are not very representative of the world's people. The two examples above—the Müller-Lyer illusion and the fish study—both demonstrate how seemingly basic human processes can work differently in different cultural contexts.

When psychology researchers operate in theory-testing mode, they do not prioritize external validity, and they may even test their theories only on WEIRD people. However, cultural psychologists raise the alarm, reminding researchers that their theories, when tested on only WEIRD people, may not apply to everyone (Arnett, 2008; Henrich et al., 2010; Sears, 1986).

To Be Important, Does a Study Have to Take Place in a Real-World Setting?

Another assumption people often make is that studies conducted in a real-world setting are more important to people's daily lives than studies that take place in an artificial, laboratory setting. For example, read the following descriptions of psychological studies, and ask yourself whether each study is important.

1. A researcher dressed an undergraduate student in black from head to toe and placed small lights on her wrists, elbows, shoulders, hips, knees, and ankles (as shown in **Figure 13.11**). The researcher then turned out

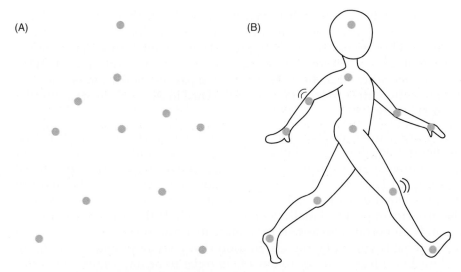

(A)   (B)

FIGURE 13.11 Recognizing a human form. Johansson (1973) placed small lights on the joints of a model and showed people either still photos of the model or movies of the model walking in a dark room. The results indicated that people cannot recognize the human form from points of light alone—the model has to be moving. In the "real world," we never observe people walking around in the dark with only small lights illuminating their joints. Is Johansson's study therefore unimportant?

the lights and made a movie of the student walking across the room. Later, the researcher showed either the movie or a still photograph of the model to a set of undergraduate students, asking them what they saw. Observers of the movie reported that the movie depicted a person walking, while observers of the photograph saw a meaningless jumble of dots (Johansson, 1973).

2. In studies of split-brain patients (see Chapter 12), Michael Gazzaniga (2005) put patients in front of a computer, asked them to fixate on a dot in the center, and then flashed two images for a fraction of a second—one picture on the right and a different picture on the left. The people he studied could name any object presented on the right side of the computer screen but could not name objects presented on the left side.

3. A group of researchers studied whether people in a library would intervene when a thief started rummaging through someone else's bookbag. In a staged event, a student (really an actor) sat down to study next to a library patron. After a few minutes, the student got up, leaving his or her bag at the table. Then another person—a "thief" (also an actor)—came along, rummaged through the abandoned bag, and removed either $20 or

a wristwatch. The researchers were interested in whether the real student sitting at the table would say anything to stop the thief. When only the real student witnessed the theft, the real student intervened in the theft 32% of the time. However, when the real student was sitting at the table with one other "student," who was really a passive confederate of the researchers, the real student *never* intervened in the theft (Shaffer, Rogel, & Hendrick, 1975).

Are these three studies important? You might argue, for instance, that the lights study does not tell us anything about the real world; after all, how often do we see someone walking around in a dark room with lights taped to his or her knees? For the split-brain study, you might argue that most of us never have our corpus callosum severed, so the study does not apply to the majority of people. Finally, you might conclude that the library study is the most important, because it took place in a real-world setting. If so, you were probably guided by the assumption that a study should be similar to real-world contexts and day-to-day life in order to be important. But is this always true?

External Validity and the Real World

When you interrogate external validity, you ask whether the study's results can generalize not only to other participants but also to other settings. When a study takes place in the real world—sometimes called a **field setting**—it has a built-in advantage for external validity, because it clearly applies to real-world settings. As mentioned previously, ecological validity is a type of external validity that refers to how similar a study's manipulations and measures are to the kinds of situations participants might encounter in their everyday lives. The library study has excellent ecological validity because it did take place in a real-world setting. However, the ecological validity of a setting is only one aspect of the setting's generalizability; just because a setting seems realistic does not mean that it represents all possible settings a person might encounter. Would the results of the library study also apply in a coffee shop, a doctor's office, or a movie theater?

Furthermore, the situation a scientist creates in a research laboratory is just as real a situation as one that occurs in a café or workplace. Although it may be easy to dismiss a study that does not seem realistic, remember that in daily life people find themselves in many different settings, all of which are "real." These settings can include not only libraries, theaters, and coffee shops but also classrooms and research laboratories.

And indeed, the emotions and behaviors generated by a laboratory manipulation (for example, the anxiety about evaluation caused by seeing red ink, or the cell phone conversation a person conducts during a driving simulator task) can also be quite real, visible, and meaningful. That is, many laboratory experiments are high in **experimental realism**—they create settings in which people experience authentic emotions, motivations, and behaviors.

To what extent does the real-world similarity—the ecological validity—of a study affect our ideas about the study's importance? It depends on the mode it is conducted in: generalization mode or theory-testing mode.

Generalization Mode and the Real World

Because external validity is of primary importance when researchers are in generalization mode, they might strive for a representative sample of a population. But they might also try to enhance the ecological validity of their study in order to ensure its generalizability to nonlaboratory settings. By the time Shaffer and colleagues studied helping behavior, several authors had already tested theories of helping in laboratory settings. Specifically, other researchers had learned in a laboratory setting that when undergraduate students heard what sounded like a woman falling in a nearby room (it was actually a realistic audio recording), the students were more likely to investigate the accident if they were alone. When students were with even one other person, rates of helping went down dramatically. The results from these lab studies supported a theory of bystander intervention known as *diffusion of responsibility* (Darley & Latané, 1968; Latane & Nida, 1981). The theory predicts that as the number of witnesses to an emergency event increases, the likelihood that each individual will offer to help decreases.

After reading about laboratory research supporting the diffusion of responsibility theory, Shaffer and colleagues wanted to know whether the diffusion of responsibility theory would work in the real world, so they conducted the library study. And indeed, the theory was also supported there. People were more likely to report the theft when they were sole witnesses than when another person was there. By conducting the study in a real-world setting, Shaffer and his colleagues were operating in generalization mode. Their results provided evidence for the theory's generalizability to other real-world settings.

Theory-Testing Mode and the Real World

When a researcher is in theory-testing mode, external validity and real-world applicability are lower priorities. Take, for instance, Johansson's study, in which the model had lights on her joints. Of course, no one is going to encounter this kind of situation in the real world, but the ecological validity of the situation did not matter to the researcher. He was testing a research question: How much information do people need before they can conclude that they are looking at a human being? By keeping the room dark and attaching lights only to the model's joints, the researcher was able to cut out all other visual information; only the location of the joints was visible. Johansson was concerned with internal validity—eliminating alternative explanations for people's interpretations. It was not enough just to see the lights on the joints, however. People could not detect a human form from a still photo; instead, the lights had to be moving in a coordinated way. To narrow down exactly what visual information people needed in order to detect a human form, Johansson had to create an extremely artificial situation.

Was Johansson's study important? In terms of the theory he was testing, it was invaluable, because he was able to show that both joint location and movement are necessary and sufficient for people to detect a human form. But what about generalizability and real-world applicability? On the one hand, both the model and the study's participants were drawn haphazardly, not randomly, from a narrow group of North American college students. In addition, the situation created in the laboratory would never occur in a real-world setting. On the other hand, the ability to recognize human gestures and postures is undoubtedly crucial to aspects of human social life. The theoretical understanding gained from this seemingly artificial study contributes to our understanding of a basic perceptual process involved in social cognition.

Gazzaniga and his colleagues' studies of split-brain patients are another example of research done in theory-testing mode (Gazzaniga, 2005; Turk et al. 2003). Gazzaniga designed his two-sided, flashing pictures so he could better understand where language was localized in the brain. Do the situations he created in his laboratory occur in the real world? Absolutely not. They do not even occur in the everyday lives of the split-brain patients in the study, who can usually move their eyes from right to left. If an image falls on the left side of the visual field, they can shift the input from the right side of the brain to the left with a quick movement of the eye.

The stimuli Gazzaniga presented to his participants were therefore about as unnatural as can be imagined. But Gazzaniga specifically created these artificial conditions to test a theory, and, despite the lack of real-world similarity in his methods, he was able to confirm an important theory about how the brain is organized—knowledge that has many real-world implications.

Finally, consider the study design that many people (quite correctly) respect as a pinnacle of behavioral research: the randomized, double-blind, placebo-controlled study, introduced in Chapter 10. In such a study, an experimenter goes to extreme artificial lengths to assign people at random to carefully constructed experimental conditions that control for placebo effects, experimenter bias, and experimental demand. Such studies have virtually no equivalent in everyday, real-world settings, yet their results can be among the most valuable we have in science.

In short, theory-testing mode often demands that experimenters create artificial situations that allow them to minimize distractions, eliminate alternative explanations, and isolate individual features of some situation. Theory-testing mode prioritizes internal validity at the expense of all other considerations, including ecological validity. Nonetheless, such studies often provide crucial knowledge to the field of psychology. **Table 13.4** summarizes the nuanced approach to external validity that has been emphasized in this chapter.

Say this:	Not that:
"Is that result statistically significant?"	"This single study is definitive!"
"Was that result replicated?"	"This study has nothing to do with the real world."
"That is a single study. How does the study fit in with the entire literature?"	"That's only a theory."
"How well do the methods of this study get at the theory they were testing?"	"This is a bad study because they didn't use a random sample."
"Was the study conducted in generalization mode? If so, were the participants sampled randomly?"	"This is a bad study because they used only North Americans as participants."
Would the results also apply to other settings?"	"They used thousands of participants. It must have great external validity."
"Would that result hold up in another cultural context?"	"That psychological principle seems so basic, I'm sure it's universal."

Check Your Understanding

1. In your own words, describe the difference between generalization mode and theory-testing mode.

2. Which of the three types of claims (frequency, association, or causal) is almost always conducted in generalization mode? Which of the three claims are usually conducted in theory-testing mode?

3. Explain why researchers who are operating in theory-testing mode might not attempt to use a random sample in their research. What validity are they prioritizing? What aspects of their research are they emphasizing (for now)?

4. Summarize the goal of cultural psychology. What does this field suggest about working in theory-testing and generalization modes?

5. When an experiment tests hypotheses in an artificial laboratory setting, it does not necessarily mean that the study does not apply to the real world. Explain why not.

1. See pp. 387–390. 2. See pp. 389–390. 3. See pp. 390–391. 4. See pp. 387–389. 5. See pp. 396–398.

Summary

The first step to establishing a study's importance is to use inferential statistics or replication studies to determine whether the findings are replicable. If inferential statistics show that a study result is significant, we can conclude that if we ran the study in exactly the same way again, we would probably obtain the same result. Replication studies are a concrete way of establishing a study's replicability. There are three main types of replication studies. Direct replications attempt to repeat the original study exactly. Conceptual replications have the same conceptual variables as the original study, but they operationalize the variables differently. Replication-plus-extension studies repeat the original study but introduce new participant variables, situations, or levels of the independent variable.

Meta-analyses collect the effect sizes from all published (and, when possible, unpublished) studies that have tested the relationship between a set of variables, using statistical tools to compute the average effect size for a particular research question. Meta-analyses are powerful tools that help quantify whether an effect exists in the literature and, if so, how large the effect is and what moderates it.

When researchers are in generalization mode, they care whether the samples they are studying are representative—whether the data from sample A are applicable to population A (and even whether the data might be applicable to population B). In contrast, when researchers are in theory-testing mode, they do not care as much about using representative samples. In theory-testing mode, researchers design studies that test a theory—to find out whether the study turns out the way the theory predicts it should. If not, the theory must be modified, and the new theory must be tested in a new study. In theory-testing mode, researchers leave the generalization step for later studies, which will test whether the theory holds in a sample that is representative of another population.

This chapter questioned two assumptions about generalization to populations: first, that important research should use random samples from populations, and second, that important research should apply to people from both sexes and all ethnicities, social classes, states, provinces, countries, and so forth. In some studies, it is important to use random samples and a variety of people, but diverse, representative samples are primarily important when researchers are in generalization mode. In theory-testing mode, researchers do not (yet) consider whether their samples are representative of some population, so external validity is much less important than internal validity. Researchers who make frequency claims are always in generalization mode, but they are also in generalization mode when they ask whether an association or causal claim can be generalized to a different group of people.

Cultural psychologists have documented how psychological discoveries are not always applicable cross-culturally. Even seemingly basic cognitive or visual processes may not operate the same way in different cultural contexts. The work of cultural psychologists serves as a potent reminder that when researchers collect data only from WEIRD (Western, educated, industrialized, rich, and democratic) samples, they cannot assume that the theories they develop in theory-testing mode will apply to all human beings.

Finally, this chapter questioned the assumption that to be important, research must be conducted in settings that resemble the real world. Some research has high ecological validity—it takes place in settings that are similar to common real-world settings. Other research (conducted in theory-testing mode) takes place in laboratories. While such studies might be high in experimental realism, they may not resemble other real-world settings outside of the lab. Nonetheless, the data from such artificial settings help researchers test theories in the most internally valid way possible, and their lessons usually apply to other real-world situations.

Key Terms

conceptual replication, p. 378
cultural psychology, p. 390
direct replication, p. 377
ecological validity, p. 387
experimental realism, p. 396
external validity, p. 387
field setting, p. 396
file drawer problem, p. 384

generalization mode, p. 389
inferential statistics, p. 376
meta-analysis, p. 381
replicable, p. 376
replication-plus-extension, p. 379
scientific literature, p. 381
theory-testing mode, p. 387

 **NEED HELP STUDYING?**
wwnorton.com/studyspace

Visit StudySpace to access free review materials such as:

- Diagnostic Review Quizzes
- Study Outlines

Learning Actively

1. Consider Elliot and colleagues' (2007) study on the color red and achievement (see Chapter 9). Describe how you might design a study to be each of the following:

   a. A direct replication of Elliot and colleagues' Study 1
   b. A replication-plus-extension study
   c. A conceptual replication with excellent ecological validity

2. Now consider Zhong and Leonardelli's (2008) research, which manipulated social exclusion and measured feelings of warmth or coldness (see Chapter 9). Consider how you might design a study that would be

   a. A replication-plus-extension study
   b. A conceptual replication with excellent ecological validity

3. For each short study description below, indicate whether you think the study would have been conducted in theory-testing mode or in generalization mode, or whether it could be done in either mode. Explain your answer.

   a. A study found that most Holocaust survivors struggle with depression, sleep disorders, and emotional distress. The conclusion was based on a government data set that has tracked 220,000 Holocaust survivors ("Most Holocaust Survivors Battle Depression," 2010).
   b. A neuropsychologist exposed mice to radio waves from cell phones. In a pretest/posttest design, their cages were exposed to a typical cell phone's electromagnetic field for about 1 hour a day, for about 9 months. Later, the researchers tested each mouse's memory and found that the mice had better memory after their exposure to the electromagnetic fields than before, and better memory compared with the control group of mice that was not exposed (Hamzelou, 2010).
   c. A group of researchers (Ostrovsky, Meyers, Ganesh, Mathur, & Sinha, 2009) studied three men in India who were born blind. At ages 7, 12, and 29, respectively, each man received surgery and treatment to correct his vision. (In all three cases, the families of the men had been too poor to afford treatment for the blindness.) After the patients regained their sight, the researchers studied how these three people developed their newly acquired abilities to decode the visual world. At first, each patient thought that a two-dimensional picture, such as the one marked "B," depicted three objects instead of two. With several months of experience, however, they all learned to interpret the images appropriately. By moving

the objects apart from each other on some of the trials, the researchers discovered that the three individuals could use motion cues to decode what lines belonged to which object (similar to how people in Johansson's study could identify that a lighted model was walking only when she was moving). The researchers concluded that as the brain learns about the visual world, it uses motion cues to decide which lines belong to which objects.

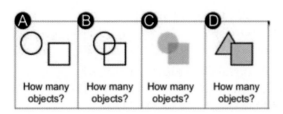

4. Apply lessons from this chapter, using the questions in the left-hand column of Table 13.4, to evaluate the following study:

> One week after the terrorist attacks on the World Trade Center and the Pentagon on September 11, 2001, the researcher William Hirst and his colleagues (2009) asked a convenience sample of more than 3,000 people in seven U.S. cities what they remembered about the event. The respondents were asked where they were and what they were doing when they heard about the attack. They were asked factual questions about the event, too, such as how many planes were involved and what airlines were involved. Eleven months later and 35 months later, many of the same respondents were located by the researchers and asked the same questions. The researchers compared the early reports (1 week after the event) to the later reports (11 or 35 months after the event) to test each person's accuracy. One of the many findings of the study was that people do not remember their emotional reactions very well: People's memories of their emotions were less accurate than their memories of nonemotional features of the event. In addition, even though people were not always accurate about the event 11 months later, their confidence in their memories was nevertheless rather high.

Appendix A
Overview of Descriptive Statistics

In everyday language, the word *statistics* is used to describe quantitative records, such as a baseball player's batting average or the average life span of a country's citizens. But in science, the word *statistics* refers to the set of tools researchers use to make sense of data that they have collected in a study. This appendix provides a very brief overview of one set of such statistical tools: **descriptive statistics**, used to organize and summarize the properties of a set of data. The other set of statistical tools, inferential statistics, is covered in Appendix B.

Describing Data

Recall that when a researcher collects data from a group of people or animals, the group is often a sample from a larger population. If we tested 5 rhesus monkeys on their ability to discriminate blue from green, and the 5 came from a larger population of 25 monkeys in the lab, then the 5 monkeys would be our sample. If we tested 50 students on their anagram skills, the 50 students might be a sample from a larger population of students who could have signed up for the research. However, we do not always study a sample from a larger population. If we give a midterm exam to 31 students, the 31 students are a complete set of cases; they are not a sample, because they are the whole population we care about. Or we might collect data on the air temperature and teen pregnancy rates in all of the 50 United States. These 50 states are not a sample, either; they are a population. Or we might simply have a batch of scores—perhaps a set of prices from the local supermarket, or some data on reading speed from a group of third graders. Regardless of whether our data are best described as a sample, a population, or a simple set of scores, we can still apply the descriptive techniques explained in this appendix.

Variables (introduced in Chapter 3) are what researchers measure or manipulate in a study. If we study 31 students' grades on a midterm exam, then exam score is the variable. In other studies, variables might be the ability to discriminate blue from green, the average air temperature, or the pregnancy rate among teenagers. Variables vary: They take on different levels, or values, for the different members of a sample. Thus, the values for an exam score might range from 16 to 33 on a 35-point scale. Ability to discriminate blue from green might have the categorical values of "yes" or "no." Average air temperature might have quantitative values ranging from 50 to 81 degrees Fahrenheit and anything in between.

For a review of categorical and quantitative variables, see Chapter 5, p. 118.

Student name	Exam score
Henry	17
Emma	29
Caitlyn	19
Lonnie	27
Lalia	22
Alek	27
Rohan	22
Max	20
Shane	29
Yukiko	29
Alexi	18
Marianna	30
Mira	21
Cristina	27
Emmanuel	26
Raul	30
Ian	19
Sena	29
Jordan	27
Ayase	32
Luke	25
Miguel	32
Jon	30
Gabriel	31
Rhianna	32
Juniper	24
Malika	25
Shawn	30
Adhya	24
Harriet	33
Lucio	25

FIGURE A.1 **A data matrix of exam scores.** A data matrix is the starting point for computing most statistics.

Data Matrices

When we collect a set of data, we start by entering the data into a **data matrix**, usually using a computer program such as Excel, SPSS/PASW Statistics, SYSTAT, SAS, or STATA. Computer programs can make it easy to calculate formulas, make graphs, and organize data. All computer programs start with a data matrix, a grid that contains data from our cases. **Figure A.1** shows a data matrix that contains the scores of 31 students who took a short-answer exam containing 35 items. The first column identifies each person by name (this column might contain simple ID numbers, instead). The second column shows the person's score on the exam. In a data matrix, each column represents a variable, and each row represents a case (such as a person, an animal, a state, a price, or any other case under study).

Frequency Distributions and Stemplots

Frequency distributions and *stemplots* are techniques for organizing a column of data in a data matrix. At first glance, the data matrix shows a disorganized list of scores. However, we can quickly bring some order to the scores by making a **frequency distribution**—a table that gives a visual picture of the observations on a particular variable: It clearly shows how many of the cases scored each possible value on the variable. To make a frequency distribution, we list possible values for the variable from lowest to highest and tally how many people obtained each score, as in **Figure A.2.A**. Normally, we do not leave the tally marks there—we count them and enter the value in the table, as in **Figure A.2.B**.

(A)

Possible value	Number of cases
17	I
18	I
19	II
20	I
21	I
22	II
23	
24	II
25	III
26	I
27	IIII
28	
29	IIII
30	IIII
31	I
32	III
33	I

(B)

Possible value	Number of cases
17	1
18	1
19	2
20	1
21	1
22	2
23	0
24	2
25	3
26	1
27	4
28	0
29	4
30	4
31	1
32	3
33	1

FIGURE A.2 **A frequency distribution for exam scores.** To create a frequency distribution, start by listing the possible values in one column and tallying the number of times each value occurs in the data set in the next column (Panel A). Then convert the tallies to numerals. The final frequency distribution appears in Panel B.

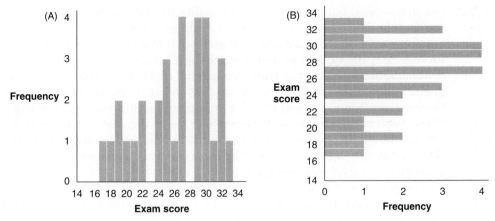

FIGURE A.3 Frequency histogram of the scores in Table A.1. Exam scores are on the x-axis in Panel A and on the y-axis in Panel B.

Based on the data from a frequency distribution, it is a fairly simple step to create a **frequency histogram** (often just called a *histogram*), as in **Figure A.3.A**. Note that the possible exam scores are on the x-axis, while the frequency of each score is on the y-axis. We could also draw the histogram the other way, as in **Figure A.3.B**.

Instead of giving individual numerical scores, we could group the exam score values. For example, if we call any score between 30 and 33 an A, any score between 25 and 29 a B, and so on, the frequency histogram looks simpler, as in **Figure A.4**.

Another option for organizing data is a **stemplot**, also known as a *stem-and-leaf plot*. **Figure A.5** depicts the data from the midterm exam in stemplot form. The values on the left of the line are called *stems*, and the values on the right are called *leaves*. To make a stemplot, we would first decide the units for

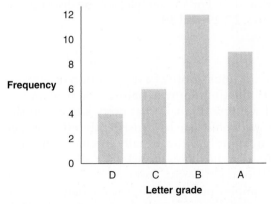

FIGURE A.4 Grouped frequency histogram of the scores in Table A.1.

Stem	Leaves
10	7 8 9 9
20	0 1 2 2 4 4 5 5 5 6 7 7 7 7 9 9 9 9
30	0 0 0 0 1 2 2 2 3

FIGURE A.5 Stemplot of the 31 short-answer test scores. A stemplot serves as a table and a figure at the same time, allowing you to see all of the scores in a batch and how they are distributed.

the stems—tens, hundreds, thousands—using the most appropriate level for the data. In this example, tens are used as the unit for the stems, because the possible scores on the exam could range from 0 to 35. After listing the stems (in this case, 10, 20, 30), we would enter the leaves, which represent each individual score. For example, there is one score of 17, so on the stem 10 there is one leaf marked with "7." There are two scores of 19, so on the stem 10 there are two leaves marked "9." The stemplot is useful because it is a table and a graph at the same time. It is simple to see all the scores in a stemplot. A grouped frequency distribution might tell us that five students got an A in the class, but we would not know what the students' exact scores were. In contrast, a stemplot reveals this information.

Compared with a disorganized list of scores, a frequency distribution, frequency histogram, or stemplot makes it easier to visualize the scores we collected.

Describing Central Tendencies (Mode, Median, and Mean)

Imagine that I come into class carrying a bundle of exams in my hand, and a student asks me, "How did the class do?" I start to read off the individual exam scores, but the student says, "Too much information. What was a *typical* score?" The student is asking for a measure of **central tendency**—a measure of what value the individual scores tend to center on. Three measures of central tendency are commonly used to determine the central tendency of the class's test scores: the mode, the median, and the mean.

Mode

The **mode** is the value of the most common score—the score that was received by more members of the group than any other. To find the mode, we can look at the frequency histogram (as in Figure A.3) and find the highest peak. The value below the peak on the x-axis is the mode. Or we can look at the stemplot and find the value with the most leaves. Some distributions have more than one mode (they are called **bimodal** or **multimodal**). For an example, see the distribution in Figure A.3, which has three modes: 27, 29, and 30.

Median

The **median** is the value at the middlemost score of a distribution of scores—the score that divides a frequency distribution into halves. The median is a typical score in the sense that if we were to guess that every student in the class received the median score, we would not be consistently off in either direction. We would guess too high and too low equally often. To find the median of 31 scores, we would line up the scores in order (smallest to greatest) and find the value of the 16th, or middlemost, score. A stemplot makes it easy to find the median. In the stemplot in Figure A.5, the median is a score of 27, because if we count the leaves starting from the lowest score, the 16th leaf is the score of 27.

Mean

To find the **mean**, also called the *average*, we add up all the scores in the batch and then divide by the number of scores. We abbreviate the mean with the symbol M. The formula for the mean looks like this:

$$M = \Sigma \frac{X}{N}$$

The X in this formula stands for each student's score on the test. The sigma (Σ) means "the sum of." So ΣX means that we must sum all of the values of X—all of the scores. The N stands for the number of scores. In our example, we would find the mean by adding up 33, 32, 32, 32, 31, 30, 30, 30, 30, 29, 27, 27, 27, 27, and so on (down to 17), and then we would divide by 31, the number of people who took the exam. We would find that the mean exam value in this class is 26.16.

Mode, Median, Mean: Which to Use?

The mean is by far the most common measure of central tendency. However, when a set of scores contains a few extreme scores on one end (outliers—see Chapter 7), the median or mode may be a more accurate measure of central tendency. For example, imagine we want to know the typical annual income in a community of only five families—four with modest incomes and a fifth that is very wealthy. Let's say that the incomes are

$20,000
$30,000
$40,000
$50,000
$1,000,000

The mean of these five incomes would be $228,000—a very misleading idea of the community's income. In such a case, the median income—$40,000—would be a better estimate of what is typical for the community as a whole. In short, the mean is usually the most appropriate measure of central tendency, but when a set of data has outliers, the median (or sometimes the mode) may provide a better description.

When a distribution has a clear mode, the mode can be a good choice for describing central tendency. For example, a class's evaluations of a professor's teaching performance might be distributed as follows:

Overall, this professor's teaching was:	Number of respondents
1 = poor	0
2 = average	0
3 = good	1
4 = very good	4
5 = excellent	10

In this example, the professor's mean rating would be 4.56, but this professor might also wish to report the modal response—that the overwhelming majority of the students rated him or her "excellent," or 5.

FIGURE A.6 Two sets of scores with the same mean but different variability. The set on the top has less variability than the one on the bottom, but the two sets have the same mean and the same number of scores.

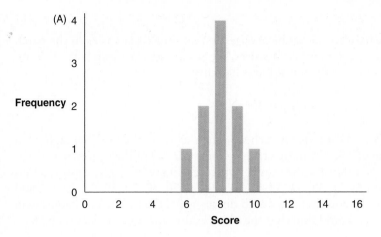

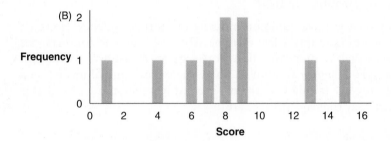

Describing Variability (Variance and Standard Deviation)

Besides describing the central tendency of a set of scores, we can also describe how spread out the scores are. In **Figure A.6**, compare the top set of scores to the bottom set. Notice that both sets have the same number of scores, and both have the same mean as well. However, the top set has less variability than the bottom one. In the top set, scores are, on average, closer to the mean. In the bottom set, scores are, on average, farther from the mean.

The two most common descriptive techniques that capture the relative spread of scores are the **variance** (sometimes abbreviated as SD^2) and the **standard deviation** (abbreviated SD). It's worth taking the time to fully understand the logic behind these computations, because the logic applies to some other statistics, as well.

When computing the variability of a set of scores, we start by calculating how far each score is from the mean. The first two columns of **Table A.1** present the set of scores that goes with the top panel of Figure A.6.

The first step is to calculate the mean of this set of 10 scores. That is, we add up all the scores in the second column, divide by 10, and get the mean: 8.0. Next, we create a deviation score for each participant. That is, we subtract the mean, 8.0, from each score. The deviation scores are in the third column. One possible way to figure out the "average" deviation score would be simply to add up all the deviation scores in the third column and divide by 10. However, because some of the deviation scores are positive and some are negative, they would cancel each

TABLE A.1 Variance and Standard Deviation Computations for the Set of Scores in Figure A.6.A

Participant	Score	Deviation (score – **mean**)	Deviation squared
A	6	$6 - 8.0 = -2$	4
B	7	$7 - 8.0 = -1$	1
C	7	$7 - 8.0 = -1$	1
D	8	$8 - 8.0 = 0$	0
E	8	$8 - 8.0 = 0$	0
F	8	$8 - 8.0 = 0$	0
G	8	$8 - 8.0 = 0$	0
H	9	$9 - 8.0 = 1$	1
I	9	$9 - 8.0 = 1$	1
J	10	$10 - 8.0 = 2$	4
	Sum = 80		Sum = 12
	Mean = 80/10 = **8.0**		Variance = 12/10 = 1.20
			$SD = \sqrt{1.20} = 1.09$

other out when added up. They would add up to zero for any distribution of scores, so merely summing them would not give us any sense of the variability in the scores.

To eliminate this problem, we square each deviation score, since the square of either a positive or a negative number is a positive number. The squared deviations are given in the fourth column of Table A.1. We now compute the average of the squared deviations by summing them (to get 12) and dividing by the number of scores (10). The result is the variance. Finally, to reverse the step in which we squared the scores, we take the square root of the variance to find the standard deviation, or *SD* (1.09).

The mathematical formula for the variance is therefore as follows:

$$SD^2 = \frac{\Sigma(X - M)^2}{N}$$

This formula can be explained as follows:

1. From each score X, we subtract the mean: $(X - M)$
2. We square each of the resulting deviation scores: $(X - M)^2$
3. We add up all the squared deviation scores: $\Sigma(X - M)^2$ (This quantity is called the "sum of squares" because we *sum* all of the *squar*ed deviation scores.)
4. We divide the sum of squares by the number of scores to get the mean squared deviation, called the variance:

$$SD^2 = \frac{\Sigma(X - M)^2}{N}$$

Finally, if we take the positive square root of the variance, we get the standard deviation:

$$SD = \sqrt{SD^2}$$

The standard deviation is more commonly reported than the variance because it better captures how far, on average, each score is from the mean. When the standard deviation is large, there is a great deal of variability in the set—the scores are spread out far from the mean, either above or below. When the standard deviation is small, there is less variability in the set—most of the scores are closer to the mean, above or below. Indeed, the standard deviation for Figure A.6.A is 1.09, but the *SD* for Figure A.6.B is 3.82. (The standard deviation computations for the scores are shown in **Table A.2**.) The more spread out the scores are, the higher the standard deviation value will be.

How Mean and Standard Deviation Are Represented in Journal Articles

When you read an empirical journal article, you are likely to see mean and standard deviation information presented either within the text of the Results section or as part of a table. Following are a couple of examples of mean and standard deviation data that appeared in actual journal articles.

First is an example of how mean and standard deviation information can be presented in a text. Read the following excerpt from Bushman's (2002, p. 728) article on using a punching bag to express anger (discussed in Chapter 2 of this book):

TABLE A.2 Variance and Standard Deviation Computations for the Set of Scores in Figure A.6.B

Participant	Score	Deviation (score − **mean**)	Deviation Squared
A	1	$1 - 8.0 = -7$	49
B	4	$4 - 8.0 = -4$	16
C	6	$6 - 8.0 = -2$	4
D	7	$7 - 8.0 = -1$	1
E	8	$8 - 8.0 = 0$	0
F	8	$8 - 8.0 = 0$	0
G	9	$9 - 8.0 = 1$	1
H	9	$9 - 8.0 = 1$	1
I	13	$13 - 8.0 = 5$	25
J	15	$15 - 8.0 = 7$	49
	Sum = 80		Sum = 146
	Mean = 80/10 = **8.0**		Variance = 146/10 = 14.6
			$SD = \sqrt{14.6} = 3.82$

Table 2. Larger Containers Influence Consumption Volume of Both Fresh and Stale Popcorn (Means ± Standard Deviations)

	Medium Container (120 g) n = 77		Large Container (240 g) n = 80			Statistical Significance of Container Size, Freshness, and Their Combined Impact	
	Fresh Popcorn	Stale Popcorn	Fresh Popcorn	Stale Popcorn	F Values (df = 154)	Container Size	Container Size × Freshness
Popcorn eaten, g	58.9 ± 16.7	38.0 ± 16.1	85.6 ± 19.8	50.8 ± 14.1	52.4**	101.8**	7.4**
"This popcorn tasted good"†	7.7 ± 1.4	3.9 ± 2.4	6.8 ± 1.5	2.2 ± 1.7	19.5**	201.1**	2.5**
"This popcorn was of high quality"†	7.3 ± 2.1	3.1 ± 1.5	6.8 ± 1.9	2.1 ± 2.1	5.6*	194.0**	0.4

†Means were measured on a 9-point scale (1 = strongly disagree; 9 = strongly agree).
*P < .05; **P < .01.

FIGURE A.7 Table from Wansink and Kim (2005) giving mean and standard deviation.

How hard the punching bag was hit. The intraclass correlation between experimenter and participant ratings of how hard the bag was hit was 0.69 (Shrout & Fleiss, 1979). The same pattern of results also was found for the two ratings. Thus, the two ratings were averaged.

Overall, men hit the punching bag harder than did women, $M = 6.69$, $SD = 2.05$, and $M = 4.73$, $SD = 1.88$, $F(1, 396) = 99.14$, $p < .0001$, $d = 1.00$. No other effects were significant ($ps > .05$).

Number of times punching bag was hit. Participants who thought about becoming physically fit hit the punching bag more times than did participants who thought about the person who insulted them, $M = 127.5$, $SD = 63.5$, and $M = 112.2$, $SD = 57.5$, $F(1, 396) = 6.31$, $p < .05$, $d = 0.25$. In other words, participants in the rumination group vented less than did participants in the distraction group. No other effects were significant ($ps > .05$).

Even if all of the statistical symbols are not familiar to you, look for the mean (*M*) and standard deviation (*SD*).

Test Yourself 1

In the excerpt above, can you find the average force with which men hit the punching bag? Can you find the average force with which women hit the punching bag? Which group, males or females, has the higher variability? How can you tell?

The second example, involving amount of popcorn eaten and size of container (from Wansink & Kim, 2005) shows how mean and standard deviation information can be presented in table form. In **Figure A.7**, focus on finding the mean and standard deviation, even if you do not recognize all of the statistical notation. Depending on the article and the journal, the tables will differ, but you can use the column labels or table captions to locate the means and standard deviations of particular cells.

Test Yourself 2

In Figure A.7, how much stale popcorn, on average, did people eat from a large container? What was the mean and standard deviation of how much fresh popcorn people ate from a medium container?

Describing Relative Standing (z Scores)

So far, this appendix has covered, among other tools, frequency distributions, means, and standard deviations. If we combine some of these techniques, we can also describe where an individual score stands in relation to the whole batch of scores. A **z score** describes whether an individual's score is above or below the mean and how far it is from the mean, in standard deviation units.

Describing Relative Standing in Standard Deviation Units

Let's start with the exam scores we used to illustrate frequency distributions, in Figure A.1. Imagine that Max, who has a score of 20, wants to know how good his exam score was in relation to the scores of the rest of the class. Because we already know that the mean score was 26.16, we can tell Max that his score, 20, was 6.16 points below the mean.

But perhaps Max also wants to know whether 6.16 points was far below mean or just a little below the mean. We might answer Max's question by using standard deviation units of distance.

The standard deviation for this group of test scores was 4.59—meaning that on average scores were 4.59 points away from the mean. So now we can tell Max that his score was 6.16 points below the mean and that the standard deviation was 4.59. Therefore, Max's score was 1.34 standard deviation units below the mean. Now Max has learned that he did worse than average, by a fairly large margin. His score was more than one standard deviation below the mean.

Computing z Scores

To describe people's relative standing in standard deviation units, we compute z scores using the following formula:

$$z = \frac{(X - M)}{SD}$$

We start with the individual score, X, and subtract the mean from that score. Then we divide the difference by the standard deviation. When we follow the z score formula, any score below the mean (like Max's) will have a negative z score. Any score above the mean will have a positive z score. Any score that is directly at the mean will have a z score of zero.

Test Yourself 3

Can you compute the z score for Emma, who got a 29 on the same exam that Max took?

Using z Scores

One of the useful qualities of a z score is that it allows us to compare individual cases' relative standing on variables that might have been measured in different units. (For this reason, the z score is sometimes referred to as a *standardized score*.) Suppose, for example, that the first exam was a mid-semester exam with only 35 questions on it, and Max's score was 20. Now imagine that the final exam has 100 questions on it, and Max's score was 65. Was Max's score on the final, relative to those of his classmates, better than his relative score on the mid-semester exam? We could use z scores to find out.

If the mean score on the final was 80, with a standard deviation of 14 points, we can use this information to compute Max's z score on the final exam:

$$z = \frac{(65 - 80)}{14} = -1.07$$

Max's z score for the first exam was -1.34, and his z score for the final exam was -1.07. Both scores are below average, but his final exam score was closer to the mean than his first exam score. Therefore, Max's performance on the final was a little better, relatively, than his performance on the mid-semester test.

In this way, to describe the relative standing of the scores in a set, we can convert each score to a z score. The z score allows us to describe how far any individual's score on a variable is from the mean, in standard deviation units. In addition, if we convert each person's scores on two or more variables to z scores, we can meaningfully compare the relative standings of each person on those variables, even when the variables are measured in different units. For example, one variable might be height, measured in centimeters, and the other variable might be weight, measured in kilograms. If a person's z score for height is $z = 0.58$ and his z score for weight is $z = 0.00$, for example, we could conclude that he is above average in height but at the mean in weight (and as a result, we can infer that he is probably a rather thin person). Or perhaps one variable, such as a state's air temperature, is measured in degrees Fahrenheit, and the other variable, teen pregnancy rate, is measured as the number of pregnancies per 100,000 teens. The z scores can tell us whether a state is relatively warm or cool and whether its teen pregnancy rate is higher or lower than average.

Describing Associations Using Scatterplots or the Correlation Coefficient, r

Three previous chapters (Chapters 3, 5, and 7) introduced the logic of scatterplots and the correlation coefficient, r. We use scatterplots and r to describe the association between two variables that are measured in the same set of cases. For example, we might want to describe the association between 2-year-old height and adult height (an example used in Chapter 3; see Figure 3.6). Or we might want to describe the association between small talk and well-being (an example used in Chapter 7).

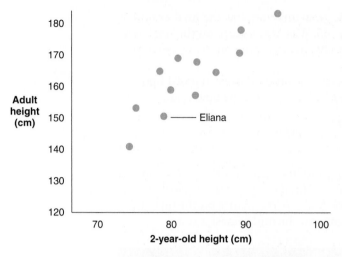

FIGURE A.8 **Scatterplot of adult height and 2-year-old height.**

Scatterplots

As discussed in previous chapters, one way to describe associations between two variables is to draw a scatterplot. To do so, we place one variable on the x-axis and one variable on the y-axis and plot each case as a dot on the scatterplot, placing the dot on the graph so that it represents the person's score on both variables.

Figure A.8 shows a hypothetical scatterplot for the association between 2-year-old height and adult height. The marked dot represents Eliana, one member of the group. The scatterplot shows that Eliana was fairly short at age 2 and is also fairly short as an adult. Other dots on the scatterplot represent other members of the group, showing their height at the two different ages.

Similarly, **Figure A.9** shows a scatterplot of the association between small talk and well-being, based on a study by Matthias Mehl and his colleagues (2010), which was introduced in Chapter 7. The black dot represents Rhoslyn, a person who does not engage in much small talk and who falls in the middle of the well-being scale. The other dots on that scatterplot represent other members of the batch, showing how much they engage in small talk and how high they rate on well-being.

By inspecting a scatterplot, we can describe two important aspects of an association: the *direction* of the relationship between two variables (positive, negative, or zero) and the *strength* of the positive or negative relationship (strong or weak).

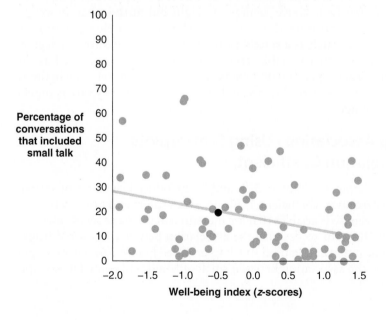

FIGURE A.9
Scatterplot of well-being and small talk.
Source: Adapted from Mehl and colleagues (2010).

Direction of Association: Positive, Negative, or Zero. In Figure A.8, notice that the cloud of points on the scatterplot slopes upward from left to right. The slope of the dots is positive—mathematically speaking, the line we would draw through the center of that cloud of points would have a positive slope. Because the slope is positive, we call the association between the two variables positive. In a positive association, high scores on one variable go with high scores on the other variable, and low scores on one variable go with low scores on the other variable. In a positive association, "high goes with high and low goes with low."

In contrast, in Figure A.9 notice that the cloud of points on the scatterplot slopes downward from left to right. Because the slope of the dots is negative—mathematically speaking, the line we would draw through the center of that cloud of points would have a negative slope—we call the association between the two variables negative. (Another name for a negative association is an *inverse* association.) In a negative association, high scores on one variable go with low scores on the other variable. In a negative association, "high goes with low and low goes with high."

Finally, we might draw a scatterplot like the one in **Figure A.10.** Here, the cloud of points does not slope clearly upward or downward. The slope of the dots is zero—mathematically speaking, the line we would draw through the center of that cloud of points would be flat, or have a zero slope. We therefore say that there is no association, or zero association.

Strength of Association. Looking at Figures A.8 and A.9, notice that the data points in Figure A.8 hang together closer to a straight line; in contrast, the data points in Figure A.9 are spread out wider. The spread of points in a scatterplot represents the relationship's *strength*. When the data points are closer to a straight line (either positive or negative in slope), we say that the association is strong. When the data points are spread out more along a positively or negatively sloped line, we say that the association is weak. Therefore, the data in Figure A.8 depict a strong, positive association, while the data in Figure A.9 depict a weak, negative association.

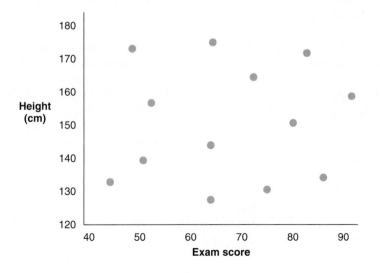

FIGURE A.10
Fictional scatterplot of test score and height.

Correlation Coefficient r

Usually, researchers do not describe associations using scatterplots. Instead, they describe the direction and strength of a relationship between two variables using the correlation coefficient r (introduced in Chapters 3, 5, and 7). The correlation coefficient r is a statistical computation that captures the direction and strength of a relationship. The value of r can range from -1.0, which represents the strongest possible negative correlation, to 1.0, which represents the strongest possible positive correlation. For example, the relationship depicted in Figure A.8 above is $r = 0.64$; the relationship depicted in Figure A.9 is $r = -0.33$.

The sign of r tells us the direction of the relationship. If r is positive (such as $r = 0.64$), the relationship between the two variables is positive. If r is negative (such as $r = -0.33$), the relationship between the two variables is negative. If r is zero, or very close to zero (such as $r = 0.02$), then the relationship between the two variables is essentially zero.

The magnitude of the absolute value of r tells us the strength of the relationship: If r is large (such as 0.64), the relationship between two variables is strong (the dots on the scatterplot would be closer together). If r is smaller (such as -0.33), the relationship between two variables is weaker (the dots on the scatterplot would be more spread out). The strength of a correlation is independent of its sign, so an r of -0.85 would represent a stronger correlation than an r of 0.35.

Computing r. The formula for computing the correlation coefficient r can be represented in many ways. But the simplest formula is

$$r = \frac{\sum z_x z_y}{N}$$

Let's break down this formula step by step. First, we have two variables per case (often that means two variables per person). **Table A.3** shows how we might carry out the steps in calculating r for a set of seven people. Notice that the first three columns of Table A.3 represent a data matrix for this data set—including one column for each variable (X and Y) and one row for each person. The three right-hand columns of the table show the computations for r. In the formula, the variables are labeled X and Y. If we are computing the correlation between 2-year-old height and adult height, for example, 2-year-old height would be variable X (column 2), and adult height would be variable Y (column 3).

The second thing the formula directs us to do is to convert each person's scores on X and Y to z scores, z_X and z_Y, using the formula for z from the previous section (page A10). If someone's 2-year-old height was above the mean, his or her z score (z_X) would be positive, but if someone's 2-year-old height was below the mean, his or her z score (z_X) would be negative (see columns 4 and 5 of Table A.3). The next step is to multiply these two z scores, z_X and z_Y, for each person (see column 6 of Table A.3). Next, we sum the products of the z scores and divide by the number of cases—in this example, seven people.

TABLE A.3 Computing r

(1) Person	(2) Score on X (2-year-old height, in cm)	(3) Score on Y (adult height, in cm)	(4) z_X (z score for 2-year-old height)	(5) z_Y (z score for adult height)	(6) $z_X z_Y$
Eliana	78	150	−1.00, or (78 − 83.3) / 5.3	−1.73, or (150 − 165.2) / 8.15	−1.73, or (−1.00 * − 1.73)
Ella	80	160	−0.62	−0.54	0.34
Eshaan	91	170	1.46	0.65	0.94
Ava	84	168	0.14	0.41	0.06
Annamaria	79	165	−0.81	−0.54	0.44
Oscar	90	175	1.27	1.24	1.58
Oliver	81	169	−0.43	0.53	−0.23
	$M = 83.3$	$M = 165.2$			$\Sigma z_X z_Y = 4.86$
	$SD = 5.3$	$SD = 8.15$			$\Sigma z_X z_Y / N = 0.64$
					$r = 0.64$

The Logic of the r Formula. It is worth reflecting on two aspects of the formula for r. First, notice that r can easily capture the association between adult height and 2-year-old height, even though the two variables have very different ranges of scores. That is, 2-year-old height ranges from 78 to 91 centimeters, but adult height ranges from 150 to 175 centimeters. However, the formula for r converts each height value to its z score first. That way, it does not matter that the two heights fall within very different ranges.

Second, think about what it means that r multiplies the two z scores for each person. Take Eliana, for example. Her height is below average at age 2 and below average at adulthood, so both of her z scores are negative. When we multiply them together, we get a positive number. Now consider Oscar, who is above average at age 2 and above average at adulthood. Both of his z scores are positive, so when we multiply them, we also get a positive number. In Table A.3, most of the products are positive, though some are negative. After adding up all these products and dividing by N, we get an r value of 0.64—a positive r, meaning that "high goes with high and low goes with low." That makes sense—people with high 2-year-old heights tend to have high adult heights, and people with low 2-year-old heights tend to have low adult heights.

In contrast, if the relationship between two variables is negative, high goes with low and low goes with high. In this situation, when we compute the r, positive z scores for one variable will tend to be multiplied with negative z scores for the other variable, so the products will be mostly negative. When we add up these negative products and divide by N, the result will be a negative number, or a negative r, meaning that "high goes with low and low goes with high."

Normally you will use computers to calculate r values. However, knowing the mathematics behind the formula for r can help you understand what r values represent.

Describing Effect Size

Because the value of r indicates the strength of the relationship between two variables, many researchers use r as a measure of *effect size*, a computation that describes the magnitude of a study's result. In fact, there are several measures of effect size, and the more you study statistics, the more effect size measures you will learn. But all measures of effect size are used for the same purpose: When a study has found a relationship between two variables, the effect size describes how weak or strong the relationship is. For example, when a study has found a difference between two groups, the effect size describes how large or small that difference is.

Take the example of Wansink and Kim (2005), who found that people ate more fresh popcorn out of large containers than they did out of medium-sized containers (see Figure A.7). If we were to ask about this study's effect size, we would ask how *much* more popcorn people ate from the large containers. Was it just a little more or a lot more? We are asking: Is the effect size large or small?

Describing Effect Size with Cohen's *d*

When a study involves group or condition means (such as the mean amount of popcorn consumed from a large bucket compared with the mean amount of popcorn consumed from a smaller bucket), we can describe the effect size in terms of how far apart the two means are, in standard deviation units. This will tell us not only how far apart the two group means are but also how much overlap there is between the two sets of scores. This commonly used effect size measure is called *d*, also known as **Cohen's *d*.**

For simplicity, we will focus on the results for the *fresh* popcorn condition in Wansink and Kim's study:

From the medium container, people ate a mean of 58.9 grams of popcorn, with a standard deviation of 16.7 grams.

From the large container, people ate a mean of 85.6 grams of popcorn, with a standard deviation of 19.8 grams.

If we want to know how far apart these two means are in standard deviation units, we use the following formula for d:

$$d = \frac{M_1 - M_2}{SD_{(pooled)}}$$

In this formula, the numerator is the mean of one group minus the mean of the other group. The denominator is the SD of these two groups, "pooled." The pooled SD is an average of the two standard deviations for the two groups. If the two groups are the same size, we can take a simple mean of the two standard deviations, but when the two groups are different sizes, we need to compute a weighted mean of the two standard deviations. That is, we weight the SD of the larger group more.[1]

---

[1] The general formula for a pooled SD is as follows, where n_1 and n_2 are the number of observations in the two groups, and SD_1^2 and SD_2^2 are the variances of each group.

$$SD_{(pooled)} = \sqrt{\frac{(n_1 - 1)SD_1^2 + (n_2 - 1)SD_2^2}{n_1 + n_2}}$$

If we apply this formula to Wansink and Kim's data, the numerator is simply the mean difference between the two groups (the large-bucket group and the medium-bucket group), or $58.9 - 85.6$. The denominator is the pooled SD, which, in this example, is 18.3. So, for the fresh popcorn condition, we would compute the effect size for bucket size as follows:

$$d = \frac{58.9 - 85.6}{18.3} = \frac{-26.7}{18.3} = -1.45$$

In other words, the effect size of the bucket manipulation is $d = 1.45$. (We can omit the negative sign when it is clear which group is higher than the other.)

Effect Size Conventions for Cohen's d. What does a d of 1.45 mean? It means that the average of the large-bucket group is 1.45 standard deviations higher than the average of the medium-bucket group. But is that large or small? One way to tell is to consult the conventions for interpreting effect size, such as those shown in **Table A.4**.

According to this table, the effect size in Wansink and Kim's study was very large—it was well above $d = 0.80$, which Cohen describes as "strong/large." Therefore, we can conclude that package size makes a large difference in the amount of popcorn people eat.

The effect size d could also be used to measure the difference between the red ink and green ink groups in Elliot and colleagues' study of ink color and anagram performance. As discussed in Chapter 9, Elliot and his colleagues manipulated the color in which an identification number was written on a test booklet and then measured how many anagrams people could solve. The effect size in that study was about $d = 0.64$—the mean of the red ink group and the mean of the green ink group were 0.64 of a standard deviation apart. According to Cohen's conventions, this represents a medium to large effect of ink color on performance.

Effect Size d and Group Overlap. Another way of looking at group-difference effect sizes such as d is to know that d represents the amount of overlap between two groups. Panels A and B of **Figure A.11** show how two groups might overlap at different effect sizes in our examples. The larger the effect size, the less overlap between the two experimental groups; the smaller the effect size, the more overlap. If the effect size is zero, there is full overlap between the two groups, as in Figure A.11.C.

TABLE A.4 Cohen's Conventions for Effect Size d. Is the Effect Size Weak, Moderate, or Strong?	
d	Strength of relationship
0.20	Weak/small
0.50	Moderate/medium
0.80	Strong/large

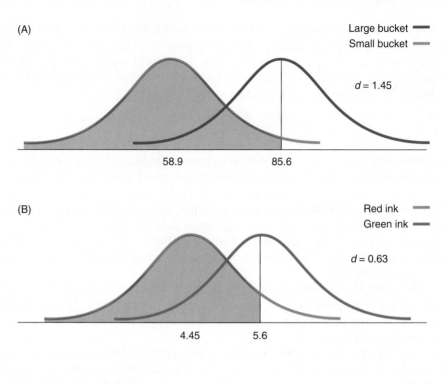

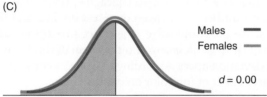

FIGURE A.11 The larger the effect size, the less overlap between the two experimental groups. (A) At an effect size of 1.45, 92% of the small-bucket group members in Wansink and Kim's study ate less popcorn than the average member of the large-bucket group. (B) At an effect size of 0.63, about 73% of the red-ink group members solved fewer anagrams than the average member of the green-ink group. (C) At an effect size of $d = 0.0$, there is full overlap between the two groups: the greatest possible overlap. That is, 50% of Group 1 members (males) fall below the average member of Group 2 (females).

r or *d*? Which Effect Size Measure Should You Use?

We usually use the effect size *r* to determine the strength of the relationship between two quantitative variables. We usually use the effect size *d* when one variable is categorical. The two measures of effect size, *r* and *d*, are based on different scales: *r* can only range between 1 and −1, but *d* can be higher than 1 or lower than −1. Therefore, the size conventions for *r* are different from those for *d* (see **Table A.5**). In psychology, if a study finds an *r* of 0.50 or higher, that relationship (that effect size) is considered to be strong. If the *r* is 0.10 or lower, that effect is considered small, or weak.

Other Effect Size Measures

As you read empirical journal articles, you may notice other indicators of effect size. One common effect size is Hedge's *g*. Hedge's *g* is very similar to *d*. Like *d*, it gives the distance between two means in standard deviation units, but it is computed with a different formula. The conventions for small, medium, and large for Hedge's *g* are the same as they are for Cohen's *d*.

TABLE A.5 Cohen's Conventions for Two Measures of Effect Size: *d* and *r*

d	Strength of relationship	*r*
0.20	Weak/small	0.10
0.50	Moderate/medium	0.30
0.80	Strong/large	0.50

Another effect size measure you might encounter is η^2, or "eta squared." This effect size may be used when researchers describe differences among several groups (that is, more than two means) or when they describe the effect sizes of interaction effects. There are no published size conventions for η^2.

Thinking About Effect Size

Effect Size and Importance. Chapters 7 and 9 explored the relationship between effect size and importance. Generally speaking, the larger an effect size is, the more important a result seems to be. However, the converse is not always true: A small effect size is not always an unimportant one. Chapter 7 introduced the example of a very small effect size ($r = 0.03$) for the relationship between taking aspirin and risk of heart attack. This small effect size, however, translates into a very real decrease in deaths in the study's aspirin treatment group. Therefore, small effect sizes are generally less important than large ones—but sometimes even small effect sizes are important and valuable. It depends on the theoretical and real-world context of the research.

Effect Sizes and Practical Numbers. Effect sizes can certainly help indicate whether a study's result is strong, moderate, or weak. But in some cases, we may not need to compute an effect size to assess the magnitude of some intervention. For example, Elliot's study on ink color found an effect size of $d = 0.63$. But we could have noted simply that people whose identification numbers were written in red solved 1.2 fewer anagrams (out of a possible 15), on average, than people whose identification numbers were written in green. In addition, for Wansink and Kim's study, instead of calculating the effect size, 1.45, we could have simply looked at the mean differences and found that people eating out of large buckets ate 26.7 more grams of popcorn (about one ounce), on average.

In these two examples, it is relatively easy to evaluate the strength of the manipulation's impact. Elliot's red ink color caused people to solve about 1.2 fewer anagrams. Wansink and Kim's large bucket caused people to eat 26.7 more grams of popcorn. (Depending on the fat content, that could contain as many as 140 calories.) These results may seem substantial and important enough to us—even without their effect size values.

Sometimes, however, we must rely on effect size values to put a result in perspective. Effect sizes are especially useful when we are not familiar with the scale on which a variable is measured. For example, imagine that we conduct an experiment in which we praise the appearance of one group and say something neutral to members of another group. Then we ask each group to take a self-esteem test whose scores can range from 1.0 to 5.0. We compute the two group means and find a mean of 4.10 ($SD = 1.46$) for the people whose appearance was praised and a mean of 3.58 ($SD = 1.5$) for the people who were not praised.

Because measures of self-esteem are abstract and subjective, it would be hard to put the difference between these two means into practical terms. Praising people's appearance seems to have made their scores on self-esteem increase about half of a point (0.52) on the 5-point self-esteem scale, so we might say that the two group means were about one-half of a "self-esteem unit" apart. But is a half-point difference on the self-esteem scale a large difference or a small one? Indeed, it is difficult to translate this self-report scale into a practical difference—it is not the same as counting correctly solved anagrams or grams of popcorn.

Now imagine that we compute the effect size, d, for the two groups and come up with $d = 0.35$. We know this means that the groups are about 0.35 of a standard deviation apart, and we know that this conventionally represents a medium effect size, so we have a somewhat better understanding of its magnitude. In isolation, of course, this might still not be very informative, so we might even compare the effect size to something else we know. For example, we might say that the effect size of praising someone's appearance on self-esteem is $d = 0.35$, but the effect size of praising someone's personal qualities is even larger, say $d = 0.45$ (these d values are fabricated for the purpose of illustration).

In addition, the effect size from one study can be compared to the effect size from another study—even a study using different variables. In one article, Brad Bushman and Craig Anderson (2001) were summarizing the evidence that violent media can cause aggressive behavior. They compared the average magnitude of the effect size for studies of the relationship between violent media and aggressive behavior, which is about $r = 0.31$ (obtained from a meta-analysis, described in Chapter 13), to studies of the impact of smoking on lung cancer, the effect of exposure to lead on IQ, and other effects whose scientific acceptance is more widely known among the general public (see **Figure A.12**). With the

Figure 2
Comparison of the Effect of Violent Media on Aggression With Effects From Other Domains

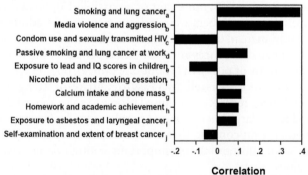

FIGURE A.12 Comparison of effect sizes. Effect sizes allow us to compare the magnitude of different studies—even ones that do not investigate the same interventions or risk factors. *Source:* Bushman and Anderson (2001).

Note. All correlations are significantly different from zero. a = the effect of smoking tobacco on lung cancer, as estimated by pooling the data from Figures 1 and 3 in Wynder and Graham's (1950) classic article. The remaining effects were estimated from meta-analyses: b = Paik and Comstock (1994); c = Weller (1993); d = Wells (1998); e = Needleman and Gatsonis (1990); f = Fiore, Smith, Jorenby, and Baker (1994); g = Weiten, Kemper, Past, and van Staveren (1995); h = Cooper (1989); i = Smith, Handley, and Wood (1990); j = Hill, White, Jolley, and Mapperson (1988).

studies lined up in such a way, the authors were able to make a more convincing argument that violent media constitute a public health risk.

TEST YOURSELF 1 The average force for men was 6.69. The average force for women was 4.73. Men had a slightly higher *SD* on this variable (2.05) than women (1.88).

TEST YOURSELF 2 On average, people ate 50.8 grams from a large container. The mean was 58.9 grams, with a standard deviation of 16.7 grams.

TEST YOURSELF 3 Emma's *z* score on the mid-semester test was 0.64. Her score is less than one standard deviation above the mean.

TEST YOURSELF 4 Emma's *z* score on the final was 1.0, so she did better on the final than she did on the first exam—relative to the rest of the class, at least.

Key Terms

bimodal, p. A4
central tendency, p. A4
Cohens *d*, p. A16
data matrix, p. A2
descriptive statistics, p. A1
frequency distribution, p. A2
frequency histogram, p. A3
mean, p. A5

median, p. A4
mode, p. A4
multimodal, p. A4
standard deviation, p. A6
stemplot, p. A3
variance, p. A6
z score, p. A10

Appendix B
Inferential Statistics

Appendix A provides some background on descriptive statistics, a set of tools for describing certain characteristics of a sample. This appendix introduces **inferential statistics**, a set of techniques that uses chance and probability to help researchers make decisions about what their data mean and what inferences they can make from it.

The Logic of Statistical Inference

Inferential statistical techniques are not so much a process of mathematics (although some basic algebra is involved) as a process of *logic*—a way of thinking through a logical set of steps. Inferential statistical thinking involves theories about how chance operates: What kinds of results can happen just by chance? How often do results like these happen just by chance? For example, imagine that we conduct a study in which we test a new drug for schizophrenia. This randomized, controlled study finds that the group taking the drug showed an improvement in symptoms. When we use inferential statistics, we follow a set of steps to decide whether the result from our study is "statistically significant." That is, we estimate the probability that we would get a similar result just by chance, even if the drug does not work.

Even though there are many statistical tests (this appendix covers *t* tests, *F* tests, correlations, and beta), all of them share the same underlying logical steps. Therefore, once you understand the process of inferential statistics, you can understand most other statistical tests, because they follow the same logic.

When researchers decide to investigate a phenomenon (such as whether the color red affects achievement or whether religiousness is related to depression), they do not test every possible individual to whom the phenomenon might apply. Instead, they conduct the study on a sample of individuals. Based on the results in that sample, they make an inference about what would happen if they tested the whole population.

Therefore, inferential statistics is (most commonly) the logical process of using data from a *sample*, whose characteristics are known, to make inferences about some *population*, whose characteristics are often unknown. We may never be able to study every person in a population. But we can use the tools of inferential statistics to make decisions about what the population's values probably are and about what our data really mean.

An Example

Here is a fictional story that illustrates the process of inferential statistics. Imagine that you encounter a woman named Sarah, who claims that in any crowd, she can pick out smart people—that is, she can identify people with high IQs. Her claim might seem a bit preposterous, so at first you are skeptical and assume she does not have this power. But you are open to testing Sarah's claim. As a psychology major, you know that across a large sample of people, IQ as it is usually measured has a mean of 100, with a standard deviation of 15, as depicted in **Figure B.1**. In addition, IQ is *normally distributed*, meaning that if you plot the IQ scores of a very large random sample on a frequency histogram, you will notice that about 68% of people fall between one standard deviation above and one standard deviation below the mean. About 14% of people fall between one and two standard deviations above the mean, and 14% of people fall between 1 and two standard deviations below the mean. Furthermore, 2% fall higher or lower than two standard deviations. Armed with this basic knowledge, you decide to put Sarah to the test.

You bring Sarah to a professional basketball stadium in your city. It is full of people from all walks of life, both smart and dull, and their IQs span the usual range—with an average of 100 and a standard deviation of 15. You ask Sarah to pick out a smart person. She looks around and chooses a woman in the 18th row. You take the woman to a private room and, after obtaining her permission, administer an IQ test with the help of a school psychologist. You find out that the woman's IQ is 115.

Are you convinced by this datum that Sarah has a special ability to detect smart people? Intuitively, you might think, "115 is a higher-than-average IQ, but it is not *that* much higher than average." So you may not be convinced that Sarah has special talents.

If you were to unpack this (correct) intuition, you would reason like this: Even if Sarah does not have special abilities, she could have selected a person

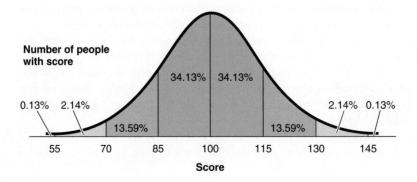

FIGURE B.1 A normal distribution of IQ scores, where *M* = 100 and *SD* = 15.

with an IQ of 115 or higher just by chance about 16% of the time. According to the normal distribution in Figure B.1, 16% of the people in the stadium should have an IQ score of 115 or higher. Sarah could have selected a person at random with an IQ that high or higher 16% of the time, even if she is not special in any way. And 16% seems too high to rule out the possibility that she just happened to choose a smarter-than-average person by chance.

Now let's imagine the scenario has produced a different result. Suppose you bring Sarah to the stadium and ask her to identify a smart person. This time, however, she identifies a person who, when tested, has an IQ of 130. Are you convinced now?

If you are thinking probabilistically, then you should find this second outcome much more convincing, because now there is a much smaller probability that Sarah could have guessed correctly just by chance. As Figure B.1 shows, only 2% of the people in the stadium are likely to have an IQ of 130 or higher. You can interpret this 2% as follows: If Sarah does not have special powers, she would have to be extremely lucky to have picked a person with an IQ that high or higher—only 2% of the time would she be so lucky. Of course, it could happen. But because the chance of her getting lucky is very low, you feel confident that she does, in fact, have a special ability to detect smart people. In other words, the assumption you started with—the skeptical assumption that Sarah cannot identify smart people—is probably wrong. (This example is adapted from Aron, 2009.)

Incidentally, Sarah's ability to identify intelligent people is actually not uncommon. An entire line of research on this phenomenon finds that most people are fairly accurate at judging certain traits, such as extraversion, agreeableness, and intelligence, just by looking at other people for a few seconds. This phenomenon is called *zero-acquaintance accuracy* (Borkenau & Liebler, 1993; Kenny & West, 2008).

The Steps of Inferential Statistics

The steps described in our example illustrate those taken by researchers when they use inferential statistics, also known as **statistical hypothesis testing**. Although there are a few forms of statistical hypothesis testing, **null hypothesis testing** is the most common form used today. To apply the steps of null hypothesis testing to the scenario in which Sarah chose a person with an IQ of 130, we would proceed as follows.

Step 1: Assume There Is No Effect (the Null Hypothesis)

When we tested Sarah's abilities, we started with the skeptical assumption that she was not able to identify smart people. In statistical hypothesis testing, this kind of starting assumption is known as a **null hypothesis**. *Null* means "nothing," and colloquially, a null hypothesis means "assume that nothing is going on." Depending on the research question, the null hypothesis can mean that a person does not have special abilities, that an independent variable does not have an effect on the dependent variable, or that two variables are not correlated with each other. A null hypothesis states that the data were generated just by chance, and this usually carries the meaning that just by chance, there would be no difference, no relationship, or no effect in our data.

Step 2: Collect Data

To test Sarah's ability to identify smart people, we asked her to demonstrate it by locating a smart person in the crowd. We then gave the person she chose an IQ test to see whether she was correct. That was the datum: She correctly identified a person with an IQ of 130.

Step 3: Calculate the Probability of Getting Such Data, or Even More Extreme Data, If the Null Hypothesis Is True

In this step, we calculated a probability: We used our knowledge of the normal distribution to compute the probability that Sarah could have chosen a person with an IQ of 130 or greater, just by chance, if the null hypothesis is true. That is, what is the probability that Sarah could have chosen a person this smart or smarter by chance if she is not in fact able to identify smart people?

In making the calculations, we used what we know about IQ—that it is normally distributed with a mean of 100 and a standard deviation of 15—to estimate what percentage of people in the stadium would have each range of IQ scores. We also used our understanding of chance. Combined, these two pieces of knowledge directed us to predict that if Sarah had chosen a person at random, she would have chosen a person with an IQ of 130 or higher about 2% of the time.

Step 4: Decide Whether to Reject or Retain the Null Hypothesis

In the fourth step, we made a decision based on the probability we obtained in Step 3. Since the probability of choosing a person with an IQ of 130 or higher just by chance is so small, we rejected our original assumption. That is, we rejected the null hypothesis that Sarah is not able to identify smart people.

The Decision to Reject the Null Hypothesis. The probability we obtained in Step 3 was so small that we rejected the null hypothesis assumption. In other words, we concluded that our data on Sarah's abilities were statistically significant.

When we reject the null hypothesis, we are essentially saying that

Data like these could have come about by chance,

but

Data like these happen very rarely by chance;

therefore

We are pretty sure the data were not the result of chance.

The Decision to Retain the Null Hypothesis. To clarify this decision, consider a situation in which we would retain the null hypothesis: the first scenario, in which Sarah identified a person with a score of 115. The probability that Sarah would identify a person who is at least that smart just by chance even if she is not special, is 16%, or 0.16. That probability seemed high enough that we would not reject our initial assumption that she is not able to detect smart people (the null hypothesis).

When we retain the null hypothesis, we are saying that

Data like these could have happened just by chance;

in fact

Data like these are likely to happen by chance 16% of the time;

therefore

We conclude that we are not confident enough, based on these data, to reject the null hypothesis.

Finally, at what probability level should we decide to reject the null hypothesis? Why did we reject the null hypothesis at $p = 0.02$ but not at $p = 0.16$? In psychology, the level that researchers typically use is 5% or less, or $p < 0.05$ (see **Table B.1**). This decision point is called the **alpha level**—the point at which researchers will decide whether the p is too high (and therefore will retain the null hypothesis) or very low (and therefore will reject the null hypothesis).

Samples, Populations, and Inference

The previous section outlined the four basic steps for drawing a conclusion based on statistical inference. The process involves using data from a sample (in the example, a sample of one of Sarah's guesses) to make an inference about the nature of a population (in this case, the population of all possible guesses Sarah

TABLE B.1 The Decision to Reject or Retain the Null Hypothesis

This term	Means the same as:	In other words:	You may see, in published work:	In a research context, may mean:
Rejecting the null hypothesis	The result is statistically significant.	The probability of getting a result this extreme, or more extreme, by chance, if the null hypothesis is true, is less than 5%.	$p < 0.05$ * (asterisk)	The difference is significantly larger than zero. The association is significantly stronger than zero.
Retaining the null hypothesis	The result is not statistically significant.	The probability of getting a result like this by chance, if the null hypothesis is true, is greater than or equal to 5%.	$p \geq 0.05$ n.s.	We cannot conclude that the difference is larger than zero. We cannot conclude that the relationship is stronger than zero.

could have made). In other words, we did not ask Sarah to demonstrate that she could classify every person in the basketball stadium as smart or not smart—that is, we did not collect data on the entire *population* of possible guesses in the stadium. Instead, we measured a *sample* of the population of guesses.

Almost all research studies a sample of some population. For example, when researchers conduct a political poll, they do not attempt to telephone every member of the voting population; instead, they select a sample of the voting population and make inferences about the voting population based on what the sample tells them. In the average experiment, researchers draw samples from populations such as monkeys, college students, or children in third grade. Often, these samples are not selected randomly, but they are still drawn from a population.

For details on sampling techniques, see Chapter 6, pp. 164-176.

Understanding Inference: Type I and Type II Errors

Recall that the process of statistical hypothesis testing requires us, in Step 4, to make a decision. We decide whether to reject the null hypothesis or to retain the null hypothesis. In the example of Sarah, if we reject the null hypothesis, we would conclude, based on this sample of data, that Sarah really is able to identify smart people. If we retain the null hypothesis, we would decide that we have insufficient evidence, based on this sample of data, to conclude that Sarah is able to identify smart people.

Because we are studying only a sample of Sarah's behavior, not the full population of her behavior, the decision we make about her abilities could be right, or it could be wrong. Therefore, when we follow the process of inferential statistics, there are two possible ways to be right and two possible ways to be wrong. These four possibilities come from the two decisions we might make, based on the sample, and the two possible states of affairs in the population.

Two Possible Correct Choices. There are two ways to make a correct decision: (1) We could conclude from the sample of behavior that Sarah has a special ability to identify smart people (reject the null hypothesis), and in truth, Sarah really does—so our conclusion is correct. (2) We could decide that we cannot confidently conclude that Sarah can identify smart people (retain the null hypothesis), and in truth, she really cannot. Again, our conclusion would be correct.

Two Possible Mistakes. There are also two ways to make an incorrect decision: (1) We could conclude that Sarah probably has special abilities, when she really does not. This kind of mistake is known as a **Type I error**, a "false positive." (2) We could conclude that Sarah probably does not have special abilities, when she really does. This kind of mistake is known as a **Type II error**, or a "miss" (see **Table B.2**).

Which Error Is Worse? In the research context, the two types of errors can lead to different types of problems. On the one hand, if we make a Type I error, we may conclude that we have found something interesting in our study, which could encourage other researchers or practitioners to follow a false lead. For example, we might conclude from a study that a particular drug is effective

TABLE B.2 Two Possible Errors and Two Possible Correct Conclusions from the Process of Statistical Inference

Decision based on the sample:	True nature of the population	
	There is really no effect in the population.	There is really an effect in the population.
Reject the null hypothesis (conclude that there is an effect).	Type I error	Correct conclusion
Retain the null hypothesis (conclude there is not enough evidence of an effect).	Correct conclusion	Type II error

Decision based on the sample:	True nature of Sarah's abilities	
	Sarah really cannot identify smart people.	Sarah really can identify smart people.
Reject the null hypothesis (conclude that Sarah is able to identify smart people).	Type I error: We conclude that Sarah is able to identify smart people, but she really is not.	Correct conclusion: We conclude that Sarah is able to identify smart people, and she really can.
Retain the null hypothesis (conclude that there is not enough evidence that Sarah is able to identify smart people).	Correct conclusion: We have not shown that Sarah is able to identify smart people, and she really does not have this ability.	Type II error: Sarah really is able to identify smart people, but we have failed to show it.

Decision based on the sample:	True nature of the drug	
	The drug does not improve schizophrenia symptoms.	The drug does improve schizophrenia symptoms.
Reject the null hypothesis (conclude that the drug does work).	Type I error: We conclude that the drug works, but it really does not.	Correct conclusion: We conclude that the drug works, and it really does.
Retain the null hypothesis (conclude that there is not sufficient evidence that the drug works).	Correct conclusion: We have not shown that the drug works, and it really does not work.	Type II error: The drug really does work, but we have failed to show it.

The first table shows the general case; the second and third tables repeat the information in terms of two examples.

against schizophrenia when it is not (a Type I error). This Type I error might be a costly mistake in terms of false hopes, unneeded side effects, or fruitless follow-up research.

On the other hand, we might conclude that a drug is not effective when it really is (a Type II error). This might be a costly mistake, too. Imagine that the new schizophrenia drug is, in fact, effective, but an early study incorrectly finds that it is not effective. These results could delay the availability of the drug to people who could benefit from it—or even prevent it from ever becoming available.

Deciding which error is more costly depends on the context. We might decide that it is important to be conservative—in which case avoiding Type I errors might be our priority. Especially if the schizophrenia drug is expensive or has troublesome side effects, we may not want to conclude that it works when it actually does not (that is, we do not want to make a Type I error). We may not want to spend the money or make people endure side effects by prescribing a drug that is useless. To be conservative in this way, we would design our study to minimize the probability of making a Type I error.

In other situations, we might decide that we do not want to overlook an effect that is really there, so our priority would be to avoid Type II errors (that is, to be sure to reject the null hypothesis if in fact it is false). We might decide that if the drug for schizophrenia really does work, we want to be able to detect that. Perhaps the disease we are treating is particularly desperate and there are no other cures. Or perhaps we are running the first study on a research question, and we want to find the effect if it is really there; if there is an effect, we do not want to miss it, because we are thinking about investing time in a promising research direction. In such cases, we want to reduce the chances of missing something important, so we design our study to reduce the probability of making a Type II error.

Finally, no matter how we design our study, there is always the possibility that no matter what we conclude, we might make an error, because the true relationship, true difference, or true state of affairs in the population is often unknowable. Our schizophrenia drug either has an effect or does not—but because we cannot evaluate the entire population of people who might use this drug, we will never know. However, we can choose the probability that we will make a Type I error, and we can estimate the probability of making a Type II error. We can design studies in order to minimize these probabilities.

Preventing Type I Errors

Only one aspect of a study affects our likelihood of making a Type I error: the level of probability (or p) at which we decide whether or not to reject the null hypothesis. As mentioned earlier, that decision point is called the *alpha level*. Researchers set the alpha level for a study in advance. They decide in advance that if the probability of their result happening just by chance (assuming the null hypothesis is true) is *less* than alpha, they will reject the null hypothesis. If the probability of their result happening just by chance (assuming the null hypothesis is true) is *greater* than alpha, they will retain the null hypothesis. In psychology, the convention is to set the alpha level at 5%, or alpha = 0.05.

To understand alpha level better, recall how we evaluated Sarah's abilities. In doing so, we used the conventional alpha level of alpha = 0.05. When Sarah identified a person with a 115 IQ, we knew that the probability of her doing so by chance was $p = 0.16$ even if she was not really able to identify smart people. Because that probability was "high"—higher than 0.05—it seemed too high for us to conclude that Sarah did not make a lucky guess this time. In other words, because the probability of the result turned out to be higher than 0.05, we retained the null hypothesis. In contrast, when Sarah identified someone with an IQ of 130, we knew that the probability of her doing so by chance, even if she has no skill, was 0.02. Because that probability was "low"—less than 0.05—we assumed that she probably did not identify that person by chance, and therefore we rejected the null hypothesis.

Alpha Is the Type I Error Rate. The alpha we set in advance is also the probability of making a Type I error if the null hypothesis is true. Returning to our example, when we computed that the probability of Sarah choosing someone with a 130 IQ by chance was 0.02 (if the null hypothesis is really true), we rejected the null hypothesis. However, it is still possible that Sarah does not have special abilities and that she simply got lucky this time. In this case, we would have drawn the wrong conclusion.

When we set alpha in advance at alpha = 0.05, we are admitting that 5% of the time, when the null hypothesis is true, we will end up rejecting the null hypothesis anyway. Because we know how chance works, we know that if we asked someone who has no special abilities to select 100 people in the stadium at random, 5% of them will have an IQ of 125 or higher (the IQ score associated with the top 5% of people). However, we are admitting that we are comfortable with the possibility that we will make this particular mistake—a Type I error—5% of the time when the null hypothesis is true.

Alpha Conventions. Even though alpha level is conventionally set at alpha = 0.05, researchers can set it at whatever they want it to be, depending on the priorities of their research. If they prioritize being conservative, the researchers will set alpha lower than 5%—perhaps at 1%, or 0.01. By setting alpha lower, they are trying to minimize the chances of making a Type I error—of accidentally concluding that there is a true effect or relationship when there actually is none.

In contrast, there may be situations in which researchers choose to set alpha higher—say, at alpha = 0.10. In this case, the researchers would be comfortable making false conclusions 10% of the time if, in truth, there is no effect. By setting alpha higher, they are also increasing the probability of making a Type I error. Researchers may wish to set alpha higher as one of the strategies to avoid missing an effect of a drug or intervention—that is, to avoid a Type II error, as explained in the next section.

Preventing Type II Errors (Power, Effect Size, and Alpha)

Whereas preventing a Type I error involves only one factor (alpha level), preventing a Type II error depends on a set of factors, collectively known as **power**. Formally defined, *power* is the probability of not making a Type II error when the null hypothesis is false. In positive terms, it is the probability that a researcher will be able to reject the null hypothesis if it should be rejected (that is, if there is really some effect in the population). If we are testing a schizophrenia drug that, in truth, does reduce the symptoms of schizophrenia, then power refers to how likely a study is to detect that effect by finding a significant result.

The following analogy might help you understand Type II errors. Imagine that the electricity goes out in your house, and all the rooms are dark. You think you left something important in the bedroom, so you go upstairs with a flashlight and shine the light around the room. Assuming that the object is really there, can you find it?

If, in truth, the object is in the room, two things could happen. First, you might find the object with your flashlight. Finding the object is analogous to making a correct research decision: You have rejected the null hypothesis (so in effect, you have decided, "The object is in this room"), and indeed, the object is there. Second, you might *not* find the object with your flashlight. Failing to find the object is analogous to making a Type II error: You have retained the null hypothesis (you retained the assumption that the object is not in the room, implying "The object is not here"). Power is about the first case, being able to detect the object when it is really there.

In this example, one factor that will help you detect the missing object is to have a good, strong flashlight. If the flashlight puts out a lot of light, you will be able to find the object in the room much more easily. But if the flashlight's batteries are running low and its beam is weak, you might not see the object—and you might erroneously conclude that it is not in the room when in fact it is there. That would be a Type II error.

Another factor that influences the Type II error rate is the size of the object. If you are looking for something large (your pet elephant, perhaps), you will probably find it, even if the flashlight is very weak. However, if you are looking for something very small (a lost earring), you may not detect it—even if the flashlight is bright.

Similarly, when researchers predict the chance of making a Type II error, they consider several factors simultaneously. The alpha level, the sample size, the effect size, the degree of variability in the sample, and the appropriate statistical test all have an impact on the power of a study.

Alpha Level. Alpha level is the first factor that influences the Type II error rate. Alpha (usually set at alpha = 0.05) is the point at which researchers decide whether or not to reject the null hypothesis. When researchers set alpha lower in a study (say, at 0.01), it will be more difficult for them to reject the null hypothesis. But if it is harder to reject the null hypothesis, it is also more likely that they will *retain* the null hypothesis even if it deserves to be rejected. Therefore, when researchers set the alpha level low (usually to avoid Type I errors), they increase the chances of making a Type II error. In this one sense, Type I and Type II errors compete: As the chance of Type I errors goes down, the chance of Type II errors goes up.

Because of this competition between Type I and Type II errors, alpha levels are conventionally set at 0.05. According to most researchers, this level is low enough to keep Type I error rates in control but high enough that they can still find a significant result (keeping Type II error rates down).

Sample Size. A second determinant of power is the sample size used in a study. All else being equal, a study that has a larger sample will have more power to reject the null hypothesis if there really is an effect in the population. A large sample is analogous to carrying a big, powerful flashlight, and a small sample is analogous to carrying a candle. The big flashlight will enable you to find what you are looking for more easily than the candle. If you carry a candle, you might mistakenly conclude that your missing object is not in the dark room when it really is (a Type II error). Similarly, if a drug really improves the symptoms of schizophrenia in the population, we are more likely to detect that effect in a study with a larger sample than with a smaller sample. (You will see how sample size works mathematically later in this appendix.)

Effect Size. A third factor is the size of the effect in the population. All else being equal, when there is a large effect size in the population, there is a greater chance of conducting a study that rejects the null hypothesis. As an analogy, no matter what kind of light you use, you are much more likely to find an elephant than an earring. Elephants are just easier to see. Similarly, if, in the population, a drug has a large effect on schizophrenia symptoms, we would be likely to detect that effect easily, even if we used a small sample and a low alpha level. But if the drug has a small effect on schizophrenia symptoms in the population, we are less likely to find it easily, and we might miss it in our sample. When there is a small effect size in the population, Type II errors are more likely to occur.

Sample Size and Effect Size. It is a common misconception that a study should have the largest sample size possible. Say you come across a study that found a significant result but had a very small sample size—only 10 participants. Should the researchers conducting this study have used twice as many participants? Or maybe 50 more?

In fact, sample size and effect size interact. Large samples are necessary *only* when researchers are trying to detect a small effect size. In contrast, if they are trying to detect a large effect size, a small sample may be all that is necessary. Think again about the lost object analogy. If, on the one hand, you are looking for a lost elephant, you can find it easily, even if you only have a small candle in the dark room. If the elephant is there (like a large effect size), your candle (like a small sample) is all you need to detect him. (Of course, you would also find him with a powerful flashlight, but all you need is the candle.) On the other hand, if you are looking for a lost earring, you may not be able to find it with the small candle, which is not powerful enough to illuminate the darkest corners. You need a big flashlight (like a large sample) to be sure to find the earring (like a small effect size) that is there.

Therefore, the smaller the effect size in the population, the larger the sample needed to reject the null hypothesis (and therefore to avoid a Type II error). But as the effect size in the population gets larger, researchers can get away with a smaller sample and still detect it.

Degree of Unsystematic Variability. A fourth factor that affects the Type II error rate is the amount of unsystematic variability in a sample's data. All else being equal, when a study's design introduces more unsystematic variability into the results, researchers have less power to detect effects that are really there. Unsystematic variability in the data prevents researchers from seeing a clear effect resulting from their experimental manipulation.

See Chapter 10 for more on systematic and unsystematic variability and how a study's design can reduce unsystematic variability.

Three sources of unsystematic variability are measurement error, individual differences, and situation noise. Measurement error occurs when the variables are measured with a less precise instrument or with less careful coding. Individual differences among study participants can also obscure the difference between two groups and thus reduce power. Using a repeated-measures design in an experiment reduces the impact of individual differences and improves the study's power. Situation noise can reduce power by adding extraneous sources of variability into the results. Researchers can conduct experiments and studies in controlled conditions to avoid such situation noise.

Statistical Choices. A fifth aspect of power involves the statistical choices the researcher makes. A researcher selects a statistical test (such as a sign test, a chi square test, a *t* test, an *F* test, analysis of covariance, or multiple regression) to compute the results from a sample of data. Some of these tests make it more difficult to find significant results and thus increase the chance of Type II errors. Researchers must carefully decide which statistical test is appropriate. (Some of the commonly used statistical tests are explained in the next section of this appendix.)

Another statistical choice that affects power is the decision to use a "one-tailed" versus a "two-tailed" test. The choice is related to the researcher's hypothesis. For example, if we are only interested in finding out whether the schizophrenia drug significantly *improves* symptoms, we use a one-tailed test. But if we are interested in finding out whether the schizophrenia drug significantly improves *or* significantly worsens symptoms, we use a two-tailed test. In general, a one-tailed test is more powerful than a two-tailed test when we have a good idea about the direction in which the effect will occur.

In summary, power is the probability of not making a Type II error: It is the probability that a researcher will be able to reject the null hypothesis if it deserves to be rejected. Researchers have more power to detect an effect in a population if:

1. They select a larger (that is, less stringent) alpha level.
2. The effect size in the population is large rather than small.
3. The sample size is large rather than small.
4. The data have lower levels of variability.
5. They use the most appropriate statistical test.

Common Inferential Techniques in Psychology

There are dozens of statistical tests. Researchers use different tests depending on whether they are testing frequency, association, or causal claims. They also use different tests depending on whether the variables are categorical (such as sex or political party affiliation), numeric (such as test grade or height), or a combination of the two.

This section describes four of the inferential tests commonly used in psychology research, all of which follow the same set of four logical steps outlined earlier. (A full-length statistics book will provide more detail on these and other statistical tests.)

Is That Difference Significant? the *t* Test

One common inferential test is the *t* test for independent groups. This inferential device allows researchers to test whether the difference between two group means in an independent-groups design is statistically significant. For example, in a study by Bargh, Chen, and Burrows (1996), introduced in Chapter 13, students were asked to complete one of two sets of puzzles. The researchers were investigating whether semantic priming of a stereotype could affect people's behavior as well as their cognitions and emotions. One group of 15 students worked on puzzles whose answers were associated with stereotypes for elderly people (words such as *forgetful, old, gray, wise, careful*). The other group of 15 students worked on puzzles whose answers were neutral (words such as *thirsty, clean, private*). After the students worked on the puzzles, the researchers timed how long it took each student to walk to the elevator at the end of the experiment.

Bargh and colleagues found the following results:

Mean walking time for students in the elderly puzzle group: 8.28 seconds
Mean walking time for students in the neutral puzzle group: 7.30 seconds

To conduct inferential statistics for this study, we would ask whether these two means, 8.28 and 7.30, are significantly different from each other. In other words, what is the probability that this difference, or an even larger one, could have been obtained by chance alone, even if there's no difference?

Stating the Null Hypothesis (Step 1)

We would begin by stating the null hypothesis for Bargh and colleagues' study. Here, the null hypothesis would be that there is no difference between the mean of the elderly puzzle group and the mean of the neutral puzzle group.

Computation of the *t* Test for Independent Groups (Step 2)

The next step is to organize the data and decide which test to use. The appropriate inferential test to use in this case is the *t* test for independent groups. The *t* test helps us estimate whether the difference in scores between two samples is significantly greater than zero.

As discussed in the section on effect size in Appendix A, two features of the data influence the distance between two means. One is the difference *between* the two means themselves, and the other is how much variability there is *within* each group. The *t* test is a ratio of these two values. The numerator of the *t* test is the simple difference between the means of the two groups: Mean 1 minus Mean 2. The denominator of the *t* test contains information about the variance within each of the two means, as well as the number of cases (n) that make up each of the means. Here is the formula:

$$t = \frac{M_1 - M_2}{\sqrt{\left(\dfrac{SD_1^2}{n_1} + \dfrac{SD_2^2}{n_2}\right)}}$$

As you can see, t will be larger if the difference between M_1 and M_2 is larger. The value of t will also be larger if the SD^2 (variance) for each mean is smaller. The less the two groups overlap—either because their means are farther apart or because there is less variability within each group—the larger the value of t will be. Sample size (n) also influences t. All else being equal, if n is larger, then the denominator of the t formula becomes smaller, making t larger.

Bargh and colleagues obtained a t value from their study of 2.86. Once we know this t value, we must decide whether it is statistically significant (Step 3).

Calculating the Probability of the Result, or One Even More Extreme, If the Null Hypothesis Is True (Step 3)

In Step 3, we calculate the probability of getting this result, or a result even more extreme, if the null hypothesis is true. To do so, we compare the t value from our sample of data to the types of t values we are likely to get if the null hypothesis is true.

By far the most common way to estimate this probability is to use a **sampling distribution** of t. This method estimates the probability of obtaining the t we got, just by chance, from a null-hypothesis population.

Sampling Distribution of t. To start, it helps to know that we never actually create a sampling distribution; however, we can estimate what its properties will be. To do so, we theorize about what values of t we would get if the null hypothesis is true in the population. If we were to run the study many, many times, drawing different random samples from this same null-hypothesis population, what values of t would we get? Most of the time, we should find only a small difference in the means, so t would be close to zero most of the time (that is, the numerator of the t test would be close to zero, making t close to zero). Therefore, the average of the t values should be around 0.00. Half of the time, just by chance, t might be a little higher than 0.00. And just by chance, half the time, t might be a little lower than 0.00. Sometimes, we might even get a t that is *much* higher or lower than 0.00. Thus, when the null hypothesis is true, we will still get a variety of values of t, but they will average around zero.

Sampling distributions of t are always centered at zero, because they are always created based on the assumption that the null hypothesis is true. But the width of the sampling distribution of t will depend on the sample size (that is, the sample size of the study that we hypothetically run many times). As shown in **Figure B.2**, when the sample size in our study is small, the sampling distribution will be wider and will result in more values at the extremes. This occurs in part because a small sample is more likely, just by chance, to obtain t values that are far from the mean because of sampling error. In contrast, in a large sample, the sampling distribution will be thinner.

Sampling distributions are created based on sample size, but they do not use sample sizes directly; instead, they use a slightly smaller number called *degrees*

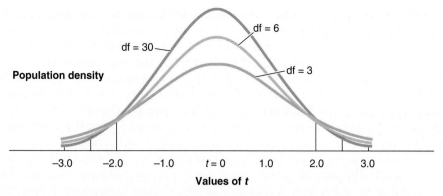

FIGURE B.2 **Sampling distributions of t for small samples (degrees of freedom = 3 and 6) and large samples (degrees of freedom = 30 or larger).** As the sample size increases, the t distribution gets thinner and approximates a normal distribution.

of freedom. A full-length statistics book will tell you more about this value. In the present example, the degrees of freedom are computed from the number of people in the first group, minus 1, plus the number of people in the second group, minus 1: $(15 - 1) + (15 - 1) = 28$. The sampling distribution of t for the example from Bargh and colleagues (1996) would look like **Figure B.3**.

This sampling distribution of t tells us what values of t we would be likely to get if the null hypothesis is true. In addition, this figure tells us that occasionally it is possible (but very rare) to get t values of 1.8, 2.0, or even larger, just by chance.

Using the Sampling Distribution to Evaluate Significance, or p. Why did we go to the trouble of estimating that sampling distribution anyway? Doing so helps us complete Step 3 of the null hypothesis testing process: Now that we have derived the sampling distribution, we can use it to evaluate the probability of getting the t obtained in Bargh and colleagues' study (2.86), or an even more extreme value of t, if the null hypothesis is true in the population.

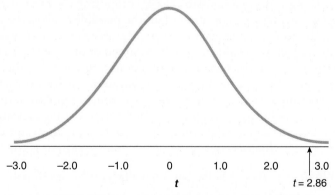

FIGURE B.3 **The sampling distribution of t for degrees of freedom of 28.** If the null hypothesis is true and we ran a study many times with a same number of people, these are the values of t we would expect. The average is zero; half of the t values are above zero, and half of them are below zero. The t obtained in Bargh and colleagues' study, 2.86, is marked with the small black line.

One way to determine this probability is to find where our obtained t falls on the x-axis of the sampling distribution. Then we use calculus to determine the area under the curve from that point outward, which gives us the probability of obtaining a t as large as, or larger than, 2.86 when the null hypothesis is true. Researchers typically compute this probability using a computer program, such as SPSS/PASW, STATA, or SYSTAT. The p that the computer reports is the exact probability of getting a t that extreme or more extreme if the null hypothesis is true. In Bargh and colleagues' case, the computer reported that the probability of obtaining a t value of 2.86, with 28 degrees of freedom, is exactly 0.0079.

Another way to determine the probability of a particular t value is to use the table in Appendix F. This table shows the probability of obtaining different values of t for different degrees of freedom. A critical t table like the one in Appendix F does not give the exact area under the curve, as the computer can do. However, using that table, we can look up the **critical value** of t—that is, the t value that is associated with our alpha level. For example, in Appendix F, we can look up the critical t value associated with a 0.05 alpha level and 28 degrees of freedom: 2.05. (As an analogy, this is like establishing that the IQ score associated with the 0.05 alpha level was 125.) The critical value of t means that in a sampling distribution of t based on 28 degrees of freedom, we would get a t of 2.05 or higher 5% of the time, just by chance. In Step 4, we will compare the critical value of t to the t we actually obtained, 2.86.

Using Randomization Tests to Evaluate Significance. To evaluate the probability of getting our results by chance if the null hypothesis is true, we could use a sampling distribution, as explained earlier, in which we evaluate the chances of randomly sampling the t we got from a null-hypothesis population, using either a computer or a critical values table. However, a different way to estimate the power of chance is by conducting a randomization test (Edgington & Onghena, 2007). In a randomization test, researchers use a computer to determine all of the possible ways the study could have come out (all possible permutations) if only chance were operating. For Bargh and colleagues' study, the computer would take the 30 scores actually obtained in the study and randomly assign them to the two groups in all possible ways, computing the t test after each permutation. This creates a distribution of all the possible t values the researchers could get in the study, just by chance. Using this distribution, they can see how often they would get the t value that they obtained or one more extreme, just by chance. Randomization tests are much less commonly used, but they are in fact more appropriate than the method of using sampling distributions when samples in an experiment are not drawn randomly from a population (Bear, 1995). However, both methods—sampling distributions and randomization tests—allow researchers to estimate the probability of obtaining the t value they got, or a larger one, if only chance is operating (if the null hypothesis is true).

Deciding Whether to Reject or Retain the Null Hypothesis (Step 4)

Now we are ready for Step 4 of the hypothesis-testing process. Again, according to the computer, the probability of Bargh and colleagues obtaining the t of 2.86 in a study with 30 people was $p = 0.0079$. This p is much smaller than the conventional alpha level of 0.05, so we reject the null hypothesis and conclude that the difference between the two puzzle groups is statistically significant.

In other words, we said:

It is possible to get a *t* of 2.86 just by chance,

but

The probability of getting a *t* of that size (or larger) is very small—only 0.0079;

therefore

We assume that the difference between the two means did not happen just by chance.

When we use a table of critical values of *t* such as in Appendix F, we compare the *t* we obtained to the critical value of *t* we looked up. Because the *t* we obtained (2.86) is greater than the critical *t* associated with the alpha level of 0.05 (2.05), we conclude that the result is statistically significant. Because our *t* is even more extreme than the *t* associated with the 0.05 alpha level, we can reject the null hypothesis. This means that the probability of getting the *t* we got is something less than 0.05 if the null hypothesis is true.

Notice that the two methods—the computer-derived probability and the critical value method—lead to the same conclusion from different directions. When using the computer's estimate of probability, we decide whether or not the computer's estimate of *p* is *smaller* than our alpha level of 0.05. In contrast, when we use the critical values table, we are assessing whether our obtained *t* is *larger* than the critical value of *t*. *Larger* values of *t* are associated with *smaller* probabilities.

Is That Difference Significant? The *F* Test (or ANOVA)

The *t* test is the appropriate test for evaluating whether two group means are significantly different, but when a study compares two *or more* groups to each other, the appropriate test is the *F* test, obtained from an analysis of variance, or ANOVA.

Another study conducted by Bargh, Chen, and Burrows (1996) provides an example of research for which the *F* test is appropriate. Again, the researchers were testing the hypothesis that semantic primes of stereotypes can affect people's behavior. There were two stages in the study. In the first stage, three groups of students each worked on word puzzles. One group worked on puzzles that primed the concept of rudeness (words such as *aggressively, bold, rude, bother, disturb*). A second group worked on puzzles that primed the concept of politeness (words such as *appreciate, honor, respect, cordially, behaved*). A third group worked on puzzles that were neutral (words such as *exercising, rapidly, send*). In the second stage, the participants were placed in a situation in which they needed to get the attention of the experimenter, who was having a long, staged conversation with another person. Bargh, Chen, and Burrows measured how long it took each participant to interrupt the experimenter.

The researchers obtained three group means (representing the average time it took each group to interrupt the conversation):

Mean of rude puzzle group: 326 seconds
Mean of neutral puzzle group: 519 seconds
Mean of polite puzzle group: 558 seconds

To conduct inferential statistics for this study, we need to ask whether these three means, 326, 519, and 558, are significantly different from one another. Could this difference plausibly have been obtained just by chance? The authors used an F test, or ANOVA, to find out.

The F test helps us decide whether the differences among the three groups are statistically significant. Just as with the t test, two sources of variability will influence the distances between these three groups. One is the variability *between* the three means themselves. The other is how much variability there is *within* each of the groups. Like t, the F test is a ratio of these two values. The numerator contains the value representing the variability between the means, and the denominator contains the value representing the variability within the groups.

The computations of the F ratio are not that complicated, but they are also beyond the scope of this appendix. In brief, when the F ratio is large, it means that there is more variability between the groups than there is within the groups; that is, the groups' scores are far apart and do not overlap much. When the F ratio is small, it means that there is about the same (or even less) variability between the groups than there is within the groups—that is, the groups overlap more.

Next let's walk through how we would use an ANOVA in the example.

Stating the Null Hypothesis (Step 1)

To go through the hypothesis-testing steps for Bargh, Chen, and Burrows's second study, which compared rudeness cues, politeness cues, and neutral cues, we would start by assuming the null hypothesis. In this case, we assume that there is no difference among the three groups (Step 1). In other words, the null hypothesis is that the difference between the means of the groups will be zero—all possible differences among the three means result in zero.

Computation of the F Ratio (Step 2)

Next, we would calculate the F ratio for the study (Step 2). In their article, the researchers reported that they obtained an F value of 5.76 for their results. We will not discuss the computations here, but this means that the variability between the three means was 5.76 times larger than the variability within the three means. That sounds like a large ratio. But is it statistically significant?

Calculating the Probability of the F Value We Obtained, or an Even Larger Value, If the Null Hypothesis Is True (Step 3)

Next, we compare the F we obtained in Step 2 to a sampling distribution of F values, similar to the way we did for the t value.

Samplng Distribution of F. We derive the sampling distribution of F by assuming that the null hypothesis is true in the population and then imagining that we run the study many more times, drawing different samples from that null-hypothesis population. If we use the same design and run the study again and again, what values of F would we expect from such a population if the null hypothesis is true?

If there is no difference between means in the population, then most of the time the variance between the groups will be about the same as the variance within the groups. When these two variances are about the same, the F ratio will be close to 1 most of the time. Therefore, the sampling distribution of F is centered on 1.0—most of the F values we get from the null-hypothesis population will be close to 1.0.

The sampling distribution of F is not symmetrical (see **Figure B.4**). While it is possible to get an F that is lower than 1 (for example, when the between-groups variance is smaller than the within-groups variance), it is not possible to get an F that is less than zero. Zero is the lowest that F can be. However, F can be very large sometimes, such as when the between-groups variance is much larger than the within-groups variance.

Just like t, the sampling distribution of F will take on slightly different shapes, depending on the degrees of freedom for F. The degrees of freedom for the sampling distribution of F contain two values. The degrees of freedom value for the numerator (that is, for the between-groups variance) is the number of groups minus 1 (in this example, $3 - 1$, or 2). The degrees of freedom value for the denominator (that is, for the within-groups variance) is computed from the number of participants in the study, minus the number of groups. (So if there were 36 students in Bargh and colleagues' study, or 12 in each group, the degrees of freedom would be $36 - 3 = 33$.)

By deriving the sampling distribution, a computer program will calculate the probability of getting the F we got, or one more extreme, if the null hypothesis is true. The larger the F we obtained, the less likely it is to have happened just by chance if the null hypothesis is true. In Bargh and colleague's case, the computer reported that value to be $p = 0.008$. This means that if the null hypothesis is true, we could get an F value of 5.76 only 0.8% of the time, just by chance.

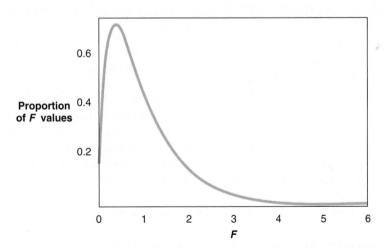

FIGURE B.4 A sampling distribution of F. The sampling distribution of F is centered on 1.0 and is not symmetrical. If the null hypothesis is true, most of the F values would be close to 1.0. The F value cannot be lower than zero, but it can be infinitely large. The exact shape of the F distribution will differ slightly, depending on the degrees of freedom.

Usually we use a computer to tell us the exact probability of getting the F we got if the null hypothesis is true. But if a computer is not available, we would use a table like the one in Appendix G to look up the critical value of F. The critical value of F is the F value associated with our alpha level. According to Appendix G, the critical value of F at 2 and 33 degrees of freedom is 3.28. This means that if we ran the study many times, we would get an F of 3.28 or higher 5% of the time when the null hypothesis is true.

In step 4, we will compare this critical value (3.28) to the one we obtained in our study (5.76).

Deciding Whether to Reject or Retain the Null Hypothesis (Step 4)

We are now at Step 4. When we use the computer, we simply compare the computer's estimated p value, $p = 0.008$, to the conventional alpha level of 0.05. In this case, we will reject the null hypothesis and conclude that there is a significant difference among the means of the three groups in Bargh, Chen, and Burrows's study.

If we used the critical values table, we would compare the value we obtained, 5.76, to the critical value we looked up, 3.28. Because the F we obtained is even *larger* than the critical value, we can also reject the null hypothesis and conclude that there is a significant difference among the means of the three groups in Bargh, Chen, and Burrows's study.

Just as with the t test, the two decision techniques lead to the same conclusion from different directions. When we use the computer's estimate of probability, we are assessing whether the computer's estimate of p is *smaller* than our alpha level of 0.05. But because larger F values are associated with smaller probabilities, when we use the critical values table, we are assessing whether our obtained F is *larger* than the critical value of F.

Is That Correlation Significant? Inferential Statistics with r

Chapter 7 and Appendix A both discussed the correlation coefficient r in detail. The correlation coefficient is considered a descriptive test because it describes the direction and strength of a relationship between two numeric variables.

In addition to using r to describe an association, we can also evaluate the statistical significance of a correlation coefficient. As with t and F, we follow the steps of null hypothesis testing: We assume that there is no relationship in the population (Step 1). We collect some data and calculate r (Step 2). We estimate the probability of getting the r we got, or one more extreme, if the null hypothesis is true (Step 3). We decide whether to reject or retain the null hypothesis (Step 4). When we reject the null hypothesis, we are concluding that the relationship (the r) we observed in our sample is statistically significant—in other words, that r we obtained is unlikely to occur just by chance in a null-hypothesis population.

Sampling Distribution of r

Just as t and F had sampling distributions, so does the correlation coefficient. The sampling distribution of r is developed to show the probable values of r we would get if we ran the study many times on random samples from a population in which the null hypothesis is true. If the null hypothesis is true, most of the values of r would be around 0.00. Some would be greater than 0.00, and some would be less than 0.00, but they would average at (or near) 0.00. If the null hypothesis is true and there is a large sample (greater than 30), then the sampling distribution of r is shaped very much like the t distribution. It is centered on zero, and it varies in width depending on degrees of freedom—that is, the number of cases in the sample.

The larger our study's r is (the closer it gets to 1.0 or -1.0), the less likely it becomes that we would get that value, just by chance, if the null hypothesis is true. (Therefore, the larger r is, the more likely it will be that r is statistically significant.)

When we use a computer program to test r, the computer usually reports the value of r in the sample, along with an exact p value. That exact p tells us the probability of obtaining the r we got or a more extreme r if the null hypothesis is true. As in most statistical tests, when the p value is below alpha (usually, below a p of 0.05), we conclude that the result is statistically significant.

Sample Size and r

A larger (that is, stronger) r is more likely to be statistically significant. However, the statistical significance of a value of r depends heavily on the sample size in a study. When a study has a very small sample (say, fewer than 15 people), it requires a large value of r to be statistically significant. But when a study has a very large sample—say, more than 1,000 people—a small r (for example, even an r of only 0.09 or -0.09) will be statistically significant. Therefore, it is important to remember that r can also be used as a measure of effect size. That is, an r of 0.09 may be statistically significant, but it still represents a very small, or weak, effect size (see Table A.5).

For more on statistical significance, see Chapter 7, pp. 193–195.

Therefore, as you evaluate the meaning of a correlation coefficient, recall what you have learned in this book about statistical significance, effect size, and practical importance.

As you consider these three elements, you will be interrogating statistical validity.

Is That Regression Coefficient Significant? Inferential Statistics for Beta

Chapter 8 introduced beta, a value obtained from the multiple regression process. Beta is similar to r in that both are used to estimate the association between two variables. However, beta goes further than r, because it usually represents the relationship between a predictor variable and a dependent variable, *controlling for* other, "third" variables. Chapter 8 used the example of a study that estimated the relationship between recess and school behavior problems, controlling for other variables such as poverty, class size, and the percentage of boys in the classroom.

We can evaluate the statistical significance of beta by following a series of mathematical steps that leads to a t value. We find the t value that is associated with a beta and then use the sampling distribution of t to evaluate the statistical significance of that beta. The sampling distributions of the t that are used to evaluate beta are the same as the sampling distributions of t used to evaluate the difference between two samples. (Recall that these sampling distributions vary in width depending on their degrees of freedom.)

Other than that, the steps are the same as for all other statistical tests. We assume that there is no relationship in the population (Step 1). We collect some data and calculate beta (Step 2). We estimate the probability of getting the beta we got or one more extreme, if the null hypothesis is true (Step 3). We decide whether to reject or retain the null hypothesis (Step 4).

When you see a multiple-regression table in an empirical journal article, it will usually have a column in the table that indicates whether each beta is statistically significant. As discussed in Chapter 8, sometimes the significance column will contain the actual t value associated with that beta, along with the p value associated with that t. Alternatively, it might contain only the p value associated with the beta and its t. Or this column may simply contain an asterisk (*), which indicates that the beta is statistically significant, or the letters $n.s.$, which indicate that the beta is not significant.

Other Statistical Tests: Same Process, Different Letters

This appendix has introduced you to four inferential statistical tests: the t test, the F test, and tests of the significance of r and beta. These four tests were developed for different research designs. The t test is for evaluating the difference between two group means. The F test is for evaluating the differences between two or more group means. The correlation coefficient, r, and its sampling distribution (based on t) are used for evaluating whether an association between two variables is statistically significant. And the t test evaluates whether an association between two variables, controlling for some other variable(s), is statistically significant. **Table B.3** presents a more comprehensive list of inferential statistical tests.

Although these tests are used for different research situations, they all follow the same general steps:

Step 1: We assume the null hypothesis.
Step 2: We collect data and calculate a statistical test (a t, F, r, or beta).
Step 3: We create a sampling distribution of that statistic—the distribution of the values of t, F, z, or beta we would get if we ran the study using many samples from a null-hypothesis population. We then use the sampling distribution to evaluate the probability of getting the t, F, r, or beta that we got in our data, or one even more extreme, if the null hypothesis is true.
Step 4: We decide whether to reject or retain the null hypothesis based on this probability.

No matter what the test is, the inferential process is the same. In the future, you may see a statistical test that you have not encountered before. If it is an inferential statistic, you can assume that it will follow the same logic—the same

TABLE B.3 Which Statistical Test Do I Use?

	One variable is:	The other variable is:	Example research questions	The test to use is:
Testing the significance of a difference between two groups (comparing two group means)	Categorical/nominal e.g., sex e.g., experimental versus control group	Quantitative e.g., exam score e.g., severity of symptoms	Did girls score significantly higher than boys? Did the experimental group show a significant reduction in symptom severity?	t test for independent groups (returns a t value)
Testing the significance of a difference between two groups (comparing group percentages)	Categorical e.g., Sex e.g., experimental and control group	Categorical (2 levels) e.g., Pass/fail rate e.g., recovery rate (recovered, or not?)	Are girls more likely to pass than boys? Is the experimental group more likely to recover than the control group?	Most common: chi-square test of goodness of fit (returns a χ^2 value)
Testing the significance of a difference between two or more groups (comparing group means)	Categorical e.g., major (chemistry, psychology, or biology)	Quantitative e.g., exam score	Is there a significant difference in exam score among the three groups?	One-way ANOVA (returns an F value)
Testing the significance of a difference between two or more groups (comparing group percentages)	Categorical e.g., grade level (Grade 1, 3, and 5)	Categorical (2 levels) e.g., pass/fail rate	Is there a significant difference in the passing rate among the three groups?	Most common: chi-square test of goodness of fit (returns a χ^2 value)
Testing a difference between two means, measured in the same sample	Categorical e.g., kind of cola (regular or diet; people taste both kinds of cola)	Quantitative e.g., rating of flavor on a scale of 1 to 10	Which of the two colas do people rate the highest?	Paired-samples t test (also known as t test for dependent groups) Also used: sign test
Testing a difference between two or more means, all measured in the same sample	Categorical e.g., kind of cola (regular, diet, caffeine-free, or vitamin-fortified; people taste all kinds)	Quantitative e.g., rating of flavor on a scale of 1 to 10	Which of the four colas do people rate the highest?	Repeated-measures ANOVA (returns an F value)

(continued)

	One variable is:		The other variable is:	Example research questions	The test to use is:
Testing two or more independent variables at a time and their interaction (see Chapter 11)	First independent variable is categorical e.g., size of box (large or small)	Second independent variable is categorical e.g., price of product (cheap or expensive)	Dependent variable is quantitative e.g., grams of spaghetti poured from the box	Do people use more spaghetti from large or small boxes? Do people use more spaghetti when it is cheap, rather than expensive? Does the effect of box size depend on the price of the product? Do people use more spaghetti from a large box only when it is on sale?	Factorial analysis of variance (returns F values for each main effect and each interaction)
Testing an association between two variables	Quantitative e.g., hours of study for exam		Quantitative e.g., grade on exam	Do people who study longer get better grades?	Correlation coefficient (returns an r value)
Testing an association between two variables, controlling for a third variable	Quantitative e.g., hours of study for exam	Quantitative e.g., preference for material	Quantitative e.g., grade on exam	Do people who study longer get better grades, even when their preference for the material is controlled for?	Multiple regression (returns beta values or b values). Sampling distribution of beta and b is the t distribution.
Testing an association between two variables	Categorical e.g., class year: freshman, sophomore, junior, senior		Categorical e.g., form of transportation to campus: bike, bus, car	Do people in different class years differ systematically in what form of transportation they use?	Chi-square test of independence (returns a χ^2)

Note: Not all of these statistical tests are explained in this appendix.

null hypothesis testing process. For example, imagine that a researcher reports a test you have never heard of, called "Q." If the test is accompanied by a p value, you are safe to assume that the researchers derived a sampling distribution of Q and then used the sampling distribution to evaluate the probability (p) of getting the Q they got in their sample, if the null hypothesis is true.

In the future, as you read about psychological research in empirical journal articles, you will encounter new statistical tests. These statistical tests have been developed for different kinds of data and for different research designs. However, no matter what the test is, it will probably be accompanied by a p value, and in most cases, the p value will tell you whether or not the results are statistically significant.

Key Terms

alpha level, p. A27
critical value, p. A38
inferential statistics, p. A23
null hypothesis, p. A25
null hypothesis testing, p. A25

power, p. A31
sampling distribution, p. A36
statistical hypothesis testing, p. A25
Type I error, p. A28
Type II error, p. A28

Appendix C
Presenting Results
APA-Style Research Reports and Poster Presentations

Scientists make their results public in order to tell others about the advances they have made or the phenomena they have documented. The dissemination of research results can involve all four of the scientific cycles discussed in Chapter 1.

First, publication contributes to the theory-data cycle because the researcher will write about the results in terms of how well they support a theory. Published data also become the basis for theory development and theory revision. Second, through the peer-review process, a scientist's methods and results are scrutinized by peers who evaluate the quality of the research and the importance of its findings. Published data may also contribute to the basic and applied research cycle because basic research findings can later be adapted to applied settings. In turn, when applied research is made public, basic researchers may be inspired to refine or develop new theories. Finally, data published in scientific settings may also be transmitted to the general public through the journal-to-journalism cycle, if the findings seem interesting and valuable enough. A well-written report can help ensure that journalists interpret and present scientific findings accurately.

This appendix covers two forms in which psychological scientists publicize their data: the written research report and the conference poster.

Writing Research Reports in APA Style

As part of your psychology studies, you will probably be required to prepare a research report. This appendix introduces you to the most common format for report writing: APA style, outlined in the *Publication Manual of the American Psychological Association* (6th edition, 2009). In a classroom setting, your research reports will be read only by your professors and fellow students. However, psychological scientists use the same APA style to write research reports that may become empirical journal articles.

APA Style Overview

A scientific research report is different from other kinds of nonfiction writing you may have tried so far. All APA-style research reports contain the same sections (including an introduction and Method and Discussion sections), presenting particular kinds of information. As Chapter 2 explains, when you know what is contained in each section of an empirical journal article, it is simpler to locate the study's hypotheses, background, and methodological details. In turn, when you write an APA-style report, you will be expected to include certain information in each section for your readers to find easily. An APA-style report includes the following elements:

Title
Abstract
Introduction
Method
Results
Discussion
Reference list

APA style prescribes not only the content that belongs in each of these sections but also the format you must use to present it. That is, it specifies what margins to use, how headings must be formatted, and how to present statistical tests.

Title

By reading the title alone, readers should understand the main idea of the manuscript. The APA manual recommends that the title be no more than 12 words long.

Table C.1 presents some examples of titles of research papers cited in this textbook. You can see that, overall, they are informative and concise. In some cases, they even communicate their message with style. Most of the titles in Table C.1 contain a colon and a subtitle. Often the words before the colon are

TABLE C.1 Some Titles of Empirical Journal Articles

Article Title	Authors
A longitudinal study of children with day-care experiences of varying quality	Vandell et al., 1988
Television viewing and aggressive behavior during adolescence and adulthood	Johnson et al., 2002
Profiles in driver distraction: Effects of cell phone conversations on younger and older drivers	Strayer & Drews, 2004
Superbowls: Serving bowl size and food consumption	Wansink & Cheney, 2005
Eavesdropping on happiness: Well-being is related to having less small talk and more substantive conversations	Mehl et al., 2010
The do-re-mi's of everyday life: The structure and personality correlates of music preferences	Rentfrow & Gosling, 2003

intended to attract readers' interest, and the words after the colon specify the article's content.

- Titles should communicate the purpose of the research in about 12 words or less.
- Titles do not typically contain abbreviations.
- Titles do not use the words "method," "results," "a study of," or "An experimental investigation of."
- In an APA-style manuscript, the title is centered and presented in uppercase and lowercase letters; it is not boldfaced. It appears in two places in the typed manuscript: on the cover page and on the first page of the introduction (see the sample paper, pp. A68 and A70).

Abstract

The abstract is a summary of the article's content. It does not present the nuances and details of the research—for that, readers will consult the full report. However, the abstract should clearly communicate the report's main research question, the methods used to test it, the major results, and an indication of why the results are important—for example, how the results support or shape a theory.

The abstract is the first section of your paper that most readers will encounter, but it is often the last thing you will write. After you complete the other sections of the paper, you can easily create an abstract by adapting one or two sentences each from the introduction and the Method, Results, and Discussion sections. Above all, abstracts should be concise, accurate, and clear. Readers should be able to get a good sense of your research question and the results you obtained by reading the abstract alone.

- Abstracts clearly and accurately summarize the research question, methods used, primary results, and interpretation of the results in terms of some theory or application.
- Abstracts should be about 150 words long. (Different journals have different word limits for abstracts, so the APA manual does not specify the abstract length; ask your professor how long he or she would like your abstract to be.)
- In an APA-style manuscript, the abstract is presented on its own page. The page is labeled with the word Abstract in plain text at the top center. The abstract itself should be typed as a single paragraph with no indentation (see the sample paper, p. A69).

Introduction

The first major section of your paper will be the introduction.

The Content of an Introduction. The main body of the introduction introduces the problem you studied and explains why it is important—usually because it tests some element of a theory. Your study may also be important because your particular approach or method has not been used in past research. Therefore, the bulk of your introduction will be an explanation of the theory or theories that your study is testing, as well as an explanation of any past research that is pertinent to the problem that you studied. In the introduction, you will describe what other researchers have found and explain why their research is relevant to yours.

In the last paragraph of the introduction, you will briefly introduce the method you used. (Was it a correlational study? Was it a single-N design? Was it an experiment? Did you use a factorial design?) The introduction is not the place to explain all the methodological details, such as how many participants you used or what questionnaires or tasks they completed—that information belongs in the Method section. However, you will need to tell your readers whether your method was correlational or experimental and what your primary variables were. Then, usually in the same paragraph, you will state your hypothesis or research question. If you had a clear prediction about what would happen in the study, that is your hypothesis. If you conducted a study to see which of several interesting outcomes might happen (Will A happen? Or will B?), that is your research question. The hypothesis or research question will be stated in terms of the variables you mentioned when you described the brief method.

Here is an example of how you can combine a brief description of the method with a statement of hypothesis. These are the last two sentences of the introduction from an article by Barros, Silver, and Stein (2009), described in Chapter 8, on school recess and behavior:

> Therefore, this study examined the amount of recess that children 8 to 9 years of age receive in the United States and compared the group classroom behavior of children of the same age receiving daily recess or not receiving recess. We hypothesized that children who received recess would behave better in the classroom as a group, compared with those who did not receive recess. (p. 431)

Here is an example of how you might state an exploratory research question. This is the last paragraph of the introduction to an article by Wansink and Kim (2005). Earlier paragraphs had reviewed relevant literature.

> Past research in this area by Wansink and Park has not been conclusive because it did not objectively manipulate the palatability of food. The study described in this article directly manipulates the palatability of popcorn (fresh versus stale) and then presents it to moviegoers in either medium- or large-size containers. Although people tend to believe that how much they eat is largely based on the taste of food, this study investigated whether this was true or whether environmental factors could instead influence a food's intake independent of its palatability. (p. 243)

A Process for Writing the Introduction. For many students, the introduction is the hardest section to write. Typically, you will have read several background sources— either review articles or empirical journal articles—that inspired your study. But writing about these sources to create a coherent introduction is a challenge.

If you are writing an introduction for the first time, try writing the end of your introduction first. Write about the method you used and the variables you studied. State your research question or hypothesis.

Next, try writing the first paragraph of your introduction. In this paragraph, you introduce the main area of research (perhaps it is stereotyping, eating preferences, cultural differences, or brain activity during reading). You may introduce your topic in a creative way to describe why this area of research is potentially interesting. However, the balance can be tricky. It might be appropriate to link your topic to contemporary events, but it is not appropriate to explain why you personally became interested in the research topic. And for your readers' sake, you should avoid being too broad in this opening paragraph, lest you sound trite or say things you cannot back up (such as "From the dawn of time, stereotypes have plagued humankind" or "Cultural differences are a common source of tension in our society today"). You also want to avoid jumping into technical waters too early. A good balance is to link your topic to a concrete story—but to do so briefly. For example, here is how Brad Bushman (2002) introduced his report of an experimental study on venting anger, described in Chapter 2:

> The belief in the value of venting anger has become widespread in our culture. In movies, magazine articles, and even on billboards, people are encouraged to vent their anger and "blow off steam." For example, in the movie *Analyze This*, a psychiatrist (played by Billy Crystal) tells his New York gangster client (played by Robert De Niro), "You know what I do when I'm angry? I hit a pillow. Try that." The client promptly pulls out his gun, points it at the couch, and fires several bullets into the pillow. "Feel better?" asks the psychiatrist. "Yeah, I do," says the gunman. (p. 724)

It can be particularly challenging to organize the middle portion of the introduction—the paragraphs following the opening paragraph and before those containing the statement of your hypothesis or research question. It generally is not effective simply to summarize each empirical journal article in isolation, one after another. Instead of describing the studies this way, you should attempt to use past studies to build an argument that leads up to your hypothesis. Therefore, the central portion of your introduction requires planning. Reread the background articles you have. Write each article's results and arguments on separate index cards, summarizing its main point, and move the index cards around on your desk as you explore the most logical way to arrange them. What order of presentation will allow you to explain the past research so that it leads up to your hypothesis? Then you can turn your index card arrangement into an outline and start writing.

As you write your introduction, alternate between summaries of past research, including brief citations (e.g., "In one study, Wansink and Cheney [2005] prepared bowls of chips in a party setting that were either large and small, and found that people ate more out of large bowls") and statements that reflect your own interpretations and arguments (e.g., "This study demonstrated that serving bowl size can affect how much people eat, but it was conducted with junk food; it does not indicate whether serving bowl size will affect how much people eat healthy food"). It might help to think of the descriptions of past research as the "bricks" of your introduction and to think of the interpretations, arguments, and transitions you provide as the "mortar." As you build your introduction, you will arrange the bricks in a logical order and then provide the mortar that connects them. By the end of your introduction, it should be very clear to the reader why you conducted your study the way you did and why you formed your hypothesis.

Introduction Checklist

- Follow the typical introduction format:
  - The first paragraph of the introduction describes the general area of research.
  - The middle paragraphs summarize past research studies (the "bricks") and give your interpretation of their meaning and importance (the "mortar"), arranged in a way that logically leads to your hypothesis.
  - The last paragraphs briefly describe the method used and the primary variables studied, and they state the hypothesis or research question.
- Document the sources you are summarizing by listing the authors' last names and year of publication, using parentheses or a signal phrase, as described in the section "Citing Sources in APA Style" (see pp. A65–A67). You do not need to type out the full titles of the articles you describe.
- Describe past research by paraphrasing or summarizing the research, not by quoting. When you paraphrase and summarize, be careful to avoid plagiarizing (see pp. A63–A64), and be sure to cite each article you describe.
- Describe completed research in the past tense. Most of the time, it is appropriate to write the entire introduction in the past tense.
- When appropriate, break up the introduction using section headings.
- In your opening paragraph, avoid phrases that are vague and undocumentable, such as "in our society today" and "since the beginning of time."
- In APA-style manuscript format, the introduction begins at the top of page 3 (the Title page is page 1, and the Abstract is on page 2). You should retype the paper's title at the top of the introduction and begin the text on the next line. (The introduction does not need the heading "Introduction.") Do not insert any extra line breaks or extra spacing throughout the introduction. If you insert additional subheadings to organize a long introduction, the subheads should be boldfaced, capitalized, and flush left.

Method

The Method section explains, in concise and accurate detail, the procedures you followed in conducting your study. When you write the Method section, your goal should be to communicate the details of your study so completely that a reader who had only your report to go on could conduct an exact replication study.

A conventional Method section contains about four subsections. Depending on the study, the exact sections you include will differ, but possible subsections include Design, Participants, Measures, Apparatus, and Procedure.

Design. If you conducted a factorial experiment, it can be helpful to open the Method section with a statement of the study's design, naming its independent and dependent variables. You would state whether the independent variables were manipulated as between subjects or within subjects. For example, you might write, "We conducted a 3 (serving bowl size: small, medium, or large) × 2 (type of food: healthy or unhealthy) between-subjects factorial experiment. The dependent variable was the amount of food participants consumed."

If your study is a simple experiment or if you conducted a correlational study, the Design subsection may not be necessary. But a complex correlational study may require a section headed Overview, in which you describe the variables measured and the procedure you followed.

Participants (or for Animals, Subjects). Describe the number, type, and characteristics of the people or animals you studied. For human participants, you must describe how many people participated, as well as relevant demographic information such as sex, ethnicity, socioeconomic group, age range, immigrant status, and native language. In addition, other characteristics may be relevant to report. Participants' intellectual abilities or disabilities may be relevant for a study on educational techniques; participants' sexual orientation may be relevant for a study on dating behaviors. In describing human participants, you will also indicate how the participants were selected (randomly? by convenience?), recruited (by e-mail? in a shopping mall? in psychology classes?), and compensated (Were they paid? Did they get course credit? Did they volunteer?).

When describing animal subjects, it is conventional to give the species' common name and taxonomic name (e.g., "We observed 10 piping plovers [*charadrius melodus*] in their natural environment") and indicate for laboratory animals the strain and provider used.

Materials (or Apparatus). In this subsection you will describe in detail the instruments you used to measure or manipulate the variables in your study. If you presented information on a computer screen, indicate how large the screen was and how far participants sat from it. If you used a commercially available computer program, specify the program you used. If animals were exposed to a particular piece of equipment, give its dimensions, manufacturer, and model.

If you used questionnaires or published scales to measure well-being or self-esteem (for example), you would devote one paragraph to each measurement scale. Indicate who wrote the items by citing the authors who first published the scale. Give one or two sample items from the questionnaire and indicate what the response scale was (e.g., "a 5-point scale ranging from 1 [*strongly disagree*] to 5 [*strongly agree*]"). You should also indicate the scale's reliability and validity. For example, you might indicate the Cronbach's alpha value you obtained in your own study and indicate the extent to which past researchers have validated the measure.

Although the Materials section should be complete and detailed, you do not need to describe obvious features, such as what kind of paper a questionnaire was printed on (unless there was something special about it) or whether the participants used pens or pencils to record their answers.

See Chapter 5 for types of reliability and validity that might be relevant.

Procedure. The Procedure subsection tells what happened in your study, in what order. Did participants come to a laboratory or classroom, or did they participate online? What did participants do first, next, and last? If there was a series of trials, what happened in each trial? If there were counterbalanced orders of presentation, what were they, and how were participants assigned to each order? How were participants assigned to independent variable groups (randomly or not?). Were participants or experimenters blind to conditions in the study? If so, how was this achieved? If there was a confederate in the study, what did the confederate say (exactly), and when?

In writing the Procedure section, take care not to repeat information you already described in other sections. In a Method section, each element is presented only once, in the most appropriate section and in the most appropriate order. Often it makes sense to put the Procedure section last, but in some cases it may need to be placed earlier in the Method section for more clarity.

Method Checklist

- The reader should be able to use your Method section to conduct an exact replication study, without asking any further questions.
- In APA style, the heading should be "Method," not "Methods."
- Use subheadings such as Design, Participants, Materials, and Procedure, presented in the order that is most appropriate and clear.
- Do not put the same information in more than one section. If you describe a measure in the Materials section, do not describe it again or give more detail about it in the Procedure section.
- If you used published questionnaires, describe each one in its own short paragraph, citing its source, sample items, and response options. Indicate relevant reliability and validity results for each questionnaire.
- In an APA-style manuscript, the Method section is labeled **Method** in boldface, centered. The Method section does not start on a new page; it begins directly after the introduction with no extra spaces. Subheadings for Participants, Apparatus, or Procedure should be typed flush left, boldfaced, and capitalized. Do not insert extra spaces between subsections.

Results

The Results section of a research report presents the study's numerical results, including any statistical tests and their significance, sometimes in the form of a table or figure. Do not report the values for individual participants; instead, present group means or overall associations. In a Results section, you will type out numerals for means, standard deviations, correlation coefficients, effect sizes, or other descriptive statistics. You will also type out the results and symbols for any statistical tests you calculated. APA style provides precise guidelines about how to present these values. Generally, the symbols for statistical computations and means (such as M for mean, SD for standard deviation, t for t test, and F for ANOVA) are presented in italics, but the numerals themselves are not (e.g., $M = 3.25$).

A well-organized Results section is systematic, and its sentence structure may even be a little repetitive. The priority is to be crystal clear. It is often best to begin with simple results and then move to more complicated ones. For example, if you included a manipulation check in an experiment, begin with its results. Then move to group means, followed by tests of significance. If your study was correlational, begin by presenting the simple bivariate correlations and then present multiple regression results. If your study was a factorial design, present main effects first and then interactions. If your study included multiple dependent variables, present the results for each one in turn, but try to keep the sentence structure the same for each dependent variable; that way, the reader can follow a predictable pattern.

It might also be appropriate to refer to your study's hypothesis and expectations as you write your Results section. For example, you might write, "As predicted, people were less affected by bowl size when eating healthy food than when eating unhealthy food."

Tables and Figures. It is good practice to present certain results in a table or figure. While a sentence is appropriate for presenting one to three numerical values, a table can helpfully summarize a larger set of descriptive statistics—four or more means and standard deviations—much more clearly and easily than you could do in a sentence. Tables are also appropriate for presenting multiple-regression results.

Tables must follow APA style guidelines. They may be single- or double-spaced, but they must include only horizontal lines as spacers, not vertical lines. You should never simply copy and paste tables of output from a statistical program into your manuscript. Instead, you will need to reformat them in APA style, usually retyping the numbers and formatting them appropriately. Tables are not included within the main body of the text. They are placed near the end of the paper, after the reference list. If you have more than one table, number each one consecutively (Table 1, Table 2, and so on) and place each on its own page. A title for each table appears at the top of the page. The label (e.g., Table 1) is printed in plain text, and the title itself appears on the next line, italicized, in upper- and lower-case letters. In the text of the Results section, refer to each table you created (e.g., "Means and standard deviations for the main dependent variables are presented in Table 1"). An example of an APA-style table is provided in the sample paper (see p. A80).

A figure can often highlight your data's strongest result. For example, if your factorial design found a predicted interaction, you might wish to present the result as a line graph or bar graph. Figures should be created using a computer program such as Excel. Each figure should have clearly labeled axes and should be presented in black and white whenever feasible. Like tables, figures do not appear in the body of the Results section; they are placed at the very end of the printed manuscript. If you have more than one figure, number each one consecutively (Figure 1, Figure 2, and so on) and place each on its own page. You must refer to each figure that you are including in the text of the Results section (e.g., "Figure 1 depicts the effect of food quality and bowl size on amount of food consumed"), and you should provide a descriptive caption for each figure. The figure caption is typed on the same page as the figure, appearing below it. The label (e.g., *Figure 1*) appears in italics followed by a period. The caption follows on the same line, in plain text.

If you present results in a table or figure, do not repeat the same numerical values (such as the same group means) in the text of the Results section. Mention the general pattern in the text, and refer readers to the table or figure for the full story (e.g., "As Figure 2 depicts, people ate more food from the largest bowl, especially when the food was unhealthy").

The key guideline for the Results section is to state the numerical findings clearly, concisely, and accurately, and then stop writing. The Results section is likely to be the shortest section of a student research report.

Results Checklist

- A good Results section is well organized and crystal clear. Present simple results first, and use repetitive sentence structures when presenting multiple, related results.
- Use a table to present multiple values such as means, correlations, or multiple inferential tests.
- Figures are always called figures, not graphs. Use figures to present the strongest results in your study. Do not overdo it—most papers contain only one to three figures.
- Call out all tables and figures in the text of the Results section, but place the tables and figures themselves at the end of the manuscript.
- Do not present the same results twice. If you present a result in the text, do not repeat it in a table or figure.
- In APA style, the Results section begins right after the Method section, with no page break or extra lines. It is labeled with the word **Results** in boldface. You may insert additional subheadings to organize a long Results section; such subheads should be boldfaced, capitalized, and flush left.
- Check the APA style manual or the sample paper on pages A68–A82 for examples of how to present statistical results.

Discussion

A well-written Discussion section achieves three goals. First, you will summarize the results of your study and describe the extent to which the results support your hypothesis or answer your research question. You will tell the reader how well the results fit with the theory or background literature that you described in the introduction. Second, you will evaluate your study, advocating for its strengths and defending its weaknesses. Third, you will suggest what the next step might be for the theory-data cycle.

Summarize Your Study and Link to the Theory-Data Cycle. The first paragraph or two of the Discussion section should contain a summary of the hypotheses and major results of your study. As you summarize the study, indicate clearly which results supported your hypothesis and which did not. Tie the results back to the literature and theories you mentioned in the introduction. In this sense, the Discussion section and introduction are like bookends to your paper—they both address the theory-data cycle. In this summary section, indicate how these results support the broader theory and why (or why not). If the results support the theory you were testing, you should explain how.

If the results do not support your theory, it will mean one of two things (as depicted in Figure 1.4): Either the theory is incorrect (and therefore must be modified in some way), or your study was flawed (and therefore a better study should be conducted). The Discussion is the place to explore these options and explain what you think is going on. For example, if you conducted an experiment that found a null effect, What factors might be responsible?

See Table 10.2 on p. 305 for some common reasons for a null result.

Evaluate Your Study. In the next paragraphs of the Discussion section, you will evaluate the choices you made in conducting your study. Generally speaking, authors advocate for the strengths of their own studies and anticipate criticisms that others might make so that they can deflect them in advance. An excellent strategy is to write about the four big validities one by one. First, address the construct validity of your study—explain whether your variables were manipulated or measured well, and explain how you know (review the evidence). Then, if you conducted an experiment, assess how well your study addressed potential internal validity threats. If your study was correlational, you might remind your readers that your data do not allow you to make a causal statement, and explain why. Address the statistical validity of your study by discussing the statistical choices you made. Finally, you might address the study's external validity. Because many student papers are not based on random samples of participants, however, you need to consider how much this matters in your case. Maybe it does not—if you were in theory-testing mode, for example. Reviewing your study in terms of the four big validities is an excellent way to make sure you have thoroughly evaluated and defended your study. The average student paper can probably include about one paragraph for each of the four big validities.

See Chapter 13 for more on balancing research priorities.

Specify the Next Step. In the last paragraph or two, it is common to indicate some directions for further research. However, it is not sufficient to conclude with a vague statement such as "Future research is needed." Instead, suggest a specific, theory-driven direction for the next study to take. If your study was flawed in some way, could specific steps be taken to correct the flaws, and what results would you expect? If your study was conducted well, what part of the theory should be tested next? How could you test it, what results would you expect, and what would such results mean? If your study was correlational, could you conduct an experiment next? If so, how would you do so, what results would you expect, and what would those results mean? Could the next study be a conceptual replication? If so, what new contexts might you test, what results would you expect, and what would those results mean?

Push yourself to answer these questions so that you can write thoughtful suggestions about the next step. Who knows—you might even inspire yourself to conduct another study.

Discussion Checklist

- The Discussion section contains three sections of content.
  - The first one or two paragraphs summarize the results and interpret how the results fit with the theory and literature discussed in the introduction.
  - The middle paragraphs evaluate your study. Work through each of the four big validities in turn, explaining the extent to which your study has fulfilled each one.

- The last one or two paragraphs give suggestions for future research. For each suggestion, explain four things: Why you would study that question, how you would study it, what your results might be, and what those results would mean.
- Do not report new statistical findings in the Discussion section—numerals and statistics belong in the Results section.
- The Discussion section and introduction are bookends—they both describe how your particular study fits in with the larger body of literature on a topic. If you opened your paper with a real-world example or story, you might consider closing your paper by reflecting on how your findings can help interpret that same example.
- In an APA-style manuscript, the Discussion section starts directly after the Results section with no page break or extra lines. Head the section with the word **Discussion**, boldfaced and centered. You may insert additional subheadings to organize a long Discussion section; such subheads should be boldfaced, capitalized, and flush left.

Reference List

In the course of writing the introduction and the Discussion section, you undoubtedly consulted and summarized articles written by other authors. You cited these papers within the text using the authors' last names and the year of publication. Near the end of your paper, in a section titled "References," you will provide the full bibliographic information for each of the sources you cited. The format for documentation is described on pages A65–A67.

Formatting an APA-Style Manuscript

When you prepare a research report in APA style, you will follow a number of specific guidelines. It can be difficult to assimilate all of the rules the first time. A good strategy is to use the sample paper on pages A68–A82. Pay attention to every detail; small details such as line spacing, font, and boldface and italicized terms matter. Here is an introductory list of APA format rules that apply to all sections of the paper:

- In an APA-style paper, everything is double-spaced, with the exception of tables and figures, which may contain single-spaced text.
- All text is in the same-sized font (usually 12-point) and printed in black. Section headings are the same font size and color as the main text.
- Margins on all sides should be 1 inch (2.54 centimeters). Do not right-justify the text. That is, do not have the right side of the text line up in a straight line; leave it ragged.
- The paper's title is not boldfaced but is centered and capitalized, both on the first page and at the top of page 3.
- Headings are boldfaced. The first-level heading—used for section headings such as Method, Results, and Discussion—is centered and capitalized. The second-level heading is boldfaced and flush left, and the first letters of major words are capitalized; the text following the heading begins on the next line. The third-level heading, if any, is boldfaced and indented and is followed by a period; only the first letter of the heading and any proper nouns are capitalized, and the text following the heading begins on the same line.

- The title page of the paper contains the title, the authors' names, the authors' institutional affiliations, an author note with contact information, and a running head—a shortened version of the title that appears on the top of each page.
- The following sections start on a new page: abstract, introduction, and reference list. (The Method, Results, and Discussion sections do not start on new pages.)
- The order of pages is as follows: title page, abstract, main body of paper (including introduction and Method, Results, and Discussion sections), reference list, footnotes (if any), appendixes (if any), tables, figures. Tables and figures should be presented one per page.
- The top of each page should include the three- to four-word shortened title (running head), printed in all capitals and flush left, as well as the page number, which goes on the same line but flush right. In most word processors you will open "view header" to insert this information.

Writing Style: Five Suggestions

An APA-style research report should be written in clear, concise language. This is not the place to use long, complex sentences or show off a large vocabulary. In general, research writing is straightforward, not fancy.

Such writing is easier said than done: It takes practice, feedback, and attention. Here are five suggestions that can go a long way toward making your research report writing more sophisticated and clear. Your course instructor may have further suggestions to help you improve your writing.

Write in the First Person

In APA style, the first person (*I*, *we*) is permitted because it can make a sentence more readable. The first person sounds especially natural and clear when there are two or more authors on a paper. Compare the following sentences:

> The authors presented participants with three bowl sizes: large, medium, and small. It was expected that participants would consume more food from the larger bowls.

> We presented participants with three bowl sizes: large, medium, and small. We expected that participants would consume more food from the larger bowls.

Whereas the first-person singular pronoun *I* can be acceptable in report writing, it can sound awkward, so use it sparingly. In addition, the second person (*you*) is considered too casual for report writing: In a research report, do not refer to the reader directly.

Choose the Most Appropriate Subject for Each Sentence

Sometimes, when you are comparing competing theories or briefly describing past research, it makes sense to use the theorists' names as the subject of your sentences, as in the following example:

Darley and Latané's (1968) laboratory studies supported a theory of bystander intervention known as diffusion of responsibility, but Shaffer and colleagues (1975) wanted to test the theory in a real-world context.

Often, however, when you are primarily describing the behavior of people, children, students, or animals, it is better to start a sentence with them, not with the researchers who studied them. Compare the following two sentences:

Latané and Darley (1970) have found that in an emergency, people are less likely to help others when there are other people around who might also offer help.

In an emergency, people are less likely to help others when there are other people around who might also offer help (Latané & Darley, 1970).

The first sentence emphasizes the researchers' *names*, whereas the second sentence more appropriately emphasizes the *findings*: what people do in an emergency. Emphasizing the findings will make your descriptions of past research more vivid and interesting. Notice that in the second sentence above, the citation in parentheses makes it clear that the preceding statement is a research finding by Latané and Darley.

Prefer the Active Voice

The subject you use for a sentence can also determine whether the sentence is written in the active voice or the passive voice. Sentences in the active voice are usually easier to read, so you should strive to write in the active voice as much as possible. Compare the following examples:

Passive: The target actions were never seen by the children.

Active: The children never saw the target actions.

Passive: Some of the action sequences were verbally commented upon by the adults.

Active: The adults verbally commented on some of the action sequences.

In these examples, both options are grammatically correct, but the active sentences are clearer, shorter, and easier to read.

Sometimes, however, the passive voice makes the most sense. For example:

The rats were injected with ethanol 2 hours before each trial.

This sentence is passive, but it appropriately places the focus of the sentence on the rats, not the people who injected them.

Use Strong Verbs

A precise verb can improve a sentence's clarity and style. Search your paragraphs for linking verbs such as *is, are,* and *be.* Try to replace them with stronger verbs, as in the following examples:

Our results are consistent with past research on eating behavior.

Our results replicate past research on eating behavior.

Portion size is an important influence on how much people eat.

Portion size influences how much people eat.

The manual was the guide for how to conduct the study.

The manual explained how to conduct the study.

Cut Clutter

Concise writing is more readable. You can often write clearer sentences simply by cutting needless words. For example, the following sentence originally appeared in earlier drafts of this very appendix:

> A precise verb can improve a sentence's clarity and make your writing easier to read. (15 words)

But this shorter sentence conveys the same meaning without being repetitive:

> A precise verb can improve a sentence's clarity. (8 words)

> In the next example, the writer streamlined a long sentence by trimming unnecessary words:

> When challenged to do so by their professors, most students find they can cut out 20% of their manuscript's length simply by taking out a few extra words from each sentence. (31 words)

> Most students can shorten their manuscript by 20% simply by removing unnecessary words from each sentence. (16 words)

Your writing becomes more readable when you cut redundant phrases and replace strings of short words with a single, effective one.

Avoiding Plagiarism*

When you use the words or ideas of others, you need to acknowledge them; if you don't credit your sources, you are guilty of plagiarism. Plagiarism is often unintentional—as when a writer paraphrases someone else's ideas in language that is close to the original. It is essential, therefore, to know what constitutes plagiarism: (1) using another writer's words or ideas without in-text citation and documentation, (2) using another writer's exact words without quotation marks, and (3) paraphrasing or summarizing someone else's ideas using language or sentence structures that are too close to the original—even if you cited the source in parentheses. The following practices will help you avoid plagiarizing:

- **Take careful notes**, clearly labeling quotations and using your own phrasing and sentence structure in paraphrases and summaries.

---

* "Avoiding Plagiarism" and "Using Appropriate Paraphrasing": From *The Norton Field Guide to Writing Second Edition* by Richard Bullock. Copyright ©2009, 2006 by W. W. Norton & Company, Inc. Used by permission of W. W. Norton & Company, Inc. This selection may not be reproduced, stored in a retrieval system, or transmitted in any form or by any means without the prior written permission of the publisher.

- **Know what sources you must document**, and credit them both in the text and in the reference list.
- **Be especially careful with online material**—copying material from a web browser directly into a document you are writing is all too easy. Like other sources, information from the web must be acknowledged.
- **Check all paraphrases and summaries** to be sure they are in your words and sentence structures—and that you put quotation marks around any of the source's original phrasing.
- **Check to see that all quotations are documented**; it is not enough just to include quotation marks or indent a block quotation. (Remember, however, that in APA style it is not conventional to quote; you should paraphrase instead.)

Whether deliberate or accidental, plagiarism has consequences. Students who plagiarize may automatically fail a course or even be expelled from school. If you are having trouble completing an assignment, seek assistance from your instructor or your school's writing center.

Using Appropriate Paraphrasing

When you paraphrase, you restate information from a source in your own words, using your own sentence structures. Paraphrase when the source material is important but the original wording is not. Because it includes all the main points of the source, a paraphrase is usually about the same length as the original.

Here is an excerpt from a source, followed by three paraphrases. The first two demonstrate some of the challenges of paraphrasing:

Original Source

In 1938, in a series of now-classic experiments, exposure to synthetic dyes derived from coal and belonging to a class of chemicals called aromatic amines was shown to cause bladder cancer in dogs. These results helped explain why bladder cancers had become so prevalent among dyestuffs workers. With the invention of mauve in 1854, synthetic dyes began replacing natural plant-based dyes in the coloring of cloth and leather. By the beginning of the twentieth century, bladder cancer rates among this group of workers had skyrocketed, and the dog experiments helped unravel this mystery.

—Sandra Steingraber, 2008, p. 976

Unacceptable Paraphrase: Wording Too Close

<u>Now-classic experiments</u> in 1938 showed that when dogs were exposed to aromatic amines, chemicals used in <u>synthetic dyes derived from coal</u>, they developed bladder cancer. Similar cancers were <u>prevalent among dyestuffs workers</u>, and these experiments <u>helped</u> to <u>explain why</u>. Mauve, a synthetic dye, was invented in 1854, after which <u>cloth and leather</u> manufacturers replaced most of the natural plant-based dyes with synthetic dyes. <u>By the</u> early <u>twentieth century</u>, <u>this group of workers had skyrocketing</u> rates of

bladder cancer, a <u>mystery</u> <u>the dog experiments helped to unravel</u> (Steingraber, 2008).

This paraphrase borrows too much of the language of the original or changes it only slightly, as the underlined words and phrases show.

Unacceptable Paraphrase: Sentence Structure Too Close

In 1938, several path-breaking experiments showed that being exposed to synthetic dyes that are made from coal and belong to a type of chemicals called aromatic amines caused dogs to get bladder cancer. These results helped researchers identify why cancers of the bladder had become so common among textile workers who worked with dyes. With the development of mauve in 1854, synthetic dyes began to be used instead of dyes based on plants in the dyeing of leather and cloth. By the end of the nineteenth century, rates of bladder cancer among these workers had increased dramatically, and the experiments using dogs helped clear up this oddity (Steingraber, 2008).

This paraphrase uses different language but follows the sentence structure of Steingraber's text too closely.

Acceptable Paraphrase

Biologist Sandra Steingraber (2008) explains that path-breaking experiments in 1938 demonstrated that dogs exposed to aromatic amines (chemicals used in coal-derived synthetic dyes) developed cancers of the bladder that were similar to cancers common among dyers in the textile industry. After mauve, the first synthetic dye, was invented in 1854, leather and cloth manufacturers replaced most natural dyes made from plants with synthetic dyes, and by the early 1900s textile workers had very high rates of bladder cancer. The experiments with dogs proved the connection.

Use your own words and sentence structure. If you use a few words from the original, put them in quotation marks.

Citing Sources in APA Style

As you write, you must briefly document the sources you used within the text, and you must document the full source in the reference list.

Brief Documentation in Text

When you are describing another researcher's ideas, words, methods, instruments, or research findings in your research report, you will cite the source by indicating the author's last name and the year of publication. There are two ways to provide in-text documentation: by using a signal phrase or by placing the entire citation in parentheses.

When you use a signal phrase, you present the last names as part of the sentence and place only the year of publication in parentheses:

Results by Wansink and Cheney (2005) indicate . . .

According to Elliot and his colleagues (2006), . . .

Alternatively, you can provide in-text documentation by putting both the author name(s) and the date in parentheses:

> One study showed that people eat more junk food when it is presented in a large bowl (Wansink & Cheney, 2005).

When you use the second method, remember to use an ampersand (&) and to place the sentence's period outside the parentheses.

In APA-style papers, you will not usually quote directly; instead, you should paraphrase the research in your own words. However, if you do quote directly from another author, you must use quotation marks and indicate the page number:

> "Although a small bowl of raw carrots might make a good afternoon snack, a large bowl might be even better " (Wansink & Kim, 2005, p. 244).

When a source is written by either one or two authors, you will cite their names and the date every time you refer to that source, as in the previous example. When a source is written by three or more authors, you will cite all of the names and the date the first time. The next time you cite the source, you will use the first author's name followed by "et al." and the date:

> The color red can affect our motivation (Elliot, Maier, Moller, Friedman, & Meinhardt, 2007). Even the color of paper on which a set of puzzles is printed can cause people to score worse if it is red (Elliot et al., 2005).

These are the rules for sources with obvious authors—the most common types of sources used by psychology students. You might need to cite other sources, such as websites with no author or government agency reports. In those cases, consult the APA manual for the correct documentation style.

Full Documentation in the Reference List

The reference list contains an alphabetized list of all the sources you cited in your paper—and only those sources. If you did not cite an article, chapter, or book in the main body of your text, it does not belong in the reference list. Do not list the sources in the order in which you cited them in the text; instead, alphabetize them by the first author's last name.

In the following examples, note the capitalization patterns for the titles of different types of publications—articles, journals, books, and book chapters—and whether they are italicized or formatted as plain text. Also pay attention to the placement of periods and commas.

Journal Articles with One Author. Here and in the next set of examples, note that only the volume number of a journal, not the issue, is included and that the volume number is italicized along with the journal title.

> Gernsbacher, M. A. (2003). Is one style of autism early intervention "scientifically proven"? *Journal of Developmental and Learning Disorders, 7,* 19–25.
>
> McNulty, J. K. (2010). When positive processes hurt relationships. *Current Directions in Psychological Science, 19,* 167–171.

Journal Articles with Two or More Authors. These examples follow the same pattern as a single-authored article. Note how a list of authors is separated with commas in APA style.

> Mueller, C. M., & Dweck, C. S. (1998). Intelligence praise can undermine motivation and performance. *Journal of Personality and Social Psychology, 75,* 33–52.

> Elliot, A. J., Maier, M. A., Moller, A. C., Friedman, R., & Meinhardt, J. (2007). Color and psychological functioning: The effect of red on performance in achievement contexts. *Journal of Experimental Psychology: General, 136,* 154–168.

Books. In the next two sets of examples, pay attention to how the publisher and its location are listed.

> Tomasello, M. (1999). *The cultural origins of human cognition.* Cambridge, MA: Harvard University Press.

> Wansink, B. (2005). *Marketing nutrition: Soy, functional foods, and obesity.* Champaign: University of Illinois Press.

Chapters in Edited Books. Here, compare the way the chapter authors' names and those of the book editors are given, and note how and where the page numbers appear.

> Geen, R. G., & Bushman, B. J. (1989). The arousing effects of social presence. In H. Wagner & A. Manstead (Eds.), *Handbook of psychophysiology* (pp. 261–281). New York, NY: John Wiley.

> Kitayama, S., & Bowman, N. A. (2010). Cultural consequences of voluntary settlement in the frontier: Evidence and implications. In M. Schaller, A. Norenzayan, S. J. Heine, T. Yamagishi, & T. Kameda (Eds.), *Evolution, culture, and the human mind* (pp. 205–227). New York, NY: Psychology Press.

Checklist for Documenting Sources

- In the reference list, entries are listed in alphabetical order by the author's last name. They are not listed in the order in which you mentioned them in the paper.
- Within a source entry, the order of the authors matters—often the first author contributed the most to the paper, and the last author contributed the least. Therefore, if an article or book chapter has multiple authors, list them all in the same order that they appeared in the publication.
- The entry for each source starts on a new line, using a hanging indent format (see the examples and the sample paper). Do not insert extra spaces between entries.
- The reference list is double-spaced and starts on a new page, after the Discussion section. The heading References appears at the top of the page, in plain text and centered. (Do not label this section "Bibliography" or "Works Cited.")

A short version of the title appears on the top of every page, in all caps. To edit this, view the "headers" area in your word processor.

Page numbers start with 1 on the title page and appear on the right corner of each page.

The Effect of Negative "Child of Divorce" Stereotypes on

Thinking About Future Romantic Relationships

Kristina Ciarlo

Muhlenberg College

Author Note

Kristina Ciarlo, Psychology Department,

Muhlenberg College

Correspondence concerning this article should be addressed to:

123 Main Street, Bloomville, NY, 12000

kciarlo@college.edu

Abstract

This study investigated whether negative stereotypes about children with divorced parents extend to beliefs about their romantic relationships. Specifically, we looked at whether people would use information about the level of conflict of a child's parents, as well as information about the marital status of the child's parents, in predicting a child's future relationship success. Undergraduates read a vignette about a child and his or her family and then predicted the child's future romantic relationships. We found that participants predicted the future relationships of children from divorced families to be more negative than those from married parents, and predicted that the relationships of children from high-conflict families would be more negative than those from low-conflict families. The results suggest that people use both the marital status of a child's parents and the conflict level of the child's parents to predict the child's future success in romantic relationships.

The word Abstract is centered and not bold. The abstract begins on page 2.

The abstract text is not indented.

It is appropriate to use the first person (I, we) in a research report. This student is presenting the results of a group project, so "we" is appropriate.

Avoid sexist language by using both "his and her" or by using plural rather than singular.

The abstract should be about 150 words long; some journals allow an abstract to be as long as 250 words.

The introduction begins on Page 3.

Repeat the title of the manuscript at the top of the introduction.

There is no extra space or heading between the title and the introduction text.

Citation format for a paper with three or more authors, first citation

Citation format for a paper with three or more authors, second citation

Citation format for a direct quotation—includes quotation marks and the page number

Parenthetical citation format for a single-authored source

Signal phrase citation format

The Effect of Negative "Child of Divorce" Stereotypes on

Thinking About Future Relationships

People use categories to simplify the task of processing the enormous amount of stimuli that confronts us (Gilovich, Keltner, & Nisbett, 2006). In social interactions, categorization may involve stereotypes, which are defined as "beliefs about attributes that are thought to be characteristic of particular groups" (Gilovich et al., 2006, p. 432). Even though stereotypes are not always accurate, we still knowingly or unknowingly use them as we interact with the social world. Stereotypes can apply to people from different ethnic populations, genders, or social classes, as well as other categories. The present study investigated the stereotype content and effects of one social category: children from divorced parents.

Past research has established that people hold stereotypes about children from divorced families, at least at the implicit level (Amato, 1991). In three studies, Amato (1991) assessed people's implicit beliefs about offspring of divorce. The first study demonstrated that people hold implicit negative stereotypes about individuals from divorced families, including the beliefs that they are distrustful, insecure, rebellious, prone to delinquency, shy, unpopular, have trouble relating to the opposite sex, and have nontraditional attitudes about marriage and family life. The results of the second study showed how these stereotypes work: Participants recalled fewer favorable facts about children from divorce than individuals from intact families. That is, participants implicitly ignored information that did not go along with the "child of divorce" stereotypes. However, when participants were explicitly asked if they thought that divorce caused negative effects for children, most responded that they thought divorce had few effects on children. Amato concluded that negative "child of divorce" stereotypes are widespread but implicit. They affect people's implicit beliefs even if they do not want them to.

One stereotype documented by Amato's study is that people perceive children of divorce as having trouble relating to the opposite sex. This particular stereotype is based upon some truth. Segrin, Taylor, and Altman (2005) found that children who come from divorced parents are more reluctant to enter into relationships because of the negative observations they made regarding their parents' committed relationship. The researchers also found that these children are less intimate even when they do enter into romantic relationships. The experimenters believe that this is the case because good communication skills were never modeled for them.

Although divorce may predict poor romantic relationships at an overall level, the context of the divorce seems to matter, too. The amount of parental conflict before the divorce moderates divorce's consequences for children (Kaslow & Schwartz, 1987). Some studies have shown that sometimes divorce has severe negative effects on children, and sometimes it has minimal effects or no consequences at all (Bartell, 2006). This discrepancy is partly due to the level of parental conflict that occurred prior to the divorce. Parental hostility and conflict have a stronger influence on children than the actual family structure does (Ensign, Scherman, & Clark, 1998). Furthermore, the cognitive-developmental model of the influence of parental divorce on romantic relationships explains that the level of parental conflict and proper modeling of relationships determines if children experience negative effects from the divorce or not (Bartell, 2006). Hence, the context surrounding the divorce matters more than the actual divorce does when considering the effects on future romantic relationships.

In the present study, we tested whether undergraduates' stereotypes about divorced children would be sensitive to the contextual factor of parental conflict. We predicted that although parental conflict matters in actual divorce cases, people's stereotypes would not be sensitive to this factor. Instead, we

Citation format for a two-author source

When possible, do not simply discuss past research articles one at a time; integrate them into an argument, as the student has done here.

The final paragraph of the introduction describes the method briefly and explains the hypotheses of the study in terms of this method.

hypothesized that people would ignore the context of the divorce and perceive overall negative effects of divorce across situations, because people fail to notice or tend to discard information that does not confirm their previous stereotypes (Amato, 1991). To test this prediction, we used a factorial design that manipulated both parental conflict and parental marital status in a set of vignettes. Participants read a high- or low-conflict vignette about parents who were married or divorced, and then responded to statements about the future romantic relationships of the couple's child. Due to overall negative stereotypes about individuals whose parents are divorced, we predicted that participants would perceive more harmful outcomes for such individuals' romantic relationships than for those who came from intact families (a main effect for marital status). However, we predicted that participants would fail to consider the effect of conflict, predicting that participants would not make any distinction between the low- and high-parental conflict vignettes (no main effect for conflict). We hypothesized that these predictions will hold true for all the participants regardless of their own family situations because of how far-reaching negative "child of divorce" stereotypes are.

Method

Design

We conducted a 2 × 2 between-subjects factorial experiment. The independent variables were the level of parental conflict in the vignette, either low conflict or high conflict, and the marital status of the parents in the passage, either married or divorced. Furthermore, the dependent variable of the study was the participants' responses to the statements regarding the romantic relationships of the children.

Participants

Participants were nine male students and 29 female students from upper-level psychology classes at Muhlenberg College. Thirty-three participants came from parents who were married, three came from divorced parents, one came from parents who were separated, and one came from a single parent. In terms of class year, one was a first-year student, 20 were sophomores, 12 were juniors, and five were seniors. All the participants participated to fulfill a requirement in their psychology courses.

Materials

We randomly assigned each participant to read one of four vignettes and answer several dependent-variable questions.

Vignettes. We used four different vignettes representing each cell of the 2 × 2 design, specifically: high-conflict/divorced, high-conflict/married, low-conflict/divorced, and low-conflict/married (see Appendix). Each scenario described two parents, John and Elizabeth, who were involved in either a high-conflict or a low-conflict relationship. The last line of the passage stated if the couple remain married or had gotten divorced.

We confirmed the effectiveness of the vignette manipulation by conducting a pilot test. Subjects answered questions pertaining to a passage thought to portray either high parental conflict or low parental conflict. Participants used a 5-point scale to rate the level of conflict that they felt the vignette represented (1 = *very low conflict* to 5 = *very high conflict*). In addition, students were asked to rate how realistic they thought the scenario was using a 5-point scale (1 = *extremely unrealistic* to 5 = *extremely realistic*). We found a significant effect for level of conflict, $t(9) = 6.43$, $p < .001$. The students rated the high-conflict scenario as containing much more conflict than the low-conflict scenario (see Table 1 for the means). Hence, we determined that the parental conflict manipulation was effective. Furthermore, there was not a significant effect for realism, $t(9) = -0.98$, $p = .35$. The participants did not rate the low-conflict scenario as being significantly more realistic than the

Format for a third-level heading: indented, bold-faced, sentence case, followed by a period; the text starts on the same line.

Refer to appendices in the main text. Place appendices after any figures or tables.

It is appropriate to present construct validity results, such as these pilot-tested manipulation checks, in the Method section.

Format for presenting a t test

Call out all tables in the text. Do not repeat values presented in a table in the text.

Indicate rating scales and anchors when describing self-report scales.

Use numerals for the point numbers and anchors of scales, and italicize scale anchors.

Give example items when describing self-report scales.

There is no extra space between the end of the Method section and the Results heading.

Call out all figures in the text. Do not repeat values in the text if they also appear in a figure.

Format for presenting an F statistic

high-conflict scenario. From these results, we concluded that the vignettes were equally realistic.

Dependent variables. The vignettes were followed by nine statements that addressed predictions about the future romantic relationships of John and Elizabeth's child. Each statement was assessed using a 5-point scale (1 = *strongly disagree* to 5 = *strongly agree*). We asked the students to circle the number that most appropriately corresponded with their feelings regarding the statements about the child from the previous passage. Examples of the statements include "This child will have difficulty sustaining a long term relationship" and "Their child will be able to effectively communicate with a significant other." After appropriate recoding, higher scores on the survey indicate a more negative view of the child's future romantic relationships. Possible scores could range from 9 to 45.

One survey question reassessed the construct validity of the vignettes, as we did in the pilot testing. Specifically, we asked, "What level of parental conflict does this vignette represent?" This statement was assessed using a different 5-point scale than the rest of the survey (1 = *very low conflict* to 5 = *very high conflict*).

The final four questions of the survey evaluated demographic information, including age, class year, sex, and parents' marital status.

Results

A factorial analysis of variance was calculated to determine if level of parental conflict or marital status had an effect on the students' perceptions of the children's future romantic relationships. Figure 1 presents the pattern of means. There was a significant main effect for level of conflict, $F(1, 34) = 55.88$, $p < .001$. The romantic relationships of children coming from high-conflict situations were rated more negatively than relationships of those coming from low-conflict situations. There was also a significant main effect for parents' marital status, $F(1, 34) = 5.95, p = .02$. The romantic relation-ships of individuals coming from divorced parents were rated more nega-tively than children coming from married parents. Finally, there was not a significant interaction between level of conflict and marital status, $F(1, 34) = 0.09, p = .76$. Thus, the relationship ratings did not depend on the combined effects of parental conflict and marital status.

In addition, there was not a significant effect for the sex of the partici-pant.[1] The female subjects rated the relationships ($M = 25.17, SD = 7.06$) slightly worse than the males ($M = 20.67, SD = 6.28$); however, this differ-ence was not statistically significant, $t(36) = -1.71, p = .095$.

To reassess construct validity, as was done in the pilot test, we computed another independent-samples t test to determine if the ratings of conflict level differed between the high- and low-conflict vignettes. The results replicated the findings from the pilot test: There was a statistically significant difference between the two scenarios, $t(36) = 8.68, p < .001$. Students rated the high-conflict vignette ($M = 4.53, SD = 0.61$) as containing much more conflict than the low-conflict vignette ($M = 2.37, SD = 0.90$).

Discussion

Due to globally negative "child of divorce" stereotypes, we hypothesized that people would ignore the context of divorce and perceive overall negative effects across situations. Our results supported this hypothesis; students rated the romantic relationships of the children from divorced parents more negatively than the relationships of those coming from married parents. This result repli-cates past research showing that negative "child of divorce" stereotypes include negative perceptions about their future romantic relationships (Amato, 1991). We had also hypothesized that participants' ratings would not be affected by the conflict level of the parents, but the results showed otherwise. Students rated the

Report exact p values between .001 and .99. If p is less than .001, report p < .001.

Use a repetitive sentence structure when describ-ing related results.

Use a zero before a decimal fraction when the statistic can be greater than 1 (e.g., F and t values). Do not use a zero before a decimal fraction when the sta-tistic cannot be greater than 1 (e.g., correlations, proportions, and p values).

Footnotes should be used sparingly. They appear on a new page titled Footnotes after the reference list.

There is no extra space between the end of the Results section and the Discussion heading.

The first paragraph of the Discussion section summarizes the hypoth-eses and major results.

romantic relationships of children coming from high-conflict situations much more negatively than those coming from low-conflict circumstances. Hence, even though negative "child of divorce" stereotypes were activated, participants also took the context of the situation into account, contrary to predictions.

In our study, the contextual factor of conflict may have mattered because the vignettes were so extreme. The high-conflict passage contained an excessive amount of conflict, including verbal and physical violence, while the low-conflict vignette contained almost no conflict at all. The scenarios were made to represent opposite ends of a conflict spectrum in order to ensure that the manipulation was effective—it had good construct validity. However, this may also have increased demand characteristics. Participants may have realized what we were trying to study after reading such extreme situations. Thus, future studies should use vignettes that are more subtle in their differences and maybe even include a greater variety of conflict levels.

Our study was designed with good internal validity. We used a between-subjects design so that participants would not be easily aware of the comparisons we were making between divorced and married parents, or low- and high-conflict families. The vignette paradigm made it easy to keep extraneous variables controlled.

On the one hand, our external validity was not strong in this study; we recruited most of the participants from upper-level psychology classes, which means that they have all probably been taught a lot about stereotypes and biases. Additionally, all the subjects were college students and probably know someone whose parents are divorced. These individuals may realize that the effects of divorce depend on the context because of their personal experience. Such students may be better at controlling their implicit beliefs because they are aware of the automatic activation of certain stereotypes. Even so, they showed evidence of stereotypes that favor the children of married parents

When the results do not support the hypothesis, offer an explanation.

The middle paragraphs of the Discussion section evaluate the study's strengths and weaknesses.

and low-conflict parents. Such stereotypes may, if anything, be even stronger among a non-student population.

We originally wanted to look at the difference between the relationship ratings of participants coming from married, divorced, separated, and single parents. However, the sample size was small and most of the students came from an intact family. Consequently, we could not run statistical tests to identify if there was a difference between the participants based on their family structure. However, we examined other sample characteristics, like participant sex, to look for discrepancies. Females rated the relationships more negatively than the males across all the conditions, but this difference was not statistically significant.

A future study could examine the possible dissimilarities between the perceptions of people coming from married versus divorced parents. We predict that children of divorce would be even more sensitive to contextual factors because of their own personal experiences—that is, we would predict an interaction between the participant's own family status and the experimental factor of parental conflict.

At the end of the discussion, point to future research questions, explain what you would expect, and explain why they would be important.

The reference list begins on a new page. Its heading is not boldfaced. Sources are listed in alphabetical order by first author.

Reference format for an empirical journal article with one author

Reference format for a chapter in an edited book

Reference format for an empirical journal article with more than one author

Reference format for a book

Within a single source, preserve the order of authorship; do not list authors alphabetically unless they originally appeared that way.

References

Amato, P. R. (1991). The "child of divorce" as a person prototype: Bias in the recall of information about children in divorced families. *Journal of Marriage and the Family, 53*, 59–69.

Bartell, D. (2006). Influence of parental divorce on romantic relationships in young adulthood: A cognitive-developmental perspective. In M. A. Fine & J. H. Harvey (Eds.), *Handbook of divorce and relationship dissolution* (pp. 339–360). London, England: Psychology Press.

Ensign, J., Scherman, A., & Clark, J. J. (1998). The relationship of family structure and conflict to levels of intimacy and parental attachment in college students. *Adolescence, 33*, 575–582.

Gilovich, T., Keltner, D., & Nisbett, R. E. (2006). *Social psychology*. New York, NY: W. W. Norton & Company.

Kaslow, F. W., & Schwartz, L. L. (1987). *The dynamics of divorce: A life cycle perspective*. Philadelphia, PA: Brunner/Mazel.

Segrin, C., Taylor, M. E., & Altman, J. (2005). Social cognitive mediators and relational outcomes associated with parental divorce. *Journal of Social and Relationships, 22*, 361–377.

Footnotes

Footnotes heading is not bold.

[1]We originally intended to test the effect of the participants' own family status, but we did not have enough participants in each category for this analysis.

Tables are numbered consecutively and placed one per page.

Table titles are presented in italics and are printed in title case.

Do not simply copy output from a statistical program into a table. Retype the data and its labels in the APA format.

Tables may be double- or single-spaced.

Table format can include horizontal separation lines, but no vertical lines.

Use the table note to describe any abbreviations used in the table or explain the nature of measures used in the table. The table note should be double-spaced.

Table 1

Pilot Testing Data

Rating	High-conflict vignette M *(SD)*	Low-conflict vignette M *(SD)*
Conflict	4.40 (0.55)	2.33 (0.52)
Realism	3.50 (0.55)	3.20 (0.45)

Note. n = 10 for all values. Conflict ratings ranged from 1 (*very low conflict*) to 5 (*very high conflict*). Realism ratings ranged from 1 (*extremely unrealistic*) to 5 (*extremely realistic*).

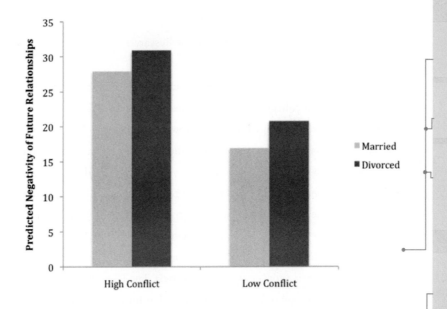

Figure 1. Predicted negativity of a child's future romantic relationships as a function

of the parents' relationship conflict and marital status.

Prepare figures in a computer program, not by hand.

Do not use gridlines (horizontal lines across the figure).

Label both the x-axis and the y-axis clearly. Use shades of gray, not color, to represent levels of a variable.

Each figure goes on its own page and is numbered consecutively. Figure labels are italicized.

Figure captions are double-spaced and appear in plain text below each figure.

An appendix is appropriate for presenting the full text of research materials, when such information is too long to present in the Method section.

If there is more than one appendix, they are called Appendix A, Appendix B, and so on.

Appendix

Vignettes Used in the Research

High Conflict:

John and Elizabeth have a child who just graduated from high school and is about to leave for college. Growing up, their child noticed that John and Elizabeth weren't always affectionate towards each other. They rarely hugged or held hands. The parents often fought over what was to be served for dinner, sometimes to the point that dinner was only served at 10:30 at night when they had finally settled on what to have. Their child had seen one parent or the other storm out of the house from time to time after a fight. Sometimes their verbal arguments turned violent, with either John hitting Elizabeth or Elizabeth hitting John. They would eventually apologize to each other only to get into another argument the next day. Their child often heard them yelling after going to bed, and it seemed that John and Elizabeth had more difficulties getting along than other parents.

Note. The vignette was followed by either of the following statements: "John and Elizabeth divorced about 1 year ago" or "John and Elizabeth remain married."

Low Conflict:

John and Elizabeth have a child who just graduated from high school and is about to leave for college. Growing up, their child noticed that John and Elizabeth were often affectionate towards each other. The parents sometimes had disagreements about what was to be served for dinner, but these problems were always resolved and dinner was served at 6:00 every evening. Their child had occasionally seen one parent or the other storm out of the room after a fight. However, they would apologize to each other soon after and the argument would be resolved. The child also noticed that John and Elizabeth could always make each other laugh and knew how to cheer each other up.

Note. The vignette was followed by either of the following statements: "John and Elizabeth divorced about 1 year ago" or "John and Elizabeth remain married."

Preparing Posters for Conferences

If you become involved in conducting original research—whether as part of a class project, for a student thesis, or as a research assistant for a professor—you may have the opportunity to present your research in a poster session. A **poster** is a brief summary of a research study, typed in a large, easy-to-read font and printed on a page as large as 4 to 5 feet wide. Poster sessions, in which several researchers present their posters simultaneously, are a common part of psychology conferences, both at undergraduate psychology conferences (where undergraduate research is the sole focus) and at regional and national psychology conferences (where faculty and graduate student research is the primary focus).

The Purpose of a Poster Session

A poster session is an informal way to share research results with the scientific community. At a typical poster session, dozens of researchers stand next to their posters in a large conference room (as in **Figure C.1**). Other researchers mingle, stopping to read posters that attract their interest, and perhaps talking one-on-one with the poster authors about the research.

FIGURE C.1 **A poster session at a local conference.**

Besides sharing results with the scientific community, the other goal of a poster session is to allow researchers to talk informally. The one-on-one conversations and the nonthreatening context allow people to talk to potential collaborators, meet people they admire, or simply learn more about research conducted at other colleges and universities.

Preparing the Poster

An APA-style research report will be the starting point for your poster, which should contain sections labeled "Introduction," "Method," "Results," "Discussion," and "References." But the poster format lends itself to less text and more images, as shown in the sample poster on pages A86–A87.

Keep the Text Short

A poster should give only a *brief* summary of the study you conducted. Many posters contain more text than most people are willing to read as they walk by. Instead, keep the text short. Limit yourself to one or two paragraphs (perhaps even bulleted statements) for the introduction and the Discussion section. Keep the Method section focused on the bare minimum of information (such as the number of participants and the operationalizations of the primary variables). And let your tables and figures tell the story of your results.

Show, Don't Tell

Present as much information as you can in tables, images, and figures. Art attracts an audience: People are more likely to stop by a poster that contains a large, interesting photo or a colorful graph. Tables and figures can also help you talk about your results in an interactive way. (For example, while pointing to your poster, you could explain, "Here are the large and small bowls we used. And you can see in this figure that the large-bowl group ate about twice as much as the small-bowl group.")

Make the Poster Readable and Attractive

The typeface and formatting rules for a poster are flexible. Any text should be in a font that is large enough to read from a distance—at least 20-point. The title of your poster (printed across the top edge) should be even larger—at least 40-point. You can combine a variety of font sizes, colors, and backgrounds if you wish, as long as the poster is readable. (Be careful not to go overboard with too many visual effects.)

Attending a Poster Session

When you participate in a poster session, you will find your assigned space, hang up your poster with the pushpins provided, and stand next to it wearing your best outfit and a friendly expression. As people approach your poster, give them a moment to look it over, and then offer to explain your work. Some people prefer to read silently, but most of your audience will appreciate the chance to talk one-on-one.

It is a good idea to practice delivering a "poster talk," in which you describe your research in 1 minute or less. Using your poster's images as props, practice delivering the key points—the purpose of the study, the method, and the results—in this very short time period. After your brief description, a visitor can ask follow-up questions, and you can begin a conversation about the research. Congratulations—you are now participating in the scientific community!

In addition to preparing your poster, you should bring handouts to the session—regular-sized pages on which you have printed the text and images from your poster. You can offer handouts to interested people. Be sure to include your name and email address, so people can contact you with questions.

Finally, during a poster session, it is perfectly appropriate to leave your poster for a few minutes to mingle and look at the other posters. This is especially important if your conference contains only one poster session. You should not miss this chance to learn about others' research as well as show off your own.

Effect of Negative "Child of Divorce" Stereotypes

Kristina Ciarlo, Muhlenberg College

Introduction

People hold negative stereotypes about children from divorced families; for example, they make negative predictions about such children's future relationships (Amato, 1991). For real families, studies show that divorce on its own is not the main factor in actual outcomes. Family conflict moderates the outcomes of divorce for children (Bartell, 2006).

The present study investigated whether people would stereotype children of divorced families as having less positive romantic relationships, and whether people would stereotype differently depending on whether the relationship had been high or low in conflict. We predicted that parental marital status alone, not marriage conflict, would affect people's predictions about a child's future relationships.

Method

Participants were 38 college students (29 female).

We used a 2 (marital status: divorced or married) × 2 (relationship conflict: high or low) between-subjects factorial design. Each student read one version of the story and predicted the child's future relationship success (see the vignettes to the right).

Statements about future relationships included "This child will have difficulty sustaining a long term relationship" and "Their child will be able to effectively communicate with a significant other."

Each statement was assessed using a 5-point scale (1 = strongly disagree to 5 = strongly agree)

Vignettes

HIGH CONFLICT:

John and Elizabeth have a child who just graduated from high school and is about to leave for college. Growing up, their child noticed that John and Elizabeth **weren't always affectionate towards** each other. **They rarely hugged or held hands.** The parents often fought over what was to be served for dinner, sometimes to the point that **dinner was only served at 10:30 at night** when they had finally settled on what to have. Their child had seen one parent or the other storm out of the house from time to time after a fight. Sometimes **their verbal arguments turned violent**, with either John hitting Elizabeth or Elizabeth hitting John. They would eventually apologize to each **other only to get into another argument the next day**.

Note. The vignette was followed by one of the following statements: "John and Elizabeth divorced about 1 year ago" or "John and Elizabeth remain married."

LOW CONFLICT:

John and Elizabeth have a child who just graduated from high school and is about to leave for college. Growing up, their child noticed that John and Elizabeth were **often affectionate toward each other**. The parents sometimes had disagreements about what was to be served for dinner, but these problems **were always resolved and dinner was served at 6:00 every evening**. Their child had occasionally seen one parent or the other storm out of the room after a fight. However, **they would apologize to each other soon after and the argument would be resolved**. The child also noticed that John and Elizabeth **could always make each other laugh and knew how to cheer each other up.**

Note. The vignette was followed by one of the following statements: "John and Elizabeth divorced about 1 year ago" or "John and Elizabeth remain married."

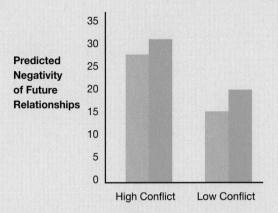

FIGURE 1. Predicted negativity of a child's future romantic relationships as a function of the parents' relationship conflict and marital status.

Table 1 *Pretesting data on the vignettes*

Rating	High Conflict Vignette	Low Conflict Vignette
Conflict	4.40	2.33
	(0.55)	(0.52)
Realism	3.50	3.20
	(0.55)	(0.45)

The pretest was conducted on a sample of 10 undergraduates, using only the high- and low-conflict versions of the vignettes.

Results

There were main effects for conflict, $F_{(1,34)} = 55.88$, $p < .001$, and marital status, $F_{(1, 34)} = 5.95$, $p = .02$, but no interaction.

Discussion

The results suggest that people used both marital status and marriage conflict when they predicted the future relationships of a child. As hypothesized, people predicted worse relationships for children of divorced parents than children of married parents. But counter to predictions, people also predicted worse relationships for children whose parents had high levels of conflict. These results suggest that people may, in fact, be sensitive to the level of conflict in a marriage, as well as marital status, when applying stereotypes to children of divorced parents.

References

Amato , P. R. (1991). The "child of divorce" as a person prototype: Bias in the recall of information about children in divorced families. *Journal of Marriage and the Family, 53*, 59–69.

Bartell , D. (2006). Influence of parental divorce on romantic relationships in young adulthood: A cognitive-developmental perspective. In M. A. Fine & J. H. Harvey (Eds.), *Handbook of divorce and relationship dissolution* (pp. 339–360). London, England: Psychology Press.

Appendix D
Random Numbers and How to Use Them

There are two uses of the term *randomization* in psychology, and it is important not to confuse them. Sometimes the term refers to *random sampling* from a population, and sometimes it refers to *random assignment* of participants to groups in a between-subjects experiment. Whereas random sampling is a method for selecting participants from some population in an unbiased way, random assignment is a method for assigning participants to two or more experimental conditions in an unbiased way. Random sampling enhances a study's external validity, and random assignment enhances a study's internal validity.

Table D.1 contains a random series of two-digit numbers, from 00 to 99. This kind of random number table is useful for both random sampling and random assignment, but they are used differently for the two.

For more on random sampling, see Chapter 6. For more on random assignment, see Chapter 9.

Random Sampling

Suppose we have a classroom with no more than 100 people in it; that is our population. And suppose we want to sample 20 cases from this population using *simple random sampling*. The first step is to assign a number to each member of the population, from 00 to 99. Then we would take the random number table and select a starting value haphazardly—by dropping a pen onto the page, perhaps. Starting with this value, we would then read across the rows. For example, if the pen dropped on the third entry on the first row, 78, person number 78 would be sampled in our study. Then we would continue moving along the row from there—persons 71, 21, 28, and so on—until we sampled 20 cases. If a number is duplicated, we would just ignore the duplicate and go to the next number. And if the population has fewer than 100 people in it—say, only 60 people—we would ignore any random numbers that are greater than 60.

The example assumes we have a population of no more than 100 cases. If the population is larger than 100, we would take the numbers in pairs, making the first entry on the table 7917. By using two columns at a time, we can handle populations up to 10,000 members.

We can also use the random number table for *systematic random sampling*, another variation of random sampling. We would drop a pen on Table D.1 and choose a value—say, 98. We would split this into two digits, 9 and 8. Then we would count off—starting with the ninth person in a group, we would select every eighth person after that until we had a full sample.

Random Assignment

Now let's assume we have already selected some sample of people who are going to be subjects in an experiment, and we are ready to assign participants to each experimental condition.

Suppose we plan to have 30 participants in our study, which includes three groups (say, red, green, and black). Thirty participants have agreed to be in our study, and we decide that red will be Group 1, green will be Group 2, and black will be Group 3. We can start anywhere on the random number table (perhaps by dropping a pen on it) and read along the row, considering only the digits 1, 2, and 3; we ignore any other numbers.

We will assign our participants in sets of three. If we had a prearranged list of participant names, we would start with the first three on the list. If we did not have names in advance, we could set up a schedule based on the order in which participants show up for the experiment and start with the first three participants who arrive. Suppose we drop the pen on a part of the table that starts with the following row of random numbers:

93   94   17   15   28   07   16   87   22   06

Starting with the 9 in 93 and reading across, the first value of 1, 2, or 3 we encounter is a 3. That means the first person in the first set of three people will be in Group 3—black. The next value we encounter is 1, so the second person will be in Group 1—red. Therefore, by elimination, the final person in this group of three will be in Group 2—green.

Now we would start again with the next set of three people. The next appropriate value we encounter is a 1, so the fourth person is in Group 1. Next is a 2, so the fifth person will be in Group 2, and, by elimination, the sixth person will be in Group 3. And so on.

Of course, if we had four experimental groups, we would consider the numbers 1, 2, 3, and 4. If we had two experimental groups, we might consider numbers 1 and 2. Or we could consider odd and even numbers—any odd number would mean an assignment to Group 1, and any even number would mean an assignment to Group 2. (In the case of two groups, we can also flip a coin to assign people to conditions.)

TABLE D.1 Random Numbers

79	17	78	71	21	28	49	08	47	79
17	33	72	97	86	45	44	65	97	29
27	65	06	82	98	28	36	03	72	93
33	57	70	34	39	91	78	99	64	53
76	81	31	42	31	04	00	10	82	13
27	72	54	77	94	97	92	56	20	98
97	95	39	36	02	43	10	08	19	00
87	84	51	57	65	03	46	70	94	69
40	80	05	81	12	90	02	90	44	38
21	90	78	37	47	61	92	69	35	30
40	61	04	23	42	76	72	13	08	83
59	02	28	10	82	77	75	89	13	34
91	37	80	64	61	39	19	38	91	28
24	42	44	77	45	44	03	46	25	94
66	49	81	89	88	40	81	60	25	26
57	55	52	54	53	31	49	38	14	72
83	26	59	05	42	05	89	74	68	10
16	97	26	84	41	14	94	94	94	03
53	16	08	29	29	28	19	28	01	83
87	73	84	55	94	57	52	68	56	90
56	55	60	96	53	21	18	59	55	86
83	59	56	38	86	84	07	40	77	20
37	39	88	49	43	00	49	13	02	51
14	20	68	04	90	94	70	05	83	10
11	16	82	54	39	36	56	00	52	07
46	97	32	82	63	13	42	30	20	64
25	04	76	44	88	19	61	20	56	97
05	54	35	78	93	94	17	15	28	07
16	87	66	77	22	06	50	76	95	09
67	78	65	43	99	96	82	04	48	30
50	70	46	81	33	52	89	59	09	49
57	90	31	77	96	04	97	17	87	54
51	85	26	99	70	46	88	58	00	99
45	07	47	13	64	79	44	06	15	07
46	72	46	81	14	12	17	48	07	33
04	62	90	98	01	48	00	54	91	65
75	83	67	58	01	28	14	42	41	00
84	72	63	83	39	67	62	67	28	05
61	91	27	17	24	76	64	22	20	75
01	05	20	78	51	19	23	31	44	61
71	71	55	10	29	62	30	90	52	04
08	98	57	51	73	55	96	67	02	36
57	83	20	73	45	93	21	48	23	95

Source: Reprinted from Mook (2001, pp. 517–519).

33	51	57	26	11	16	82	56	63	55
10	35	48	50	12	09	09	83	81	46
26	07	34	35	97	89	11	71	88	75
94	08	05	65	43	55	83	00	20	64
03	80	52	12	55	86	62	79	39	72
50	86	61	36	18	43	48	01	71	04
24	58	31	51	91	55	43	43	17	27
76	96	32	12	33	99	74	96	26	65
41	63	83	68	38	74	97	45	30	82
22	25	34	52	80	38	18	62	53	15
79	88	43	73	32	02	38	51	22	47
28	37	38	51	44	13	10	03	18	97
95	09	89	59	94	87	96	44	55	82
53	37	57	01	72	33	79	00	85	10
84	83	02	29	98	81	77	79	49	28
86	67	93	57	32	17	50	69	42	12
18	61	05	12	59	12	71	25	42	60
26	09	16	23	90	39	33	49	11	64
48	83	61	38	67	06	46	03	18	83
88	46	69	96	53	83	10	91	06	15
89	34	46	69	45	65	42	29	04	04
58	06	18	26	65	07	55	36	54	05
85	87	13	15	14	37	25	31	61	36
01	81	81	80	61	99	67	81	14	25
14	46	11	80	94	45	75	84	92	28
17	04	08	18	02	51	04	84	31	76
79	72	38	16	74	54	22	00	51	22
71	17	12	26	47	03	30	51	27	95
08	64	24	69	14	90	49	53	37	89
65	79	53	49	56	27	20	15	10	59
33	13	86	60	94	48	27	27	98	84
14	78	26	31	01	57	02	92	55	81
56	57	03	39	92	45	53	36	69	25
42	54	21	57	40	71	99	66	91	48
93	10	88	86	67	14	03	16	38	89
32	61	47	42	04	94	25	65	84	76
60	44	66	51	94	34	21	32	12	86
06	70	13	90	90	05	68	01	98	87
76	38	70	73	55	62	94	24	47	06
66	22	83	26	59	77	97	79	04	97
80	38	89	80	14	96	13	64	16	12
51	16	75	12	20	77	85	30	59	76
87	74	55	86	74	38	76	81	30	94

00	16	08	49	50	55	59	33	65	93
75	61	81	62	03	92	94	27	41	67
23	87	37	06	08	56	34	86	06	86
41	48	68	45	23	89	04	83	37	38
84	34	63	36	22	31	02	53	42	53
35	20	23	20	76	56	73	88	60	17
80	49	38	13	41	00	93	37	62	53
70	35	78	06	05	91	52	81	98	14
33	14	40	54	94	39	20	69	69	15
54	42	74	80	12	98	76	28	42	91
30	55	14	38	26	06	33	44	94	24
96	28	58	93	82	45	63	13	15	79
85	46	30	34	09	39	37	55	46	01
53	57	10	83	57	51	79	05	90	76
17	19	89	90	27	01	50	84	55	09
40	09	81	67	07	32	52	40	68	71
49	17	66	61	97	30	20	66	54	53
22	32	35	81	47	32	70	73	87	77
89	97	08	70	87	39	11	40	15	46
46	74	00	02	80	39	85	92	57	65
42	75	86	23	09	75	28	28	40	73
94	43	80	48	64	63	01	02	80	22
54	72	93	31	34	07	50	42	60	66
55	16	04	74	47	21	43	16	70	89
07	92	33	15	38	36	86	79	95	71
54	11	73	86	13	49	10	10	89	36
05	52	32	81	69	27	76	65	87	73
93	65	64	46	20	42	68	34	85	95
09	38	86	01	19	06	94	71	04	16
71	01	97	48	42	07	38	90	53	56
37	65	03	46	22	79	31	84	70	20
04	81	54	72	34	51	85	03	07	83
13	57	23	30	11	58	68	32	83	96
67	61	33	63	86	59	14	58	99	17
60	35	99	45	88	44	76	17	69	96
22	03	82	01	22	27	58	50	89	24
87	30	73	72	02	93	22	09	27	89
99	94	97	86	75	02	95	33	44	88
45	52	41	35	79	56	51	82	60	26
41	94	12	01	61	24	15	62	89	77
52	14	05	73	11	94	46	70	97	64
60	00	84	59	49	21	31	13	02	92
39	68	23	26	03	47	31	65	19	44

Appendix E
Areas Under the Normal Curve (Distribution of z)

How to Use This Table

After computing a z score, you can use this table to look up the percentage of the scores between that z score and the mean in a normal distribution or the percentage of scores that lie beyond that z score in a normal distribution.

The percentage of scores in the entire normal distribution is 100%, or an area of 1.00. A score that is directly at the mean would have a z score of 0.00, in the exact center of the distribution. Therefore, 0% of the scores fall between a z score of 0.00 and the mean, and 50% (that is, half) of them fall beyond that z score.

For a z score of 1.11, using the table you can see that 36.65% of the scores fall between that z score and the mean, and 13.35% fall beyond that z score.

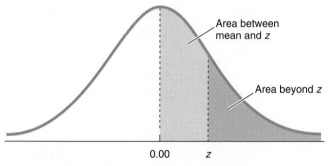

The normal distribution is symmetrical, so if your z score is negative, you will use the absolute value of z to look up the relevant areas.

z Score	Area between mean and z	Area beyond z	z Score	Area between mean and z	Area beyond z
0.00	0.0000	0.5000	0.04	0.0160	0.4840
0.01	0.0040	0.4960	0.05	0.0199	0.4801
0.02	0.0080	0.4920	0.06	0.0239	0.4761
0.03	0.0120	0.4880	0.07	0.0279	0.4721

Continued on A96

z Score	Area between mean and z	Area beyond z	z Score	Area between mean and z	Area beyond z
0.08	0.0319	0.4681	0.43	0.1664	0.3336
0.09	0.0359	0.4641	0.44	0.1700	0.3300
0.10	0.0398	0.4602	0.45	0.1736	0.3264
0.11	0.0438	0.4562	0.46	0.1772	0.3228
0.12	0.0478	0.4522	0.47	0.1808	0.3192
0.13	0.0517	0.4483	0.48	0.1844	0.3156
0.14	0.0557	0.4443	0.49	0.1879	0.3121
0.15	0.0596	0.4404	0.50	0.1915	0.3085
0.16	0.0636	0.4364	0.51	0.1950	0.3050
0.17	0.0675	0.4325	0.52	0.1985	0.3015
0.18	0.0714	0.4286	0.53	0.2019	0.2981
0.19	0.0753	0.4247	0.54	0.2054	0.2946
0.20	0.0793	0.4207	0.55	0.2088	0.2912
0.21	0.0832	0.4168	0.56	0.2123	0.2877
0.22	0.0871	0.4129	0.57	0.2157	0.2843
0.23	0.0910	0.4090	0.58	0.2190	0.2810
0.24	0.0948	0.4052	0.59	0.2224	0.2776
0.25	0.0987	0.4013	0.60	0.2257	0.2743
0.26	0.1026	0.3974	0.61	0.2291	0.2709
0.27	0.1064	0.3936	0.62	0.2324	0.2676
0.28	0.1103	0.3897	0.63	0.2357	0.2643
0.29	0.1141	0.3859	0.64	0.2389	0.2611
0.30	0.1179	0.3821	0.65	0.2422	0.2578
0.31	0.1217	0.3783	0.66	0.2454	0.2546
0.32	0.1255	0.3745	0.67	0.2486	0.2514
0.33	0.1293	0.3707	0.68	0.2517	0.2483
0.34	0.1331	0.3669	0.69	0.2549	0.2451
0.35	0.1368	0.3632	0.70	0.2580	0.2420
0.36	0.1406	0.3594	0.71	0.2611	0.2389
0.37	0.1443	0.3557	0.72	0.2642	0.2358
0.38	0.1480	0.3520	0.73	0.2673	0.2327
0.39	0.1517	0.3483	0.74	0.2704	0.2296
0.40	0.1554	0.3446	0.76	0.2764	0.2236
0.41	0.1591	0.3409	0.77	0.2794	0.2206
0.42	0.1628	0.3372	0.78	0.2823	0.2177

z Score	Area between mean and z	Area beyond z	z Score	Area between mean and z	Area beyond z
0.79	0.2852	0.2148	1.15	0.3749	0.1251
0.80	0.2881	0.2119	1.16	0.3770	0.1230
0.81	0.2910	0.2090	1.17	0.3790	0.1210
0.82	0.2939	0.2061	1.18	0.3810	0.1190
0.83	0.2967	0.2033	1.19	0.3830	0.1170
0.84	0.2995	0.2005	1.20	0.3849	0.1151
0.85	0.3023	0.1977	1.21	0.3869	0.1131
0.86	0.3051	0.1949	1.22	0.3888	0.1112
0.87	0.3078	0.1922	1.23	0.3907	0.1093
0.88	0.3106	0.1894	1.24	0.3925	0.1075
0.89	0.3133	0.1867	1.25	0.3944	0.1056
0.90	0.3159	0.1841	1.26	0.3962	0.1038
0.91	0.3186	0.1814	1.28	0.3997	0.1003
0.92	0.3212	0.1788	1.29	0.4015	0.0985
0.93	0.3238	0.1762	1.30	0.4032	0.0968
0.94	0.3264	0.1736	1.31	0.4049	0.0951
0.95	0.3289	0.1711	1.32	0.4066	0.0934
0.96	0.3315	0.1685	1.33	0.4082	0.0918
0.97	0.3340	0.1660	1.34	0.4099	0.0901
0.98	0.3365	0.1635	1.35	0.4115	0.0885
0.99	0.3389	0.1611	1.36	0.4131	0.0869
1.00	0.3413	0.1587	1.37	0.4147	0.0853
1.02	0.3461	0.1539	1.38	0.4162	0.0838
1.03	0.3485	0.1515	1.39	0.4177	0.0823
1.04	0.3508	0.1492	1.40	0.4192	0.0808
1.05	0.3531	0.1469	1.41	0.4207	0.0793
1.06	0.3554	0.1446	1.42	0.4222	0.0778
1.07	0.3577	0.1423	1.43	0.4236	0.0764
1.08	0.3599	0.1401	1.44	0.4251	0.0749
1.09	0.3621	0.1379	1.45	0.4265	0.0735
1.10	0.3643	0.1357	1.46	0.4279	0.0721
1.11	0.3665	0.1335	1.47	0.4292	0.0708
1.12	0.3686	0.1314	1.48	0.4306	0.0694
1.13	0.3708	0.1292	1.49	0.4319	0.0681
1.14	0.3729	0.1271	1.50	0.4332	0.0668

Continued on A98

z Score	Area between mean and z	Area beyond z	z Score	Area between mean and z	Area beyond z
1.51	0.4345	0.0655	1.88	0.4699	0.0301
1.52	0.4357	0.0643	1.89	0.4706	0.0294
1.54	0.4382	0.0618	1.90	0.4713	0.0287
1.55	0.4394	0.0606	1.91	0.4719	0.0281
1.56	0.4406	0.0594	1.92	0.4726	0.0274
1.57	0.4418	0.0582	1.93	0.4732	0.0268
1.58	0.4429	0.0571	1.94	0.4738	0.0262
1.59	0.4441	0.0559	1.95	0.4744	0.0256
1.60	0.4452	0.0548	1.96	0.4750	0.0250
1.61	0.4463	0.0537	1.97	0.4756	0.0244
1.62	0.4474	0.0526	1.98	0.4761	0.0239
1.63	0.4484	0.0516	1.99	0.4767	0.0233
1.64	0.4495	0.0505	2.00	0.4772	0.0228
1.65	0.4505	0.0495	2.01	0.4778	0.0222
1.66	0.4515	0.0485	2.02	0.4783	0.0217
1.67	0.4525	0.0475	2.03	0.4788	0.0212
1.68	0.4535	0.0465	2.04	0.4793	0.0207
1.69	0.4545	0.0455	2.06	0.4803	0.0197
1.70	0.4554	0.0446	2.07	0.4808	0.0192
1.71	0.4564	0.0436	2.08	0.4812	0.0188
1.72	0.4573	0.0427	2.09	0.4817	0.0183
1.73	0.4582	0.0418	2.10	0.4821	0.0179
1.74	0.4591	0.0409	2.11	0.4826	0.0174
1.75	0.4599	0.0401	2.12	0.4830	0.0170
1.76	0.4608	0.0392	2.13	0.4834	0.0166
1.77	0.4616	0.0384	2.14	0.4838	0.0162
1.78	0.4625	0.0375	2.15	0.4842	0.0158
1.80	0.4641	0.0359	2.16	0.4846	0.0154
1.81	0.4649	0.0351	2.17	0.4850	0.0150
1.82	0.4656	0.0344	2.18	0.4854	0.0146
1.83	0.4664	0.0336	2.19	0.4857	0.0143
1.84	0.4671	0.0329	2.20	0.4861	0.0139
1.85	0.4678	0.0322	2.21	0.4864	0.0136
1.86	0.4686	0.0314	2.22	0.4868	0.0132
1.87	0.4693	0.0307	2.23	0.4871	0.0129

z Score	Area between mean and z	Area beyond z	z Score	Area between mean and z	Area beyond z
2.24	0.4875	0.0125	2.61	0.4955	0.0045
2.25	0.4878	0.0122	2.62	0.4956	0.0044
2.26	0.4881	0.0119	2.63	0.4957	0.0043
2.27	0.4884	0.0116	2.64	0.4959	0.0041
2.28	0.4887	0.0113	2.65	0.4960	0.0040
2.29	0.4890	0.0110	2.66	0.4961	0.0039
2.30	0.4893	0.0107	2.67	0.4962	0.0038
2.32	0.4898	0.0102	2.68	0.4963	0.0037
2.33	0.4901	0.0099	2.69	0.4964	0.0036
2.34	0.4904	0.0096	2.70	0.4965	0.0035
2.35	0.4906	0.0094	2.71	0.4966	0.0034
2.36	0.4909	0.0091	2.72	0.4967	0.0033
2.37	0.4911	0.0089	2.73	0.4968	0.0032
2.38	0.4913	0.0087	2.74	0.4969	0.0031
2.39	0.4916	0.0084	2.75	0.4970	0.0030
2.40	0.4918	0.0082	2.76	0.4971	0.0029
2.41	0.4920	0.0080	2.77	0.4972	0.0028
2.42	0.4922	0.0078	2.78	0.4973	0.0027
2.43	0.4925	0.0075	2.79	0.4974	0.0026
2.44	0.4927	0.0073	2.80	0.4974	0.0026
2.45	0.4929	0.0071	2.81	0.4975	0.0025
2.46	0.4931	0.0069	2.82	0.4976	0.0024
2.47	0.4932	0.0068	2.84	0.4977	0.0023
2.48	0.4934	0.0066	2.85	0.4978	0.0022
2.49	0.4936	0.0064	2.86	0.4979	0.0021
2.50	0.4938	0.0062	2.87	0.4979	0.0021
2.51	0.4940	0.0060	2.88	0.4980	0.0020
2.52	0.4941	0.0059	2.89	0.4981	0.0019
2.53	0.4943	0.0057	2.90	0.4981	0.0019
2.54	0.4945	0.0055	2.91	0.4982	0.0018
2.55	0.4946	0.0054	2.92	0.4982	0.0018
2.56	0.4948	0.0052	2.93	0.4983	0.0017
2.58	0.4950	0.0050	2.94	0.4984	0.0016
2.59	0.4952	0.0048	2.95	0.4984	0.0016
2.60	0.4953	0.0047	2.96	0.4985	0.0015

Continued on A100

z Score	Area between mean and z	Area beyond z	z Score	Area between mean and z	Area beyond z
2.97	0.4985	0.0015	3.31	0.4995	0.0005
2.98	0.4986	0.0014	3.32	0.4995	0.0005
2.99	0.4986	0.0014	3.33	0.4996	0.0004
3.00	0.4987	0.0013	3.34	0.4996	0.0004
3.01	0.4987	0.0013	3.36	0.4996	0.0004
3.02	0.4987	0.0013	3.37	0.4996	0.0004
3.03	0.4988	0.0012	3.38	0.4996	0.0004
3.04	0.4988	0.0012	3.39	0.4997	0.0003
3.05	0.4989	0.0011	3.40	0.4997	0.0003
3.06	0.4989	0.0011	3.41	0.4997	0.0003
3.07	0.4989	0.0011	3.42	0.4997	0.0003
3.08	0.4990	0.0010	3.43	0.4997	0.0003
3.10	0.4990	0.0010	3.44	0.4997	0.0003
3.11	0.4991	0.0009	3.45	0.4997	0.0003
3.12	0.4991	0.0009	3.46	0.4997	0.0003
3.13	0.4991	0.0009	3.47	0.4997	0.0003
3.14	0.4992	0.0008	3.48	0.4997	0.0003
3.15	0.4992	0.0008	3.49	0.4998	0.0002
3.16	0.4992	0.0008	3.50	0.4998	0.0002
3.17	0.4992	0.0008	3.51	0.4998	0.0002
3.18	0.4993	0.0007	3.52	0.4998	0.0002
3.19	0.4993	0.0007	3.53	0.4998	0.0002
3.20	0.4993	0.0007	3.54	0.4998	0.0002
3.21	0.4993	0.0007	3.55	0.4998	0.0002
3.22	0.4994	0.0006	3.56	0.4998	0.0002
3.23	0.4994	0.0006	3.57	0.4998	0.0002
3.24	0.4994	0.0006	3.58	0.4998	0.0002
3.25	0.4994	0.0006	3.59	0.4998	0.0002
3.26	0.4994	0.0006	3.60	0.4998	0.0002
3.27	0.4995	0.0005	3.70	0.4999	0.0001
3.28	0.4995	0.0005	3.80	0.4999	0.0001
3.29	0.4995	0.0005	3.90	0.49995	0.00005
3.30	0.4995	0.0005	4.00	0.49997	0.00003

Note. This table is included for basic statistical reference. It is not discussed in detail in this book.

Appendix F
Critical Values of *t*

To use this table, first decide whether a one- or a two-tailed test is appropriate. Decide the level of significance. Then read down the corresponding column to the number of degrees of freedom. The tabled entry gives the value of *t* that must be *exceeded* in order to be significant. For example, if we do a two-tailed test with 20 degrees of freedom, our *t* must be greater than 2.086 to be significant at the 0.05 level.

df	One-tailed tests			Two-tailed tests		
	.10	.05	.01	.10	.05	.01
1	3.078	6.314	31.821	6.314	12.706	63.657
2	1.886	2.920	6.965	2.920	4.303	9.925
3	1.638	2.353	4.541	2.353	3.182	5.841
4	1.533	2.132	3.747	2.132	2.776	4.604
5	1.476	2.015	3.365	2.015	2.571	4.032
6	1.440	1.943	3.143	1.943	2.447	3.708
7	1.415	1.895	2.998	1.895	2.365	3.500
8	1.397	1.860	2.897	1.860	2.306	3.356
9	1.383	1.833	2.822	1.833	2.262	3.250
10	1.372	1.813	2.764	1.813	2.228	3.170
11	1.364	1.796	2.718	1.796	2.201	3.106
12	1.356	1.783	2.681	1.783	2.179	3.055
13	1.350	1.771	2.651	1.771	2.161	3.013
14	1.345	1.762	2.625	1.762	2.145	2.977
15	1.341	1.753	2.603	1.753	2.132	2.947
16	1.337	1.746	2.584	1.746	2.120	2.921
17	1.334	1.740	2.567	1.740	2.110	2.898

Continued on A102

Continued from A101

df	One-tailed tests			Two-tailed tests		
	.10	.05	.01	.10	.05	.01
18	1.331	1.734	2.553	1.734	2.101	2.897
19	1.328	1.729	2.540	1.729	2.093	2.861
20	1.326	1.725	2.528	1.725	2.086	2.846
21	1.323	1.721	2.518	1.721	2.080	2.832
22	1.321	1.717	2.509	1.717	2.074	2.819
23	1.320	1.714	2.500	1.714	2.069	2.808
24	1.318	1.711	2.492	1.711	2.064	2.797
25	1.317	1.708	2.485	1.708	2.060	2.788
26	1.315	1.706	2.479	1.706	2.056	2.779
27	1.314	1.704	2.473	1.704	2.052	2.771
28	1.313	1.701	2.467	1.701	2.049	2.764
29	1.312	1.699	2.462	1.699	2.045	2.757
30	1.311	1.697	2.458	1.698	2.042	2.750
35	1.306	1.690	2.438	1.690	2.030	2.724
40	1.303	1.684	2.424	1.684	2.021	2.705
45	1.301	1.680	2.412	1.680	2.014	2.690
50	1.299	1.676	2.404	1.676	2.009	2.678
55	1.297	1.673	2.396	1.673	2.004	2.668
60	1.296	1.671	2.390	1.671	2.001	2.661
65	1.295	1.669	2.385	1.669	1.997	2.654
70	1.294	1.667	2.381	1.667	1.995	2.648
75	1.293	1.666	2.377	1.666	1.992	2.643
80	1.292	1.664	2.374	1.664	1.990	2.639
85	1.292	1.663	2.371	1.663	1.989	2.635
90	1.291	1.662	2.369	1.662	1.987	2.632
95	1.291	1.661	2.366	1.661	1.986	2.629
100	1.290	1.660	2.364	1.660	1.984	2.626
∞	1.282	1.645	2.327	1.645	1.960	2.576

Appendix G
Critical Values of *F*

This table can handle up to seven independent treatment groups. To use it, decide your level of significance (.01, .05, or .10). Determine degrees of freedom for the numerator (number of groups minus 1) and degrees of freedom for the denominator (sum of the number of subjects, minus 1 in each group). The table then gives the value of F that must be *exceeded* to be significant at the specified level.

Thus if we have three treatment groups with 10 subjects each, we have 2 *df* for the numerator and $9 + 9 + 9 = 27$ *df* for the denominator. If we set our significance criterion at .05, we need an *F* larger than 3.36 to reject the null hypothesis.

Denominator df	Significance level	Numerator degrees of freedom					
		1	2	3	4	5	6
1	.01	4,052	5,000	5,404	5,625	5,764	5,859
	.05	162	200	216	225	230	234
	.10	39.9	49.5	53.6	55.8	57.2	58.2
2	.01	98.50	99.00	99.17	99.25	99.30	99.33
	.05	18.51	19.00	19.17	19.25	19.30	19.33
	.10	8.53	9.00	9.16	9.24	9.29	9.33
3	.01	34.12	30.82	29.46	28.71	28.24	27.91
	.05	10.13	9.55	9.28	9.12	9.01	8.94
	.10	5.54	5.46	5.39	5.34	5.31	5.28
4	.01	21.20	18.00	16.70	15.98	15.52	15.21
	.05	7.71	6.95	6.59	6.39	6.26	6.16
	.10	4.55	4.33	4.19	4.11	4.05	4.01
5	.01	16.26	13.27	12.06	11.39	10.97	10.67
	.05	6.61	5.79	5.41	5.19	5.05	4.95
	.10	4.06	3.78	3.62	3.52	3.45	3.41
6	.01	13.75	10.93	9.78	9.15	8.75	8.47
	.05	5.99	5.14	4.76	4.53	4.39	4.28
	.10	3.78	3.46	3.29	3.18	3.11	3.06
7	.01	12.25	9.55	8.45	7.85	7.46	7.19
	.05	5.59	4.74	4.35	4.12	3.97	3.87
	.10	3.59	3.26	3.08	2.96	2.88	2.83

Continued on A104

Denomi-nator df	Signifi-cance level	Numerator degrees of freedom					
		1	2	3	4	5	6
8	.01	11.26	8.65	7.59	7.01	6.63	6.37
	.05	5.32	4.46	4.07	3.84	3.69	3.58
	.10	3.46	3.11	2.92	2.81	2.73	2.67
9	.01	10.56	8.02	6.99	6.42	6.06	5.80
	.05	5.12	4.26	3.86	3.63	3.48	3.37
	.10	3.36	3.01	2.81	2.69	2.61	2.55
10	.01	10.05	7.56	6.55	6.00	5.64	5.39
	.05	4.97	4.10	3.71	3.48	3.33	3.22
	.10	3.29	2.93	2.73	2.61	2.52	2.46
11	.01	9.65	7.21	6.22	5.67	5.32	5.07
	.05	4.85	3.98	3.59	3.36	3.20	3.10
	.10	3.23	2.86	2.66	2.55	2.45	2.39
12	.01	9.33	6.93	5.95	5.41	5.07	4.82
	.05	4.75	3.89	3.49	3.26	3.11	3.00
	.10	3.18	2.81	2.61	2.48	2.40	2.33
13	.01	9.07	6.70	5.74	5.21	4.86	4.62
	.05	4.67	3.81	3.41	3.18	3.03	2.92
	.10	3.14	2.76	2.56	2.43	2.35	2.28
14	.01	8.86	6.52	5.56	5.04	4.70	4.46
	.05	4.60	3.74	3.34	3.11	2.96	2.85
	.10	3.10	2.73	2.52	2.40	2.31	2.24
15	.01	8.68	6.36	5.42	4.89	4.56	4.32
	.05	4.54	3.68	3.29	3.06	2.90	2.79
	.10	3.07	2.70	2.49	2.36	2.27	2.21
16	.01	8.53	6.23	5.29	4.77	4.44	4.30
	.05	4.49	3.63	3.24	3.01	2.85	2.74
	.10	3.05	2.67	2.46	2.33	2.24	2.18
17	.01	8.40	6.11	5.19	4.67	4.34	4.10
	.05	4.45	3.59	3.20	2.97	2.81	2.70
	.10	3.03	2.65	2.44	2.31	2.22	2.15
18	.01	8.29	6.01	5.09	4.58	4.25	4.02
	.05	4.41	3.56	3.16	2.93	2.77	2.66
	.10	3.01	2.62	2.42	2.29	2.20	2.13
19	.01	8.19	5.93	5.01	4.50	4.17	3.94
	.05	4.38	3.52	3.13	2.90	2.74	2.63
	.10	2.91	2.61	2.40	2.27	2.18	2.11

Denomi-nator df	Signifi-cance level	Numerator degrees of freedom					
		1	2	3	4	5	6
20	.01	8.10	5.85	4.94	4.43	4.10	3.87
	.05	4.35	3.49	3.10	2.87	2.71	2.60
	.10	2.98	2.59	2.38	2.25	2.16	2.09
21	.01	8.02	5.78	4.88	4.37	4.04	3.81
	.05	4.33	3.47	3.07	2.84	2.69	2.57
	.10	2.96	2.58	2.37	2.23	2.14	2.08
22	.01	7.95	5.72	4.82	4.31	3.99	3.76
	.05	4.30	3.44	3.05	2.82	2.66	2.55
	.10	2.95	2.56	2.35	2.22	2.13	2.06
23	.01	7.88	5.66	4.77	4.26	3.94	3.71
	.05	4.28	3.42	3.03	2.80	2.64	2.53
	.10	2.94	2.55	2.34	2.21	2.12	2.05
24	.01	7.82	5.61	4.72	4.22	3.90	3.67
	.05	4.26	3.40	3.01	2.78	2.62	2.51
	.10	2.93	2.54	2.33	2.20	2.10	2.04
25	.01	7.77	5.57	4.68	4.18	3.86	3.63
	.05	4.24	3.39	2.99	2.76	2.60	2.49
	.10	2.92	2.53	2.32	2.19	2.09	2.03
26	.01	7.72	5.53	4.64	4.14	3.82	3.59
	.05	4.23	3.37	2.98	2.74	2.59	2.48
	.10	2.91	2.52	2.31	2.18	2.08	2.01
27	.01	7.68	5.49	4.60	4.11	3.79	3.56
	.05	4.21	3.36	2.96	2.73	2.57	2.46
	.10	2.90	2.51	2.30	2.17	2.07	2.01
28	.01	7.64	5.45	4.57	4.08	3.75	3.53
	.05	4.20	3.34	2.95	2.72	2.56	2.45
	.10	2.89	2.50	2.29	2.16	2.07	2.00
29	.01	7.60	5.42	4.54	4.05	3.73	3.50
	.05	4.18	3.33	2.94	2.70	2.55	2.43
	.10	2.89	2.50	2.28	2.15	2.06	1.99
30	.01	7.56	5.39	4.51	4.02	3.70	3.47
	.05	4.17	3.32	2.92	2.69	2.53	2.42
	.10	2.88	2.49	2.28	2.14	2.05	1.98
35	.01	7.42	5.27	4.40	3.91	3.59	3.37
	.05	4.12	3.27	2.88	2.64	2.49	2.37
	.10	2.86	2.46	2.25	2.11	2.02	1.95

Continued on A106

Continued from A105

Denomi-nator df	Signifi-cance level	Numerator degrees of freedom					
		1	2	3	4	5	6
40	.01	7.32	5.18	4.31	3.83	3.51	3.29
	.05	4.09	3.23	2.84	2.61	2.45	2.34
	.10	2.84	2.44	2.23	2.09	2.00	1.93
45	.01	7.23	5.11	4.25	3.77	3.46	3.23
	.05	4.06	3.21	2.81	2.58	2.42	2.31
	.10	2.82	2.43	2.21	2.08	1.98	1.91
50	.01	7.17	5.06	4.20	3.72	3.41	3.19
	.05	4.04	3.18	2.79	2.56	2.40	2.29
	.10	2.81	2.41	2.20	2.06	1.97	1.90
55	.01	7.12	5.01	4.16	3.68	3.37	3.15
	.05	4.02	3.17	2.77	2.54	2.38	2.27
	.10	2.80	2.40	2.19	2.05	1.96	1.89
60	.01	7.08	4.98	4.13	3.65	3.34	3.12
	.05	4.00	3.15	2.76	2.53	2.37	2.26
	.10	2.79	2.39	2.18	2.04	1.95	1.88
65	.01	7.04	4.95	4.10	3.62	3.31	3.09
	.05	3.99	3.14	2.75	2.51	2.36	2.24
	.10	2.79	2.39	2.17	2.03	1.94	1.87
70	.01	7.01	4.92	4.08	3.60	3.29	3.07
	.05	3.98	3.13	2.74	2.50	2.35	2.23
	.10	2.78	2.38	2.16	2.03	1.93	1.86
75	.01	6.99	4.90	4.06	3.58	3.27	3.05
	.05	3.97	3.12	2.73	2.49	2.34	2.22
	.10	2.77	2.38	2.16	2.02	1.93	1.86
80	.01	6.96	4.88	4.04	3.56	3.26	3.04
	.05	3.96	3.11	2.72	2.49	2.33	2.22
	.10	2.77	2.37	2.15	2.02	1.92	1.85
85	.01	6.94	4.86	4.02	3.55	3.24	3.02
	.05	3.95	3.10	2.71	2.48	2.32	2.21
	.10	2.77	2.37	2.15	2.01	1.92	1.85
90	.01	6.93	4.85	4.01	3.54	3.23	3.01
	.05	3.95	3.10	2.71	2.47	2.32	2.20
	.10	2.76	2.36	2.15	2.01	1.91	1.84

Source: Reprinted from Mook (2001, pp. 514–516).

Appendix H
r to z' Conversion

r	z'	r	z'	r	z'
0.00	0.0000	0.25	0.2554	0.50	0.5493
0.01	0.0100	0.26	0.2661	0.51	0.5627
0.02	0.0200	0.27	0.2769	0.52	0.5763
0.03	0.0300	0.28	0.2877	0.53	0.5901
0.04	0.0400	0.29	0.2986	0.54	0.6042
0.05	0.0500	0.30	0.3095	0.55	0.6184
0.06	0.0601	0.31	0.3205	0.56	0.6328
0.07	0.0701	0.32	0.3316	0.57	0.6475
0.08	0.0802	0.33	0.3428	0.58	0.6625
0.09	0.0902	0.34	0.3541	0.59	0.6777
0.10	0.1003	0.35	0.3654	0.60	0.6931
0.11	0.1104	0.36	0.3769	0.61	0.7089
0.12	0.1206	0.37	0.3884	0.62	0.7250
0.13	0.1307	0.38	0.4001	0.63	0.7414
0.14	0.1409	0.39	0.4118	0.64	0.7582
0.15	0.1511	0.40	0.4236	0.65	0.7753
0.16	0.1614	0.41	0.4356	0.66	0.7928
0.17	0.1717	0.42	0.4477	0.67	0.8107
0.18	0.1820	0.43	0.4599	0.68	0.8291
0.19	0.1923	0.44	0.4722	0.69	0.8480
0.20	0.2027	0.45	0.4847	0.70	0.8673
0.21	0.2132	0.46	0.4973	0.71	0.8872
0.22	0.2237	0.47	0.5101	0.72	0.9076
0.23	0.2342	0.48	0.5230	0.73	0.9287
0.24	0.2448	0.49	0.5361	0.74	0.9505

Continued on A108

r	z′		r	z′		r	z′
0.75	0.9730		0.84	1.2212		0.93	1.6584
0.76	0.9962		0.85	1.2562		0.94	1.7380
0.77	1.0203		0.86	1.2933		0.95	1.8318
0.78	1.0454		0.87	1.3331		0.96	1.9459
0.79	1.0714		0.88	1.3758		0.97	2.0923
0.80	1.0986		0.89	1.4219		0.98	2.2976
0.81	1.1270		0.90	1.4722		0.99	2.6467
0.82	1.1568		0.91	1.5275			
0.83	1.1881		0.92	1.5890			

Note. This table is included for basic statistical reference. Its use is not discussed in detail in this book.

Glossary

A

abstract a concise summary of a **journal** article.

acquiescence or *yea-saying* answering "yes" or "strongly agree" to every item in a questionnaire or interview.

alpha level the value, determined in advance, at which researchers decide whether a *p* is low enough that they can reject the **null hypothesis** or too high (and therefore they retain the null hypothesis).

applied research research whose goal is to find a solution to a particular real-world problem.

association claim a **claim** about two **variables**, in which the level of one variable is said to vary systematically with the level of another variable, such that when one variable changes, the other variable tends to change, too.

attrition threat in a **repeated-measures experiment** or **quasi-experiment**, a threat to **internal validity** that occurs when a systematic type of participant drops out of a study before it ends.

autocorrelation the **correlation** of one **variable** with itself, **measured** at two different times.

availability heuristic *see* **pop-up principle**.

B

basic research research whose goal is to enhance the general body of knowledge, without regard for direct application to practical problems.

behavioral measure *see* **observational measure**.

beneficence an ethical principle from the Belmont Report stating that researchers must take precautions to protect participants from harm and to promote participants' well-being.

between-subjects design or *between-groups design* *see* **independent-groups design**.

bimodal having two **modes**, or most common scores.

bivariate association or *bivariate correlation* an association that involves exactly two **variables**.

blind design or *masked design* a study design in which the observers are unaware of the experimental **conditions** to which participants have been assigned.

C

carryover effect *see* **order effect**.

categorical variable a **variable** whose levels are categories (e.g., male/female).

causal claim a **claim** arguing that a specific change in one **variable** is responsible for influencing the level of another variable.

ceiling effect an experimental design problem in which **independent variable** groups score almost the same on a **dependent variable**, such that all scores fall at the high end of their possible distribution. (*See also* **floor effect**.)

cell a **condition** in an **experiment**. A cell can represent the level of one **independent variable** in a simple experiment or one of the possible combinations of two independent variables in a **factorial design**.

census a set of observations that contains all members of the **population** of interest.

central tendency a value that the individual scores in a data set tend to center around.

claim the argument an author or scientist is trying to make.

cluster sampling a sampling method in which researchers randomly select clusters of participants within the **population** of interest and then collect data from all of the participants in each selected cluster.

Cohen's *d* a measure of **effect size** that tells how far apart two group **means** are, in **standard deviation** units.

comparison group a group in an **experiment** whose levels on the **independent variable** differ from those of the **treatment group** in some intended and meaningful way.

conceptual definition a researcher's definition of a **variable** at an abstract level.

conceptual replication a replication study in which researchers examine the same research question (the same concepts) but use different procedures for **operationalizing** the **variables**.

concurrent-measures design an **experiment** using a **within-groups design** in which participants are exposed to all the levels of an **independent variable** at roughly the same time, and a single attitudinal or behavioral preference is the **dependent variable**.

concurrent validity an empirically supported type of measurement **validity** that represents the extent to which a measure is related to a concrete, simultaneous outcome that it should be related to.

condition one of the levels of the **independent variable** in an **experiment**.

confederate an actor who is directed by the researcher to play a specific role in a research study.

confirmatory hypothesis testing the tendency to ask only the questions that will lead to the expected answer.

confound a potential alternative explanation for a research finding (a threat to **internal validity**).

constant something that could potentially vary but that has only one level in the study in question.

construct validity a measure of how well a **variable** was **measured** or **manipulated** in a study.

content validity the extent to which a measure captures all parts of a defined construct.

control for holding a potential third **variable** steady while investigating the association between two other variables.

control group a level of an **independent variable** that is intended to represent "no treatment" or a neutral **condition**.

control variable a potential **variable** that an experimenter holds constant on purpose.

convenience sampling choosing a **sample** based on those who are easiest to access.

convergent validity an empirically supported type of measurement **validity** that represents the extent to which a measure is associated with other measures of a theoretically similar construct.

correlate or *covary* to occur or vary together systematically (as two **variables**).

correlation coefficient (*r*) a single number, ranging from –1.0 to 1.0, used to indicate the **strength** and **direction** of an association.

counterbalancing presenting the levels of the **independent variable** to participants in different orders to control for order effects.

covariance one of the three rules for establishing causation, stating that the proposed causal **variable** must vary systematically with changes in the proposed outcome variable.

covary *see* **correlate**.

criterion variable the **variable** in a **multiple regression** that the researchers are most interested in understanding or predicting. (May also be called the **dependent variable**.)

critical value a value of a statistic that is associated with a desired **alpha level**.

Cronbach's alpha or *coefficient alpha* a correlation-based statistic that measures a scale's **internal reliability**.

crossed factorial design a study in which researchers cross two or more **independent variables**, or *factors*, and study each possible combination of the levels of the variables.

cross-lag correlation in a **longitudinal design**, a correlation between an earlier measure of one **variable** and a later measure of another variable.

cross-sectional correlation in a **longitudinal design**, a correlation between two **variables** that are measured at the same time.

cultural psychology a subdiscipline of psychology concerned with how cultural settings shape a person's thoughts, feelings, and behavior and how these in turn shape cultural settings.

curvilinear association an association in which, as one **variable** increases, the level of the other variable changes its pattern (such as increasing and then decreasing).

D

data (*plural*; *singular* **datum**) a set of observations representing the **values** of some **variable**, collected from one or more research studies.

data fabrication an ethical problem that occurs when researchers invent data that fit their **hypotheses**.

data falsification an ethical problem that occurs when researchers influence a study's results, perhaps by deleting observations from a data set or by influencing their research subjects to act in the hypothesized way.

data matrix a grid presenting collected **data**.

debrief to inform participants afterward about a study's true nature, details, and **hypotheses**.

deception the withholding of some details of a study from participants (deception through *omission*) or the act of actively lying to them (deception through *commission*).

demand characteristics cues that lead participants to guess a study's **hypotheses** or goals.

dependent variable in an **experiment**, the **variable** that is measured, or the outcome variable. In a regression analysis, the single outcome, or **criterion variable**, that the researchers are most interested in understanding or predicting.

descriptive statistics a set of statistics used to organize and summarize the properties of a set of **data**.

design confound a second **variable** that happens to vary systematically along with the **independent variable** and therefore is an alternative explanation for the results.

directionality problem a situation in which it is unclear which **variable** in an association came first.

direct replication or *exact replication* a replication study in which researchers repeat the original study as closely as possible to see whether the original effect shows up in the newly collected **data**.

discriminant validity or *divergent validity* an empirically supported type of measurement **validity** that represents the extent to which a measure does not associate strongly with measures of other, theoretically different constructs.

double-blind placebo control study a study that uses a **treatment group** and a **placebo group** and in which neither the research assistant nor the participants know who is in which group.

double-blind study a study in which neither the participants nor the researchers who evaluate them know who is in the **treatment group** and who is in the **comparison group**.

E

ecological validity or *mundane realism* the extent to which the tasks and manipulations of a study are similar to real-world contexts.

effect size the magnitude of a relationship between two or more **variables**.

empirical journal article a scholarly article that reports for the first time the results of a research study.

empiricism or *empirical method* or *empirical research* using verifiable evidence as the basis for conclusions; collecting **data** and using it to develop, support, or challenge a **theory**.

error variance *see* **noise**.

exact replication *see* **direct replication**.

experiment a study in which one **variable** is **manipulated** and the other is **measured**.

experimental demand *see* **demand characteristics**.

experimental realism the extent to which a laboratory **experiment** is designed so that participants experience authentic emotions, motivations, and behaviors.

external validity a measure how well the results of a study generalize to, or represent, individuals or contexts besides those in the study itself.

F

F test a statistical test based on analysis of variance that determines degree of difference among two or more group **means**.

face validity the extent to which a measure is subjectively considered a plausible operationalization of the **conceptual variable** in question.

factorial design a study in which there are two or more **independent variables**, or factors.

faking bad a situation that occurs when survey respondents give answers that make them look worse than they really are.

faking good *see* **socially desirable responding**.

falsifiable a quality of a **theory** that applies when it is possible to collect **data** that will prove the theory wrong.

fence sitting a situation that occurs when respondents play it safe by answering in the middle of the scale for every question in a questionnaire or interview.

field setting a real-world setting for a research study.

file drawer problem the idea that studies finding **null effects** are less likely to be published than studies finding significant results.

floor effect an experimental design problem in which **independent variable** groups score almost the same on a **dependent variable**, such that all scores fall at the low end of their possible distribution. (*See also* **ceiling effect**.)

forced choice a question type in which respondents give their opinion by picking the best of two or more options.

frequency claim a **claim** that describes a particular rate or level of a single **variable**.

frequency distribution a table or figure that shows how many of the cases in a batch of data scored each possible **value** on the **variable**.

frequency histogram a figure that shows how many of the cases in a batch of **data** scored each possible **value** or range of values on the **variable**.

full counterbalancing a method of **counterbalancing** in which all of the possible **condition** orders are represented.

G

generalizability the extent to which the subjects in a study represent the **populations** they are intended to represent; how well the settings in a study represent other settings or contexts.

generalization mode the intent of researchers to generalize the findings from the **samples** and procedures in their study to other **populations** or contexts. (*See also* **theory-testing mode**.)

H

history threat a threat to **internal validity** that occurs when it is unclear whether a change in the **treatment group** is caused by the treatment or by a historical event that affects everyone or almost everyone in the group.

hypothesis or *prediction* a statement of the specific relationship between a study's variables that the researcher expects to observe if a **theory** is accurate.

I

independent-groups design an experimental design in which different groups of participants are exposed to different levels of the **independent variable** such that each participant experiences only one level of the independent variable.

independent variable a **variable** that is **manipulated** in an **experiment**. In a regression analysis, it is the variable used to explain variance in the **criterion variable**.

inferential statistics a set of techniques that uses chance and probability to help researchers make decisions about what their **data** mean and what inferences they can make from them.

informed consent research participants' right to learn about a research project, know its risks and benefits, and decide whether to participate.

institutional review board (IRB) a committee responsible for ensuring that research on humans is conducted ethically.

instrumentation threat a threat to **internal validity** that occurs when a measuring instrument changes over time from having been used before.

interaction in a **factorial design**, a situation that occurs when the effect of one **independent variable** differs depending on the level of the other independent variable.

internal reliability in a measuring instrument that contains several items, the consistency in a pattern of answers, no matter how a question is phrased.

internal validity the ability to rule out alternative explanations for a causal relationship between two **variables**.

interrater reliability the degree to which two or more coders or observers agree in their ratings of a set of targets.

interrupted time-series design a **quasi-experiment** in which people are measured repeatedly on a **dependent variable** before, during, and after the "interruption" caused by some event.

interval scale a quantitative measurement scale that has no "true zero" and in which the numerals represent equal intervals (distances) between levels (e.g., temperature in degrees). (*See also* **ordinal scales**, **ratio scales**.)

J

journal a monthly or quarterly periodical containing peer-reviewed articles on a specific academic discipline or subdiscipline, written for a scholarly audience.

journalism news and commentary published or broadcast in the popular media and produced for a general audience.

justice an ethical principle from the Belmont Report calling for a fair balance between the kinds of people who participate in research and the kinds of people who benefit from it.

L

Latin square a formal system of **partial counterbalancing** that ensures that each **condition** appears in each position at least once.

Likert scale a scale containing multiple response options that are anchored by the terms *strongly agree, agree, neither agree nor disagree, disagree*, and *strongly disagree*. A scale that does not follow this format exactly may be called a *Likert-type scale*.

longitudinal design a study in which the same **variables** are measured in the same people at different points in time.

M

main effect in a **factorial design**, the overall effect of one **independent variable** on the **dependent variable**, averaging over the levels of the other independent variable.

manipulated variable a **variable** in an **experiment** that researchers control by assigning participants to its different levels.

manipulation check an extra **dependent variable** that researchers can include in an **experiment** to determine how well an experimental manipulation worked.

marginal means in a **factorial design**, the **means** for each level of an **independent variable**, averaging over the levels of another independent variable.

masked design *see* **blind design**.

matched-groups design an experimental design in which participants who are similar on some **measured variable** are grouped into sets and the members of each matched set are then randomly assigned to different experimental **conditions**.

maturation a threat to **internal validity** that occurs when an observed change in an experimental group could have emerged more or less spontaneously over time.

mean a measure of **central tendency** computed from the sum of all the scores in a set of **data**, divided by the total number of scores.

measured variable a **variable** in a study whose levels are observed and recorded.

median a measure of **central tendency** that is the value at the middlemost score of a distribution of scores, dividing the **frequency distribution** into halves.

mediating variable or *mediator* a **variable** that helps explain the relationship between two other variables.

meta-analysis a way of mathematically averaging the results of all the studies that have tested the same **variables** to see what conclusion that whole body of evidence supports.

mode a measure of **central tendency** that is the most common score in a set of **data**.

moderator a third **variable** that, depending on its level, changes the relationship between two other variables.

multimodal having two or more **modes**, or most common scores.

multiple-baseline design a **small-*N* design** in which researchers stagger their introduction of an intervention across a variety of contexts, times, or situations.

multiple regression or *multivariate regression* a statistical technique used to test for the influence of third **variables**.

multistage sampling a method of sampling in which two **random samples** are taken from some **population**: a random sample of clusters and then a random sample of people within those clusters.

multivariate design a study designed to test an association involving more than two **measured variables**.

mundane realism *see* **ecological validity**.

N

nay-saying answering "no" or "strongly disagree" to every item in a questionnaire or interview.

negative association an association in which high levels of one **variable** go with low levels of the other variable.

nested factorial design a study with more than one **independent variable,** in which levels of one independent variable are nested under, and unique to, the levels of another, higher-order independent variable.

noise or *error variance* the **unsystematic variability** among the members of a group in an **experiment**.

nonequivalent control group design a **quasi-experiment** that has at least one **treatment group** and one **comparison group**, but participants have not been randomly assigned to the two groups.

nonequivalent groups interrupted time-series design a **quasi-experiment** with two or more groups in which (1) participants have not been randomly assigned to groups; (2) participants are measured repeatedly on a **dependent variable** before, during, and after the "interruption" caused by some event; and (3) the presence or timing of the interrupting event differs among the groups.

null effect a finding that an **independent variable** did not make a difference in the **dependent variable**—that there is no significant **covariance** between the two.

null hypothesis in a common form of statistical hypothesis testing, the assumption that there is no difference, no relationship, or no effect in a population.

null hypothesis testing a common form of **statistical hypothesis testing** in which researchers calculate the probability of obtaining their result if the **null hypothesis** is true; they then decide whether to reject or retain the null hypothesis based on their calculations.

O

observational measure or *behavioral measure* a **variable** measured by recording observable behaviors or physical traces of behaviors.

observational research the process of watching people or animals and systematically recording what they are doing.

observer bias a bias that occurs when observers' expectations influence their interpretation of the subjects' behaviors or the outcome of the study.

observer effects or *reactivity* a term referring to people or animals changing their behavior (reacting) because they know another person is watching.

one-group, pretest/posttest design a study in which a researcher recruits one group of participants; measures them on a pretest; exposes them to a treatment, intervention, or change; and then measures them on a posttest.

open-ended question a question that allows respondents to answer in any way they see fit.

operational definition or *operationalization* the specific way in which a concept of interest is measured or manipulated as a **variable** in a study.

order effect a threat to **internal validity** that occurs when being exposed to one **condition** changes how people react to a later condition.

ordinal scale a quantitative measurement scale whose levels represent a ranked order, in which it is unclear whether the distances between levels are equivalent (e.g., a 5-star rating scale). (*See also* **interval scale**, **ratio scale**.)

outlier one or a few cases that stand out as either much higher or much lower than most of the other scores in a **sample**.

oversampling a variation of **stratified random sampling** in which the researcher intentionally overrepresents one or more groups.

P

parsimony the degree to which a **theory** provides the simplest explanation of some phenomenon.

partial counterbalancing a method of **counterbalancing** in which some, but not all, of the possible **condition** orders are represented.

participant variable a **variable** such as age, gender, or ethnicity whose levels are selected (or **measured**), not **manipulated**.

phi coefficient a statistical test designed to evaluate the association between two **categorical variables**.

physiological measure a **variable** measured by recording biological data.

pilot study a study completed before (or sometimes after) the study of primary interest, usually to test the effectiveness or characteristics of the **manipulations**.

placebo effect an effect that occurs when people receiving an experimental treatment experience a change only because they believe they are receiving a valid treatment.

placebo group a **control group** that is exposed to an inert treatment (e.g., a sugar pill).

plagiarism the representation of the ideas or words of others as one's own.

point-biserial correlation a statistical test used for evaluating the association between one **categorical variable** and one **quantitative variable**.

population some larger group from which a **sample** is drawn, which the sample is intended to represent.

pop-up principle or *availability heuristic* the tendency to rely predominantly on evidence that easily comes to mind rather than use all possible evidence in evaluating some conclusion.

positive association an association in which high levels of one **variable** go with high levels of the other variable, and low levels of one variable go with low levels of the other variable.

posttest-only design an **experiment** with an **independent-groups design** in which participants are tested on the **dependent variable** only once.

power the probability that a study will show a **statistically significant** result when some effect is truly present in the **population**.

practice effect a type of **order effect** in which people's performance improves over time because they become practiced at the dependent measure (not because of the **manipulation** or treatment).

prediction *see* **hypothesis**.

predictive validity an empirically supported type of measurement **validity** that represents the extent to which a measure is related to a concrete, future outcome that it should be related to.

predictor variable a **variable** in an analysis using **multiple regression** that is used to explain variance in the **dependent** or **criterion variable**. The predictor variable may also be called the **independent variable**.

present/present bias the tendency to rely only on what is present (e.g., instances in which both a treatment and a desired outcome are present) and ignore what is absent (e.g., instances in which a treatment is absent or the desired outcome is absent) when evaluating the evidence for a conclusion.

pretest/posttest design an **experiment** with an **independent-groups design** in which participants are tested on the key **dependent variable** twice—once before and once after exposure to the **independent variable**.

probabilistic a description of the empirical method, stating that science is intended to explain a certain proportion (but not necessarily all) of the possible cases.

probability sampling the process of drawing a **sample** from a **population** of interest in such a way that each member of the population has an equal probability of being included in the sample (e.g., randomly).

purposive sampling the inclusion of only certain kinds of people in a **sample**.

Q

quantitative variable a variable whose **values** can be recorded as meaningful numbers.

quasi-experiment a study that is similar to an **experiment** except that the researchers do not have full experimental control (e.g., they may not be able to randomly assign participants to the **independent variable** conditions).

R

r see **correlation coefficient**.

random assignment the use of a random method (e.g., flipping a coin) to assign participants into different experimental groups.

random sampling see **probability sampling**.

ratio scale a quantitative scale of measurement in which the numerals have equal intervals and the value of zero truly means "nothing" (e.g., weight). (See also **interval scale**, **ordinal scale**.)

regression threat a threat to **internal validity** related to regression toward the **mean**, by which any extreme finding is likely to be closer to its own typical, or mean, level the next time it is measured (with or without the experimental treatment or intervention).

reliability the consistency of a measure.

repeated-measures design an **experiment** with a **within-groups design** in which participants respond to a **dependent variable** more than once, after exposure to each level of the **independent variable**.

replicable pertaining to a study whose results are obtained again when the study is repeated.

replication-plus-extension a replication study in which researchers replicate their original study but add **variables** to test additional questions.

respect for persons an ethical principle from the Belmont Report stating that research participants should be treated as autonomous agents and that certain groups deserve special protections.

response set a shortcut respondents may use to answer the items in a **self-report measure** with multiple items, rather than responding to the content of each item.

reversal design a study in which a researcher observes a problem behavior both before and during treatment and then discontinues the treatment for a while to see if the problem behavior returns.

review journal article an article summarizing all the studies that have been done in one research area.

S

sample the group of people, animals, or cases used in a study.

sampling distribution a theoretical prediction about the kinds of statistical outcomes likely to be obtained if a study is run many times and the **null hypothesis** is true.

scatterplot a graphical representation of an association, in which each dot represents one participant in the study measured on two **variables**.

scientific literature/literature a series of related studies, conducted by various researchers, that have tested similar **variables**.

selection effect a threat to **internal validity** that occurs when the kinds of participants at one level of the **independent variable** are systematically different from those at the other level of the independent variable.

selection-history threat a threat to **internal validity** in which a historical or seasonal event systematically affects only the subjects in the **treatment group** or only those in the **comparison group**— not both.

self-report measure a method of measuring a **variable** in which people answer questions about themselves in a questionnaire or interview.

self-selection a form of sampling bias that occurs when a **sample** contains only people who volunteer to participate.

semantic differential a **self-report** response scale whose numbers are anchored with contrasting adjectives (e.g., *easy* and *hard*).

simple random sampling the most basic form of **probability sampling**, in which the **sample** is chosen completely at random from the **population**, perhaps by drawing names out of a hat.

single-N design a study in which researchers gather information from only one animal or one person.

situation noise irrelevant events, sounds, or distractions in the external situation that create **unsystematic variability** within groups in an **experiment**.

slope direction the upward, downward, or neutral slope of the cloud of points in a **scatterplot**.

small-N design a study in which researchers gather information from just a few cases.

snowball sampling a variation on **purposive sampling** in which participants are asked to recommend acquaintances for the study.

socially desirable responding or *faking good* giving answers to a self-report measure that make one look better than one really is.

spurious an association that is attributable only to systematic **mean** differences on subgroups within the **sample**.

stable-baseline design a study in which a researcher observes behavior for an extended baseline period before beginning a treatment or other intervention; if behavior during the baseline is stable, the researcher is more certain of the treatment's effectiveness.

standard deviation a computation that captures how far, on average, each score in a **data** set is from the **mean**.

statistical hypothesis testing the steps taken by researchers when they use **inferential statistics**.

statistically significant a conclusion that a result is extreme enough that it is unlikely to have happened by chance if the **null hypothesis** is true.

statistical validity or *statistical conclusion validity* the extent to which statistical conclusions derived from a study are accurate and reasonable.

stemplot or *stem-and-leaf plot* a graphical representation of the **values** obtained on some **variable** in a **sample** of data.

stratified random sampling a sampling method in which the researcher identifies particular demographic categories of interest and then randomly selects individuals within each of the categories.

strength a description of an association indicating how closely the data points in a **scatterplot** cluster along a line of best fit drawn through them.

systematic sampling a method of **random sampling** in which the researcher counts off to achieve a **sample** (e.g., choosing every *n*th person in a population, where *n* is a randomly chosen number).

systematic variability in an **experiment**, the situation that occurs when the levels of a **variable** coincide in some predictable way with **experimental group** membership, creating a potential **confound**. (*See also* **unsystematic variability**.)

T

***t* test** a statistical test used to evaluate the size and significance of the difference between two **means**.

temporal precedence one of the three rules for establishing causation, stating that the proposed causal **variable** comes first in time, before the proposed outcome variable.

testing threat in a **repeated-measures experiment** or **quasi-experiment**, a kind of **order effect** in which scores change over time just because participants have taken the test more than once.

test-retest reliability the consistency in results every time a measure is used.

theory a statement or set of statements that describes general principles about how **variables** relate to one another.

theory-testing mode the testing of **association claims** or **causal claims** to investigate support for a **theory**. (*See also* **generalization mode**.)

third-variable problem a situation in which plausible alternative explanations exist for the association between two **variables**.

third-variable rule one of the three rules for establishing causation, referring to the ability to rule out alternative explanations for a proposed causal relationship between two **variables**.

translational research studies that use knowledge derived from **basic research** to develop and test solutions to real-world problems.

treatment group the participants in an **experiment** who are exposed to the level of the **independent variable** that involves a drug, therapy, or intervention.

Type I error a "false positive" result from a statistical inference process, in which researchers conclude that there is an effect in a **population** when there really is none.

Type II error a "miss" in the statistical inference process, in which researchers conclude that there is no effect in a **population** when there really is an effect.

U

unobtrusive observation an observation made indirectly, through physical traces of behavior, or made by someone who is hidden or is posing as a bystander.

unsystematic variability in an **experiment**, the levels of a **variable** occurring independently of **experimental group** membership, contributing to variability within groups. (*See also* **systematic variability**.)

V

valid/validity the appropriateness of a conclusion or decision. (*See also* **construct validity**, **external validity**, **internal validity**, **statistical validity**.)

value one of the possible variations, or levels, of a **variable**.

variable an attribute that varies, having at least two levels, or **values**.

variance the square of the **standard deviation** of a set of data, measuring how spread out the score of a **sample** are around their **mean**.

W

weight of the evidence a conclusion drawn from reviewing **scientific literature** and considering the proportion of studies that is consistent with a **theory**.

within-groups design or *within-subjects design* a study design in which each participant is presented with all levels of the **independent variable**.

Z

z score a computation that describes how far an individual score is above or below the **mean**, in **standard deviation** units.

zero association or *zero correlation* a lack of systematic association between two **variables**.

Guidelines for Selected Learning Actively Exercises

Chapter 1

Answers will vary.

Chapter 2

Selected answers

1. A.

   a. How close would you feel, without texting?

   b.

	Send text messages (treatment)	No text messages (no treatment)
Feeling emotionally close (outcome present)		
Feeling emotionally distant (outcome absent)		

   c. Could it be that I only text with the friends with whom I already feel emotionally close? Is it the texting or some third variable, such as a similar class schedule that allows us to send more texts between classes as well as see each other more often?

   C.

   a. Are older teachers just as good with students? (Older teachers are the comparison group.)

   b.

	Younger teachers ("treatment" group)	Older teachers (comparison group)
Good rapport with students (outcome present)		
Poor rapport with students (outcome absent)		

   c. What else might be confounded with young teacher age that would account for rapport with kids? Perhaps younger teachers are more common in a school, and it's familiarity, not their age. Perhaps younger teachers are more likely to teach early grades, and early-grade children act more friendly anyway.

2. a. This statement reflects intuitive reasoning, specifically the pop-up principle, or availability heuristic. The speaker bases the conclusion on evidence that comes easily to mind (what he or she sees the cousin eating). The speaker also shows some overconfidence ("I'm positive...").

   b. RAND is a well-respected research institution, which means that the conclusion your friend is talking about is most likely supported by empirical evidence. But you might also wish to ask her where she read about the research study and whether that source reported the research findings accurately.

   c. This statement is an example of cherry-picking the evidence: While watching the debate, the speaker was more motivated to notice the preferred candidate's successes and to ignore the candidate's lapses.

   d. This speaker is relying on an online source. How good is the science on which this website's conclusions are based, and is the website reporting the science accurately? Is the website presenting only some of the research and not others?

   e. This statement is an example of the pop-up principle: Dogs tend to be outdoors more than cats, especially in a city. But being more visible does not necessarily mean that they are more plentiful.

f. The speaker relies on personal experience to conclude that tanning beds are not dangerous. In addition, the speaker is thinking what he or she wants by disregarding research evidence linking tanning beds and cancer.

g. This statement reflects faulty intuition and the pop-up principle. Because airplane crashes get so much attention in the media, the speaker erroneously concludes that they are frequent. (Statistically, driving a car is much more dangerous than flying.)

h. This statement is based on a research study, so it is more credible. Did the journalist report the research findings accurately?

3. Answers will vary.

4. Answers will vary.

Chapter 3

Selected answers

1.

Variable	Conceptual level (marked in bold in the description)	Levels of this variable	Measured or manipulated?	Operational definition of the variable
A questionnaire study asks for various demographic information, including **participant sex**.	Participant sex	Male, female	Measured	Asking participants to circle "male" or "female" on a form
A questionnaire study asks about **self-esteem**, measured on a 10-item Rosenberg self-esteem scale.	Self-esteem	Self-esteem from low to high, numerical scores from 1 to 10	Measured	Score on 10-item Rosenberg self-esteem scale
A study of readability gives people a passage of text. The passage to be read is printed in one of three **colors of text** (black, red, or blue).	Color of text	Black, red, blue text	Manipulated	Printed color of the text of a passage
A study of school achievement requests each participant to report his or her SAT score, as a measure of **college readiness**.	College readiness	SAT score, from 400 to 1600	Measured	SAT score
A professor who wants to know more about **study habits** among his students asks students to report the number of minutes they studied for the midterm exam.	Study habits	Number, from 0 to longest possible study time	Measured	Self-reported time spent studying
A researcher studying self-control and **blood glucose levels** asks participants to come to an experiment at 1:00 pm. Some of the students are asked not to eat anything before the experiment; others are told to eat lunch before arriving.	Blood glucose levels	High glucose (after lunch), low glucose (fasting)	Manipulated	Coming to the experiment after lunch versus fasting
In a study on **self-esteem**'s association with self-control, the researchers give a group of students a self-esteem inventory. Then they invite participants who score in the top 10% and the bottom 10% of the self-esteem scale to participate in the next step.	Self-esteem	Top 10% and bottom 10% of scores on self-esteem inventory groups	Measured (They did not make people have high or low self-esteem—they just measured it)	Students scoring in upper 10% or lower 10% on a self-report self-esteem inventory

2. a. Causal. Variables: fasting (or not), degree of jet lag

b. Causal. Variables: reliving trauma (or not), severity of PTSD

c. Frequency. Variable: stress level

d. Causal. Variables: GPA, private vs. public college

e. Association. Variables: ADHD diagnosis, amount of work done in 1 year

f. Causal. Variables: mother's level of criticism, father's level of baby care

g. Frequency. Variable: number of underweight babies

h. Causal. Variables: MMR shot (or not), autism diagnosis

i. Causal. Variables: breastfeeding status, child's IQ

j. Frequency. Variable: breastfeeding rate

k. Association. Variables: child's weight, heart disease risk

l. Causal. Variables: texting and IM-ing frequency, spelling ability

m. Association. Variables: use of Facebook, college grades

3. a. • How well was ADHD measured in this study? How well was bullying measured in this study? (construct validity questions)

• What is the probability that these researchers are making a "false alarm" conclusion? How strong is the effect size—the relationship between these two variables? (statistical validity questions)

• Was a random sample or something else used? Does this relationship generalize to urban and rural children? To older or younger children? (external validity questions)

b. • How well was IQ measured in this study? How well was breastfeeding manipulated in this study? (construct validity questions)

• Did the researchers conduct an experiment? Did they make sure that the breastfeeding group was the same as the control group, in terms of how educated the mothers were, the sex of their babies, the health of their babies, and so on? (internal validity questions)

• Will the study's pattern generalize to another country or another age group? (external validity questions)

• What is the probability that these researchers are making a false alarm conclusion? How large is the effect of breastfeeding on IQ? Is the association statistically significant? (statistical validity questions)

c. • How well was stress measured in this study? (construct validity question)

• Did the researchers randomly sample people in lower Manhattan? (external validity question)

4. Your study would need to manipulate the causal variable (distributing studying versus cramming) and measure the outcome variable (long-term retention of information). For example, you could assign people to study some psychology material for three 20-minute sessions versus one 60-minute session. Then you could test them on the material 10 weeks later using a psychology test (recording the percentage of items correct).

The first variable is distributed studying versus crammed studying. This is a manipulated variable. The second variable is the score on the psychology test. This is a measured variable.

The causal claim here is that distributed studying causes people to remember information for a longer time.

1. *Covariance*: If your study finds that the distributed studying group scores higher on the test than the crammed studying group, your study has demonstrated covariance.

2. *Temporal precedence*: Because participants in your experiment were assigned to study in a particular way before they took the test, you have established temporal precedence.

3. *Internal validity*: If you ensured that the distributed studying group and the crammed studying group were the same in every way except the key distinction (distribution of study time), you have internal validity. For example, the two groups should have studied the same total amount of time (in this example, both groups studied 60 minutes total) and must have similar kinds of participants. Was the number of psychology majors equal in both groups? Were students' average SAT scores roughly equivalent in both groups? If all these things are equal, you have controlled for alternative explanations for the results, so you have achieved internal validity.

Chapter 4

1. The IRB members might consider that publicly observable behavior is usually exempt from informed consent requirements, but children are considered a "vulnerable population." Children may not be able to give informed consent, and they may not monitor their public behavior to the same extent as adults do. Depending on the case, the IRB may require the researcher to request informed consent from parents in the play area before proceeding. In addition, the researcher has not yet explained what the purpose of the study will be. The IRB, in its evaluation of the research proposal, should consider the benefits of the knowledge to be gained from the study.

2. Normally, researchers using anonymous, low-risk questionnaires may be exempted from informed consent procedures, but a review board might be concerned about the risk of coercion in this situation. The IRB might wonder if students in

the professor's class will feel coerced to complete the questionnaire, even if they do not wish to. (However, if there is truly no way to link responses back to the participants, then a student who does not wish to participate might be instructed to turn in a blank questionnaire.) In a small class, the students' handwriting might be recognized by the professor, so the surveys may not be truly anonymous. The IRB would probably evaluate this proposal more negatively if the questions on the survey were about personal values or private behaviors, rather than study habits.

3. You might have listed some of the following costs and benefits: Deception might harm participants by making them feel tricked or embarrassed. Such negative feelings may make participants less likely to participate in future research and may make them less willing to accept or read research findings in the future. On the one hand, people might become aware of negative information about themselves, such as what kinds of actions they will perform (in Milgram's study, delivering shocks to the "learner")—knowledge that may not be welcome or comfortable. On the other hand, deceived research participants may gain some valuable self-knowledge from their participation and may feel that they are contributing to the enterprise of science through their participation.

Deception studies may be valuable to society because, as noted in the chapter, the results of such studies may provide important lessons about obedience, helping behavior, subliminal persuasion, or other research topics. In addition, human welfare might be improved when scientists or practitioners apply the knowledge from a deception study. However, when members of society read or hear about deceptive research studies, they may begin to mistrust scientists. They may also become more suspicious of others around them. (Text from this question and answer is based on an analysis by Dunn, 2009.)

4. Prisoners are considered vulnerable to coercion. Being in prison makes people dependent on the behavior of powerful others for important outcomes; therefore, prisoners may not feel that they can freely decline to participate in a research study. Therefore, if researchers choose to study prisoners, they must attempt to reduce all possible coercion for participation. (Most IRBs require that a prisoner, or prisoner representative, be invited to IRB meetings at which research involving pris-

oners is discussed.) However, it might be important—and even necessary—to study prisoners if the outcome of the research question can uniquely benefit prisoners. Certain diseases or disorders may be more likely to affect prisoners; in addition, a researcher may find it valuable to investigate certain social patterns, coping styles, or relationships that are unique to a prison population.

5. Answers will vary.

Chapter 5

1. a. quantitative—ratio
   b. quantitative—ratio
   c. quantitative—ordinal
   d. categorical
   e. categorical
   f. quantitative—interval
2. a. Scatterplot D
   b. Scatterplot B
   c. Scatterplot C
   d. Scatterplot A
3. a. The interrater reliability of the coders should be evaluated. You should observe a positive correlation on a scatterplot, with Rater 1's rating on one axis and Rater 2's rating on the other axis.

   Test-retest reliability may also be relevant. If you assume that children's video game playing is stable over time, you should observe a positive relationship on a scatterplot, or a strong, positive correlation coefficient. The labels on the scatterplot should be "gaming level at recording time 1" on one axis and "gaming level at recording time 2" on the other axis.
   b. Test-retest reliability may be relevant. If you assume that panic disorder is a stable diagnosis over time, you should observe a positive relationship on a scatterplot, or a strong, positive correlation coefficient. The labels on the scatterplot should be "panic disorder scale score time 1" on one axis and "panic disorder scale score time 2" on the other axis. Each dot will represent one person.

   Internal reliability will also be relevant. The seven items should be correlated with one another. The standard evidence for internal reliability is Cronbach's alpha, which is difficult to sketch on a scatterplot
   c. Interrater reliability of the timing measure is the most relevant here.
   d. If the restaurant owner wants to use the card to rate the overall quality of his restaurant,

then he might be interested in combining these items into a single scale. If he does this, then internal reliability is the most relevant. However, if he plans to treat the four items as separate aspects of quality, then he will not combine them, and internal reliability will not be relevant.

e. Interrater (interteacher) reliability is relevant here. So is test-retest reliability, assuming that shyness is stable over time.

4. To measure concurrent validity, you would see whether the teacher ratings correlated with some behavioral measure of classroom shyness. For example, you might see if the shyness ratings correlated (negatively) with the number of times the student was seen to raise his hand in a classroom setting during the day. For concurrent validity, you would administer the shyness rating and the hand-raising measure on the same day.

To measure predictive validity, you would administer the shyness rating on one day and collect the hand-raising measure from the same children some time later.

For convergent validity, you would want to show that the classroom shyness rating is correlated with other ratings of shyness, perhaps parent ratings of shyness in the children, or therapist ratings of shyness. You might also expect shyness to be correlated with a measure of introversion.

5. Answers will vary.

Chapter 6

1. Answers will vary.

2. Many people are frustrated that opinion pollsters never call them, and they may even volunteer to contribute polling data for opinion polls during an election. But of course, the polling organizations cannot accept volunteer respondents. If they did, their polls would have poor external validity—or at least, they would only be able to generalize to other people who voluntarily call pollsters to share their opinions.

One reason this woman has not been called by pollsters is that each poll needs to sample only about 1,000 to 2,000 voters. With hundreds of millions of voters in the population, the chance of being selected by a poll is rather small.

3. a. The sample is the 200 books you select, and the population is the entire store of 13,000 titles.

b. To collect a random sample, you would make a list (perhaps on the computer) of all 13,000 titles. You could assign each book a random number, use the computer to sort the books into a list with the smallest numbers on top, and select the first 200 books on the sorted list. For each of the 200 books in the sample, you would record the price and take the average. That sample average would be a good estimate of the average price of the full book population in the store.

c. To collect a stratified random sample, you would first choose some strata that might be important to you. For example, you might stratify the sample into textbooks and trade books. If the population includes 60% textbooks and 40% trade books, you could select a stratified random sample of 120 textbooks and 80 trade books (so that your sample is proportional to the true strata). Or you might, instead, stratify on whether the books are paperback or hardback, fiction or nonfiction, or you might even stratify by topic (literature, foreign language, self-help, and so on).

d. A convenience sample would involve recording the price of the first 200 books you can pick up in the store, simply walking around and choosing books. (This would bias your sample toward books on the most reachable shelves.) Or you could stand by the cash register and record the price of the next 200 books sold at that store. (This convenience sample might bias your sample to include mainly the cheaper books, or mainly the sale books, or mainly the popular books.)

e. To conduct a systematic random sample, you would select two random numbers (say, 15 and 33). You would list the 13,000 books in the store, start with the 15th book, and then count off, selecting every 33rd book in the list until you get 200 books. Record the prices and take the average of the 200 books in the sample.

f. To conduct a cluster sample, you could make a list of all the display shelves in the store (say there are twenty bookshelves). You could select four of the twenty bookshelves at random and then record the price of all the books on each of the four selected shelves. Alternatively, you could randomly sample 50 books from each of the four selected shelves.

4. a. A representative sample is essential here.
   b. A nonrepresentative sample is probably okay, because people's reasons for volunteering to rate the movie online may not be relevant to their rating of the movie.
   c. A representative sample of scores from each school is essential here.
5. Answers will vary.
6. Your decisions will depend on where you are planning to code, but the one thing to attend carefully to is interrater reliability. To establish interrater reliability, you will need to have two coders each rate each person so that you have two ratings per observation. The association between the two coders' ratings is the interrater reliability.

Chapter 7

1. a. Measured variables: conscientiousness and health precautions. Can be plotted with a scatterplot.
   b. Measured variables: depression and chocolate consumption. If depression is considered categorical (depressed versus not depressed), it could be plotted as a bar graph, but if it is considered quantitative (level of depression), then a scatterplot is appropriate.
   c. Measured variables: private (versus public) college and GPA. Best plotted with a bar graph, because private versus public college is a categorical variable.
2. a. To interrogate construct validity, you could ask how well the researchers measured each of the two variables in this study: the level of physical activity and the object(s) the child was playing with. For physical activity, was there interrater reliability when the observers evaluated how vigorous each child's physical activity was? And was the measure valid: Did the observers' ratings of physical activity really measure how vigorous the activity was? For instance, if children's behavior was rated as "vigorous," was their heart rate elevated compared to when the children's behavior was rated "sedentary"? For the second variable, did observers agree on the kinds of activities children were engaged in—whether they were playing with balls and toys versus fixed equipment? (Measuring what kind of equipment a child is playing with is probably easy to do in a reliable and valid way.)

   For statistical validity, you might start by asking how large the effect size was—the difference in physical activity between children play-ing with balls and toys versus children playing with fixed equipment. You could ask whether the association might be attributable to subgroups: Could it be that the children playing with balls and toys were all boys, who also tended to play more vigorously, while girls tended to play both less vigorously and on fixed equipment? You could ask whether the association could be due to an outlier—perhaps one child who played with balls and toys extremely vigorously.

   For external validity, you might ask how representative the children are of the average U.S. preschooler. However, keep in mind that even if the study did not use a random sample (and thus has lower external validity), you would not necessarily dismiss the results. The association still holds in the sample, and to explore how it generalizes to other samples you would have to see if other studies conducted with different samples had similar results.

   b. To interrogate construct validity, you could ask how well the researchers measured each of the two variables in this association: level of ADHD and level of bullying. You could first ask how the ADHD diagnosis was made. If a professional psychologist diagnosed each child, you could feel more confident in the construct validity of this measure. You would then ask about the measure of bullying. How was this variable measured? The article mentions only that the researchers asked the children about bullying. You might wonder how valid a child's report of his or her own bullying behavior would be. Would a child's self-ratings correlate with teachers' ratings?

   For statistical validity, you could ask about effect size first. The article reports that children with ADHD are "four times more likely to bully" than non-ADHD children, which seems like a strong effect size. You might ask, as well, about subgroups—perhaps children from one socioeconomic group are more likely both to bully and to have an ADHD diagnosis. Finally, when the variables are categorical, as they seem to be in this study (children either have ADHD or they don't, and they are either bullies or not), outliers are typically not a problem, because a person cannot have an extreme score on a categorical variable.

   For external validity, the article reports that all of the children in one grade level were studied. This study used a census, not a sample, so the findings clearly generalize to children in this Swedish town.

3. For the first example, you might be tempted to suggest that children will exercise more vigorously if they are given balls and toys to play with on the playground. Is this causal claim justified?

1. *Covariance:* There is an association between the equipment and the level of physical activity.
2. *Temporal precedence:* It is not clear from this study whether the children's level of activity came first or whether they chose the equipment to play on first and the physical activity followed. (Were the more active children running around first and then picked up balls and toys? Or did they pick up the balls and toys first and then start running with them?)
3. *Internal validity:* There might be an alternative explanation—a third variable that is associated with both activity level and equipment. If children's sex is a subgroup (if boys both play more actively than girls and play with balls and toys more than girls), that would mean that sex is the real reason that equipment is correlated with activity intensity.

4. a. This strong correlation means that scientists who drank more beer published fewer articles.
   b. This means that the correlation is statistically significant—it is unlikely to have occurred by chance if there is really no relationship.
   c. The correlation would become stronger with this outlier.
   d. Answers will vary.
   e. No, the result establishes covariance, but it does not establish temporal precedence (it could also be the case that the scientists drank beer to cope with a lower publication rate). It does not establish internal validity, either: A third variable might be institution type; scientists working at universities might publish more and socialize less with beer, while scientists at working companies might publish less and socialize more with beer.

Chapter 8

1. a. The two variables are the degree of Facebook use and grades in college. It seems that college grades would be straightforward to measure by asking students or by looking at their transcripts. Students could self-report on their Facebook use, or researchers could observe the students' computer records somehow to track their usage more accurately.
   b. If "use of Facebook" is a quantitative variable (e.g., number of minutes of Facebook use per day), a scatterplot should show a negative slope, with Facebook use on one axis and GPA on the other axis. However, if "use of Facebook" is categorical (e.g., Do students use Facebook or not?), a bar graph would show the Facebook group with a lower mean GPA.
   c. 1. *Covariance*: Yes, the study does show an association between Facebook use and grades.
      2. *Temporal precedence*: No, it could be that students use Facebook first and then their grades drop, or it could be that students start with low grades and then turn to Facebook to distract themselves or to cope with their low grades.
      3. *Internal validity*: A third variable could be the explanation for this relationship. Perhaps better students both get higher grades and avoid Facebook in favor of more intellectual pursuits. Perhaps students in engineering majors both get lower grades and are more likely to use networking sites. Or perhaps very social students tend to use any kind of social outlet (including Facebook), and they are more distracted from studying by their busy social lives.

2. This sentence would mean that the original academic preparedness of these students is not a third variable that would explain the Facebook/GPA relationship. The researchers used multiple regression to control for SAT scores, and the beta for the Facebook/GPA relationship was still statistically significantly different from zero.

3. a. The dependent variable is perceived risk of using marijuana, found at the top of the table.
   b. There were five: age, gender, impulse control, body and self-image, and mastery of the external world.
   c. As age increases, perceived risk of using marijuana decreases, controlling for gender, impulse control, students' body and self-image, and students' sense of mastery of the external world.
   d. There is no relationship between body and self-image and perceived risk of using marijuana, when controlling for age, gender, impulse control, and sense of mastery of the external world.
   e. If you imagine a scatterplot in which gender is on the x-axis (with males at 0 and females at 1) and perceived risk of using marijuana is

on the y-axis, the positive slope of this beta means that females score higher than males on this variable. However, in this table, the gender difference is not statistically significant when controlling for the other predictors.

4. a. **Cross-Sectional Correlations**

Responsiveness Time 1	Responsiveness Time 2

Fussiness Time 1	Fussiness Time 2

Autocorrelations

Responsiveness Time 1	Responsiveness Time 2

Fussiness Time 1	Fussiness Time 2

Cross-Lag Correlations

Responsiveness Time 1	Responsiveness Time 2

Fussiness Time 1	Fussiness Time 2

b. A significant correlation between responsiveness at Time 1 and fussiness at Time 2 would suggest that responsiveness causes less fussiness. A significant correlation between responsiveness at Time 2 and fussiness at Time 1 would suggest that infant fussiness causes less responsiveness. A mutually reinforcing relationship would be indicated if both cross-lag correlations were significant.

5. a. Modeling is a mediator.

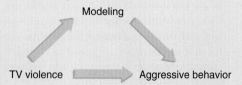

Modeling

TV violence → Aggressive behavior

b. Parent leniency is a third variable.

Parent leniency → TV violence
Parent leniency → Aggressive behavior

c. Age is a moderator.

Age	Relationship between TV violence and aggression
Teenager	Stronger r
Young adult	Weaker r

d. Education is a third variable.

Education → Cognitively demanding job
Education → Later cognitive skills

e. Gender is a moderator.

Gender	Relationship between having a cognitively demanding job and later cognitive skills
Male	Significant r
Female	Nonsignificant r

f. The increase in connections in the brain is a mediator

Increased connections in brain

Cognitively demanding job 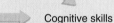 Cognitive skills

g. Nationality is a moderator.
h. Teasing is a mediator.
i. Socioeconomic class is a third variable.

Chapter 9

1. a. measured
   b. measured
   c. manipulated
   d. measured
   e. manipulated
   f. measured
   g. measured
   h. manipulated
   i. measured
   j. measured
   k. manipulated

2. (*Sample answer*) a. You could randomly assign students to two groups. Both groups will be taught the same material, using the same teaching methods, homework, and examples. However, you would train a teacher to act either friendly or stern as he or she teaches the two

groups of students. After the teaching unit, students would take the same school achievement test.

The bar graph should look something like this:

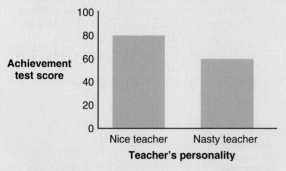

The independent (manipulated) variable is teacher's personality, with two levels (friendly and stern). The dependent (measured) variable is the achievement test score. The control variables might include the teacher's appearance, the content taught, the teaching method, the examples used, and the homework used.

Your assessment of covariance will depend on how your graph is prepared; however, this study would show covariance if the results came out as depicted in the graph shown above, in which the achievement test scores covary with the teacher's personality. This study also shows temporal precedence: The teacher's personality was manipulated, so it came first in time, followed by the achievement test. This study would also have internal validity if the researchers controlled for potential alternative explanations—for example, by keeping the teaching methods and homework the same. If the study has met all three causal rules, you can make a causal statement that a friendlier teacher causes students to score higher on school achievement tests.

3. (*Sample answer*) a. If you manipulated the temperature of a stranger's hand as independent groups, you would have some participants shake the hand of a stranger with a warm hand and other participants shake the hand of a stranger with a cold hand. You would randomly assign people to the two groups.

If you manipulated the temperature of a stranger's hand as within-groups, you would have participants shake the hands of two strangers— one with warm hands and one with cold hands. You would counterbalance the presentation, so that some participants shake the warm hand first and others shake the cold hand first.

For this independent variable, the advantage to using the independent-groups design is that you could use the same stranger at both levels and merely manipulate the temperature of his or her hand (perhaps by placing it in warm water or cool water ahead of time). If you manipulated this variable as within-groups, you could use fewer participants; however, having people shake the same person's hand twice—once when it's warm and once when it's cold—might increase suspicions in your participants. Using different strangers in the warm and cold conditions might help avert these suspicions but might also introduce confounds caused by the two different strangers' appearance, clothing, voice, mannerisms, height, and so forth. One way to avoid such confounds is to counterbalance your two strangers (as well as the presentation order), such that some participants see stranger A with warm hands and stranger B with cold hands, whereas other participants see stranger A with cold hands and stranger B with warm hands. Overall, the independent-groups design may be simpler to carry out. The within-groups design does retain the advantage, however, that each participant will be serving as his or her own control for the two experimental conditions.

4. a. The independent variable is whether participants were doing their questionnaires alone or with a passive confederate. The dependent variable was whether people stopped filling out their questionnaires to investigate the "accident" or help the "victim." The control variables were the tape recording of the accident (always the same), the room in which the study was held, the appearance and behavior of the female experimenter, and the questionnaires participants completed.

b.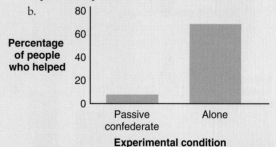

c. This was an independent-groups manipulation.

d. For construct validity, you would ask whether getting up to help is a good measure of helping behavior. You would also ask whether participating alone or with a passive confederate is a reasonable manipulation of the presence of bystanders. For internal validity, you would make sure that the experimenters used random assignment (they did) and appropriate control variables to avoid confounds. Are any other control variables unaccounted for? For external validity, you would ask how the experimenters gathered their sample: Was it a random sample of some population? You can also ask if this situation—helping a woman falling from a chair in another room—would generalize to other emergencies, such as helping a man bleeding on the street, helping somebody who fainted, or helping in other kinds of situations.

For statistical validity, you could ask how large the effect size was. Indeed, the difference was 7% versus 70%, and this is an extremely large effect size. You would make sure it was statistically significant, too. (An effect size that large probably is.)

5. Your friend is asking about the internal validity of this study, because she is proposing an alternative explanation for the results. However, her criticisms are inappropriate, because Darley and Latané used random assignment to place people in the two groups. This process would have ensured that the most helpful people in a sample were equally distributed across the different experimental conditions.

Chapter 10

1. a. IV: Exposure to alcohol advertising. DV: Reported level of drinking
   b. Design: One-group, pretest/posttest design (a within-groups design)
   c.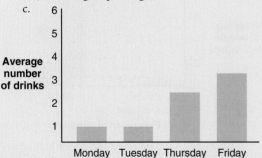
   d. IV threats: Because this is a one-group, pretest/posttest design, it is subject to multiple inter-

nal validity threats. Perhaps the most obvious is history—it is plausible that students drank more after exposure to the advertising simply because the posttest was on a weekend.
   e. To redesign the study, Jack could add a comparison group that is also tested on the same days but does not see the alcohol advertising.

2. a. IV: The use of the categorization strategy. DV: the memory rate
   b. Design: one-group, pretest/posttest (a within-groups design)
   c.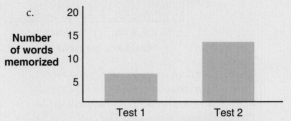
   d. Because this is a one-group, pretest/posttest design, it is subject to multiple internal validity threats. Perhaps the most obvious here is testing: The students probably recalled more words the second time because they had a second chance to learn the same list of words.
   e. To fix this problem, the student presenters should use a new word list the second time—when categorization is used as a mnemonic. To control for the possibility that one word list might be more difficult than the other (which would be a design confound), the presenters should also counterbalance the use of the two word lists.

3. a. IV: Exposure to positive or negative adjectives in Stage 1. DV: Rated positivity of the adventures of fictional people
   b. Design: Posttest-only design
   c.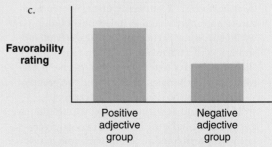
   d. No obvious internal validity threats in this design
   e. No redesign would be needed.

4. *Between-group differences:* Was 3 ounces of chocolate enough to cause a difference in well-being? Was the well-being questionnaire sensitive enough to detect differences in this variable?

   Within-group differences: With such a small sample, Dr. Dove might need to use a within-groups design, because there are likely to be individual differences in well-being. Otherwise, she might try using a larger number of participants (30 in each group might be better) so that the impact of measurement errors or individual differences will be muted. The participants in this study also seemed to be going about their normal routines in real-world settings. There may have been innumerable sources of situation noise in their lives over this 4-week period. In a future study, Dr. Dove might consider quarantining participants for some period of time.

5. Choosing an appropriate number of participants for an experiment is a statistical validity consideration, but a study does not always need to have a large sample size. Small samples (of even 15 or fewer participants) can usefully show group differences in within-groups designs when measurement error is small, individual differences are few, and situation noise is absent. Also, when effect sizes are large—that is, when there are large, real differences between two groups—small samples are sufficient to detect statistically significant group differences. It may seem counterintuitive, but the larger the difference you are looking for, the smaller the sample you need to find it.

Chapter 11

1. In the driving example, there does appear to be a main effect for driver age, such that older drivers are slower to brake. And there does appear to be a main effect for the cell phone condition, such that drivers using cell phones are slower to brake. Although we would need statistics to confirm that these differences are significant we know that in the actual study, both main effects were statistically significant (see p. 336).

DV: Brake onset time (ms)	IV$_1$: Cell phone condition		
	On cell phone	Not on phone	Main effect for IV$_2$: Driver age
IV$_2$: Driver age — Younger drivers	912	780	848
IV$_2$: Driver age — Older drivers	1066	912	999
Main effect for IV$_1$: Cell phone condition	1086	846	

In the memory test example, there does not appear to be a main effect for the testing condition, since the two marginal means are almost the same. There also does not appear to be a very large main effect for the learning condition, since the two marginal means are almost the same here, too. We would need inferential statistics to tell us if the difference between 11.05 and 9.90 is a statistically significant difference.

DV: Number of words memorized	IV$_1$: Testing condition		
	Water's edge	Underwater	Main effect for IV$_2$: Learning condition
IV$_2$: Learning condition — Water's edge	13.5	8.6	11.05
IV$_2$: Learning condition — Underwater	8.4	11.4	9.9
Main effect for IV$_1$: Testing conditions	10.95	10	

2. a. This is a 3 × 2 within-groups factorial design.
   b. The independent variables are cell phone condition (two levels) and testing condition (three levels). The dependent variable is the number of collisions.
   c. Both independent variables are within-groups variables.
   d. Notice that you could put either independent variable on the x-axis; either would be correct, and you can detect interactions equally well from either graph.

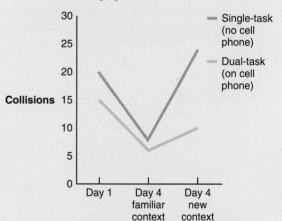

   e. There is a main effect for cell phone condition, such that talking on a cell phone causes more collisions. (We can say "cause" here because this was an experimental design with no confounds.) There is also a main effect for testing day: People had the fewest collisions on Day 4, familiar context, and the most collisions on Day 4, new context. There appears to be an interaction: The difference between single and dual task is about the same on Day 1 and Day 4, familiar context, but the difference is greater on Day 4, new context.

f. The results of this study seem to show that regardless of experience level, using cell phones impairs people's driving skill.

3. a. This design would have 6 cells. There would be two main effects and one two-way interaction.

b. This design would have 24 cells. There would be three main effects, three two-way interactions, and one three-way interaction.

c. This design would have 120 cells. There would be four main effects, eight two-way interactions, four three-way interactions, and one four-way interaction.

4. *Construct Validity*

- *Was the manipulation of package size a good one?* The large package was twice as large as the small package, so this seems to be a very straightforward manipulation.

- *Was the manipulation of product price a good one?* You do not have enough information, but Wansink might ideally say that a manipulation check showed that the sale-priced package was estimated to be significantly less expensive than the regular-price package, so this was a good manipulation.

- *Was the measure of how much spaghetti people used a reliable and valid measure of that variable?* Counting spaghetti strands is an objective measure of product usage, subject to very little measurement error. It is also a straightforwardly valid measure of product use.

Internal Validity

- *Were the two independent variables manipulated without confounds?* In the case of product price, this independent variable does not appear to have confounds; the participants were told a price for each product, and the price was different in each case. In the case of package size, the amount of product was kept constant across the two size conditions. However, this control variable introduces the potential confound that the large package was only half full, whereas the small package was completely full. Therefore, we are not sure if people used more from the large package because it was larger or because they were reacting to a perception that the smaller package was "almost empty."

- *Were people randomly assigned to each cell of the design?* You do not have enough information, but Wansink should have randomly assigned participants to each cell. In fact, if you read Wansink's original article, you find that the people were randomly assigned.

External Validity

- *To whom can the results of the study generalize?* You do not have enough information. Ideally, Wansink could answer that he used a random sample of participants from a community, so his results may generalize to that same community. In fact, the participants in this study were a nonrandom sample of PTA members in New Hampshire and Vermont. They may not generalize to other kinds of people. However, Wansink has replicated the results, showing that other types of participants in other studies also tend to use more of a product from a larger package.

- *Do the results of this study generalize to products other than spaghetti?* As you read in the chapter, the article that reported the spaghetti study also reported similar studies involving Crisco oil, Mr. Clean cleanser, Clorox bleach, and bottled water. These replications across a range of products provide good evidence for external validity.

Statistical Validity

There are three statistical results from this factorial design: two main effects and one interaction. For each of these main effects and interactions, you can ask: *How large is the effect size?* and *Is the effect size statistically significant?* You might be interested in how many people participated in the study, but only if the results are not statistically significant: A small sample size is a problem only when the results are not significant, because adding more participants is one way of increasing the chance of a significant result. For Wansink's study, you would not need to question the sample size because the effects are significant.

5. Participant variables are usually independent-groups variables. In the case of gender, participants cannot be both male and female—they are one or the other. Ethnicity, too, is an independent-groups variable. Sometimes personality traits (such as high self-esteem versus low self-esteem or introversion versus extroversion) are used as participant variables; these, too, are independent-groups variables. Age, however, could go either way. Strayer and his colleagues recruited some people in their 20s and other people in their 70s, so age was an independent-groups variable in his design. However, if a researcher recruits one sample of

people and tests them in their 20s, 30s, 40s, and 50s, age becomes a participant variable that is studied as a repeated-measures variable. (This kind of design is called a longitudinal study; see Chapter 8.)

Chapter 12

1. a. This is a nonequivalent control group design.

   b.
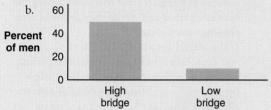

   c. The causal claim would be that being on the high bridge caused men to call the female experimenter (presumably because they thought they were attracted to her). This design has co-variance (the participants from the high bridge called more than those from the low bridge) and temporal precedence (the participants crossed the bridge before they called the woman). How-ever, in this experimental design, it is possible that a selection effect is threatening internal validity. Different kinds of men might choose to cross a precarious high bridge versus a safer low bridge. Furthermore, a man who would cross the exciting bridge might also be more likely to take the risk of calling an attractive woman. Therefore, the internal validity is questionable in this study.

   You could redesign this study by somehow studying only the men who chose to cross the bridge but studying them either before they were about to cross it or after they had already crossed it. (In fact, Dutton and Aron ran a second study to rule out the selection effect problem. Specifically, in the second study, the female experimenter approached only men who had crossed the tall bridge. However, half of the men she approached had just crossed the bridge, and the other half were approached after they had taken a significant rest—so that their heart rates had returned to normal. The results showed that the men approached while in the middle of the bridge were more likely to call than the men who had rested—helping the researchers rule out the selection effect expla-nation for the first study.)

   d. Construct validity of the dependent variable: How well does a phone call operationalize a man's attraction to a woman? (Probably very well.) External validity: How well does the situation of crossing a bridge represent other situations in which a person might be aroused? (The researchers could also study other arous-ing activities, such as exercising or watching a scary movie.)

3. There are two possible nonequivalent control group designs. One would compare concern for physical appearance among students who are in fraternities or sororities versus those who are not. The results might look like this:

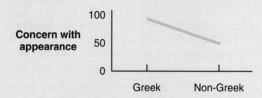

Even if there was a difference between the two groups, you could not be sure that the fraternity/sorority membership caused the concern with physical appear-ance. There is a possible selection effect: Students who are concerned with their physical appearance might be more likely to join a fraternity or sorority.

Therefore, you might be better off design-ing a nonequivalent control group design with a pretest and a posttest (measuring concern with appearance both before and after the time when people join sororities). The results might look like this:

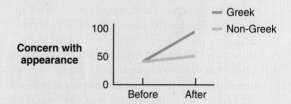

These results would help rule out a selection ef-fect, because the groups started out with the same concern about appearance.

An interrupted time-series design might measure students monthly, both before and after they joined a fraternity or sorority. The re-sults might look like this (this example assumes that students join fraternities and sororities in February):

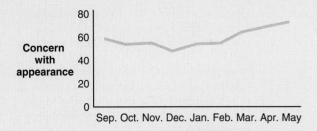

These results would suggest that sorority membership causes an increased concern with appearance. However, it could be the season: Perhaps all students are more concerned with appearance as the spring approaches and the weather grows warmer. (That would be a history threat.)

Therefore, you might be most convinced by a nonequivalent-groups interrupted-time-series design that follows both students who are in fraternities and sororities and students who are not in them over the course of the year. The results might look like this:

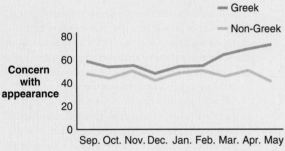

These results suggest that fraternity and sorority membership causes an increased concern with appearance, because the season affects all students. Even though, in this pattern, the students who eventually join fraternities and sororities are more concerned with their appearance initially, they become even more concerned with appearance after they pledge, whereas the other students' concern with appearance does not increase.

4. a. Either the stable-baseline design or the reversal design might be appropriate here. Since there is only one context for the growling behavior, the multiple-baseline design might not be appropriate.
   b. If you used a stable-baseline design, you would observe and record your dog's growling behav-

ior daily in the presence of other dogs for a long period of time (perhaps two or three weeks). Then you would continue to observe and record your dog's growling behavior daily as you began to implement the behavioral technique.
   c. The graph would look similar to Figure 12.10, except the growling behavior would be consistently high (rather than low) during the baseline period and would then decrease after the intervention starts.
   d. If the results were as depicted in the graph you drew, you could rule out maturation and regression explanations for the dog's behavior, because the stable-baseline period shows that the dog's behavior has not changed on its own. A history threat might still apply to your data if some other change (such as a change in diet) happened to occur in the dog's life at the same time you started using the behavioral technique. However, in the absence of some other explanation, you could infer the causal success of the therapy if the dog's growling behavior began to decrease at the time you started the therapy.

Chapter 13

1. Answers will vary.
2. Answers will vary.
3. a. This study could be conducted in theory-testing mode, because it tests a theory that exposure to a very stressful event is a potential cause of mental suffering. However, this study is more likely to be conducted in generalization mode, since it appears to be testing a frequency claim about the population of Holocaust survivors. (What percentage of survivors experience mood or sleep disorders?) Frequency claims are always in generalization mode.
   b. This study appears at first to be conducted in theory-testing mode. It is testing a link between electromagnetic radiation and brain activity. (Does this kind of radiation affect the brain?) However, because the type of radiation is tied to cell phones, the researchers may be interested, eventually, in generalizing the results to humans who use cell phones and may be worried about the technology's long-term benefits and risks.

c. This study used a restricted sample of a special kind of person—few individuals are born blind and later regain their sight—so it is unlikely this study was conducted in generalization mode. It is a good example of theory-testing mode because the results from this special sample allowed the researchers to learn that the brain uses motion (more than color or lines) to decode the visual world.

4. Although this was a study of a real-life event, it appears to have been conducted in theory-testing mode because the authors were testing theories about "flashbulb" memories, such as people's relative memory for emotional versus nonemotional events and the relationship between the accuracy of people's memory and their confidence in their memories.

   You could ask whether the results of this study are replicable: Are they statistically significant? Do the results from each of the seven cities resemble one another, suggesting that the results are replicable? You could ask how well the measures allowed the researchers to test the theories. You might be critical of the study's sampling techniques; after all, the 3,000 people they studied were not selected randomly, and they were selected from seven convenient U.S. cities (close to the authors' friends). However, since the researchers were testing theories about flashbulb memories rather than attempting to generalize, you might be satisfied despite the lack of external validity in this study. You might also ask whether the results would hold up in another cultural context. Although people in other countries probably reacted to the events of September 11 differently from Americans, a future study could use some other flashbulb event (such as an earthquake, storm, or political event) to investigate the same conceptual variables.

References

Abelson, R. P. (1995). *Statistics as principled argument.* Hillsdale, NJ: Erlbaum.

American Psychological Association. (1994). Resolution on Facilitated Communication by the American Psychological Association Adopted in Council, August 14, 1994, Los Angeles, CA.

American Psychological Association. (2002). *Ethical principles of psychologists and code of conduct.* Retrieved from http://www.apa.org/ethics/code/index.aspx

American Psychological Association. (2010). *Publication manual of the American Psychological Association* (6th ed). Washington, DC: American Psychological Association.

Anderson, C. A., Berkowitz, L., Donnerstein, E., Huesmann, L. R., Johnson, J., Linz, D., . . . Wartella, E. (2003). The influence of media violence on youth. *Psychological Science in the Public Interest, 4,* 81–110.

Anderson, C. A., Shibuya, A., Ihori, N., Swing, E. L., Bushman, B. J., Sakamoto, A., . . . Barlett, C. P. (2010). Violent video game effects on aggression, empathy, and prosocial behavior in Eastern and Western countries: A meta-analytic review. *Psychological Bulletin, 136,* 151–173.

Answerbag.com. (2005). How can a person release built-up tension, anger, and stress . . . ? Retrieved from http://www.answerbag.com/q_view/32657

Arnett, J. (2008). The neglected 95%: Why American psychology needs to become less American. *American Psychologist, 63,* 602–614.

Aron, A. (2009). *Instructor's manual with tests for Statistics for Psychology* (5th ed.). New York, NY: Pearson.

Associated Press. (2008). Half of Americans struggle to stay happy. Retrieved from http://www.msnbc.msn.com/id/24376037/ns/health-mental_health/

Back, M. D., Schmuckle, S. C., & Egloff, B. (2008). Becoming friends by chance. *Psychological Science, 19,* 439–440.

Bakalar, N. (2005, May 3). Ugly children may get parental short shrift. *The New York Times.* Retrieved from www.nytimes.com

Bargh, J. A., Chen, M., & Burrows, L. (1996). Automaticity of social behavior: Direct effects of trait construct and stereotype activation on action. *Journal of Personality and Social Psychology, 71,* 230–244.

Barnett, W. S. (1998). Long-term effects on cognitive development and school success. In W. S. Barnett & S. S. Boocock (Eds.), *Early care and education for children in poverty: Promises, programs, and long-term outcomes* (pp. 11–44). Buffalo, NY: SUNY Press.

Baron, R. (1997). The sweet smell of . . . helping: Effects of pleasant ambient fragrance on prosocial behavior in shopping malls. *Personality and Social Psychology Bulletin, 23,* 498–503.

Baron, R. M., & Kenny, D. A. (1986). The moderator-mediator variable distinction in social psychological research: Conceptual, strategic and statistical considerations. *Journal of Personality and Social Psychology, 51,* 1173–1182.

Barros, R. M., Silver, E. J., & Stein, R. E. K. (2009). School recess and group classroom behavior. *Pediatrics, 123,* 431–436.

Baumrind, D. (1964). Some thoughts on the ethics of research: After reading Milgram's "Behavioral Study of Obedience." *American Psychologist, 19,* 421–423.

Bear, G. (1995). Computationally intensive methods warrant reconsideration of pedagogy in statistics. *Behavior Research Methods, Instruments, and Computers, 27,* 144–147.

Beck A. T., Ward C., & Mendelson M. (1961). Beck Depression Inventory (BDI). *Archives of General Psychiatry, 4,* 561–571.

Beck, A. T., Ward, C. H., Mendelson, M., Mock, J., & Erbaugh, J. (1961). An inventory for measuring depression. *Archives of General Psychiatry, 4,* 53–63.

Beecher, H. K. (1955). The powerful placebo. *Journal of the American Medical Association, 159*(17), 1601–1606.

Belly fat linked to dementia, study shows (2010, May 10). Retrieved from http://www.msnbc.msn.com/id/37283683/ns/health-diet_and_nutrition/

Benedetti, F., Amanzio, M., Vighetti, S., & Asteggiano, G. (2006). The biochemical and neuroendocrine bases of the hyperalgesic nocebo effect. *The Journal of Neuroscience, 26,* 12014–12022.

Berkowitz, L. (1973, July). The case for bottling up rage. *Psychology Today, 7,* 24–31.

Berkowitz, L., & Donnerstein, E. (1982). External validity is more than skin deep: Some answers to criticisms of laboratory experiments. *American Psychologist, 37,* 245–257.

Bick, J., & Dozier, M. (2008, May). *Mother-child interactions and maternal oxytocin production: The role of biological relatedness.* Poster presented at the Association for Psychological Science, Chicago, IL.

Blaine, B., & Crocker, J. (1995). Religiousness, race and psychological well-being: Exploring social psychological mediators. *Personality and Social Psychology Bulletin, 21,* 1031–1041.

Blass, T. (2002). The man who shocked the world. *Psychology Today, 35,* 68–74.

Bogg, T., & Roberts, B. W. (2004). Conscientiousness and health-related behaviors: A meta-analysis of the leading behavioral contributors to mortality. *Psychological Bulletin, 130,* 887–919.

Borkenau, P., & Liebler, A. (1993). Convergence of stranger ratings of personality and intelligence with self-ratings, partner ratings, and measured intelligence. *Journal of Personality and Social Psychology, 65,* 546–553.

Bothwell, R. K., Deffenbacher, K. A., & Brigham, J. C. (1987). Correlations of eyewitness accuracy and confidence: Optimality hypothesis revisited. *Journal of Applied Psychology, 72,* 691–695.

Bowker, A., Boekhoven, B., Nolan, A., Bauhaus, S., Glover, P., Powell, T., & Taylor, S. (2009). Naturalistic observations of spectator behavior at youth hockey games. *The Sport Psychologist, 23*(3), 301–316.

Boys with unusual names more likely to break the law. (2009, January 28). Retrieved from http://www.foxnews.com/story/0,2933,484585,00.html

Brewer, M. (2000). Research design and issues of validity. In H. Reis & C. Judd (Eds.), *Handbook of research methods in social and personality psychology.* Cambridge, England: Cambridge University Press.

Brewer, N., & Wells, G. L. (2006). The confidence-accuracy relationship in eyewitness identification: Effects of lineup instructions, foil similarity, and target-absent base rates. *Journal of Experimental Psychology: Applied, 12,* 11–30.

Brice, G. C. Gorey, K. M., Hall, R. M., & Angelino, S. (1996). The STAYWELL program: Maximizing elders' capacity for independent living through health promotion and disease prevention activities. *Research on Aging, 18,* 202–218.

Bröder, A. (1998). Deception can be acceptable. *American Psychologist, 53*(7), 805–806. doi:10.1037/0003-066X.53.7.805.b

Brown, R., & Hanlon, C. (1970). Derivational complexity and order of acquisition in child speech. In J. R. Hayes (Ed.), *Cognition and the development of language* (pp. 11–54). New York, NY: Wiley.

Brown, W. H., Pfeiffer, K. A., McIver, K. L., Dowda, M., Addy, C. L., & Pate, R. R. (2009). Social and environmental factors associated with preschoolers' nonsedentary physical activity. *Child Development, 80,* 45–58.

Bushman, B. J. (2002). Does venting anger feed or extinguish the flame? Catharsis, rumination, distraction, anger and aggressive responding. *Personality and Social Psychology Bulletin, 28,* 724–731.

Bushman, B. J., & Anderson, C. A. (2001). Media violence and the American public: Scientific facts versus media misinformation. *American Psychologist, 56,* 477–489.

Bushman, B. J., Baumeister, R. F., & Phillips, C. M. (2001). Do people aggress to improve their mood? Catharsis beliefs, affect regulation opportunity, and aggressive responding. *Journal of Personality and Social Psychology, 81,* 17–32.

Campos, B., Graesch, A. P., Repetti, R., Bradbury, T., & Ochs, E. (2009). Opportunity for interaction? A naturalistic observation study of dual-earner families after work and school. *Journal of Family Psychology, 23*(6), 798–807. doi:10.1037/a0015824

Carey, B. (2007, June 22). Research finds firstborns gain the higher IQ. *The New York Times.* Retrieved from www.nytimes.com

Carlson, N. (2009). *Physiology of behavior* (10th ed.). New York, NY: Allyn & Bacon.

Carroll, L. (2008, January 29). Kids with ADHD may be more likely to bully. Retrieved from http://www.msnbc.msn.com/id/22813400/

Centers for Disease Control. (2000). Clinical growth charts. Retrieved from http://www.cdc.gov/growthcharts/clinical_charts.htm

Centers for Disease Control. (2008). Youth risk behavior surveillance—United States 2007. Retrieved from http://www.cdc.gov/mmwr/preview/mmwrhtml/ss5704a1.htm

Childress, J. F., Meslin, E. M., & Shapiro, H. T. (2005). *Belmont revisited: Ethical principles for research with human subjects.* Washington, DC: Georgetown University Press.

Christian, L., Keeter, S., Purcell, K., & Smith, A. (2010). Assessing the cell phone challenge. Pew Research Center. Retrieved from http://pewresearch.org/pubs/1601/assessing-cell-phone-challenge-in-public-opinion-surveys

Cicirelli, V. G., & Associates. (1969). *The impact of Head Start: An evaluation of the effects of Head Start on children's cognitive and affective development* (Vols. 1–2) (Report to the Office of Economic Opportunity). Athens, OH: Ohio University and Westinghouse Learning Corporation.

Cocaine exposure during pregnancy leads to impulsivity in male, not female, monkeys (2009, October 24). Retrieved from http://www.sciencedaily.com/releases/2009/10/091022114309.htm

Cohen, J. (1992). A power primer. *Psychological Bulletin, 112,* 155–159.

Cohen, S., Kamarck, T., & Mermelstein, R. (1983). A global measure of perceived stress. *Journal of Health and Social Behavior, 24,* 385–396.

Coile, D. C., & Miller, N. E. (1984). How radical animal activists try to mislead humane people. *American Psychologist, 45,* 1304–1312.

Coleman, N. (2008, September 13). Hockey moms? Hockey dads set the example. *Star Tribune.* Retrieved from http://www.startribune.com

Conner Snibbe, A., & Markus, H. R. (2005). You can't always get what you want: Educational attainment, agency, and choice. *Journal of Personality and Social Psychology, 88,* 703–720.

Cooper, J., & Strayer, D. L. (2008). Effects of simulator practice and real world experience on cell-phone-related driver distraction. *Human Factors, 50,* 893–902.

Copeland, J., & Snyder, M. (1995). When counselors confirm: A functional analysis. *Personality and Social Psychology Bulletin, 21,* 1210–1220.

Cozby, P. C. (2007). *Methods in Behavioral Research* (9th ed.). New York, NY: McGraw-Hill.

Cronbach, L. J., & Meehl, P. E. (1955). Construct validity in psychological tests. *Psychological Bulletin, 52,* 281–302.

Crowne, D. P., & Marlowe, D. (1960). A new scale of social desirability independent of psychopathology. *Journal of Consulting Psychology, 24,* 349–354.

Darley, J. M., & Latané, B. (1968). Bystander intervention in emergencies: Diffusion of responsibility. *Journal of Personality and Social Psychology, 8,* 377–383.

Deary, I. J., Penke, J., & Johnson, W. (2010). The neuroscience of human intelligence differences. *Nature Reviews: Neuroscience, 11,* 201–212.

DeNoon, D. J. (2008, May 7). Perk of a good job: Aging mind is sharp. Retrieved from http://www.webmd.com/brain/news/20080507/perk-of-good-job-aging-mind-is-sharp

Diener, E., & Diener, C. (1996). Most people are happy. *Psychological Science, 7,* 181–185.

Diener, E., Horwitz, J., & Emmons, R. A. (1985). Happiness of the very wealthy. *Social Indicators, 16,* 263–274.

Do experiences or material goods make us happier? (2009, February 23). Esciencenews.com. Retrieved from http://esciencenews.com/articles/2009/02/23/do.experiences.or.material.goods.make.us.happier

Doyle, A. C. (1892/2002). Silver blaze. In *The complete Sherlock Holmes.* New York, NY: Gramercy.

Dunn, D. (2009). *Research methods for social psychology.* New York, NY: Wiley-Blackwell.

Dunn, L. M., & Dunn, L. M. (1981). *PPVT: Revised manual.* Circle Pines, MN: American Guidance Service.

Dutton, D. G., & Aron, A. P. (1974). Some evidence for heightened sexual attraction under conditions of high anxiety. *Journal of Personality and Social Psychology, 30,* 510–517. doi:10.1037/h0037031

Ebbinghaus, H. (1913). *Memory: A contribution to experimental psychology.* New York, NY: Columbia University Press. (Original work published 1885)

Edgington, E. S., & Onghena, P. (2007). *Randomization tests* (4th ed). London, England: Chapman and Hall/CRC.

Eisenberg, L. (1977). The social imperatives of medical research. *Science, 198,* 1105–1110.

Elliot, A. J., Maier, M. A., Moller, A. C., Friedman, R., & Meinhardt, J. (2007). Color and psychological functioning: The effect of red on performance in achievement contexts. *Journal of Experimental Psychology: General, 136,* 154–168.

Ericsson, K. A., Chase, W. G., & Faloon, S. (1980). Acquisition of a memory skill. *Science, 208,* 1181–1182.

Eron, L. D., Huesmann, L. R., Lefkowitz, M. M., & Walder, L. O. (1972). Does television violence cause aggression? *American Psychologist, 27,* 253–263.

Federal Register. (2000, December 6). FR Doc 06de00-72. Federal Research Misconduct Policy. Washington, DC: Department of Health and Human Services.

Federal Register. (2001). FR Doc 01-30627. Washington, DC: Department of Health and Human Services.

Feshbach, S. (1956). The catharsis hypothesis and some consequences of interaction with aggression and neutral play objects. *Journal of Personality, 24,* 449–462.

Fleary, S. A., Heffer, R. W., McKyer, E. L. J., & Newman, D. A. (2010). Using the bioecological model to predict risk perception of marijuana use and reported marijuana use in adolescence. *Addictive Behaviors, 35*(8), 795–798.

Frey, D., & Stahlberg, D. (1986). Selection of information after receiving more or less reliable self-threatening information. *Personality and Social Psychology Bulletin, 12,* 434–441.

Gabriel, T. (2010, May 1). Despite push, success at charter schools is mixed. *The New York Times.* Retrieved from www.nytimes.com

Gallup-Healthways. (2009). *Gallup-Healthways Well-Being Index: Methodology report for indexes.* Retrieved from http://www.well-beingindex.com/methodology.asp

Gay, P. (Ed.). (1989). *A Freud reader.* New York, NY: Norton.

Gazzaniga, M. (2005). Forty-five years of split-brain research and still going strong. *Nature Reviews Neuroscience, 6,* 653–649.

Gazzaniga, M. S., Bogen, J. E., & Sperry, R. W. (1962). Some functional effects of sectioning the cerebral commissures in man. *Proceedings of the National Academy of Science, 48,* part 2, 1765–1769.

Geen, R. G., & Quanty, M. B. (1977). The catharsis of aggression: An evaluation of a hypothesis. *Advances in Experimental Social Psychology, 10,* 2–39.

Gernsbacher, M. A. (2003). Is one style of autism early intervention "scientifically proven"? *Journal of Developmental and Learning Disorders, 7,* 19–25.

Gidus, T. (2008, June 19). Mindless eating [Web log post]. Retrieved from http://www.healthline.com/blogs/diet_nutrition/2008/06/mindless-eating.html

Gilbert, D. (2005). *Stumbling on happiness.* New York, NY: Vintage.

Godden, D. R., & Baddeley, D. (1975). Context-dependent memory in two natural environments: On land and underwater. *British Journal of Psychology, 66,* 325–331.

Goldacre, B. (2008, September 6). Cheer up, it's all down to random variation [Web log post]. Retrieved from http://www.guardian.co.uk/commentisfree/2008/sep/06/medicalresearch

Gottfredson, L. S. (Ed.). (1997). Intelligence and social policy. *Intelligence, 24* (Special Issue).

Gould, S. J. (1981). *The mismeasure of man.* New York, NY: Norton.

Gould, S. J. (1996). *The mismeasure of man* (revised and expanded). New York, NY: Norton.

Gray, F. D. (1998). *The Tuskegee syphilis study: The real story and beyond.* Montgomery, AL: River City Publishers.

Greenberg, A. G., Spangenberg, E. R., Pratkanis, A. R., & Eskenazi, J. (1991). Double-blind tests of subliminal self-help audiotapes. *Psychological Science, 2,* 119–122.

Greenwald, A. G., Nosek, B. A., & Banaji, M. R. (2003). Understanding and using the Implicit Association Test: I. An improved scoring algorithm. *Journal of Personality and Social Psychology, 85,* 197–216.

Gross, J. J., & John, O. P. (2002). Wise emotion regulation. In L. F. Barrett & P. Salovey (Eds.), *The wisdom in feeling: Psychological processes in emotional intelligence* (pp. 297–319). New York, NY: Guilford Press.

Halavis, A. (2004, August 29). The Isuzu experiment. Retrieved from http://alex.halavais.net/the-isuzu-experiment

Hamzelou, J. (2010, January). Cell phone radiation is good for Alzheimer's mice. New Scientist Health. Retrieved from http://www.newscientist.com/article/dn18351-cellphone-radiation-is-good-for-alzheimers-mice.html

Harlow, H. (1958). The nature of love. *American Psychologist, 13,* 673–685.

Harvey, E. (1999). Short-term and long-term effects of early parental employment on children of the National Longitudinal Survey of Youth. *Developmental Psychology, 35,* 445–459.

Hastorf, A., & Cantril, H. (1954). They saw a game: A case study. *Journal of Abnormal and Social Psychology, 49,* 129–134.

Heine, S. J. (2008). *Cultural psychology.* New York, NY: Norton.

Heller, J. (1972, July 26). Syphilis victims went untreated for 40 years. *The New York Times.* Retrieved from www.nytimes.com

Hennigan, K. M., Del Rosario, M. L., Heath, L., Cook, T. D., Wharton, J. D., & Calder, B. J. (1982). Impact of the introduction of television on crime in the United States: Empirical findings and theoretical implications. *Journal of Personality and Social Psychology, 42,* 461–477.

Henrich, J., Heine, S. J., & Norenzayan, A. (2010). The weirdest people in the world? (Target article, commentaries, and response). *Behavioral and Brain Sciences, 33,* 61–83.

Hertsgaard, D., & Light, H. (1984). Anxiety, depression, and hostility in rural women. *Psychological Reports, 55,* 673–674.

Herzog, H. A., Jr. (1993). "The movement is my life": The psychology of animal rights activism. *Journal of Social Issues, 49,* 103–119.

Hirst, W., Phelps, E. A., Buckner, R. L., Budson, A. E., Cuc, A., Gabrieli, J. D. E., . . . Chandan J. (2009). Long-term memory for the terrorist attack of September 11: Flashbulb memories, event memories, and the factors that influence their retention. *Journal of Experimental Psychology: General, 138,* 161–176.

Holmes, T. H., & Rahe, R. H. (1967). The social readjustment rating scale. *Journal of Psychosomatic Research, 11,* 213–218.

Hsu, J. (2009, April 12). Facebook users get worse grades in college. Retrieved from http://www.livescience.com/culture/090413-facebook-grades.html

Hubbard, F. O. A., & van Ijzendoorn, M. H. (1991). Maternal unresponsiveness and infant crying across the first 9 months: A naturalistic longitudinal study. *Infant Behavior and Development, 14,* 299–312.

Jacobson, J. W., Mulick, J. A., & Schwartz, A. A. (1995). A history of facilitated communication: Science, pseudoscience, and antiscience. (Science Working Group on facilitated communication). *American Psychologist, 50,* 750–765.

Janzen-Wilde, M. L., Duchan, J. F., & Higginbotham, D. J. (1995). Successful use of facilitated communication with an oral child. *Journal of Speech and Hearing Research, 38,* 658–676.

Johansson, G. (1973). Visual perception of biological motion and a model for its analysis. *Perception and Psychophysics, 14,* 201–211.

Johnson, J. G., Cohen, P., Smailes, E. M., Kasen, S., & Brook, J. S. (2002). Television viewing and aggressive behavior during adolescence and adulthood. *Science, 295,* 2468–2471.

Jones, J. H. (1993). *Bad blood: The Tuskegee syphilis experiment* (Rev. ed.). New York, NY: Free Press.

Jonsen, A. R. (2005). On the origins and future of the Belmont Report. In J. F. Childress, E. M. Meslin, & H. T. Shapiro (Eds.), *Belmont revisited: Ethical principles for research with human subjects* (pp. 3–11). Washington, DC: Georgetown University Press.

Kagay, M. (1994, July 8). Poll on doubt of Holocaust is corrected. *The New York Times.* Retrieved from www.nytimes.com

Kenny, D. A. (2008). Mediation. Retrieved from http://davidakenny.net/cm/mediate.htm

Kenny, D. A. (2009). Moderator variables. Retrieved from http://davidakenny.net/cm/moderation.htm

Kenny, D. A., & West, T. V. (2008). Zero acquaintance: Definitions, statistical model, findings, and process. In J. Skowronski & N. Ambady (Eds.), *First impressions* (pp. 129–146). New York, NY: Guilford Press.

Kienle, G. S., & Kiene, H. (1997). The powerful placebo effect: Fact or fiction? *Journal of Clinical Epidemiology, 50*(12), 1311–1318.

Kimmel, A. J. (1998). In defense of deception. *American Psychologist, 53,* 803–805.

Kimmel, A. J. (2007). *Ethical issues in behavioral research* (2nd ed.). Malden, MA: Blackwell.

Kirsch, I., & Sapirstein, G. (1998). Listening to Prozac and hearing placebo: A meta-analysis of antidepressant medication. *Prevention & Treatment, 1*(2). doi: 10.1037/1522-3736.1.1.12a

Klayman, J., & Ha, Y.-W. (1987). Confirmation, disconfirmation, and information in hypothesis testing. *Psychological Review, 94,* 211–228.

Klewe, L. (1993). An empirical evaluation of spelling boards as a means of communication for the multihandicapped. *Journal of Autism and Developmental Disorders, 23,* 559–566.

Kringelbach, M. L., & Berridge, K. C. (2009). Towards a functional neuroanatomy of pleasure and happiness. *Trends in Cognitive Sciences, 13,* 479–487.

Langer, E. J., & Abelson, R. P. (1974). A patient by any other name . . . clinician group differences in labeling bias. *Journal of Consulting and Clinical Psychology, 42,* 4–9.

Langer, E. J., & Rodin, J. (1976). The effects of choice and enhanced personal responsibility for the aged: A field experiment in an institutional setting. *Journal of Personality and Social Psychology, 34,* 191–198. doi:10.1037/0022-3514.34.2.191

Latané, B., & Darley, J. M. (1968). Bystander "apathy." *American Scientist, 57,* 244–268.

Latané, B., & Nida, S. (1981). Ten years of research on group size and helping. *Psychological Bulletin, 89,* 308–324.

Lee, J. (1993). *Facing the fire: Experiencing and expressing anger appropriately.* New York, NY: Bantam.

Leppik, P. (2005, December 1). How authoritative is Wikipedia? Retrieved from http://66.49.144.193/C2011481421/E652809545/index.html

Liberman, R. P., & Raskin, D. E. (1971). Depression: A behavioral formulation. *Archives of General Psychiatry, 24,* 515–523.

Likert, R. (1932). A technique for the measurement of attitudes. *Archives of Psychology, 22,* 1–55.

Lohr, J. M., Olatunji, B. O., Baumeister, R. F., & Bushman, B. J. (2007). The psychology of anger venting and empirically supported alternatives that do no harm. *The Scientific Review of Mental Health Practice, 5,* 54–65.

Luk, R., Ferrence, R., & Gmel, G. (2006). The economic impact of a smoke-free bylaw on restaurant and bar sales in Ottawa, Canada. *Addiction, 101,* 738–745. doi:10.1111/j.1360-0443.2006.01434.x

Lutsky, N. (2008). Arguing with numbers: A rationale and suggestions for teaching quantitative reasoning through argument and writing. In B. L. Madison & L. A. Steen (Eds.), *Calculation vs. context: quantitative literacy and its implications for teacher education* (pp. 59–74). Washington, DC: Mathematical Association of America.

Lyubomirsky, S., King, L. A., & Diener, E. (2005). The benefits of frequent positive affect. *Psychological Bulletin, 131*, 803–855.

Markus, H. R., & Hamedani, M. G. (2007). Sociocultural psychology: The dynamic interdependence among self systems and social systems. In S. Kitayama & D. Cohen (Eds.), *Handbook of cultural psychology* (pp. 3–39). New York, NY: Guilford Press.

Markus, H. R., & Kitayama, S. (1991). Culture and the self: Implications for cognition, emotion, and motivation. *Psychological Review, 98*, 224–253.

Marshall, B. J., & Warren, J. R. (1983). Unidentified curved bacillus on gastric epithelium in active chronic gastritis. *Lancet, 1*(8336), 1273–1275.

Marshall, B. J., & Warren, J. R. (1984). Unidentified curved bacilli in the stomach patients with gastritis and peptic ulceration. *Lancet, 1*(8390), 1311–1315.

Martin, D. S. (2007). If you see it, you'll eat it, expert says. Retrieved from http://www.cnn.com/2007/HEALTH/diet.fitness/09/21/kd.mindless.eating/index.html

Masuda, T., & Nisbett, R. E. (2001). Attending holistically vs. analytically: Comparing the context sensitivity of Japanese and Americans. *Journal of Personality and Social Psychology, 81*, 922–934.

McCallum, J. M., Arekere, D. M., Green, B. L., Katz, R. V., & Rivers, B. M. (2007). Awareness and knowledge of the U.S. Public Health Service syphilis study at Tuskegee: Implications for biomedical research. *Journal of Health Care for the Poor and Underserved, 17*, 716–733.

McCartney, K., & Rosenthal, R. (2000). Effect size, practical importance, and social policy for children. *Child Development, 71*, 173–180.

McKey, R., Condelli, L., Ganson, H., Barrett, B., McConkey, C., & Plantz, M. (1985). *The impact of Head Start on children, families, and communities.* (Final report of the Head Start Evaluation, Synthesis, and Utilization Project). Washington, DC: U.S. Department of Health and Human Services.

McNulty, J. K. (2010). When positive processes hurt relationships. *Current Directions in Psychological Science, 19*, 167–171.

Mehl, M. R., & Pennebaker, J. W. (2003). The sounds of social life: A psychometric analysis of students' daily social environments and natural conversations. *Journal of Personality and Social Psychology, 84*(4), 857–870. doi:10.1037/0022-3514.84.4.857

Mehl, M. R., Vazire, S., Holleran, S. E., & Clark, C. S. (2010). Eavesdropping on happiness: Well-being is related to having less small talk and more substantive conversations. *Psychological Science, 21*, 539–541.

Mehl, M. R., Vazire, S., Ramirez-Esparza, N., Slatcher, R. B., & Pennebaker, J. W. (2007). Are women really more talkative than men? *Science, 317*, 82.

Milgram, S. (1963). Behavioral study of obedience. *Journal of Abnormal and Social Psychology, 67*, 371–378.

Milgram, S. (1974). *Obedience to authority.* New York, NY: Harper & Row.

Miller, G. E. (1956). The magic number seven plus or minus two: Some limits on our capacity for processing information. *Psychological Review, 63*, 81–97.

Moffat, N. J. (1989). Home-based cognitive rehabilitation with the elderly. In L. W. Poon, D. C. Rubin, & B. A. Wilson (Eds.), *Everyday cognition in adulthood and late life* (pp. 659–680). Cambridge, England: Cambridge University Press.

Mook, D. (1989). The myth of external validity. In L. W. Poon, D. C. Rubin, & B. A. Wilson (Eds.), *Everyday cognition in adulthood and late life* (pp. 25–43). Cambridge, England: Cambridge University Press.

Mook, D. (2001). *Psychological research.* New York, NY: Norton.

Mueller, C. M., & Dweck, C. S. (1998). Intelligence praise can undermine motivation and performance. *Journal of Personality and Social Psychology, 75*, 33–52.

Mundell, E. J. (2007, July 5). Science quiets myth of "chatterbox" females. Sexualhealth.com. Retrieved from http://sexualhealth.e-healtsource.com/index.php?p=news1&id=606134

Myers, D. (2000). The funds, friends, and faith of happy people. *American Psychologist, 55*, 56–67.

National Institutes of Health, Office of Human Subjects Research. (1979). *The Belmont Report.* Retrieved from http://ohsr.od.nih.gov/guidelines/belmont.html

National Research Council. (2011). *Guide for the care and use of laboratory animals* (8th ed.). Washington, DC: National Academies Press.

Nisbett, R. E., & Wilson, T. (1977). Telling more than we can know: Verbal reports on mental processes. *Psychological Review, 84*, 231–259.

Ortmann, A., & Hertwig, R. (1997). Is deception acceptable? *American Psychologist, 52*(7), 746–747.

Ostrovsky, Y., Meyers, E., Ganesh, S., Mathur, U., & Sinha, P. (2009). Parsing images via dynamic cues. *Psychological Science, 20*(12), 1484–1491.

Paik, H., & Comstock, G. (1994). The effects of television violence on antisocial behavior: A meta-analysis. *Communication Research, 21*, 516–546.

Pavot, W., & Diener, E. (1993). Review of the Satisfaction with Life Scale. *Psychological Assessment, 5*, 164–172.

Pew Research Center. (2008, December 18). Calling cell phones in '08 pre-election polls. Retrieved from http://pewresearch.org/pubs/1061/cell-phones-election-polling

Pew Research Center. (n.d.). Random digit dialing—Our standard method. Retrieved from http://people-press.org/methodology/sampling/#1

Pezdek, K. (2004). Event memory and autobiographical memory for the events of September 11, 2001. *Applied Cognitive Psychology, 17*, 1033–1045.

Piaget, J. (1923). *The language and thought of the child* (M. Worden, trans.). New York, NY: Harcourt, Brace, & World.

Pietschnig, J., Voracek, M., & Formann, A. K. (2010). Mozart effect—Shmozart effect: A meta-analysis. *Intelligence, 38*, 314–323.

Pittenger, D. J. (2002). Deception in research: Distinctions and solutions from the perspective of utilitarianism. *Ethics & Behavior, 12*(2), 117–142.

Plous, S. (1996a). Attitudes toward the use of animals in psychological research and education: Results from a national survey of psychologists. *American Psychologist, 51*, 1167–1180.

Plous, S. (1996b). Attitudes toward the use of animals in psychological research and education: Results from a national survey of psychology majors. *Psychological Science, 7*, 352–358.

Plous, S. (1998). Signs of change within the animal rights movement: Results from a follow-up survey of activists. *Journal of Comparative Psychology, 112*, 48–54.

Plous, S., & Herzog, H. A., Jr. (2000). Poll shows researchers favor lab animal protection. *Science, 290*, 711.

Pope, T. (2009, February 24). The three R's? A fourth is crucial, too: Recess. *The New York Times*, p. D4.

Rampell, C. (2010, April 19). Want a higher GPA? Go to a private college [Web log post]. Retrieved from http://economix.blogs.nytimes.com/2010/04/19/want-a-higher-g-p-a-go-to-a-private-college/

Raskin, R., & Terry, H. (1988). A principle components analysis of the Narcissistic Personality Inventory and further evidence of its construct validity. *Journal of Personality and Social Psychology, 54*, 890–902.

Rauscher, F. H., Shaw, G. L., & Ky, K. N. (1993). Music and spatial task performance. *Nature, 365*, 611.

Reiss, J. E., & Hoffman, J. E. (2006). Object substitution masking interferes with semantic processing: Evidence from event-related potentials. *Psychological Science, 17*, 1015–1020.

Religion can spur goodness (2008, April 28). World-science.net. Retrieved from http://www.world-science.net/othernews/081002_religion

Rentfrow, P. J., & Gosling, S. D. (2003). The do-re-mi's of everyday life: The structure and personality correlates of music preferences. *Journal of Personality and Social Psychology, 84*, 1236–1256.

Reverby, S. (2009). *Examining Tuskegee: The infamous syphilis study and its legacy.* Chapel Hill: University of North Carolina Press.

Roberts, B. W., & Robins, R. W. (2000). Broad dispositions, broad aspirations: The intersection of personality traits and major life goals. *Personality and Social Psychology Bulletin, 26*, 1284–1296.

Ropeik, D., & Gray, G. (2002). *Risk: A practical guide for deciding what's really safe and what's really dangerous in the world around you.* New York, NY: Houghton Mifflin.

Rosenberg, M. (1965). *Society and the adolescent self-image.* Princeton, NJ: Princeton University Press.

Rosenthal, R., & Fode, K. (1963). The effect of experimenter bias on the performance of the albino rat. *Behavioral Science, 8*, 183–189.

Saxe, L. (1991). Lying: Thoughts of an applied social psychologist. *American Psychologist, 46*(4), 409–415.

Schellenberg, G. (2004). Music lessons enhance IQ. *Psychological Science, 15*, 511–514.

Sears, D. O. (1986). College freshmen in the laboratory: Influences of a narrow data base on social psychology's view of human nature. *Journal of Personality and Social Psychology, 51*, 515–539.

Seeing red affects achievement. (2007, March 2). World Science. Retrieved from http://www.world-science.net/othernews/070301_red.htm.

Segal, D. L., Coolidge, F. L., Cahill, B. S., & O'Riley, A. A. (2008). Psychometric properties of the Beck Depression Inventory-II (BDI-II) among community-dwelling older adults. *Behavior Modification, 32*, 3–20.

Segall, M. H., Campbell, D. T., & Herskovits, M. J. (1966). *The influence of culture on visual perception.* Indianapolis, IN: Bobbs-Merrill.

Shadish, W. R., & Luellen, J. K. (2006). Quasi-experimental design. In J. L. Green, G. Camilli, & P. B. Elmore (Eds.), *Handbook of complementary methods in education research* (pp. 539–550). Mahwah, NJ: Erlbaum.

Shaffer, D. R., Rogel, M., & Hendrick, C. (1975). Intervention in the library: The effect of increased responsibility on bystanders' willingness to prevent a theft. *Journal of Applied Social Psychology, 5*, 303–319.

Sharpe, D., Adair, J. G., & Roese, N. J. (1992). Twenty years of deception research: A decline in subjects' trust? *Personality and Social Psychology Bulletin, 18,* 585–590.

Should cell phone use by drivers be illegal? (2009, July 18). *The New York Times.* Retrieved from www.nytimes.com

Shweder, R. (1989). Cultural psychology: What is it? In J. Stigler, R. Shweder, & G. Herdt (Eds.), *Cultural psychology: The Chicago symposia on culture and development* (pp. 1–46). New York, NY: Cambridge University Press.

Smith, G. T. (2005a). On construct validity: Issues of method and measurement. *Psychological Assessment, 17,* 396–408.

Smith, G. T. (2005b). On the complexity of quantifying construct validity. *Psychological Assessment, 17,* 413–414.

Smith, S. S., & Richardson, D. (1983). Amelioriation of deception and harm in psychological research: The important role of debriefing. *Journal of Personality and Social Psychology, 44,* 1075–1082.

Smith, T. B., McCullough, M. E., & Poll, J. (2003). Religiousness and depression: Evidence for a main effect and the moderating influence of stressful life events. *Psychological Bulletin, 129,* 614–636.

Snyder, M., & Campbell, B. (1980). Testing hypotheses about other people: The role of the hypothesis. *Personality and Social Psychology Bulletin, 6,* 421–426.

Snyder, M., & Swann, W. B. (1978). Hypothesis-testing processes in social interaction. *Journal of Personality and Social Psychology, 36,* 1202–1212.

Snyder, M., & White, M. (1981). Testing hypotheses about other people: Strategies of verification and falsification. *Personality and Social Psychology Bulletin, 7,* 39–43.

Social isolation may have a negative effect on intellectual abilities (2007, October 30). Medicalnewstoday.com. Retrieved from http://www.medicalnewstoday.com/articles/87087.php

Sperry, R. W. (1961). Cerebral organization and behavior. *Science, 133,* 1749–1757.

Spiegel, A. (2010, June 28). "Mozart effect" was just what we wanted to hear. National Public Radio transcript. Retrieved from http://www.npr.org/templates/story/story.php?storyId=128104580

Stanovich, K. E. (2010). *How to think straight about psychology* (9th ed.). Boston, MA: Allyn & Bacon.

Steenhuysen, J. (2010, April 26). Depressed? You must like chocolate. MSNBC mental health. Retrieved from http://www.msnbc.msn.com/id/36786824/ns/health-mental_health/

Stein, R. (2009, June 22). Positive is negative. *Washington Post.* Retrieved from www.washingtonpost.com

Steingraber, S. (2008). Pesticides, animals, and humans. In L. H. Peterson & J. C. Brereton (Eds.), *The Norton Reader* (11th ed., pp. 971–982). New York, NY: Norton. (Reprinted from *Living downstream: An ecologist looks at cancer and the environment,* by S. Steingraber, 1997, New York, NY: Perseus Books.)

Strauman, T. J., Vieth, A. Z., Merrill, K. A., Woods, T. E., Kolden, G. G., Klein, M. H., . . . Kwapil, L. (2006). Self-system therapy as an intervention for self-regulatory dysfunction in depression: A randomized comparison with cognitive therapy. *Journal of Consulting and Clinical Psychology, 74,* 367–376.

Strayer, D. L., & Drews, F. A. (2004). Profiles in distraction: Effects of cell phone conversations on younger and older drivers. *Human Factors, 46,* 640–650.

Strayer, D. L., Drews, F. A., & Crouch, D. J. (2006). A comparison of the cell phone driver and the drunk driver. *Human Factors, 48,* 381–391.

Strayer, D. L., Drews, F. A., & Johnston, W. A. (2003). Cell phone induced failures in visual attention during simulated driving. *Journal of Experimental Psychology: Applied, 9,* 23–52.

Tavris, C. (1989). *Anger: The misunderstood emotion.* New York, NY: Simon & Schuster.

Turk, D. J., Heatherton, T. F., Macrae, C. N., Kelley, W. M., & Gazzaniga, M. S. (2003). Out of contact, out of mind: The distributed nature of the self. *Annals of the New York Academy of Sciences, 1001,* 65–78.

Tversky, A., & Kahneman, D. (1974). Judgments under uncertainty: Heuristics and biases. *Science, 185,* 1124–1131.

Twachtman-Cullen, D. (1997). *A passion to believe: Autism and the facilitated communication phenomenon.* Boulder, CO: Westview Press.

Van Orden, K. A., Witte, T. K., Cukrowicz, K. C., Braithwaite, S. R., Selby, E. A., & Joiner, T. E. (2010). The interpersonal theory of suicide. *Psychological Review, 117,* 575–600.

Vandell, D., Henderson, L. V., & Wilson, K. S. (1988). A longitudinal study of children with day-care experiences of varying quality. *Child Development, 59,* 1286–1292.

Wansink, B. (1996). Can package size accelerate usage volume? *Journal of Marketing, 60,* 1–14.

Wansink, B., & Cheney, M. M. (2005). Superbowls: Serving bowl size and food consumption. *Journal of the American Medical Association, 293,* 1727–1728.

Wansink, B., & Kim, J. (2005). Bad popcorn in big buckets: Portion size can influence intake as much as taste. *Journal of Nutrition Education and Behavior, 37,* 242–245.

Webb, E., Campbell, D., Schwartz, R., & Sechrest, L. (1966). *Unobtrusive measures: Nonreactive research in the social sciences.* Chicago, IL: Rand McNally.

Wechsler, D. (2004). *The Wechsler Intelligence Scale for Children* (4th ed.). London, England: Pearson Assessment.

Weisz, J. R., McCarty, C. A., & Valeri, S. M. (2006). Effects of psychotherapy for depression in children and adolescents: A meta-analysis. *Psychological Bulletin, 132*(1), 132–149.

Westman, M., & Eden, D. (1997). Effects of a respite from work on burnout: Vacation relief and fade-out. *Journal of Applied Psychology, 82,* 516–527.

Wilson, D. C. (2006, December). Framing the future of race relations. *Public Opinion Pros.* Retrieved from www.publicopinionpros.norc.org

Wilson, D. C., Moore, D. W., McKay, P. F., & Avery, D. R. (2008). Affirmative action programs for women and minorities: Support affected by question order. *Public Opinion Quarterly, 73,* 514–522.

Ybarra, O., Burnstein, E., Winkielman, P., Keller, M. C., Manis, M., Chan, E., & Rodriguez, J. (2008). Mental exercising through simple socializing: Social interaction promotes general cognitive functioning. *Personality and Social Psychology Bulletin, 34,* 248–259.

Zajonc, R. B., Heingartner, A., & Herman, E. M. (1969). Social enhancement and impairment of performance in the cockroach. *Journal of Personality and Social Psychology, 13,* 83–92.

Zhong, C., & Leonardelli, G. J. (2008). Cold and lonely: Does social exclusion literally feel cold? *Psychological Science, 19,* 838–843.

Credits

Chapter 1

Page 1: (Grand Theft Auto): Landov; (credit card): iStockphoto; (kid): Dreamstime: p. (2): Dreamstime; (baby): iStockphoto; **p. 5:** Courtesy Carthage College; **p. 7:** Stringer/AFP/Getty Images; **p. 10:** Harlow Primate Lab, Madison, WI; **p. 15 (left):** Courtesy Anglia Vision Research, Anglia Ruskin University; **p. 15 (right):** Courtesy Vision Research Corporation; **p. 17:** PHD Comics. com; **p. 18:** Jim Wilson/The New York Times/Redux.

Chapter 2

Page 22 (middle): Landov; (top): Alamy; **p. 22 (bottom):** iStockphoto; **p. 24 (punching bag):** MBI/ Alamy; **p. 24 (video game):** David Pearson/Alamy; **p. 25:** Rue des Archives/The Granger Collection; **p. 35:** PhotoStock-Israel/Alamy; **p. 39:** Bushman, Brad J., Does Venting Anger Feed or Extinguish the Flame? Catharsis, Rumination, Distraction, Anger, and Aggressive Responding. *Personality and Social Psychology Bulletin.* Sage Publications, 06/01/2002. ©2002, Society for Personality and Social Psychology, Inc.; **p. 47:** http:// www.psychwiki.com/wiki/Catharsis.

Chapter 3

Page 52 (credit card): iStockphoto; **p. 52 (teen):** Richard Hutchings/Digital Light/Newscom; **p. 52 (man):** Dreamstime; (texture): Shutterstock; **p. 56 (therapist):** Mary Kate Denny/PhotoEdit; **p. 56 (scale):** Radloff, L. S. (1977). The CES-D Scale: A self-report depression scale for research in the general population. *Applied Psychological Measurement*, 1, 385-401; Janine Wiedel Photolibrary/Alamy; **p. 63:** AP Photo; **p. 70:** Schellenberg, G. (2004). Music lessons enhance IQ. *Psychological Science*, 15, 511–514; **p. 72 (top):** Design Pics/Alamy; **p. 72 (bottom):**

Kevin Lamarque/Reuters/Corbis; **p. 76 (left):** J. Carlee/Bullshotz Photography; **p. 76 (right):** Creatas/ Photolibrary.

Chapter 4

Page 83 (crowd): David Grossman/Alamy; **p. 83 (man):** iStockphoto; **p. 84:** David Grossman/Alamy; **p. 84:** Akira Suwa/Philadelphia Inquirer/Newscom; **p. 84 (texture):** Swisshippo/Dreamstime; **p. 84 (sign):** W.W. Norton; **p. 86:** NARA; **p. 87:** Paul J. Richards/ AFP/Getty Images; **p. 88:** Courtesy Alexandra Milgram; **p. 89:** Courtesy Alexandra Milgram; **p. 92:** © Bill Aron/Photo Edit; **p. 94:** The APA website screenshot is reproduced with permission. Copyright © 2011 by the American Psychological Association, all rights reserved; **p. 99:** Corbis Flirt/Alamy; **p. 102:** Courtesy PETA; **p. 103:** Courtesy Foundation for Biomedical Research; **pp. 108–110:** Copyright © 2010 by the American Psychological Association. Reproduced with permission. The official citation that should be used in referencing this material is: American Psychological Association. (2010a). *Ethical principles of psychologists and code of conduct (2002, amended June 1, 2010)*. Retrieved from http://www.apa.org/ethics/code/index.aspx. No further reproduction or distribution is permitted without written permission from the American Psychological Association.

Chapter 5

Page 112 (man): iStockphoto; **p. 112 (texture):** Shutterstock; **p. 116:** From *Intelligence and How to Get It* by Richard Nisbett. Copyright © 2009 by Richard E. Nisbett. Used by permission of W.W. Norton & Company, Inc. This selection may not be reproduced, stored in a retrieval system, or transmitted in any form or by any means without the prior written permission of the publisher; **p. 117:** Reading Stories Activates Neural Representations of Visual and Motor Experiences, Nicole K. Speer, Jeremy R. Reynolds, Khena M. Swallow, Jeffrey M. Zacks, *Psychological Science*, 8/1/2009. Fig.2 ©2009, Association for Psychological Science; **p. 136:** Table 2, p.167, from Pavot, W., & Diener, E. (1993). Review of the Satisfaction With Life Scale. *Psychological Assessment*, 5(2), 164–172. doi:10.1037/1040-3590.5.2.164.

Chapter 6
Page 143 (woman): Dreamstime; **p. 143 (boy):** Shutterstock; **p. 144 (woman):** Dreamstime; **p. 144 (computer):** W.W. Norton; **p. 144 (boy):** Shutterstock; **p. 147:** © 2011 Zappos.com, Inc; p. 155: eNed Frisk/AgeFotostock; **p. 157 (a):** Courtesy Matthias Mehl, University of Arizona; **p. 157 (b):** Mehl, Vazire, Ramirez-Esparza, Slatcher, & Pennebaker, 2007. Are women really more talkative than men? *Science* 6 July 2007: Vol. 317 no. 5834, p. 82; **p. 160:** Toppham/The Image Works; **p. 161:** Spencer Grant/Photo Researchers; **p. 162:** Reprinted with permission from A.Bowker, B. Boekhoven, A. Nolan, et al., 2009, Naturalistic observations of spectator behavior at youth hockey games. *The Sport Psychologist*, 23(3) 301–316. ©2009 Human Kinetics, Inc; **p. 163:** Campos, B., et al. Opportunity for interaction? A naturalistic observation study of dual earner families after work and School. *Journal of Family Psychology* 2009, Vol. 23, No.6, 798–807; **p. 165:** Paul J. Richards/AFP/Getty Images; **p. 167:** RayArt Graphics/Alamy; **p. 168:** Newscom.

Chapter 7
Page 181 (woman headphones): Jason Stitt/Dreamstime; **p. 181 (kids):** H. Mark Weidman Photography/Alamy; **p. 181 (texture):** Artur Marciniec/Dreamstime; **p. 182 (mom and son):** Drz400/Dreamstime; **p. 182 (woman headphones):** Jason Stitt/Dreamstime; **p. 182 (texture):** Panom Bounak/Dreamstime; **p. 192:** i love images/Alamy; **p. 194:** Eavesdropping on happiness: Well-being is related to having less small talk and more substantive conversations. *Psychological Science* April 2010 21: 539–541, first published 2/18/10. Table 1. With permission of Matthias Mehl and Sage Publications.

Chapter 8
Page 208 (remote): Diego Vito Cervo/Dreamstime; **p. 208 (kids):** H. Mark Weidman Photography/Alamy; **p. 208 (texture):** Artur Marciniec/Dreamstime; **p. 214:** Andia/Alamy; **p. 225:** Megapress/Alamy; **p. 227:** David

J. Green-Lifestyle/Alamy; **p. 233:** Barros et al. (2009). School recess and group classroom behavior. *Pediatrics* 123, 431–436. © 2009, American Academy of Pediatrics.

Chapter 9
Page 240 (man): Bloomimage/Corbis; (2) iStockphoto; **p. 242 (stop sign):** Elopaint/Dreamstime.com; **p. 242 (sign):** (radioactive): Batman2000/FeaturePics; **p. 242 (cones):** devon/FeaturePics.

Chapter 10
Page 276 (man): Geoff Manasse/Getty Images; **p. 276 (texture):** istockphoto.

Chapter 11
Page 310 (fries): Eyewave/Dreamstime; (keyboard): Novastock Stock Connection Worldwide/Newscom; **p. 310 (woman):** Fred Prouser/Reuters; **p. 317:** Strayer, D. L., & Drews, F. A. (2004). Profiles in driver distraction: Effects of cell phone conversations on younger and older drivers. *Human Factors*, 46, 640–649. Photo courtesy David Strayer.

Chapter 12
Page 343 (woman): Shutterstock; **p. 343 (fish):** iStockphoto; **p. 344 (dice):** iStockphoto; **p. 344 (drop):** Shutterstock; **p. 352:** Paul Conklin/PhotoEdit; **p. 365:** Mendil/Photo Researchers; **p. 368 (left):** Michael Newman/Photo Edit; **p. 368 (right):** Farrell Grehan/Corbis.

Chapter 13
Page 374 (survey): Shutterstock; **p. 374 (counseling):** Barbara Davidson/Los Angeles Times; **p. 374 (texture):** iStockphoto; **p. 377:** Bargh et al., (1996). Automaticity of social behavior: Direct effect of trait construct and sterotype activation on action. *Journal of Personality and Social Psychology*, 71, 230–244; **p. 382:** Robert Harding Picture Library/Alamy; p. 392: Masuda & Nisbett (2001), *JPSP*, 81, 922–934. ©Takahiko Masuda, All rights Reserved; **p. 393:** Masuda & Nisbett (2001), *JPSP*, 81, 922-934. ©Takahiko Masuda, All rights Reserved; **p. 403:** Ostrovsky et al., Visual parsing after recovery from blindness. *Psychological Science*, March 2, 2010, vol. 20 no. 12 1484–1491.

Appendix A
A.7: B. Wansink, J. Kim, Bad popcorn in big buckets: Portion size can influence intake as much as taste. *Journal of Nutrition Education and Behavior*, Volume 37, Issue 5, Pages 242–245. Table 2. **A.12:** Bushman, B. J., & Anderson, C. A. (2001). Media violence and the American

Name Index

Subject Index

Belmont Report
    about, 90–91
    principle of beneficence, 92–93, 95
    principle of justice, 93, 95
    principle of respect for persons,
        91–92, 95
beneficence
    APA ethical principles on, 95
    Belmont Report, 92–93, 95
    defined, 92
    Tuskegee Syphilis Study and, 87
beta
    inferential statistics for, A43–A44
    interpretation of, 220
    predictor variables and, 219–220,
        223
    process steps, A44–A46
    statistical significance of,
        221–222
between-subjects designs
    defined, 254
    in factorial designs, 328
    null effects and, 295–299
biases
    observer, 159, 288, 293, 357
    present/present, 31–32
    sample, 165–166
    thinking the easy way, 30–33
    thinking what we want to think,
        30, 33–35
    when asking questions, 34–35
bimodal distributions, A4
Binet, Alfred, 14–15
bivariate correlations (associations)
    construct validity and, 190
    defined, 183–184
    external validity and, 201–204
    internal validity and, 199–201
    introduction to, 184–189
    statistical validity and, 190–198
blind studies
    defined, 161
    observer effects and, 288–289
blogs, finding research in, 48
Buxton, Peter, 87

carryover effects, 261
categorical variables
    defined, 118, 187
    describing associations with,
        187–189

catharsis
    defined, 28
    managing anger via, 24, 28–29, 39
    steam engine metaphor for, 31
causal claims
    about, 241
    defined, 63–64
    determining, 64
    examples of, 57, 244–245
    generalization mode and, 390
    interrogating, 69–74, 77,
        265–271
    see also experiments
causal temptation, 199–201
ceiling effects, 296–298, 305
cells
    cell phones study, 312–318,
        323–336, 379–380
    defined, 315
census, defined, 164
central tendency, A4–A5
CES-D (Center for Epidemiologic
    Studies Depression) scale,
    134–135
Cham, Jorge, 17
cherry-picking evidence, 33–34
chi-square tests, A45–A46
citing sources in APA-style research
    reports, A65–A67, A70–A71
claims, 57, see also association
    claims; causal claims;
    frequency claims
Clever Hans the horse, 160
Clinton, Bill, 87
cluster sampling, 169
Cohen's d
    defined, 271, A16
    effect size and, A17–A19
color associations, 7, 16
comparison groups
    anger management study, 28–29
    attrition threats and, 286
    bleeding cure example, 25–27
    defined, 25
    Head Start study, 346–347
    personal experience and, 27
    testing threats and, 287
concept maps, 37
conceptual replication, 378–379
conceptual variables
    defined, 55, 114

operational versus, 55–56,
    114–118
concurrent-measures designs, 258
concurrent validity
    of association claims, 191
    correlational evidence for,
        129–131
    defined, 129
    known-groups paradigm,
        131–132
conditions, 246
confederates, 28
confirmatory hypothesis testing, 34
confounds
    controlling for, 29
    defined, 27, 249
    design, 249–250
    in experiments, 249–250
    null effects and, 298–299
    threats to internal validity and,
        278, 292
conservation of mass theory, 368
constants, 54
construct validity
    of association claims, 66–67, 77,
        190–191
    of behavioral observations,
        156–163
    of causal claims, 73, 77, 265–267
    defined, 66, 68
    of experiments, 266–267
    of frequency claims, 65–66, 77
    interrogating as a consumer,
        135–138
    measuring, 127–128
    of multivariate designs, 232
    in quasi-experiments, 359
    in small-N designs, 370
    of surveys and polls, 146–156
consumers of research information
    about, 4
    importance of, 5–6
contact-comfort theory, 9–10,
    387–388
content validity
    of association claims, 191
    defined, 128–129
context-dependent learning,
    320–321
context-sensitivity study, 393–394
control for (term usage)

intuition
  empirical research versus, 35–36
  as source of information, 30–31
  thinking the easy way bias, 30–33
  thinking what we want to think
    bias, 30, 33–35
inverse association, 60, A13
IQ (intelligence quotient) test
  Binet developing, 14–15
  music lessons enhancing, 70–71
  predictive validity and, 131
IRB (institutional review board),
    96, 108
it depends (term usage), 337–338

journal articles
  consulting, 38–40
  empirical, 38
  mean and standard deviation in,
    A8–A9
  reference lists in, A66–A67
  review, 38
journalism
  defined, 16
  journal-to-journalism cycle and,
    16–19
journals
  about psychological science, 48
  defined, 15
  journal-to-journalism cycle and,
    16–19
  peer reviewed, 15
  psychology-related, 40
journal-to-journalism cycle
  about, 16
  benefits and risks of, 16–18
justice, principle of
  APA ethical principles, 95
  Belmont Report on, 93, 95
  defined, 93
  Tuskegee Syphilis Study and, 87

known-groups paradigm, 131–132

Lao Tzu, 381
large-N designs, 361
Latin square, 262–263
leading questions, 148
lie detectors, 131
Likert scale, 147

longitudinal designs
  defined, 211
  experiments versus, 215
  interpreting results from, 211–213
  rules for causation and, 214
low-price theories, testing, 319–320

magazines, finding research in, 48
main effects
  defined, 321
  interactions and, 325–327
  marginal means and, 321–322
  statistical significance of, 322
  three-way designs and, 331–332
manipulated variables
  construct validity of, 265–266
  defined, 54
  in experiments, 245
  factorial designs and, 316
  measured versus, 54–55
manipulation checks, 266
marginal means, 321–322
margin of error, 175
masked study, 161
matched-group designs
  defined, 252
  selection effects and, 252–253
maturation threats
  in experiments, 280–281, 292
  in quasi-experiments, 352–353
maze rats, 160
McCain, John, 167
mean
  defined, A5
  in journal articles, A8–A9
measured variables
  construct validity of, 265
  defined, 54
  in experiments, 245–246
  manipulated versus, 54–55
  scales of measurement, 118–119
  types of, 116–118
  see also bivariate correlations
    (associations); measurement in
    research; multivariate designs
measurement error, 300–301, 305
measurement in research
  applied review, 135–138
  measuring variables, 114–119
  reliability of, 119–126
  validity of, 126–135

median, A4–A5
mediating variables
  defined, 229
  moderators versus, 231
  reverse-mediation model, 230
  testing for, 229–230
  third variables versus, 230–231
memories of events, 156
memory theories, testing, 320–321
meta-analysis
  defined, 381
  important features of, 384–385
  psychotherapy effectiveness
    example, 382–384
  religion and depression example,
    381–382
  in review journal articles, 381
  in scientific literature, 381–385
meta-analysis in review journal
    articles, 39
Method section
  in APA-style research reports,
    A54–A56, A72–A74, A86
  in empirical journal articles, 43,
    335–336
Milgram obedience studies, 88–90
Ming, Yao, 63
mixed factorial designs, 329
mode, A4–A5
moderators
  association example, 202–204
  defined, 202
  interactions and, 318
  mediators versus, 231
  testing for, 383
mother-infant attachment, 9–10
Mozart effect, 18
Müller-Lyer illusion, 391–392
multimodal distributions, A4
multiple-baseline designs, 365–366
multiple regression
  adding predictors to, 222–223
  defined, 216
  in popular press articles, 223–225
  recess and classroom behavior
    study, 215–226
  third-variable problem, 216–222
multistage sampling, 169
multivariate designs
  causal rules and, 210–211
  defined, 210